1976

This book may be kept

FOU

W9-CMN-479

The Middle East:
A Geographical Study

The Middle East:
A Geographical Study

Peter Beaumont
Senior Lecturer in Geography, University of Durham

Gerald H. Blake
Senior Lecturer in Geography, University of Durham

J. Malcolm Wagstaff
Lecturer in Geography, University of Southampton

JOHN WILEY & SONS

London · New York · Sydney · Toronto

Library of Congress Cataloging in Publication Data:

Beaumont, Peter.
  The Middle East.

  Bibliography: p.
  Includes index.
  1. Near East—Description and travel. I. Blake, Gerald Henry, joint author. II. Wagstaff, John Malcolm, (date)   joint author. III. Title.
DS49.7.B36 1975   330.9′56′04   74–28284

ISBN 0 471 06117 4 (Cloth)

ISBN 0 471 06119 0 (Pbk)

Photosetting in India by Thomson Press (India) Ltd., New Delhi. Printed in Great Britain by J. W. Arrowsmith Ltd., Bristol.

Acknowledgements

Copyright material is reproduced by kind permission of the following whose cooperation we gratefully acknowledge: *Nature* (Macmillan Journals Ltd), (Figures 1.2 and 1.4); Oxford University Press, (Figure 1.3); Ministry of Agriculture, Republic of Turkey, (Figure 1.7); United Nations Food and Agriculture Organisation, (Figure 1.8); British Society of Soil Science, (Figure 1.9); Institute of Land Reclamation, Alexandria University, (Figure 1.10); Iranian Meteorological Organisation, (Figure 2.1); The Geographical Association, (Figure 2.7); C. W. Thornthwaite Associates, Centerton, New Jersey, (Figures 2.12 and 2.15); United Nations (UNESCO–FAO), (Figure 2.13); National Water Well Association, (Figure 2.16); American Association for the Advancement of Science, (Figure 3.4); Koninklijk Nederlands Aardrijskundig Genootschap, (Figure 3.5); Wolf Hütteroth, (Figures 3.6, 4.3 and 4.4(a)); Department of Surveys, Tel Aviv, Israel, (Figure 3.8); World Meteorological Organisation, (Figures, 4.1 and 13.2); American Geographical Society, (Figures 4.5 and 13.3); Douglas L. Johnson, (Figure 4.7); Editor, *Middle East Journal*, (Figure 4.8); Lars Eldblom, (Figure 4.9); Israel Exploration Journal, (Figure 4.10); David F. Darwent, (Figure 6.5); The Controller of Her Majesty's Stationery Office, (Figure 6.7); University of London Press Limited, (Figure 6.8); M. M. Azeez, (Figure 6.9); Keter Publishing House, Jerusalem, Limited, (Figure 10.2); Associated Book Publishers, (Figure 10.5); University of Chicago Press, (Figure 12.5); Institut de Géographie Alpine, (Figure 14.1); Société de Géographie de Lyon, (Figure 14.2); Soil Conservation Society of America, (Figure 15.3); Plan Organisation of Iran, (Figures 18.2 and 18.3); Institute of British Geographers, (Figure 18.7); and *Middle East International*, (Figure 20.2).

We also thank the following for permission to quote from previously published tables: Iranian Meteorological Organisation, (Table 2.1); The Controller, Her Majesty's Stationery Office, (Tables 2.2, 2.3, 2.4, 2.5, and 2.6); World Meteorological Organisation, Geneva, (Table 2.7); Royal Meteorological Society, (Table 2.8); The Geographical Association, (Table 2.10); American Philosophical Society, (Table 5.1); Regents of the University of California, (Table 6.2); Petroleum Press Bureau, (Table 9.1); Institute of Petroleum, (Tables 9.2 and 9.3); The British Petroleum Co. Ltd., (Table 9.4); Middle East Economic Digest Ltd., (Table 9.6); United Nations Educational Scientific and Cultural Organisation, (Tables 12.2 and 12.3); and Echo of Iran, (Table 18.1).

All sources are fully cited in the chapter references and in the bibliography.

Preface

This book is the outcome of nearly a decade of teaching and research, in the course of which we have received much practical assistance and generous hospitality from numerous friends and associates in various parts of the Middle East and North Africa. We hope that their kindness will be rewarded at least in some measure by any contribution we may make to a better understanding of the problems and aspirations of the people of the region. We are equally indebted to many colleagues in this country, notably to Professor W. B. Fisher, Head of the Department of Geography, and Professor H. Bowen-Jones, Director of the Centre for Middle Eastern and Islamic Studies in the University of Durham who have done so much to foster Middle East studies. We are grateful to the Centre for Middle Eastern and Islamic Studies and other institutions which have enabled us to conduct fieldwork in the Middle East on many occasions.

We wish to thank all those who have commented on parts of the text at various stages, particularly Mr. C. G. Smith of Keble College Oxford, Professor J. I. Clarke, Mr. J. C. Dewdney, Dr. R. I. Lawless, and Mr. M. El-Mehdawi of Durham University, Dr. S. A. Khater of the University of Kuwait, and Dr. B. S. Hoyle of Southampton University who also suggested useful sources for Chapter 11. In addition we owe a great deal to several generations of students, including many from the Middle East, who asked most of the questions this book seeks to answer, and many more which we have been unable to tackle adequately.

In the production stage, Mr. A. S. Burn of the Cartographic Unit at Southampton University was responsible for drawing all the maps, and Mrs. J. E. Munro typed the manuscript, and we are extremely grateful to them for their skills and infinite patience. We also wish to pay tribute to our publishers who have accepted alarming increases in the cost of production with equanimity in the belief that the volume may be of lasting value, and we hope their faith will prove justified.

Above all, we are greatly indebted to our families for putting up with our many absences from home during the preparation of this book.

Durham, June 1975
                                                   P. B.
                                                   G. H. B.
                                                   J. M. W.

A NOTE ON NAMES, UNITS AND MEASURES

One of the problems encountered in studying a foreign region is the spelling of names. This is compounded where languages are written in the unfamiliar Arabic script and different systems of transliteration have been employed to turn names into European languages. Although T. E. Lawrence gloried in the variety of forms which could be produced, most readers are likely to be confused unless some standardization is achieved. Three principles have directed the choice for this book. As far as possible, place names have been spelt in the form used by *The Times Atlas of the World* since this is generally accessible, but where an English version is already in common use that spelling has been preferred. For example, Taurus Mountains is preferred to Toros Dağlari and Euphrates to al-Fūrat or Firat. Where reference is made to places not marked on the maps of *The Times Atlas*, the versions employed in the English language literature have generally been accepted, though for places in Turkey the modern Romanized spelling is used (J. C. Dewdney, *Turkey*, Chatto and Windus, London, 1971, pp. 8–10). For other names, the practice adopted by the *Encyclopaedia of Islam* has been followed, even though this has sometimes created inconsistencies in the text. To avoid the inconvenient term 'Persian/Arabian Gulf', 'the Gulf' has been adopted throughout.

The metric system has been adopted for most quantities, in line with current British practice. For financial matters, however, a variety of currencies are used. Standardization over a long period of time is virtually impossible in a situation of inflation and rapidly changing exchange rates.

Contents

6. Towns and Cities 189

7. Problems of Economic Development 222

8. Industry and Trade 238

9. Petroleum 268

Introduction

0.1 Terms and definitions

The term 'Middle East' was coined in 1902 by the American naval historian, A. T. Mahan, in a discussion of British naval strategy in relation to Russian activity in Iran and a German project for a Berlin to Baghdād railway.[1] He was referring to a region centred on the Persian Gulf, for which the current terms 'Near East' and 'Far East' seemed inadequate. The new term was taken up by *The Times* correspondent in Tehrān, V. Chirol, for a series of articles on the lands forming the western and northern approaches to India,[2] the defence of which had been a sensitive issue for more than a century and became more and more crucial as the strategic centre of the British Empire, no less than British trade, became centred upon the subcontinent (Figure 0.1). 'Middle East' was given respectability when it was used in the House of Lords on 22 March, 1911 by Lord Curzon when opening a discussion of 'the state of affairs in Persia, the Persian Gulf, and Turkey in Asia, in relation . . . to the construction of railways. . .'[3] (Figure 0.1).

Clearly, the term 'Middle East' was one of strategic reference, developed in a Eurocentred world, just as the older terms 'The East', 'Far East' and 'Near East' had been. It was employed again during the First World War when the expeditionary force in Iraq, directed through New Delhi, was described as 'Middle East Forces' and distinguished from 'Near East Forces' based on Cairo.[4] Although Curzon had already given the term a wider application than the lands centred about the Gulf, this only became permanent by a series of accidents in military organization. In 1932 the existing Royal Air Force Middle Eastern Command, in Iraq, was amalgamated with Near Eastern Command, in Egypt, but the new command retained the title 'Middle East'. When the Italian threat to the Suez Canal at the beginning of the Second World War led to the establishment of a military headquarters in Cairo, the army followed the R.A.F. in calling this 'G.H.Q. Middle East'. Between 1940 and 1943, the Cairo headquarters controlled British and Allied operations over a very wide region (Figure 0.1). The constant use of 'Middle East' to describe this region in communiqués and amongst military personnel made the term familiar to a large public. Continued political ferment in the region and its basic strategic importance have maintained the term in use, though not without some pleas for the retention of the old term 'Near East'.[5] Indeed, so useful has the term 'Middle East' become that it is employed by the Russians

1

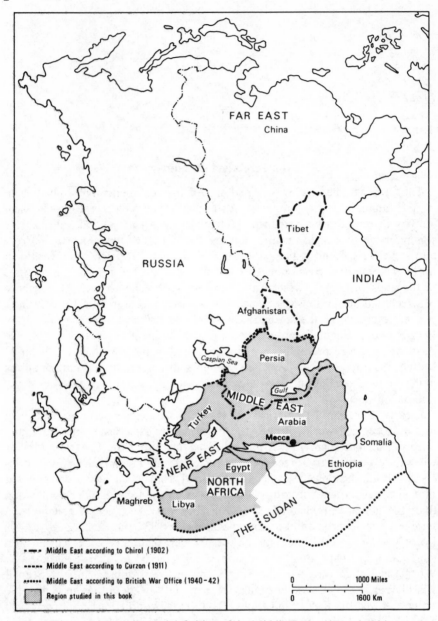

Figure 0.1 Location and definition of the Middle East and North Africa

and even the inhabitants of the region itself, though sometimes with reference to slightly different areas.

In an effort to gain clarity, two other terms are now widely used in the literature to refer to subregions of the 'Middle East' and will be so employed here. 'Southwest Asia' is a term originally devised by American commentators to cover that part of the region lying east of the Isthmus of Suez and north of the eastern Mediterranean Sea, thus excluding North Africa. 'North Africa' itself was used during the Second World War to designate the subregion of the 'Middle East' where fighting between Allied and Axis troops was actually taking place, particularly the Western Desert of Egypt and Libya. Later the term was extended to the whole of Africa between the Mediterranean Sea and the steppe lands of the Sudan, including the Sahara Desert and the north-western corner of the continent which the Arab geographers had called *Jezira al-Maghreb* ('Island of the West') and Europeans had known as *Barbary*. Although the Maghreb states of Morocco, Algeria and Tunisia are not given detailed consideration in this book, some reference to them is made as part of the wider context necessary to certain of the thematic chapters. On these occasions, the term 'North Africa' may be understood in its widest sense, but, generally, usage will be restricted to Libya and Egypt.

The regional and subregional definitions employed in this book are thus essentially pragmatic. The macro-region itself is defined in terms of modern states, since today these may be regarded as constituting distinctive socio-economic systems, despite a number of shared characteristics. Iran and Turkey form the northern tier, with frontiers shared with the Soviet Union. To the south lie the Arab states of Lebanon, Jordan, Syria and Iraq, as well as the Jewish state of Israel. Further south is the heartland of Arabia, consisting of Saudi Arabia, a fringe of small states along the Gulf and the larger units of Oman and the two Yemens. Libya and Egypt form the south-western corner of the region (Figure 0.1).

Apart from political frontiers, there are no clear boundaries around the region defined in this way. The sea, which penetrates deeply into the region, is as much a medium for movement as a barrier, and it is easily crossed at the Red Sea, between Africa and Arabia, and the Turkish Straits, between Europe and Asia. The upland which forms much of eastern Iran may retard movement, but well-defined corridors lead through it into central Asia and northern India. On the south, deserts interpose not so much an impassable barrier between the Middle East, on the one hand, and the Maghreb and the Sudan, on the other, as a difficult and exhausting zone of transition.

0.2 Unity and Diversity[6]

Certain shared characteristics give a degree of unity to the region. The most fundamental is climate. The region is characterized by extremely arid summers and a winter–spring maximum of precipitation. Continental effects are so marked in the centre of the main land masses—Asia Minor, Iran, Arabia and North Africa—and the precipitation so low that population is confined to oases or thinly scattered as nomadic groups. Human activity throughout the region is closely adapted to climatic conditions. The seasonal rhythm in farming and herding is dependent upon the incidence of precipitation, and all human life requires successful harvests of wheat and barley. Nomads and settled cultivators have been mutually dependent here for millenia, and though similar patterns are found in northern India, central Asia and sub-Saharan Africa, they do not appear to have been so well developed or so closely interdependent. In the Middle East, the towns, situated at nodes on natural route ways, have been the organizational centres of the region, closely influencing land use patterns and mediating high cultural developments.

The culture of the region today is fundamentally Muslim and deeply penetrated by the Arabic language. Arabic is the language of God's revelation in the Qur'ān and of the suppliant's prayers. It spread as Islam itself spread throughout the region, partly by conquest but largely by the slower process of conversion. The close identification of Islam with everyday life and administration has ensured the transference of Arabic words and phrases into the other languages of the region. Islam itself is a major integrating force. It stresses the equality of men before the mercy and power of God. Although the Middle East forms only a part of the *Dar al-Islam* ('House of Islam'), it constitutes the core about the major pilgrimage centre of Mecca, which all the faithful are commanded to visit at least once in their lives.[7] The Great Pilgrimage has bestowed considerable unity on the region, for until recently the lands closest to Mecca sent most people to the Ka'ba and the diffusion of Islamic influence backwards was correspondingly great. However, not all the population of the Middle East is Muslim, even after the population movements of the last fifty years. Nonetheless, the culture of Jews and Christians has been powerfully shaped by centuries of life as 'People of the Book' within the Muslim theocracy.

Diversity is as characteristic of the Middle East when examined at a detailed level, as unity appears to be at the regional scale. In many ways the lack of unity looms very large. In detail, a variety of terrain and climate exists in the region, and human response is not uniform. The presence of several races has been recognized. Three major languages—Arabic, Persian and Turkish—are spoken in different parts of the region, but their dominance was often slow in developing and a number of more ancient languages are still spoken by particular groups, whilst recent Jewish immigration has revived Hebrew as the language of Israel (Figure 0.2). The rise of nationalism has weakened many of the old sympathies and relationships, so that much of the cultural unity of the region appears to be disintegrating, whilst political regimes spread through a wide spectrum from patriarchal monarchy to people's democracy. States vary greatly in size, from the virtual city states of the United Arab Emirates to Saudi Arabia, which is about twelve times the size of England. Population densities range from minimal figures for this desert kingdom and much of Libya to over 800 per km² in the Nile valley. Finally, the region does not yet constitute a unifield trading bloc, since intraregional trade is poorly developed, except between the contiguous states of Lebanon, Syria and Jordan.

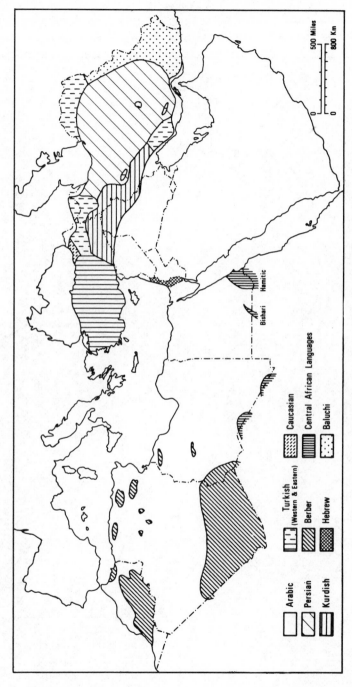

Figure 0.2 Major languages of the Middle East and North Africa

6

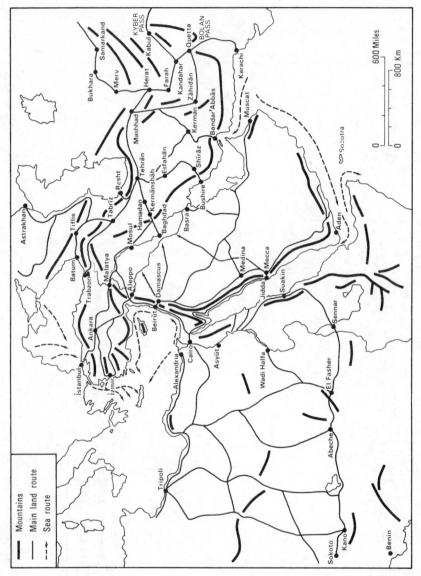

Figure 0.3 Historic trade routes in the Middle East and North Africa

0.3 Geopolitical significance

The region centres around the junction of Africa, Asia and Europe, where the land mass is deeply penetrated by the sea. Maritime trade has long been important and control of ports and constrictions in the seaways has alternately supported cities and disrupted commerce. The four great isthmuses which lie between the arms of the ocean and the inland Caspian Sea have been crossed by major routes for millenia (Figure 0.3), and their control has been of considerable geopolitical concern. This may be illustrated briefly with reference to the nineteenth century. In sailing ship days, when the sea passage from Britain to India via the Cape of Good Hope took anything between five and eight months, the quicker land routes were of vital importance. One ran from Alexandria through Cairo to Suez and thence by ship down the Red Sea, but it was super- seded in 1869 by the Suez Canal, so vital to British imperial strategy, particularly in two World Wars. An alternative route ran across Syria from the eastern Mediterranean to the Euphrates and followed the river as far as the latitude of Baghdād. There one branch continued to Basra and the Gulf, whilst the other struck across Persia and reached northern India via the Bolan or the Kyber passes. A comparatively little used route also ran through Persia, but came down through Tabriz from Batum or Trabzon on the Black Sea. Ease of movement between the Gulf, on the one hand, and the eastern Mediterranean or the Caspian Sea, on the other, made this area one of great concern to both Britain and Russia in the nineteenth century, as well as to the Allies and Germany during the First and Second World Wars. Other routes, of course, converged in the region. Mention might be made of the romantic-sounding but arduous Silk Road, which entered the region from Samarkand and ultimately China through the valleys of the Atrek and Kashaf rivers, and of the slave route which ran from the vicinity of Lake Chad through the Saharan oases to the Mediterranean coast at Tripoli in what is now Libya.

Land and sea routes tied the region into the rest of the world. Along them came people, ideas and plants, as well as the trade which nurtured cities and enriched empires. The region was one great transit zone, a major crossroads in the world. Indeed, *Crossroads* is the apt title of G. B. Cressey's book on the region.[8] The Middle East flourished economically and politically as long as the ancient routes were used, but decayed when they were either closed, often by political change, or bypassed, as when the Dutch and English began to ship large cargoes from India and the Far East via the Cape. Although the region is now both the source and destination of important commercial and passenger movements, the ancient transit routes have retained some of their former significance. Caravan trails have been replaced by all-weather roads and railways, but both carry a surprising amount of international traffic. Their geopolitical value was emphasized during the Second World War, when sea routes were hazardous and Allied forces had to be supplied by land. Some of them flourished again after the closure of the Suez Canal in 1967. Pipelines across the great isthmuses are already of major importance in the movement

8

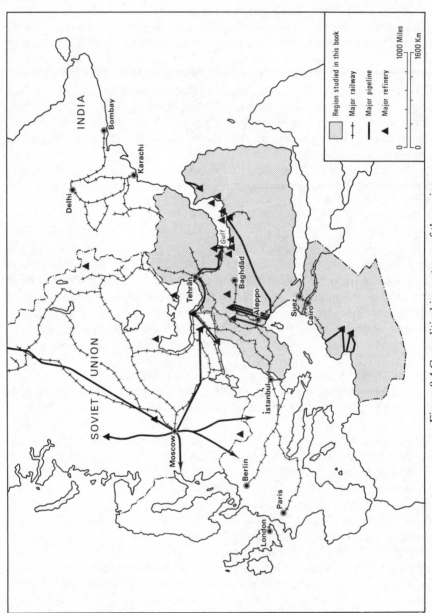

Figure 0.4 Geopolitical importance of the region

Parts of the Middle East have immense tourist potential:

The international festival at Baalbek in Lebanon, 1968. (National Council of Tourism in Lebanon. Photograph by Manoug)

10

An international hotel in Beirūt, Lebanon. (National Council of Tourism in Lebanon. Photograph by Yetenegian).

of oil from the Gulf region and northern Iraq (Figure 0.4), and in future will carry much of the transit trade once shipped via Suez. In particular, Egypt's SUMED and Israel's pipeline from Eilat to Ashqelon will become vital supply lines to Europe. When the canal reopens, there will be many ships ready to use it, doubtless including units of the Soviet Navy. Meanwhile, tanker traffic in the Gulf, the Red Sea, the northern Indian Ocean and the eastern Mediterranean makes the peripheral seas some of the most important highways in the world. International air traffic between Europe and India, Southeast Asia, the Far East and Australia crosses the region, partly to take advantage of approximations to great circle routes, partly to benefit from clear air and fairly stable weather conditions, and partly because of the restrictions on flying over the Soviet Union. Cairo and Beirūt have emerged as major civil airports, while Iran's interest in the Concorde aeroplane is to some extent a recognition of the commercial possibilities arising from geographical location. Military staging posts maintained at various times in Libya, Cyprus, Egypt, southern Turkey and the Gulf testify to the same basic facts.

International tourist traffic is increasing, but perhaps the most significant feature is the steady rise in movements between the countries of the Middle East. An important element in this is the movement of pilgrims to and from Mecca, the rapid increase of which can be attributed to relatively cheap and easy air transport to Jiddah. Tourists from the United States and Europe have declined in number since the Six Days War of June, 1967, except to Israel, but a sharp increase may be expected in the future. The cumulative effect of this first hand knowledge could be a powerful force in the creation of better international understanding of the region. Real and lasting peace and cooperation will come to the Middle East only when technological developments and economic pressures together create powerful internal interaction. One optimistic forecast sees a common market, a network of international motorways, universities linked by computer systems and a high degree of scientific and cultural cooperation by the end of this century.[9] In the meantime, friction and strife continue in the region.

Military control of the region may be less important in the age of the intercontinental ballistic missile than it was in the 1940's or even 1950's, but, as 'Russia's back garden'[10] and the world's major source of oil, the Middle East retains a world significance (Figure 0.4). Russian eastward expansion in the eighteenth and nineteenth centuries gave Moscow an interest in the northern parts of the region, and she was particularly concerned about control of the Turkish Straits and Persia. In large measure, this became the reverse side of the same coin as British concern with the approaches to India, once protection had been extended to the native princes, and the Gulf had been brought under control. The causes of Russian concern have changed, but Turkey's involvement with NATO, as well as her alliance with Iran in CENTO, and the presence of units of the American Sixth Fleet in the eastern Mediterranean, have constituted a threat to Soviet security. Like the United States, the Soviet Union has developed a forward defensive strategy which has sought to increase her influence in the region. To some extent Turkey and Iran have now been neutralized by economic aid and trade agreements, while Russian friendship with several Arab states has prospered on the bases of anti-western feeling, manipulation of the Arab-Israeli conflict and the supply of arms and some technical assistance. The growth of Soviet sea power and the presence of naval units in the Mediterranean Sea and the Indian Ocean have increased Russian influence. They have also made Egypt an important pivot in Soviet world strategy.

Soviet interest in the Middle East has been increased during the 1970's by the need for oil, both for Russia's own needs and to supply to the other members of COMECON. Although the Soviet Union has vast resources of her own (Figure 0.4), demands are rising rapidly as industry and transport are modernized, whilst there is a continuing need to sell crude oil abroad to earn the foreign exchange now vital for continued economic development at home. Most Russian imports were shipped from Iran via the Red Sea and the Eilat–Ashdod pipeline, but since 1971 the quantity imported from Libya has more than doubled. Russia is also interested in developing Iraqi and Syrian oil reserves.

The United States, Western Europe and above all Japan are dependent upon the Middle East for supplies of crude oil. Following the Arab–Israeli war of October, 1973 technical and commercial agreements were reached which seem to guarantee the interdependence of industrial Europe and the oil-rich states for at least a decade.

Apart from oil, Europe is becoming linked with the region in other ways. Preferential agreements with the European Economic Community have been signed by Turkey, Tunisia, Morocco and Israel, while in 1973 negotiations with Algeria, Cyprus, Egypt and Lebanon were in progress. One can perhaps foresee a strengthening of these links between Europe and the non-oil exporting countries of the Mediterranean basin, with Turkey eventually becoming a full member of the Community. It is important to remember that Europe is physically united with the Middle East by the Mediterranean Sea and that this facilitates seaborne trade, as well as the movements of a growing number of cruise ships. The Mediterranean itself is one of the seas seriously at risk from pollution, and there is a need for all the bordering states to cooperate in the management of its waters and resources.[11] Another connection with Europe is being forged by large numbers of migrant workers, chiefly from Algeria and Turkey, employed in Western Europe. While the economic and social consequences of labour migrations are arguably damaging to the home economies, Turkish workers in West Germany sent home over £12 million a month in remittances in 1973,[12] and it is abundantly clear that the economy of Western Europe is dependent upon immigrant labour.

0.4 Middle East: Image and Reality

The understanding of mundane issues like these is complicated by the region's historic role in the clash of western and eastern civilizations. The West often sees the Middle East in terms of romantic, slightly unfocused stereotypes which have been fostered by childhood familiarity with some of the tales from the *Arabian Nights* and novels like John Buchan's *Greenmantle*. Knowledge of the region's languages, and thus of much of its history, literature and philosophy, has been confined to the few. Understanding of the region's peoples has been clouded by religious prejudice, stretching back at least as far as the Crusades, and befogged by the West's recently attained military and economic superiority.[13] While the Middle East's great social and economic leap forward is only just gathering momentum, many of the region's advances over the last decade have gone largely unnoticed in the western world. If this volume succeeds in dispelling some of the myths and misunderstandings and in introducing some of the changes taking place in the region today, its appearance will be justified.

Although the Middle East has had an enormous impact on the history and culture of Western Europe, the region receives extraordinarily little attention in English-speaking schools and universities. Absence of reliable information was perhaps a valid excuse for such neglect, but, in recent years, governments and other agencies have produced a mass of statistical and other material, whilst a large body of serious academic research has been published on all aspects of the region. A number of regional geographies, pioneered by W. B. Fisher, are already available, but there is room for much more geographical research. Work at the local level has often been limited in scope and patchy in coverage; hundreds of topics remain untouched. In the field of human geography, for example, several of the priority areas for research identified by the Social Science Research Council would have particular significance in the Middle East: perception studies; population and migration; regional taxonomy; and the processes of regional economic and social development.[14]

During the next two or three decades new horizons will open up, as the offshore waters of the Middle East are explored and exploited to a degree inconceivable a few years ago. The offshore oilfields of the Gulf and Red Sea already yield substantial quantities of oil, and output is likely to increase. Offshore exploration is also taking place in the Black Sea, the Aegean Sea and off the Libyan coast. New techniques and the moderate depths of the Red Sea and the Gulf may soon lead to the recovery of mineral deposits from the sea-bed. The variety of marine life is considerable and most Mediterranean and Middle Eastern countries are making strenuous efforts to develop their fisheries. At the same time, the tourist potential of the coasts and seas is being developed for the benefit of an increasingly mobile and prosperous local population, as well as anticipated increases in overseas visitors. Parts of the eastern Mediterranean have already developed beach tourism, but other parts, notably in the Red Sea and the Gulf, could evolve entirely new types of holiday which might combine the desert safari with coastal cruises to places of historical interest. Interest in archaeology throughout the Middle East and North Africa gains momentum all the time, both on account of the region's glorious past and because of the appeal of its superb ruins. Significantly, the nascent discipline of underwater archaeology has developed in the waters of the Middle East where so much remains to be discovered.[15] Several Arab countries in Southwest Asia have not encouraged tourism, but it is to be hoped that one day visitors will be welcomed. Tourist revenues will be relatively insignificant, except perhaps in Syria, Lebanon and Jordan, so that many of the host countries have a unique opportunity to confine the number of visitors to the absolute capacity of the amenities they come to enjoy.

The Middle East is beginning to experience some of the environmental problems associated with advanced industrial economies. Rapid growth of urban centres since the end of the Second World War has produced a few cities, often national capitals, which dwarf all others in the state. Accompanying this process has been a rise in urban standards of living, with the introduction of modern methods of industrial production and transportation. The number of cars and lorries in towns and cities has increased enormously, while sprawling industrial development is now characteristic of the outskirts of the larger urban centres.

The serious effects of such rapid growth on the environment have not always been appreciated. Large areas of cultivated or potentially cultivable flat land have been swallowed up by the expansion of many cities. The growing concentrations of population have severely strained locally available resources, particularly of fresh water. This has necessitated large-scale capital investment in new projects in an attempt to overcome the severe water shortages often experienced during the summer. Linked to fresh water supply is the problem of sewage disposal. Until about 1960, most of the cities of the region did not possess any form of organized sewage removal or treatment system. A decade later the situation has been little improved in many countries, for while new and efficient sewage systems are being built for the largest cities, most others are not likely to obtain sewage treatment facilities within the next ten years. It is increasingly likely that water supplies will be polluted

In many places, especially where industrial development has become important, new pollutants are beginning to cause ecological damage. Petrochemicals and other chemical waste products present the greatest dangers to what are often very fragile ecosystems. Pollution by solid waste from urban centres is another growing problem throughout the region. Waste disposal methods are generally primitive. The usual practice is either to throw domestic and industrial refuse into the nearest water course, whether dry or flowing with water, or to tip it indiscriminately just outside the city boundaries. Once again, the risk of disease is very real.

Regrettably, atmospheric pollution is already characteristic of the Middle Eastern urban environment. Exhaust fumes from automobiles are probably the greatest single cause of this nuisance, but domestic and industrial consumption of hydrocarbons is also an important contributory factor. In winter, Ankara is frequently blanketed by a thick brown smog which collects in its enclosed basin as a result of temperature inversions and the use of lignite in central heating systems. Photochemical smog is now apparent in the larger cities during the hot summer months, and it is likely to grow worse because of the lax regulations governing automobile exhaust emissions. Closely associated with automobile and air pollution is the growing amount of urban noise and its deleterious effect on the inhabitants. From this point of view, cities such as Cairo, Tehrān, Tel Aviv, Beirūt and İstanbul are now as unpleasant to visit and work in as London or New York. The tranquillity and charm which recently characterized Jerusalem and Esfahān, for example, have been lost, possibly for ever.

0.5 Perspective

The authors of this book cannot claim to be free from prejudice or to have attained perfect knowledge, but in discussing the geography of the Middle East they hope to display reasonable sympathy with the people of the region. Their object is to deal with the region as it is today. An historical perspective is used only where it has direct bearing on the present situation. The contention is that the region is as vital in world affairs towards the end of the twentieth century as it ever was. It is still one of the major stages of the 'Great Debate' between West and East, and the source of considerable political friction, as well as a danger to world peace. But the Middle East is a region eminently worth studying in its own right. It was one of the major hearths of civilization and the birthplace of Judaism, Christianity and Islam. Man/land relationships are particularly close, and, whilst the physical environment has affected human activity profoundly, man has in turn left a deep imprint on the land in his struggle for survival. The settlement history of the region has demonstrated both man's destructive capacity and his ability to derive a reasonable living, when he adjusts to his environment with skill and ingenuity. The testimony of the Middle Eastern landscapes should be more widely known in an age of ecological concern. Although the region's social and economic life was once markedly more advanced than that of Europe, the Middle East is now one of the less-developed parts of the world. The long decay experienced by the region and its recent efforts to revive itself are a fascinating study.

The approach to regional geography used here is broadly conventional. The first part of the book deals with themes on a regional scale. It begins with discussions of the fixed and dynamic elements in the physical environment and man's interaction with them over time. This provides the setting for an analysis of socio-economic activity, including land use. General problems of population growth and economic development are discussed as a prelude to an outline of modern industrial development and contemporary trading patterns and an evaluation of the role of petroleum in the region. The final section, introduced by an essay on the political geography of the region, consists of ten studies which explore the geography of the modern states comprising the region as functional subregions. The approach in these chapters is thematic. Themes of human geography outlined in the first half of the work are studied in some detail and are chosen to illuminate the personality and

16

evolution of the countries concerned. Physical geography is largely assumed in these chapters, but its role has frequently been crucial in this often ecologically fragile region.

References

1. R. H. Davidson, 'Where is the Middle East?', *Foreign Affairs*, **38**, 665–675 (1960).
2. V. Chirol, 'The quest for the Middle East', *The Times*, beginning 14 October 1902, reprinted as *The Middle East Question, or Some Political Problems of Indian Defence*, John Murray, London, 1903.
3. *Parliamentary Debates, House of Lords*, 5th Series, **7**, col. 575.
4. C. G. Smith, 'The emergence of the Middle East', *Journal of Contemporary History*, **3**, 3–17 (1968).
5. P. Lorraine, 'Perspectives of the Near East', *Geogr. J.*, **102**, 6–13 (1943).
   L. Martin, 'The miscalled Middle East', *Geogr. Rev.*, **34**, 355–356 (1944).
6. (a) W. B. Fisher, 'Unity and diversity in the Middle East', *Geogr. Rev.*, **37**, 414–435 (1947).
   (b) R. Patai, 'The Middle East as a culture area', *Middle East Journal*, **6**, 1–21 (1952), reprinted in *Readings in Arab Middle East society and cultures*, A. M. Lutfiyya and C. W. Churchill (Eds), Mouton, Paris and The Hague, 1970,187–204.
7. *Qur'ān*, II, 192f.
8. G. B. Cressey, *Crossroads: Land and Life in Southwest Asia*, J. B. Lippincott Co., Chicago, 1960.
9. The Association for Peace, *The Middle East in the Year 2000*, Tel Aviv, 1969, 1–40.
10. W. Laqueur, *The Struggle for the Middle East. The Soviet Union and the Middle East 1958–69*, Penguin, Harmondsworth, 1972, 221.
11. 'Conservation du milieu maritime Méditerranéen', *Telex Méditerranée* (Supplement to No. 41), Brussels, 1–6 (11 February 1974).
12. J. Power, 'Threat to rural life and economy from large labour migration', *The Times*, 24 September 1973.
13. (a) N. Daniel, *Islam, Europe and Empire*, Edinburgh University Press, Edinburgh, 1966.
    (b) B. Lewis, *The Middle East and the West*, Weidenfeld and Nicolson, London, 1964.
14. M. Chisholm, *Research in Human Geography*, Social Science Research Council, Heinemann, London, 1971, 71–72.
15. UNESCO, *Underwater Archaeology*, Paris, 1972.

CHAPTER 1

Relief, Geology, Geomorphology and Soils

1.1 Relief

In a region as large and diverse as the Middle East, it is difficult to describe topographical conditions in a simple way. However, relief factors have played an important and often directly controlling role on the human occupancy of the region, and it is, therefore, essential that at least a brief sketch is given of the major features. For convenience the region can be divided into a northern mountainous belt, comprising the states of Turkey and Iran, and a southern zone made up largely of plains and dissected plateaus (Figure 1.1).

In Turkey, two major, though not continuous, mountain belts are usually recognized. The Pontus Mountains are an interrupted chain of highlands paralleling the Black Sea coast. They rise in altitude in an easterly direction to heights of more than 3,000 m south of Rize. Inland from the southern coast of Turkey is the much more formidable range of the Taurus Mountains. Being less dissected by river systems than their northern counterparts, these uplands have always presented a considerable barrier to human movement, so focusing routes through passes such as the Cilisian Gates, to the northwest of Adana. Between the two ranges the central or Anatolian Plateau lies sandwiched. This is almost everywhere about 500 m in height and relatively isolated from the coastal regions.

In eastern Turkey the Pontus and Taurus ranges coalesce in a complex upland massif near Mount Ararat (5,165 m) where crest elevations surpass 3,000 m. From here eastwards into Iran the mountain chains divide once more. In the north along the southern shore of the Caspian Sea are the Elburz Mountains, which in Mount Damavand (5,610 m) contain the highest peak of the region. Although these uplands are relatively narrow in a north to south direction, they present the greatest barrier to human movement anywhere in the Middle East. Southwards from Mount Ararat, overlooking the Tigris-Euphrates lowlands and the Gulf, stretch the broad Zagros Mountains. They attain a maximum height of 4,548 m in Zard Kuh. These parallel ranges with their wide upland valleys have never presented the same degree of difficulty of movement as the Elburz.

In eastern Iran, on the borders of Afghanistan, a very complex pattern of mountain ranges, usually described as the Eastern Iranian Highlands, are found. These are lower than both the Elburz and Zagros Mountains, attaining only 2,500 m in altitude. Surrounded by these highlands is the Central Plateau of Iran. This, like the Anatolian Plateau, is almost everywhere above 500 m

17

18

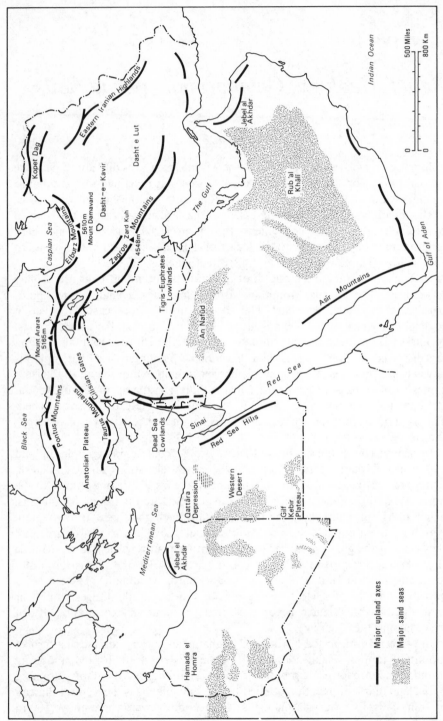

Figure 1.1 Major relief features of the Middle East

in height, and is subdivided into two major basins both of inland drainage. The Dasht-e-Kavir forms a huge salt desert in the north, while the term Dasht-e-Lut is used for the southern basin.

In the southern region of plains and dissected plateaus a useful east/west division can be made along the line of the Red Sea and the Suez Canal. In eastern Egypt the Red Sea Hills are the major upland area, while the Nile delta forms the major lowland. To the west, a relatively simple topographical picture can be drawn, with narrow lowlands along the coast rising inland to upland plateaus along the southern margins of Libya and Egypt. Even on these interior plateaus heights of more than 1,000 m are rarely surpassed. Large sand seas form important landscape features in this zone. An important exception to this general description is the existence of a small upland zone, the Gebel el Akhdar, in northeast Libya. Although only some 1,000 m in height this region has played an important role in the human settlement of the region.

To the east of the Red Sea the highest land in this zone is found at the southwestern corner of the Arabian peninsula. Here in Yemen altitudes of more than 3,700 m are attained. Highland also occurs along the whole of the western part of Arabia, with the general level of the land declining to the north and east. In central Arabia, characteristic features of the relief are a series of westward facing escarpments, in arc-like form around the main highland mass of the west coast. Although none of these landforms are particularly high they have concentrated the routes across the peninsula towards the regions of most easy access. In the Levant, upland areas are found in proximity to the coast, with a gradual decline in altitude towards the interior. Heights here too can be considerable, reaching almost 3,000 m at Mount Hermōn. The pattern of relief in this region is complicated by the existence of the north-south fault zone of the Dead Sea Lowlands, which has dissected the upland belt to form a trough-like region descending to 300 m below sea level.

Stretching from northern Iraq to the coast of the Indian Ocean in Oman is the largest lowland belt of the region. In Iraq it is crossed by the large rivers Tigris and Euphrates and in the southern parts relief is minimal. Some of the oldest human settlement in the world is found here. The lowland belt continues as an attenuated zone along the western shore of the Gulf to broaden into an extensive plain in southeastern Arabia. In this latter zone the largest sand sea in the world, the Rub'al Khālī, is situated. Here some of the dunes are more than 200 m in height. At the easternmost tip of Arabia, a belt of uplands, also called Gebel al Akhdar ('Green Mountain') reach a maximum height of more than 3,000 m. This region has always been an extremely isolated part of the region cut off by both sand and water from adjacent areas.

1.2 Geology

Over the last decade our knowledge of the evolution of the continental masses has increased tremendously owing to detailed geological and geophysical investigations in many parts of the world. As a result of this work new theories of sea floor spreading and plate tectonics have been put forward, and widely accepted by most earth scientists.[1] The basic idea of these new theories is that the continental masses are embedded in huge plates which move over the denser material beneath the earth's crust. These plates, and the continents on top of them, travel across the surface of the earth probably as the result of convectional currents acting deep within the earth. This movement can lead to the plates coming into contact with one another, so producing crush zones, or mountain ranges. In such contact zones, parts of one or other of the colliding plates are dragged down towards the centre of the earth, along what are termed Benioff or subduction zones. In contrast, where two plates are moving away from one another, upwelling of magma occurs usually beneath the ocean floors, to produce sea floor spreading.

Geologically speaking, the Middle East and North Africa is a particularly complex region, as a number of different continental plates have come into contact here. North Africa and Arabia represent the remnants of an ancient continental landmass in the southern hemisphere known as Gondwanaland. During the Mesozoic period this landmass, composed mainly of Palaeozoic and older rocks, began to split up and drift northwards. Eventually these moving continental plates made contact with a similar landmass in the northern hemisphere, known as Laurasia. When this occurred, probably during the Tertiary period, the younger sediments which had formed between and over-lapped onto the ancient and stable continental platforms in the Tethyan Sea, buckled and contorted as the result of compressive stresses to produce the mountain ranges which stretch through the region from the Alps to the Himalayas. Although this simple picture of events gives a reasonable idea of what happened, a glance at a detailed geological map illustrates just how complex the real situation is. Indeed, it is still true to say that the exact inter-relationships of the different continental plates in the region are not known with any degree of certainty.

In the Mediterranean and Middle Eastern region three major plates can be identified. These are the African, Eurasian and Arabian plates, and the boundaries between them are the Azores-Gibraltar ridge and its extension across North Africa, the Red Sea, and the Alpide zone of Iran (Figure 1.2).[2] Seismic activity in Yugoslavia, Greece and Turkey is much more pronounced than in the western Mediterranean. The reason for this appears to be the existence of two small, but rapidly moving plates, named the Aegean and Turkish plates respectively. Observations reveal that the Aegean plate is moving towards the southwest relative to both the European and African plates. As a result of its motion, it is overthrusting the Mediterranean Sea floor south of the Cretan arc and thus causing it to sink beneath the Aegean Sea.

The Turkish plate is moving almost due westwards with respect to the Eurasian and African plates. Its northern boundary is the North Anatolian fault, but the southern limit is not fully defined. The existence of these two small plates and the role they play in the regional tectonics is possibly explained

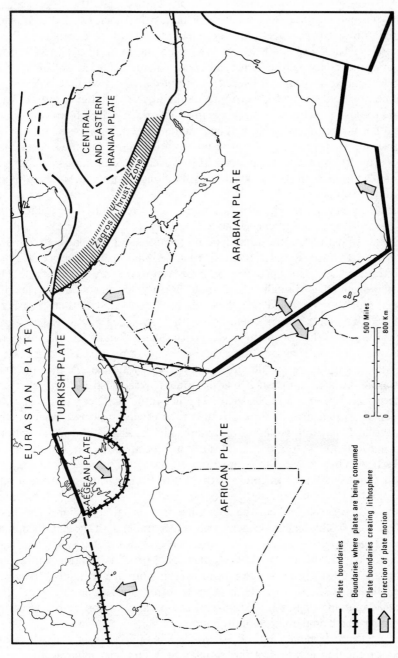

Figure 1.2 Structural units in the Middle East (Modified by permission of *Nature* 1970, 1970)

by differences in behaviour between continental and oceanic lithosphere. Material forming the continents is light in density and, therefore, cannot be drawn down into the denser mantle of the earth. When two plates of such material come into contact tremendous energy has to be expended against gravitational forces to thicken the continental crust and so permit crustal shortening. In contrast, the same end result can be achieved and much less energy expended if oceanic lithosphere, composed of denser material, can be consumed by being dragged down into the mantle. This latter is indeed what appears to be happening with the Aegean and Turkish plates, for their motion is such that further overthrusting of continental material is avoided in Turkey, and, instead, Mediterranean Sea floor is consumed in front of the Cretan arc.[3] In this way the observed movements of the Aegean and Turkish plates are such as to minimize the work which must be done to move the African plate towards the Eurasian one.

Further south in the region it has been discovered that three plates also meet towards the southern end of the Red Sea. These are the African, Arabian and Somalian plates.[4] In this area it would seem that all the plates are moving away from each other, and that the Red Sea and Gulf of Aden have been formed as the result of sea floor spreading as Arabia moved away from Africa. The rate of movement is thought to be about 1 cm/yr on each side of the rift. Detailed work in the Dead Sea lowlands has revealed that there has been about 100 km left lateral movement on the Dead Sea Fault system since Miocene times.[5] What seems to have occurred here is that the Arabian plate has moved northward relative to the small and apparently fixed Sinai plate.[6]

In Iran it would appear that the northwards motion of Arabia towards Eurasia has been accomplished by widespread overthrusting in a belt from southern Iran to the central Caspian. The net result has been to thicken the continental crust over large areas. Iran can be divided into two regions: the Zagros folded belt, and the rest of the country. In the Zagros region continuous sedimentation under tranquil conditions has occurred from Cambrian to late Tertiary times, when the sediments were folded into a series of parallel anticlines and synclines.[7] In contrast, the rest of Iran has suffered more severe epeirogenic movements, as well as considerable igneous and metamorphic activity. Three provinces can be identified in this latter region. The first, the Reza'īyeh–Eşfandegheh orogenic belt runs parallel with the Zagros mountains and unites with the Taurus orogenic belt of Turkey. It is separated from the Zagros Mountains by the Zagros crush zone, which is an area of thrusting and faulting. Central and eastern Iran, a fault bounded, roughly triangular shaped region with its apex in the south, forms the second province. The Elburz Mountains of northern Iran and the parallel region to the south of them make up the final division of the country.

The northward movement of Africa and Arabia during the Mesozoic caused a reduction in width of the Tethyan Sea. This was achieved by a subduction zone which consumed oceanic crust. Eventually at some time during the late Cretaceous all the oceanic crust disappeared into the mantle and the leading edges of the African and Arabian plates reached the subduction zone. When this occurred ophiolites were emplaced along the Zagros crush zone at the leading margin of the Arabian plate.[8] The Zagros sedimentary basin, the present Zagros Mountains, continued as the shelf of the old Afro-Arabian continent, with continuing sedimentation, mostly of a carbonate nature.

Although relatively little drift occurred in Eurasia during the Mesozoic period, it was sufficient to cause a partial break-up of the northern continents. This led to the formation of micro-continents, such as central and eastern Iran, which were separated by narrow oceanic areas of the Red Sea type. Continued northerly drift of the African and Arabian plates during the early Tertiary resulted in the closure of these basins and the emplacement of melange complexes along their former axes. Eventually, therefore, the continental plates of Eurasia, Africa and Arabia became connected by a series of micro-continents, with only a few shelf seas still existing in the region. At this time, to the east, the northward movement of the Indian plate was underthrusting Eurasia, and giving rise to the Himalayan ranges.

Yet another period of compression occurred in the late Tertiary period, associated with the formation of the Red Sea and Gulf of Aden, and also the southeastwards movement of Eurasia. These movements, which are continuing at the present day, led to the underthrusting of Iran by the Arabian plate and resulted in the complex folding of the Zagros Mountains, together with folding and faulting in other parts of the country.

Bearing the above outline in mind, the distribution of rocks of different ages is relatively simple to explain, at least in general terms. The oldest rocks, of Pre-Cambrian and Palaeozoic age, are found on the stable masses of both North Africa and Arabia, with occasional smaller outcrops occurring in other places throughout the region. These basement complex rocks are only exposed, however, on a large scale in eastern Egypt and western Saudi Arabia (Figure 1.3).

Northwards, progressively younger rocks, mostly of sedimentary origin, which have overlapped onto the basement complex, as it was downwarped during its northwards passage, are found. In general the older sedimentary rocks of both North Africa and Arabia tend to be of continental origin and are represented by such rock types as the famous Nubian Sandstone. Further north still, as one moves into the Levant region and also southern Iran, marine sediments, in particular limestones and marls of Mesozoic age, make up a much larger proportion of the outcrop. These sediments, it is believed, were deposited in the Tethyan Sea, between the respective remnants of Gondwanaland and Laurasia. Calcareous sediments such as these have tremendous importance in the economic life of the region, for it is in these rocks that the oil reserves are concentrated. For example, in Iran, the Asmari Limestone is the most important reservoir rock for petroleum accumulation.

Rocks of Tertiary age, mostly marine sands, clays, marls and limestones, although some continental deposits also do occur, tend to be confined to the lowest lying areas of the region. In particular, sediments of this period are

24

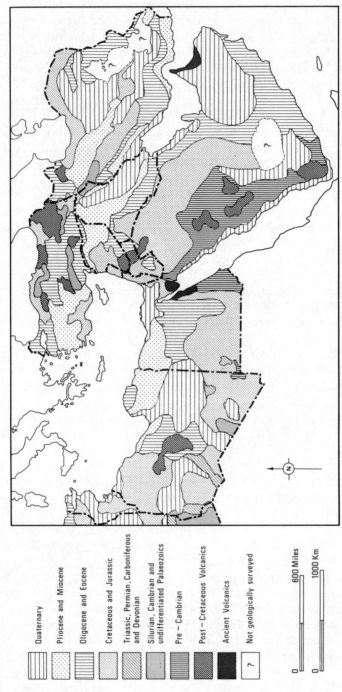

Figure 1.3 Geology of the Middle East (Reproduced by permission of Oxford University Press)

Quaternary

Pliocene and Miocene

Oligocene and Eocene

Cretaceous and Jurassic

Triassic, Permian, Carboniferous and Devonian

Silurian, Cambrian and undifferentiated Palaeozoics

Pre – Cambrian

Post – Cretaceous Volcanics

Ancient Volcanics

Not geologically surveyed

0 600 Miles

0 1000 Km

found extensively along the North African coast in Libya and Egypt, as well as along a wide zone paralleling the Gulf. More restricted outcrops of Tertiary rocks also occur in the inland basins of Iran and Turkey.

Thick Quaternary sediments, almost all of which are unconsolidated, are confined to the upland basins of the highland zone, and the major valley systems of such rivers as the Tigris–Euphrates and the Nile.

A characteristic feature of the region is the widespread occurrence of eruptive rocks, chiefly basalts. They are found associated with zones of structural weakness, especially in the highland zones of Turkey and Iran, and also adjacent to the major faulting zones of the Dead Sea Lowlands and Red Sea regions.

Perfectly formed volcanic peaks, from which lava flows radiate, are seen in Mount Ararat and Mount Damavand in Turkey and Iran respectively. In other places lava upwelling has occurred along fissures rather than from single vents. Such is the case around the Jebel ed Druze in Syria, and in the uplands of western Saudi Arabia. Although all the different lava fields have not been investigated in detail, most of them appear to be geologically young, dating from the Tertiary to the historical period.

Owing to the tectonic instability of much of the region, earthquakes, with epicentres along the major plate boundaries, are of common occurrence (Figure 1.4). Throughout history these natural hazards have had considerable impact on human activity in those regions affected by them.

1.3 Geomorphology

In the Middle East catastrophic geomorphic events play an important role in the evolution of landforms, and at the same time greatly influence human activity. Most of these events occur during the season of maximum precipitation, and are a direct result of water action. In upland areas, landslides and mudflows are common occurrences on unstable slopes with little vegetation cover, while more generally, floods can devastate river valleys and lowland areas.

Despite the aridity which prevails over much of the region, fluvial action tends to be the most important geomorphic process, even though it might operate on only a few days per year in the more desertic parts. The effect of the wind, however, should not be ignored, although the results of its action are rarely spectacular. Large sand seas do exist in Arabia, Libya, Egypt and Iran, but their total area is only a small proportion of the region. With the long dry season which prevails almost everywhere during summer, wind action often plays a significant role in the movement of large quantities of fine grained material, leaving behind concentrations of coarse grained sediments. Loessic deposits are common throughout the eastern parts of the Middle East.

The study of weathering within the region, as with the study of landforms, is still limited. In Iran salt weathering has been discovered to be an important process in the breakdown of rocks crossing the alluvial fans and plains on the margin of the Dasht-e-Kavir.[9] Further evidence of the importance of

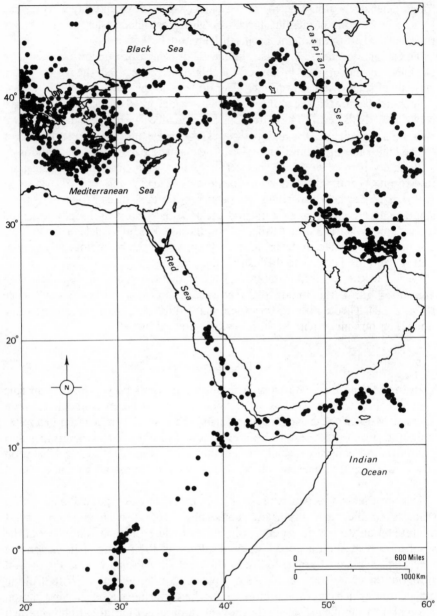

Figure 1.4 Epicentres of recent earthquakes in the Middle East (Reproduced by permission of *Nature*)

such a process is found in a description of parallel stone cracking on pavement surfaces in the Sinai desert.[10] Here, as in the Iranian example, the growth of gypsum and salt crystals in fine crevices seems to be the prime cause.

The complex physical nature of the Middle East makes it extremely difficult to generalize about landform types. It is, however, useful to employ the concept of a simple basin model to provide a framework with which to look at both the physical and the human environment. In its simplest form the basin is divided into four zones (Figure 1.5). These are upland, alluvial fan, alluvial plain, and salt lake or salt desert.

The upland zone is characterized by the outcrop of usually resistant rock types and very steep slopes. The amplitude of relief may be hundreds or even thousands of metres. Weathering profiles are thin or absent, and coarse scree-like material mantles the lower slope segments. The river valleys tend

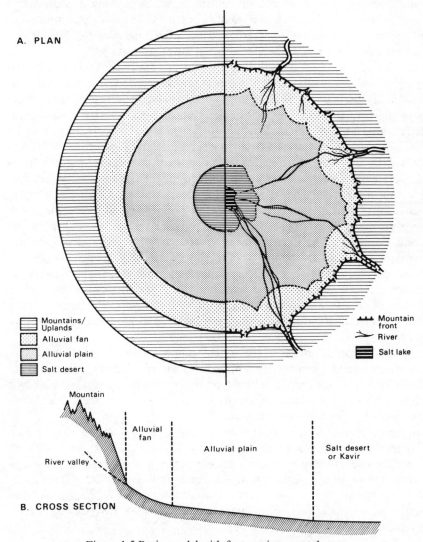

Figure 1.5 Basin model with four environmental zones

to be flat floored, owing to the deposition of material eroded from the adjacent slopes. Freeze–thaw action is an important weathering phenomenon, and consequently angular debris is common. In general, this is a zone of maximum erosive activity as the result of severe weathering conditions, mass movement on the steep slopes, and considerable fluvial activity along the major valley systems.

The three other morphological zones are essentially depositional in nature. The alluvial fan zone is situated at the margin of the upland zone and is characterized by slopes with angles between about 15 degrees and three degrees. Amplitude of relief is usually very low. Coarse material, both angular and rounded, makes up most of the alluvial fan zone. Deposition of sediment is brought about by both fluvial and mudflow activity. In most cases, mudflows from the upland areas only penetrate to the upper parts of the fan region, while river flows often continue onto the two lower zones as well.

The alluvial plain and the salt desert zones are really continuations of the alluvial fan zone. The alluvial plain possesses lower angle slopes than the fans, and, in many parts of the Middle East, forms the major morphological zone. It is chiefly formed by the depositional action of running water, but aeolian activity is also important here. The finer surface material is commonly removed by the wind, leaving a stone or desert pavement behind. The sediment carried or moved by the wind is subsequently redeposited as loess or as sand dunes in the lower parts of this zone, or on the margins of the adjacent salt desert.

The salt lake, or salt desert zone, only occurs in basins with no drainage outlets. Material in this zone is normally fine grained, of silt or clay size, with the coarser material having been deposited during its passage over the alluvial fan and plain zones. Salt crusts are often found on the ground surface and saline deposits occur in the soil profile. Slopes are very gentle, usually less than one degree, and as a consequence water bodies are very shallow and cover extensive areas. Water movement into this zone from adjacent uplands takes place mostly in late winter and early spring as the snow pack begins to melt. By late summer all standing water has normally evaporated and salt crusts are formed.

In any one region, not all of the zones outlined above may be found. Undoubtedly the model can be best applied in Iran and Turkey, but elsewhere also the ideas and concepts generated by it are of value. The Dasht-e-Kavir of central Iran and the basin of the River Jordan provide excellent environmental units for illustrating the model.

Our knowledge of environmental and climatic changes in the Middle East during the Quaternary era is still fragmentary. This makes it extremely difficult to correlate events there with those taking place in northwestern Europe at the same period. In this latter region, an accumulation of evidence from many sources has shown that the last glacial period, known as the Wisconsin–Würm–Weichsel, occurred between about 70,000 years and 10,000 BP (Before Present), and was followed by the Holocene Period.

During the latter part of the Wisconsin–Würm–Weichsel period, between 25,000 years and 15,000 years ago approximately, a major ice advance occurred, which, at its maximum, covered a large proportion of the northern hemisphere. The nature of the changes which occurred beyond the ice front, in places such as the Middle East, still remain largely unknown, owing to the paucity of research work which has been carried out there.

Early workers postulated climatic changes on a large scale, which they claimed had a fundamental effect on the geomorphic processes operating in the region. Pluvial periods, that is times with higher precipitation than at present, were considered to have occurred in the Middle East contemporaneously with glacial activity in northwest Europe. More recent work, however, has shown that the pattern is much more complex than this, and that perhaps different conditions prevailed in different areas at the same period.[11] The lack of evidence from large large parts of the region makes it difficult, though, to be precise in drawing detailed conclusions.

Information on the Nile Valley has been greatly enhanced over the last few years as the result of work on the Aswân High Dam as well as by continued archaeological investigations.[12] Studies of alluvial deposits in Egypt have been used for two main purposes. Small wadi deposits provide an indication of local climatological conditions, while flood-plain sediments of the Nile record environmental events, particularly summer monsoonal rainfall, in Ethiopia. Evidence of pluvial conditions in southern Egypt, possibly about 60,000 years ago, is provided by the Wadi Floor Conglomerate, which overlies bedrock along many wadi floors. At the time of the accumulation of this deposit there is no evidence for higher Nile flood levels, which would be indicative of pluvial conditions in Ethiopia.

The Korosko Formation, consisting of Nile silts, was deposited between 50,000 and 25,000 years ago. During the first part of this cycle, pluvial conditions still continued in southern Egypt, while at the same time increased precipitation in Ethiopia produced greater floods along the Nile. Later, pluvial activity in Egypt declined, although even higher flood levels were recorded down the Nile river system. This lack of complete agreement between environmental conditions in south Egypt and the source of the Blue Nile in Ethiopia seems characteristic of the latter part of the Pleistocene Period.

During the time of maximum Wisconsin–Würm–Weichsel glaciation in northwest Europe, that is between 25,000 to 15,000 years BP, the climate in southern Egypt appears to have been arid, as it is today, while at the same time comparatively wet conditions prevailed in Ethiopia. In the 10,000 years following 15,000 years BP, the discharge of the Nile apparently increased, as too did wadi incision in southern Egypt. This latter fact is taken to indicate the return of pluvial conditions in that region.

Nile flood levels began to decrease in the third millenium BC, and local wadi activity also declined in intensity. Since this period the climate of southern Egypt has remained intensely arid. The lowest Nile floods appear to have been recorded between 2,350 BC and 800 BC, with slightly less arid conditions prevailing since that time.

Although similar sequences of alluvial deposits exist throughout the Tigris-Euphrates basin, their chronological significance has not yet been deciphered in any detail. So far the most detailed work on the Euphrates comes from Syria, where late Pleistocene and Holocene terraces have been described.[13] Terrace suites on the Tigris above Baghdād are also known to exist.[14]

Pleistocene stratigraphy has been particularly well studied in the basin of the River Jordan.[15] Here, the main sequence of sediments, known as the Lisan Marls, are believed to be late Pleistocene in age and to have been deposited in a huge lake over 300 km in length, which possessed a water level about 200 m above that of the present Dead Sea. Following the maximum development of the lake, more arid conditions occurred, and the lake decreased in size. With a lowering of water surface elevation a sequence of shorelines were cut in the Lisan Marls at many different heights down to the present level of the Dead Sea.

Glacial activity at the present day is confined to a few small corrie glaciers and permanent snow patches in the Pontus and Taurus ranges and the Armenian Plateau of Turkey, as well as on Mounts Savalan, Suleiman and Damavand in the Elburz Mountains of Iran. In Turkey the contemporary snowline reaches a minimum height of about 3,200 m in the northern part of the Pontus Range, rising inland to more than 4,000 m, while in Iran it appears to be slightly higher at between 4,000 and 4,300 m.[16] During the Pleistocene it seems that the glaciers grew larger and that new ones came into being in other upland regions. The actual amount by which the snowline was depressed during this period is still the subject of considerable controversy. Values of 800 to 1,200 m have been reported for Turkey,[17] while in parts of the Zagros it is claimed to have been at least 1,200 m.[18] Morphological evidence for such advances remains in the form of numerous retreat moraines along the higher valleys of Turkey[19] and of the Elburz range of Iran.[20]

In the Zagros Mountains, Pleistocene shorelines have been identified around Lake Rezā'īyeh up to 20 m above the present lake level.[21] From hydrological studies it was concluded that a 5°C lowering of mean annual temperature would be sufficient to explain a lake volume 10 times that found today, without the necessity of any increase in precipitation.

One of the most important works of regional geomorphological significance in an upland region concerns the origin of transverse drainage lines in the Zagros Mountains.[22] In this work it was postulated that the transverse gorge systems are the result of normal fluvial development in certain structural–lithological environments. The critical type of environment seems to be a succession of limestones and flysch deposits which have been subjected to orogenic activity to produce *en echelon* anticline groups. With this view older ideas suggesting single mechanisms operating on a regional scale, such as superimposition of a drainage pattern, or the development of antecedent drainage, are considered incorrect.

In western Saudi Arabia a well-developed pediplain, the Najd, developed on Pre-Cambrian crystalline rocks with isolated inselbergs rising above it, has been mapped.[23] As parts of the pediplain are covered with early Tertiary lavas, the surface must predate this period. Parts of it may well be a Pre-Cambrian surface which has been buried and subsequently exhumed. An important period of erosion and planation seems also to have occurred in middle Tertiary times and this has caused modifications to the forms of the earlier surfaces.

Erosion surfaces have also been identified further north along the rift of the Dead Sea Lowlands.[24] Three high level surfaces at 1,650 m, 1,200 m and 900 m are found, with the lowest, the Sinai or Arabia surface, extending far into central Arabia. This lowest surface is thought to have been formed prior to the formation of the main rift system, and to be of most probably Upper Oligocene age. A series of much smaller surfaces and terraces are described below 600 m, mostly identifiable along the margins of the rift system.

Salt deserts have been studied in detail in Iran by a number of workers. The classic work in this field is on the Dasht-e-Kavir of the Central Plateau.[25] In this it is claimed that the Kavir is not a relict landform, but one which is actually forming under present day environmental conditions. To prove this assertion a number of examples of where kavir fill of silt and clay sized material is transgressing over the adjacent eroded surfaces of *dasht* (gravel desert) are quoted. This rise in the level of the kavir fill, it is suggested, has been caused by a climatic change which has resulted in more humid conditions. The date of such a change is unknown, but it is believed to have been preceded by earlier drier periods, when erosional processes dominated. Early views on the origin of the Dasht-e-Kavir considered it to have been an enormous lake or closed-in part of a Tertiary sea, which was later reduced to a mudfilled basin as hydrological conditions changed.[26] More recent research, however, revealed that most of the marginal surfaces of the Kavir were erosional in origin with series of anticlines and synclines truncated by the processes of erosion. Further work in the same region confirms the idea that no widespread lakes existed in the Dasht-e-Kavir during the Pleistocene period.[27] It is also concluded that the Pleistocene climate of northern Iran was similar to that of the present day, with the exception that the precipitation evapotranspiration ratio was higher owing to lower summer temperatures.

A considerable body of research has been carried out in the Middle East on alluvial deposits of Tertiary and Quaternary age fringing the major upland regions. These deposits are often of very great thicknesses, upwards of 300 m, and would seem to indicate continued continental sedimentation over very long periods of time. In a series of papers dealing with alluvial deposits along the southern slopes of the Elburz Mountains three major alluvial formations of post-Upper Miocene age have been identified.[28] The oldest, between 100 and 120 m in thickness, is named the Hezardarrah Formation. It has often been subjected to folding and is correlated with the Mio-Pliocene or Pliocene Bakhtiari Formation of the main oil producing region of Iran. Overlying this is the Kahrizak Formation. This is much thinner, rarely more than 60 m in thickness, but it too has been subjected to folding and faulting. Its age is estimated to be mid-Quaternary. Finally, the youngest formation, the Tehrān Alluvium, is generally less than 35 m in thickness and has been relatively unaffected by orogenic activity.

The dating of recent alluvial material, and the land forms to which they give rise, still poses considerable problems. Two phases of alluvial deposition are widely recognized in the Middle East.[29] In Iran, the earlier phase began no more than 50,000 years ago and had probably ended by the fourth millenium BC. This was followed by a period of erosion, after which a second phase of deposition occurred during the Middle Ages. At the present time this deposit is being eroded. Detailed work on a number of alluvial fans near Tehrān suggests that sedimentary deposition over the last 750 years has been of only minor importance, and that optimum conditions for fan formation probably occurred during the glacial phases of the Quaternary.[30] Almost all the fans, particularly the larger ones, show evidence of fan-head trenching. This has meant that the upper portions of the fans cannot be alluviated under present conditions. Some deposition is currently occurring on the lower parts of the fans but the dominant processes appear to be largely erosional in nature.

In the Konya basin of central Turkey, research suggests that present environmental conditions are not responsible for the major geomorphological features.[31] Such features, including abandoned shorelines, wave-cut cliffs, sandspits and deltas, all testify to lacustrinal conditions during the recent geological past. Studies of the fauna of the lacustrinal sediments suggest that the water was fresh, even though it had no outlet. Archaeological evidence shows that the basin was largely dry by 8,500 years ago. At present depositional processes appear to be confined to alluvial fan formation along the margins of the basin. The total thickness of sediments within the basin is unknown, but boreholes have revealed that in some places it is at least 400 m.

Sea level changes also occurred during the Pleistocene period leaving behind well marked raised beaches in the Mediterranean Sea, Red Sea, and the Gulf. As yet few attempts have been made to correlate the differing levels which have been described in studies of local significance. An exception is found in the Mediterranean, where published work in the region has been reviewed over the last decade by the Mediterranean and Black Sea Shorelines Subcommission of INQUA, with the objective of trying to separate out reliable observations from those of a more doubtful character.[32]

In the Black Sea region eight distinct Quaternary shorelines have been re-recognized, ranging in height from 105 m to the present sea level.[33] A much more complex situation exists in the Mediterranean with no general agreement about correlation between the different areas, owing to the absence of diagnostic faunal assemblages. Shorelines have been described ranging from 200 m to 2 m above the present sea level, with many of these levels being recognized in the eastern Mediterranean region. In the Lebanon, high-level shorelines have been identified at 180–190 m, 110–120 m and at 60 m, together with a series of lower ones.[34]

1.4 Soil

Soil is one of the most vital natural resources of any region, for without it agricultural activity is not possible. It is also relatively easily destroyed by the careless actions of man. Certain basic factors can be thought of as controlling soil formation.[35] These are climate, parent material, vegetation, slope, hydrology, micro-organisms, man, and time. In a given region any one of these factors may have a dominating influence on the soil type produced, but, in general, parent material and climatic conditions are usually the most significant.

In a region like the Middle East, where arid conditions and in particular summer drought prevail almost everywhere, climate produces a characteristic stamp on the soils. One of the crucial climatically controlled factors in soil formation is the predominant direction of moisture in the soil profile. When it is downwards, the soluble products of weathering are carried through the soil and into streams and rivers. Such soils are known as pedalfers. In contrast, in arid climates these same weathering products accumulate in the upper layers of the soil, as water evaporates from the surface, to form salt, gypsum and calcium carbonate layers or nodules. The soils produced under these conditions are termed pedocals. In the Middle East, pedocal soils predominate in the more arid regions of the south, whilst pedalfers are commonly developed in the northern highland regions of Turkey and Iran, as well as in the Black and Caspian Sea lowlands where high annual precipitation totals occur.

Soil classification is still the subject of much controversy, even though increasing standardization is being introduced. Until recently, the Russian genetic classification into great soil groups, with subsequent modifications by North American workers, has been most used in the western world. As new information became available it was obvious that the modified Russian genetic classification, often known as the Great Soil Group classification, with its three major orders of zonal, intrazonal and azonal soils, was inadequate for detailed survey and research work. It was therefore decided in the United States that a new scheme should be established, and so there appeared in 1960 a publication entitled *Soil Classification: A Comprehensive System (7th Approximation)*.[36] This system, which is now the chief one employed in many parts of the world, is based on the morphological characteristics of the soil profile, particularly diagnostic horizons, and the sequence of occurrence of different horizons. The aim of the classification is to ensure that soils from any part of the world can be placed in their proper relation to each other. To facilitate this, an entirely new nomenclature has been introduced and ten major global orders recognized.

The final classification which has to be mentioned in the Middle East context is that established by FAO/UNESCO as the basis for their 1 : 5,000,000 soil map of the world.[37] This scheme includes ideas and information from both the major classifications already outlined, together with data on the suitability of a particular soil as a production resource. In this respect it has similarities with other methods employing land capability approaches. In all 103 soil units are recognized, which are grouped into 23 higher categories.[38]

All the above mentioned classification systems have been utilized at some time or other in the Middle East. By far the majority of the earlier soil studies made use of the Great Soil Group classification, but later work has tended to utilize either the 7th Approximation system or the FAO/UNESCO approach. For exploratory surveys in unknown areas land capability studies have often been the only feasible method.

In the Middle East, a number of soil types stand out as being of exceptional importance with regard to either their total area of occurrence or their agricultural productivity. In terms of the Great Soil Group classification these are Red Desert soils (including lithosols and sand); Sierozems (including lithosols and sand); Reddish Prairie, Reddish Chestnut and Reddish Brown soils; Terra Rossa, and Rendzinas; Chestnut and Brown soils; and alluvial soils (Figure 1.6).

The most widely occurring soils in the region are without doubt, the Red Desert soils, found throughout North Africa, much of Arabia and southern Iran. Owing to the dryness of the regions in which these soils are found, animal and plant growth within them is minimal and, as a consequence, the humus content is very low. Soil horizons are only poorly developed and the texture is coarse with many unweathered fragments of rock present.

Closely related to the Red Desert soil are the Sierozems, or Grey Desert soils. These soils are of more limited occurrence than their red counterparts, and are confined mainly to the northern and central parts of Iran where temperature conditions are cooler. They lack a marked profile, but are usually characterized by the accumulation of calcium carbonate just below the surface. In some cases, this has built up into a resistant layer known as caliche. Neither the Red Desert nor the Grey Desert soils are usually of great agricultural significance.

Reddish Prairie, Reddish Chestnut and Reddish Brown soils are found in the region of the 'Fertile Crescent' of northern Iraq and Syria. The Reddish Prairie soils represent a transitional type between the pedocals and the pedalfers. They appear to have been developed under grassland conditions and are usually extremely productive agriculturally, particularly for cereals. In slightly drier areas Reddish Chestnut and Reddish Brown soils occur. These seem to form under a range of vegetation conditions, but all show the development of a calcium carbonate horizon at depth.

Of exceptional agricultural importance are Terra Rossa soils. These develop on hard, pure crystalline limestones under a Mediterranean climatic regime, and occur extensively in Turkey, Syria, Lebanon, Jordan, Israel and Libya. Although found on limestone parent material, they possess little or no free

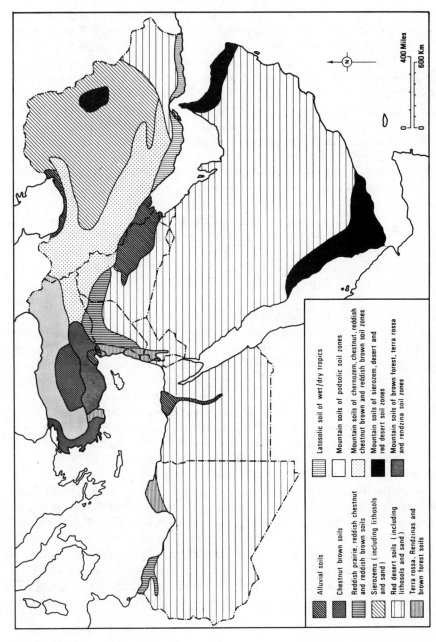

Figure 1.6 Soil groups of the Middle East

lime and their pH values are between seven and eight. The deep red colour of these soils is thought to be due to the presence of sesquioxides of iron in considerable quantities. Their clay content is commonly above 50 per cent and, because of this, their moisture holding capacity is good. The structure of the soil is particularly unstable when water is added, breaking down to a paste-like consistency, which greatly reduces the infiltration capacity of the underlying soil layers. These soils are, therefore, very susceptible to erosion when the vegetation cover is removed. Following long continued erosion, bare limestone hills remain in many parts of the region, with only traces of soil being found in the deeper joints between the limestone blocks.

The actual soil-forming processes associated with Terra Rossa development are still not fully understood.[39] Chemical weathering of the limestone to produce an insoluble residue is the fundamental process, and this occurs mainly during the wet winter season, along cracks and fissures in the rock. Soil water charged with carbon dioxide in the form of carbonic acid is believed to be the major chemical agent. A characteristic feature of Terra Rossa soils is the very sharp weathering front between the base of the soil profile and the underlying limestone.

Rendzina soils possess dark grey or black surface layers overlying lighter coloured material which is highly calcareous. Such soils are found only on soft limestones and marls, usually in association with Terra Rossa soils which form on more resistant calcareous formations.

In the transitional zone between the true prairie or grassland soils and the arid or desert soils, Chestnut and Brown soils are found. They are best developed in central Anatolia. The Chestnut soils are similar in type to Chernozem soils with a well-developed A horizon, but one which lacks the high humus content of a true black earth. This horizon grades down into a lighter brown B horizon, followed across a sharp line of demarcation by a light coloured C horizon. In more arid regions, the Chestnut soils are replaced by Brown soils, which are similar in profile characteristics, but contain less humus and consequently are of a lighter colour. Both these soils tend to be found in regions which are marginal for dry-land farming.

Alluvial soils are amongst the most fertile soils found in the Middle East. They occur along all the major river systems, and are especially well developed along the Nile Valley and in the Tigris-Euphrates lowlands. The texture of this type of soil varies considerably, depending upon local sediment supply conditions. In the larger river basins silty-clays, silty-loams, and silty-clay-loams tend to predominate. Where poor drainage occurs, salinity can be a problem. As these soils are often added to annually, their profiles are not well developed. Occasionally, a horizon of calcium carbonate deposition can be distinguished.

1.4.1 Soil surveys

For illustrative purposes summaries of soil surveys carried out in four countries of the region are included. The countries selected, Turkey, Iran, Israel and Egypt, were chosen with a view to providing details of the differing soil types which commonly occur throughout the Middle East and North Africa.

1.4.1.1 Turkey

The only comprehensive survey of soils in Turkey is that made by Oakes in 1957, in which 18 major soil types were recognized.[40] Over about one-fifth of the area of the country, particularly the mountains of the east, it did not prove possible to classify the soils adequately. In these regions the soils are usually thin and discontinuous, with igneous and metamorphic rocks forming the parent material (Figure 1.7).

Pedalfers cover approximately one third of the country and are represented by Red and Grey–Brown Podsolic soils, and Brown Forest soils. These soils types tend to occur in the wetter upland regions, with the Brown Forest soils developed on calcareous strata. The soil profiles are often thin and truncated, owing to the erosion of the steep mountain slopes. In total these three soil types cover almost 40 per cent of Turkey.

An intermediate grouping of soil types, which are difficult to classify as either pedalfers or pedocals, are the non-calcic Brown soils, Rendzinas and Grumusols. The non-calcic Brown soils are similar to the Red Podsolic soils, but less strongly leached. Rendzinas and Grumusols are both azonal types found in similar climatic zones to those of the non-calcic Brown soils. The former are highly calcareous and are usually developed on soft or marly limestones, while the latter tend to be deeper, and to contain a higher clay content, although they too are associated with calcareous parent material. The remaining soil types can be broadly classed as pedocals, with the exception of the alluvial soils. These latter occur along the major valley systems of the country, and tend to be the most productive soils agriculturally. They exhibit considerable variations in lithology and are all characterized by a relatively immature profile development, and marked lateral variations over short distances. Where drainage is poor, alluvial hydromorphic soils occur. Some of these soils are characterized by severe salinity build-up.

Brown and Reddish Brown soils are found in the semi-arid areas of central Anatolia and the southeast of Turkey near the Syrian border, and are usually developed on a calcareous substrate. They cover one-fifth of the country, mostly rolling terrain, and are important soils for the dry farming of cereals. In wetter areas the Brown soils grade into calcareous Chestnut soils.

Within the regime of the Mediterranean climate proper, Terra Rossa and Red Prairie soils predominate. They are developed as the result of limestone weathering, with the Red Prairie soils tending to be located in the warmer and damper areas. Although they are very distinctive soils, they cover only a very small proportion of Turkey.

Finally, in the most arid parts of central Turkey, particularly in the southern

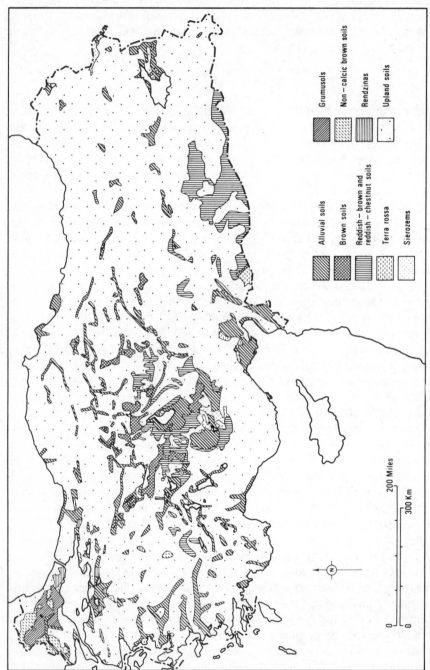

Figure 1.7 Soil map of Turkey (Modified by permission of Ministry of Agriculture, Turkey)

part of the Konya basin, Sierozem soils are found. These semi-desert soils are highly calcareous, but are often extremely productive under irrigation, if carefully managed.

An attempt has also been made to group the soils of Turkey in terms of their suitability for arable forming. Fifteen groups are distinguished on the basis of altitude, slope, and drainage as well as the intrinsic properties of the soils themselves. Eighty per cent of the total area of the country is classed in groups 11 to 15, which are considered as unsuitable for arable farming.

1.4.1.2 Iran

A detailed soil map of Iran at a scale of 1:2,500,000 has been prepared jointly by the Iranian Ministry of Agriculture and FAO.[41] Nineteen soil associations were identified and used as a basis of mapping. For convenience these mapping units were grouped into four physiographic units. These were soils of the plains and valleys, soils of the plateau, soils of the Caspian Piedmont, and soils of the dissected slopes and mountains.

The soils of the plains and valleys are formed on material which has been deposited mainly by water or wind. Alluvial soils are composed of the sediments of terraces and flood plains. They lack marked horizon differentiation and are usually medium to fine textured. Where drainage is poor, saline soils are found. Coarser grained alluvial soils are associated with alluvial fans along foothill regions. Sand dunes are commonly found in lowland basins in Iran. Hydromorphic soils, dark in colour and high in humus content, are well developed in the paddy lands of the Caspian Lowlands.

Solonchak and Solonetz are saline and alkali soils found in the drier areas of the country. They are either poorly drained or have developed under impeded drainage conditions, contain large quantities of soluble salts and are low in organic matter. Solonetz soils are produced by the partial leaching of Solonchak soils when irrigation is practised without proper drainage. They have a light coloured surface layer over a heavy dark coloured subsoil. Both soil types are commonly found in the basins of central Iran, where they can also be associated with salt marsh soils.

The soils of the plateau have been formed under modified continental climatic conditions with marked aridity at heights of around 1,000 m. Grey Desert and Red Desert soils are common in this region. They are characterized by a thin surface crust of compacted or cemented material which produces the typical desert pavement. These soils are always alkaline in reaction, possess a high calcareous content, and are very low in humus. Sierozem soils are light grey in colour and extremely calcareous. The surface layer is usually powdery and organic matter content is minimal. Such soils are common in desert steppe areas. Closely related to the Sierozems are the Brown Steppe soils, which are probably the most widespread soils in Iran. These are brown in colour and usually overlie calcareous horizons. They have been developed beneath grass vegetation under semi-arid climatic conditions.

40

The soils of the Caspian Piedmont have climatic conditions different from any other part of Iran, being characterized by precipitation throughout the year and an almost subtropical temperature regime. Vegetation is abundant, and chemical weathering of the outcropping Mesozoic sediments intense. Many different soil types, including Brown Forest, Red–Yellow Podsolic, Grey–Brown Podsolic, and Red-Brown Mediterranean soils, have been described. The total area of these soils, however, is only 0·2 per cent of the country.

The soils of the dissected slopes and mountains are stony, shallow and lack profile development. They are described mainly as lithosols. In total they occupy almost half the area of the country.

To make the soil map more useful for planning purposes it was decided to group the classes to indicate the limitations of the soils for agricultural productivity. Five broad groups with ten divisions in all, were employed ranging from soils with no or only slight limitations, to those with almost no potentiality whatsoever (Figure 1.8).

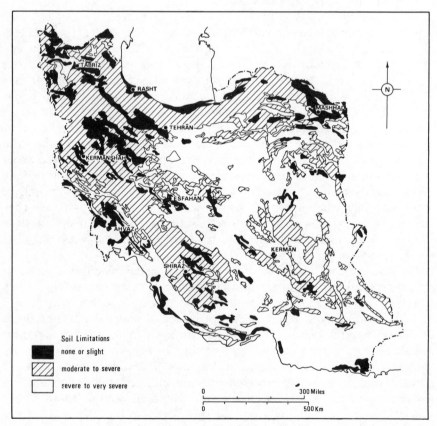

Figure 1.8 Simplified soil potentiality map of Iran (Modified from Dewan and Famouri, *The Soil of Iran*, FAO, Rome, 1964).

1.4.1.3 Israel

The soils of Palestine were the subject of a study by Reifenberg prior to the Second World War.[42] In this work he divided the country into four regions and described the soils within each (Table 1.1). For agricultural purposes, alluvial soils, Terra Rossa soils, and Mediterranean Steppe soils were by far the most important types.

TABLE 1.1
The Soils of Palestine

1. Arid region
    Desert soils
    Lisan Marl soils
    Loess
2. Semi-arid region
    Mediterranean steppe soils
    Dune sands
3. Sub-humid region
    Kurkar soils
    Red sandy soils
    Nazzaz soils
    Alluvial soils and Aclimatic Black Earths
    Peat
4. Humid region
    Terra Rossa
    Red earths on volcanic rocks
  Mountain marl soils

Source: After Reifenberg A, 1947

This work has now been superseded by more detailed Israeli surveys.[43] For descriptive purposes the country has been divided into three terrain types: a coastal region, a mountain and hill region, and a valley, plains and plateau region. Each of these is then further subdivided with respect to moisture availability, and lithology (Figure 1.9).

The soils of the coastal region are formed on sandy sediments, and belong to three great soil groups. Non-calcic Brown soils are found in the north under Mediterranean climatic conditions. Further south the soils become calcareous. In the semi-arid zone Reddish Chestnut soils occur, while in the arid zone proper coarse textured Burozems (arid brown soils) are common.

In the mountain and hill region, the parent material on which the soils have developed consists mainly of hard limestone, dolomite, and marl. Under the Mediterranean regime, Terra Rossa soils have formed on the more resistant calcareous strata with brown Rendzinas on the marly limestones. With increasing aridity, brown Rendzinas first become the predominant soil on all parent materials, to be replaced under even drier conditions by calcareous desert-steppe lithosols.

Quaternary sediments of differing textures form the material on which most of the soils of the valleys, plains, and plateaus have been formed. In the wettest or Mediterranean zone, dark coloured Grumusols predominate, giving way

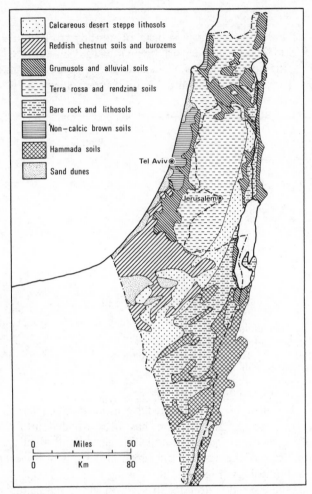

Figure 1.9 Soil map of Israel (Modified from Dan and Koyumdjisky 1963, by permission of British Society of Soil Science)

to more silty soils with accumulation horizons of calcium carbonate as precipitation decreases. Burozems also occur here. Finally, under true desert conditions, usually gravel plains, soils termed hammadas predominate. These possess a stone cover, beneath which finer material, often with a marked saline layer, is seen. In areas of poor drainage a range of soil types, including peats, Planosols and Hydrohalomorphic soils, are found.

1.4.1.4 Egypt

A recent soil survey of Egypt has been carried out using the FAO/UNESCO classification of soils which was adopted for the project on the Soil Map of

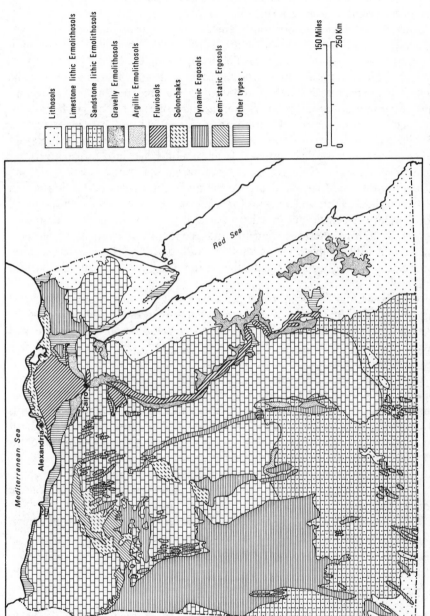

Figure 1.10 Soil map of Egypt (Reproduced by permission of Institute of Land Reclamation, Egypt)

the World.[44] Altogether, eighteen soil associations were identified, but of these, six associations accounted for more than 85 per cent of the surface area of the country (Figure 1.10).

Lithosols cover a large portion of the country, approximately 17 per cent, especially in the Eastern Desert, south Sinai and on the Gilf Kebir plateau. The parent material is usually the Basement Complex, consisting mostly of Pre-Cambrian igneous and metamorphic rocks with some more recent volcanic rocks. The soil profiles are shallow and stony, and possess only a weakly developed A horizon. Rock outcrops are common, and slopes nearly everywhere steep.

A new soil unit, termed Ermolithosol, was introduced for this survey to describe the characteristic desert formations usually referred to in the literature as 'desert pavements'. The unit was further subdivided into three categories, lithic, gravelly, and argillic, on the basis of parent material.

Limestone Lithic Ermolithosols are the most important subdivision within the Ermolithosol unit, and account for a quarter of all the soils of the country, especially in the central and northern parts of the western desert. These soils are developed on limestone plateaus and are merely thin crusts of physical weathering which have been smoothed and polished by aeolian activity. Some fine material occurs beneath the weathered stones, making the surface very level.

Sandstone Lithic Ermolithosols are developed on the Nubian Sandstone and cover some 20 per cent of the country, mainly in the southern part of the western desert. These soils produce a very bare and smooth form of desert pavement which has been intensely affected by wind action. Again no profile development is seen.

Another new unit, Ergosols, was introduced for the mapping of sand dune complexes. Shifting sand dunes are classified as Dynamic Ergosols, while semi-stabilized dunes are known as Semistatic Ergosols. Dynamic Ergosols cover 15 per cent of the country in a series of scattered zones throughout the main plateau region. The best known occurrence of these soils is undoubtably the great sand sea of the Western Desert.

All other soil types cover only very small parts of the country. However, it must be realized that almost all the cultivated area is restricted to one of these groups, namely Fluviosols, which occur extensively throughout the Nile Valley and Delta region. These soils, which cover only 2.5 per cent of Egypt, are developed on Nile silt, and, as a consequence, are heavy textured. Gleying is common, and in badly drained areas salinity is a problem.

1.4.2 Soil management

In most countries of the Middle East two major problems exist with regard to man's utilization of soil resources. These are soil erosion and soil salinity.

1.4.2.1 Soil erosion

Soil erosion occurs when the vegetation cover is disturbed or removed, permitting the upper soil layers to be subjected to the direct action of water or wind. The problem is compounded when the soil structure is such that it is unstable when water is present, and also when slopes are steep (Chapter 15).

Throughout most of the region water erosion predominates. Gully erosion is especially spectacular on soft and unconsolidated materials, while almost imperceptible sheet erosion occurs nearly everywhere. Although water action reaches its maximum during the wet winter months, the converse is true of the wind. The greatest effect of this is felt in the dry summer, when surface soils become dust-like and so are easily transported in strong winds.

Control measures against soil erosion are usually difficult to implement as well as expensive. Two major approaches, often carried out together, are utilized.

The first, and most simple method is to attempt to establish a continuous vegetation cover over the soil which is being subjected to erosion. One of the major causes of soil erosion in the Middle East is the practice of bare fallowing the land between the cereal harvest and the first rains of the winter. This means that large quantities of soil are lost as a result of sheet erosion from what are often the most fertile and productive regions. A simple, though as yet not widely used remedy, is to strip plant grasses in belts parallel to the contours between areas of cereal cultivation. Deforestation also accentuates erosion by removing foliage which dissipates the effects of rain drop impact. Afforestation programmes throughout the region are helping to combat this problem with pioneering work being carried out by both Israel and Turkey.

The second method of erosion control is the construction of physical barriers which reduce the speed of surface runoff. Throughout the Middle East the most widely used soil conservation technique is terracing. Terraces are constructed by hand labour and have been a feature of rural agriculture in many parts of the region for millenia. They are particularly well developed in the eastern Mediterranean littoral.

Since the Second World War modern conservation methods have been increasingly introduced. These include gradoni terracing, contour walling, and gully-plug or check-dam construction (Chapter 15).

1.4.2.2 Soil salinity

The major effects of soil salinity are most clearly seen in lowland and riverine areas where irrigated agriculture is practised and drainage systems are inadequate (Chapter 12). The major cause of soil salinity is the presence of groundwater, often though not necessarily saline, close to the surface. Under these conditions water is drawn upwards to the surface by capillary action, and from there it evaporates into the atmosphere. When it does so, it leaves behind any dissolved chemicals to form a surface crust, or saline horizon, in the top few centimetres of the profile. Salt can also be added directly to the soil through poor quality irrigation water, even though satisfactory drainage systems are in existence, if insufficient water to permit full leaching is not utilized.

The major salts found in soils are chlorides and sulphates of sodium, calcium and magnesium. In arid soils, sodium ions tend to present the greatest problem as they cause the breakdown of soil structure and a great reduction in permeability. These ions are also toxic to most plant species when present in large quantities. The reclamation of saline soils is a straightforward process if sufficient water is available for leaching away the soluble salts, and provided that an adequate drainage system exists (Chapter 12).

References

1. R. S. Dietz and J. C. Holden, 'The Breakup of Pangaea', *Scient. Am.*, **233**, 30–41 (1970).
2. D. P. McKenzie, 'Plate Tectonics of the Mediterranean Region', *Nature, Lond.*, **226**, 239–243 (1970).
3. D. P. McKenzie, 'Plate Tectonics of the Mediterranean Region', *Nature, Lond.*, **226**, 242 (1970).
4. D. P. McKenzie, D. Davies and P. Molnar, 'Plate Tectonics of the Red Sea and East Africa', *Nature, Lond.*, **226**, 243–248 (1970).
5. A. M. Quennell, 'The structural and geomorphic evolution of the Dead Sea Rift', *Q. Jl. geol. Soc. Lond.*, **114**, 1–24 (1958).
6. D. P. McKenzie, D. Davies and P. Molnar, 'Plate Tectonics of the Red Sea and East Africa', *Nature, Lond.*, **226**, 247 (1970).
7. M. Takin, 'Iranian Geology and Continental Drift in the Middle East', *Nature, Lond.*, **235**, 147–150 (1972).
8. M. Takin, 'Iranian Geology and Continental Drift in the Middle East', *Nature, Lond.*, **235**, 149 (1972).
9. P. Beaumont, 'Salt weathering on the margin of the Great Kavir, Iran', *Bull. geol. Soc. Am.*, **79**, 1683–1684 (1968).
10. D. H. Yaalon, 'Parallel stone cracking, a weathering process on desert surfaces', *Geological Institute Technical and Economic Bulletins, Series C, Pedology, Bucharest*, **18**, 107–111 (1970).
11. K. W. Butzer, *Quaternary stratigraphy and climate in the Near East*, Bonner Geog. Abh., **24**, 1958, 157 pages.
12. K. W. Butzer, and C. L. Hansen, *Desert and River in Nubia*, The University of Wisconsin Press, Madison, 1968, 562 pages.
13. W. J. Van Liere, 'Observations on the Quaternary of Syria', *Berichten, Rijksdienst Oudheidkundig Bodemonderzoek*, **10–11**, 1–69 (1961).
14. P. Buringh, *Soils and soil conditions in Iraq*, Ministry of Agriculture, Republic of Iraq, Baghdād, 1960, 322 pages.
15. K. W. Butzer, *Quaternary stratigraphy and climate in the Near East*, Bonner Geog. Abh., **24**, 1958, 157 pages.
16. (a) B. Messerli, 'Die eiszeitliche und die gegenwärtige Vergletscherung im Mittelmeeraum', *Geographica helv.*, **3**, 105–228 (1967).
    (b) B. Frenzel, 'Die Vegetations und Landschaftszonen Nord-Eurasien während der letzten Eiszeit und während der postglazialen Wärmezeit', *Abh. Akad. Wiss. Liter. (Mainz) Math.—Naturw. Kl.*, **13**, 164 pages (1959) and **6**, 167 pages (1960).
17. B. Messerli, 'Die eiszeitliche und die gegenwärtige Vergletscherung im Mittelmeeraum', *Geographica helv.*, **3**, 105–228 (1967).
18. H. E. Wright, 'Pleistocene glaciation in Kurdistan', *Eiszeitalter Gegenw.*, **12**, 131–164 (1962).
19. J. H. Birman, 'Glacial reconnaissance in Turkey', *Bull. geol. Soc. Am.*, **79**, 1009–1026 (1968).

20. H. Bobek, 'Die Rolle der Eiszeit in Nordwestiran', *Z. Gletscherk, Glacial geol.*, **25**, 130–183 (1937).
21. H. Bobek, 'Nature and implications of Quaternary Climatic changes in Iran', in *Changes in Climate*, UNESCO, Paris, 1963, Arid Zone Research, **20**, 403–413.
22. T. M. Oberlander, *The Zagros Streams: A new interpretation of transverse drainage in an orogenic zone*, Syracuse Geographical Series No. 1, Syracuse, 1965, 168 pages.
23. G. F. Brown, 'Geomorphology of Western and Central Saudi Arabia', *Report of XXI International Geological Congress, Copenhagen*, **21**, 150–159 (1960).
24. A. M. Quennell, 'The Structural and geomorphic evolution of the Dead Sea Rift'. *Q. Jl. geol. Soc. Lond.*, **114**, 1–24 (1958).
25. H. Bobek, *Features and Formation of the Great Kavir and Masileh*, Arid Zone Research Centre, University of Tehrān, Publication No. 2, Tehrān 1959, 63 pages.
26. W. T. Blandford, 'On the nature and probable origin of the superficial deposits in the valleys and deserts of Central Persia', *Q. Jl. geol. Soc. Lond.*, **29**, 495–503 (1873).
27. D. B. Krinsley, 'Geomorphology of Three Kavirs in Northern Iran', in *Playa Surface Morphology: Miscellaneous Investigations* (Ed. J. T. Neal), USAF, Office of Aerospace Research, Environmental Research Papers, No. 283, 1968, 105–130.
28. (a) E. H. Rieben, *Geological observations on alluvial deposits in Northern Iran*, Geological Survey, Iran, Report 9, 1966, 41 pages.
    (b) E. H. Rieben, *Les Terrains Alluviaux de la région de Tehrān*, Publication No. 4, Arid Zone Research Centre, Tehrān, 1960, 41 pages.
    (c) E. H. Rieben, 'The Geology of the Tehrān Plain', *Am. J. Sci.*, **253**, 627–639 (1955).
29. (a) C. Vita-Finzi, 'Late Quaternary alluvial chronology of Iran', *Geol. Rdsch.*, **58**, 951–973 (1968).
    (b) C. Vita-Finzi, *Mediterranean Valleys*, Cambridge University Press, Cambridge, 1969, 140 pages.
30. P. Beaumont, "Alluvial fans along the foothills of the Elburz Mountains, Iran', *Palaeogeography, Palaeoclimatology, Palaeoecology*, **12**, 251–273 (1972).
31. N. A. De Ridder, 'Sediments of the Konya Basin, Central Anatolia, Turkey', *Palaeography, Palaeoclimatology, Palaeoecology*, **1**, 225–254 (1965).
32. R. W. Hey, 'Quaternary shorelines of the Mediterranean and Black Seas', *Quaternaria*, **XV**, (VIII Congrés INQUA—Les Niveaux Marins Quaternaires), II—Pleistocene, 273–284 (1971).
33. P. V. Federov, 'The marine terraces of the Black Sea Coast of the Caucasus and the problem of the most recent vertical movements'. *Dokl. Acad. Nauk. USSR*, **144**, 431–434 (1969), (in Russian).
34. (a) P. Sanlaville, 'Sur les niveaux marins quaternaires de la région de Tabarja (Liban)', *Comptes Rendues Somm. Soc. Geol. Fr.*, 157–158 (1967).
    (b) P. Sanlaville, 'Sur le Tyrrhènien libanais', *Quaternaria*, **XV** (VIII Congrés INQUA—Les Niveaux Marins Quaternaires), II—Pleistocene, 239–248 (1971).
35. H. Jenny, *Factors of Soil Formation*, McGraw-Hill Book Co., New York, 1941, 281 pages.
36. Soil Survey Staff, Soil Conservation Service, United States Department of Agriculture, *Soil Classification: A Comprehensive System (7th Approximation)*, U.S. Government Printing Office, Washington D.C., 1960.
37. FAO, *Definitions of soil units for the Soil Map of the World*, Soil Map of the World; FAO/UNESCO Project, World Soil Resources Office, Land and Water Development Division, FAO, Rome, 1968, 72 pages.
38. FAO, *Key to soil units for the Soil Map of the World*, Soil Map of the World, FAO/UNESCO Project, Soil Resources, Development and Conservation Service, Land and Water Development Division, FAO, Rome, 1970, 16 pages.
39. K. Atkinson, 'The dynamics of Terra Rossa soils', *Bulletin of the Faculty of Arts, University of Libya, Benghazi*, **3**, 15–35 (1969).

48

40. H. Oakes, *The Soils of Turkey*, Republic of Turkey, Ministry of Agriculture, Soil Conservation and Farm Irrigation Division, Ankara, Division Publication No. 1, 1957, 180 pages.
41. M. L. Dewan, and J. Famouri, *The Soils of Iran*, Food and Agricultural Organisation of the United Nations, Rome, 1964, 319 pages.
42. A. Reifenberg, *The Soils of Palestine* (Translated by C. L. Whittles). Thomas Murby and Sons, London, 1947, 179 pages.
43. J. Dan and H. Koyumdjisky, 'The Soils of Israel and their distribution', *J. Soil Sci.*, **14,** 12–20 (1963).
44. M. M. Elgabaly, I. M. Gewaifel, N. N. Hassan, and B. G. Rosanov, *Soil map and land resources of U.A.R.*, Institute of Land Reclamation, Alexandria University, Research Bulletin, Alexandria, No. 22, 1969, 14 pages.

CHAPTER 2

Climate and Water Resources

2.1 Climate

2.1.1 Introduction

No single climatic regime prevails throughout the Middle East. Indeed, as in so many other respects the region is a transitional zone, in this case between equatorial and mid-latitude climates. A characteristic feature of all subtropical latitudes, of which the Middle East forms a substantial part, is the prevalence of aridity, with a marked precipitation minimum, over both the oceans and continents, centred on 30 degrees of latitude. The fact that aridity is found over the oceans as well as the land, suggests the operation of some mechanism which inhibits the precipitation process, as there is obviously no shortage of water for replenishing atmospheric moisture.[1] In oceanic regions, annual evaporation can attain values of more than 200 cm/annum, making these areas one of the most important sources for atmospheric water recharge.[2] Given these facts there can be little doubt that the aridity of subtropical latitudes can only be accounted for by dynamical factors related to the general circulation of the atmosphere. Although it is possible to outline a number of phenomena which help to explain the arid zone, it is difficult, if not impossible, to point to a single factor which can be regarded as the ultimate control of the whole system.

Much of the subtropical region is characterized by divergent air flow in the atmosphere at low levels. In turn, this implies the presence of converging and subsiding air aloft, which being subjected to dynamical warming, will produce a lowering of relative humidities and the creation of stable atmospheric conditions. Under these circumstances, convectional activity, capable of producing precipitation, is reduced to a minimum.

Closely related with both the surface divergent flow of air and widespread air subsidence, is the occurrence of a normally well developed high pressure zone near the 30th parallel, which separates the tropical easterlies from the circum-polar westerlies. In both the regimes of the tropical easterlies and mid-latitude westerlies, a large proportion of the precipitation is the result of moving wave disturbances, which play such a crucial role in the distribution of heat, water vapour and momentum. The intensity of these disturbances, and hence the amounts of precipitation, decline as the subtropical high pressure belt is approached from either a northerly or a southerly direction. Although clearly detectable at sea level over the oceanic areas, the high pressure belt is usually

49

only well developed over land above heights of two to three kilometres owing to surface heating effects.

A belt of strong westerlies, known as the subtropical jet stream, is found in the upper atmosphere in the Middle East, above the light and variable winds associated with the subtropical high pressure system which occurs at the earth's surface. The position of the core, or line of maximum velocity, of the jet stream varies over 10 to 15 degrees of latitude from summer to winter, especially over the eastern part of the region (Table 2.1). In July it is centred over the Caspian Sea, while by January it has moved southwards to lie over the northern part of the Gulf.[3] In the west over the Mediterranean Sea the jet stream core reveals a much more restricted latitudinal movement (Figure 2.1).

TABLE 2.1
Average speed and latitude of subtropical jet stream along 45°E

Month	J	F	M	A	M	J	J	A	S	O	N	D
Knots	120	120	100	90	90	80	70	60	50	60	70	90
Latitude	30	29	29	29	T	39	40	40	39	T	30	30

T = transitional period

Source: Weickman, L. 1961 'Some characteristics of the subtropical jet stream in the Middle East and adjacent regions'. Meteorological Publications Series A-No. 1 Ministry of Roads, Iranian Meteorological Department, Tehrān, p. 4

This seasonal shift of the subtropical jet stream in the Middle East parallels the movement of the major climatic belts between their summer and winter positions. Observation of the jet stream has shown that the movement between the two positions is normally abrupt. The winter position, over the northern part of the Gulf, is maintained for approximately six to seven months from mid-October to April. This is followed by a rapid shift to the summer position over the Caspian Sea, which is held for three to four months from June to the end of September.

The reasons for the rapid shift of the jet-stream core position are not known with certainty. It has been discovered, however, that it appears to be related to atmospheric conditions generated by the existence of the high mountain belt of the Himalayas. Observations have revealed that the change in position of the jet-stream, together with the related sudden climatic change from winter to summer and vice versa, is associated with a jet-stream movement from one side of the Himalayan range to the other. The Himalayas apparently retard the movement of the jet-stream core in some direct or indirect manner, until a certain threshold value is exceeded. There then follows a sudden movement of the jet-stream core to the opposite side of the Himalayan chain, and the subsequent establishment of a new equilibrium position.

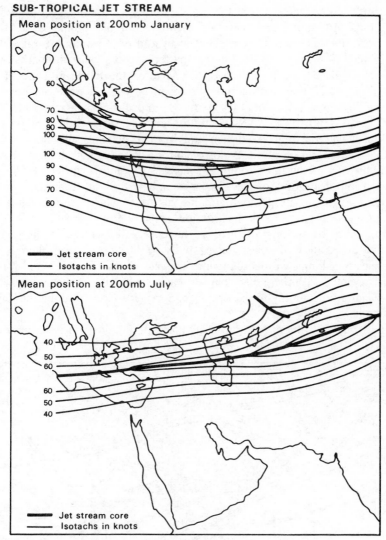

SUB-TROPICAL JET STREAM

Mean position at 200mb January

Jet stream core
Isotachs in knots

Mean position at 200mb July

Jet stream core
Isotachs in knots

Figure 2.1 Position of the jet-stream core in winter and summer (Reproduced
by permission of Iranian Meteorological Organisation)

2.1.2 Weather systems

The weather patterns of the Middle East can best be explained by reference
to the succession of cyclones which pass over the region. Cyclones are wave
disturbances generated along the polar front, separating polar and tropical
air masses. They develop over the North Atlantic and especially the Mediterranean Sea, and travel westwards over the Middle East.[4]

During summer the paths of the cyclones tend to pass north of the Pontus and Elburz Mountains, and, therefore, their effect on the climate of the Middle East, with the exception of northern Turkey and the Caspian littoral of Iran, is minimal. In winter a quite different pattern occurs, with the paths of the cyclones displaced southwards over the Mediterranean Sea and the Middle East (Figure 2.2). Even at this time, however, very few depressions penetrate south of 30 degrees north and their frequency of occurrence increases markedly as one travels northwards. As winter progresses, very cold air masses are developed over the high Anatolian and Iranian plateaus and these tend to exercise a steering effect on the cyclones, causing them to pass either northwards or southwards of the main mountain masses. For much of the Middle East the most important cyclone track is across northern Syria, Iraq, and southern Iran, as it is disturbances moving along this route which account for a very large proportion of the total precipitation of the region.

Three types of cyclonic disturbance have been recognized in the region.[5] The first are shallow waves moving rapidly in the upper troposphere, which cross the area along a west-east corridor between southern Turkey and Jordan. Rain associated with these disturbances reaches a maximum during the winter months, and falls mainly in the Lebanon, Syria, Jordan and along the Zagros Mountains.

Cold troughs in the upper atmosphere, creating almost stationary cyclones

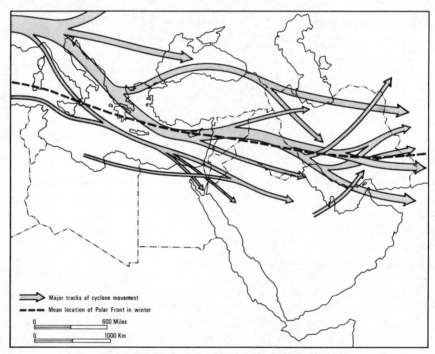

Figure 2.2 Cyclone tracks over the Middle East

in certain regions, form the second type of the group. The best known area for this kind of disturbance is centred on the island of Cyprus, where cyclones moving through the Mediterranean slow down, and often become part of a semi-permanent low pressure system. Such slow moving cyclones bring considerable precipitation to the lands fringing the Levant coastline. Moving further east these disturbances tend to become semi-stationary once again over the steppe region of northern Iraq, or over the Turkish mountains to the north, where they draw in moist air from the Gulf region and cause precipitation along the line of the Zagros Mountains and northwestern parts of the Iranian Plateau. Maximum precipitation associated with these systems occurs during spring.

The final type of cyclone, sometimes known as the 'Khamsin type', originates over the northern Sahara and moves eastwards over the southern part of the Middle East. Occasionally they come into contact with a cold upper air trough and under such conditions can give rise to appreciable rainfall amounts.

The Middle East comes under the influence of five air masses at different times of the year. During the summer months there is relatively little air movement throughout the region, and a cT (continental tropical) air mass, which is very hot and dry, prevails. A very different situation occurs in winter when air masses from four major source areas can enter the region as the result of cyclonic activity. The most important air mass is mP (maritime polar) air, originating over the North Atlantic. This contains large amounts of moisture and provides most of the precipitation experienced throughout the Middle East.

With the passage of a depression cP, (continental polar) air is drawn into the region from eastern Europe and Siberia. This is very cold and dry and with its progression across the area temperatures can drop rapidly. Associated with the warm sectors of cyclones is cT (continental tropical) air from North Africa, or mT (maritime tropical) air from the Red Sea, the Gulf and the Indian Ocean. The former is hot, even in winter and very dry, while the latter is warm and moist. The relative penetration of these two air masses into the Middle East depends to a large degree on the form and stage of development of the cyclone, together with the path of its movement.

During the winter months it is sometimes possible to distinguish a fifth air mass to which the term 'Mediterranean' is sometimes given. This is normally maritime polar air originating over the North Atlantic which has been stationary over the Mediterranean Sea for a considerable period. In general it is considerably milder than the maritime polar air, but it is equally as moist since water vapour is added to it during its sojourn over the Mediterranean. With the passage of a cyclone, this air is drawn into the general circulation system and can penetrate eastwards to the Gulf and Iranian plateau region.

2.1.3 Pressure and winds

During the summer months a relatively simple pattern of pressure conditions predominates throughout the region. The main feature at this time is a large belt of low pressure formed over the Gulf and the adjacent lowlands of Iraq. Smaller and less permanent low pressure centres also occur over Anatolia, central Iran and the southern Red Sea. Although these low pressure zones can often be identified on synoptic charts, the pressure gradients tend to be slight throughout the whole region and winds gentle. To the southeast of the region, very low pressure develops over northern India as the monsoonal circulation is established in mid-summer. This system, however, only affects the extreme southern fringe of the Middle East.

Despite the gentle pressure gradients, remarkably persistent local winds can develop at this time of year, blowing towards the low pressure centres. In the Tigris–Euphrates lowlands the *shamal* is a dry north or northwesterly wind which blows throughout much of the summer. A similar wind in the **Sistan** basin of southeast Iran is known as the *sad-ou-bist bad* (120-day wind). This, too, blows from the north and northwest, is extremely hot, and, owing to its high velocities, heavily dust laden.

Along the coastal areas of the Mediterranean, and in particular in western Turkey, land–sea breezes are well developed during the summer months. These blow onshore during the day, especially in the afternoon, bringing cooler but more humid conditions to narrow coastal areas. At night, these winds decline markedly in intensity and are sometimes replaced by offshore winds. Where they are funnelled along valley systems they can often attain high velocities. In summer, locally very strong pressure gradients can also be developed as the result of intense solar heating, producing a range of small dust storms characteristic of the interior deserts of Iran and Saudi Arabia.

In winter, it is much more difficult to speak of average pressure conditions, for this is the period when the region is crossed by a succession of cyclones. In general, one can identify a tendency for low pressure conditions to be dominant over the eastern Mediterranean, centred on Cyprus, and also over the Black Sea. Similarly, high pressure systems develop commonly over Anatolia and central Iran, as a result of the very cold winter temperatures.

With the passage of depressions locally steep pressure gradients can result, and, if associated with favourable topographic conditions such as a sharp altitudinal change over a short distance or else a funnelling effect, these can produce the various types of local winds for which the Mediterranean and Middle East region is so well known.

Similar local winds are also caused by particular air masses being drawn into a region with the passage of a cyclone and its associated frontal systems. For example, hot dry winds, with differing local names, such as *khamsin* in Egypt; *ghibli* in Libya; *shlour* in Syria and Lebanon; *shargi* in Iraq; and *simoon* in Iran, develop when tropical continental air from over North Africa and Arabia, is brought into a region in the warm sector of a travelling cyclone. Such winds are often strong, and, therefore, frequently give rise to dust and sand storms in desert regions, especially during autumn and spring. As they are associated with moving weather systems, these winds last only for three or four days, at most. A sudden rise in temperature is associated with their arrival, while an equally rapid fall in temperature and increase in humidity witnesses the passage of the following cold front and the subsequent invasion of cooler polar maritime air.

Pronounced adiabatic warming of air masses is also a common phenomenon in the Middle East in areas where high mountains are found in close proximity to lowlands. Warm winds produced by this mechanism are common in spring along both the Mediterranean and Black Sea shores of Turkey, in the Tigris-Euphrates and Khuzestan lowlands bordering the Zagros Mountains, and along the Caspian Sea coast of Iran.

During the winter months, the intense cold which develops over Anatolia and central Iran, means that outbursts of air from these regions still reach adjacent lowland regions as very cold winds, despite the adiabatic warming effect. This is particularly true in western Turkey where very low temperatures can be experienced in the İzmir region as the result of cold air movement down the valleys of the Gediz and Büyük Menderes rivers.

2.1.4 Temperatures

Throughout the Middle East summer temperatures are high almost every-where. The highest mean daily temperatures at this period, of more than 30°C,

TABLE 2.2
July temperatures at stations with mean daily temperatures greater than 30°C

	Average daily max.	min.	Mean daily range °C	Absolute max.	min.
Coastal stations					
Quseir (Egypt)	34	26	8	40	23
Jiddah (Saudi Arabia)	38	26	12	42	21
Aden (South Yemen)	36	28	8	40	23
Muscat (Oman)	36	30	6	45	25
Bahrain (Bahrain)	37	29	8	44	24
Kuwait (Kuwait)	40	30	10	48	26
Būshehr (Iran)	35	29	6	44	23
Bandar 'Abbās (Iran)	38	29	9	45	26
Interior stations					
Ghadames (Libya)	43	22	21	54	15
Kufra (Libya)	38	24	14	43	17
Aswân (Egypt)	42	26	16	51	21
Riyadh (Saudi Arabia)	42	25	17	45	19
Baghdād (Iraq)	43	24	19	50	17
Mosul (Iraq)	43	22	21	51	15
Tehrān (Iran)	37	22	15	43	15
Sīstan (Iran)	40	26	14	48	17

Source: Meteorological Office, London. 1966. 'Tables of Temperature, Relative Humidity and Precipitation for the World', Part V—Asia, HMSO. Meteorological Office, London. 1967. 'Tables of Temperature, Relative Humidity and Precipitation for the World'. Part IV—Africa, the Atlantic Ocean south of 35°N and the Indian Ocean, HMSO.

56

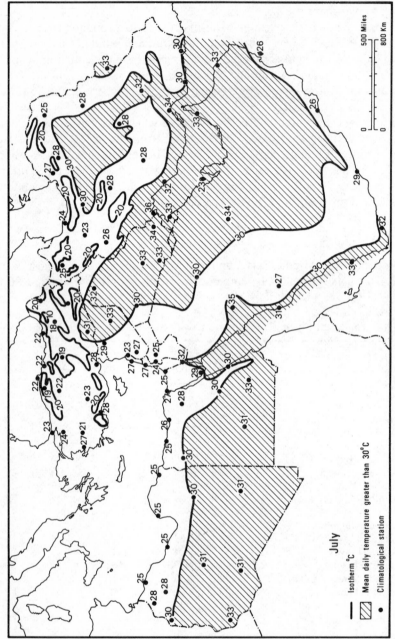

Figure 2.3 Mean daily temperatures for July

TABLE 2.3
July temperatures of stations in northern highland regions °C

	Average daily max.	min.	Mean daily range °C	Absolute max.	min.
Ankara (Turkey)	30	15	15	38	7
Uşak (Turkey)	29	14	15	38	3
Konya (Turkey)	30	15	15	38	7
Sivas (Turkey)	27	10	17	37	3
Erzurum (Turkey)	25·5	11·5	14	34	3
Mashhad (Iran)	33	17	16	41	8
Kermānshāh (Iran)	37	13	24	42	3·5
Eşfahān (Iran)	38	19	19	42	9
Damascus (Syria)	35·5	18	17·5	42·5	13
Amman (Jordan)	31·5	18	13·5	40	13
Jerusalem (Israel)	30	17	13	38	10

Source: Meteorological Office, London. 1966. 'Tables of Temperature, Relative Humidity and Precipitation for the World'. Part V—Asia. HMSO.

are recorded in the southern desert areas of Libya and Egypt, the Red Sea coastlands, the Gulf coastlands and adjacent lowlands and parts of the central plateau of Iran (Figure 2.3). In the coastal regions diurnal temperature ranges tend to be smaller than in the interior stations (Table 2.2). During the summer months very few places, however, are free from the relentless heat during the middle of the day. Even on the high plateaux of northern Iran and central Anatolia day-time maxima can often surpass 35°C (Table 2.3). Indeed, it

TABLE 2.4
July temperatures in coastal locations °C

	Average daily max.	min.	Mean daily range °C	Absolute max.	min.
Tripoli (Libya)	29·5	21	8·5	45	15
Benghazi (Libya)	29	21·5	8·5	40	11
Alexandria (Egypt)	29	23	6·0	40	17
Haifa (Israel)	31	24	7·0	35·5	17
Beirūt (Lebanon)	30·5	23	7·5	40	13
Antalya (Turkey)	34	22·5	11·5	43·5	15
Izmir (Turkey)	33	20·5	12·5	42·5	11
Sinop (Turkey)	24	18	6·0	34	13
Trabzon (Turkey)	25·5	19	6·5	32·5	15
Bandar-e Pahlavī (Iran)	29·5	21	8·5	—	—
Bābol Sar (Iran)	29·5	22	7·5	—	—
Masīra Island (Oman)	31·0	23	7·0	38	20·5
Salālah (Oman)	27·5	24	2·5	32	21

Source: Meteorological Office, London. 1966. 'Tables of Temperature, Relative Humidity and Precipitation for the World'. Part V—Asia. HMSO. Meteorological Office, London. 1967. 'Tables of Temperature, Relative Humidity and Precipitation for the World'. Part IV—Africa, the Atlantic Ocean south of 35°N and the Indian Ocean. HMSO.

58

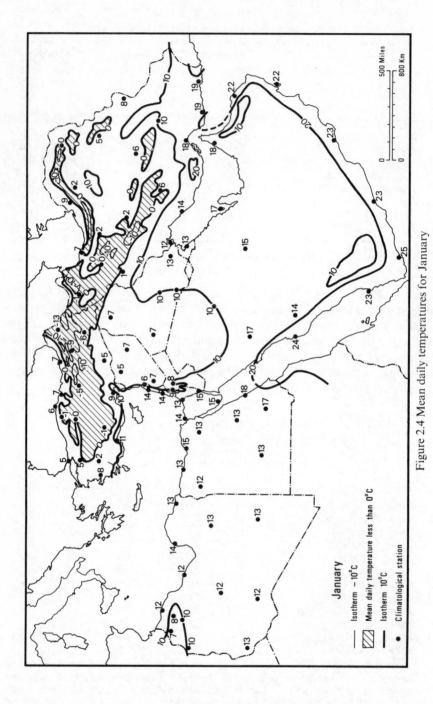

Figure 2.4 Mean daily temperatures for January

January

— Isotherm – 10°C

Mean daily temperature less than 0°C

— Isotherm 10°C

• Climatological station

TABLE 2.5
January temperatures in the southern part of the region °C

	Average daily max.	min.	Mean daily range °C	Absolute max.	min.
Coastal					
Tripoli (Libya)	16	8·5	7·5	28	1
Benghazi (Libya)	17	10	7·0	24·5	3·5
Alexandria (Egypt)	18	10·5	7·5	28	3
Beirūt (Lebanon)	16·5	10·5	6·0	25	−0·5
Kuwait (Kuwait)	16	9·5	6·5	27·5	0·5
Būshehr (Iran)	17·5	10·5	7·0	26·5	0
Bandar'Abbās (Iran)	23	13	10·0	28	3
Sharjah (United Arab Emirates)	23	12	11·0	29·5	2·5
Interior					
Sebra (Libya)	17·5	5	12·5	28·5	−2
Kufra (Libya)	20·5	6	14·5	32	−3·5
Dakhla (Egypt)	21	5	16·0	35·5	−0·5
Aswân (Egypt)	23	10	13·0	38	3
Riyadh (Saudi Arabia)	21	8	13·0	30	−7
Hā'il (Saudi Arabia)	16·5	4	12·5	26·5	−2·5
Bam (Iran)	16·5	5	11·5	—	—

Source: Meteorological Office, London. 1966. 'Tables of Temperature, Relative Humidity and Precipitation for the World'. Part V—Asia. HMSO. Meteorological Office, London. 1967. 'Tables of Temperature, Relative Humidity and Precipitation for the World'. Part IV—Africa, the Atlantic Ocean south of 35°N and the Indian Ocean, HMSO.

TABLE 2.6
January temperatures in the northern part of the region °C

	Average daily max.	min.	Mean daily range °C	Absolute max.	min.
Eṣfahān (Iran)	10	−2	12	20	−16
Tehrān (Iran)	9	−1	10	19	−16
Mashhad (Iran)	8	−2	10	24	−24
Kermānshāh (Iran)	8	−4	12	19	−21
Tabrīz (Iran)	4	−5	9	17	−25
Ankara (Turkey)	4	−5·5	9·5	15	
Konya (Turkey)	4	−5	9	16	−27
Sivas (Turkey)	−0·5	−9·5	9	10·5	−31
Erzurum (Turkey)	−5·5	−13	7·5	5·5	−30
Kars (Turkey)	−4	−18	14	5	−36

Source: (a) Meteorological Office, London. 1966. 'Tables of Temperature, Relative Humidity and Precipitation for the World'. Part V—Asia. HMSO.
(b) Ganji, M. H. 'Climate', Chapter 5, in *The Land of Iran*, Ed. W. B. Fisher, Vol. 1, Cambridge History of Iran, Cambridge University Press.

is only in the highest upland areas of Turkey, Iran and the coastal Mediterranean region where day-time maxima do not normally rise above 30°C at this time of year. Along the narrow strip bordering the Black, Caspian, and Mediterranean Seas, together with a similar zone along the Indian Ocean in southern Arabia, summer temperatures are moderated by the proximity of large water bodies (Table 2.4). A few miles inland this influence quickly declines and temperatures soar to values approaching those found in inland regions.

Much stronger contrasts in temperatures are noted between different regions in winter. In general, a regional gradient, with temperatures declining in a northerly direction, tends to dominate the picture, and this pattern is intensified by the location of the major mountain masses in the northern parts of the region running through Turkey and Iran. During the coldest month it is possible to divide the Middle East into two major zones, north and south respectively of the 10°C mean monthly January isotherm (Figure 2.4).

To the south of this line mean daily temperatures are above 10°C, and, with the exceptions of the southern coastal areas of Arabia and southeast Egypt, less than 20°C. Strong temperature gradients, therefore, are absent from this region. The mean daily values, however, do tend to conceal variations in the magnitude of diurnal ranges which exist between coastal and interior locations (Table 2.5). Nearly everywhere on the coast this range is much smaller than inland.

North of the 10°C mean January isotherm, daily temperatures decline rapidly across the Taurus and Zagros Mountains to give mean daily minimum values of less than −10°C over parts of the plateau regions of eastern Turkey, and in smaller pockets along the Elburz and Zagros chains. Few people live in such areas and, as a consequence, climatological stations are rare. However, a number of the high plateau and mountain stations in both Turkey and Iran clearly indicate the severity of conditions during the winter (Table 2.6). For example, in the interior of eastern Turkey the mean maximum daily temperatures of January are below freezing point.

As a consequence of these regional differences in temperature between the summer and winter months, the mean annual range of temperatures reveals marked variations between the northern and southern limits of the area. The greatest mean annual temperature range, of more than 30°C, is found in the mountainous areas of eastern Turkey (Figure 2.5). Much of eastern Turkey and northern Iran experiences a range of more than 25°C, particularly over the enclosed plateau regions. To the north of this zone, a sharp downward gradient is experienced toward both the Caspian and Black Sea coastlands, while a much more gentle reduction in the mean annual range is noted to the south. The lowest mean annual temperature range of less than 5°C is found along the southeastern coastline of Oman. Most of the Red Sea coastline, together with the coastal area of South Yemen, have an annual range of less than 10°C.

The temperature regimes of individual stations can best be illustrated in terms of diagrams showing mean maximum and mean minimum monthly

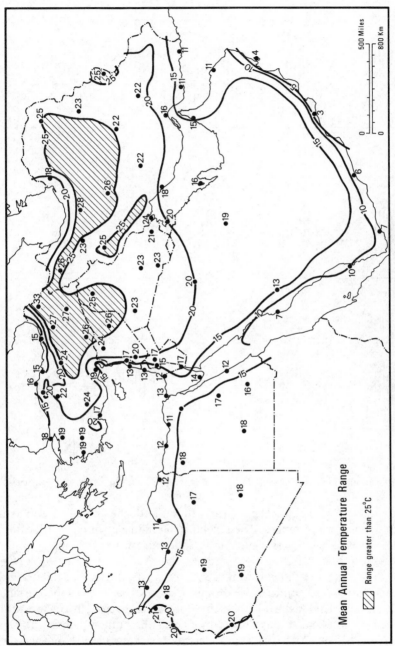

Figure 2.5 Mean annual temperature range

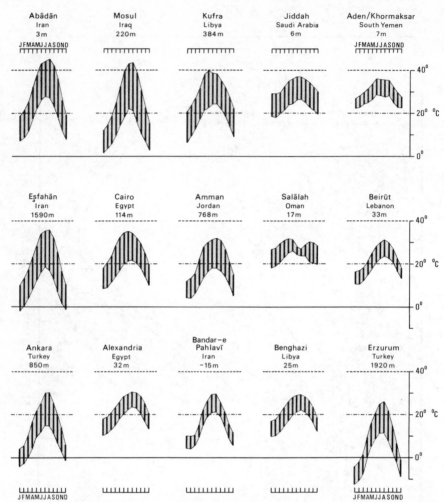

Figure 2.6 Diagrams of mean maximum and mean minimum monthly temperatures for selected stations

temperatures (Figure 2.6). These clearly reveal both the annual as well as the monthly temperature ranges. The ameliorating influence of coastal locations, and the extreme severity of winters in the interiors of Anatolia and Iran stand out markedly.

Features which are difficult to illustrate, owing to the lack of data, are the sharp meteorological contrasts which can occur over relatively short distances at a given time. An illustration of such a contrast is given by two temperature traverses on consecutive days made by one of the authors across the Dead Sea Lowlands from Amman to Jerusalem and back again.[6] Along this route, a distance of 80 km, the road descends from about 1,000 m above sea level near Amman to almost 400 m below sea level, the lowest point on earth, and then ascends to 700 m above sea level in the vicinity of Jerusalem. The tempera-

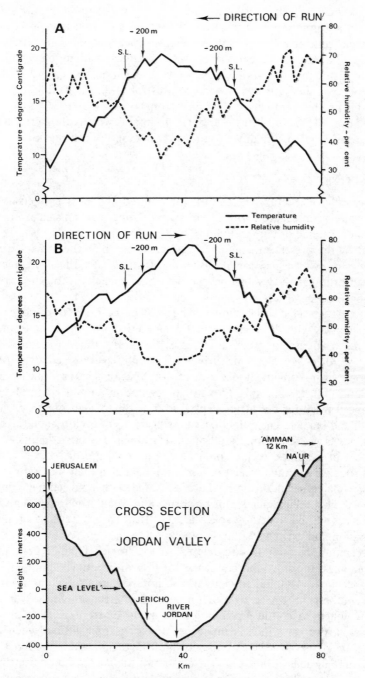

Figure 2.7 Temperature and relative humidity variations in
a transect across the Dead Sea lowlands (Reproduced from
Geography, **53**, 1968)

ture and humidity changes along this route are registered in Figure 2.7. Variations in absolute temperature of 11·5° and 12·5°C, and in relative humidity of 38 per cent and 35 per cent respectively were recorded on the two days. Such studies clearly reveal the considerable local climatological differences which exist within the Middle East in areas which possess considerable amplitude of relief. Perhaps the greatest contrast of all in the Middle East is to be found in northern Iran along a traverse from the well-watered Caspian Sea lowlands, over the summits of the Elburz Mountains which attain crest heights of more than 3,000 m, and down to the arid salt desert of central Iran.

2.1.5 Precipitation

Precipitation occurs when moist air is lifted above its condensation level and water droplets are formed. The major lifting mechanisms are of an orographic, cyclonic or convectional nature. Orographic lifting is usually brought about by the presence of highland regions over which the moving air masses have to rise. As the position of mountain ranges is fixed, this lifting mechanism is in operation all the year round, though whether it actually produces precipitation or not depends upon dynamic factors in the atmosphere.

Lifting associated with cyclones is the result of the interaction and intermixing of air masses with different thermal characteristics along frontal boundaries. The net result is that warm air masses, especially those associated with the warm sector of a cyclonic disturbance, are uplifted to the condensation level. Cyclonic lifting obviously occurs over all types of terrain, both lowland and highland, but its effects, in terms of precipitation amounts, are often greatly enhanced when further lifting is produced by the movement of a cyclone over a highland barrier. The individual paths or tracks of cyclones tend to be highly variable. However, if one studies statistically the average paths of a large number of cyclones, certain preferred routeways appear to exist, and along such routeways annual precipitation amounts reach their maximum values.

The final type of lifting is that associated with convectional, or thermal activity. This occurs chiefly during spring and summer in lowland and plateau regions subjected to strong solar heating. It often gives rise to thunderstorm formation and extremely intense precipitation.

Precipitation amounts are related to two major factors, first, proximity to the major moisture sources of the Mediterranean, Black and Caspian Seas, and, secondly, altitude. In general, precipitation totals decline in an easterly and southerly direction away from the Mediterranean Sea. Over much of the region most of the precipitation is caused by frontal lifting of moist air masses, a process which is intensified by orographic lifting, when highland zones are crossed. In the extreme north of the region, along the Black Sea and Caspian Sea coasts, precipitation occurs all the year round since this region always falls under the influence of mid-latitude cyclonic disturbances. Not surprisingly, therefore, this part of the Middle East receives some of the highest precipitation totals within the region (Figure 2.8).

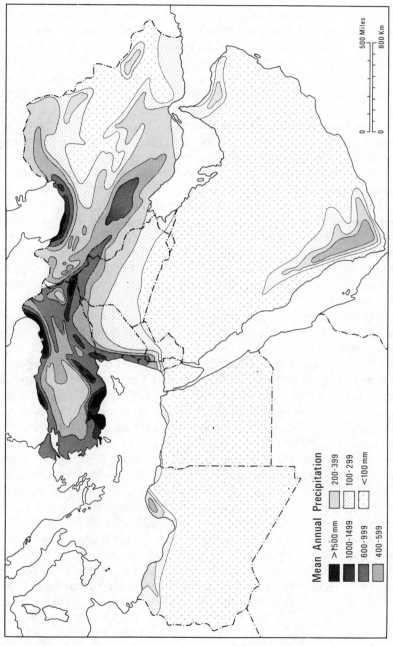

Figure 2.8 Mean annual precipitation totals

Areas receiving more than 600 mm/annum of precipitation are extremely restricted in the Middle East. With only one major exception, they are confined to a few narrow coastal belts backed by mountain ranges. In Turkey both the northern, or Black Sea coast and the southern, or Mediterranean coast possess regions where precipitation totals are in excess of 1,000 mm/annum. Even in these areas, though, the belt of high rainfall is not continuous. The eastern shoreline of the Mediterranean, in Syria, Lebanon and Israel, together with the mountains behind it, is another favoured region in terms of precipitation amounts. Maximum values are recorded in the northern highlands, and precipitation totals tend to decline southwards.

Along the Caspian Sea lowlands of Iran high precipitation values, commonly over 1,000 mm/annum in the western area, are recorded. A very marked gradient is found in an easterly direction along the coast with annual values dropping at the eastern margin of the lowlands to less than one half of those recorded in the west. A similar and perhaps somewhat surprising decrease in precipitation amounts is seen as one ascends southwards from the Caspian lowlands towards the crest line of the Elburz Mountains.

The final zone of high precipitation is a long and discontinuous belt commencing in eastern Turkey and running southeastwards parallel with the crest of the Zagros Mountains. Only rarely do precipitation totals rise above 800 mm/annum, but the sheer size of the area gives it tremendous importance in the water balance of the region. Although the highland regions continue eastwards to the Pakistan border, precipitation totals begin to fall off rapidly south of 30 degrees north.

Of all the countries of the Middle East, only two, Turkey and Lebanon, do not possess areas of extreme aridity, where precipitation falls below 200 mm/annum. In contrast, well over three quarters of the total areas of Libya, Egypt and Arabia receive annual precipitation totals of less than 200 mm. All other states experience a range of variations between these two extremes.

The seasonal distribution of precipitation in the Middle East, reflects, as one might expect, the passage of winter cyclones (Figure 2.9). Winter precipitation maxima predominate almost everywhere with the exception of parts of the southern coastlands of Arabia where summer monsoon conditions often penetrate. Along the Black and Caspian Sea littorals summer rain occurs, but here also an autumn/winter maximum is normally observed.

Throughout the upland areas of the Middle East, particularly in Turkey, northern Iran and the higher parts of the Levant, a considerable proportion of the precipitation falls as snow. This means that large quantities of water are stored in the highlands as snow pack during the winter period to be released, often as flood discharges, when temperatures begin to rise in spring and early summer.

Even over relatively short distances, relief and rain shadow influences can produce considerable variations in precipitation. For example, in the eastern Mediterranean region of Israel and Jordan daily precipitation totals for selected stations forming a west to east transect from the coast to the

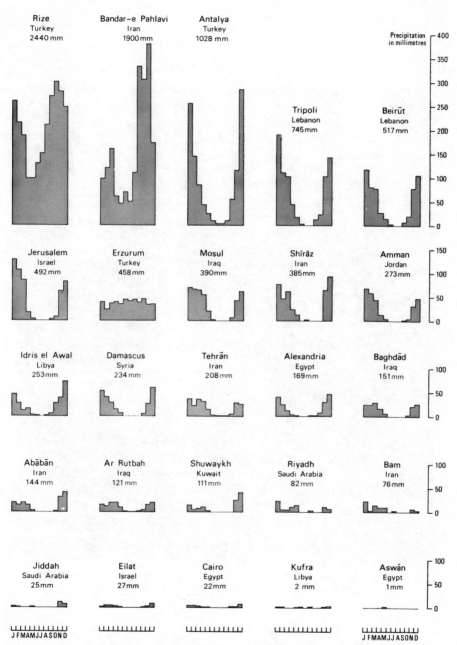

Figure 2.9 Diagrams of mean monthly precipitation for selected stations

Snowfalls can be heavy in some areas; winter conditions in a refugee camp near Amman, Jordan. (UNRWA photograph by John Bonar).

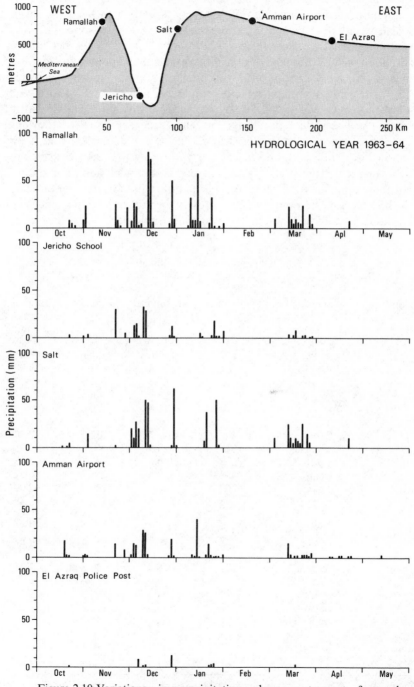

Figure 2.10 Variations in precipitation along a transect from the Mediterranean Sea to the Jordanian desert

interior desert, clearly reveal both these effects (Figure 2.10). Analysis of the precipitation records show rain-day sequences of two to five days duration associated with the passage of depressions separated by longer periods of dry weather. At the drier stations, the number of rain days per annum is fewer, and the daily amounts of precipitation less than at the wetter stations.

One of the characteristic features of precipitation amounts in the arid zone is the high annual variability. Unfortunately, however, the short records available for most climatological stations make it difficult to utilize statistical methods to assess this variability with any accuracy. Two of the longest precipitation records within the Middle East, for Jerusalem and Tehrān, are shown in Figure 2.11, and these clearly illustrate the very marked changes which can occur from year to year. A study of the maximum, minimum and mean annual precipitation values for selected stations indicates that the stations with the lowest mean annual rainfall show the greatest difference between the maximum and minimum annual recorded fall (Table 2.7).

TABLE 2.7
Annual precipitation in millimetres

Region	Station	Mean	Maximum	Minimum	Ratio of maximum to minimum
Egypt	Alexandria	169	313·6	33·2	9·45
	Port Said	63	129·6	13·0	9·97
	Cairo	22	63·4	1·5	42·27
	Asyût	5	25·0	0·0	—
	Dakhla	Trace	11·0	0·0	—
Turkey	Rize	2440	4045·3	1757·5	2·30
	Antalya	1028	1644·9	560·8	2·93
	İzmir	695	1116·5	441·2	2·53
	Erzurum	458	829·6	253·7	3·27
	Ankara	362	500·8	247·5	2·02
	Konya	316	500·5	143·7	3·48
Israel	Jerusalem	529	957·7	273·1	3·51
	Eilat	27	96·9	5·5	17·62
Jordan	Amman	273	476·5	128·3	3·71
Iraq	Mosul	390	585·2	208·2	2·81
	Baghdād	151	336·0	72·3	4·65
	Ar Rutbah	121	269·9	46·9	5·75
Arabia	Bahrain	76	169·4	10·1	16·77
	Aden	39	93·0	7·6	12·24

Source: World Meteorological Organisation 1971, 'Climatological Normals (Clino) for Climat and Climate Ship Stations for the Period 1931–1960. WMO/OMM—No. 117 TP52

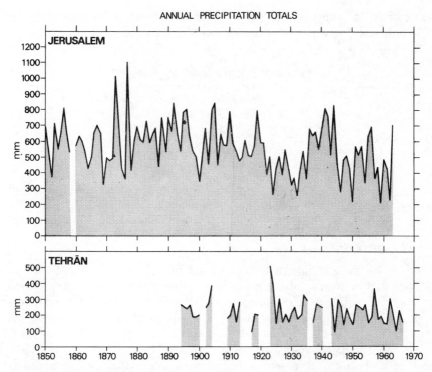

ANNUAL PRECIPITATION TOTALS

Figure 2.11 Annual precipitation variability at Jerusalem and Tehrān

More sophisticated types of analysis, involving calculations of relative interannual variability of precipitation, have been made as part of a study of agroclimatology in the Near East.[7] This work showed that the relative interannual variability of annual precipitation in per cent within the region studied increased as the mean annual total decreased. Using these data, together with mean annual precipitation values, it was concluded that a mean annual rainfall of 240 mm, with a relative interannual variability of 37 per cent, was the normal minimum requirement for dryland farming in the region. In mountainous areas, where the relative interannual variability was particularly high, a greater mean annual rainfall total was necessary to ensure regular dryland farming than in the lowland regions.

Information on the intensity of rainfall in the Middle East is also very meagre since recording rain gauges have only been introduced on a large scale within the last few years. The most generally available data which can be used to gain some indication of precipitation intensity are daily precipitation figures which are normally collected from all precipitation stations. To date, relatively little of this information has been subjected to analysis. At Tehrān, however, daily precipitation data going back to 1898 have been analysed to discover the return periods of falls of a given magnitude.[8] For the winter season this work revealed that a daily fall of 35 mm of precipitation would be expected to occur once in every ten years on average, whilst a daily fall of 75 mm would be expected only once in 1,000 years (Table 2.8).

TABLE 2.8
Maximum daily precipitation—Tehrān

| | Daily precipitation (mm) likely to be equalled or exceeded once in: | | | | | | |
	10 yrs	20 yrs	50 yrs	100 yrs	200 yrs	500 yrs	1000 yrs
Winter season	35	41	49	55	61	69	75

Source: Gordon A. H. and Lockwood J. G. 1970.

These results clearly indicate that torrential downpours over long periods of time, that is of 24 hours or longer, are of relatively rare occurrence in the Tehrān situation.

2.1.6 Evapotranspiration

In any climatic regime, temperature and precipitation data often do not provide a clear picture of the prevailing moisture conditions as experienced by plants. To obtain such information a number of empirical formulae have been devised which attempt to measure the combined effects of evaporation and transpiration, and thus permit a detailed water balance for a region to be drawn up. The best known formulae are those of Penman and Thornthwaite, both of which measure potential evapotranspiration (PET).[9] This is defined as the maximum amount of evaporation and transpiration which would occur from a vegetated surface (grass) if an abundant and continuous supply of moisture is available in the upper soil layers. Because a continuously available supply of water is assumed, potential evapotranspiration is really a measure of the available energy in the atmosphere. In contrast, actual evapotranspiration is the amount of moisture which is lost from a vegetated or ground surface under normal conditions. This is always less than, or equal to, the figure of potential evapotranspiration, and is governed by the amount of soil moisture storage, as well as by air temperature conditions. Of the two methods, the Penman formula produces results which agree most closely with field measurements of potential evapotranspiration. However, the amounts of meteorological data required for its calculation mean that the formula can only be applied at relatively few climatological stations in the Middle East, where detailed records are available. As a result, the simpler Thornthwaite method, relying only on mean monthly temperature and precipitation data, together with information on latitude, has been most widely used throughout the region.

By using calculated potential evapotranspiration and precipitation data it is possible to draw up water balance diagrams for climatological stations which reveal periods of water surplus and water deficit in the annual cycle. Water surplus occurs when precipitation and available soil moisture reserves exceed potential evapotranspiration for a given month, while water deficit

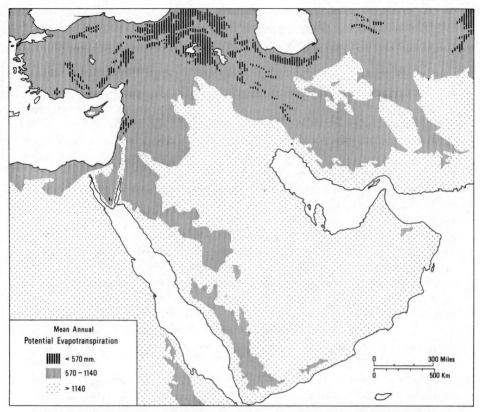

Figure 2.12 Mean annual potential evapotranspiration in the Middle East (after Thornthwaite, Mather and Carter, 1958).

results when precipitation and available soil moisture reserves are less than potential evapotranspiration.

Detailed work on potential evapotranspiration amounts in the Middle East revealed marked variations throughout the region (Figure 2.12).[10] The highest values of mean annual potential evapotranspiration, of more than 1,140 mm, are confined to the lower lying areas south of 30 degrees north. Medium values, between 570 and 1,140 mm/annum, occur throughout much of Turkey, the eastern Mediterranean coastal region, Syria, northern Jordan, northern Iraq and in the highlands of Iran, while figures below 570 mm are found only in the highest upland regions of Turkey and in northern Iran.

2.1.7 Climatic classification

In the geographical study of the environment of a region, it is always useful to have some simple framework within the confines of which a number of related factors can be studied. Climatic classifications provide such a framework, in so far as they integrate information concerning, in particular, temperature and precipitation. In turn, these parameters are important controls of soil development, vegetation patterns and man's use of the environment.

One of the better known climatic classifications is that proposed by Köppen, and later elaborated by Geiger.[11] Köppen realized that the major vegetation belts were determined by important climatic controls, and, therefore, placed his climatic boundaries at the margins of the major vegetation regions. These lines were then empirically defined in terms of mean monthly temperatures and precipitation amounts and their seasonal distribution (Table 2.9).

In the Middle East the only climatic types which occur on a large scale are the B and C types. Much of the region, however, does possess mountainous regions which do not fit easily into a climatic classification owing to the very large changes which can occur over relatively short distances.

Throughout North Africa, Arabia and much of Iran, BW (arid) climates predominate. BS (semi-arid) climates occur in the Levant and in an arc paralleling the Taurus and Zagros Mountains, as well as in the northwestern margin of the Iranian plateau, while C climates are confined largely to Turkey, parts of northern Syria and the Caspian littoral of Iran.

A more comprehensive division of the Middle East into climatic zones has been carried out by FAO/UNESCO, as part of their arid zone research programme.[12] This classification, based on temperature, precipitation totals, number of rain days, and amounts of atmospheric humidity, mist and dew, was designed to synthesize the effects of the climatic factors of particular importance for living organisms.

The initial division of climates is into three broad groupings on the basis of the mean temperature of the coldest month (t). With hot, warm temperate, and temperate climates the mean temperature of the coldest month is always more than $0°C$, whereas for cold and cold temperate climates the mean temperature of the coldest month is less than $0°C$. Finally in glacial climates mean monthly temperatures for all the months of the year are less than $0°C$.

A second division, again into three groups, is then made on the basis of the distribution, nature and intensity of the drier periods, making use of a 'xerothermic index'. This term denotes the number of 'biologically' dry days during the dry season and seeks to integrate information on precipitation amounts, number of rain days and atmospheric humidity conditions. Using the xerothermic index, 31 separate climatic types have been distinguished within the major divisions of hot and warm temperate climates. A simplified

TABLE 2.9
Köppen climatic classification

A —	humid climates—no winter
B —	dry climates (subtypes BS—semi-arid; BW—arid)
C —	climates with mild winter
D —	climates with severe winter
E —	polar climates—no true summer.

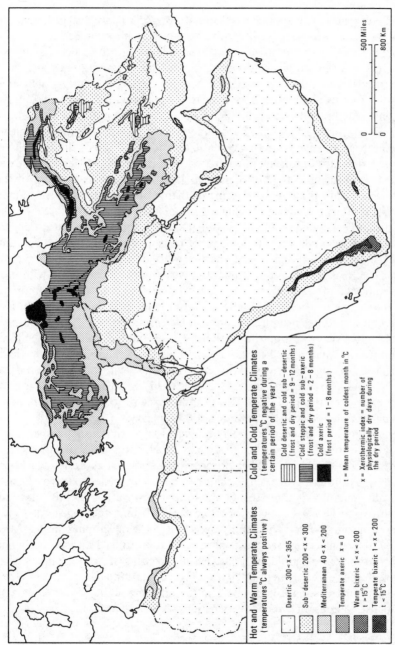

Figure 2.13 Simplified bioclimatic map of the Middle East (Modified from UNESCO–FAO, 1963)

Hot and Warm Temperate Climates
(temperatures °C always positive)

Deseric 300 < x < 365

Sub – deseric 200 < x < 300

Mediterranean 40 < x < 200

Temperate axeric x = 0

Warm bixeric 1 < x < 200
t > 15°C

Temperate bixeric 1 < x < 200
t < 15°C

Cold and Cold Temperate Climates
(temperatures °C negative during a
certain period of the year)

Cold desertic and cold sub–desertic
(frost and dry period = 9 – 12 months)

Cold steppic and cold sub – axeric
(frost and dry period = 2 – 8 months)

Cold axeric
(frost period = 1 – 8 months)

t = Mean temperature of coldest month in °C

x = Xerothermic index = number of
physiologically dry days during
the dry period

500 Miles
800 Km

map of the differing climatic types in the Middle East using this classification is seen in Figure 2.13.

The actual human response to a climatic regime is still very difficult to quantify with any accuracy, yet it is obviously of vital importance in a developing country when new industrial and urban development is being planned. Although some general works do exist, as yet little research appears to have been carried out on this topic in the Middle East.[13] Recently, interesting works of a biomedical nature have appeared dealing with Libya and Kuwait, which have attempted to access all factors affecting human life, including local climate conditions.[14] One of the simplest methods for outlining comfort conditions for humans in differing climatic regimes is the use of climographs.[15] With these diagrams, monthly plots are made of relative humidity against wet bulb temperatures, and they do permit at least a rough classification of the major cities within the region in terms of their general suitability for human activity (Figure 2.14). From this figure it can be seen that very few of the large cities possess what would be classified as an 'ideal' climate, except during only a few months per year. Indeed, some coastal stations, such as Bahrain, experience 'uncomfortable' conditions for most of the year, whilst interior stations, such as Tehrān and Ankara, reveal marked extremes, with raw winters and scorching summers. Only Shīrāz possesses a climate which approximates the ideal climatic range, and even here the temperatures of the summer months can sometimes produce uncomfortable conditions.

Climate also plays an important, though often indirect role in agricultural production and planning. For example, following analysis of wheat yields in Iran over the last few years and comparing these with precipitation data, it is now possible to forecast the next season's yields on the basis of the preceeding winter precipitation totals.[16] This technique seems to produce satisfactory results in the arid and semi-arid regions of the country.

Interestingly, it has been found that there is a correlation between local weather conditions and upsurges of locusts.[17] Such happenings obviously have a tremendously deleterious effect on crops; in some cases destroying them completely. Although much still remains to be discovered about why locusts swarm and migrate, it does seem that local moisture availability plays an important role. This is because, for successful breeding, the locust has to lay her eggs in ground which will supply moisture to the developing larvae. After hatching, the small wingless locusts need vegetation to feed on, so once again a water supply is essential. For successful breeding it would appear that moisture in the soil equivalent to 20 mm of precipitation is necessary.[18] When a series of wet seasons follow one another, the possibility of an explosion in the locust population becomes very real.

2.1.8 Conclusions

Although mean monthly and mean annual temperature and precipitation data permit a general picture of average conditions to be drawn up for the

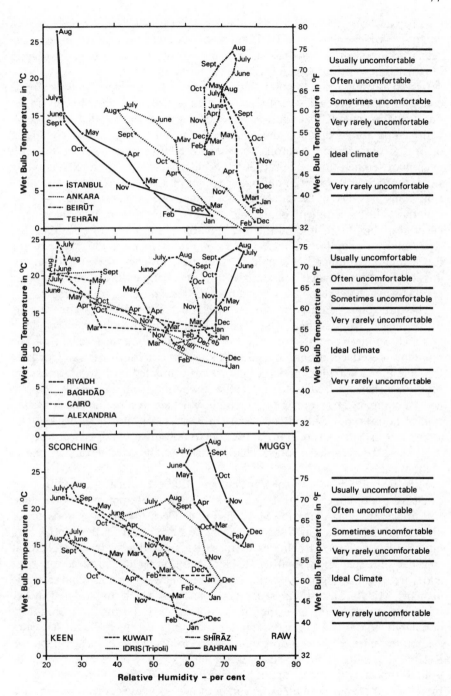

Figure 2.14 Climographs for selected cities in the Middle East

region as a whole, they tend to conceal the wide range of extreme meteorological conditions which can prevail. To the inhabitants of the Middle East, an 'average' year is soon forgotten, whereas an extreme year of flood or drought lives long in the memory of the peoples, owing to its devasting effects.

It is equally important to point out that in such a large region, similar extreme conditions rarely prevail over the whole area at the same time. For example, during 1973, while Khuzestan was experiencing an exceptionally hot August, with temperatures of 50°C and above, and with many people collapsing of heat stroke, central Anatolia was having relatively cool conditions with maximum temperatures of only 30°C. Similarly, while widespread flooding swept through northern Iran during the winter of 1968 to 1969, almost rainless conditions prevailed at the same time over much of Egypt and Libya.

Perhaps the most difficult of all meteorological factors to assess is the general effect of a climatic regime on the local inhabitants in terms of both their life styles and an adaption of their living conditions to meet the requirements of a harsh environment. It should be admitted, however, that it is often impossible to separate what is a cultural trait of a people developed in another region from a direct response of a group to the local physical environment.

The flat roofed, courtyard house so characteristic of the southern part of the region, with its thick whitewashed brick or mud walls, small windows and high-ceilinged rooms, provides cool indoor conditions as a relief from the scorching desert conditions outside (Chapter 6). In southern Iran, lowland Iraq and the Gulf region, underground rooms ventilated from wind towers are often constructed in houses, to protect the inhabitants from the fierce oppressive heat of summer. High precipitation conditions have resulted in the construction of house types with pitched roofs in western and northern Turkey and along the Caspian coast of Iran. In Iran, such roofs are often thatched, whereas in Turkey the red-tiled roof so characteristic of the Mediterranean region predominates.

Modern buildings, now so prevalent in Middle Eastern cities, with their extensive use of concrete, steel, and glass, often do not appear to be designed with any particular climatic regime in mind. Occasionally one finds tower blocks with balconies which shade the windows beneath from the midday sun, but mostly the internal climates of these large buildings are controlled, at considerable expense, by sophisticated air conditioning units. Indeed, the buzz and whine of air conditioners during summer is a new urban noise characteristic of many Middle Eastern cities. In the large cities which are situated in dry inland locations, simple evaporative coolers have become tremendously popular over the last 20 years. These work on the principle that as water evaporates, energy is given up from the air, producing a cooler temperature. Relative humidity is increased, however, and so these coolers can only be utilized successfully where summer humidities of less than 30 per cent prevail. In Tehrān, there has been an explosion in the sale of these coolers over the last five years, and this is now beginning to give rise to concern owing to the very large quantities of water being consumed.

A meteorological phenomenon of increasing importance in the Middle East is air pollution. To some extent this occurs in all the larger cities of the region, although its cause and season of maximum incidence varies. For example, serious air pollution in Ankara is largely a winter phenomenon. It occurs because the city is situated in a large basin which experiences very cold still conditions during the winter period. To combat the cold, the urban population, which now numbers more than 1·3 million, utilize numerous small and generally inefficient lignite and oil burning stoves. As the quality of the lignite which is used is often very poor, the amount of pollution is considerable and visibility is often reduced to a few tens of metres. This problem has become so severe that the government, with the aid of the Middle East Technical University, Ankara, is now attempting to devise a strategy using better quality coal and more efficient combustion methods which will at least alleviate the pollution problem. The fact that the population of Ankara is expected to rise to about five million by the year 2000 clearly illustrates the potential seriousness of the issue in future.

Tehrān, like Ankara, also has a serious air pollution problem, though here the situation is most pronounced during the hot summer period. The basic cause is the accumulation of exhaust gases from the many vehicles which crowd the streets of this city of more than three million inhabitants. These gases, and in particular the reactive hydrocarbons, undergo photochemical reactions under the strong sunlight of the summer period, which result in the conversion of nitric oxide into nitrogen dioxide. This gas may have adverse effects on plants, animals and humans if high concentrations occur. Other products reduce visibility and some can cause eye irritation. These phenomena are usually termed 'smog', and their effects are best known from the city of Los Angeles, U.S.A. The first symptom of this form of pollution is visibility reduction, followed by damage to plants and finally eye irritation. In central Tehrān, on hot summer days, the eye irritation stage has now been reached. The problem here is compounded also by the fact that, unlike California, no emission control regulations as yet exist for automobile exhaust systems. Consequently, badly tuned engines, burning incorrect octane fuels and spewing out noxious gases are a common sight in the streets of Tehrān.

Although Tehrān, on account of its huge size, has been singled out to illustrate the photochemical air pollution problem created by automobiles, it is by no means the only large city in the area to suffer in this way. Indeed Beirūt, Tel Aviv, Baghdād, Cairo, and İstanbul all suffer this same type of pollution to varying degrees. With the expected growth of all these cities, together with the associated rise in the standard of living of the inhabitants, there can be little doubt that the problem will become much worse in the future, unless regulations controlling exhaust emissions are introduced quickly.

Finally, mention must be made of one of the most controversial issues relating to the environment of the Middle East, which is the question of whether the region has been subjected to marked changes of climate during the Quaternary era (Chapter 1). Although climate change during the Pleistocene period is now widely accepted as having occurred in the Middle East, the nature of climatic change during the Holocene is still a matter of considerable dispute and the subject of a considerable research effort. Recently, a number of works have appeared treating the issue of climatic change on a world scale.[19] These have emphasized the fact that any major breakthrough in our knowledge of the climatic changes which may have occurred during the last 10,000 years, is more likely to come from our increasing understanding of the general circulation of the atmosphere, than from detailed local and regional works. Certainly, the present range of literature dealing with Holocene climatic changes in the Middle East reveals a dearth of information which can be interpreted in a number of different ways.[20] Unfortunately, it would seem that man's impact on the Middle East has been so great, that it is probably now impossible, from the evidence remaining, to separate environmental changes caused by variations in climate from those induced by human activity.

2.2 Water resources

2.2.1 Introduction

A reliable supply of water for both domestic and agricultural use is one of the prerequisites for human survival. As a result, perennial water sources have played a crucial role in the siting of settlement and the growth of economic activity in the Middle East. In the past, water resource development has tended to take place at a local level, with the aim of supplying immediate agricultural and domestic needs from either surface or groundwater sources. With increasing populations, and in particular the rapid growth of large cities, local water sources are often totally inadequate to supply the new demands. As a result, individual countries have had to resort to the implementation of a number of large water resource projects, often at least partially financed from overseas sources.

2.2.2 Available water resources

The two major dimensions of water are quantity and quality. The former can usually be adequately described with the aid of precipitation and runoff data, but the latter, owing to the lack of detailed observations, is often a neglected aspect of water resource studies. Water quality is normally assessed in terms of its chemical, physical and bacteriological characteristics. The quality requirements for water depend largely upon the use to which it is to be put. Highest standards are associated with drinking water, while many industrial processes can utilize water of a low quality. For irrigation purposes, a detailed knowledge of water quality is also essential, if serious soil problems are to be avoided. A classification of irrigation waters is normally made in terms of the salinity hazard, and the sodium (alkali) hazard.[21]

The total water supply within a region is best studied by means of a map

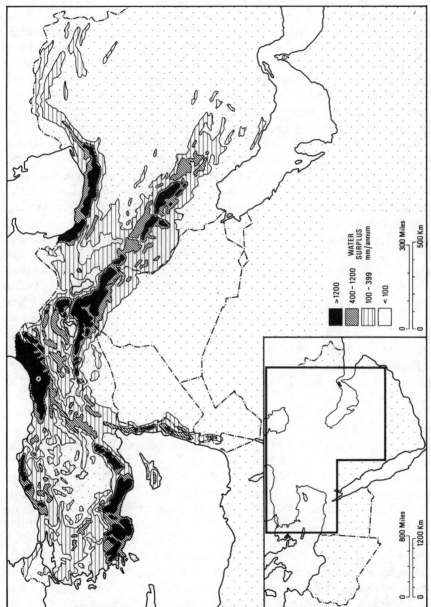

Figure 2.15 Mean annual water surplus in the Middle East (after Thornthwaite, Mather and Carter, 1958)

of annual precipitation. Such a map, however, is not necessarily a good indication of water availability, in terms of the water supply which can be utilized by man for beneficial purposes. In the hot and arid regions of the world, a large proportion of the precipitation is lost through evapotranspiration, from water and vegetation surfaces, with little or no economic gain. To obtain more accurate assessments of water availability, maps of water surplus have been constructed for parts of the Middle East[22] (Figure 2.15). These maps, constructed from monthly data, show the annual water surplus which represents the sum of the monthly differences between precipitation and potential evapotranspiration. Water surpluses are often transported from their places of origin to other regions by river flow. As a result the mean annual discharge from a drainage basin is equivalent to the mean annual water surplus. Although most of the water surplus normally occurs within a restricted period of the year, its export is often delayed as a result of infiltration and subsequent discharge as groundwater, or by snow storage. Water surpluses, whether abstracted from surface water sources, or from groundwater, permit irrigated agriculture throughout much of the Middle East.

The map of water surplus, constructed by use of the Thornthwaite method, clearly illustrates that surpluses are confined to the northern part of the region, and are closely associated with upland areas. The greatest water surplus of 2,400 mm/yr is found at the eastern edge of the Black Sea in northeastern Turkey. Other large surplus regions occur in mountains fringing the Black Sea and the Mediterranean coasts of Turkey, in the coastal uplands of Syria and Lebanon, in the Elburz mountains along the margin of the Caspian Sea, in the mountain regions of eastern Turkey, and in scattered regions throughout the Zagros Mountains. Egypt, much of Syria, Jordan, Iraq and Arabia, together with central and western Iran, are characterized by the absence of a water surplus.

Despite the great size of the Middle East, there are only three rivers, the Nile, Euphrates and Tigris, which can be classed as large by world standards. Of these, the Nile receives most of its discharge from precipitation falling well outside the Middle East on the upland plateau areas of East Africa and the highlands of Ethiopia. In contrast, the watersheds of both the Euphrates and Tigris are situated within the Middle East, dominantly in the countries of Turkey, Syria and Iraq. Elsewhere, perennial river systems are confined to the more northern upland regions of Turkey and Iran, together with the coastal highlands of the Levant.

Owing to the general aridity within the region, a very large proportion of the total area consists of endoreic or inland drainage. Included in this zone is most of North Africa south of the coastal fringe, almost all of Arabia, with the exception once again of a narrow coastal strip, a large part of central Iran and, finally, smaller zones in Turkey, Iraq and the Levant.

Even though maximum precipitation occurs during the winter period, almost all the larger rivers of the northern part of the region are characterized by regime hydrographs with maximum discharge in spring and early summer.

This is the result of the superimposition of a large snow-melt component onto the direct runoff discharge pattern.[23] The larger the proportion of upland within a catchment, the more pronounced the spring and early summer discharge peak tends to be. Further south in the region and also at lower altitudes the regime hydrograph peak more closely reflects the pattern of precipitation distribution throughout the year. From June through to September, owing to the absence of precipitation over most of the region, the rivers are fed almost entirely from groundwater reserves and, as a result, the rivers reveal well developed recession curves.

The total amounts of river water which are available in the countries of the Middle East are still not known with any degree of certainty, although recently an attempt has been made to tabulate existing data[24] (Table 2.10). The favoured position of Egypt, Turkey and Iraq is clearly seen. No comparable data are yet available for Saudi Arabia or Libya, but in both these countries river discharges are small and unreliable.

Average data on the amounts of runoff per unit area are still scarce within the Middle East, since river discharge gauging stations have only recently been established. In Iran, however, a country with a wide range of climatic conditions, recent work has revealed runoff figures of up to 550,000 $m^3/km^2/$ annum, or the equivalent of a water depth of 550 mm/annum, for some of the river systems.[25] Amongst the larger rivers of Iran, for which reliable data are

TABLE 2.10
River water available in Middle Eastern countries

Country	Estimate of total mean annual flow of major rivers (in 10^9 m^3)	
U.A.R.	84	$18 \cdot 5 \times 10^9$ m^3 of this can be used by Sudan
Turkey	80	About 40×10^9 m^3 of this is in Euphrates and Tigris
Iraq	76	Of which only $20-30 \times 10^9$ m^3 originates in Iraq
Syria	28	Of which 24×10^9 m^3 is in Euphrates
Iran	42	22×10^9 m^3 in Kārūn and Dez systems in Khuzestan
Israel	1	Includes Jordan flow
Jordan	0·5	Excludes main Jordan
Lebanon	1·0	Excludes the upper Orontes ($0 \cdot 5 \times 10^9$ m^3)

Source: Smith C. G., 'Water Resources and Irrigation development in the Middle East', *Geography*, **55**, p. 424 (1970).

available, the Kārūn catchment has by far the largest runoff potential, with a value of 255,000 m³/km²/annum.

2.2.3 Irrigation

Irrigation consists of the controlled application of water to the soil with the objective of making good any soil moisture deficiencies which limit the optimum growth of crops. Actual irrigation methods vary with respect to topography, soils, crops, available water supplies and the prevailing cultural pattern within a region. Surface, sub-surface, and sprinkler irrigation are the three basic methods by which water can be added to the soil. In the Middle East, surface irrigation methods continue to be the most important, although there is now an increasing use of sub-surface and sprinkler irrigation methods on the newer schemes.

Surface irrigation can be divided into two main types, flood irrigation and furrow irrigation, both of which are extensively used throughout the region. With flood, or basin irrigation as it is sometimes known, fields are levelled, and surrounded by earth dykes. Water is then rapidly applied to the basin and held there until it all soaks into the ground. This type of irrigation is widely used for cereal cultivation. In furrow irrigation, water is led in trenches, either along or down the slope between individual crop rows. It requires a considerable input of labour to maintain the furrow systems, and, consequently, tends to be utilized only for high value vegetable and fruit crops.

One of the earliest known sites in the Middle East where irrigation appears to have played an important role in the establishment of human settlement, is to be found at the town of Jericho adjacent to the Dead Sea. Here an arid climate prevails, with precipitation totals of less than 150 mm/annum. The water source at this site is a perennial spring, '*Ain es Sultan*, situated at the foot of the western escarpment of the Dead Sea lowlands. The earliest occupation of the site was apparently by Mesolithic hunters and food gatherers in the period around 9000 BC.[26] From this date, almost continuous occupation seems to have occurred leading to the establishment of a walled settlement by about 8000 BC, during the Pre-pottery Neolithic A period. This settlement is believed to have covered an area of about four hectares and to have probably contained a population of between 2,000 to 3,000 inhabitants. By the time the walled city came into being, it would seem that an organized community with a strong leadership must have existed in Jericho. Equally, it seems likely that to feed this relatively large population in such an arid environment, some form of irrigated cultivation of the Jordan valley, using water from the adjacent spring, must have been practised.

The distribution of water in irrigation systems has traditionally been achieved by the use of hand-dug canals, usually in alluvial materials. These canals, some of which, for example the Nahrawān canal in lowland Iraq, were many metres in width, formed the lifelines on which the local agricultural economies relied. In many cases, these canal systems were extremely complex

Two types of irrigation: (top) traditional, using mud walls for diversion purposes (Libyan Embassy, London); (bottom) sprinkler system (Libyan Embassy, London).

Modern river regulator under construction on the Zayandeh River near Esfahan for irrigation purposes. (Peter Beaumont)

and designed to irrigate areas of many hundreds of square kilometres (Chapter 12). Even today intricate irrigation systems, almost exclusively hand constructed, are found. One of their main problems is that water losses through seepage can result in the loss of up to 50 per cent of the water passing through the canal intake. Although such wastage sounds excessive, it should be remembered that in these regions groundwater is often also widely utilized, and that the canal seepage losses are sometimes a very useful method of groundwater recharge.

At the present time it is the usual practice when new irrigation systems are being built, or traditional ones modernized, to construct concrete-lined, trapezoidal, primary canals, as the main arteries of the system. Much more variety exists at the secondary and tertiary distribution levels, including such variates as concrete canalets, underground PVC pipes or, in the majority of cases, still the hand-dug canal.

In the more arid parts of the region, water supply in the past was largely obtained from groundwater sources, either from springs in foothill regions or from hand-dug wells along river valleys or on gravel plains. For centuries, Mecca was dependant upon water from the well of Zam Zam.[27] Later, new wells were sunk and then, as the population of the town expanded and the numbers of people visiting Mecca on pilgrimage increased, water was led into the town along aqueducts from springs adjacent to the town. The most famous of these, *Aine Zubeda*, was about 16 km in length, and brought water from the springs of Zubeda, in the Arafat Hills northeast of the city. It was built in the early part of the ninth century, under the instigation of Queen Zubeda, the wife of Hārūn-al-Rashīd. At Medina, too, water was largely obtained from a shallow aquifer, with about seventy wells in existence during the lifetime of the Prophet Muhammad.[28] A number of aqueducts brought water from springs and wells on the margins of the town.

Further east in Arabia, groundwater has also played an important role in rural life. Between Al Kharj, some 100 km to the southeast of Riyadh, and Al Aflaj, are a series of spectacular solution cavities in calcareous strata. Some of the pits at Al Kharj are 100 m in diameter and more than 130 m in depth, with pools of fresh water forming their floors.[29] At Al Aflaj, the largest pit is almost 0·75 km in diameter. Here it has been claimed that the remains of three irrigation ditches indicate that the water-table has been lowered nine metres in the last millenia, perhaps owing to climatic changes. Water from these pits is utilized for the irrigation of date gardens and cereals.

Al Hufūf, which is the largest oasis in Saudi Arabia, is situated about 100 km west of the Gulf coast. Here groundwater reaches the surface by way of nine prolific springs at a rate of more than 5·6 m^3/sec.[30] Over the years huge date gardens have been planted close by to make use of this water. The sheer volume of available water, however, has led to a serious drainage problem, and, in a number of places, salinity build-up within the soil has taken place.

Comparisons of the proportion of irrigated land within the countries of

TABLE 2·11
Cultivated and irrigated areas in the countries of the Middle East

	Cultivated area (temporary and permanent crops) (ha)	Irrigated area (ha)	Irrigated area as per cent of cultivated area
Turkey	27,378,000	1,549,000	5·75
Iran	16,560,000	4,651,000	28·1
Iraq	10,163,000	3,675,000	31·2
Syria	5,899,000	450,000	7·6
Lebanon	316,000	68,000	21·5
Israel	423,000	174,000	41·1
Jordan	1,300,000	60,000	4·6
Saudi Arabia	809,000	131,000	16·2
Kuwait	500	500	100·0
Egypt	2,843,000	2,843,000	100·0
Libya	2,515,000	124,000	4·9

Source: FAO 1972, *Production Yearbook 1971*, FAO (UN), Rome, Tables 1 and 2.

the Middle East are extremely difficult to make owing to the differing interpretations as to what constitutes cultivated land, and indeed, what is implied by the term irrigation. Nevertheless, accepting that these problems do exist, it is possible to note major differences in the areas under irrigation within the countries of the region (Table 2.11). In terms of the absolute size of the irrigated area, Iran, Iraq, Egypt and Turkey stand out as the most important countries, whilst in Egypt and Kuwait cultivation is not possible without irrigation. The relatively low proportion of irrigated lands in the very arid countries of Libya and Saudi Arabia is largely caused by the use of a very broad definition as to what constitutes the cultivated area.

2.2.4 The *Qanāt*

Throughout much of Iran, groundwater is extracted by means of an unusual engineering construction known as a *qanāt*. This consists of a gently sloping tunnel which conducts water from an infiltration section beneath the watertable to the ground surface by gravity flow. In the construction of a *qanāt* a shaft or well is initially sunk to prove the presence of groundwater at depth. An outlet point for the water is selected, and then a tunnel is dug back into the hillside to link up with the original shaft, or mother well (Figure 2.16). To aid in construction a series of vertical shafts are sunk along the line of the tunnel. These permit the extraction of spoil and provide a measure of air circulation to the workers below. Eventually, the tunnel will intersect the watertable, but construction continues beyond this point, as it is only in this section that water penetrates into the *qanāt*.

The construction of *qanāts* is carried out by a team of workers known as

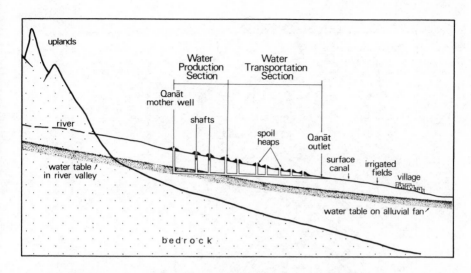

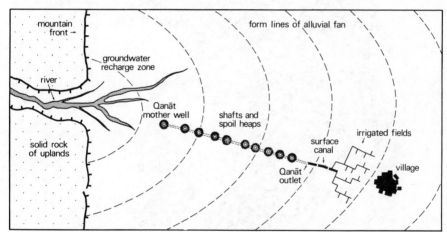

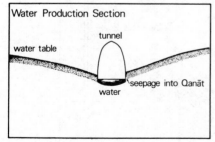

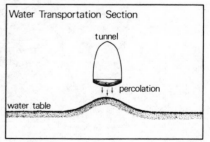

Figure 2.16 A *qanāt*: cross-section and plan (Reproduced by permission of The National Well Water Association)

90

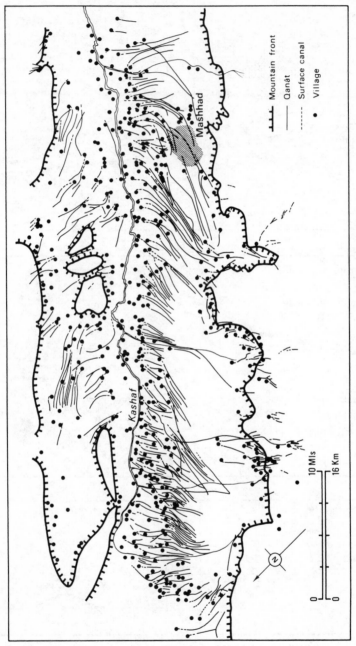

Figure 2.17 *Qanāt* system around Mashhad, Iran

muqannis. All work is carried out by hand and so progress, even in unconsolidated material, is slow. As a consequence, it normally takes many years to construct a single *qanāt*.[31] Almost all *qanāts* are constructed in alluvial material where the water-table is relatively close to the surface. This means that tunnel collapse is often a serious problem, which necessitates the lining of the tunnel with baked clay rings, known as *kavulls*. The average tunnel dimensions are 1·2 m in height by 0·8 m in width. Frequent caving of the roof and sides of the gallery in unlined *qanāts* means that actual dimensions vary considerably.

The great advantage of the *qanāt*, is that once constructed, it will continue to supply water for long periods with little energy input, apart from annual cleaning and maintenance operations. Its largest drawback is that the water discharge is uncontrollable. This means that water runs to waste during the winter season when irrigation is not required. Even during the summer months, water flow during the night is unused, unless a storage reservoir is constructed downslope from the point where the tunnel reaches the ground surface.[32]

Large *qanāt* systems, often with more than a 100 individual *qanāts*, are found throughout Iran[33] (Figure 2.17). These are commonly located on huge alluvial fans in foothill regions, where precipitation totals average between 100 and 300 mm/annum. Groundwater recharge is believed to occur in the better watered adjacent high mountain regions.

Although *qanāts* with lengths of more than 50 km have been described from the Kermān region, it would seem that the vast majority are between one and five kilometres in length.[34] The depths of the mother wells also reveal great variations. A number of *qanāts* in the Jūymand region of eastern Iran have mother wells which are more than 250 m deep.[35] These, however, are exceptional, and in most large *qanāt* systems the majority of the mother well depths range between 10 and 50 m.[36]

The discharge of water from *qanāts* exhibits seasonal variations, as well as longer period trends dependent upon climatic fluctuations, so that discussion of average values is somewhat difficult. Nevertheless, the available measurements for Iranian *qanāts* reveal that the majority of discharge values fall between 0 and 80 m³/hr, although occasionally, values of over 300 m³/hr have been recorded.[37]

Many of the *qanāt* systems have been affected by gradual changes in the methods of groundwater extraction. For example, on the Varāmīn Plain, Iran, numerous wells have been drilled since 1955. Pumping from these wells, together with the effects of a long dry period, has meant that the water-table has fallen appreciably in many parts of the region. The result has been that many of the *qanāts* irrigating the plain have had their discharge reduced and some have even ceased flowing altogether[38] (Chapter 18).

In the Qasvīn area of Iran, a large irrigation and water resource development project has been planned with the aid of Israeli consultants. The main feature of this project has been that the traditional means of groundwater extraction by *qanāt* has gradually been replaced by a number of pumped wells. The method employed has been to pump the aquifer heavily so that the water-table falls and the *qanāts* decrease in water discharge and eventually dry up. In this way, the waters which used to be wasted by *qanāt* discharge during the winter months would remain in ground water storage to be utilized when needed. Technically the plan was very sound, but, unfortunately, little attempt was made to enlist the cooperation of the peasants in the early stages or to tell them the purposes and details of the plan. As a result, the peasant farmers tended to regard the development authority as akin to a new landowner and a widespread resistance to change was generated, which greatly hindered the implementation of the project.[39]

2.2.5 Multi-purpose water resource schemes

The type of water resource development which has been most common in the Middle East since the Second World War has been the construction of a large dam on a river system with the objective of serving a number of purposes. These have usually included the provision of irrigation water, domestic and industrial water supply, hydro-electric power generation, and flood control. Only rarely, however, have the dams been part of an integrated scheme with the aim of the unified development of a river basin system, such as was achieved in the United States of America with the establishment of the Tennessee Valley Authority (T.V.A.). Even within a country, it is rare for comprehensive river basin management to be implemented. All too often in the past, a dam has been constructed with the sole aim of providing benefits to a particular area without any consideration of the likely impacts on the rest of the basin. To some extent this type of development is understandable, as international loan or fund granting agencies, for example, the United Nations or the World Bank, have always been more willing to give financial support to what appears to be a single, well-defined and relatively easily costed project, such as a dam, rather than become involved in the broad and often costly, intangible problems of river basin management.

Of all the major water resource projects completed or under construction in the Middle East, the one which has most captured the imagination of the West is the Aswân High Dam project on the River Nile (Figure 2.18). Although the idea of a large dam on the Nile to control its waters and to provide 'century storage' dates back to the late nineteenth century, finance for the dam was only arranged between Egypt and the U.S.S.R. in the late 1950's and the project was officially inaugurated by President Nasser in 1960.[40]

Before the High Dam project could begin it was essential that a new agreement between Egypt and the Sudan was reached on the distribution of the waters of the Nile. This was achieved by a treaty signed in 1959 which increased the total water rights of the Sudan, previously negotiated in 1929, from 4,000 million m³/annum to 18,500 million m³/annum. It was also agreed that Egypt should pay the Sudan £15 million compensation for the flooding of parts of the Nile valley within the Sudan brought about by the construction of the High Dam.

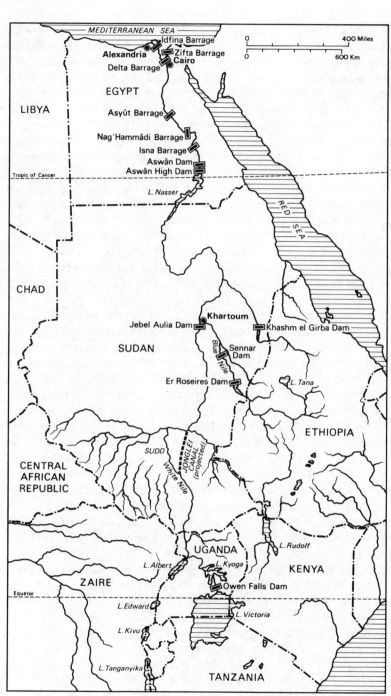

Figure 2.18 Hydraulic works along the Nile

The dam is sited seven kilometres upstream from the earlier Aswân Dam, which was built in 1902 and further heightened in 1921 and 1933. The storage capacity of Lake Nasser, the reservoir held up by the Aswân High Dam, is 164,000 million m³, or approximately thirty times larger than the storage of the heightened Aswân Dam.[41] The High Dam provides a controlled mean annual discharge of 84,000 million m³ downstream from Aswân, which is considered to represent the mean flow of the Nile over a 60 year period.[42]

The great advantage of the High Dam, compared with earlier structures on the Nile, is that it has the capacity to store the flood waters moving down the river and to hold them for use in succeeding years. This is enabling an expansion of the cultivated area by 1·3 million feddans, and a conversion of 700,000 feddans from basin to perennial irrigation. Navigation conditions along the Nile have been improved, and an estimated 10,000 million kWh of hydroelectric power will be generated annually. Flood protection along the lower Nile is now guaranteed, and the productivity of the land has been increased in many areas by a lowering of the water-table. To all intents and purposes, the Nile below Aswân has now been reduced to the status of an irrigation canal.

The construction of the High Dam at Aswân has given rise to a number of problems, some of which were only vaguely appreciated before building began. For example, the dam has prevented the continued movement of silt down the River Nile. With less sediment load to carry below the dam, this has meant that the water has become more erosive, and has begun to undermine the foundations of some of the older bridges and hydraulic structures.[43] The absence of silt in the Lower Nile valley also appears to have damaged the Nile fishing industry by reducing the supply of nutrients, and consequently the number of plants and animals on which the fish feed. Similarly the decline in sardine landings in the eastern Mediterranean over the last few years has been attributed to the same cause.[44]

The spread of bilharzia is being blamed on the High Dam, as well. This disease, carried by parasites living on freshwater snails in irrigation canals, will, it is claimed, increase in incidence with the spread of perennial irrigation and the construction of new canal systems.[45] It should be stressed in fairness, however, that bilharzia was already rampant before the High Dam was built.

The potential loss of water by seepage from Lake Nasser was considered by some engineers to be so serious as to make the whole project a failure. Although such losses are probably considerable, the lake level is now beginning to rise. With continued silt deposition in the lake, seepage losses are likely to be progressively reduced. Seepage and evaporation losses from Lake Nasser when it reaches its maximum level, are expected to be of the order of 15,000 million m³/year.[46]

An objective assessment of the Aswân High Dam and its environmental, social and economic effects is an extremely difficult task. A voluminous literature already exists on the subject, but with many of these works it is hard to separate fact from prejudice. Given a population increase of 2·8 per cent/

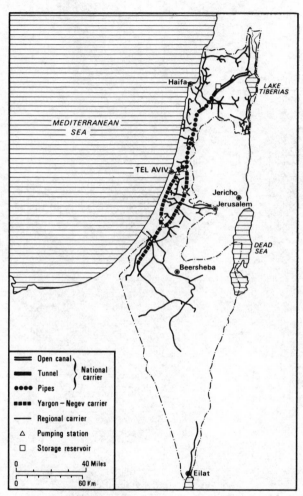

Figure 2.19 Water distribution networks in Israel

Desalination plant on the Gulf of Aqaba at Eilat, Israel, (Israel Embassy, London).

annum, there was little doubt that something had to be done to try and alleviate the falling standards of living of the masses (Chapter 19). The government chose to build the Aswân High Dam. By doing so, it did not solve the basic Egyptian problem of ever increasing human pressure on resources, but it did at least buy a period of time in which more fundamental social and economic changes could be attempted. Many people, with the benefit of hindsight, have claimed that the price Egypt has paid for this privilege has been much too high, and yet the alternatives are scarcely considered. One thing does seem certain; in Egyptian eyes the Aswân High Dam is a huge symbol of progress. The psychological impact on the nation might be just the stimulus which is needed to spur on the Egyptian economy in the future.

The most comprehensive schemes for water resource management in the Middle East are undoubtably found within the small state of Israel (Figure 2.19). Following the establishment of the state in 1948, the government decided to undertake a comprehensive plan for water resource development based on the ideas outlined in Lowdermilk's *Palestine: Land of Promise*.[47] Two factors had considerable importance in the initial stages of development. The first was the lack of capital in the new state, and the second, the urgent necessity to provide water supplies for the many immigrants pouring into the country. It was decided, therefore, that a highly integrated water system should be established, and that emphasis should be placed on the maximum conservation of water, as well as on strict water allocations.[48] To achieve these ends, the water resources of the state were nationalized and a series of water laws and regulations drawn up.

Initially, attention was concentrated on low cost projects, such as the drilling of wells, which produced quick results. These pumped wells permitted the irrigation of new lands in the coastal plain and northern Negev.

With medium term development projects, schemes were chosen which provided the minimum investment per unit of water supplied, which were not technically complex, and which were capable of having the investment divided into a number of stages. At the same time, the idea evolved that every project within the country, no matter what its size, should be capable of being integrated into a nationwide hierarchical water supply system.

A number of long-term projects, which possessed a regional, rather than local significance, were also implemented. One of the largest of the early schemes was the Yarqon-Negev Project, which diverts water from the River Yarqon at the Rosh Ha'ayin springs near Tel Aviv southwards towards the Negev desert. With the output of numerous wells integrated into the project, the total water delivered is 270 million m^3/yr.[49]

Another large development was the Western Galilee-Kishon Project. In this, water from western Galilee was transported to the fertile, but dry Jezreel Plain. In all, 85 million m^3/yr are carried by the system. This is made up largely of surface water supplies during the winter months, when these are relatively abundant, and ground water during the drier summer period.

An unusual project is located in the Beit She'an Valley. Here abundant water is available from saline springs, but by itself, it is too salty to be used for irrigation purposes. However, it has been found possible to utilize this water by diluting it with purer water obtained from Lake Tiberias.

The largest water resource development project in Israel is the National Water Carrier, which is a huge aqueduct and pipeline network carrying the waters of the River Jordan southwards along the coastal plain region. This scheme stems from earlier ideas and concepts for the integrated development of all the waters of the River Jordan for the mutual benefit of the states of Lebanon, Syria, Jordan and Israel. In the earlier 1950's, discussions took place between Israel and the adjoining Arab states in an attempt to reach an understanding as to how the waters of the River Jordan might be most fairly allocated amongst the four states. This plan, which was drawn up for the United Nations is usually referred to as the 'Main Plan'.[50] After prolonged negotiations, modifications to the original plan were made and this new version became known as the 'Johnston Plan', named after the American mediator, Eric Johnston. This gave Israel 36 per cent of the utilizable waters of the Jordan, estimated at 1,380 million m³/yr, compared with 52 per cent for Jordan, seven per cent for Syria, and three per cent for Lebanon. It is widely assumed that the technical experts of the various countries involved agreed upon the details of this plan, although soon afterwards the governments rejected it for political reasons.

With the failure of these negotiations, both Israel and Jordan decided to proceed with water projects situated entirely within their own boundaries. As a result Israel began work on the National Water Carrier in 1958. The major storage reservoir, and also the starting point for the scheme, is Lake Tiberias. From here water is pumped through pipes from 210 m below sea level, to a level from where it flows by gravity to a reservoir at Tsalmon. After a further lift, the water flows via a canal to a large storage reservoir at Beit Netofa, which forms a key part of the system. South of Beit Netofa, the water is carried in a 270 cm pipeline to the starting point of the Yarqon-Negev distribution system at Rosh Ha'ayin. In the initial stages 180 million m³/yr of water were carried. This capacity was increased to 360 million m³/yr in 1968, and it is now believed that the maximum capacity approaches 500 million m³/yr.[51] This has, however, not yet been attained owing to water salinity problems. At the present time, the national water grid interconnects all the major water demand and supply regions of the country, with the exception of a number of desert regions in the south. In total, it supplies approximately 1400 m³/yr, or about 90 per cent of all Israel's easily available water resources. This allows more than 116,000 ha of land to be irrigated compared with a figure of 28,000 ha when Israel was established in 1948.[52] More than half of the water is obtained from the River Jordan and its tributaries, with a further 14 per cent from the River Yarqon. The largest groundwater contribution is produced from coastal aquifers and amounts to 29·5 per cent of the total. Approximately five per cent of the supply is obtained by the reclamation of waste waters from the Tel Aviv metropolitan area.

Israel is now rapidly approaching the time when all her easily available water resources will be fully utilized. Once this occurs, the continued development of the nation can only continue if stringent policies of water control and use are introduced. These are likely to include attempts, first, to obtain even higher yields, if possible, from the present system; secondly, to ensure the transfer of water use from low value to high value production; thirdly, to increase the efficiency of water utilization; and finally, to introduce on a large scale the widespread desalination of sea water.

2.2.6 Industrial and domestic demands for water

The growth of the large cities in the Middle East has imposed a tremendous burden on the water supply facilities of the urban centres for domestic and industrial use. In the past, drinking water was obtained from local sources such as wells and streams. The increase in population numbers of the last 30 years or so has meant that such supplies have now become totally inadequate, and the water catchment regions have had to be continuously enlarged in an attempt to cope with water demands. Even with these tremendous efforts, it is true to say that almost every large city in the Middle East has water supply problems, and that these are likely to increase before the end of the century.

Tehrān, the capital of Iran, over the last few years, has experienced growing problems with both domestic water supply and sewage disposal. Since 1922, the population of greater Tehrān has grown from 210,000 to an estimated 3·4 million in 1971,[53] and it has been this phenomenal growth which has strained the water resources of the area to their limit. With no perennial streams close by, Tehrān has been dependent on 34 local *qanāts* for its water supply until very recently.[54]

With growing water demand during the 1920's, a canal was constructed to carry water from the River Karaj, in the west, to Tehrān. This project was completed in 1930, and had a capacity of 1·3 m^3/sec.[55] By 1950, water was once again in short supply, and so a well-drilling programme in the city was initiated. At the same period, the installation of a piped water system was commenced to replace the prevailing open ditch distribution system, but the rapid rate of growth of the city meant that large areas still received their supply by traditional methods.

In the early 1960's, the severity of the Tehrān water shortage was alleviated by the construction of the Amir Kabir (Karaj) Dam and of two pipelines for transporting the water to the city. This scheme provided Tehrān with an extra 144 million m^3/annum of water, to make a total available supply of 184 million m^3/annum.[56] With the continued expansion of the capital still further water was needed. This time it was provided by the construction of the Farahnaz Pahlavi (Latian) Dam on the River Jaji to the east of Tehrān, which was opened in 1967, and supplied an extra 80 million m^3/yr.[57]

Even the total water supply from these two large projects, has now become insufficient to satiate the rising need for water in Tehrān beyond 1973. As a result, new and even larger schemes to provide water are at present under review. Although no final decision has yet been made, the most likely project to be implemented involves the diversion of the headwaters of the River Lar, which flows into the Caspian Sea, southwards in a huge tunnel beneath the Elburz Mountains and into the River Jaji (Figure 2.20). The water would then flow into the reservoir behind the Farahnaz Pahlavi (Latian) Dam from which it could be distributed to the Tehrān network through existing pipelines.

Related to the problem of water supply is that of sewage disposal. Until very recently, Tehrān has possessed no integrated sewage system, and human wastes were discharged untreated into the ground or into the nearest water course. As a result, the shallow aquifers became contaminated, but, fortunately, the deeper and at present more important ones, have remained unpolluted. With the construction of a modern sewage disposal system, which is at present under way, it is hoped that the potential danger of disease will be prevented, or at least substantially reduced, and that water pollution can be controlled.

İstanbul is another large city which is suffering from severe water supply and waste water disposal problems at the present time. Large parts of the city are not provided with a public water supply, while industrial expansion both within the city and in the region to the east has been hampered by lack

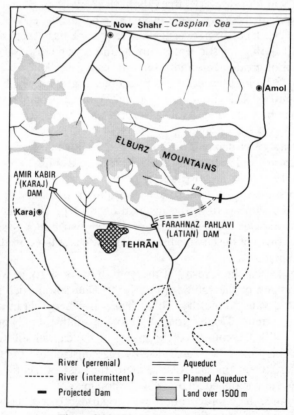

Figure 2.20 Tehrān: water supply

of water. Groundwater has been contaminated locally due to an inadequate sewage system and beaches and waterways around the city have been grossly polluted by domestic and industrial effluents. Here, as elsewhere, the major problem has been population growth, coupled with a rise in the per capita demand for water. In 1965, the Greater İstanbul region had a population of 2·5 million. By the early 1970's it reached three million and official estimates predict a figure of nine million by the year 2020. At present the water supplied to the region is approximately 120 million m³/yr, although the actual demand is estimated to be nearer 170 million m³/yr. This clearly illustrates the deficiencies of both the present distribution system and also the resources available.

Detailed work carried out by, and for, the Turkish government has shown that an adequate water supply for the Istanbul city region can be supplied from within a radius of 100 km to meet the anticipated demands of the early part of the twenty first century. However, it does entail the construction of a number of large reservoir projects to control surface water runoff, and, naturally, involves a very large capital investment programme.

Waste and effluent disposal within the area is also causing concern, as the waters of the Sea of Marmara, the Bosporus and İzmit Bay, all of which possess great value from aesthetic, recreational and other utilitarian stand-points, become increasingly polluted. Throughout much of the region sewage works are rare, and the waste waters are usually discharged untreated into the nearest water course. Within the city of İstanbul, a sewage system, with parts dating back to the Byzantine and Ottoman administrations, does exist, but it is estimated to serve only one quarter of the city's area.

The Government is now well aware of the severity of the pollution problem within the region, and planning and construction of an integrated sewage system with separate storm and foul water sewers has recently begun. The problem of efficient disposal is made particularly difficult by the fact that İstanbul is a linear coastal city, and, therefore, sewage has to be collected over a very wide area. Outfalls for the system will be into the Sea of Marmara and the Bosporus.

All other cities in the region face, to a greater or lesser degree, the sort of problem outlined in the case studies for Tehrān and İstanbul. Indeed, in the future it seems that the supply of water to cities, and the disposal of waste and contaminated water is likely to cause much greater problems in the Middle East than those generated by the provision of irrigation waters to supply agricultural needs. Whether they can be efficiently and economically overcome in the immediate future is still uncertain.

References

1. F. K. Hare, 'The causation of the arid zone', in *A History of Land use in Arid Lands*, Arid Zone Research, **17**, UNESCO, Paris, 1961, 35–50.
2. M. I. Budyko, N. A. Yefimova, L. I. Aubenok and L. A. Strokina, 'The heat balance of the surface of the earth'. *Soviet Geogr.*, **3**, 3–16 (1962).
3. L. Weickman, *Some characteristics of the sub-tropical jet-stream in the Middle East*

102

and adjacent regions, Meteorological Publications, Series A, No. 1, Ministry of Roads, Meteorological Department, Tehrān, Iran, 1961, 29 pages.
4. Meteorological Office, *Weather in the Mediterranean*, **1** *(Second edition)*, *General Meteorology*, London, Her Majesty's Stationery Office, 1962, 32.
5. G. Perrin de Brichambaut, and C C. Wallén, *A Study of Agroclimatology in semi-arid and arid zones of the Near East*, World Meteorogical Organisation, Technical Note No. 56, Geneva 1963, 8.
6. P. Beaumont, 'The Road to Jericho—A Climatological Traverse across the Dead Sea Lowlands', *Geography*, **53,** 170–174 (1968).
7. G. Perrin de Brichambaut and C. C. Wallén, *A study of Agroclimatology in semi-arid and arid zones of the Near East*, World Meteorological Organisation, Technical Note No. 56, Geneva, 1963, 10 et seq.
8. A. H. Gordon and J. G. Lockwood, 'Maximum one day falls of precipitation in Tehrān', *Weather, Lond.*, **25,** 2–8 (1970).
9. (a) H. L. Penman, 'Natural evaporation from open water, bare soil and grass', *Proc. R. Soc. Series A.*, **193,** 120–145 (1948).
   (b) C. W. Thornthwaite and J. R. Mather, *Instructions and tables for computing the potential evapotranspiration and the water balance.* Publs. Clim. Drexel Inst. Technol., **X,** 1957, 311 pages.
10. C. W. Thornthwaite, J. R. Mather and D. B. Carter, *Three water balance maps of southwest Asia*, Publs. Clim. Drexel Inst. Technol., **XI,** 1958, 57 pages.
11. J. E. Van Riper, *Man's Physical World*, McGraw-Hill Book Company, New York, 1971, 627–630.
12. UNESCO–FAO, *Bioclimatic Map of the Mediterranean Zone*, Arid Zone Research, **XXI,** UNESCO, Paris, 1963, 58 pages.
13. UNESCO–FAO, *Environmental Physiology and Psychology in Arid Regions—Review of Research*, Arid Zone Research, No. **21,** UNESCO, Parıs, 1963, 345 pages.
14. (a) H. Kanter, *Libya*, **1,** Geomedical Monograph Series, Geomedical Research Unit of the Heidelberg Academy of Sciences, Springer-Verlag, Berlin, 1967, 188 pages.
   (b) G. E. Ffrench and A. G. Hill, *Kuwait*, **4,** Geomedical Monograph Series, Geomedical Research Unit of the Heidelberg Academy of Sciences, Springer-Verlag, Berlin, 1971, 124 pages.
15. G. Taylor, *Australia*, Methuen and Co. Ltd., London, 1955, 72–74.
16. J. Lomas, 'Forcasting wheat yields from rainfall data in Iran', *World Meteorological Bulletin*, **XXI,** 9–14 (1972).
17. D. E. Pedgley and P. M. Symmons, 'Weather and the locust upsurge'. *Weather, Lond.*, **XXIII,** 484–492 (1968).
18. D. E. Pedgley and P. M. Symmons, 'Weather and the locust upsurge', *Weather, Lond.*, **XXIII,** 485 (1968).
19. (a) H. H. Lamb, *Climate: Present, Past and Future, Vol. 1. Fundamentals and Climate Now*, Methuen & Co. Ltd., London, 1972, 613 pages.
   (b) Royal Meteorological Society, *World Climate from 8000 to 0 B.C.*, Proceedings of the International Symposium held at Imperial College, London, 18 and 19 April 1966, Royal Meteorological Society, London, 1966, 229 pages.
   (c) W. C. Sherbrook and P. Paylore, *World Desertification: Cause and Effect*, Arid Lands Resource Information Paper No. 3, University of Arizona, Office of Arid Lands Studies, Tucson, Arizona, 1973, 168 pages.
20. UNESCO-FAO, *Changes of Climate*, Arid Zone Research, **XX,** UNESCO, Paris, 1963, 488 pages.
21. L. V. Wilcox, *Classification and use of irrigation waters*, U.S. Dept. Agric. Circular No. 969, Washington, 1955, 7.
22. C. W. Thornthwaite, J. R. Mather and D. B. Carter, *Three water balance maps of southwest Asia*, Publs. Clim. Drexel Inst. Technol., **XI,** 1958, 57 pages.
23. P. Beaumont, *River regimes in Iran*, Occasional Publications (New Series) No. 1, Department of Geography, University of Durham, 1973, 29 pages.

24. C. G. Smith, 'Water resources and irrigation development in the Middle East', *Geography*, **55**, 424 (1970).
25. P. Beaumont, *River regimes in Iran*, Occasional Publications (New Series) No. 1, Department of Geography, University of Durham, 1973, 10–13.
26. K. Kenyon, 'The origins of the Neolithic', *Advmt. Sci., Lond.*, **26**, 155 (1969).
27. N. A. Jiabajee, 'Saudi Arabia—water supply of important towns', *Pakist. J. Sci.*, **9**, 192 (1957).
28. N. A. Jiabajee, 'Saudi Arabia—water supply of important towns', *Pakist. J. Sci.*, **9**, 197 (1957).
29. K. S. Twitchell, 'Water resources of Saudi Arabia', *Geogrl. Rev.*, **34**, 380 (1944).
30. K. S. Twitchell, 'Water resources of Saudi Arabia', *Geogrl. Rev.*, **34**, 384 (1944).
31. P. W. English, 'The origin and spread of qanats in the Old World', *Proc. Am. phil. Soc.*, **112**, 174 (1968).
32. D. J. Flower, 'Water use in north-east Iran', in *The Land of Iran* (Ed. W. B. Fisher), **1**, The Cambridge History of Iran, Cambridge University Press, Cambridge, 1968, Chapter 19, 603.
33. P. Beaumont, 'Qanāt systems in Iran', *Bull. int. Ass. scient. Hydrol.*, **XVI**, 39–59 (1971).
34. (a) P. W. English, 'The origin and spread of qanāts in the Old World', *Proc. Am. phil. Soc.*, **112**, 170 (1968).
   (b) P. Beaumont, 'Qanāt systems in Iran', *Bull. int. Ass. scient. Hydrol.*, **XVI**, 43 (1971).
35. P. Beaumont, 'Qanāt systems in Iran', *Bull. int. Ass. scient. Hydrol.*, **XVI**, 46 (1971).
36. P. Beaumont, 'Qanāt systems in Iran', *Bull. int. Ass. scient. Hydrol.*, **XVI**, 45 (1971).
37. P. Beaumont, 'Qanāt systems in Iran', *Bull. int. Ass. scient. Hydrol.*, **XVI**, 47 (1971).
38. P. Beaumont, 'Qanāts on the Varāmīn Plain, Iran', *Trans. Inst. Br. Geogr.*, **45**, 177 (1968).
39. A. K. S. Lambton, *The Persian Land Reform*, Clarendon Press, Oxford, 1969, 281.
40. United Arab Republic, Ministry of the High Dam, Aswân High Dam Authority, *Aswân High Dam—Commissioning of the First Units—Transmission of Power to Cairo*, Ministry of the High Dam, Aswân, Egypt, 1968, 6.
41. Arab Republic of Egypt, Ministry of Culture and Information, State Information Office, *The High Dam*, State Information Office, Cairo, Egypt, 1972, 11.
42. United Arab Republic, Information Department, *The High Dam—Bulwark of our Future*, Information Department, Cairo, Egypt, 1963, 6.
43. C. Hollingworth, 'Egypt's Aswân balance-sheet', *The Times*, London, 15 January (1971).
44. Arab Report and Record, 'Dam devastates Mediterranean fishing', *Arab Report and Record*, Issue 23, 1–15 December, 677 (1970).
45. J. McCaull, 'Conference on the ecological aspects of international development', *Nature and Resources* (UNESCO), **V**, 6 (1969).
46. T. Little, 'Why cry havoc at Aswân?', *Middle East International*, June, No. 3, 5 (1971).
47. W. C. Lowdermilk, *Palestine—Land of Promise*, Victor Gollancz Ltd., London, 1944, 167 pages.
48. A. Wiener, *The Role of Water in Development*, McGraw-Hill, New York, 1972, 403.
49. Y. Prushansky, *Water development*, Israel Digest, Israel Today, No. 11, Jerusalem, 1967, 24.
50. C. T. Main, *The Unified Development of the Water Resources of the Jordan Valley Basin*, Boston, Massachusetts, 1953.
51. (a) C. G. Smith, 'The disputed waters of the Jordan', *Trans. Inst., Brit. Geogr.*, **40**, 122 (1966).
   (b) E. Orni and E. Efrat, *Geography of Israel*, Israel Universities Press, Jerusalem, 1971, 451.

52. A. Weiner, *The Role of the Water in Development*, McGraw-Hill, New York, 1972, 404–405.
53. Echo of Iran, *Iran Almanac 1971*, Echo of Iran, 1971, 101.
54. X. De Planhol, 'Geography of Settlement', in *The Land of Iran* (Ed. W. B. Fisher), **1,** The Cambridge History of Iran, Cambridge University Press, Cambridge, 1968, 452.
55. Plan Organisation, *Dam construction in Iran*, Bureau of Information and Reports, Tehrān, 1969, 69.
56. Plan Organisation, *Dam construction in Iran*, Bureau of Information and Reports, Tehrān, 1969, 69.
57. M. Vahidi, *Water and Irrigation in Iran*, Plan Organisation and Bureau of Information and Reports, Tehrān, 1969, 69.

CHAPTER 3

Landscape Evolution

3.1 Introduction

Over millenia wind and weather have shaped a variety of landscapes from the rocks of the Middle East, though locally tectonic movements and volcanic eruptions have been important. Man's basic demands for food, fuel and raw materials played their part, particularly through their effects upon vegetation.[1] Palaeolithic man no doubt had some effect upon his environment, especially through the use of fire.[2] However, it was with the domestication of plants and animals, what Childe called the 'Neolithic Revolution', that man began to clear vegetation on an increasing scale and to initiate far-reaching, even irrevocable changes in his environment. Crucial developments after initial domestication were the emergence of peasant farming and nomadic pastoralism, together with the diffusion of their characteristic techniques throughout the region. Farming and pastoralism have gradually worn away the surface of the natural landscape, leaving only its bare bones behind in many districts. On the margins of the region's deserts, man's work has been assisted by irregular fluctuations of precipitation, for in such marginal zones any interference with the delicate natural balance can produce havoc, though, as Lamb has pointed out, climatic and human effects are often inextricably confused in this sensitive zone.[3]

The result of physical and human interaction by the closing decades of the twentieth century has been the production of a variety of landscapes. Some of these are mapped in Figure 3.1, but particular emphasis has been given to the 'humanized' landscapes. The most obvious 'natural' landscapes include the mountains above 3000 to 4000 m in Iran and Turkey, where corrie glaciers and permanent snow fields are found, and the great sand seas of the Nafūd and the Rub'al Khālī in Arabia. At least as impressive are the blackened lava tracts and barren, stone-strewn surfaces of Arabia and Egypt, as well as the shimmering salt flats of central Iran. Towns, especially those above 500,000 in population, contain the clearest man-made landscapes in the region, but the gold and green landscapes of dry- and irrigated-farming are equally human creations, as are the burnt and overgrazed pastures of many districts. But man, plants and animals are sustained by water, and its availability is a fundamental constraint in this arid region, while relief even today exerts a profound effect upon spatial organization and distributional systems. Olive, fig and other tree plantations sometimes constitute veritable man-made forests, just as much as deliberately afforested areas, but both cover only a small proportion of

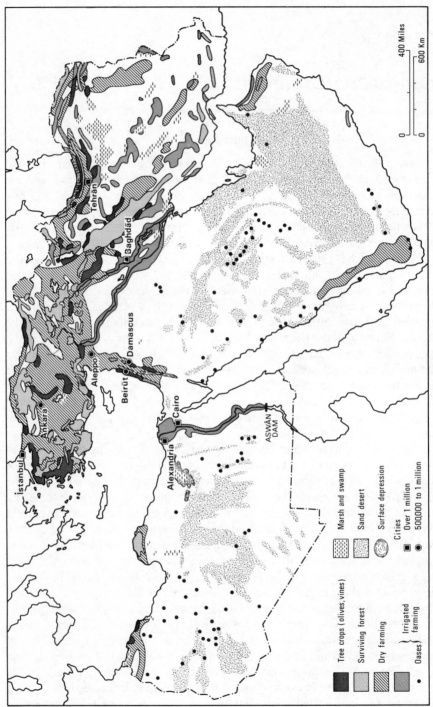

Figure 3.1 Contemporary landscapes of the Middle East

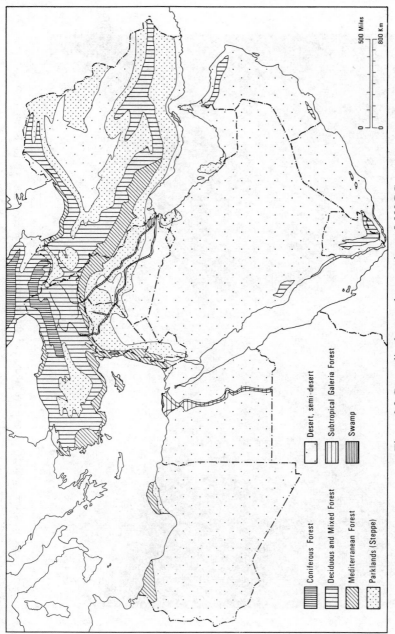

Figure 3.2 Generalized natural vegetation c. 8,000 BC

Coniferous Forest

Deciduous and Mixed Forest

Mediterranean Forest

Parklands (Steppe)

Desert, semi-desert

Subtropical Galeria Forest

Swamp

500 Miles

800 Km

Dense forest along the southern margin of the Plain of Mazanderan, Iran (Peter Beaumont)

the region which, over the centuries, has been either completely denuded of vegetation or severely ravaged by human activity. Very little 'natural' vegetation survives. A reconstruction of the 'natural' vegetation associated with present climates will provide a base from which to gauge the effects of human activity upon the landscape. The effects of man on the 'natural' environment provide the theme for this chapter.

3.2 'Natural' vegetation

Vegetational assemblages are generally related to physical conditions, particularly the prevailing climate. Variations in the types of deposit (aeolian or alluvial) in certain areas of the Middle East have been interpreted as indicating drier or wetter conditions than those prevailing at the present. The period around 3,000 BC, for example, may have been moister than the present, while markedly arid conditions may have prevailed around 2,350 BC.[4] Certainly, within the period of direct evidence from instruments, precipitation across the region was between two and 11 mm lower during the 1920's and 1930's than during the period 1891 to 1910 and temperatures were up to 0·75°C higher.[5] However, Butzer has argued that the main precipitation and temperature characteristics of the present were established by 8,000 BC.[6] 'Natural' vegetation over the region must be adjusted to these conditions (Figure 3.2).

Butzer stated that about 8,000 BC the high mountains of Kurdistan were covered predominantly with coniferous forest,[7] but the accuracy of this view has been contested. Wright has suggested that the Alpine vegetation characteristic there today was already in existence about 10,000 years ago.[8] At lower elevations, where conditions were less severe but precipitation comparatively heavy, as over the Taurus and the western Zagros, a mixed forest of deciduous and coniferous species was found in which black pine *(Pinus pinea)*, juniper *(Juniperus communis)* and the holm or evergreen oak *(Quercus ilex)* were predominant. The mixture varied from area to area so that, for example, the deciduous Persian oak *(Quercus persica)* was common in the western Zagros, while in southwestern Turkey the main components of the forest were juniper and pine.[9] In Lebanon and parts of the maritime Taurus, stands of cedar were found *(Cedrus Libanus)*. At still lower altitudes lay a zone of Mediterranean forest consisting of evergreen, drought-resistant species, such as the Aleppo pine *(Pinus halpensis)*, valonia, holm and kermes oaks *(Quercus macrolepis/aegilops, Q. ilex, Q. coccifera)*, lentisc *(Pistacia lentiscus)*, carob *(Ceratonia siliqua)*, wild olive and wild vine. The whole assemblage was probably fairly open and may have contained a variety of grasses, including the early domesticates—two-rowed barley *(Hordeum distichum)*, emmer and einkorn wheat *(Triticum dicoccum, T. monococcum)*.

Precipitation over central Asia Minor, northern Arabia, much of Iran, and along the Libyan and Egyptian coasts was insufficient to support forest; steppe grasslands punctuated by occasional trees were probably characteristic. With a further decline in precipitation over Arabia and the Sahara even grassland was impossible. It was replaced by grass tufts, shrubs and low bush, which became wider and wider apart until vegetation virtually disappeared as annual precipitation faded away to nearly nothing and the expected frequency became extremely low. Even so, an irregular shower would produce a miraculous flush of vegetation.

Cutting across the desert and semi-desert were linear oases along the valleys of the Nile, the Tigris and the Euphrates. Before their occupation by agricultural communities, these valleys were probably marked by subtropical galeria forest containing species such as tamarisk *(Tamarix gallica, T. mannifera)*, aspen *(Populus tremula)* and oleander *(Nerium oleander)*. Swamps probably existed in low-lying areas where floodwater accumulated, especially in the southern parts of the Tigris–Euphrates lowland and in the Nile delta. Indeed, swamps so impressed the early population of Egypt that such an environment became the epitome of the underworld through which the souls of the dead were required to pass on their way to reincarnation on the eastern horizon. Islands and lines of riverine woodland must also have existed in desert and semi-desert areas wherever a spring, stream or permanent pool occurred. The abundant food supplies of these watery environments were so attractive to early man that agriculture was slow to penetrate, once the initial stages of domestication had been accomplished elsewhere.

3.3 Domestication

Domestication of plants and animals represented a considerable change in the ways by which men secured their subsistence. It is perhaps best summarized as the introduction of deliberate management and control into food production, though, as Flannery has pointed out, the subsistence base was not necessarily more stable or more reliable than a hunting-fishing-gathering economy under Middle Eastern conditions.[10] The chief advantages of farming were that it greatly increased the carrying capacity of a given unit of land[11] and made more intensive use of time and space.[12]

Several theories have been advanced to account for domestication.[13] Most of them are unsatisfactory and proof is difficult, especially since the available archaeological evidence is so equivocal. Explanation based solely on climatic change has been popular in the past, but now seems unacceptable. Man's food supply is unlikely to have been so insecure for famine to be the spur to domestication, while the study of other mammals suggests that, far from starvation acting as the principal regulator of human populations, social behaviour may be a mechanism for maintaining human populations in harmony with the carrying capacity of their inhabited space.[14] Whatever the true explanation, at the time of writing there is a concensus of opinion that the final steps towards recognizable domestication in the west Eurasian tradition were taken at the end of a gradual, almost imperceptible process of developing human control over selected plants and animals within a context provided by an original symbiosis of plants, animals and man. These final steps appear

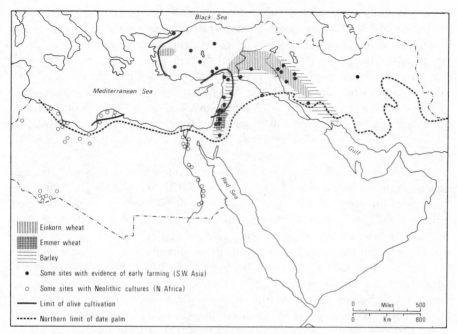

Figure 3.3 Natural distribution of early domesticates: early farming sites

to have been taken within the uplands of, in Darlington's words, 'a single connected region'.[15] Certainly, a fully developed agricultural complex, involving the cultivation of wheat and barley, as well as the keeping of sheep and goats, was widespread by the end of the eighth millenium BC in an arc from Khuzestan through the intermontane valleys of the Zagros and the Taurus mountains into central and western Asia Minor, on the one hand, and southwards into Syria and Palestine, on the other (Figure 3.3). Virtually nothing is known at present of the cultivation techniques employed by the first farmers, though the recovery of flint sickle blades from early contexts in Palestine indicates a specialized range of implements. Even if its use may be considerably older, the appearance of the plough in the archaeological record about 3,000 BC marks the final transition to dry farming of the type which has existed in the Middle East for several millenia down to the present and which seems so well adjusted to the region's soil and water conditions. Wheat and barley, however, were not the only plants which were domesticated. Fruit trees were probably brought into regular cultivation at later dates, but by the fourth millenium the growing of vines and olives had created the triad so characteristic of the Mediterranean fringes of the region down to the present, and so basic to the development of a type of civilization markedly different from those found in the interior parts of the Middle East.

Farming spread from the uplands of the Middle East into the Tigris–Euphrates lowland, the Nile valley and parts of North Africa. Progress was slow. Part of the reason was the existence of resilient collecting economies based on the comparatively rich resources of the rivers and their banks, or, in the case of North Africa, of the comparatively damp mountain areas of the interior. Also important, however, was the need to master techniques of irrigation so that the lack of adequate rainfall could be compensated. Irrigated farming had spread into the Tigris–Euphrates lowland by the late fifth millenium BC and throughout the Nile valley by the fourth millenium BC. Cultivation may have spread to the coastal areas of North Africa independently of Egypt and dry farming was apparent in several places before 5,000 BC. Another 2,000 years passed, however, before cultivation was established in the mountain valleys and oases of the interior.

Pastoralism appears to have developed later than cultivation, though goats were probably domesticated before 7,000 BC. Although cultivators continued to keep animals, specialist forms of pastoralism soon developed (before 6,000 BC in North Africa), perhaps as a means of using different, but adjacent environments to meet the needs of settled cultivators for cheese, hides and draught animals. Important developments were the domestication of the Bactrian camel *(Camelus bactrianus)* and the dromedary *(Camelus dromedarius)*. The Bactrian camel appears to have been domesticated in central Asia between the third and second millenium BC, but was introduced to the northern parts of the Middle East much later. The dromedary may have been first broken in southern Arabia before 1,000 BC, but its effective use as a beast of burden and the basis of 'desert power' came with the adaptation of horse saddles in northern Arabia some time before the ninth century BC when the first evidence appears.[17] Use of the dromedary allowed fully nomadic pastoralism to develop in Arabia and adjacent areas and to appear into North Africa. Various forms of pastoralism and cultivation have co-existed in the Middle East and North Africa for several millenia, alternately expanding and contracting their domains in response to political and economic conditions, as well as to fluctuations in precipitation. Both economies have slowly transformed the 'natural' landscapes of the region.

3.4 Effects of domestication

Domestication itself initiated widespread, radical and perhaps irreversible changes in the uplands. Woodland was thinned and even cleared in various ways to allow cereals to grow. The extent of the cultivated area required would depend upon the size of the community which had to be fed, but the support of even quite small numbers could result in extensive clearance. For example, to support the 125 to 175 people at the famous site of Jarmo, which flourished around 6,000 BC, it has been estimated that a crop area of between 45·0 and 91·2 ha would have been necessary.[18] Forest and bush fallowing techniques, which may have been used by early cultivators, would have required a larger area. Regeneration of woodland on these cleared plots may have been prevented partly by the brousing and grubbing of domesticated animals and partly by changed soil and water conditions, so that in time quite wide areas of woodland were devastated. The net result of cultivation, then, was to provide open space in the 'natural' forest. Open ground must have become gradually more extensive around the various farming communities. Population increase meant that more land had to be cleared and may have brought in a short-fallow system of working, a development which would have expanded the area of permanently open ground. The unrelenting and steadily mounting demands of the domestic hearth must have also consumed large areas of irreplaceable woodland. Pressure and clearance undoubtedly increased when pottery began to be fired and metals worked.[19] Demand for constructional timber became immense, especially from the evolving kingdoms and empires of the region, and resulted in the deforestation of the more accessible parts of the uplands, such as the upper Euphrates catchment in southeastern Turkey from which timber was sent as rafts to southern Iraq for several thousand years,[20] and the virtual elimination from Lebanon of stands of cedar, a wood valued for its colour and perfume.[21]

Removal of the woodland and its failure to regenerate had several important effects upon the landscape. Clearance of undergrowth may have diminished the number, and perhaps the variety of plants (berries, roots), previously used as food or else forced them into peripheral locations with respect to settlements. Wild game, initially important to early farming villages, almost certainly must have been forced further and further away to become characteristic of remote districts.[22] Forest, too, survived in something approaching its original state only in the more distant and physically difficult parts of the region, such as the Taurus mountains and the High Atlas. Where woodland did not regenerate, any forest and bush-fallowing practices must have come to an end and been replaced by cultivation techniques, involving the plough and fallowing, which themselves kept land open and largely free of 'natural' vegetation. Although dry-farming techniques may help to conserve soil moisture and to some extent preserve natural fertility, the existence of large areas of bare plough soil in winter must have led to the destruction of soils by wind erosion, sheet wash and gullying. The long-term effects were almost certainly a lowering of the water-table and the gradual reduction of the cultivable area. River flow probably became more erratic, too, exposing the lower reaches of valleys to greater floods and the deposition of silt.[23]

Domestication and then peasant farming brought about changes on the human as well as on the physical side of the man–land equation. In the first place, the land area from which people lived was reduced. This may be demonstrated with reference to Iran.[24] In 1956, about 65 per cent of the surface area of Iran was classified as uninhabitable and marginal for exploitation. The remaining 35 per cent was available for some form of exploitation, but only 10 per cent was considered as arable land, actual or potential. A similar situation prevails in other parts of the Middle East (Table 4.6) Domestication, thus, meant that man became increasingly dependent upon a smaller area for subsistence and one which was being diminished by erosion initiated and perpetuated by man's own activities. A second result of domestication may have been an increase in population, perhaps stimulated by growing output, though recent theories suggest that population change is an independent variable and that output rose to meet demand.[25] Either way, the impact of man on the land would have increased. A third change resulting from domestication and the development of peasant farming was also cumulative. This was the gradual emergence of an open, regulated landscape in the uplands. It contained plough-ed fields, terraces and treeless pastures, all of which were linked by trackways and crossed locally by irrigation channels.

Although development began in the uplands, great transformations occurred in the major lowland areas of the region as a result of the spread of cultivation. Not only was 'natural' galeria forest removed, but marshes and swamps were at least partially reclaimed. They were replaced by a regulated landscape composed of basins used for irrigation and networks of irrigation canals. Irrigation, however, was confined to relatively narrow bands along the river channels or to favoured localities on the edges of the surviving marshes. Beyond the immediate vicinity of the rivers lay untamed land. In the Tigris–Euphrates lowland this was semi-arid steppe used as grazing, but scrub vegeta-tion may have survived for quite a long time between the river and the steep valley sides marking the edge of the desert in Egypt. Patterns in the hydraulic landscape changed through time, especially in the Tigris–Euphrates lowland where natural water channels were unstable, meandering and braiding.[26] Developing salination also had effects in southern Mesopotamia leading to the spread of barley growing (relatively salt tolerant) and sheep rearing, as well as to the abandonment of the most severely poisoned land (Chapter 12). The Nile valley did not suffer to the same degree because of the natural flushing of the annual flood, but some salination seems to have developed in parts of the delta by Byzantine times. In Egypt, more than in the Tigris–Euphrates lowland, cultivation responded to the annual fluctuations in the height of the flood, since this conditioned the amount of land which could be cropped in the pre-dam era.[27]

Semi-permanent or permanent settlements predate domestication, but the number grew after domestication because farming increased the carrying capacity of land by as much as 200 times.[28] The density and spacing of perma-nent settlements in Khuzestan, a region in southwestern Iran which has been well explored by archaeologists, had achieved their modern characteristics by about 3,500 BC, though the details of the patterns have changed considerably over the intervening time. The same region has also produced evidence for the emergence of towns (Figure 3.4). Around 3,500 BC many settlement sites in Khuzestan varied from one to two hectares in extent, but some had areas of four to five hectares, while a few covered as many as 20 ha. The size hierarchy strongly suggests variations in population and the possibility that the largest settlements performed some urban functions, perhaps arising not only from local marketing needs, but also from some long-distance trade.[29] Although most towns in the Middle East may have resulted from organic growth, some appear to have been created, even during the fourth millenium BC, by the

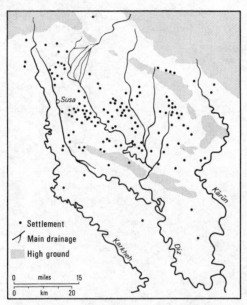

Figure 3.4 Settlement pattern in Khuzistan before about 3,500 BC (Adams, R. M., 'Agriculture and urban Life in Early Southwestern Iran', *Science*), **136,** 109–122, Figure 3 (13 April 1962). Copyright 1962 by the American Association for Advancement of Science)

Aerial view of the city of Rezaiyeh, Iran in 1956, showing the abrupt transition from the built-up area to the irrigated fields, with arid land beyond. (National Cartographic Centre, Iran).

deliberate concentration of population as an administrative and military device,[30] while their internal layout shows clear evidence of structural planning. Once they had appeared, towns became increasingly characteristic of the Middle East. Many continued to result from organic growth at some convenient central place and their importance, even their existence, depended upon the general economic health of their immediate hinterland and, in some cases, upon the flow of trade along long-distance caravan and sea routes. Other towns, however, were artificial creations, generally built for some administrative or political purpose, but they were able to perpetuate themselves because of location at a natural focus, like Baghdād or Cairo,[31] or because their administrative functions survived long enough for them to become the centres of a sustaining web of socio-economic relationships. Whatever their origins, from early times the towns of the region constituted a distinctive built environment, in which large numbers of relatively densely packed dwellings were dominated by large public buildings. They were also organizational and marketing centres, so that their demands for food, fuel and raw materials had significant effects upon the landscape of surrounding regions. In particular, the fluctuating demands of the town economy controlled the rhythm of exploitation in the countryside and thus the pace of landscape change.[32]

3.5 Spatio-temporal variations [33]

So far in this chapter a case has been made for gradual but relentless change in Middle Eastern landscapes as the result of domestication and the subsequent spread of farming and pastoralism. However, over time the direction and pace of landscape change have varied regionally. A frequent theme in the history of the whole region has been the struggle between the desert and the sown, the advance and retreat of the pastoral domain alternating with the contraction and expansion of the cultivated area. Related to this rhythm has been one of change in agricultural specialization in those areas which remained under cultivation. Such spatio-economic changes may be regarded as responses to forces, internal and external to the region, which were as much political as economic. The next few pages attempt to outline some of the major changes and their causes.

Roman rule over North Africa and much of Southwest Asia was sufficiently strong and efficient over several centuries for cultivation to expand, though in some districts at considerable cost to the physical environment. Within the bounds of modern Libya, agricultural expansion during the first and second centuries AD took place within the zone at present suitable for dry-farming, particularly the area near Tripoli and the plateau of Cyrenaica, though the coastal plain near the modern town of Sirte was also intensively developed. Careful attention was given to the control, storage and distribution of winter stream flow, leaving behind massive concrete dams at the heads of various wadis as evidence for this activity. More extensive, though, are systems of terraces running down wadi beds. These were obviously designed to trap silt, soak up runoff, irrigate land and prevent erosion. During the third century AD, following a series of military campaigns against the nomads of the interior, marginal land beyond the effective limits of dry-farming was brought into cultivation, largely through widespread use of water-conserving techniques. For example, the great wadi systems of Sofejin and Zemzem south of modern Misurata were intensively farmed by soldier-farmers living in closely spaced but small, tower-like farmsteads which were part of a deep zone of frontier defence incorporating a few very strong fortresses. Both phases of development were associated with an expansion of olive growing, partly to meet the domestic needs of a growing population and partly to supply the public baths with oil. Oleiculture was already established around the old Greek colonies in Cyrenaica before the Romans took over the territory, but under Roman rule it spread further, particularly across the hilly hinterland of Leptis Magna, where the remains of several oil presses attached to substantial farmsteads may still be seen. In neighbouring parts of modern Tunisia, oil-growing was carefully organized within a grid division of land *(centuriation)* based upon a square with a side of 710 m.[34]

Oleiculture also expanded along the western coast of Asia Minor, where the remains of ancient presses are common. Behind the coasts, though, forests in this region were ruthlessly cut for constructional and fuel purposes and much cleared hill land was brought under the plough or intensively grazed for the first time. The medium-term effects of this 'extractive economy', developed in Hellenistic times but perpetuated under Roman rule, were disastrous. Not only was some land completely ruined by erosion, but increased sedimentation led to the silting up of coastal bays (Figure 3.5), and the gradual extinction of once flourishing ports such as Ephesus and Miletus.[35] Aggradation and increased runoff modified the coastal valleys, producing derelict and marshy land.

The profound economic crisis which affected the Roman and Byzantine Empires between the third and sixth centuries resulted in some release of the exploitive pressure, and initiated a progressive contraction of the cultivated area, especially in districts where precipitation was low and uncertain. Contraction has been explained as the result of denudation and climatic change, but, though there may be an element of truth in these views, an alternative explanation is favoured here. Contemporaries firmly believed that the contraction of arable land resulted from oppressive taxation. The land tax was the basic source of revenue to the state, and it had to be progressively increased in order to pay for an expensive series of wars against Barbarian invaders in the west and Persia in the east, as well as to maintain a bureaucracy expanded as a result of Diocietian's reforms in imperial administration. The effects were to reduce the profitability of estate farming in marginal areas and to concentrate cultivation where it remained profitable, that is, in the main dry-farming areas.[36]

Although partial recovery had taken place by the end of the sixth century, and further local expansions of cultivation were to occur in subsequent centur-

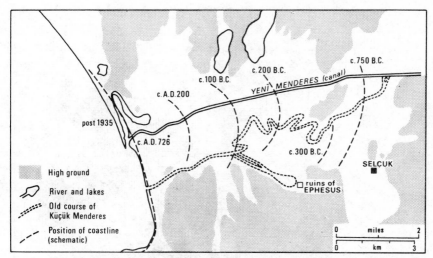

Figure 3.5 Advance of the coastline at the mouth of the Küçük Menderes (Reproduced by permission of Koninklijk Nederlands Aardrijskundig Genootschap)

ies, the period from roughly the end of the sixth century down to the end of the eighteenth century saw a marked contraction of arable land and pulsating expansions of the pastoral domain, as nomads were allowed to spill out of Arabia and the Sahara, or occasionally swept down irresistibly from central Asia. Contrary to popular opinion, the rate of deforestation may have slackened with the spread of nomadism, except close to certain coasts from which shipbuilding and other timber were taken,[37] but regeneration was prevented by the grazing of animals and radically changed soil and water conditions. Irrigation works became too expensive to maintain both in North Africa and Syria, for example, and were allowed to decay, though some canals were breached in the frequent military campaigns. Although some towns were founded by new rulers, whether Arab, Mongol or Turk, generally towns and villages lost population. Many villages were deserted altogether, while the ruins of once magnificent public buildings dwarfed the black tents of nomads in the vicinity of important towns like Baalbek and Jarash in Southwest Asia and Leptis Magna in North Africa.

Various explanations have been offered for such widespread and long-lasting decay. The situation obviously varied locally, but the keys very often appear to have been the degree of administrative control and long-term investment which a particular government and a particular society were capable of making. Thus, the earlier Caliphs restored prosperity to the former frontier provinces of Iraq and Syria, which had been devastated by a series of bitter wars between the Roman and Persian empires. From the ninth century onwards, however, falling tax receipts indicate declining agricultural production, especially in the Tigris–Euphrates lowland where cultivation was precariously dependent upon the maintenance of an elaborate system of flood control

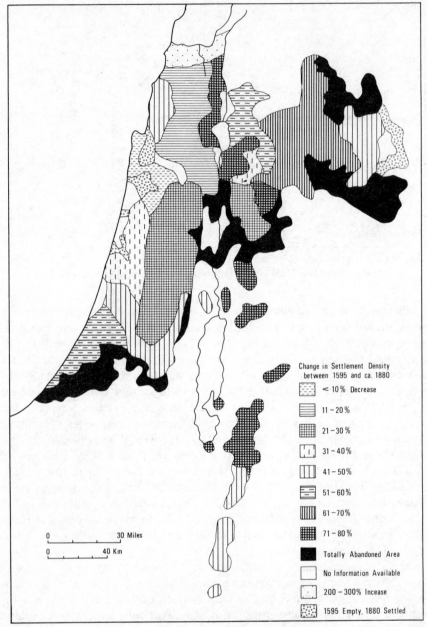

Figure 3.6 Desertion of settlements in Palestine and Transjordan, 1595 to 1880
(Reproduced by permission of Wolf Hütteroth, 1969)

and irrigation works (Chapter 12). Contemporary evidence suggests that
the system was simply neglected. Consequently, canals and distributaries
silted up, while floods created extensive damage which was seldom made good.

At the same time, the peasants were squeezed by an inefficient tax farming system to support a luxurious court and to fight interminable wars, which could no longer pay for themselves in booty. Invasions and ruthless exploitation by foreign rulers completed the process of decay.[38] A similar story can be told for Palestine and Transjordan, which appeared so prosperous when the Crusaders invaded, but which already had acquired a desolate character by 1516, when the territory was incorporated into the Ottoman Empire. Turkish rule did not improve conditions, and the desertion of villages was quite considerable over the next 300 years, especially east of the Jordan (Figure 3.6), where nomadism was allowed to expand.[39]

Western travellers to the Middle East during the eighteenth and early nineteenth centuries painted sad and sorry pictures of the lands which they crossed. Although their views may have been exaggerated, travellers were struck by the widespread devastation and desertion which they saw, as well as the dominant position of the ubiquitous nomad. In Iraq, settled life had ceased altogether along the Tigris north of Baghdād and along the Euphrates north of Al Hillah, while cultivation in Syria had shrunk back to the wetter parts of the region, largely lying west of the road from Aleppo to Damascus. Palestine seemed particularly deserted and devastated to many travellers, familiar with its milk-and-honey landscapes from their reading of the Bible. They came probably expecting too much, but from their accounts it is clear that settled life had contracted into the hills, where a largely subsistence economy based on cereal-growing was maintained. The plains were generally empty and left as grazing to the nomadic tribes which had penetrated from the east during the seventeenth and early eighteenth centuries. Neglect of springs and streams lead to swamp development and its expansion in several areas, notably the Hula Valley.[40]

Change, however, was already underway. In favoured retreat areas, especially Mount Lebanon, agricultural expansion began in the eighteenth century (Chapter 14), while Druze colonists were settling in the upland area further east which subsequently became known as Jebel ed Druze (Chapter 13). Rising demands for food and raw materials from the industrializing countries of western Europe produced a steady, if spatially scattered expansion in the cultivated area of the Middle East during the nineteenth century. Coastal areas were affected first, but the frontier of recolonization moved inland as roads were constructed, railways built and river navigation improved. Thus, the building of the road from Beirūt to Damascus between 1858 and 1863 stimulated cereal growing in the valley of El Beq'a, while the Ankara branch of the Anatolian Railway carried five times as much grain in 1911 as it had in its first full year of operation (1893), an increase which almost certainly resulted from an expansion in the cultivation area in districts accessible to the line. Completion of a narrow gauge railway from Beirūt to Damascus in 1895 further stimulated grain production in the Hauran district of Syria, though the wave of agricultural expansion had begun some sixty years before during the stable period of Egyptian rule (Chapter 13).[41] The introduction of steam navigation to the Tigris in the 1830's cut freight rates and allowed the country to supply markets in India with wheat and barley much more easily than in the past, thereby making it worthwhile for small-scale irrigation projects to begin and extend the cultivated area. Larger irrigation schemes were attempted in the 1850's in Iraq, but without very much success. The expansion of irrigated farming was much more marked in Egypt during the course of the nineteenth century. It began in the 1820's with the construction of small barrages on river channels in the delta to hold back some of the annual flood and use the water for extending the temporal and spatial limits of cultivation. The first major step in developing irrigation took place in 1843 when work began on the construction of barrages at the bifurcation of the two main channels of the Nile. The delta barrages were completed in 1861 and subsequently improved. They allowed extensive reclamation in the delta and the extension of perennial irrigation. Barrages were subsequently built further and further up the valley, but traditional forms of basin irrigation tended to persist here well into the inter-war period. Towards the end of the nineteenth century, however, it came to be realized that effective use of the barrage system really depended upon storing as much of the flood as possible and gradually using it as the flow of the river dropped through the year. The most obvious site for a dam to control the irrigation system of the Nile valley was at the First Cataract. The first Aswân Dam was constructed at this point in 1902 and was subsequently raised in 1912 and 1933. The building of the dam had tremendous effects, but in particular it initiated the penultimate stage in the transformation of Egypt's irrigation system from one dependent upon the direct use of the flood in basins to a perennial system in which water was made available through canals and distributaries. Intensive cropping thus became feasible.

Much of the new land made available in Egypt was put down to cotton, which gradually came to dominate both the economy and the landscape of Egypt during the nineteenth century. Commercial cropping also expanded elsewhere in the Middle East during the century. Cotton growing came to dominate the reclaimed lands of the Çukorova in southeastern Asia Minor. Silk production expanded in Lebanon and mulberry trees became very characteristic of the Mountain. In western Asia Minor, railways opened up the valleys near Smyrna from 1863 and reinforced the development of local specialisms in dried grapes, dried figs and tobacco.

Parallel with these developments ran improvements in administration and political control. Their clearest effect lay in the control which was gradually extended over the nomads and which either assisted in sedentarization or forced nomadic pastoralism into topographically difficult and climatically hazardous districts. Security and stability allowed the growth and the spread of settlements. Old sites were occupied, notably in Syria and Transjordan,[43] and numbers of completely new settlements were established in many districts. A few villages grew organically into towns as the rural economy prospered, as in the case of Zahle which became a collecting centre for the grain of the

Beq'a valley as well as a stopping place on the Beirūt to Damascus road. Some towns, however, were deliberately planted, like Elâziğ, the lowland successor to the citadel-town of Harput (Kharpout) in eastern Turkey.[44] New ports, like Haifa, appeared and old ones, such as Beirūt and Smyrna, expanded considerably in population and extent. Many other towns grew beyond their ancient walls and spatious suburbs were sometimes laid out on European lines. Sedentarization of the nomads and the expansion of permanent, cultivating settlements and market towns were responsible in turn for a renewed assault upon the surviving forests of the region, especially where access was improved by railways and modern roads. A rapid retreat of the forest was a result.[45]

The landscape changes described so far may be represented as the indirect effects of growth in the European market during the nineteenth century. European influence was much more direct in parts of North Africa. A large French territory was carved out of the Maghreb in the decades following the capture of Algiers in 1830, and French colonists were introduced from 1838 onwards, with the greatest flow in between 1860 and 1900.[46] French experience influenced the Italian government after its conquest of Libya in 1911. Much of Tripolitania at that time was seen as empty or under-used land which was ripe for development using techniques already in use in Italy and reviving Roman irrigation systems. Colonization began in an experimental way in 1914, only to be ended by the First World War. A more active colonization and development policy was pursued after 1922, initially by establishing large estates worked with local sharecroppers but, after 1928, by attracting peasant farmers from Italy. By 1940, when colonization again stopped, some 15 per cent of the total productive land of Libya was being used by Italians. In both the Maghreb and Libya, Europeans were largely interested in cash crops. By experimenting with new methods of dry farming and then introducing machines, the French were able to increase the area devoted to cereals, though extensively eroded land was often the long-term result in the steppe region of the Maghreb.[47] Vines and olives were grown in Maghreb and Libya on a larger scale than at any time since the Roman period. Irrigation was extended in both regions by the construction of dams and the partial restoration of ancient flood control works, but the rate of progress was slow, mainly because of the technical problems and the vast expense involved. The net effect was the production of enclaves of European landscape characterized by rectangular field patterns and alien architecture. Except in the case of a few large estates, which followed the European example, indigenous farming was affected chiefly by the appropriation of land which, in some cases at least, upset traditional extensive land use practices and increased poverty. Pastoralism was completely disrupted by increasing mechanization, the ploughing up of traditional pastures and continual attempts at containment and sedentarization. Restrictions on the range of pastoral activities was one reason for the rapid reduction in the forest cover of the Maghreb under French rule, though the demand for constructional timber by the *colons* and for export to France was also important.

The Middle East has experienced profound political and economic changes since the end of the First World War. The inter-war period saw the establishment of mandates over Syria, Palestine, Transjordan and Iraq, and the consequent aggrandizement of European power and influence. After the end of the Second World War came gradual retreat. Independence resulted in the emigration of European colonists from the Maghreb and Libya, as well as the expropriation of European property in many countries, though not the total eradication of a European imprint from local landscapes. Population increased considerably, especially after the Second World War, bringing greater pressure than ever before on natural resources. The World Wars and the depression were major causes of shifts in world commodity prices to which land use in the Middle East responded, often painfully. However, in the history of landscape evolution, the period since the end of the First World War may be visualized largely as one in which previous developments continued, but at an accelerating pace. The only major new departures have been the addition of distinctive industrial buildings to the rapidly expanding towns, especially to the port and capital cities, and the appearance of derricks, flares, pipes and storage tanks in all the places where petroleum is produced, refined and exported, but with an important concentration on the Gulf (Chapter 9). Elsewhere, continued development has produced less weird landscapes. These are discussed systemmatically in Chapters 4 to 8, and in more detail in the regional essays (Chapters 11 to 20). Only a brief general sketch need be given here.

In the age-old struggle between the desert and the sown, victory seems declared for the cultivator. Sedentarization of the nomads has proceeded rapidly, often as a result of changed economic and land-use conditions, rather than the application of military force, though this has not been wanting on occasion. Nomadic populations are now very small. In Iraq, for example, the proportion of nomads in the population fell from about 35 per cent in 1867 to 1·1 per cent in 1947.[49] Although numbers have fallen dramatically, and continue to decline throughout the region, there is a growing demand for the traditional nomadic products of wool, hair and cheese. The herds can now be kept mainly in the high mountains of eastern Turkey and the Zagros and some parts of Arabia, with the result that concentration and overstocking leads to overgrazing, further pressure on woodland, destruction of the grazing and an increase in erosion (Chapter 4).

As pastoralism has retreated, so cultivation has expanded its area (Chapter 4). Much of the effort has been devoted to the recolonization of territory which was once cultivated, but has been used largely by nomads for centuries. In some districts, though, advance has been across land which is, in effect, new. In the plains and valleys especially, the land now being brought into cultivation is frequently composed of silts laid down in late-Roman and post-Roman times and made available by the post-medieval resumption of downcutting.[50] Reclamation and recolonization, however, have meant that the once attractive hill land is being abandoned; fields lie idle and terraces are allowed to collapse. Some of the upland, of course, is being managed as forest in an attempt to

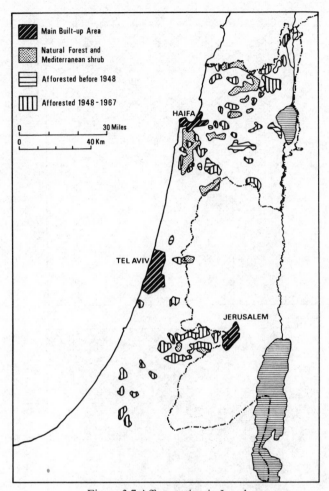

Figure 3.7 Afforestation in Israel

contain erosion, as well as to conserve and extend local timber resources (Figure 3.7).

Much of the new land in the valleys and plains is suitable for irrigation. In consequence, large dams with their associated hydraulic networks and continuously cropped fields are very much a part of modern landscapes in the Middle East.[51] In some countries, though, as land is expensively gained for cultivation in one district, neglect of drainage means that a certain amount is lost by salination in another area. Irrigation is also associated with large-scale regional planning and the production of highly formal landscapes of rectangular fields, straight roads and planned settlements. Nowhere is this type of development more apparent than in Israel, which has been fortunate not only in having sufficient capital, but also in possessing the necessary technology and skilled manpower. Figure 3.8 shows a particularly striking example of

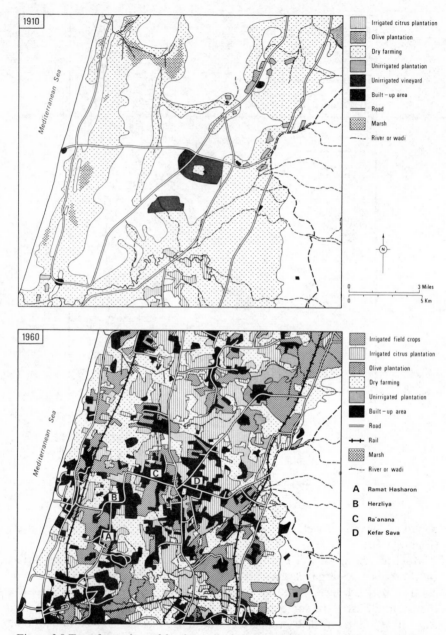

Figure 3.8 Transformation of landscapes of the southern plain of Sharon, 1910 to 1960 (Modified by permission of Department of Surveys, Tel Aviv, Israel)

how a landscape has been transformed over a period of fifty years. But even in Israel, where recovery has been greatest, centuries of human misuse of natural resources are still apparent. They are expensive, if not always impossible to put right. Everywhere in the region badlands and bare hillsides are reminders of the long history of human occupation and of the importance of care and conservation in a precarious environment. The difficulties of that environment are reiterated in the next chapter (Chapter 4), which outlines the patterns and systems involved in using the countryside today.

References

1. W. L. Thomas (Ed), *Man's Role in Changing the Face of the Earth*, Chicago University Press, Chicago, 1956.
2. D. A. E. Garrod, 'Primitive man in Egypt, western Asia and Europe in Palaeolithic times', in *The Cambridge Ancient History*, **1,** 3rd ed., Cambridge University Press, London, 1970, 70–89.
3. H. H. Lamb, 'Climatic background to the birth of civilisation', *Advt. Sci. Lond.*, **25,** 103–120 (1968).
4. K. W. Butzer, *Environment and Archaeology*, 2nd ed., Methuen, London, 1972.
5. N. Rosenam, 'Climatic fluctuations in the Middle East during the period of instrumental record', in *Changes of Climate, Proceedings of the Rome Symposium organised by UNESCO and the World Meteorological Organisation, Arid Zone Research 20*, UNESCO, 1963, 67–73.
6, 7. K. W. Butzer, 'Physical conditions in eastern Europe, western Asia and Egypt before the period of agricultural and urban settlement', in *The Cambridge Ancient History*, **1,** 3rd ed., Cambridge University Press, London, 1970, 35–69.
8. H. E. Wright, 'Natural environment of early food production north of Mesopotamia', *Science, N.Y.*, **161,** 334–339 (1968).
9. W. van Zeist, 'Reflections on prehistoric environments in the Near East', in *The Domestication and Exploitation of Plants and Animals* (Ed. P. J. Ucko and G. W. Dimbleby), Duckworth, London, 1970, 35–46.
10. K. V. Flannery, 'Origins and ecological effects of early domestication in Iran and the Near East', in *The Domestication and Exploitation of Plants and Animals* (Ed. P. J. Ucko and G. W. Dimbleby), Duckworth, London, 1970, 73–100.
11. W. Allan, 'The influence of ecology and agriculture on non-urban settlement', in *Man, Settlement and Urbanism* (Ed. P. J. Ucko, R. Tringham and G. W. Dimbleby), Duckworth, London, 1972, 211–226.
12. T. Carlstein, 'Development as a packing process in space and time', Department of Geography, University of Lund, 1972 (mimeographed).
13. (a) E. Isaac, *Geography of Domestication*, Prentice-Hall, Eaglewood Cliffs, N.J., 1970.
   (b) P. J. Ucko and G. W. Dimbleby (Eds), *The Domestication and Exploitation of Plants and Animals*, Duckworth, London, 1970.
14. K. V. Flannery, 'Origins and ecological effects of early domestication in Iran and the Near East', in *The Domestication and Exploitation of Plants and Animals* (Ed. P. J. Ucko and G. W. Dimbleby), Duckworth, London, 1970, 73–100.
15. C. D. Darlington, 'The silent millenia in the origin of agriculture', in *The Domestication and Exploitation of Plants and Animals* (Ed. P. J. Ucko and G. W. Dimbleby), Duckworth, London, 1970, 67–72.
16. (a) K. W. Butzer, *Environment and Archaeology*, 2nd ed., Methuen, London, 1972, 563, 585–595.
   (b) J. D. Clark, 'The spread of food production in sub-Saharan Africa', *Journal of African History*, **3,** 211–228 (1962).
   (c) J. D. Clark, 'The prehistoric origins of African culture', *Journal of African History*, **5,** 161–183 (1964).
   (d) J. D. Clark, *Atlas of African Prehistory*, University of Chicago Press, Chicago, 1967.

128

17. (a) W. Dostal, 'The evolution of bedouin life', in *L'Antica Società Bedouina* (Ed. F. Gabrielli), Studi Semitici No. 2, Centro de Studi Semitici, Universita di Roma, 1959, 11–34.

(b) M. W. Mikesell, 'Notes on the dispersal of the dromedary', *Southwestern Journal of Anthropology*, **11**, 231–245 (1955).

18. R. J. Braidwood and C. A. Reed, 'The achievement and early consequences of food-production: a consideration of the archaeological and natural historical evidence', *Cold Spring Harbor Symposia on Quantitative Biology*, **22**, 19–31 (1957).

19. F. R. Matson, 'Power and fuel resources in the ancient Near East', *Advmt. Sci., Lond.*, **23**, 146–153 (1966).

20. M. B. Rowton, 'The woodlands of ancient Asia', *Journal of Near Eastern Studies*, **26**, 261–277 (1967).

21. M. W. Mikesell, 'The deforestation of Mount Lebanon', *Geogrl. Rev.*, **58**, 1–28 (1969).

22. K. V. Flannery, 'Origins and ecological effect of early domestication in Iran and the Near East', in *The Domestication and Exploitation of Plants and Animals* (Ed. P. J. Ucko and G. W. Dimbleby), Duckworth, London, 1970, 73–100.

23. V. B. Proudfoot, 'Man's occupance of the soil', in *Man and his Habitat. Essays Presented to Emyr Estyn Evans* (Ed. R. H. Buchanan, E. Jones and D. McCourt), Routledge and Kegan Paul, London, 1971, 8–37.

24. K. V. Flannery, 'Origins and ecological effects of early domestication in Iran and the Near East', in *The Domestication and Exploitation of Plants and Animals* (Ed. P. J. Ucko and G. W. Dimbleby), Duckworth, London, 1970, 73–100.

25. (a) E. Boserup, *The Conditions of Agricultural Growth: The Economics of Agrarian Change under Population Pressure*, Allen and Unwin, London, 1965.

(b) P. E. L. Smith, 'Land-use, settlement patterns and subsistence agriculture: a demographic perspective', in *Man, Settlement and Urbanism* (Ed. P. J. Ucko, R. Tringham and G. W. Dimbleby), Duckworth, London, 1972, 409–425.

26. (a) R. M. Adams, 'Factors influencing the rise of civilisation in the alluvium illustrated by Mesopotamia', in *City Invincible* (Ed. C. H. Kraeling and R. M. Adams), University of Chicago Press, Chicago, 1960, 24–34.

(b) R. M. Adams, 'Patterns of Urbanism in early southern Mesopotamia', in *Man, Settlement and Urbanism* (Ed. P. J. Ucko, R. Tringham and G. W. Dimbleby), Duckworth, London, 1972, 735–749.

27. (a) K. W. Butzer, 'Archaeology and geology in ancient Egypt', *Science, N.Y.*, **132**, 1617–1674 (1961).

(b) G. Hamdan, 'Evolution of irrigation agriculture in Egypt', in *A History of Land Use in Arid Regions* (Ed. L. D. Stamp), *Arid Zone Research* **17**, UNESCO, 1961, 119–142.

(c) T. Jacobsen and R. M. Adams, 'Salt and silt in ancient Mesopotamian agriculture', *Science, N.Y.*, **128**, 1251–1257 (1958).

(d) R. O. Whyte, 'Evolution of land use in south-western Asia', in *A History of Land Use in Arid Regions*, (Ed. L. D. Stamp), *Arid Zone Research* **17**, UNESCO, 1961, 57–118.

28. (a) K. V. Flannery, 'The origins of the village as a settlement type in Mesoamerica and the Near East: a comparative study', *Man, Settlement and Urbanism* (Ed. P. J. Ucko, R. Tringham and G. W. Dimbleby), Duckworth, London, 1972, 23–53.

(b) W. Allan, 'The influence of ecology and agriculture on non-urban settlement', in *Man, Settlement and Urbanism* (Ed. P. J. Ucko, R. Tringham and G. W. Dimbleby), Duckworth, London, 1972, 211–226.

29. R. M. Adams, 'Agriculture and urban life in early southwestern Iran', *Science, N.Y.*, **136**, 109–122 (1962).

30. R. M. Adams, 'Patterns of urbanism in early southern Mesopotamia', in *Man, Settlement and Urbanism*, (Ed. P. J. Ucko, R. Tringham and G. W. Dimbleby), Duckworth, London, 1972, 735–749.

31. (a) Abu-Lughod, *Cairo: 1001 Years of the City Victorious*, Princeton University Press, Princeton, 1972.

(b) C. H. Kraeling and R. M. Adams (Eds), *City Invincible. A Symposium on Urbanisation and Cultural Development in the Ancient Near East*, University of Chicago Press, Chicago, 1960.

(c) J. H. G. Lebon, 'The site and modern development of Baghdād', *Bull. Soc. Géogr. Egypte*, **2**, 7–32 (1956).

(d) P. Marthelot, 'Bagdād; notes de géographie humaine', *Annls Géogr.*, **74**, 24–37 (1965).

32. (a) P. W. English, *City and Village in Iran. Settlement and Economy in the Kirman Basin*, University of Wisconsin Press, Madison, 1966, 87–110.

(b) G. E. von Grünebaum, 'The Muslim town and the Hellenistic town', *Scientia*, **90**, 364–370 (1955).

(c) P. Lampl, *Cities and Planning in the Ancient Near East*, Studio Vista, London, 1968.

33. (a) J. Despois, 'Development of land use in northern Africa', in *A History of Land Use in Arid Regions* (Ed. L. D. Stamp), *Arid Zone Research* **17**, UNESCO, 1961, 219–237.

(b) R. O. Whyte, 'Evolution of land use in south-western Asia', in *A History of Land Use in Arid Regions* (Ed. L. D. Stamp), *Arid Zone Research* **17**, UNESCO, 1961, 57–118.

34. (a) *Atlas des Centuriations romaines de Tunisie*, Institut Géographique National, Paris, 1954.

(b) J. Baradez, *Fossatum Africae*, Arts et Métiers Graphiques, Paris, 1949.

(c) A Caillemer and R. Chevalier, 'Les centuriations romaines de l'Africa vetus', *Annales, Économies, Sociétés, Civilisations*, **9**, 433–460 (1954).

(d) A. Caillemer and R. Chevalier, 'Centuriations romaines de Tunisie', *Annales Economies, Sociétés, Civilisations*, **12**, 275–286 (1957).

(e) R. G. Goodwood, 'Farming in Roman Libya', *Geogr. Mag.*, **25**, 70–80 (1952).

(f) R. G. Goodwood, 'The mapping of Roman Libya', *Geogr. J.*, **118**, 142–152 (1952).

35. (a) W. C. Brice, *Southwest Asia*, University of London Press, London 1966, 96–98.

(b) W. C. Brice and A. N. Balci, 'The history of forestry in Turkey', *Orman Fakültesi Dergisi, Istanbul Universitesi*, **5**, 19–42 (1955).

(c) R. J. Russell, 'Alluvial morphology of Anatolian rivers', *Ann. Ass. Am. Geogr.*, **44**, 363–391 (1954).

36. A. H. M. Jones, *The Decline of the Ancient World*, Longmans, London, 1966, 304–310.

37. (a) M. B. Rowton, 'The woodlands of ancient Asia', *Journal of Near Eastern Studies*, **26**, 261–277 (1967).

(b) M. Lombard, 'Les bois dans la méditerranée musulmane', *Annales, Economies, Sociétés, Civilisations*, **14**, 234–254 (1959).

38. R. M. Adams, *Land Behind Baghdād*, University of Chicago Press, Chicago, 1965, 69–71.

39. (a) M. Benvenisti, *The Crusaders in the Holy Land*, Israel Universities Press, Jerusalem, 1970.

(b) U. Heyd, *Ottoman Documents on Palestine, 1552–1615*, Oxford University Press, London, 1960.

(c) W. Hütteroth, 'Schwankungen von Siedlungsdichte und Siedlungsgrenze im Palästina und Transjordanien seit dem 16. Jahrhundert', in *Deutscher Geographentag Kiel, 21–26 Juli, 1969*, 463–475.

(d) G. Le Strange, *Palestine Under the Muslims, 650–1500*, London, 1890.

40. (a) M. A. Hachicho, 'English travel books about the Arab Near East in the eighteenth century', *Die Welt der Islam*, **9**, 1–206 (1964).

130

(b) A. Hourani, 'The changing face of the Fertile Crescent in the eighteenth century', *Studia Islamica*, **8**, 89–122 (1957).

(c) H. Margalit, 'Some aspects of the cultural landscapes of Palestine during the first half of the nineteenth century', *Israel Explor. J.*, **13**, 208–223 (1964).

(d) M. C. F. Volney, *Voyage en Syrie et en Égypte pendant les années 1783, 1784 et 1785*, Paris, 1786.

41. (a) G. Hamdan, 'Evolution of irrigation agriculture in Egypt', in *A History of Land Use in Arid Regions* (Ed. L. D. Stamp), *Arid Zone Research* **17**, UNESCO, 1961, 119–142.

(b) J. H. G. Lebon, 'The new irrigation era in Iraq', *Econ. Geogr.*, **31**, 47–59 (1955).

42. (a) Z. Y. Hershlag, *Introduction to the Economic History of the Middle East*, Brill, Leiden, 1964.

(c) C. Issawi (Ed), *The Economic History of the Middle East, 1800–1914*, University of Chicago Press, Chicago, 1966.

(c) D. S. Lander, *Bankers and Pashas. International Finance and Economic Imperialism in Egypt*, Heinemann, London, 1958.

(d) E. R. J. Owen, *Cotton and the Egyptian Economy, 1920–1914. A Study in Trade and Development*, Oxford University Press, London, 1969.

43. (a) N. E. Lewis, 'Malaria, irrigation and soil erosion in central Syria', *Geogrl. Rev.*, **39**, 278–290 (1949).

(b) N. E. Lewis, 'The frontier of settlement in Syria, 1800–1950', *International Affairs*, **31**, 48–60 (1955).

44. V. Cuinet, *La Turquie d'Asie. Géographie administrative, statistique, descriptive et raisonnée de chaque province d'Asie Mineure*, **2**, Paris, 1892, 355–356.

45. M. B. Rowton, 'The woodlands of ancient Asia', *Journal of Near Eastern Studies*, **26**, 261–277 (1967).

46. (a) S. Amin, *L'économic du Maghreb*, **1**, *Colonisation et la Décolonisation*, Editions de Minuit, Paris, 1966.

(b) N. Barbour (Ed), *A Survey of North-West Africa*, 2nd ed., Oxford University Press, London, 1962.

(c) J. Despois, 'Development of land use in northern Africa', in *A History of Land Use in Arid Regions* (Ed. L. D. Stamp), *Arid Zone Research* **17**, UNESCO, 1961, 219–237.

(d) M. M. Knight, 'Economic space for Europeans in French North Africa', *Economic Development and Cultural Change*, **1**, 360–375 (1952–1953).

47. (a) G. L. Fowler, 'Italian colonisation of Tripolitania', *Ann. Ass. Am. Geogr.*, **62**, 627–640 (1972).

(b) R. G. Hartley, 'Libya: economic development and demographic responses', in *Populations of the Middle East and North Africa* (Ed. J. I. Clarke and W. B. Fisher), University of London Press, London, 1972, 316–318.

48. J. Despois, 'Development of land use in northern Africa', in *A History of Land Use in Arid Regions* (Ed. L. D. Stamp), *Arid Zone Research* **17**, UNESCO, 1961, 219–237.

49. M. S. Hasan, 'Growth and structure of Iraq's population, 1867–1947', *Bull. Oxf. Univ. Inst. Statist.*, **20**, 339–352 (1958).

50. C. Vita-Finzi, *The Mediterranean Valleys. Geological Changes in Historical Times*, Cambridge University Press, Cambridge, 1969, 119.

51. C. G. Smith, 'Water resources and irrigation development in the Middle East', *Geography*, **55**, 407–425 (1970).

CHAPTER 4

Rural Land Use: Patterns and Systems

4.1 The importance of cultivation and pastoralism

Although agriculture and pastoralism are not the only types of land use in the Middle East, their role is of fundamental importance in the life of the region. Table 4.1 gives some of the indicators for the role of agriculture, which is more measurable than pastoralism and indeed essential to its support. Over the whole region, agriculture contributed directly about 15 per cent of G.D.P. in 1968–69, compared with three per cent in the case of the United Kingdom. Iran, Iraq, Jordan and Lebanon occupied roughly the average position, but the contribution of agriculture to G.D.P. varied considerably amongst the other countries of the region. An insignificant contribution was made by agriculture in Israel, where manufacturing industry is particularly well developed, and in Kuwait, Libya and Saudi Arabia, where oil production almost completely dominates the economy. A significantly greater than average contribution was made by agriculture in Egypt, where irrigated farming has reached a high level of development, and in the largely rain-fed agricultural countries of Syria and Turkey.

The real contribution of cultivation and pastoralism to the economy, however, is greater than these figures suggest. Not only does much of the region's manufacturing industry process and transform agricultural products, but rural products also contributed an average of about 65 per cent of the total non-petroleum exports of the region by value in 1970 (Chapter 9), while employing an average of 46 per cent of the economically active population. The rural contribution to the total of non-petroleum exports varied from country to country, ranging from practically nothing in the cases of Kuwait, Libya and Saudi Arabia, to 100 per cent in the case of Iraq, where dates alone contributed about 60 per cent of total non-petroleum exports by value. Iran occupied roughly the average position, whilst the contribution of cultivation and pastoralism was well below average in Israel and Jordan, and well above it in Egypt, Syria and Turkey. Estimates of the size of the active rural population vary, and some allowance should be made for the differing labour contribution of women and children, but on the basis of FAO figures for 1970, the average figure of about 46 per cent was more or less achieved in Iran, Iraq, Lebanon, Syria and, rather surprisingly, also in Libya. Lower percentages were given by FAO for Israel, Jordan and Kuwait, and much larger ones were offered for Egypt, Saudi Arabia, P.D.R. Yemen, Turkey and Yemen A.R. Taken with the contributions to G.D.P., the employment estimates suggest, despite

TABLE 4·1
Importance of Agriculture

Country (and year)	Percentage contribution to G.D.P.	Percentage contribution to exports, about 1970	Percentage of economically active population in agriculture, 1970 estimates
Egypt (1966–67)	28·0	75·3	55·0
Iran (1969)	19·0	61·8*	46·0
Iraq (1969)	19·0	100·0*	47·0
Israel (1969)	6·0	24·4	10·0
Jordan (1968)	15·0	59·8	39·0
Lebanon (1968)	10·0	30·0	47·0
Libya (1968)	3·0	0·0	43·0
P.D.R. Yemen	—	—	73·0
Saudi Arabia (1968)	6·0	0·0	60·0
Syria (1969)	26·0	78·2	49·0
Turkey (1969)	28·0	89·2	69·0
Yemen A.R.	—	—	62·0

*Total without petroleum
Source: United Nations FAO *Production Yearbook, 1971*, Rome, 1972, Table 5. *United Nations, Statistical Yearbook, 1971*, New York, 1972.

a falling proportion of the total population in the rural sector in most countries, that productivity per capita is relatively low. Low productivity is one of the region's major economic problems, and is intimately related to physical conditions.

4.2 Influence of physical conditions

Water availability is the most important constraint on rural land use in the region and the effects on cultivation are very marked. Precipitation regimes are characterized by winter or spring maxima and a long summer drought (Chapter 2). This pattern largely determines the time available for crop growth, though low temperatures in winter and high evapotranspiration in summer restrict rapid growth to the period from February to May in the so-called Fertile Crescent and from April to July in the high central parts of Turkey and Iran. Wheat and barley are the most important crops in terms of the area devoted to them as well as their large part in the diet, and, as indigenous plants, they are well adapted to local conditions. So are the fodder crops clover, lucerne and vetch, upon which draft animals—still important in the region—are dependent. The date at which the long drought is broken is crucial, for the arrival of the rain conditions the amount of land which can be sown in any one year (Chapter 15). If the rains are early, for example, then more time is available for ploughing and a greater area can be sown. Unfortunately, the rains arrive at a time when the vegetation has been dried out, and they continue over the period of ploughing. Erosion is severe and valuable soil is lost every year, while the fields may become ravaged by gullying. Run-off is rapid, resulting not only in the loss of vital soil moisture but also in the frequent flooding of the better crop land in the valleys and plains. Spring rain is vital since it falls towards the end of the growth cycle, when timing and abundance greatly affect yields. If the rain is late, or light, yields will be low and famine may threaten; it is never very far away in some parts of the region. Yields vary quite markedly from year to year (Chapter 18) and, because of the basic importance of field crops to national economies, partly explain the curious interannual fluctuations in G.D.P. characteristic of the region.

Successful long-term cereal growing without irrigation *(dry-farming* or *rainfed farming)* depends upon the relationships between the minimum amount of precipitation required for growth and the variability of precipitation from year to year. The critical conditions are met only in parts of the region where mean annual precipitation exceeds 240 mm and relative interannual variabilities are less than 37 per cent (Figure 4.1).[1] Most of the region cannot support dry-farming and permanent cultivation is dependent upon the availability of water for irrigation, and, as we have seen (Chapter 2), this is restricted.

Water availability affects livestock rearing, as well as cultivation. Although herding takes place within the same areas as rain-fed farming, it is especially associated with the margins of the dry-farming zones. Herbage here varies according to the seasonal and annual availability of precipitation. In consequence, herding has traditionally been fully or partially nomadic, while a run of unusually dry years in the past often assisted an extention of the nomadic domain deep into the core areas of dry-farming. The broad temporal and spatial movements of nomadic groups were adjusted to the observed and expected regularities in the precipitation, which determined the distribution of grazing and drinking water. Indirectly, precipitation also affects the herds themselves. The type of animals kept in particular areas is related to the amount of precipitation and drinking water to be expected there. Herd size is closely affected by the availability of these items, and thus by interannual variation in precipitation. Numbers increase in wet years and decrease in dry ones, creating a kind of dynamic equilibrium which is easily upset. For example, serious overgrazing is now widespread in the region as a result of concentrating larger numbers of animals in diminishing areas, a situation created, on the one hand, by the ploughing up of former grazing land, and, on the other hand, by increasing demand for animal products. The effects of drought in such a situation can be devastating.

If water availability exerts a dominant influence on the broad patterns of rural land use, cultivation and herding are also affected in detail by topography and soils. Extremely rocky areas may not be used at all. Steep, bare slopes can be grazed only by the agile goat, while slopes in excess of a few degrees cannot be irrigated. Slopes greater than 35 degrees cannot even be ploughed. Cultivation is possible in such circumstances only with the help of terraces, but in the past terracing was a feature of districts like Mount Lebanon and the Judaean hills where cultivable land was scarce but, for historical reasons, the

134

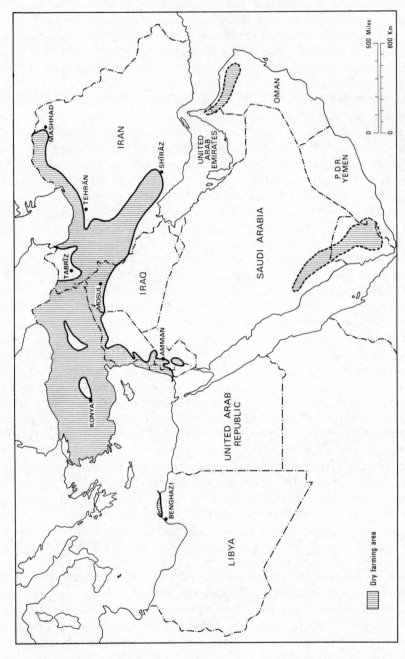

Figure 4.1 Theoretical limits of dry farming (Reproduced by permission of World Meteorological Organisation)

population became particularly dense. The soils of the region have already been described (Chapter 2), but it is important to emphasize certain of their characteristics for agriculture. They are generally deficient in humus and nitrogen so that, without the application of fertilizer, yields are low over a long period of time, though the ploughing up of old pasture has given high yields in areas like the Jezira of northeastern Syria, in the short term. In many districts, natural fertility has been reduced to a stable minimum, determined by the mineral composition of the soil, as the result of centuries, or even millenia, of almost continuous cultivation. Some soils are rich in bases and so become susceptible to salination, especially where irrigation water is carelessly applied and drainage is inefficient. Plant growth is inhibited in these conditions, and may even become impossible, as in parts of southern Iraq (Chapter 12). Partly as a result of the slow development of soils under the present climatic regimes of the region, and partly as a result of centuries of ill-treatment and mismanagement, soils away from the plains and valleys are shallow and stoney, and moisture is not retained for any length of time, thus imposing another limitation on the growing season (Chapter 15). Water percolation is often retarded and run-off increased by the tendency to puddle at the surface, which results from both precipitation characteristics and the high clay content of most soils. Puddling is also unfavourable to the early growth of cereals, while ploughing is rendered difficult by the tendencies of clayey soil to bake hard during the summer and become heavy and sticky after rain. Altogether, the farmer's task is not an easy one.

4.3 Land use organization

4.3.1 Permanent settlements

Cultivation is generally organized from, and carried on around, permanent settlements, though some completely nomadic groups in Libya grow crops. The stereotype settlement is the shapeless agglomeration of flat-roofed, single-storey, rectangular houses. Streets are narrow and winding, whilst culs-de-sac are frequent. The inhabitants are grouped spatially by kinship ties and sometimes by religious affiliation, but the entire population is often divided into at least two factions between which the normal hostility still occasionally flares into violence of such magnitude that the stability of the community seems something of a puzzle.[2]

In fact, the basic monotony of settlement type is broken in a variety of ways. Variation, for example, is quite marked in house type (Figure 4.2). The simple single-storey house is by no means universal, and two storeys are characteristic of some regions, while tower-houses are particularly characteristic of Yemen and Ḥaḍhramawt. The colour and texture of local stones and muds, the display or not of whitewash and external decoration, and the use of timber, all provide subtle variations from place to place. But the most obvious variations are in roof type. Common is the heavy flat roof, built of layers of insulating materials resting on heavy beams and topped with a layer of salted mud, but other forms are also found. Pitched roofs are characteristic of districts where precipitation is heavy, particularly the Pontic Mountains and the Caspian lowlands. Roofs consisting of several corbel-built cones are typical of the largely treeless steppe of Syria near Aleppo, but they are also found in adjacent parts of southern Turkey and occasionally in Upper Egypt. Conical roofs are also characteristic of the round huts of the coastal plain in the 'Asir and Yemen districts of southwestern Arabia, whilst barrel-vaulted roofs are a marked feature of traditional reed architecture in the marshes of southern Iraq.

Settlement form displays a basic dichotomy between the mountains and the lowland. Compact agglomerations of 100 to 2,000 houses (perhaps 400 to 8,000 people) are characteristic of lowland areas (Figure 4.3). Most are unfortified, but defensive walls were found in districts, like central Arabia (Najd), Iran and the Tigris–Euphrates lowland, which were particularly exposed to small-scale maurauding. In the open plains, settlements appear to be scattered almost at random, but they frequently occupy a mound (Arabic *tell*; Turkish *hüyük*) formed from the erosion and rebuilding of generations of mudbrick houses, though it must be pointed out that continuous occupation of the same site over several millenia is likely to be exceptional rather than the rule. In central Turkey, settlements are generally situated below the general level of the undulating plateau, so that they are almost invisible from a distance, but they are located above the floors of valleys and depressions where floods normally appear in the winter. The same situations are preferred in the Beq'a valley of Lebanon. In Iran, however, settlements are generally found around the outlet of a *qanāt* (underground aqueduct) or along the side of a water course. Linear settlements also stretch along the levees of the Tigris and Euphrates in Iraq and beside the Nile in Egypt, though desert-edge settlements are also found in Egypt, along with polynuclear forms which have developed from the growing together of once distinct settlements as a result of population increase.[3] Practically everywhere the mudbrick houses are built in the corner, or at one side, of a courtyard in which many domestic activities are carried out in warm weather and around which are gathered stores and byres. Settlements are built, in effect, from units of such courtyard houses, integrated by kinship relationships.

Mountain settlements have looser forms, though two basic types may be distinguished. On the one hand, there is the loose cluster of perhaps 10 or 20 houses and, on the other, the fragmented settlement in which smaller groups of houses are separated by ravines, rocks and steep slopes, but yet lie closer to each other than to any other settlement. Both types of settlement are generally sited on steep slopes, spurs, ridges and knolls, sometimes in such a way that the settlement has a stepped structure in which the roof of one house is the terrace in front of the house above. These difficult sites are not primarily defensive, though they may have served in this capacity on several occasions in the past, as at Maaloula in the Anti-Lebanon Mountains which successfully

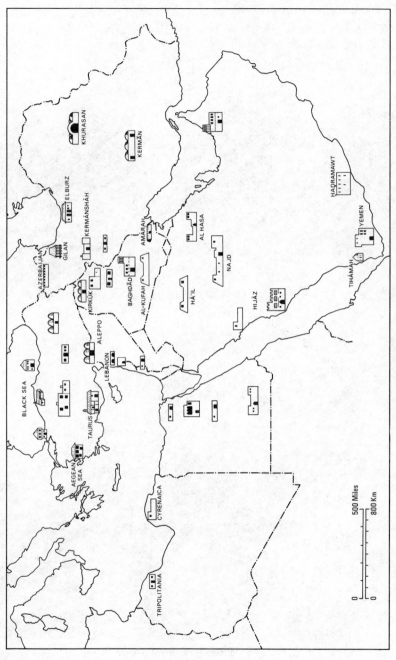

Figure 4.2 Some traditional house types

Contrasting village types: Pitched roofs made of thatch, Caspian Sea Lowlands, Iran (top); flat-roofed stone built houses, northern highlands, Jordan (bottom). (Photographs: Peter Beaumont).

Figure 4.3 An agglomerated plains settlement; Karagedik in central Turkey (Reproduced by permission of Wolf Hütteroth, 1971)

withstood full-scale sieges in 1850, 1860 and 1925.[4] The sites were chosen more often to preserve the scarce but valuable cultivable land in the vicinity. In the high mountains settlements frequently face in a southerly direction to benefit from solar warmth in the bitter winters. Houses are frequently stone-built, with flat roofs supported either by transverse arches or vaulting, instead of the timbers and mudbrick pillars characteristic of the lowland. Courtyards are generally lacking; there may not be enough space for them. Storage and stalling are provided by dividing the house itself either horizontally or vertically. In the first case people share the house with their animals, but are separated from them by their occupation of a slightly raised platform. Where vertical separation is employed, people are accommodated on the second floor, while stores and animals are kept below, often in deep cellars and even artificial caves, where the rock is soft enough to permit easy excavation.

Although Arab villages in Israel can be fitted into the simple classification outlined, Jewish agriculture is associated with very different types of settlement (Chapter 16). The earliest type, the *moshavot*, started the trend by transfering to Palestine a basically central-European settlement form, in which houses with pitched roofs were arranged on either side of a village sheet (Figure 16.1). *Kibbutzim* were a later introduction. They are communal settlements of 300 to 1,700 people, often located in regions of political insecurity or exceptional environmental difficulty. The central focus is a group of communal buildings, characterized by the separation of farm functions from the living quarters. *Moshavim* (villages of cooperative smallholders) are somewhat smaller, with populations of 200 to 450 people, but are rigorously planned. The earliest *moshavim* of the 1920's were laid out around an elliptical street with services located at the centre (Figure 16.1). This wasted valuable agricultural land and produced awkwardly shaped fields. To meet these problems, *moshavim* built after 1948 were generally laid out along a single street, or in 'T' or 'L' shaped patterns. There was also an increasing tendency to make each *moshav* a member of a completely planned pattern of settlement designed to facilitate the provision of services in a hierarchy of the type described by Christaler and Lösch. Thus, groups of up to six *moshavim* are generally served by a single rural service centre accommodating only the families of non-agriculturalists to maintain a wide range of social and economic services.

4.3.2 Land tenure

The permanent settlement is the organizational centre of the farm, but its composition, layout and pattern of working are controlled by the way in which the land itself is held. Land tenure is an important organizational structure underlying present patterns of land use.

Ultimate ownership of most of the arable land in Muslim countries is vested in the state, and state-owned land (*miri* in the Arab countries and Turkey; *khāliṣeh* in Iran) has been carefully distinguished from privately owned property (*mulk* or *milk*). The classic distinction was made originally for tax and administrative purposes, but it is of little practical significance today, since the legal tenants of the state pay no rent and their titles are inherited, mortgaged and sold, provided only that the land is not allowed to go out of cultivation for more than five years, when it can be claimed by anyone who will undertake to work it. Of more practical importance today are the existence of four other characteristic features of land tenure: mortmain land (Arabic *wakf*; Turkish *evakf*), large estates, sharecropping and the fragmentation of holdings.

Wakf is property, particularly land, which has been dedicated to God and its income allocated to some religious or charitable purpose, such as the maintainance of a particular mosque or bathhouse, or to the support of the poor of a particular locality.[5] However, it became customary for the income to be used for the maintenance of the dedicator's family over several generations before it actually devolved upon the ultimate beneficiary. This was one way in which family property could be maintained intact, since it could not be alienated by the state nor foreclosed upon in the event of debt. The management of *wakf* was put into the hands of an overseer, who was often the head of the grantor's family in successive generations, or a respected individual, or, where other managers lapsed, the ruler. Management was not very efficient, so that much *wakf* land was unproductive and the income often badly applied. The inalienable nature of *wakf* meant that consolidation and improvement schemes were often thwarted.

Much has been made of these facts by commentators, especially since it has been estimated that in the closing years of the Ottoman Empire about three-quarters of all the arable land was in *wakf*.[6] The situation has changed considerably since then. Independent governments have attempted to regulate *wakf* by establishing special ministries or agencies, and have reduced its extent by confiscation (illegal under the Sharīah), and reallocation. *Wakf* has not been totally abolished, but even by 1950, on the eve of the great land reform movements in the region, it had been reduced to about 7·0 per cent of all registered land in Egypt, 1·2 per cent in Iraq and 0·3 per cent in Jordan.[7]

The distribution of land amongst owners is far from being equal (Table 4.2). Very large estates, sometimes consisting of the whole arable area of several

TABLE 4.2
Figures illustrative of Traditional Land Ownership

	Size of holding (ha)	No. of holdings ('000)	Percentage of total holdings	Percentage of total area
EGYPT 1952	< 2	2642	94·3	35·4
	2–4	79	2·8	8·8
	4–8	47	1·7	10·7
	8–21	22	0·8	10·9
	21–42	6	0·2	7·3
	> 42	5	0·2	17·0
LEBANON 1961	< 2	92	35·0	4·0
	2–4	11	12·0	15·0
	4–20	16	13·0	38·0
	> 20	2	1·0	37·0
TURKEY 1963	< 5	2132	68·8	24·8
	2–20	853	27·5	41·7
	20–100	110	3·6	23·4
	> 100	4	0·1	10·1

Source: Central Organisation for General Mobilisation and Statistics, *Annual Statistical Abstract 1952–1966*, Cairo, 1967, pp. 50–54; Ministry of Agriculture, *Census of Agriculture, 1961*, Beirūt, 1965; B. Kayser, 'Tendances de l'économie Turque', *Information Géographique*, **36,** 26 (1972).

villages, were found even as late as the 1950's, particularly in the dry-farming areas of Syria, the irrigated districts of southern Iraq and the province of Kermān in Iran. By contrast, small-holdings were especially characteristic of two rather different subregions—mountainous terrain, like Lebanon, and the most densely populated provinces of Egypt. The situation has changed since the 1950's with the spread of effective land reform measures, but not drastically.

Development of large estates varied according to the different histories of land holding in particular subregions, but a number of common origins may be noted. Purchase was often the way in which estates were built up, particularly in recent times. Another very frequent origin, but one of greater age, was the granting of state land by the ruler (sultan, khedive or shah) to an individual who was then supported by the rents, dues and labour services of the people working the land. This arrangement is often loosely referred to as *feudal*, but it differed in a number of important respects from the classic feudalism developed in early medieval Europe. Although fiefs were granted as a way of maintaining troops (as late as the early twentieth century in Iran), the land grant in the Middle East during Islamic times was essentially a device for administering territory and raising taxes. It was not characterized by the bonds of personal loyalty and contract normal in Europe, and tokens of overlordship were few or non-existent. Moreover, the grant could not strictly be inherited, though this often happened, and could be revoked or resigned at any moment. Purchase also became characteristic. Other ways in which a large estate could be created was by the reclamation of swamp and marsh, as in the Nile delta during the second half of the nineteenth century, or by the seizure and subsequent colonization of any previously unoccupied land lying at a distance from an inhabited settlement *(mevat)*,[8] a device which was particularly common during the expansion of the cultivation frontier in Syria (Chapter 13). In these cases, cultivation provided title to the land. Some large estates developed from the registration of land under the provisions of the Ottoman Land Code (1858) by farmers in the name of a few important persons. To some extent this was the direct result of Article Eight of the Code, which prevented a community from registering its collectively owned land *(musha')* as such, but recognized only registration by individuals.[9] Under a tribal system, it was natural for the farmers to register their collective possession in the name of their chief, who was simply *primus inter pares*. Many chiefs, however, came to abuse their position of trust and, with legal right and government support, claimed the land as their own and forced the tribesmen to work it for them as tenants. At the same time, the Code allowed unscrupulous notables to ensure, by bribery and coercion, that land was registered in their name.[10] Rather similar to this was estate building by the seizure of properties to pay off debts contracted with urban merchants or wealthy farmers (the *ağas*). Most farmers could not be anything else but debtors, given their need for ready cash for such things as the brideprice, dowry, and to pay for the rituals which mark the life crises, to meet the high rates of interest charged on loans, and to counter the vagaries of the weather. The situation was exacerbated by the weak bargaining position of share-croppers. Credit and loans from government agencies have helped to relieve the situation, but it still exists. The small farmer is often refused loans and must turn elsewhere, even if it means eventual foreclosure on his property.

Whatever their ultimate origins, the large estates of the region have generally been run purely as tenancy units. Outside the Nile delta, advantage was rarely taken of the possibilities for direct exploitation or of the economies of scale offered by such large units. Land was let out as small, scattered plots in return for a share of the harvest. The arrangement is not confined to large estates, but is used commonly in the region whenever a piece of property is let, while the principle of shares is widespread and found amongst seamen as well as farmers. The proportion of the harvest taken by the lessor depends upon the relative provision of the other factors of production apart from land (labour, tools, seed, fertilizer, draught animals, and in irrigated areas, water), the type of crop grown, and the probability of a successful harvest. Thus, in Syria, the landlord's share is higher in the core areas of dry-farming than it is towards the margins of the desert, while a tree crop normally gives the tenant more rights than cereal monoculture. In Egypt, provision of labour only on the part of the tenant entitled the landlord to $\frac{4}{5}$ or $\frac{3}{4}$ of the harvest.

Sharecropping has the advantage that the landlord's share is related to the actual state of the harvest, and is not a fixed payment. On the larger estates, it also means that the tenant does not have to find the capital to supply seed, tools or even draught animals. The landlord frequently acts as an inter mediary between his tenants and the government, protecting and helping them. As Weulersse observed, the relationship of the estate owner to his tenant was normally that of the *patron* and *client*, rather than the *proprietor* and *métayer*.[11] Unfortunately, like all leasing systems, sharecropping has been abused and exploited, particularly by the larger estate owners. The lessor's share is frequently so large that the lessee is left with barely enough to support himself and his family. Accordingly, many tenants lack capital to improve the land or increase yields, and are forced to borrow to meet even bare sub-sistence. The system is thus self-perpetuating. Contracts are not normally written down, with the result that they cannot be enforced at law, but may easily be exploited by the landlord. They are renewed every year, generally on terms unfavourable to the tenant, who must have land to survive and who is already in debt to the *ağa* for previous loans. Although one family might have farmed the same land for generations, annual contracts mean that there is little incentive to improve the land, even if the capital could be raised. In the past, neglect was reinforced in some districts by a tradition of periodically redistribut-ing the holdings, sometimes by lot. The larger landlords inevitably gained control over the pattern of cropping in village territories, and are able to direct the organization of farm work, though power is usually exercised through an agent, since the more important *ağas* live in the towns and cities of the region.

Although landlords were content to draw their rents and use their tenants to support any political ambitions they might hold, they were in a position to embark upon modern commercial farming and carry out innovation when the right combination of incentives developed. The opportunity was seized in the Nile delta of Egypt following the early attempts to regulate the seasonal flow of the river, but little happened elsewhere until the tractor made its appearance; in many districts this was after the Second World War. In the Çukorova of southeastern Turkey, for example, the effect of introducing tractors has been to curtail, or completely end, the sharecropping system, since manual labour is no longer needed in large quantities for large-scale cultivation. In consequence, farmers could no longer patch together a subsistence holding from their personal properties and the land they were able to lease. They are forced either to work as wage labourers, often on a seasonal basis, when they are in competition with cheaper migrant labour from mountain villages, or to emigrate to the industrial towns of the region or to Ankara and Istanbul.[12] The situation elsewhere has not been so well documented, but throughout the region the impression gained is that machines seem to be ending the share-cropping system. In some districts, it is being replaced by money rents and written leases, but the general effect is still to assist in forcing people off the land. Other factors encouraging people to leave the land include the oppression of sharecropping, where it still survives, and the uneconomic size of farm holdings which has resulted from a combination of the ending of land surplus, population increase and the custom of equal division of property between at least the male heirs. Principles of equity combine with accidented terrain and local variations in soil and water to scatter holdings in irregular plots over village territories, thus creating a mosaic of tiny fields (Figure 4.4). Holdings may be collectively worked by members of the same family, but after several generations the degrees of kinship widen to such an extent that collectivization will no longer operate. Individual properties and shares of their joint produce become so small as to be insufficient for the support of individual families. Land may be left fallow in these circumstances, sold to some more fortunate neighbours or enter the pool of sharecropped land. Efficient use of time in modern terms is often difficult where journeys between plots become long, while consolidation and mechanization may be impossible to introduce effectively. Frustration, as well as poor living standards, is often a real impulse to migration.

The land situation is different in Israel. Although the state owned 78 per cent of all land in 1957, and the Jewish National Fund a further 18·0 per cent, individual farmers or groups of farmers were able to rent portions for nominal sums and on hereditable leases.[13] Around *kibbutzim* cultivated land is worked in large, block fields which are ideal for the efficient development of machines. Strips or long wedges in individual ownerships are more characteristic of *moshavim*, but holdings cannot be subdivided or enlarged. The situation is different around the earliest Jewish *moshavot* on the citrus-growing coastal plain. Much land here is still in private ownership and, because of the way it was acquired and divided, it is not as regularly arranged as around the other

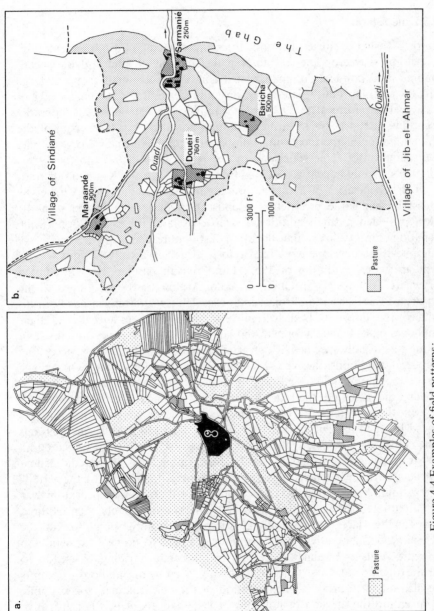

Figure 4.4 Examples of field patterns:
(a) Dry-farming, plains-type: Runkus, central Turkey (after Hütteroth, 1971)
(b) Dry-farming, mountain-type: Doueir el Akrad, western Syria (after Weulersse, 1946)

types of Jewish settlement. The situation is more akin to that found in neighbouring Muslim countries.

4.3.3 Land reform

In the Muslim countries, the difficulties engendered by farm fragmentation, the evils of sharecropping, the uneven distribution of land and the social, economic and political dominance of a comparatively small group of large estate owners all produced pressures for land reform. Before the main wave of effective land reform after 1950, most countries had already made sporadic allocations of state land to farmers, though not always to the benefit of the smallholders or of the increasing numbers of landless people. For example, the distribution of some state land by the Republic of Turkey in the 1920's and 1930's mainly benefited refugees from Europe. In the Kingdom of Iraq, the chief beneficiaries of a similar process in the 1930's were tribal sheikhs and established large proprietors. Confiscation of foreign property in the region provided a small additional source of land for distribution, while allienation of *wakf* allowed the allocation of still more land.

Despite these developments, land reform began in a really serious way in Egypt after the revolution of 1952. Land reform has not been attempted everywhere, for instance in Oman or Saudi Arabia, and was confined to the territory of the East Ghor Project in Jordan. But where reform has been introduced, the aims have been to remove the largest estates and allocate their component lands to sharecroppers and landless labourers. A maximum size of holding was usually specified. This varied from country to country, according to physical conditions, the type of farming and cultural traditions. One village was the maximum holding allowed in Iran during the first stage of reform following the passing of the Land Reform Law in January, 1962 (Chapter 18). In Egypt, the maximum size of an individual's holding has been progressively reduced from 84 ha (200 *feddans*) in 1952 to 21 ha (50 *feddans*) in 1969, but all the cultivated land is irrigated. Following agrarian reform in 1958, 500 ha (2000 Iraqi *donums*) was the limit in the dry-farming areas of Iraq and 250 ha (1000 *donums*) in irrigated districts. In every country, holdings above the permitted maximum were seized by the state for distribution. Compensation was normally offered to the landlords, while the new state tenants were required to pay for their land, but generally at prices considerably below those on the open market. Cooperatives were normally planned to provide farmers with the credit, seeds and animals necessary for successful farming, as well as to offer the direction and assistance traditionally given by the landlord. Attempts were also made to prevent fragmentation of the new holdings, for example, by preventing the division of holdings of less than about two hectares (five *feddans*) in Egypt.[14]

The success of the various land reform schemes is difficult to determine, especially since evaluation depends very much upon the criteria chosen. It is not always realized that large estates still survive and that the reforms were aimed only at the very largest holdings. In Egypt, where land reform seems to have been so thorough-going, about 17 per cent of the cultivated land was actually involved, though in Syria about 40 per cent of the arable will be effected when confiscation and reallocation is finally completed.[15] Landless labourers have tended not to benefit from the reallocation of land, which has often gone to the smaller tenants. Non-cooperation and considerable opposition from landowners, together with uncertainty about the future of landholdings, brought considerable disruption to Iraqi's agriculture so that output of wheat, barley and rice, for example, fell by 25 per cent over the first three years following confiscation (Chapter 12). This was an important factor in the sudden flood of emigration from the marsh provinces to Baghdād. The attempt to establish cooperatives is proving successful in Egypt, and has resulted in something like collective farming on the Soviet model,[16] but in Iraq and Syria, where Egyptian precedent was closely followed, the failures were considerable, partly because of the lack of trained staff but partly also because of different administrative traditions from those of the Nile valley. Credit is neither adequate nor easy to obtain, so that the old problem of debt remains, and the moneylender can still build up a moderate-sized estate by foreclosure. Attempts to curtail land fragmentation were confined to reallocated land, while sharecropping continues as the normal means of leasing land, though in Egypt money rents are now well established. On the more positive side, though, the various land reforms have improved the agrarian situation to some extent. The power of the landlords has been curtailed, although not everywhere broken. Tenure is now more secure than before, and rents may be lower. Agricultural output has increased, and this has been attributed to the greater interest in the land and the more efficient farming which reform has allowed, though factors like the growth of population and of market demand have been important, too.

4.3.4 Water rights [17]

Land is not the only aspect of cultivation which has required organization. The ownership and distribution of water for irrigation is crucial, especially beyond the limits of successful dry-farming and if any summer cropping is to be practicable. Indeed, so scarce and so vital is water that access has customarily given title to land in some parts of the region, and in villages near Eşfahān the size of land holdings is reckoned in shares of water, as measured on a time basis. In Israel water provision is highly subsidized by the state and elaborate means have been developed to secure and distribute it, but the overall shortage of this vital commodity has established a system of allocation which has been said to be similar to that which would exist if an economic land rent prevailed.[18] Ownership, access to and use of water in the Muslim countries of the region are governed by customary and codified law, often based on the Qur'ānic teaching in favour of sharing and equity.[19] Practice varies considerably from country to country and district to district, depending upon hydraulic conditions. With the exception of Egypt, where a single system prevails and there is a long tradition of government control, the irrigation systems are fragmentary and independent of each other. Generally speaking, the scarcer the water is, the more complicated are the regulations. However, two broad methods of distribution have been observed. Water is frequently allocated on a volume basis, and the recipient takes a set share of the flow from a continual supply, as in the oases of the Fezzan in Libya. A time allocation is used more widely in the region. It provides for the entire supply from a particular source to be available on a rotational basis, though the actual method of calculating time, and hence the shares, varies quite considerably. Attempts have been made to standardize practice within national boundaries, as well as to protect both users and owners, but reforms similar to those carried through for land holding are probably impossible to implement. Modifications, rather than radical changes, are characteristic also of the way in which farming itself is carried on.

4.3.5 'Peasant economy'

Farming in the Middle East may be represented as a form of *peasant economy*.[20] Most of the region's farmers own or lease only small holdings. They and their ancestors have been exploited and oppressed, contributing to the high cultural developments of the region only through their rents and their labour. The land, however held, is worked by the family as an economic unit under the direction of its oldest male. Except in Egypt, where the smaller holdings seem to have at least a seasonal need for outside help,[21] paid labour is not normally employed. The basis of subsistence is the family holding, and the product available to the farmer after the deduction of rent and other payments is largely consumed directly. The whole enterprise is more concerned with securing the subsistence of the family group than with making a profit in a capitalist sense, though the need for certain basic commodities (salt, iron), and the expenses of the rituals marking life crises, such as circumcision and marriage, require periodic sales. A balance was maintained traditionally between subsistence needs and a distaste for manual labour, a distaste probably felt more keenly where there was a periodic reallocation of holdings, and hence little opportunity to develop a sense of attachment to the land. The family would make an effort to produce more for enlarged consumption or investment only if the drudgery of labour was not pushed beyond a critical point where the increased output was outweighed by the irksomeness of the extra work. This balance occurred at different points according to the size of the family and the ratio of its working and non-working members (very young children, old adults).

Most members of the family naturally worked on the land, making an increased labour contribution as they grew from infancy to maturity. The labour imputs would then stabilize for a while before declining as the mature adults became older and less capable of manual labour. The amount of labour

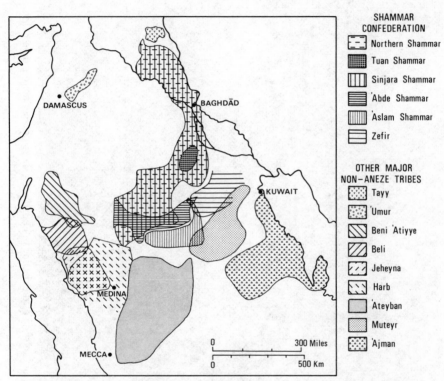

Figure 4.5 Some traditional tribal territories in northern Arabia (Reproduced by permission of *Geographical Review*)

150

Pastoralism remains important in spite of the decline in nomadism; sheep grazing among date palms near Tripoli, Libya
(An Esso photograph)

available controlled the amount of land which could be cultivated. Additional land might have been secured by bringing under the plough more of the family holding, if they had a surplus, or by reclamation, where waste land still survived, or by acquiring a larger holding, where communal systems of land tenure continued and periodic redistribution was normal, or by entering into share-cropping contracts. Thus, the optimum amount of land which a family could work would vary through its biological cycle, as would the pivot between need satisfaction and drudgery of labour.

Peasant economy has different objectives from those of capitalist farming. It is hardly surprising, therefore, that it reacts differently to certain market forces, or that the 'peasant' is reluctant to adopt new crops and new techniques. What has often been taken in the past for resistance based on ignorance and conservation may be regarded in this light as perfectly rational responses to innovations which threaten a satisfactory life-style by invoking goals which may be little appreciated or which can be purchased at too high a social price. Change may come with the acceptance of a different set of social objectives which reach the villages through the towns by personal contact and through the mass media. Modifications and change are in progress, though it may not be as devastating as that experienced in the pastoral sector of the economy, the organization of which is outlined below.

4.3.6 Pastoralism[22]

Although permanently settled communities of cultivators keep draught and herd animals, animal husbandry and cultivation are not normally integrated into a mixed farming system similar to that found in northwestern Europe. Only in Israel has mixed farming been developed to any degree, with fodder grown to supply stall-fed cattle. Everywhere else herd animals are not normally fed on fodder crops, which are saved for winter feed and for draught animals, but are kept away from the cultivated areas, as far as possible. There is spatial separation of the two activities, as well as a certain amount of traditional group specialization.

Animal husbandry in the Middle East is organized from permanent bases where food and water can be obtained in the difficult season, whether that is winter, as in the mountains with their frosts and snow, or summer, with its extreme heat and drought, as on the edges of the Saharan and Arabian deserts. Until very recently, some herders were completely mobile after they had left their base areas. In following the available grazing they produced spatial patterns which will be described below. The basic grazing unit was usually the *tent* (of perhaps five people), each moving with a group of five or six others, but in no particularly stable or permanent association, only for mutual company and help. The individual movements of a *tent* in any year were conditioned by the state of the grazing and the availability of drinking water; they were closely affected by the spatial and temporal pattern of precipitation. Over a period of years, though, they tended to follow traditional routes which themselves led through tribal areas. These are territories with well recognized if flexible limits, where a tribe has traditional rights at certain times of the year (Figure 4.5). Only in dire emergencies were the boundaries crossed, and then the pattern and extent of the trespass depended upon traditional agreements and alliances.

Animals were kept for sale, or for the sale of their produce, so that the staple foods (dates and cereals) and other necessities could be bought. Supplies were also obtained by ownership of, or control over, cultivated land, while cash was often secured as protection money from settled communities and caravans. Large herds meant prosperity and prestige, so that stealing and raiding were part of the traditional way of life.

Other groups of herders have been more restricted in their movements. They have moved from bases in their own permanent, cultivating villages to seasonal grazing land at a distance, but on which often stood a second settlement. The *shieling*, to use a Scottish term, was generally less substantial than the permanent settlement, and was used by only a section of the group for part of the year, but it provided a focus around which the herds grazed on traditional pastures according to their known advantages for different kinds of animals[23] and a place where liquid milk was made into cheese and yoghurt. In addition, a few crops might be grown. As population pressure grew, the shielings were frequently converted into permanent cultivating villages, as the many-*yayla* suffixes testify in Turkey today. Modern pressures, in a situation approaching one of land shortage, have produced severe overgrazing in many parts of the region, which has been exacerbated by the decline of more extensive forms of nomadism (Chapter 11).

4.4 Patterns of land use (Figure 4.6)

A large part of the Middle East is little used by man. The mountains are too high in places for comfortable use, and in winter they are too cold and snow-covered for permanent occupation, though Mount Lebanon and Uludag (near Bursa) are proving a joy to the skier. Small glaciers still exist in parts. Tracts of sand and stone desert provide a physical contrast, but human use is rare and limited to exceptional seasons when a flush of herbage has been produced by an occasional shower. Both the mountains and the true deserts have been the traditional haunts of outcasts, brigands and *jinns*, all characters in the region's folk stories. Nomadic pastoralists were the main organized groups to enter these negative subregions, since they have traditionally operated across the margins of the permanently settled districts, while some of them were traversed by historic caravan routes.

4.4.1 Herding

Herding has been an essentially mobile way of life induced by seasonal variations in the availability of grazing and drinking water, and by the type

153

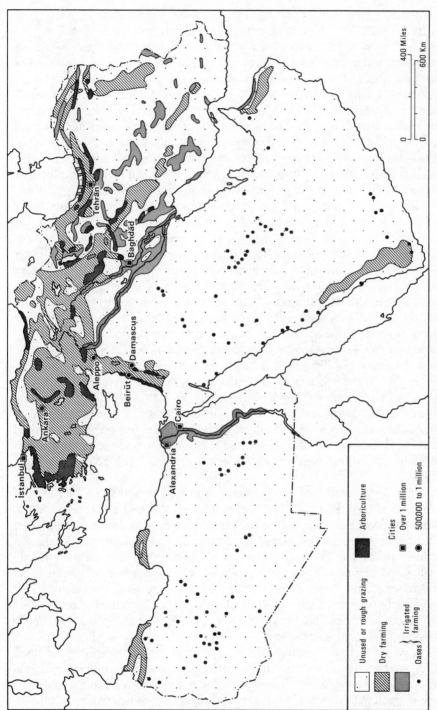

Figure 4.6 General land use in about 1970

of animal herded. Where the grazing and water resources have been good, sheep and goats have been kept, either in mixed herds or sometimes in separation. Sheep are rather fussy about what they eat and cannot graze far from permanent water, since they need to drink at least every ten days, even when the vegetation is fresh and green, and every two days, when it is old and more desiccated. Goats have reputations for being almost omniverous, and consequently very destructive of vegetation,[24] but they need less water than sheep. Their other attractions include an ability to climb where other herd animals cannot go, which means that they can graze in otherwise unusable country. Goats also have a higher rate of reproduction than sheep and a lactation period which is 50 to 100 per cent greater than that of sheep. Further deterioration in both water and grazing brings the dromedary *(camelus dromedarius)* into its own. Not only can it eat parched grass and desiccated shrub, but it will exist on such a diet for several days without being watered. However, the quantity of water consumed is closely related to the quality of the vegetation. In the extremely arid conditions of summer, dromedaries may require water every day, while just after rain, when the grazing is succulent but surface water may still be scarce, they may need water only once in a month. This ability to last without water is the great advantage possessed by the dromedary over the donkey as a transport animal for, while they will eat much the same type of vegetation, the donkey requires watering every second day. Dromedary rearing has been characteristic of nomadic pastoralists over much of Arabia, Syria, Palestine and Iraq for centuries, probably spreading from these sub-regions into North Africa from the sixth century BC. It was replaced by rearing of the Bactrian camel *(camelus bactrianus)* in Iran and Turkey. The two animals are similar in many ways, but the Bactrian camel is more adapted to the cold, snow and rocks of the high plateaus and mountains where it is required to work. Horses were traditionally bred by some nomads, and Arab stallions were famous, but they were always difficult to rear and often kept as a prestige symbol.

A minimum number of herd animals is needed to support a *tent* at subsistence level by producing a sufficient number of offspring and other products to pay for food. Estimates of the critical number have varied, but range from 25 to 60 for sheep and goats and from 10 to 25 for dromedaries. There is a tendency to build up the herds in years of good grazing in an attempt to provide a safeguard against the years of drought, when the number of stock will be reduced to a level from which it might be difficult to build up again.[25] This is especially true in the case of dromedaries, whose reproduction rate is low, and largely explains the importance of formalized raiding once common amongst north Arabian nomads.

The patterns of movement produced by animal herding have been classified by Johnson into two main types, horizontal and vertical. Horizontal movements are created by areal variations in the availability of water and grazing, and were characteristic of Saudi Arabia, with extensions into neighbouring Jordan, Syria, Iraq and Kuwait. Mixed herds were common, but traditionally dromedaries were the most important animals and allowed the long migrations associated with some nomadic groups. Movements had a marked seasonality to them, involving summer clustering about permanent wells, frequently on the fringes of cultivated areas, and winter migration from pasture to pasture. Johnson recognized two subtypes of horizontal nomadism.[26] *Pulsatory* nomadism involves movement out from a dry season base on an oasis or group of wells into the surrounding desert and then a return back along almost the same line when the grazing fails (Figure 4.7a). This is the pattern followed by sheep and camel nomads in Cyrenaica, in Libya. *Elliptical* nomadism, the second type, begins as a similar movement outward from a dry-season base, but the return is made along a markedly different route and generally along a valley where water lasts longest, even though its permanency cannot be relied upon (Figure 4.7a). The movements of the Ruwala of north Arabia provide

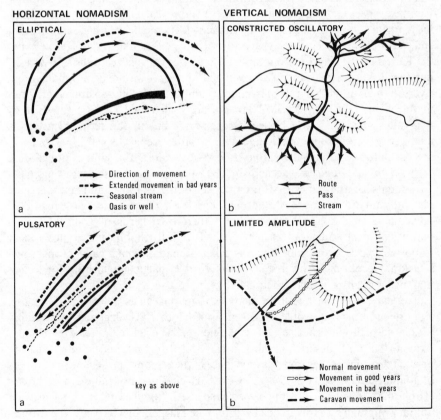

Figure 4.7 Schematic patterns of nomadic movement:
(a) horizontal nomadism
    (i) elliptical pattern, (ii) pulsatory pattern.
(b) vertical nomadism
    constricted oscillatory pattern, (ii) limited amplitude pattern
(Reproduced by permission of Douglas L. Johnson, 1969)

a classic example. They formerly spent the dry season near Damascus, but from October onwards worked southwards towards al-Jawf, and then returned between late April and June down the Wādī es Sirhān, through modern Jordan, but their movements have been greatly curtailed in modern times.

Vertical nomadism makes use of altitudinal variations in the seasonal availability of pasture and water. It is associated, of course, with mountain areas and in some districts is similar to the classic transhumance of the Alps. Again two basic subtypes have been recognized. *Constricted Oscillatory* nomadism is very widespread where mountains and lowland are juxtaposed. Sheep and goats are the main herd animals, with camels and donkeys for transport. The herders usually have a firm agricultural base, either in their own fields and villages or through a close relationship with cultivators whose territory they cross during the migrations. Movement takes place from winter pastures in the lowlands as desiccation sets in, and is directed at upland pastures. Rights of passage and grazing are held along the migratory route, which may, in fact, be anchored by a permanent settlement at either one or other end. The distances covered vary considerably. The Yürüks of Turkey and the Kurds of the Zagros Mountains generally cover relatively short distances, but the Bakhtiari of Iran travel over 500 km each way over mountains and rivers in their annual migration from the plains of Khuzestan to upland grazings in the vicinity of Eşfahān. Movements are constricted because they follow the valleys and therefore have a linear form, but at the terminal area the members of the group spread out and go their separate ways. Movements are oscillatory, because the whole tribe returns along the same route (Figure 4.7b). *Limited Amplitude* nomadism is found in the particularly harsh environments of the Tibesti Mountains in southern Libya and amongst the plateaus and mountains of southern Arabia. It is characterized by the restricted movements of individual families with their own herds of goats around a number of local water sources. The groups are fully mobile and do not appear to possess bases in the same sense as other nomads, though catch crops, sown after an exceptional shower, may tie them to a particular locality for longer than usual in any one year (Figure 4.7b).

Everywhere in the region nomadism is in retreat as a form of land use, and the number of people involved appears to have declined appreciably (Table 4.3), though precise figures cannot be secured (Chapter 5). In Saudi Arabia, the 'true' desert nomad is already hard to find, and within a decade or two there may be few nomads anywhere in the region. The decline in numbers of animals in most countries, however, is confined to camels and horses (Table 4.4). They are no longer required as draught animals or to provide military might. The caravan has been replaced largely by the truck, the dromedary and horse by the car, bus and tank. Pumps have replaced various types of animal-powered lifting devices in most districts, while ploughing and farm haulage is increasingly being done by tractors. The ploughing up of traditional grazing land, and the replacement of seasonal and annual fallow by rotational crops has diminished the grazing in the vital base areas, as well as in the seasonal

TABLE 4.3
Figures illustrative of the decline in
the numbers of nomads

	Year	Estimate (millions)
IRAN	1910	2·60
	1932	1·00
	1956	0·25
	1966	0·25
IRAQ	1867	0·50
	1947	0·20
	1957	0·06
	1965	0·06

Source: J. I. Clarke and W. B. Fisher (Eds), *Populations of the Middle East and North Africa*, University of London Press, London, 1972, pp. 82–83, 109.

pastures. Nomads find it increasingly hard to rent the grazing they need, and many have given up herding, especially after a disaster to their herds. Even in good seasons, the nomadic life is hard, while status has deteriorated as the relative wealth and military power of the tribes have declined. Some former nomads attach themselves as paid herders to established cultivating communities, where they are at the bottom of the social hierarchy. Others take advantage of various government schemes to settle on the land and be

TABLE 4.4
Selected animals
('000)

Country	Buffaloes		Camels		Cattle		Horses		Mules		Donkeys	
	a	b	a	a	a	b	a	b	a	b	a	b
Egypt	1212	2100	266	130	1356	2120	39	65	10	12	816	1330
Iran	111	280	638	175	3388	5100	358	380	126	138	1230	7000
Iraq	294	290	450	220	1495	1920	290	127	120	56	460	580
Israel	—	—	181	10	55	251	7	10	3	5	17	16
Jordan	—	—	4	10	2397	43	7	2	4	9	34	44
Lebanon	—	—	2	—	75	84	6	3	10	3	22	25
Libya	—	—	324	160	79	109	17	24	1	—	26	96
P.D.R. Yemen	—	—	75	40	60	92	—	—	—	—	7	28
Saudi Arabia	—	—	265	560	110	320	—	—	—	—	22	135
Syria	6	2	75	7	483	550	101	70	63	66	256	230
Turkey	939	1117	107	31	10121	12756	1136	1049	104	299	1696	1805
Yemen, A. R.	—	—	48	59	972	138	3	3	—	—	—	—

a = average 1947/48 to 1951/52
b = 1970–71
Source: United Nations, FAO, *Production Yearbook, 1971*, Rome 1972.

transformed into cultivators. Governments act from mixed motives. There is undoubtedly a philanthropic, even a religious motive involved, but political factors have been important also, for the strong kinship ties vital to nomadic life, tribal loyalties and skill with weapons have meant that the nomads have frequently been seen as a threat to security and ordered administration.

Animal husbandry, however, is in a somewhat paradoxical situation. Against the decline in nomadism must be set a rising demand for meat, hair, wool and dairy products from within the region and which the nomads have traditionally supplied. The number of animals in the Middle East has actually increased (Table 4.4). In Saudi Arabia even the number of camels has increased, too, perhaps because camel meat is a traditional, but formerly rare pleasure, and water supplies are now more secure. Donkeys and mules have increased in number nearly everywhere, largely to supply the farmers' need for a cheap means of travel and carriage between their villages and their plots, consequent upon the cultivation of more land and the shift towards greater intensification of use. The numbers of buffaloes and cattle have risen partly to provide traction to the greatly increased numbers of ploughs in the region, for not every farmer owns a tractor. But the increase may be chiefly explained by the demand for more milk, different types of meat and larger hides. The stall feeding of cattle is increasing throughout the region, especially near the large towns, where the requirements for liquid milk are growing. The greatest increases, though, have been in the traditional herd animals, sheep and goats. These are still ranged in traditional ways, though the movements are being curtailed as outlined above. In consequence, animals are being concentrated in areas formerly considered marginal for cultivation. Grazing has seriously deteriorated as a result. This has been helped to some extent by government philanthropic measures, deliberately or casually applied, to secure water for the surviving nomads. New wells, as along Tapline in Saudi Arabia, have focused and concentrated grazing, leading to overgrazing and the destruction of the pastures (Chapter 11). Without serious consideration of measures to conserve and improve traditional grazing lands, a great deal of land will go out of use. In that event, animal husbandry will have to be integrated more fully into the region's cultivation systems which are so fundamental to the socio-economic life of the region. Alternatively, large commercial enterprises, based on irrigated fodder, as at Kufra in Libya, may be practicable in capital-rich states.

4.4.2 Forestry

Traditional forest communities partook of the characteristics of nomadism and sedentary cultivation. Forest generally survived to any extent only in the mountains, in a zone between the plains and lower slopes, on the one hand, which were the domain of the settled cultivator, and the upland pastures, on the other, where the pastoralists spent the summer (Figure 4.5). Livestock were herded in the forest or beyond and some crops were grown, sometimes under systems reminiscent of bush fallowing. The major activities in the forests,

TABLE 4.5
Surviving forest, in about 1970

Country	Area '000 ha	Percentage area
Egypt	2	0·0
Iran	18000	11·0
Iraq	1851	4·2
Israel	109	5·4
Jordan	125	1·3
Lebanon	95	9·5
Libya	532	0·3
P.D.R. Yemen	2590	9·0
Saudi Arabia	1680	0·8
Syria	440	2·4
Turkey	18273	23·8

Source: United Nations, FAO, *Production Yearbook, 1971,* Rome, 1972, Table 1.

though, were cutting timber to provide lumber and firewood, producing charcoal for cooking and metal working, and extracting resins for adhesives, gums and paints. The specialist forest communities, like the Tahtaci of the southwestern parts of the Taurus Mountains, steadily destroyed the resources on which they depended and were thus forced to live in camps away from home and, from time to time, to shift their settlements completely. Forest destruction was aided by the activities of nomadic pastoralists who, on occasion, wilfully burnt forest to extent the open grazing and frequently had no alternative but to graze their animals amongst the trees as they passed through, thereby hindering regeneration.

Only a small amount of forest survives today (Table 4.5; Figure 4.6), and

TABLE 4.6
Agricultural land use

Country (and year)	Total land area '000 ha	Arable '000 ha	Percentage total area	Permanent crops '000 ha	Percentage arable
Egypt (1970)	100145	—	—	2725	100·0
Iran (1967)	163600	16060	9·8	500	3·1
Iraq (1970)	43492	10800	24·4	163	1·5
Israel (1970)	2032	377	16·6	86	25·5
Jordan (1970)	9774	1132	11·6	168	14·8
Kuwait (1970)	1600	0·5	0·03	—	—
Lebanon (1968)	1000	240	24·0	76	31·7
Libya (1969)	175954	2375	1·3	140	5·9
P.D.R. Yemen (1966)	28768	—	—	252	—
Saudi Arabia (1967)	214969	765	0·36	44	5·7
Syria (1970)	18493	5641	30·5	258	4·6
Turkey (1970)	77076	24793	32·2	2585	10·4

Source: United Nations, FAO, *Production Yearbook, 1971,* Rome, 1972, Table 1.

much of that consists of little more than scrub. Forest removal has increased steadily since the First World War as the demands for wood have grown and as more land has been cleared for cultivation. The consequences have not only been the loss of a valuable resource, but extensive erosion in the mountains and an increase in flooding in the valleys and plains. Governments have acted to preserve forests, prevent coastal flooding, and curtail the activities of their traditional inhabitants, whose numbers are almost certainly in decline. In some countries, notably Israel, afforestation programmes are in progress (Figure 3.7). Conservation efforts elsewhere, however, are not entirely successful because of the relentless demands for fuel and arable land.

4.4.3 Cultivation

Farming is still basic to the socio-economic life of the Middle East, despite recent attempts at industrialization (Chapter 8). Arable land, however, covers a very small part of the surface area of the region. Recent and comparative statistics are not available, but a crude estimate for 1970 would put the average arable area for countries in the region at about 14 per cent of their total surface area. The range, however, was considerable (Table 4.6).

Extremely small arable areas were found in Saudi Arabia and P.D.R. Yemen, while about 30 and 32 per cent of the total area was cultivated in Syria and Turkey respectively. The average was approached by Israel and Jordan, with about 17 and 12 per cent of their surface area reported as under arable. Everywhere the arable area has been increasing, as the later regional chapters make clear (Chapters 11–20). Former grazing land has been ploughed up in the dry-farming districts, and irrigation has been extended there and in the more arid parts of the region. The use of the cultivated area is also changing.

In 1970–71, the cropping pattern was still dominated by wheat and barley, which everywhere occupied more than 50 per cent of the field crop area and reached over 80 per cent in Iran, Iraq, Jordan, Turkey and Yemen A.R. and even 90 per cent in P.D.R. Yemen (Table 4.7). Yields, however, were below the world average of 1850 gms/ha for barley and 1850 gms/ha for wheat, though these were exceeded in a few countries, notably Egypt (Table 4.8). Wheat was generally the most important crop, grown principally for bread, but in Libya its place was taken by barley, which is tolerant of greater aridity. Maize is well adapted to the deep soil and plentiful water available in the Nile valley and delta, where it is the most important foodstuff. In Yemen A.R. and P.D.R. Yemen, by contrast, the hardy cereals, millet and sorghum, predominated (Table 4.7). Wheat and barley are generally sown after the first rains, in October or November, but millet and sorghum are normally planted as the rains end, while maize is a summer crop grown under irrigation.

Despite their predominance, cereals are rarely grown as the only crops in any district today (Table 4.7). Traditionally, vegetables have been grown on a small scale in gardens in and around the settlements, but their production as field crops has steadily grown since the Second World War. Improved communi-

TABLE 4.7
Field crops, 1970–71 ('000 ha)

COUNTRY	WHEAT	BARLEY	MAIZE	MILLET + SORGHUM	RICE	SUGAR CANE	SUGAR BEET	POTATOES	ONIONS	TOMATOES	CABBAGES	CAULI-FLOWER	BEANS	BROAD BEANS	PEAS	CUCUMBER	MELONS	WATER MELONS	CHICK PEAS	LENTILS	VETCH	PULSES	GROUND NUTS	COTTON	SESAME	SUN FLOWER	FLAX	TOBACCO	TOTAL AREA *
EGYPT	567	42	641	210	483	75	30	30	21	100	11	3	21	135	7	11	11	37	3	20	?	23	21	702	25	—	12	—	3211
IRAN	5000	1300	25	30	380	17	157	30	—	—	—	—	10	—	—	—	19	43	95	55	—	—	—	375	10	56	—	17	7557
IRAQ	1387	744	5	6	73	—	3	1	19	29	1	1	11	15	—	20	2	8	5	6	1	3	6	69	15	—	—	17	2490
ISRAEL	113	16	2	1	—	—	5	5	2	4	1	1	1	1	2	3	6	8	2	—	3	—	6	31	1	5	—	2	220
JORDAN	210	50	1	1	—	—	—	1	1	13	1	1	1	2	?	1	?	—	2	22	7	—	—	?	1	—	—	4	324
LEBANON	60	10	1	2	—	—	3	9	2	6	2	1	4	1	?	3	?	2	2	3	6	2	3	?	?	5	—	7	132
LIBYA	250	350	1	66	1	—	—	2	4	7	—	—	—	4	2	—	—	2	—	—	—	—	5	—	—	—	—	1	696
SAUDI ARABIA	100	26	—	25	1	?	—	—	—	8	—	—	—	—	—	—	—	—	—	—	—	—	—	—	20	—	—	—	180
SYRIA	1208	725	5	34	1	—	9	6	8	16	1	1	6	7	2	9	12	35	29	129	60	—	9	251	6	1	—	11	2581
TURKEY	9000	2750	660	370	65	—	124	160	78	73	?	?	145	30	4	—	—	200	100	103	175	15	16	682	67	360	18	310	15505
YEMEN A.R.	14	2	16	40	—	—	—	7	—	—	—	—	—	—	—	—	—	—	—	—	—	—	—	2	—	—	—	—	81
P.D.R. YEMEN	8	1	—	—	—	—	—	—	—	—	—	—	—	—	—	—	—	—	—	—	—	—	—	4	4	—	—	—	17

N.B. Data very incomplete.
— = No information.
? = Some production, are a unknown.
* = Sum of area under reported crops. Fodder crops are not reported by FAO.
Source: United Nations, FAO, *Production Yearbook, 1971*, Rome, 1972.

cations have been largely responsible, since perishable commodities can now quickly reach the distant urban markets, where the demand has been rising, by fast truck. Potatoes, onions, tomatoes, cucumbers, melons and water melons, as well as legumes (lentils, chick peas and beans), have expanded their areas considerably in many districts. Nonetheless, they are most important in Israel, Jordan and Lebanon where export markets have been developed in addition to the urban home market. Total areas, however, remain very small. Vetch is widely grown as a fodder crop, but its place is taken in Egypt and parts of Arabia by *berseem* (clover). Unfortunately, FAO does not include fodder crops in its statistics, though the area is proportionately large, especially when it is remembered that a portion of the cereals grown are intended for animal food, generally for the winter. The extreme is probably reached in Egypt, where up to one fifth of the entire cropped area is devoted to clover.

Some cereals and most of the vegetables are sold off the farm, but a good deal of the income is now obtained by growing specific industrial crops. The most important in terms of area is cotton. It has long been grown in the region, but its rapid expansion came in two phases. The first came during the nineteenth century, and was stimulated by rising demand from industrialized Europe. The second phase came after the Second World War, and was conse-quent upon world-wide shortages and high prices created by the Korean War (1950–1953). Although a large proportion of P.D.R. Yemen's crop area was claimed to be under cotton in 1970–1971, cotton almost certainly occupied the greatest proportion of the non-fodder crop area in Egypt (21·9 per cent), followed by Israel (14·1 per cent) and Syria (9·7 per cent). Practically everywhere the crop is grown under irrigation. But whilst cotton is the most important commercial crop in areal terms, others of at least local importance are also found. Sugar-cane is grown under irrigation in near tropical conditions in parts of Egypt and Iran. Sugar beet, by contrast, is grown in the cooler dry-farming districts of the north as part of rotations involving cereals. Tobacco has been an important industrial crop in the region since the eighteenth century, and the leading growing areas today are the Aegean and Black Sea coastlands of Turkey, the Latakia district of Syria and parts of Jordan. Sunflowers are significant in Iran and Turkey, where the opium poppy is also grown, both legally and illegally. Sesame and groundnuts are grown more widely for their oils, while flax and hemp have very limited distributions in the wetter western districts.

By contrast with the area under field or annual crops, that devoted to perma-nent crops, principally fruit trees is small (Table 4.6). Olives, vines and figs are the most numerous trees since they have the advantage of being deep-rooted and so able to draw moisture from depth in the long, arid summers characteri-stic of the region. However, the extreme aridity of the interior and the winter cold of the mountains and high plateaus make them a characteristic combi-nation only in areas adjacent to the Mediterranean, chiefly Israel, Jordan, Lebanon and coastal Turkey. Undercropping with cereals is possible here, but with distance inland and falling precipitation, olives must be planted

TABLE 4.8
Yields of Wheat and Barley in 1971
(100 gms/ha)

Country	Wheat	Barley
Egypt	27·7	23·8
Iran	7·0	6·5
Iraq	5·9	6·8
Israel	17·3	11·4
Jordan	9·0	8·0
Lebanon	8·3	10·0
Libya	2·8	2·9
P.D.R. Yemen	17·3	30·0
Saudi Arabia	15·0	13·5
Syria	7·0	3·6
Turkey	14·0	14·5
Yemen A.R.	10·7	12·5
World	15·8	18·5

Source: United Nations, FAO, *Production Yearbook, 1971*, Rome, 1972.

further apart and soil moisture is not sufficient to permit undercropping, unless irrigation is applied, as in the oasis of Damascus. Vines have a wider distribution than the other two tree crops, but, until recently, the area devoted to them had been restricted by the Muslim ban on wine-drinking. Tropical fruits, such as bananas, are grown on a small scale in Egypt, Israel and Lebanon. Oranges, which are both a subtropical and Mediterranean fruit, are grown in most countries, though production is particularly high from the coastal plain of Israel. Grapefruit and peaches are expanding in similar areas to supply the export market in western and eastern Europe. Temperate fruits (apples, pears and cherries) are widely found, but on a fairly small scale still. They are particularly associated with upland areas, where there are local specialities, such as the apples of Lebanon and the pears of Ankara. Sales are largely restricted to local or national markets, though Lebanon has built up a trade in apples with some of its more southerly neighbours. Date groves, as commercial propositions, are more restricted still. The main commercial growing area is along the Shaṭṭ al'Arab in southern Iraq, but dates are also an important crop in the oases of Arabia, Egypt and Libya. Dates are not only an important local food and a useful export. The palm trees are valuable also as a source of building materials in otherwise largely treeless areas and provide essential shade for the successful growing of cereals, vegetables and other crops under desert conditions.

Everywhere the commercial orientation of cropping patterns is increasing. Demand continues to rise, both within the region and beyond, as populations grow and incomes rise. Accessibility has been improved for many farming communities by the introduction of the truck and the construction of motor roads.[27] Marketing has become easier and quicker. The mechanization of farm work and the extension of irrigation have also been important in affecting the changes, since the necessary investments, which are comparatively high in a region where agricultural investment was once the exception rather than the rule, can only be recouped by growing industrial or high value commercial crops. The price of these changes in cropping has often been the ending of traditional sharecropping contracts and the destruction of 'peasant economy', with the consequent appearance of cash rents and unemployment in the rural areas.

Cropping patterns, however, have not only responded to commercial pressures. Considerable influence has been exerted by governments on the national scale and, at the local level, by distance from the operational centre, the village. Distance from the nucleated village exerts a profound influence on the local pattern of land use and von Thünen's location theory seems to apply.[28] Land uses which require the application of relatively large amounts of labour, such as vegetable growing for home consumption, are generally situated close about the settlement, though some distortion occurs where excentrically placed and small-scale irrigation is practised. Cereal growing is less labour intensive, and is carried out further away from the settlement (Figure 4.8). With traditional techniques the cereal and fallow belt extended for a maximum distance of between three and four kilometres from the settlement, and it seems that beyond this distance the economic return did not normally exceed the drudgery involved in cultivating plots so far away from each other. Where tree crops are important, they appear to be grown in a zone more than three or four kilometres from the settlement, since they require less labour and the fewest visits in the year. Where trees are not of commercial importance,

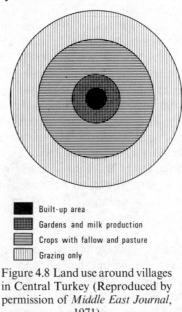

■ Built-up area

▓ Gardens and milk production

▤ Crops with fallow and pasture

▥ Grazing only

Figure 4.8 Land use around villages in Central Turkey (Reproduced by permission of *Middle East Journal*, 1971)

however, they might often be seen growing in and immediately around the village to give shade and an atmosphere of coolness. Grazing land lies beyond the commercial tree-crop zone, since the herding of animals requires comparatively little effort compared with other forms of land use, while the animals have to be kept away from the cropped areas as much as possible to prevent destruction of the vital harvest. Mechanization, of course, has extended the radius of cereal growing and, in some places, brought into existence a second cereal zone beyond the belt of tree crops, while increased demand has brought under the plough occasional tracts of common grazing found closer to the village. Such areas are divided into the long strips shown in Figure 4.3a.

Locational changes are associated also with the introduction of irrigated farming to dry-farming districts, where it is usually accompanied by a change in crop type, often in response to government plans, as well as to the needs of capital investment programmes. In addition to undertaking reclamation and irrigation schemes, providing credit and supplying new strains, government has exerted other controls over land use. Restrictions are normally imposed on the area which can be planted with cotton and tobacco in an attempt to manage the market and stabilize prices, while poppy growing is controlled as much as possible to prevent illegal drug trafficking with the West. Production of other crops is not completely free either. Cereals, for example, are often supported by guaranteed prices which are higher than those on the world market and, in consequence, the areas under wheat and barley are considerably greater than they would be if market forces were allowed something like full play. Inefficient forms of land use are thus perpetuated, as are archaic farming techniques.

Techniques of cultivation vary quite considerably across the region, but a basic distinction may be made between dry-farming and forms of irrigated farming. Dry-farming uses only the annual precipitation of the area, and the system is geared to conserving limited soil moisture in conditions of high summer evapotranspiration and relatively low winter precipitation. Fallowing of part of the cultivated area for at least one year was characteristic of the system, and is still retained widely. This was often explained by the mistaken belief that at least two seasons moisture could be accumulated and produce better crops. In fact, the use of fallow was probably more related to the relative abundance of land until recently, the shortage of fodder and the adequacy of extensive production, with traditional labour imputs, to support the population at an acceptable standard. Population growth and market demands have reduced the extent of fallowing by introducing a year of vegetables or fodder crops into a rotation with the basic cereals. Other features of the system can be more definitely explained as attempts to use available precipitation wisely.

Ploughing begins as the rains start, but after a sufficient interval has elapsed for the baked soil to soften. The traditional plough is a simple ard made of wood, frequently with a fire-hardened point, rather than an iron share. It is pulled by a pair of animals, frequently but not always, a yoke of oxen.[29]

Such an implement merely scratches the surface of the ground, but when employed with simple harrows and mattocks, it is very effective in producing a fine tilth which aids water conservation. Seeds are then sown on to this seedbed, traditionally by broadcasting, and harrowed or trodden in. The whole process might take two to three weeks under favourable conditions on an average-sized holding. Soil is still prepared in such a way in some districts, generally the remoter and more mountainous ones, where steel ploughs and tractors are not only relatively expensive but often ill-adapted to difficult terrain, awkward terraces, and thin, stoney soils. Steel ploughs, designed to turn a furrow, are almost universal, while in the plains and larger valleys multiple ploughs are commonplace. Haulage is frequently by tractors now, a fact which helps to explain the decline in the number of horses in the region since 1950. In Israel, the position has now been reached where there are more tractors per hectare than in the United States.[30] Tractors and steel ploughs have allowed more land to be ploughed with less labour. In addition, they are efficient at opening up the soil and allowing plants to get full benefit from the nutrients in the ground. But, unless contour ploughing is employed—and this is still exceptional—the soil is more dangerously exposed to erosion, especially gullying, than with traditional techniques.

In the past, artificial fertilizers were seldom applied and dunging was often by chance rather than deliberate application. Chemical fertilizers are used practically everywhere today in an attempt to maintain or improve yields, but application is still generally low, except in Egypt. This is partly because their value is not always appreciated, but it is largely because fertilizers are not readily available to the farmer. Prices are high, distribution is often inadequate to the requirement, and national output is frequently very low. Israel and Lebanon are exceptional for predominantly dry-farming countries in that their rates of application, relative to area, are greater than in the United States, but on the regional scale they are fortunate in having the raw materials, industries and infrastructure upon which the adequate use of fertilizers depends.

Harvest time varies according to the type of crop, date of sowing and elevation, but the cereal harvest begins in May and ends in August across the region. Cereals were traditionally cut with sickles, though the use of scythes has been reported from parts of Iran. These methods are still employed in difficult terrain, on irregularly-shaped fields and by poor families, but combine-harvesters operated by contractors are now widespread. A similar use of mixed techniques is apparent at threshing. If hand cut, the cereals are taken to threshing floors, often located in windy places near the village. There they are prepared for winnowing by means of a threshing sledge or similar device, consisting of heavy pieces of wood shod with flints or pieces of sharpened steel, dragged round and round the circle of the floor. Winnowing, to separate grain and chaff, then takes place by hurling spadefuls or forkfuls of the chopped material in to the wind–a skilled and tiring operation. In some districts, simple box-threshing machines, driven by tractor engines, are employed. It is at

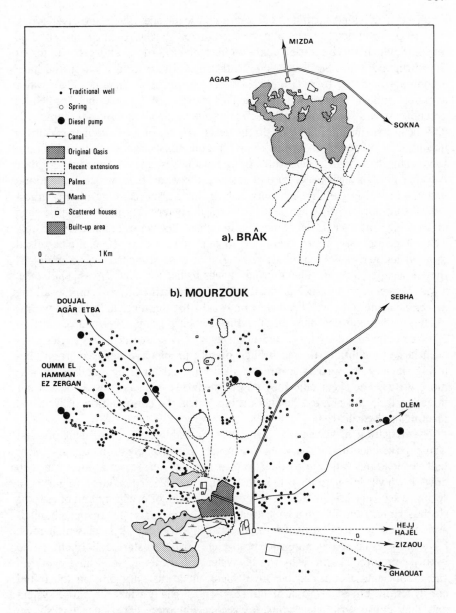

Figure 4.9 Forms of oasis in Libya:
(a) Brâk and (b) Mourzouk
(Reproduced by permission of Lars Eldblom, 1961)

the threshing floors, of course, that sharecropping contracts are fulfilled with the division of the bagged grain.

Similar implements and techniques are employed in irrigated areas, but irrigated farming as a system of land use is dominated by water supply methods. The various sources of the vital water, thus allow a four-part classification of types of irrigated farming. These are oasis, terrace, *qanāt* and river types.

Various subtypes of oasis may be recognized, but all of them are situated in areas which receive little or no regular precipitation, and grow dates as their principal crop. Some oases depend primarily on surface water and have a compact or linear form (Figure 4.9), depending upon the amount of water available and the type of source actually tapped.[31] Water may be supplied by perennial streams, as in the case of the famous oasis of Damascus (Chapter 13) and the numerous humble oases on the desert fringes of the Omani and Yemeni mountains. Other oases depend upon irregular flash floods *(seils)* which are used extensively and successfully in the wadi systems of southern Arabia. Another type of oasis makes use of springs, the water from which is fed along systems of aqueducts fanning outwards from the source. One of the largest and most complex of such oases is al Hasa in eastern Arabia. The type image of an oasis, however, is dependent upon subsurface water reached by shallow wells. Traditionally, water was lifted in one of two ways. It might be raised in great leather bags by animals pulling on a rope stretched over a pulley as they descended a ramp. The alternative was to use the *noria* (Arabic *na'oura*), a waterwheel geared in such a way that it could be turned by an animal walking in a circle around the well head. The physical effort required in lifting comparatively small quantities of water produced an essentially fragmented pattern of fields or gardens, each centred upon its well (Figure 4.9). This pattern has been largely maintained, even though diesel pumps have replaced traditional lifting devices and produced greater flexibility through their ability to raise more water. The sheer efficiency of pumps, however, has caused local water tables to fall, and created serious problems for the continuation of irrigated farming in a few districts.

The irrigation of systems of terraces is probably only a fragment of what it may have been under the Roman Empire. Terrace irrigation consists essentially of leading water on to the top of a flight of terraces and allowing it to flow downwards by gravity (Figure 4.10). The original source might be a spring, a seasonal stream diverted by dams or weirs, or even a system of cisterns storing winter runoff from a wide area. Each source, water conveyors, channels and levelled terraces constitute a separate hydrological system which must have been visualized as an entity before construction started.[32] Each system is tiny compared with the hydraulic system of the Nile valley in Egypt, yet each represents a considerable investment of labour, not only in the initial construction, but also in maintenance. Neglect easily ruins the entire system and may cause serious flooding, as recent Lebanese experience has shown (Chapter 14). Terrace irrigation is characteristic either of once densely settled areas, like ancient Judaea, where as much of the sloping ground as possible must be cultivated, or of districts where labour might have been coerced, as in parts of Libya under Roman rule (Chapter 3). Labour costs today, however, mean that the systems are expensive to maintain, and must be used to produce high value vegetables and tree crops if they are to continue in use.

Qanāt is the Persian term for a subterranean gravity canal or aqueduct

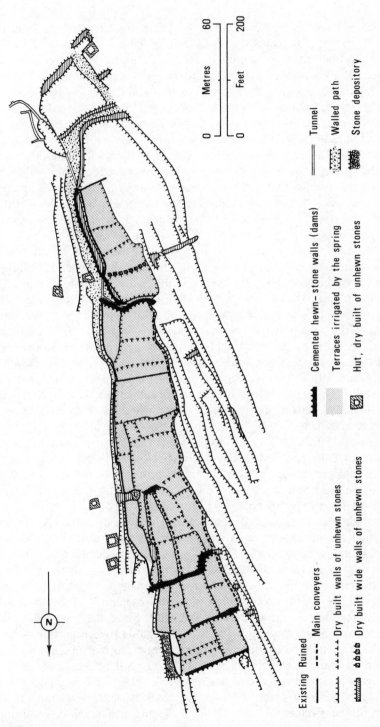

Existing Ruined

——————   Main conveyers

------- +++++ Dry built walls of unhewn stones

⚹⚹⚹⚹⚹⚹ Dry built wide walls of unhewn stones

▰▰▰▰▰ Cemented hewn–stone walls (dams)

░░░ Terraces irrigated by the spring

⬚ Hut, dry built of unhewn stones

══ Tunnel

░░░ Walled path

▓▓▓ Stone depository

Figure 4.10 Ein Khandak system of irrigated terraces, Judaea (Reproduced by permission of *Israel Exploration Journal*, 1969)

leading water from an aquifer in an alluvial fan situated up slope from the area to be irrigated (Chapter 2). Although probably developed in Iran,[33] the 'horizontal well', as it is sometimes called, is widespread in the region under a variety of local names. It is an expensive way of securing water, and it has been calculated that a median length of qanāt of about nine km gives a return in crops and water sold of only about 10 per cent.[34] Once provided, the water is allocated and used in similar ways to the water from other flow sources. Security of supply, however, is generally more uncertain. Excessive rainfall, leading to floods, can cause a roof-fall or choke the gallery with material washed in from the surface. Aquifers may dry up or the flow be reduced, either through natural events, like earth tremors, or through sinking deep bores in areas crossed by the qanāt. In any case, in many long settled areas, there is competition for underground water from other qanāts running in a variety of directions and at different depths.[35]

River irrigation is becoming more important in the region as a result of the construction of large dams across the major rivers, though its largest extent is still in the Nile valley and delta and in the Tigris–Euphrates lowland. Water is not obtained in the same way in all districts irrigated from rivers, and basic distinctions can be made between flow and lift-based types of irrigation, and between the perennial and seasonal availability of water. Until the recent advent of the motor pump, perennial irrigation was normally dependent upon lifting water out of the rivers and canals by various devices. The *shaduf* (a weighted beam with a bag on a rope at one end) is still widespread, generally used singly, though in the Qena district of Egypt sets of these devices were used at different levels of the river bank. Waterwheels were commonly used, but remained characteristic of the Orontes in the vicinity of Homs and Hama until recently (Chapter 13). The use of the *tambūr* (hand-operated Archimedean screw) was virtually confined to Egypt. Practically everywhere, these devices have been replaced and supplemented by pumps, which are not only more efficient in raising water, but, with the use of pipes, allow a much wider and more continuous strip of flood plain to be irrigated.

Flow irrigation, although found on other rivers in the Middle East, has been particularly characteristic of seasonal irrigation in the Nile valley and the Tigris–Euphrates lowland. Different systems were employed in the two subregions until the nineteenth century. Basin irrigation, using the annual flood, was characteristic of Egypt, while the use of canals and distributaries was preferred in the Tigris–Euphrates lowland, particularly where the rivers are closest together in the vicinity of Baghdād. Since the early nineteenth century, the irrigation systems in the two subregions have been transformed and made more alike. Perennial irrigation is now normal in Egypt, where greater use is made of canals and distributaries than before, while in Iraq the problems of uncontrolled and destructive flooding are being ameliorated by the use of reservoirs and diversionary works. These developments are described fully in Chapters 12 and 19, while the historical situation is outlined in Chapter 3. In Egypt, change in the irrigation system has brought more intensive forms of land use. Even in 1965, before the sluices in the Aswân High Dam were closed, an average of 1·6 crops was being taken from every *feddan*, while three crops in a year were common.[36] Intensification has been more limited in Iraq, and the traditional cereals are still dominant in extensive systems of land use.

Irrigation is being extended everywhere throughout the region,[37] as the regional chapters show. Popular devices include the sinking of deep bores and the damming of seasonal streams and perennial rivers, such as the Litāni in Lebanon and the Gediz in Turkey. Water provision is usually associated with flood control and frequently with the generation of electricity, while new farming regions are organized so that more efficient use is made of the water by colonists. Particularly striking examples are found in Iran, especially in Khuzestan where agro-business enterprises operate large territories reclaimed after the construction of large dams (Chapter 18). Mechanization is usually a feature of these developments and is integrated with large rectangular fields. The projects are increasingly expensive, and frequently require financing from abroad, with important political and economic consequences, as Egypt has discovered with the Aswân High Dam. The high levels of investment also mean that valuable industrial crops and relatively high-priced vegetables and fruits are the preferred crops, rather than low-priced but basic subsistence cereals. Local deficiencies are made good by imports. Of course, regional as well as international markets are available for industrial and commercial crops, while local demand is rising as population grows and incomes increase. But a balanced land use policy is required if the conflict is to be resolved. Unfortunately, most attention has been given to exploiting mineral resources, especially petroleum where it is available, and to the development of manufacturing industry. Both again require finance from abroad and this is secured by selling rural products on the international market, so that a kind of vicious circle exists. The whole field of economic development problems is surveyed in Chapter 7, while industrialization and petroleum exploitation are discussed in Chapters 8 and 9.

References

1. G. Perrin de Brichambaut and C. C. Wallén, *A Study of the Agroclimatology in Semi-Arid and Arid Zones of the Near East*, Technical Note No. 56, World Meteorological Organisation, Geneva, 1963.
2. C. A. O. van Nieuwenhuijze, 'The Near Eastern village: a profile', *Middle East Journal*, **16**, 295–308 (1962).
3. (a) A. Ibrahim, 'Classification and characteristic patterns of rural settlements (Egypt)', *Mediterranea*, **23–24**, 332–345 (1968).
   (b) X. de Planhol, 'Geography of settlement', in *The Cambridge History of Iran*, **1**, *The Land of Iran* (Ed. W. B. Fisher), Cambridge University Press, London, 1968, 409–467.
4. J. Weulersse, *Paysans de Syrie et du Proche Orient*, Gallimard, Paris, 1946, 281.
5. *Encyclopaedia of Islam*, **4**, E. J. Brill, Leyden, and Luzac and Co., London, 1934, 1096–1103.

172

6. *Encyclopaedia of Islam*, **4**, E. J. Brill, Leyden, and Luzac and Co., London, 1934, 1096–1103.
7. G. Baer, *Population and Society in the Arab East*, Routledge and Kegan Paul, London, 1964, 142 and note.
8. R. C. Tute, *The Ottoman Land Laws*, Jerusalem, 1927, 15–16.
9. R. C. Tute, *The Ottoman Land Laws*, Jerusalem, 1927, 17–19.
10. (a) J. Weulersse, *Paysans de Syrie et du Proche Orient*, Gallimard, Paris, 1946, 99–108.
    (b) Latron, *La Vie rurale en Syrie et au Liban*, Beirūt, 1936, 213–215.
11. J. Weulersse, *Paysans de Syrie et du Proche Orient*, Gallimard, Paris, 1946, 116.
12. J. Hinderink and M. B. Kiray, *Social Stratification as an obstacle to Development. A Study of Four Turkish Villages*, Praeger Publishers, New York, Washington, London, 1970.
13. M. Clawson, H. H. Landsberg and L. T. Alexander, *The Agricultural Potential of the Middle East*, American Elsevier Publishing Co., New York, London and Amsterdam, 1971, 60.
14. (a) E. Eshag and M. A. Kamal, 'Agrarian reform in the United Arab Republic (Egypt)', *Bulletin of the Oxford Institute of Economics and Statistics*, **30**, 73–104 (1968).
    (b) D. Warriner, *Land Reform and Development in the Middle East*, 2nd ed., Oxford University Press, London, 1962.
15. D. Warriner, *Land Reform and Development in the Middle East*, 2nd ed., Oxford University Press, London, 1962.
16. F. Fattah, 'Farming Cooperatives in Egypt', *World Marxist Review*, **15**, 96–99 (1972).
17. D. A. Caponera, *Water Laws in Moslem Countries*, FAO Development Paper No. 43, Rome, 1954.
18. M. Clawson, H. H. Landsberg and L. T. Alexander, *The Agricultural Potential of the Middle East*, American Elsevier Publishing Co., New York, London and Amsterdam, 1971, 60.
19. D. A. Caponera, *Water Laws in Moslem Countries*, FAO Development Paper No. 43, Rome, 1954, 14–18.
20. T. Shanin (Ed.), *Peasants and Peasant Societies*, Penguin Books, Harmondsworth, 1971.
21. M. Clawson, H. H. Landsberg and L. T. Alexander, *The Agricultural Potential in the Middle East*, American Elsevier Publishing Co., New York, London and Amsterdam, 1971, 50–51.
22. D. L. Johnson, *The Nature of Nomadism: A Comparative Study of Pastoral Migrations in Southwestern Asia and Northern Africa*, Department of Geography, Research Paper No. 118, Chicago, 1969.
23. A. Tanoğlu, 'The geography of settlement', *Rev. geogr. Inst. Univ. Istanb.*, **1**, 3–27 (1954).
24. J. Kolars, 'Locational aspects of cultural ecology: the case of the goat in non-western agriculture', *Geogrl. Rev.*, **56**, 577–584 (1966).
25. T. R. Stauffer, 'The economics of nomadism in Iran', *Middle East Journal*, **22**, 284–302 (1965).
26. D. L. Johnson, *The Nature of Nomadism: A Comparative Study of Pastoral Migrations in Southwestern Asia and Northern Africa*, Department of Geography, Research Paper No. 118, Chicago, 1969, 158–176.
27. J. F. Kolars, 'Types of rural development', in *Four Studies on the Economic Development of Turkey*, (Ed. F. C. Shorter, J. F. Kolars, D. A. Rustow and O. Yenal), Frank Cass and Co., London, 1967, 63–87.
28. W. A. Mitchell, 'Turkish villages in interior Anatolia and von Thünen's "Isolated State"; a comparative analysis', *Middle East Journal*, **25**, 355–369 (1971).

29. (a) L. Turkowski, 'Peasant agriculture in the Judaean Hills', *Palestine Exploration Quarterly*, **101**, 21–33, 101–112 (1969).
    (b) H. E. Wulff, *The Traditional Crafts of Persia*, M. I. T. Press, Cambridge (Mass.) and London, 1966, 260–277.
30. M. Clawson, H. H. Landsberg and L. T. Alexander, *The Agricultural Potential of the Middle East*, American Elsevier Publishing Co., New York, London and Amsterdam, 1971, Fig. 5.1.
31. L. Eldblom, *Quelques points de vue comparatifs sur les problemes d'irrigation dans les trois oases Libyennes de Brâk, Ghadamès et particuliément Mourzouk* Lund Studies in Geography, No. 22, Lund, 1961.
32. Z. Ron, 'Agricultural terraces in the Judaean mountains', *Israel Explor. J.*, **16**, 33–49, 111–122 (1969).
33. H. Goblot, 'Dans l'ancien Iran, les techniques de l'eau et la grande histoire', *Annales, Économies, Sociétés, Civilisations*, **18**, 499–520 (1963).
34. (a) P. H. T. Beckett, 'Qanāts around Kerman', *Royal Central Asian Journal*, **40**, 47–57 (1953).
    (b) E. Noel, 'Qanāts', *Royal Central Asian Journal*, **31**, 191–202 (1944).
35. P. Beaumont, 'Qanāts in the Varamin Plain', *Trans. Inst. Br. Geogr.*, **45**, 169–180 (1968).
36. P. O'Brien, *The Revolution in Egypt's Economic System, from Private Enterprise to Socialism, 1952–1965*, Oxford University Press, London, 1966, 5.
37. C. G. Smith, 'Water resources and irrigation development in the Middle East', *Geography*, **55**, 407–425 (1970).

CHAPTER 5

Population

5.1 Historic perspective

Possibly the most tantalizing gaps in our knowledge of Southwest Asia and North Africa relate to population. Many attempts have been made to estimate population sizes for parts of the region at particular periods of history, but results are inconclusive. In the region as a whole, it is clear that the population was relatively small until the demographic upsurge of the last two or three hundred years. It is also clear that the first century population was larger than at any time until the eighteenth century. Table 5.1 (which does not correspond precisely with the region discussed in this book) gives some idea of population trends based on a variety of evidence.

The 1500 AD populations shown in Table 5.1 are consistent with calculations derived from the sixteenth century Ottoman censuses of Suleiman the magnificent.[1] Estimates for Arabia and the Tigris–Euphrates region are unfortunately not shown. Arabia is estimated to have had a population of one million in 600 AD and the Tigris–Euphrates valley 9·1 million,[2] although there is more disagreement concerning the former populations of Iraq than any other part of the region. One estimate puts the population of Iraq as high as 20 million in the eighth to thirteenth centuries.[3] In general Arabia and the Tigris–Euphrates region undoubtedly experienced the same pattern of demographic decline and stagnation shown in Table 5.1. The most important causes of this decline were the disastrous plagues of the second, sixth, and fourteenth centuries which ravaged populations, though possibly on a smaller scale than in Europe. There were also local factors, usually arising from political instability. The long border struggle between the Arabs and Byzantines had a devastating effect on the populations of Syria and Iraq, and the Mongol invasion of Iraq in the thirteenth century marked the climax of a period of destruction and insecurity from which the rural areas have scarcely recovered. The most striking changes occurred in regions where high population densities could only be sustained by the painstaking upkeep of terraces or irrigation installations which were vulnerable to attack or deteriorated rapidly once neglected. Urban populations appear to have fluctuated even more markedly. Unlike today, towns were formerly subject to higher mortality than rural areas since they were more susceptible to epidemics of cholera, smallpox, and typhoid, as well as the plague.

From about the middle of the eighteenth century, for reasons that are not yet fully understood, populations in widely separated parts of the world

174

TABLE 5.1
Population estimates AD1–AD1500
(in millions)

	AD1	AD350	AD600	AD800	AD1000	AD1200	AD1340	AD1500
Asia Minor	8·8	11·6	7·0	8·0	8·0	7·0	8·0	6·0
Syria	4·4	4·0	4·0	4·0	2·0	2·7	3·0	2·0
Egypt	4·5	3·0	2·7	3·0	3·0	2·0	3·0	2·0
North Africa	4·2	2·0	1·8	1·0	1·0	1·5	2·0	3·5
	21·9	21·0	15·5	16·0	14·0	13·2	16·0	13·5

Source: M. M. Fryde in J. C. Russell, 'Late ancient and medieval population', *Trans. Amer. phil. Soc.*, **48**, Appendix B (1958).

began to show a simultaneous upward trend in their growth rates. What was the population of the Middle East on the eve of this unprecedented population increase? By backward extrapolation from the highest and lowest estimated 1920 populations of the region (including Afghanistan and Cyprus but not Egypt and Libya), J. C. Durand arrived at a 'low' estimate of 14 million for 1750 and a 'high' estimate of 44 million.[4] It now seems clear that the lowest figure for 1920 was much more accurate* and allowing for the addition of Libya and Egypt and the exclusion of Afghanistan and Cyprus, a 1750 population of 20 million is a fair estimate. By 1950 the same region contained approximately 44 million people,[5] having more than doubled in two hundred years. The significance of this increase becomes clear when it is realized that for the previous 10,000 years the world population had probably taken about one thousand years to double itself.[6] After the Second World War growth rates accelerated still further, largely in response to the widespread use of modern drugs and insecticides, and the population of the region can now double itself in 25 years or less.

5.2 Demographic characteristics

Modern demographic data for countries of the Middle East are often inadequate or unreliable or both. At the end of 1973 there were still four states which had never conducted a full national census, while only Turkey (since 1927) and Egypt (since 1897) have a long series of census records (Table 5.2).

Several factors account for the general paucity of statistical information. There is the practical problem of census taking where a high proportion of the population are nomadic, as in the Arabian peninsula. Political factors have also discouraged enumeration. In Lebanon, for example, a census would doubtless reveal radical changes in the delicate balance between Christians and Muslims. There is also much discussion as to the accuracy of figures

*The United Nations for example revised the 1950 estimated population of South West Asia *downwards* from 60 million to 44 million in the light of increasing census information. *UN Demographic Yearbook*, p. 124 (1962), p. 105 (1970).

TABLE 5.2
Population census years

Egypt	1897 to 1947, every decade; 1960, 1966, 1971
Libya	1954, 1964, 1973
Saudi Arabia	1962/63 (repudiated)
Yemen A. R.	None
P.D.R. Yemen	None (census of Aden colony only, 1946)
Kuwait	1957, 1961, 1965, 1970
Oman	None
Bahrain	1950, 1959, 1965, 1971
Qatar	1970
United Arab Emirates	1968 (then the Trucial States)
Iraq	1947, 1957, 1965
Syria	1952, 1960, 1970
Lebanon	None
Jordan	1952, 1961
Turkey	1927, 1935 to 1970, every five years
Iran	1956, 1966
Israel	1948, 1960, 1971 (Occupied areas, 1967)

for Palestine refugees. In Saudi Arabia the census of 1962/1963 apparently revealed a population of 3·9 millions compared with previous estimates of up to seven million, and has remained unpublished. The true figure is almost certainly below the eight million quoted in Table 5.3. Much population data is inaccurate on account of poor techniques, illiteracy, and false reporting of female children. There is also deep-seated suspicion since enumeration has traditionally been the prelude to taxation or conscription.[7] Nevertheless, the broad characteristics of the region's population can be deduced from available figures, while for individual countries, notably Kuwait and Israel, the statistics are generally reliable.

Table 5.3 gives vital statistics of populations by country. The grand total for the 17 states considered here was 149 million in 1972, less than four per cent of the world total, or little more than a quarter that of India. Figures for the Maghreb countries are included as a reminder that more than twice as many *Arabs* live in North Africa as in Southwest Asia. There are no particularly large populations represented; Turkey and Egypt rank seventeenth and eighteenth respectively in the world, while the Gulf states are among the world's smallest sovereign states. The range in size is strikingly illustrated by the fact that the annual increment of population in Egypt is greater than the total population of Kuwait.

5.2.1 Birth rates

Even allowing for some inaccuracies in vital statistics, it is clear that birth rates are generally high. In the last fifty years they have fluctuated but not increased markedly, though there has been a sharp decline in infant deaths before the age of one year. Gross reproduction rates are around 2·8 to 3·4, and there is

TABLE 5.3
Population statistics, 1972

	Population in thousands	Births per thousand	Deaths per thousand	Annual increase per cent	Number of years to double population	Per cent population under 15 years
North Africa						
Egypt	35,900	44	16	2·8	25	43
Libya	2,000	46	16	3·1	23	44
Arabian Peninsula						
Saudi Arabia	8,200	50	23	2·8	25	—
Yemen A.R.	6,100	50	23	2·8	25	—
P.D.R. Yemen	1,400	50	21	2·9	24	—
Kuwait	800	43	7	8·2	9	38
Oman	700	50	19	3·1	23	—
Bahrain	200	50	19	3·1	23	—
Qatar	100	50	19	3·1	23	—
United Arab Emirates	200	50	19	3·1	23	32
Fertile Crescent						
Iraq	10,400	49	15	3·4	21	48
Syria	6,600	48	15	3·3	21	47
Lebanon	3,000	27	4	2·3	30	—
Jordan	2,500	48	16	3·3	21	47
Non-Arab countries						
Turkey	37,600	40	15	2·5	28	42
Iran	30,200	45	17	2·8	25	46
Israel	3,000	27	7	2·4	29	33
TOTAL:	148,900					
Maghreb						
Morocco	16,800	50	16	3·4	21	46
Algeria	15,000	50	17	3·3	21	47
Tunisia	5,400	42	16	2·6	27	46

Source: Population Reference Bureau, *1972 World Population Data Sheet*, New York, 1972.
United Nations, *Demographic Yearbook*, New York, 1970.

so far no evidence of fertility decline.[8] Two countries with a lower birth rate are Israel and Lebanon, both with substantial non-Muslim populations. Young and universal marriages of women, together with the virtues of matrimony and fecundity were traditionally among pro-natalist influences in the Muslim world.[9]

The persistence of high birth rates can be attributed to a number of factors, not all of which apply throughout the region. Only in recent years have family planning programmes been officially adopted by Egypt (since 1962), Jordan (since 1970), and Turkey (since 1964). Even in these countries there is great difficulty in persuading devout Muslims, particularly the less well educated, that contraception is compatible with the teachings of Islam, and so far only an educated minority have benefited. Most Islamic leaders agree that there is no real religious objection, but resistance is strong among the people. In some areas children may actually be regarded as an economic asset, for cotton picking for example. With some countries committed to population control, and others giving family allowances, an increasing measure of demographic individuality is becoming evident. Equally striking are contrasts within individual states arising from differences in social, religious, and economic status. Fertility rates for uneducated city Christians and Muslims in Lebanon for example, were found to be 4·14 and 7·35 respectively, and for educated Christians and Muslims 3·44 and 5·56 respectively.[10]

5.2.2 Death rates

In the past, mortality was high in the Middle East. Today, however, death rates include some of the lowest as well as some of the highest in the world (Table 5.3). Mortality statistics are notoriously underestimated and the true levels may be higher both on account of the prevalence of disease, and as a result of periodic natural disasters and war. Countries with low death rates tend to be those with small youthful populations, most of whom have access to good health facilities, like Israel and Kuwait, while death rates remain high where large dispersed populations have not felt the impact of medical services. The trend throughout the century has been for death rates to decline and in most countries they are continuing to fall. Indeed, even in countries with relatively high mortality, remarkable reductions are already evident in the towns where better housing and sanitation and medical care are available, and city death rates may be as much as half those of rural areas. In other respects too, as with fertility, average figures tend to obscure important regional and sectoral contrasts in mortality.

TABLE 5.4
Estimated future birth and death rates and
rates of population increase, 1980–1985

	Birth rate per thousand	Death rate per thousand	Per cent increase per annum
Egypt	41·0	11·8	2·9
Libya	42·9	11·8	3·1
Syria	44·9	11·2	3·4
Jordan	44·2	11·4	3·3
Iraq	45·1	10·8	3·4
Kuwait	45·5	4·7	Kuwaitis 7·2
		Non-Kuwaitis 8·6	

Source: Cairo Demographic Centre, *Demographic measures and population growth in Arab countries*, Cairo, 1970, pp. 322–323.

The decline in death rates during the past thirty or forty years has been the chief cause of rapid population increase. This is well illustrated by Figure 20.1 showing birth rates and death rates in Egypt since 1922. The death rate throughout the region was generally over 25 per thousand in the 1920's. It is now around 17 in North Africa and 16 in Southwest Asia, and could eventually fall as low as 11 per thousand. Table 5.4 showing estimates of future birth rates, death rates and rates of increase for selected Arab countries, suggests that declining death rates will for a time at least, offset declining birth rates in maintaining high rates of increase.

5.2.3 Age structures

With declining death rates and high birth rates, the populations of the Middle East are growing rapidly. Between 1950 and 1960 the average annual increase was 2·5 per cent, whereas today it has risen to 2·8 per cent. Every state in Table 5.3 is growing at rates in excess of the world average, while annual increases of three per cent and above are among the highest in the world. In all the largest states the annual increment is due to natural increase, but in some of the smaller states, immigration accounts for some of the increase.

One characteristic of rapidly increasing populations is their youthful age structure. Age structure is important in developing countries because it indicates the ratio of dependent groups to the active population, and it also determines future population growth rates. Figure 5.1 illustrates the age pyramids of selected countries. With the exception of Israel's Jewish population, these display very broad bases associated with extreme youth, with over 40 per cent commonly under the age of 15, indicating a vast potential for future population expansion. The proportions aged 65 and over on the other hand are very small, around three to six per cent. Overall there are often as many economically inactive persons as active in the population. Most countries also show a slight predominance of males in all but the highest age groups, possibly due in part to under-registration of females, and mortality associated with frequent pregnancies.[11] Age–sex pyramids for foreign groups in Kuwait (Figure 5.1) and other Gulf states, however, reveal the classic form of an immigrant community in which male migrants form the majority.

5.3 Migration

In recent years the oil-rich Gulf states have grown rapidly as a result of large numbers of immigrants who now constitute a significant proportion of their total populations. The population of Kuwait, for example, doubled between 1957 and 1965 with the influx of Palestinians and Jordanians (amounting to over 31 per cent of all immigrants), Iranians, Iraqis, Lebanese, Omanis, Syrians and others. Non-Kuwaitis now represent well over half the total population of Kuwait.[12] Another state to have experienced high immigration

180

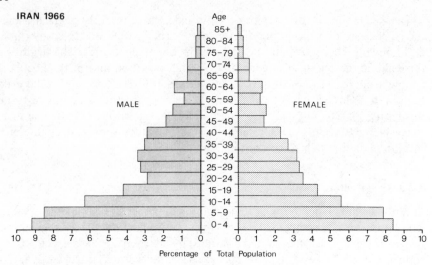

IRAN 1966

Age
85+
80-84
75-79
70-74
65-69
60-64
55-59
50-54
45-49
40-44
35-39
30-34
25-29
20-24
15-19
10-14
5-9
0-4

MALE   FEMALE

10 9 8 7 6 5 4 3 2 1 0   0 1 2 3 4 5 6 7 8 9 10

Percentage of Total Population

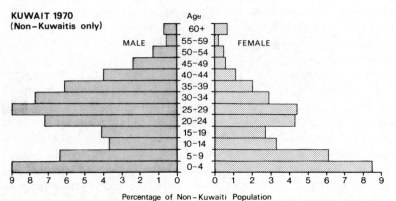

KUWAIT 1970
(Non-Kuwaitis only)

Age
60+
55-59
50-54
45-49
40-44
35-39
30-34
25-29
20-24
15-19
10-14
5-9
0-4

MALE   FEMALE

9 8 7 6 5 4 3 2 1 0   0 1 2 3 4 5 6 7 8 9

Percentage of Non-Kuwaiti Population

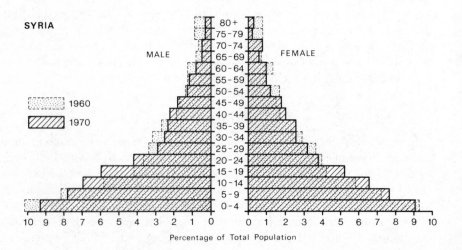

SYRIA

Age
80+
75-79
70-74
65-69
60-64
55-59
50-54
45-49
40-44
35-39
30-34
25-29
20-24
15-19
10-14
5-9
0-4

MALE   FEMALE

1960
1970

10 9 8 7 6 5 4 3 2 1 0   0 1 2 3 4 5 6 7 8 9 10

Percentage of Total Population

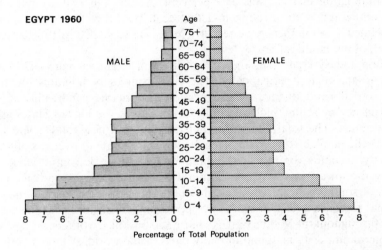

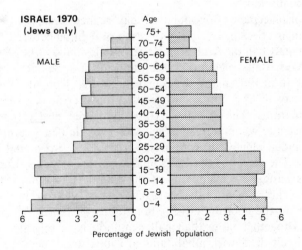

Figure 5.1 Age–sex pyramids for selected countries

rates is Israel, which received 1,407,000 Jewish immigrants between 1948 and 1971.[13] About half of these were from Muslim countries in North Africa and Southwest Asia. During the first four years of the state, the average annual rate of population increase was 23·7 per cent. At times in 1949 as many as 20,000 immigrants were arriving in Israel each month.[14] Since 1952 rates have declined, but numbers have recently increased to 42,000 in 1971, largely as a result of the exodus of Soviet Jews.

Lebanon and Syria are well known as sources of migrants, many of whom are lost to the region permanently. The chief sources of migrants are the densely settled rural districts whose peasant proprietors can readily raise passage money by selling plots of land.[15] Many go to the United States and South America. The total number of Lebanese abroad now totals some 1·5 million,[16] the number from Syria being far fewer. The rate of overseas migration partly accounts for the slow population growth in Lebanon which is currently the lowest in the region. Emigration is also an important feature of much of southern Arabia, where temporary and permanent migration is a traditional response to lack of economic opportunity. Yemenis have long been familiar throughout the Middle East as sailors and unskilled workers, and today small communities can be found in many parts of the world. A large number also migrate as seasonal harvesters, chiefly to Sudan and Iraq. Perhaps better known are the migrants from the Ḥaḍramawt in the P.D.R. Yemen, who are found chiefly as traders in the East Indies, India, East Africa and Egypt. The total number of migrants absent from southern Arabia at any one time may be near one million.

Two major displacements of population may be mentioned. In 1948, 700 to 800,000 Palestinians became refugees as a result of fighting between Arabs and Jews, approximately half the Arab population of Palestine. The largest numbers settled in the West Bank region of Jordan and in the Egyptian administered Gaza Strip. In June 1967 many were again uprooted from the West Bank, making their way to east Jordan, where they have created severe political and economic strains. The Palestine Arabs numbered nearly three million in 1973, 16 per cent of whom were in Israel, 36 per cent in Israel occupied areas, and the remainder chiefly in Jordan (28 per cent), Syria and Lebanon (12 per cent).[17] The plight of the Palestinians, particularly the 1·5 million or so classified as refugees, remains one of the Middle East's most distressing problems. The establishment of the State of Israel in 1948 also brought about radical changes in the ancient Jewish communities of North Africa and the Middle East. Altogether more than half a million have migrated to Israel, including nearly all the Jewish inhabitants of Libya, Iraq, Yemen and Aden, and a high proportion of those in Morocco, Turkey and Iran. About 95 per cent of all the Jews in the region are now in Israel, a greater degree of concentration than at any time since AD 70.

A population movement of a rather different kind occurred between 1922 and 1924 when approximately 1·6 million Greek and Armenian-speaking peoples left Turkey, the former in exchange for some 400,000 Turkish speakers from Greece.[18] After the Second World War many Muslims also left Bulgaria to settle in Turkey. The most important exodus of Europeans from the Arab world in recent years was the large French settler community of the Maghreb, but Libya has also witnessed the departure of well over 100,000 Italians (about 15 per cent of the population in 1940) since the outbreak of the Second World War.

5.4 Distribution and density of population

This large region remains overall one of the least densely populated in the world, in spite of rapid rates of population increase which have created marked local increases in density during recent decades. The chief explanation is in the large tracts of arid and semi-arid land, and the more limited areas of high altitude unsuitable for permanent settlement. Southwest Asia has an average density of 17 persons per km,^{2} and North Africa, including the Maghreb, 10 persons per km^2.[19] Table 5.5 gives average densities for each country. Such figures are of limited value since most states possess large tracts of almost uninhabited land, and over one third of the total population are urban dwellers.

TABLE 5.5
Population densities in 1970

	(A) Population density per km^2	(B) Agricultural population Number (millions)	(B) Per Cent	(C) Arable or under permanent crops (km^2)	(D) Population density per km^2 of (C)
Egypt	33·3	18·2	55	28,430	640·2
Libya	1·1	0·8	43	25,150	31·8
Saudi Arabia	3·6	3·2	60	8,090	395·5
Yemen A.R.	29·4	4·1	73	—	—
P.D.R. Yemen	4·2	0·8	62	2,520	317·4
Kuwait	44·4	0·6	1	5	—
Oman	—	—	—	—	—
Bahrain	359·5	—	—	—	—
Qatar	4·5	—	—	—	—
United Arab Emirates	2·2	—	—	—	—
Iraq	21·7	4·5	47	101,630	44·3
Syria	34·0	2·9	49	58,990	49·1
Lebanon	268·0	1·2	47	3,160	380·0
Jordan	23·7	0·9	39	13,000	69·2
Turkey	45·1	24·0	69	273,780	87·6
Iran	18·0	13·3	46	165,600	80·3
Israel	141·7	0·3	10	4,230	70·9

Source: United Nations FAO, *Production Yearbook 1971*, Rome, 1971, pp. 5–7, 22–23.
H. Fullard, *Geographical Digest*, Philip, 1972, 11–15.

Lebanon's average density of 268 persons per km^2 compares with the densely populated states of western Europe largely on account of the city of Beirūt. A more useful index is obtained by considering the density of agricultural populations on arable land, though there are problems arising from different definitions (Table 5.5). If nomadic populations are excluded from the agricultural populations, densities increase, particularly for Saudi Arabia, which recorded 858 settled persons per km^2 of agricultural land in 1964.[20] The highest densities are associated with irrigated lands of river valleys and desert oases. By far the highest densities are encountered in parts of the Nile valley and delta where entire rural governorates record over 800 persons per km.^{2} Every country, however, displays considerable contrasts in population density; even Turkey which has less obvious signs of sparsely populated regions has rural densities ranging from seven to 127 per km.^{2} In general, physical controls, notably the availability of water account for these contrasts, but historical factors may sometimes be responsible.

Figures 5.2 and 5.3 illustrate the distribution of population and the broad range of densities. Apart from the large areas of uninhabited semi-arid land, the abrupt changes in density are a notable feature, reflecting the rainshadow effect of some of the mountain ranges, and the margin between irrigated lands and desert particularly along the Nile valley and delta. It should be noted that the population distribution of the region has never been static. In certain regions the frontier between the desert and the sown has migrated in response to political and economic change. One famous example is the northern Negev, which was an area of nomadism in Old Testament times; under the Nabateans and their immediate successors a dozen flourishing cities grew up which had been largely abandoned by the seventh century AD. Today, modern technology and the needs of national security have again stimulated desert colonization in southern Israel. Of far more significance, however, are a number of large dams and barrages recently constructed in Turkey, Syria, Iraq and Iran which have brought large irrigated areas under the plough. Similarly, some impressive schemes of desert reclamation are being carried out in western Egypt (Chapter 19) and in Libya and Saudi Arabia,[21] the result of which will be to sustain larger numbers of people in formerly underpopulated regions. In a number of states an important feature of recent years has also been the slow readvance of cultivation in areas of dry farming.

5.5 Conclusion: population growth and change

The population of the Middle East is thus increasing rapidly. It is also undergoing structural changes at least as radical as those of any other developing region of comparable size. In the following chapter it is shown that approximately 35 per cent of the population could be classified as urban dwellers in 1970, compared with perhaps 10 per cent in 1900, and the proportion is increasing. The nomadic population of the region, on the other hand, is experiencing considerable pressures to sedentarize, both indirectly and by

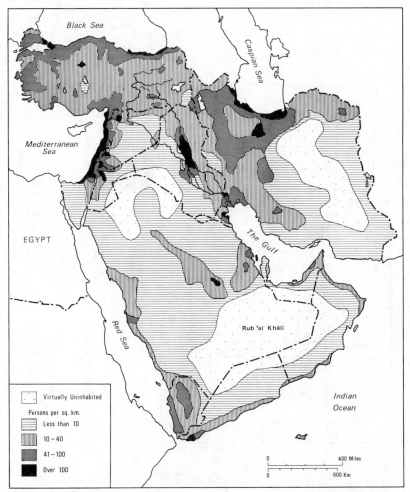

Figure 5.2 Distribution and density of population in Southwest Asia, 1972

the direct action of governments.[22] Estimates of their exact number vary greatly (Table 5.6), but there can be little doubt that they now scarcely exceed one per cent of the total population.[23] Two-thirds of the people in the region are still village dwellers, but the proportion is slowly falling because of higher natural increase in the towns and rural-urban migrations.

Important qualitative changes in the population are also occurring which generally receive far too little recognition. In recent years, great progress has been made in providing schools and educational services of all kinds but a high proportion of adults, particularly females, remain illiterate, and even among children rapid population increases have sometimes offset extensive school building programmes. Throughout the region it is still common to find about one-third of the children of school age illiterate, and two-thirds

186

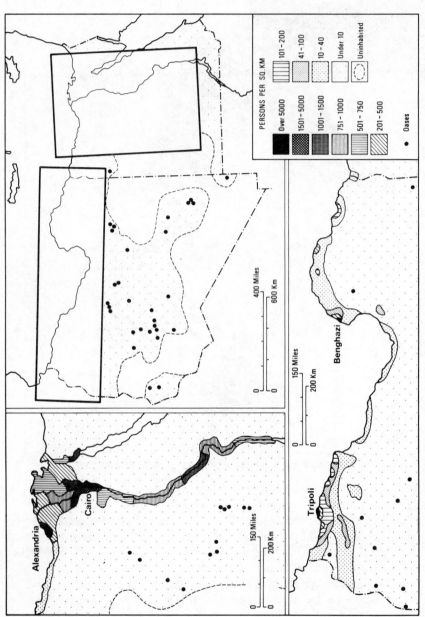

Figure 5.3 Distribution and density of population in Egypt and Libya, 1972

or more of older adults illiterate, so that illiteracy is still most common among the economically active population.

In all the larger countries, university education is well developed, though vocational training is sometimes inadequate. Growing numbers of students study abroad and do not return to their countries, thus constituting a serious 'brain drain'.[24]

The fight against illiteracy has been accompanied by progress in other spheres, notably in combatting many of the debilitating diseases from which a high proportion of the people commonly suffered. Malnutrition is now less widespread than it once was, though recent work in Arab countries indicates that dietary deficiencies and nutritional disorders are still far too common. Besides augmenting food supplies, a whole range of measures need to be taken, including more local food processing and enrichment, pest control, and general health education.[25]

TABLE 5.6
Estimated numbers of nomads in 1970

	Number	Per cent 1970 population (From Table 5.3)
Egypt	50,000	0·1
Libya	70,000	3·5
Saudi Arabia	400,000	4·9*
Rest of Arabia	200,000	14·3
Iraq	300,000	2·8
Syria	200,000	3·0
Jordan	50,000	2·0
Iran	300,000	1·0
Turkey	600,000	1·6
Israel	18,000	0·6
TOTAL	2,188,000	1·4

*Or 11 per cent based on the lower population figure for Saudi Arabia rejected in 1962–63.
Source: Calculated from a variety of estimates.

References

1. O. L. Barkan, 'Essai sur les données statistiques des registres de recensement dans l'Empire Ottoman aux XVe et XVIe siècles', J. Econ. Soc. Hist. Orient, **1**, 9–36 (1958).
2. J. C. Russell, 'Late ancient and medieval population', Trans. Amer. phil. Soc., **48**, 89 (1958).
3. R. I. Lawless, 'Iraq: changing population patterns', in Populations of the Middle East and North Africa (Ed. J. I. Clarke and W. B. Fisher), University of London Press, London 1972, 97.

4. J. D. Durand, 'The modern expansion of world population', *Proc. Amer. Soc.*, **III,** 151 (1967).
5. United Nations, *Demographic Yearbook*, New York, 1962, 124.
6. J. D. Durand, 'The modern expansion of world population', *Proc. Amer. phil. Soc.*, **III,** 137 (1967).
7. J. C. Hurewitz, 'The politics of rapid population growth in the Middle East', *J. Int. Affairs*, **19,** 27 (1963).
8. J. I. Clarke, *Population Geography and the Developing Countries*, Pergamon, Oxford, 1971, 160.
9. J. I. Clarke and W. B. Fisher (Eds) *Populations of the Middle East and North Africa*, University of London Press, London, 1972, 24.
10. D. Yaukey, 'Fertility differences in a modernising country', in *Readings in Arab Middle East societies and cultures* (Ed. A. M. Lutfiyya and C. W. Churchill), Mouton, The Hague, 1970, 165.
11. United Nations, 'Notes on some demographic characteristics', in *Studies on selected development problems in various countries of the Middle East*, New York, 1969, 53.
12. A. Hill, 'The population of Kuwait', *Geography*, **54,** 84–88 (1969).
13. State of Israel, *Statistical Abstract*, **23,** Jerusalem, 1972, 127.
14. G. H. Blake, 'Israel: immigration and dispersal of population', in *Populations of the Middle East and North Africa* (Ed. J. J. Clarke and W. B. Fisher), University of London Press, London, 1972, 185.
15. W. B. Fisher, *The Middle East*, 6th ed., Methuen, London 1971, 259.
16. J. I. Clarke, *Population Geography and the Developing Countries*, Pergamon, Oxford, 1971, 164.
17. G. H. Blake, 'The wandering Arabs', *Geogr. Mag.*, **XLV,** 179–182 (Dec. 1972).
18. J. C. Dewdney, 'Turkey: recent population trends', in *Populations of the Middle East and North Africa* (Ed. J. I. Clarke and W. B. Fisher), University of London Press, London, 1972, 42.
19. United Nations, *Demographic Yearbook*, New York, 1970, 105.
20. United Nations, 'Notes on some demographic characteristics', in *Studies on selected development problems in various countries of the Middle East*, New York, 1969, 50.
21. C. G. Smith, 'Water resources and irrigation development in the Middle East', *Geography*, **55,** 407–425 (1970).
22. (a) A. R. George, 'Processes of sedentarisation of nomads in Egypt, Israel and Syria', *Geography*, **48,** 167–169 (1973).
    (b) United Nations, 'Nomadic populations and related issues of sedentarisation and settlement', in *Studies on selected development problems in various countries of the Middle East*, New York, 1970, 105–117.
23. M. Awad, 'Living conditions of nomadic, semi-nomadic and settled tribal groups', in *Reading in Arab Middle East Societies and Cultures* (Ed. A. M. Lutfiyya and C. W. Churchill), Mouton, The Hague, 1970, 147.
24. United Nations, 'Notes on some demographic characteristics,' in *Studies on selected development problems in various countries of the Middle East*, New York, 1969, 56.
25. V. N. Patwardhan, and W. J. Darby, *The State of Nutrition in the Arab Middle East*, Vanderbilt University, Nashville, 1972, 281.

CHAPTER 6

Towns and Cities

6.1 Introduction

The importance of towns and cities in the contemporary life of Southwest Asia and North Africa has been briefly indicated in Chapter 5 by the fact that about one person in three is an urban dweller, and the proportion is increasing. Chapter 8 discusses the modern role of towns as centres of economic and social change, but the influence of urbanism has been strong throughout the region for many centuries, even at times when the actual level of urbanization has been quite low. It is true that relations between towns and country have sometimes been weak, and the two have had little in common politically, socially and culturally. Yet successive political regimes have governed their territories from the towns, and almost every major movement to have spread through the region (Christianity, Islam, westernization, and nationalism) has done so through the medium of the town. Economically, the fortunes of town dweller and countryman have probably been rather more closely interdependent than is sometimes recognized. Long-distance trade between Europe and Asia and Europe and Africa gave many of the towns of the region considerable prosperity, but their day-to-day survival often depended on the success of local agriculture.

The bulk of this chapter is devoted to an examination of the morphology and regional distribution of towns, rather than with the functions and processes of urbanization in individual countries. In the centuries following the death of Muhammad until the middle of the nineteenth century, Islam rebuilt and refashioned the towns of Southwest Asia and North Africa from their foundations, giving it one of its most distinctive elements as a single cultural region. For this reason some attention is given to the Maghreb in this chapter. With rapid urban growth over the last hundred years and the creation of a number of new towns, it has become misleading to talk of 'the Islamic town', though the impress of Islam survives to the present day. The region may still be distinguished from other developing regions of the world by its high level of urbanization, rapid rates of urban growth, and the relative significance of inland towns, in spite of the development of many ports between about 1850 and 1930. In common with other developing regions however, a high degree of urban primacy and a scarcity of medium-sized towns is often manifest, together with the first signs of the emergence of city-regions.

6.2 Pre-Islamic towns

6.2.1. Ancient towns

In ancient times the largest concentrations of population were along the valleys of the Tigris–Euphrates, the Nile, and Indus rivers. Until recently, the earliest cities were assumed to have arisen in these regions some time during the fourth millenium BC, when improved irrigation techniques combined with stock rearing and fishing began to yield surpluses of food. The availability of river transport supplemented by wheeled vehicles facilitated the concentration of surplus at a few centres, while the need to canalize water and protect habitations from flooding also encouraged the aggregation of populations. When and where the first cities grew up is not certain, but Eridu is still popularly regarded as the oldest city on earth.[1] The Neolithic town of Çatal Hüyük in Anatolia, discovered in 1961, may have a stronger claim to this distinction,[2] and it may yet be proved that the emergence of urban life in Anatolia actually *preceded* the beginnings of agriculture, which could have originated in cities.[3] It was certainly in southern Mesopotamia that a network of walled towns appeared at an earlier date than elsewhere; some are shown on Figure 6.1. Although many of their inhabitants were farmers or fishermen, these ancient towns were genuinely urban, supporting many non-agriculturalists such as priests, administrators, traders and artisans. With populations of 7,000 to 25,000 they were at least ten times larger than any contemporary villages.[4] Ornate public buildings constructed on a monumental scale have been excavated, including temples, workshops, and granaries, but knowledge of domestic building is less complete. The houses of most ordinary citizens were doubtless mud constructions which have entirely disappeared, but some impressive domestic buildings have been unearthed. At Ur, for example, a variety of house types dating from 2000 BC have been discovered, including two-storey constructions based on the courtyard principle complete with highly efficient fresh water and sewage systems. Yet more elaborate houses have been found in the Indus cities of Mohenjo-Daro and Harappa. Some possessed two storeys and an interior staircase, while wells and sophisticated drainage systems appear to have been standard. Building materials included kiln-fired bricks for the thick exterior walls, cedarwood from the Himalayas, and a damp course of bitumen.[5]

Some ancient towns, including Ur, were partially planned. A remarkable example is the Egyptian town of Kahun, laid out in 2600 BC as a colony for workmen engaged in pyramid construction. Streets were arranged in gridiron pattern, with a standard house type consisting of three rooms and an open courtyard; a few double storey houses were included for foremen and officials.[6] Such comprehensive planning is not evident in the large cities, although it seems clear that at least in Sumeria all towns were laid out along basically similar lines. Three main elements can generally be identified; a walled city;

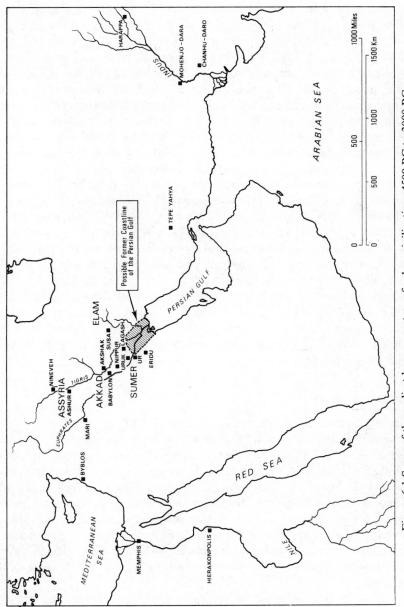

Figure 6.1 Some of the earliest known centres of urban civilization, 4500 BC to 3000 BC

suburbs, including more houses, but also fields, groves and cattle folds; and a commercial quarter. Trade between Egypt, Mesopotamia and the Indus has long been recognized as an important factor in town building in the three great river valleys civilizations. Excavations at Tepe Yahya in southern Iran in 1970 now suggest the existence of another urban, literate civilization just as early, linked with Mesopotamia and the Indus by trade, but derived from neither. The existence of a green belt of gardens and houses around many ancient cities may explain why some are alleged to have covered such vast areas. During the first millenium BC for example, Babylon is said to have occupied some 1,000 ha, Nineveh 750 ha, and Erech 450 ha.[7] Such cities were of course exceptional; probably most were more like 10 to 20 ha in area.[8]

The network of pre-Greco-Roman towns changed continually. The twin requirements of defence and commerce stimulated the growth of towns through-out the fertile crescent but particularly in the Levant. The eastern Mediterranean coast became studded with ports engaged in growing maritime trade, among them Byblos, Tyre and Sidon. The Hittites also created a few small urban centres in Asia Minor sometime after 1400 BC. While new towns grew up in Southwest Asia many old towns were abandoned as a result of some change in geographical or political fortune. The first true towns appeared in North Africa outside the Nile valley and delta after 800 BC when the Carthaginians took over a number of Phoenician trading stations which had been previously garrisoned but never colonized. After the sixth century BC Carthage itself, Tangier and Tripoli all became important cities, but the total number of towns remained comparatively few. The Romans destroyed Carthage in 146 BC and by AD 42 they controlled an unbroken zone from the Atlantic Ocean to the Red Sea.

6.2.2 Classical towns

The conquests of Alexander the Great from 334 BC marked the beginning of a phase of town-founding in Southwest Asia which has never been matched before or since. In less than two hundred years Alexander and his successors established a network of towns and roads throughout Asia Minor, Palestine, Syria, and the Tigris–Euphrates valleys and parts of Persia which has largely survived to modern times. *De novo* foundations were probably the exception, rights of self-government and city status being often conferred on existing settlements which may or may not have already possessed urban functions. Rather more than eighty towns were founded, including Alexandria in Egypt, while dozens of existing towns were rebuilt to conform with Hellenistic ideals and culture.[9]

The Romans thus inherited an extensive network of Hellenistic cities in the Middle East, and a few Carthaginian coastal towns in North Africa. In the provinces of Mesopotamia and Syria, they built a series of fortified towns to guard the eastern frontier of the empire; Aqaba, Amman and Damascus and the great cities of Jarash, Busra and Palmyra which lie in ruins today. Many new towns were built in Asia Minor for a variety of functions besides defence. Another region where extensive Roman urbanization occurred was in the North African provinces of Africa (modern Tunisia) and Numidia Tripolis. Ports, route centres, and fortified frontier towns were established, sometimes on the site of Carthaginian settlements. Both in North Africa and Southwest Asia a large number of Roman foundations were subsequently abandoned including rich and magnificent cities such as Leptis Magna and Jarash. Today, it is difficult to identify more than two dozen or so inhabited towns of genuine Roman origin in the Middle East and North Africa. Most of these are in Algeria and in Turkey, where four (Adana, Diyarbakir, Malatya and Sivas) have over 100,000 inhabitants. Persia never became part of the Roman empire, but several towns were founded there during the Sassanid dynasty (226 AD to 651 AD) most of which survive, including Ahvāz, Kermānshāh and Shīrāz.

Many Greco-Roman towns and cities declined in importance or were abandoned altogether in later centuries. W. C. Brice,[10] writing of Southwest Asia, attributes this to six major factors. First, in Asia Minor, Syria and Palestine, exploitation of soil, pasture and forest occurred in response to overseas demands for timber, grain, wool, horses, and other products of the land. By the third century AD soil erosion and overgrazing were so severe that some cities once dependent upon agriculture found themselves at the heart of an impoverished hinterland. Second, silting occurred along the coasts as a result of excessive losses of soil, leading to the abandonment of several ports such as Ephesus and Miletus. Third, hydrological changes affecting water supply through upstream diversion or silting spelt ruin as in the case of Harran in Turkey and Timgad in Tunisia. Similarly changes in the course of a stream could change the value of a site. Seleucia, for example, was deprived of its harbour with the eastward migration of the Tigris river. Fourth, many ancient towns depended on elaborate aqueducts, canals and tunnels for their water supply, and such installations were easily destroyed by raiders. The Vandals in North Africa in the fifth century, the Beni Hillal in the eleventh, the Seljuks in Asia Minor in the twelfth, and the Mongols in Iraq in the thirteenth century were all responsible for the death of towns. The sporadic raids of desert nomads also disrupted communications, destroyed effective administration, and ruined settlements. Fifth, political changes rendered Roman garrison towns obsolete both in North Africa and along the eastern frontier of the empire in Southwest Asia. Sixth, earthquakes probably dealt the final blows to some towns where economic foundations were already weak, particularly in Asia Minor where over 200 destructive earthquakes were chronicled between 33 AD and 1900.[11]

By far the most important factor however, was the changing pattern of trade and commerce following the break-up of the Roman empire. For centuries Southwest Asia in particular had derived great prosperity from transporting luxury goods between Europe and Asia, while many ports engaged in more local trade as well. The importance of the overland routes ceased as the demand for goods declined in Europe and much of Southwest Asia was plunged into years of savage warfare between Byzantium and the Persian Sassanids, depriving ports and inland towns alike of their livelihood. Thus Palmyra, Antioch, and the remarkable Nabatean cities of the Negev desert fell into ruins. The great Islamic conquests following the death of Muhammad in 632 AD further stimulated changes in the existing pattern of urbanization. While existing towns were rarely destroyed in the fighting because of the willingness of their inhabitants to come to terms with the Arab armies,[12] some declined rapidly as political and economic fortunes changed, notably in North Africa. New towns were founded, some of which took over the role of more ancient towns as regional centres; Kairouan finally displaced Carthage; Cairo rivalled Alexandria; and the rise of Baghdād brought ruin to Ctesiphon. The Arab empire was essentially land based, and all the new centres of power—Baghdād, Damascus, Cairo and Mecca—were at inland locations.

6.3 Islamic towns: seventh to eighteenth centuries

The first three centuries of Islamic domination were a period of marked urban revival and prosperity throughout Southwest Asia and North Africa. Although the early Islamic conquerors were largely desert nomads, Islam was from the beginning a religion of the towns. The religious precepts of Islam encourage the close association of believers and in many ways presuppose the existence of an urban society. The Arabs themselves added a number of new towns to the existing network, particularly in the Maghreb where nearly half the new foundations were located (Figure 6.2). Most of these towns are still prosperous, while a few which enjoyed unusual geographical advantages of site and location are among the leading cities of the region. The Islamic conquests led directly to the creation of a number of walled towns for military purposes; Kufra (638 AD), Basra (637 AD), Fustāt (old Cairo, 642 AD) and Kairouan (670 AD), for example. Some new towns were centres of pilgrimage or religious learning such as Najaf (791 AD) and Karbela (680 AD) in Iraq. Others were founded later for defence in wars between rival sultans or as the new political capital of a rising dynasty. Marrakech (1062 AD), for example, was originally founded as capital of the Almoravids, and Sāmarrā' (836 AD) was the court city of the Khalif's of Baghdād. Several centres also arose in response to commercial needs, particularly in regions like the Maghreb and the Red Sea where trade had not previously flourished; several small towns even sprang up in the Sahara at this time.

In addition to these new towns a large number of existing urban centres found themselves favourably placed to participate in the resurgence of trade which followed the spread of Islam and continued until the eleventh century. Southwest Asia again became the corridor between the storehouses of the east and the markets of Europe, and the number of trans-Saharan caravan routes suggest that North Africa also indulged in considerable transit trade (Figure 6.2). There was also highly developed trade within the Arab world, as illustrated by Maurice Lombard's work on the movement of timber.[13] The Islamic civilization created unprecedented demands for wood. It was used extensively

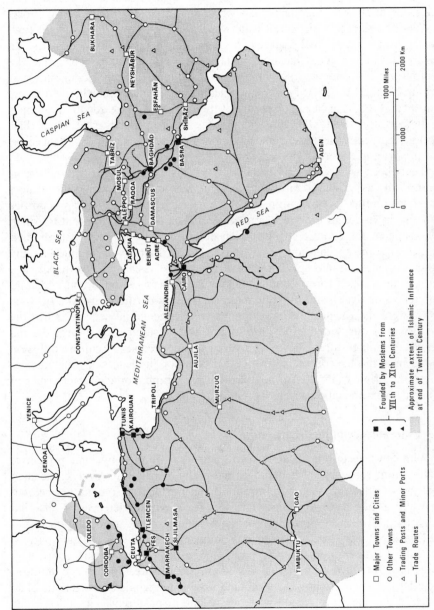

Figure 6.2 Towns of the Islamic world in the tenth to fourteenth centuries

in great buildings, particularly mosques; the famous mosque at Kairouan even contained timber from India. Ships, fishing boats and river barges on the Nile and in Mesopotamia were constructed of wood. Arab craftsmen made exquisite goods of many non-Mediterranean woods like maple, teak and ash. Wood was used in the construction of waterwheels and mills and above all for fuel. Apart from domestic fuel requirements, wood was consumed in industries like sugar refining, charcoal burning, metal working and glassblowing. Yet the Arab world from northern Syria to Tunis was almost entirely lacking in forest resources, and timber had to be imported chiefly from the northern Mediterranean and the Maghreb. The failure of the Arabs to secure adequate supplies of timber after the tenth century may have been one of the causes of their decline, but until that time some two dozen Mediterranean ports thrived on the import and export of timber.

It has been widely observed that in their basic anatomy, form and architecture, towns of the Islamic world are akin in many respects.[14] The most striking affinities occur within the Arab world and Persia, but similarities can also be traced in the towns and cities of Asia Minor. The extent to which the shape of the Islamic city has been determined by its being Islamic is a matter of some speculation,[15] but it is arguable that Islam as much as any other single factor has given towns of Southwest Asia and North Africa a basic similarity of form in spite of the uniqueness of individual sites and differences of wealth and building material. The similarities displayed by these towns were also the product of analogous environmental influences, such as the frequency of dust-laden winds, the stifling heat of summer, and large diurnal ranges of temperature. They also evolved from processes of culture diffusion along ancient trade routes and from other common influences of which insecurity is the prime example. In the following paragraphs some characteristics of Islamic towns and cities are briefly outlined.

6.3.1 Morphology of the Islamic town

With few exceptions, Islamic towns were surrounded by high protective walls, often rectangular in their ground-plans. Most walls were crenellated and possessed a series of watchtowers. Even ports were sometimes enclosed by walls, as at Salé in Morocco. The need for elaborate defences of this kind was originally for the protection of the Muslims among a population of unbelievers, but they persisted over the centuries because of dynastic quarrels, the raids of desert nomads, and piracy along the North African coast. City walls also provided climatic as well as physical protection from conditions round about by excluding the scorching sand-laden winds characteristic of so much of the region. In some towns, waste land or pasture was included inside the walls, but their effect more often was to induce uniform building densities. Cemeteries—Jewish or Muslim—were nearly always situated outside the walls, near one of the main gates of the town. Each wall was generally pierced by a gate, giving access from all directions, while inside the town two or three

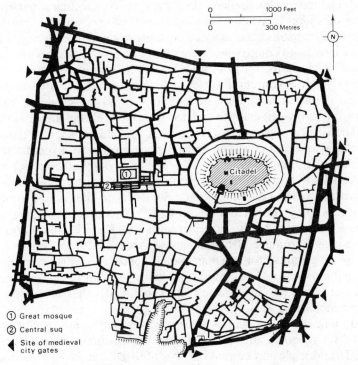

① Great mosque
② Central suq
◀ Site of medieval city gates

Figure 6.3 Old Aleppo in Syria, showing street pattern in 1941. Roman—Hellenistic influences are evident around the central *sūq*

main thoroughfares linking the gates converged on a single point, dividing the town into a number of quarters. Apart from these major axes, roads were generally narrow and winding, suitable only for pack animals, but affording welcome shade from the sun and some defence against invaders. Blind alleys were numerous, and in small towns in North Africa, roads sometimes pass through 'tunnels' beneath houses. Nevertheless, in some cities of Southwest Asia, gridiron street patterns sometimes survived from Hellenistic or Roman times, as in the southwestern quarter of Aleppo (Figure 6.3).

The focal points of towns varied. In the large town it was sometimes a citadel or *Kasba* embraced by its own wall and gates, containing the palace and gardens of the sultan with his officials and administrative officers; Rabat, Tangier and Fèz, in Morocco are all examples. In other towns, a large mosque or market place or even the ruins of an ancient citadel, as occurs in Turkey, provided the focus of main roads into the towns.

A notable feature of Islamic towns was the segregation of residential and commercial areas. The centre of the commercial quarter was usually the great mosque or Friday mosque, which in turn influenced the disposition of many activities round about. Generally there was a religious school or *medersa* associated with it. Nearby were trades to serve the needs of mosque and *medersa*—bookbinders, booksellers, furnishers of the sanctuary and so on. Next came cobblers, carpenters, tailors, carpet makers and beyond them noisy and smelly pursuits such as metal working, tanning and dyeing. Crafts primarily of interest to countrymen were often nearest the gates of the town; saddlers and blacksmiths, for example. One of the universal features of the Islamic town was the concentration of similar economic activities within a single *bazaar* or *sūq*. A number of explanations have been suggested but the practice was probably originally associated with the traditional specialization of particular tribal groups in certain activities, and this was later reinforced by the broad association of ethnic and religious groups with specific trades and professions. The guild system, one of whose functions was the preservation of trade secrets, also encouraged concentration, while security was an obvious practical reason, as the case of jewellers. Solidarity in the face of arbitrary official extortion may also have played a part.[16] This concentration is made more impressive by the density of units, most shops, stores and workshops in the *sūq* having a frontage of two or three metres only; some are no larger than an alcove big enough for one man and his goods. It is worth emphasizing that these patterns of location evolved gradually through unwritten conventions, and exceptions abounded; the remarkable fact is that there were any recognizable similarities at all.

The basic unit of the residential quarter was usually some variant of the traditional dwelling house constructed in one or two storeys around a central courtyard. The principle may be as old as town life itself, but the Arabs introduced several refinements which modern architects in semi-arid climates could well emulate. The use of wind shafts, and carved wooden screens or *mashribiya* in place of windows, together with beautiful fountains and running water created cool and pleasant living conditions. In Iraq and Iran, extremes of heat and cold also led to the adoption of an underground room suitably ventilated for use in summer. The courtyard is a simple but effective way of securing thermal comfort in hot dry climates, and is widely used throughout North Africa and as far east as the plains of India. Open courtyards are less suitable for conditions in Turkey where they tend to be rare. Since only a small courtyard can afford effective protection from the sun, large houses were often constructed with two or more courtyards, each with a set of rooms with large doors and windows opening on to them. Houses are turned inwards towards the courtyard, with openings on to the heat, dust and noise of the street reduced to a minimum. Such an arrangement incidentally conformed with the Islamic emphasis on the family unit and the seclusion of women. Wherever possible it was also the custom for successive generations to build their houses contiguously, thus creating clusters of dwellings comprising extended kinship groups. From the air, therefore, the residential quarter of an Islamic town displays a cell-like structure (Figure 6.4). A fair proportion of the built-up area was private space open to the sky. Public space on the other hand was more limited; the narrow streets which wind their way between blocks of houses sometimes give way to small open spaces suitable for groups to congregate. The cooling

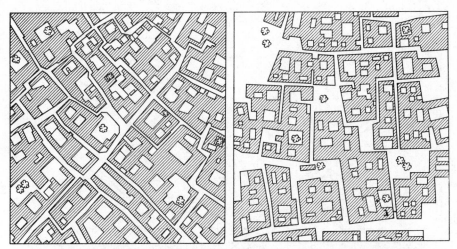

Figure 6.4 Traditional building patterns in the old city of Kuwait (left) and Misurata in Libya (right)

effect of the streets was assisted by uneven building lines, and sometimes by overhanging windows and upper storeys, resulting in compartmentalized space, full of aesthetic interest.

The residential areas of the older Islamic towns today present a formidable challenge to the urban planners seeking to provide water, electricity and sewerage, and above all access for vehicles.[17] In Iran and elsewhere the construction of broad straight avenues, sometimes crudely superimposed on a totally unrelated street pattern has been attempted in the major cities.[18] Mashhad is a particularly striking example of what has occurred in Iran since 1925 (Figure 6.5). However important such broad streets may be for the requirements of modern traffic, they are clearly less well adapted to the environment than the narrow streets of the old towns.

Residential areas were in turn divided fairly strictly into quarters (Arabic *mahalla*, or colloquially, *hara*) for peoples of differing ethnic origins and religions. Very few North African towns were without a Jewish community until their exodus in the last 25 years and the Jewish quarter was also a common element of most towns in Southwest Asia. Occasionally they were separated from other quarters by walls and most were able to close their streets at night with massive wooden doors. Originally, Jewish communities probably lived in very compact, congested quarters as in Shīrāz.[19] In the large cities however there is evidence of increasing dispersion of Jewish families around the fringes of the old *mahalla*, possibly since medieval times. Some *mahalla* had slightly narrower streets than in neighbouring quarters. The location of the *mahalla* was sometimes near the palace of the ruler as in Fèz, Tlemcen, Constantine and Marrakech. Numerous other minority groups existed besides the Jews. In the coastal towns of North Africa in recent centuries, French, Italian, Greek, Spanish and Maltese communities might be found. The importance of Christian quarters in many towns in Lebanon is discussed in Chapter 13. Throughout

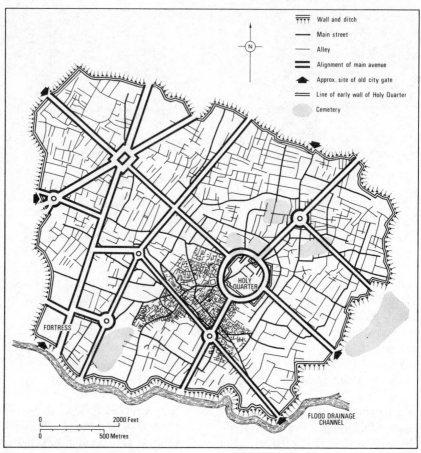

Figure 6.5 Mashhad in Iran; the superimposition of twentieth century avenues on the
ancient street pattern (Reproduced by permission of D. F. Darwent, 1965)

Southwest Asia, minorities included not only groups from within the region,
but many from outside, notably the Armenians, and Indians and Somalis
and other Africans in the ports of the Red Sea and the Gulf. Even small minorities such as foreign merchants had their own quarters, so that several dozen
quarters could exist in one city. This emphasis on kinship and ethnic groupings
reflected a vertical structure of society in which the clan was all important
as opposed to distinctions based on class or income.

The Islamic city had atmosphere, harmony and functional unity. Its public
buildings were often fine examples of Islamic architecture, exhibiting superb
craftsmanship in wood and tiles and stone, reminders of the golden age of
Persian and Arab civilization. Both Persian[20] and Arab town builders of
the early Islamic period dealt skilfully with problems of water supply for
houses, mosques, and gardens. In old Cairo every house had its own running
water and drains in the ninth century.[21] To this day in several Iranian towns,

qanāts can be found terminating in the *bazaar* or in a mosque, or sometimes in the house of the owner. Some underground rooms in houses are kept cool by the presence of running water from a *qanāt*. Although a high concentration of houses and narrow streets created a compact ground-plan in which the movement of people and pack animals was sometimes difficult, numerous small squares and gardens and courtyards with fountains and running water offered relief from the thronging streets. Here, cool air lingered long after sunrise. The renowned urban ethos of the Islamic town was derived as much from the subtle juxtaposition of buildings as from their merit as individual structures. The whole city had evolved organically over the centuries in an expressly Islamic environment and, in many ways, it was an embodiment of an Arab–Islamic culture. The centrality of the great mosque, the high status accorded to craftsmen and merchants, tolerance of minorities and the importance of family and kinship group all arose out of the precepts of Islam and more or less directly affected the morphology of the town.

In spite of their structural similarities, Islamic towns possess a rich variety of townscapes, some of extraordinary beauty. Set in contrasting geographical environments, ranging from desert and coast to river valley and mountain, many types of traditional building material are available. Oven-fired or sun-dried bricks and mud were commonly used, creating a range of colour as varied as the parent materials. In southern Morocco light brown and red predominate; in the Nile valley every shade from grey to dark brown can be seen, while the old city of Baghdād was soft yellow in colour. More striking contrasts are evident in the stone-built towns. Diyarbakir in Turkey has massive black basalt walls; Mosul is extensively constructed of speckled grey alabastrine stone, and the old city of Jerusalem is renowned for its sparkling white limestone. Building styles also differ markedly from region to region. The sloping red tiled roofs of Turkey contrast strongly with the flat roof tops of most Arab and Persian towns. Some of the dazzling whitewashed settlements of the North African coast seem to have more in common with southern Europe than the Islamic world. On the other hand the centuries old apartment buildings of the Wadi Ḥaḍhramawt, constructed without steel or concrete are peculiar to a small part of the Arabian peninsula. They average some six storeys in height, but appear higher because each floor has a double set of windows.

The one visible element common to every Islamic town is the mosque. Surprisingly, the mosque did not originate from any specific directive in the Qur'ān. In the earliest years of the faith collective prayer was probably performed in an open space rather than within a specific edifice. Mosques were first built during the Islamic conquests for the purpose of excluding unbelievers, and minarets were originally added not to call to prayer but as symbols of the presence of the people who built them.[22] The puritanical Wahhābi sect of central Saudi Arabia still frown on tall minarets, and Riyadh while a strongly Islamic city, lacks this characteristic element. Later, when the call to prayer

became common practice it seems likely that dwellings were constructed within
muezzin-call of the mosque, and when this became impossible, further mosques
were established. It is certainly evident that most parts of an Islamic town are
served by a local mosque, the total number running into several hundred in
the larger cities. Some of the important mosques of Southwest Asia, particularly
in Turkey and Iran, possess magnificent blue or golden domes, another unmistakable feature of the Islamic skyline.

6.3.2 Municipal organization

An unusual aspect of the Islamic city was the form of government. Until
the late nineteenth century, there were no councils charged with overall responsibility for town management. Occasionally the whole population might
combine for defence, but civic feeling was generally weak among town dwellers
compared with western Europe. The chief reason lay in the vertical structure
of society and the importance of the residential quarter in which men of high
and low estate were united on the basis of religion or blood. Groups cutting
across quarters were rare and ineffective, and cooperation between quarters
was consequently difficult. Most towns and cities had a governor or ruling
sultan who appointed a local sheikh to raise taxes, maintain order, and represent the quarter.[23] The custom was reinforced under the Ottomans by
the *millet* system which gave a certain degree of autonomy to religious minorities. Another instrument of administration was the trade corporations
or guilds which flourished from the ninth century until their collapse ten
centuries later. Their chief functions were the preservation of trade secrets,
the maintenance of standards, and regulation of prices. By discouraging
initiative and limiting expansion the guilds may ultimately have contributed
to the economic stagnation of certain crafts in some cities. Whether or not
this is so, the guilds provided links through their leaders, with a large proportion
of the adult male population, since most were members of some guild; even
beggars and thieves had their own.[24] The guilds also tended to perpetuate
the distinctions between quarters since economic activities were often based
upon the traditional functions and specializations of a particular tribe or
religious group. While this style of urban government probably functioned
reasonably effectively at the local level, the implementation of schemes for
the town as a whole was rendered almost impossible. Thus with very few
exceptions, chiefly in Persian cities, the Islamic period was one of unplanned
organic growth in which individualism played an important part. The physical
consequences are evident in the intricate morphology of the older towns and
cities of the region today. The first serious attempts to draw up master plans
for even the largest cities were made only in recent decades. The master plan
drawn up for Aleppo in 1932, though not generally adopted, was probably
the first in Southwest Asia[25], though the French had begun planning their
towns in the Maghreb rather earlier in the century.

6.3.3 Urban decline: fifteenth to eighteenth centuries

The full flowering of Islamic urban civilization was reached in about the eleventh century. From then until the fifteenth century a period of stagnation set in, followed by demographic and economic decline until the end of the eighteenth century. It is not possible to give precise figures, but the reality of this decline is supported by evidence from many sources. While some towns disappeared altogether, others dwindled in size and importance. The population decline of a few leading cities is illustrated in Table 6.1. The earlier figures cannot be regarded as wholly reliable; nevertheless, the differences are sufficiently large to be worth noting. Similar processes were undoubtedly widespread, though even notional figures are non-existent for the smaller towns. Asia Minor, which for centuries constituted the favoured heartland of the Ottoman empire, appears to have been an exception, the largest cities at least showing population increase from the sixteenth century. Large discrepancies frequently occur in the estimated populations of individual towns, but these are not always entirely due to inaccurate guesswork. Wars, floods,[27] fire, earthquake and epidemics in former years periodically reduced urban populations, creating enormous fluctuations over short periods. In 1969 for example, 150,000 people are estimated to have died of plague in Aleppo, and the 1831 death toll of 40 to 50,000 in Baghdād partially accounts for the sharp decline shown in Table 6.1 between 1800 and 1831.[28] Cairo has also been fearfully devastated by plague on several occasions, as in 1492, when 12,000 corpses are said to have been carried out of the city in one day.[29]

The decline of urban populations from the fifteenth to eighteenth centuries was almost certainly accompanied by a general demographic decline. A combination of complex local factors usually accounted for such decline, but three universal influences may be suggested. First, the period was marked by a

TABLE 6.1
Population change of some leading cities
(ninth to nineteenth centuries)

	Year/Period	Estimated population in thousands	Year	Estimated population in thousands
Fèz	13th century	400	1900	95
Tunis	1517	200	1881	120
Alexandria	860	100	1800	7
Cairo	14th century	300	1800	250
Damascus	14th/15th century	100	1820	120
	1520/1530	57	1840	80
Baghdād	10th century	500	1800	50–100
			1831	20
Tehrān	17th century	600	1807	45

Source: See note 26 under references.

succession of wars and political convulsions. In Southwest Asia the Crusades were followed by the repeated destructive incursions of the Mongols in the thirteenth and fourteenth centuries. During the sixteenth and seventeenth centuries the Ottomans conquered most of Southwest Asia except Persia and part of North Africa, while Persia and Turkey engaged in a succession of long and exhausting wars which left much of eastern Asia Minor, Iraq and western Persia in a state of ruin. Secondly, the Ottoman regime, and that of the oppressive Mamluks which preceded it in Syria and Egypt failed to revive industry, agriculture and trade. In the late seventeenth and eighteenth centuries the Ottomans imposed crippling taxation and arbitrary levies on merchants in the towns, thus inhibiting development. The discovery of the Cape route to the East by the Portuguese in 1498 was followed by disruption of trade in the Red Sea, the Persian Gulf, and the Indian Ocean which robbed Southwest Asia of its prosperity as the world's premier trade route. The declining standard of living and the increase of violence implicit in these events might themselves have lowered birth rates and raised death rates, but it also seems likely that during the period in question famines and epidemics became more frequent as irrigated agriculture contracted and the quality of urban life deteriorated, particularly housing and sanitation.

6.4 The nineteenth and twentieth centuries

6.4.1 Level of urbanization

Since nobody really knows the precise size of the total population, it is impossible to say whether the proportion of people living in towns rose or fell before the nineteenth century. If the level remained roughly the same as in early Islamic times, it could only have done so with the periodic influx of rural migrants to compensate for some towns abandoned altogether and to make up for high urban mortality, sometimes in excess of births. C. Issawi stresses the importance of such rural-urban migration[30] but Z. Y. Hershlag concedes little or no movement from the villages during these centuries.[31] The truth may be that it was the desert nomads who settled from time to time in the city rather than the peasant cultivator. Certainly the level of urbanization in Southwest Asia and North Africa was high during the nineteenth century, comparable with much of western Europe. In 1800 at least 10 per cent of the populations of Turkey and Egypt lived in towns of over 10,000 inhabitants; in Syria and Iraq it was probably 15 to 20 per cent. Towards the end of the century the urban population of Iran was put at 25 per cent,[32] while figures of eight to nine per cent have been suggested for Morocco and Tunisia and 16 per cent for Algeria.[33] It should be noted that many urban dwellers were agriculturalists living inside the city walls, and in this sense comparisons with Europe are not altogether valid. Nevertheless it is clear that the rapid urbanization of the last hundred years took place from a well-established demographic base.

TABLE 6.2
Per cent of population in four urban class sizes in 1970

Country	(i) 'Urban' but under 100,000	(ii) 100,000– 499,999	(iii) 500,000– 999,999	(iv) 1 Million	(v) Total urban (predicted)	(vi) Total urban (actual)
Algeria	24·6	6·4	7·2	—	38·2	42·8
Libya	2·05	26·1	—	—	28·2	26·6
Morocco	11·4	11·0	3·5	9·4	35·3	32·2
Tunisia	21·2	7·9	14·3	—	43·4	43·4
Egypt	12·7	8·0	—	23·0	43·7	43·1
North Africa	13·5	7·7	2·6	10·7	34·5	34·8
Bahrain	74·5	—	—	—	74·5	64·2
Iran	16·2	8·2	3·5	11·3	39·2	40·8
Iraq	12·6	17·2	—	13·8	43·6	47·1
Israel	26·1	24·2	30·9	—	81·2	79·5
Jordan	24·3	19·6	—	—	43·9	46·6
Kuwait	21·3	59·1	—	—	80·4	56·3
Lebanon	7·1	9·6	23·1	—	39·8	40·6
Oman	5·3	—	—	—	5·3	4·9
Qatar	68·4	—	—	—	68·4	68·3
Saudi Arabia	11·7	13·5	—	—	25·2	23·6
P.D.R. Yemen	5·0	27·5	—	—	32·5	28·7
Syria	7·7	8·7	22·1	—	38·5	43·6
United Arab Emirates	55·1	—	—	—	44·9	51·9
Turkey	12·9	5·3	2·1	10·9	31·2	41·3
Yemen A.R.	6·0	—	—	—	6·0	5·8
Southwest Asia	13·8	9·2	4·5	8·1	35·6	37·8

Sources: Columns (i)–(v): Kingsley Davis, *World Urbanisation 1950–1970, Vol. 1, Basic Data for Cities, Countries and Regions* (Berkeley: Institute of International Studies, University of California), 1969 Table C, pp. 113–130.
Column (vi): United Nations, *Statistical Yearbook*, New York, 1972, pp. 82–84.

Attempts to establish present levels of urbanization also raise problems. To begin with, there is no common definition of 'urban', and published national figures are not therefore directly comparable. Israel, for example, takes any settlement with over 2,000 inhabitants as urban, except where more than one third of the labour force is engaged in agriculture. In Saudi Arabia the urban threshold is 4,000, in Iran 5,000, and 10,000 in Turkey. Other countries such as Egypt and Syria use administrative status as criteria. Lebanon on the other hand simply classifies the eight largest cities as urban. Further difficulties arise because published figures for individual cities sometimes refer to the political city, sometimes to an urban agglomeration of the same name. Using the various definitions of the countries themselves as far as possible, Kingsley Davis forecast the proportions of their total populations in four class sizes in 1970 and with one or two exceptions his forecasts proved fairly accurate (Table 6.2). In spite of their obvious limitations, the United Nation's figures in Table 6.2 give a good impression of the present level of urbanization in the regions. With about 36 to 38 per cent urban dwellers, they are more highly urbanized than countries of South Asia or tropical Africa. It is also worth noting that the level and structure of the urban populations is very similar in North Africa and Southwest Asia. In five small states—Israel, Kuwait, Bahrain, the United Arab Emirates and Qatar—urban dwellers already constitute the majority. Israel is among the most highly urbanized countries in the world.

6.4.2 Rate of urban growth

The rate of increase of the urban population has shown almost unchecked acceleration through the twentieth century. In 1900 the overall level of urban population was probably under 10 per cent. Fifty years later it had risen to around 25 per cent, and by 1985 is forecast to have risen to 43 per cent in North Africa and 47 per cent in Southwest Asia (Table 6.3), with urban dwellers in the majority in all but half a dozen countries. These figures do not reveal the increased degree of urbanization caused by town dwelling farmers giving way to persons engaged in more truly urban occupations. Furthermore, the most rapid period of growth since the Second World War has coincided with the exodus of Jews and Europeans from the big towns, particularly in North Africa, where a high proportion of urban dwellers were non-Muslims.

The average annual urban growth rate during the period 1960 to 1970 was probably well above four per cent in North Africa and Southwest Asia, compared with a demographic growth rate of 2·6 per cent.[34] Since natural increase is often higher in towns than rural districts because of better living conditions possibly reaching three or four per cent, it can be concluded that urban growth today generally owes more to natural increase than inmigration. At times and in individual towns immigration has, however, been very important. In Algeria between 1962 and 1964 some 600,000 Europeans left the towns and their place was taken by 800,000 rural Algerians, and in this period very high rates of increase occurred in many towns. Tel Aviv, Amman and Kuwait have also experienced heavy immigration, but over the last decade it is difficult to identify more than a dozen cities among the hundred largest in the region whose migration component clearly outweighs natural increase. The great

TABLE 6.3
Urban population per cent in North Africa
and Southwest Asia

	1950	1970	1985
North Africa	24·4	34·8	43·1
Southwest Asia	25·2	37·8	46·8

Source: United Nations, Statistical Yearbook, New York, 1972, pp. 82–84.

majority of migrants settle in one or two large cities, and they and their offspring therefore make up a high proportion of the population, frequently more than two thirds.

The rapid increase of urban populations and the persistently high level of rural-urban migration has sometimes led to the conclusion that Southwest Asia and North Africa are 'overurbanized'. In the sense that migrants are often unemployed or at best undertake low productive employment the idea is valid. On the other hand, unemployment and underemployment are also common in rural areas and most migrant families enjoy higher incomes in towns than previously. While a proportion have been driven from the land by crop failure or acute population pressure, most migration occurs in response to both 'push' and 'pull' factors, the chief attraction being the steady expansion of employment opportunities since the turn of the century. Although the oil industry is capital-intensive and not labour-intensive, it has created substantial demands for labour in the oil-rich states in numerous indirect ways—in transport, services, and construction. Several states, not necessarily oil producers, have begun to establish an increasingly wide range of manufacturing industries, and these have also generated opportunities for employment. The political fragmentation of Southwest Asia following the First World War and the era of independence following the Second World War also created enormous opportunities in government service and in service industries of all kinds associated with the concentration of high spending power in the new capital cities. This does not mean that work was available for every rural migrant, but at least his motive for migration was based on more than fantasy.

6.4.3 Concentration of urban populations

The notion of 'overurbanization' is extremely complicated but its application to the region is rather doubtful. *Overconcentration* of the urban population of individual countries in one or two large cities or city regions is however an unmistakable feature of most countries of North Africa and Southwest Asia.

So far, the most heavily urbanized regions are emerging in Morocco, Tunisia, Egypt and Israel. In Morocco a zone no more than 150 km long and 50 km wide extending from Casablanca to Kénitra embraces nearly a quarter of the population of the country. Some 50 years ago the population of this small area was insignificant compared with the inland lowland regions. Similarly in Tunisia, Tunis is the heart of a strongly urbanized region extending to a radius of some 80 km, including nearly half the medium-sized towns in Tunisia. The most impressive examples however are in Egypt and Israel. Greater Cairo embraces a region more than 50 km across, including 11 towns, two of them with over 100,000 inhabitants besides Cairo itself. In Israel, nearly half of the population inhabit the Tel Aviv district, 20 km long and 8 km wide. Apart from familiar problems associated with any large city, overconcentration deprives less favoured regions of a share of new industrial units, social and economic services, and professional personnel. It is thus relevant to consider the degree of concentration of urban populations. Primacy is most evident in Kuwait and also in Tunisia, Iran, Iraq, Lebanon, Morocco and Algeria where capital cities completely outclass their rivals in size. Thus Tehrān (2,720,000 at the 1966 census) is followed in rank by Eşfahān (424,000); Baghdād (1,750,000 at the 1965 census) by Basra (313,000); and Beirūt (700,000 in 1966) by Tripoli (150,000).[35] In several other countries two cities dominate, and duality rather than primacy is the rule. Cairo and Alexandria, Damascus and Aleppo, Tripoli and Benghazi together contain at least one fifth of their respective national populations. Although İstanbul and Ankara hold a similar position in Turkey, the existence of a number of other large and medium-sized towns greatly modifies the degree of concentration in these two cities.

6.4.4 Number of towns

The number of towns in Southwest Asia and North Africa has greatly increased since the beginning of this century, both through the expansion of existing small settlements and the creation of new urban centres. It is a fair guess that in 1900 there were fewer than 100 towns with 20,000 or more inhabitants in North Africa and perhaps 150 in Southwest Asia. Table 6.4 which summarizes the position at the end of the 1960's, shows 215 such towns in North Africa and 242 in Southwest Asia. If anything, these figures are underestimates. The increase in the number of towns with over 100,000 inhabitants is remarkable. Table 6.4 shows 31 cities in this category in North Africa and 56 in Southwest Asia; by the early 1970's the total number certainly exceeded 100. In 1900 there were four towns of this size in North Africa, and fewer than a dozen in Southwest Asia. The greatest number of 100,000-plus cities are in Turkey (20), Egypt (17), Iran (14), Morocco (10) and Iraq (9). Table 6.4 also indicates six million-plus cities, whereas in 1900 there were none. The latest published population estimates for these cities are: Cairo (1970) 4·9 million; Tehrān (1966) 2·7 million; Alexandria (1970) 2·0 million; Baghdād (1970) 2·9 million; İstanbul (1970) 2·2 million; Casablanca (1970) 1·3 million. Algiers and Ankara had also achieved 'millionaire' status by 1970, while the Tel Aviv conurbation also contains over a million people in spite of the modest size attributed to the political city of Tel Aviv. The exceptionally rapid growth of these cities has been an outstanding feature of the last seventy years. They now embrace one tenth of the entire population of the region and almost one third of the urban population. All are growing more rapidly than the urban populations of their respective countries and Cairo, Tehrān, Baghdād, Casablanca and Ankara more than doubled their populations in the fifteen years preceding the most recent census. Together they account for a quarter of all million-people cities located in developing countries, and Cairo ranks about tenth in the world.

The complexities of definition renders column 1 in Table 6·3 of limited

TABLE 6.4
Number of towns in six urban class sizes

	I 10,000– 19,999	II 20,000– 49,999	III 50,000– 99,999	IV 100,000– 499,900	V 500,000– 999,999	VI 1 Million and over	Total	Sources
Algeria	24	52	12	4	1	—	93	1966 Census
Libya	8	1	—	2	—	—	11	1964 Census
Morocco (a)	22	12	5	6	1	1	47	1966 Estimate
Tunisia	22	14	3	—	1	—	40	1966 Census
Egypt (b)	200	65	20	13	—	2	300	Various–1970
Bahrain	—	1	1	—	—	—	2	1965 Census
Iran	48	41	15	11	2	1	118	1966 Census
Iraq	19	12	3	8	—	1	43	1965 Census
Israel (c)	24	15	7	4	—	—	50	1971 Estimate
Jordan (c)	7	6	1	2	—	—	16	Various–1970
Kuwait	4	3	—	1	—	—	8	1965 Census
Lebanon	4	2	1	1	1	—	9	Various–1970
Oman	1	—	—	—	—	—	1	Various–1970
P.D.R. Yemen	—	2	—	1	—	—	3	Various–1970
Qatar	1	—	1	—	—	—	2	Various–1970
Saudi Arabia	12	5	3	3	—	—	23	Various–1973
Syria	15	4	1	3	2	—	25	Various–1970
Turkey	134	77	21	17	1	2	252	1970 Census
United Arab Emirates	—	2	1	—	—	—	3	Various–1970
Yemen A.R.	1	—	1	1	—	—	3	Various–1970
TOTAL	546	314	96	77	9	7	1049	

(a) With Spanish towns of Melilla and Ceuta
(b) Including the Gaza Strip and Sinai
(c) Pre–1967 territories

value; many of the Egyptian settlements in this category are large villages with a high proportion of the population engaged in agriculture, while other figures represent strict census definitions of 'urban'. Nevertheless, the large number of small towns may be noted in Turkey, which has a relatively low level of urban population (Table 6.2).

6.4.5 New towns

Several factors explain the surprising number of new towns in the region. For the second time in its long history, the area was gradually drawn into the sphere of European commercial and political influence from the mid-nineteenth century. With the opening of the Suez Canal in 1869 the historic function of acting as the crossroads of the world was resumed, and maritime traffic received a great impetus. The export of primary products, aided in part by the development of railways and pipelines, became increasingly important and new outlets were needed to meet changing patterns of trade. Until the outbreak of the Second World War, many of the fastest growing towns and cities were in coastal locations. Besides the revival of many ancient ports, several new ones were constructed, notably in North Africa. The colonial

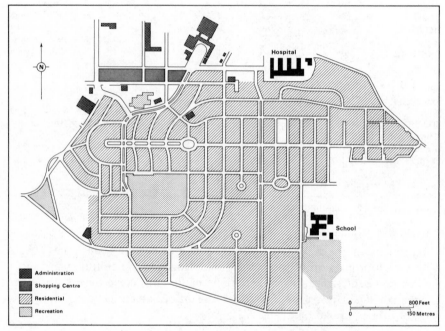

Figure 6.6 Dhahran, an oil town in Saudi Arabia

Modern townscape in the Middle East: Beirūt from the sea (National Council of Tourism in Lebanon. Photograph by Magnin)

The Nile at Cairo (The Times. Photograph by W. Harrison).

era in North Africa also stimulated a spate of town building. The French gained effective control of Algeria in 1857 and Tunisia in 1881. They partitioned Morocco with Spain in 1912, and Italy finally conquered Libya in about 1920. Many of the minor towns of the Maghreb were founded during the French occupation. A few were directly associated with mineral extraction, notably phosphates and coal, and other towns developed initially as small ports associated with mineral exports and a few were founded as resorts. A large number of towns, particularly in Algeria, were originally garrison towns with administrative functions such as Sidi-Bel-Abbès. By far the largest category however, were the village and market centres established mainly in regions of European colonization; Souk Ahras, Boufarik and Saïda are examples in Algeria; Kasba Tadla, Khemisset and Souk El Arba in Morocco. Deliberately located at the foci of discrete geographical and agricultural regions, many of them are now effective social and economic centres for the surrounding countryside in areas far removed from the large towns. One reason why so many new towns had to be created was the scarcity of indigenous centres suitable for expansion. It seems likely that the operation of weekly tribal markets at any convenient geographical foci obviated the need for permanent market towns.[36]

Israel's contribution to the number of new towns may be noted; out of a total of 77 urban centres, half are new towns.[37] Tel Aviv, which now forms the heart of a conurbation of one and a half million people, began in 1909 as a Jewish garden suburb of Jaffa.

New towns established during the last hundred years are essentially European in style and layout, owing little to local urban traditions. The oil town of Dhahran in Saudi Arabia (1970 population 10,000) provides an extreme example (Figure 6.6). Its layout is distinctly a product of the age of motor vehicles, and its culture clearly western, a transplant from the United States for the benefit of Aramco employees. Dhahran has regular streets, open spaces, cheerful gardens, air conditioned public buildings and recreational amenities including a golf course, swimming pool, tennis courts, cinema and bowling alley. Churches are not in evidence however, being forbidden by law in Saudi Arabia. The Iranian oil port of Abādān (1966 population 273,000), founded in 1910, displays a similar European impress though on a far larger scale. Besides such new towns, a number of old indigenous centres have been rebuilt on western lines following devastation by earthquakes: Sivas in Turkey (1936) and Agadir in Morocco (1960) are examples. It is astonishing how slavishly western styles of architecture and urban form are followed when traditional styles and techniques might be adapted to give greater comfort at lower cost.

6.4.6 Changes in urban form

New towns contain only a fraction of the total increase of urban dwellers in recent decades, the majority having been absorbed into expanded pre-nineteenth century foundations. The effect of rapid expansion on the structure and morphology of traditional towns and cities has varied. In the largest cities redevelopment has often been so extensive that only small parts of the old town survive, as in Algiers, Cairo, Baghdād and Tehrān. In Iran, the construction of broad avenues through most large towns has stimulated changes in the location of commercial activities and land values so that some degree of fusion between old and new has occurred. Physical change has however, been quite moderate in many other towns, expansion taking place adjacent to the original core. Even city walls have often remained substantially intact, although some have been removed to make way for much needed ring roads as in Aleppo (Figure 6.3). Within the old city or *medina* many buildings have changed their functions—hotels have replaced the old *caravanserais* and most synagogues have closed—but in general the outward appearance and atmosphere is not unlike that of a hundred years ago or more. The contrast between the old and new towns can be seen most obviously in street patterns, the one organically evolved, confused and dense, the other ruler-planned and orderly. Tetouan provides a classic example of a colonial town of this kind (Figure 6.7). There are also less tangible implications of this duality. Population densities in the *medinas* have been found to be generally higher, and different patterns of retailing and movement of people and goods have been identified. Other research has revealed higher rates of natural increase in the *medinas*, lower rates of literacy, a lower proportion of active females, and the prevalence

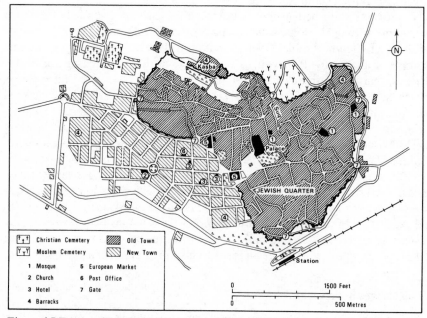

Figure 6.7 Tetouan in Spanish Morocco in about 1938, showing the old town and the new Spanish-built town (Reproduced by permission of the Controller, Her Majesty's Stationery Office)

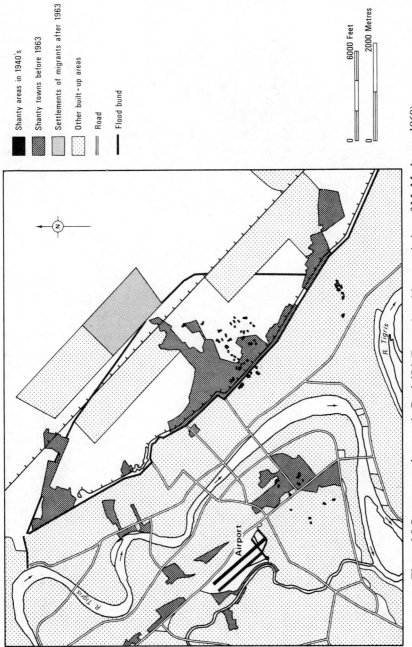

Shanty areas in 1940's

Shanty towns before 1963

Settlements of migrants after 1963

Other built-up areas

Road

Flood bund

6000 Feet

2000 Metres

Figure 6.8 Squatter settlements in Baghdād (Reproduced by permission of M. M. Ageez, 1968)

216

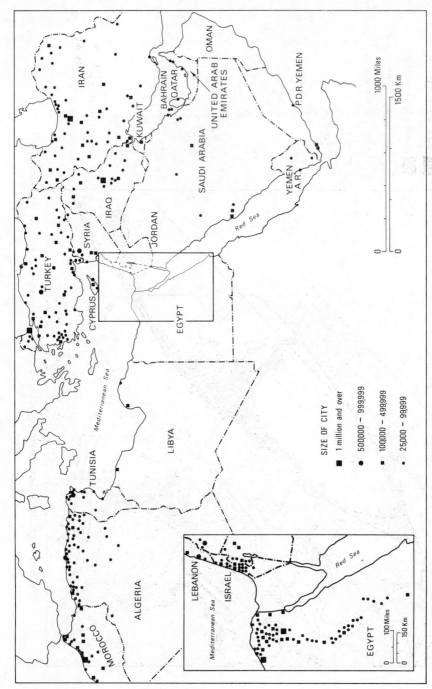

Figure 6.9 Urban centres of North Africa and Southwest Asia with over 25,000 inhabitants in the 1960's (Reproduced by permission of University of London Press Limited)

of social structures based primarily on kinship and clan groupings. Economic activity in the old town is generally unrelated to land values, while in the new town familiar processes are at work generating high values centrally, reducing towards the urban fringe.

Even where the original town has largely survived, it now represents a mere fraction of the built-up area, usually accommodating a small share of the total urban population. New and distinctly alien elements have been added to the townscape—villa development, flats, shops, garages, industrial estates, railway sidings, government offices, churches, schools and hospitals. Around the largest cities unsightly shanty towns or *bidonvilles* have sometimes been erected by poor rural immigrants. Casablanca and Baghdād (Figure 6.8) have had extensive *bidonvilles*, though partially successful efforts have been made to replace them with good housing. In most towns and cities today the characteristic Islamic skyline of domes and minarets is overshadowed by one characteristic of almost any western city with high rise apartments, chimneys and office blocks. Stone and mud have been largely replaced by bricks and concrete as building materials, and indigenous architectural forms have almost entirely disappeared. The centre of gravity has shifted from the old town to the new, and as urbanization proceeds an increasingly high proportion of the population are living in a western style of urban environment, no longer distinctly Islamic, Persian, Turkish or Arab.

6.5 The distribution of towns and cities

Figure 6.9 shows towns and cities with more than 25,000 inhabitants according to census data and other estimates made during the 1960's. Their distribution broadly corresponds with the network of medieval towns of all sizes (Figure 6.2). The largest number of towns are located in regions of over 400 mm of annual rainfall, where perennial streams and groundwater resources provide reasonably adequate water supplies and a wide choice of sites. The coast of North Africa, most of the Levant, Asia Minor and parts of northern Iraq and western Iran may be included in this category. Some towns even in these areas experience problems of water supply. A second important category with generally adequate water resources are the towns of the Nile valley and delta, and the Tigris–Euphrates lowlands where rainfall is generally less than 130 mm. Both regions possess large urban populations, but the network of towns in the Nile delta is unequalled elsewhere in North Africa or Southwest Asia. A third category of towns exist in regions with less than 400 mm of rainfall, and outside the Nile and Tigris–Euphrates valleys. In the largest of these towns the provision of an adequate water supply often presents acute problems, and in all of them the presence of a water supply in some form or other was decisive in the choice of site. Several of the most famous were caravan cities on the margins of the desert. Damascus, for example, has been described as 'the gift of the Barada', a river which rises in the mountains to the west and supplies the city with abundant water through its seven distributaries before being lost in the desert to the east.[38] Eṣfahān is another classic example.

Like most Iranian oases, it lies within sight of high mountains from which radiate scores of short streams, but the Zayandeh Rud brings water to the city and its surrounding oasis from a great distance. Not all towns in regions of rainfall deficiency are as favoured, particularly in the Arabian peninsula. Water for Jiddah has to be brought 80 km by pipeline, and about half that distance to Riyadh. Kuwait, Abū Dhabi and Dohar, the capital of Qatar, rely on desalination of sea water, and plants are also in operation at Jiddah and Eilat. Desalination plants will certainly multiply rapidly in the late 1970's.

6.5.1 Capital cities

The location of capital cities deserves some comment. In the Maghreb and Libya all capital cities are on the coast, in keeping with the fashion in the rest of the continent. Rabat, Algiers and Tunis, while not geographically central in their respective countries are well placed with regard to the most productive and populous regions. Tunis is particularly well favoured in this respect. Libya, on the other hand, suffers from a polarization of population both physically and politically between the old provinces of Tripolitania and Cyrenaica. Thus Tripoli and Benghazi were formerly regarded as joint capitals, though an ambitious scheme to build a new capital at Al Bayda' in Cyrenaica was attempted and subsequently abandoned. Since 1969, the decision has gone in favour of Tripoli. Cairo is perhaps the most rationally situated capital in the world, linking the populous delta and valley regions, standing at the natural east–west crossing point of the Nile, and at the natural focus of river traffic and north–south communications by road and rail. Baghdād and Beirūt are the only capital cities in Southwest Asia which enjoy anything like the same advantages as Cairo, and significantly both are un-rivalled in size in their own countries. Tehrān, which became capital of Persia at the end of the eighteenth century, dominates other cities in Iran despite its eccentric geographical location. Many towns have in turn fulfilled the function of capital city of Persia because of the difficulty of finding a good central site on account of the sparsely populated interior.

Ankara was a town of 30,000 inhabitants in 1923 when it was chosen as capital of Turkey in preference to İstanbul with its cosmopolitan associations. Its present population is around one million. Ankara enjoys a measure of centrality and is not unfavourably located in other respects, on an ancient east–west route, and at the focus of complementary geographical regions— forest, steppe, and cultivated land. Damascus and Aleppo had very similar geographical advantages as potential capitals for Syria after the First World War. Damascus may have been chosen partly because of its more favourable position with regard to Lebanon and the rest of the Arab world. Lebanese independence and the advent of Israel may have reduced these advantages. Certainly Aleppo remains a close rival of Damascus in size. The selection of an ideal capital for Saudi Arabia is problematic because of the marginal distribution of much of the country's population and resources. The choice of Riyadh as the Royal capital and Jiddah as administrative capital was an obvious compromise. The Yemen Arab Republic also had two capitals until 1969, but for different reasons; a Royalist capital at Şan'ā and a Republican capital at Ta'izz. Şan'ā is now the capital of a united Yemen. Jerusalem was proclaimed capital of Israel in 1950, in spite of the wishes of the United Nations that it should be internationalized. It is the seat of Israel's parliament, but most foreign embassies and certain government departments remain in Tel Aviv. It is worth noting that before June 1967, Jerusalem was a divided city, reached by a vulnerable corridor flanked by Jordanian territory, and it could one day revert to this situation.[39] Yet the emotional appeal of the city was sufficiently strong enough for it to function as Israel's capital.

6.5.2 Relations between town and country

If towns with fewer than 25,000 inhabitants could be shown on Figure 6.9, a positive relationship between rural population densities and the density of small towns would be indicated. There are perhaps 600 to 650 centres in the 10,000 to 25,000 range, the majority of which are small market towns. Many fulfil local administrative functions and possess a limited range of industrial activity, such as cotton ginning or olive pressing, and some craft industries such as leather-work or weaving. The symbiosis of town and country characteristic of these small centres may be illustrated by the functioning of Misurata in Libya, a town with less than 20,000 inhabitants in 1966. Misurata is located at the geographical centre of a small oasis, to the south of which lies a fairly extensive region of dry cereal cultivation, and enormous tracts of rough steppe pasture beyond. The total population of the surrounding region is less than 80,000, yet three times a week, each market day, about 7,000 rural dwellers, predominantly men, enter the town to buy and sell their goods. Individuals make regular visits from 30 to 40 km away, and occasional visits from as far as 300 km to the south. The entire centre of the town is devoted to open air and covered markets, and more than 800 small retail stores and craftmen's shop were counted in the town in 1966. Some countrymen were found to own workshops in Misurata while a number of townsmen also farmed land within the oasis and beyond.[40]

It is therefore appropriate to conclude by considering relationships between the countryside and the larger towns and cities of North Africa and Southwest Asia. A widely accepted view is that from early times until the nineteenth century the townsman was isolated politically, socially and culturally from his counterpart in the countryside, whom he generally despised. Furthermore, since the town was often the seat of an alien administration, antipathy between the two groups was strong. These ideas are probably exaggerated. Town and country were poles apart in wealth and culture, but they were also frequently part of a single ecosystem in which both were mutually interdependent. This was particularly true of the great cities like Marrakech, Damascus, Eşfahān and others surrounded by large oases. The peasant looked to the town for

220

protection and as a market for his produce, while the townsman depended largely upon local agriculture for food. Many farmers and landowners actually lived inside the city, and in small towns farmers may well have owned small stores and workshops as is customary in North Africa today. Some cities possessed extensive walled suburbs for gardening, such areas of green having both economic and amenity value. In fact, in many situations no absolute distinctions between urban and rural habitats could be drawn. The towns themselves were socially divided into quarters no larger than village communities, and in Egypt and Iraq canals and rivers sometimes physically separated parts of the town. Moreover, there was undoubtedly a steady trickle of rural migrants into even the meanest towns, if not a steady stream, and rural attitudes lingered in urban society. On the other hand some large villages were almost urban in character, fortified, with their own non-agriculture specialists, public baths and mosques.[41] It is probably true that those ancient towns and cities which survived the vicissitudes of interregional trade most successfully were those enjoying strong economic relations with a surrounding population of cultivators.

References

1. M. E. L. Mallowan, 'The development of cities from Al'Ubaid to the end of Uruk 5', *The Cambridge Ancient History*, **1,** Cambridge University Press, Cambridge, 1967, 6–7.
2. J. Mellaart, *Çatal Hüyük: a neolithic town in Anatolia*, Thames and Hudson, London, 1967.
3. J. Jacobs, *The Economy of Cities*, Jonathan Cape, London, 1969, 5–38.
4. V. Gordon Childe, 'The urban revolution', *Town Plann. Rev.* **21,** 3–17 (1950).
5. C. Daryll Forde, 'The ancient cities of the Indus', *Geography*, **17,** 186 (1932).
6. F. R. Hiorns, *Town-building in History*, Harrap, London, 1956, 11–14.
7. A. L. Oppenheim, 'Mesopotamian cities', in *Middle Eastern Cities*, (Ed. I. M. Lapidus), University of California, Berkeley and Los Angeles, 1969, 5.
8. R. McAdams, *Land behind Baghdād*, University of Chicago, Chicago, 1965, Figures 2, 3 and 4.
9. A. A. M. Van der Heyden and H. H. Scullard (Eds) *Atlas of the Classical World*, Nelson, London, 1959, 84.
10. W. C. Brice, *Southwest Asia*, University of London Press, London, 1966, 96–101.
11. G. B. Cressey, *Crossroads*, J. P. Lippincott Co., International University Edition, New York, 1960, 81.
12. J. B. Glubb, *The Great Arab Conquests*, Hodder and Stoughton, London 1963, 158–159, 202, 230–231.
13. M. Lombard, 'Une carte du bois dans la Méditerranée musulmane (VIIe-IXe siècles)', *Annales-Économies-Sociétés-Civilisations*, 234–254 (April–June 1969).
14. (a) G. Shiber, *The Kuwait Urbanisation*, Kuwait Planning Board, Kuwait, 1964, 15–39.
    (b) G. Marçais, 'L'urbanisme musulman', in *Mélanges d'histoire et d'archaéologie de l'occident musulman*, **1,** Gouvernement Géneral d'Algérie, Algiers, 1957, 219–231.
15. A. H. Hourani, 'The Islamic city in the light of recent research', in *The Islamic city*, (Ed. A. H. Hourani and S. M. Stern), Bruno Cassirer, Oxford, 1970, 9–24.
16. W. B. Fisher, *The Middle East*, 5th ed., Methuen, London, 1963, 132.
17. J. I. Clarke and B. D. Clark, *Kermānshāh: an Iranian Provincial city*. University of

Durham, Centre for Middle Eastern and Islamic Studies, Durham, 1969, 97–104, 127–134.

18. X. de Planhol, 'Geography of Settlement', in *Cambridge History of Iran ; The Land of Iran*, 1 (Ed. W. B. Fisher), Cambridge University Press, Cambridge 1968, 438–440.

19. J. I. Clarke, *The Iranian City of Shīrāz*, University of Durham, Department of Geography, Durham, 1963, 48–51.

20. E. E. Beaudouin and A. U. Pope, 'City Plans' in *A Survey of Persian art* (Ed. A. U. Pope), Oxford University Press, Oxford, 1939, 1398.

21. G. Marçais, 'L'urbanisme musulman', *Mélanges d'histoire et d'archéologie de l'occident musulman*, 1, Gouvernement Géneral d'Algérie, Algiers, 1957, 224–226.

22. O. Grabar, 'The Mosque', in *Middle Eastern Cities* (Ed. I. M. Lapidus), University of California, Berkeley and Los Angeles, 1969, 39.

23. I. M. Lapidus, 'Muslim cities and Islamic societies', in *Middle Eastern Cities* (Ed. I. M. Lapidus), University of California, Berkeley and Los Angeles, 1969, 49–50.

24. H. A. R. Gibb and H. Bowen, *Islamic Society and the West*, Royal Institute of International Affairs, Oxford University Press, London, 1950, 281–299.

25. N. Chechade, 'Aleppo', in *The New Metropolis in the Arab World* (Ed. M. Berger), Allied Publishers, New York, 1963, 89.

26. Table 6.1 was compiled from:
    (a) G. Hamdan, 'The pattern of medieval urbanism in the Arab world', *Geography*, **47**, 121–133 (1962).
    (b) C. Issawi, 'Economic change and urbanisation', in *Middle Eastern Cities* (Ed. I. M. Lapidus), University of California, Berkeley and Los Angeles, 1969, 102–121.
    (c) I. M. Lapidus, *Muslim Cities in the Later Middle Ages*, Harvard University Press, Cambridge, Mass. 1967, 79–87.
    (d) D. Noin, 'L'urbanisation du Maroc', *Information Géographique* **32**, 69–81 (1968).

27. J. H. G. Lebon, 'The site and modern development of Baghdād', *Bull. Soc. Géogr. Égypte*, **24**, 7–33 (1956).

28. C. Issawi, 'Economic change and urbanisation', in *Middle Eastern Cities* (Ed. I. M. Lapidus), University of California, Berkeley and Los Angeles, 1969, 106.

29. K. Baedeker, *Egypt and the Sudan*, 6th ed. Baedeker, Leipzig, 1908, 40.

30. C. Issawi, 'Economic change and urbanisation', in *Middle Eastern Cities* (Ed. I. M. Lapidus), University of California, Berkeley and Los Angeles, 1969, 105–106.

31. Z. Y. Hershlag, *Introduction to the Modern Economic History of the Middle East*, E. J. Brill, Leiden, 1964, 21.

32. 'Persia' *Encyclopaedia Britannica*, 10th ed., Edinburgh and London, 1902, 616.

33. S. Amin, *L'économie du Maghreb*, 1, Éditions de Minuit, Paris, 1966, 21–26.

34. Kingsley Davis, *World urbanisation 1950–70*, 1, Population Monograph Series No. 4, University of California, Berkeley and Los Angeles, 1969, 141–154.

35. H. Fullard, *Geographical Digest 1973*, George Philip, London, 1973, 16–26.

36. W. Fogg, 'The sūq: a study in the human geography of Morocco', *Geography*, **17**, 257–267 (1932).

37. E. Spiegal, *New Towns in Israel*, Praeger, Stuttgart and Bern, 1967.

38. J. Garrett, 'The site of Damascus', *Geography*, **21**, 283–296 (1936).

39. E. Efrat, 'The hinterland of the new city of Jerusalem and its economic significance', *Econ. Geogr.*, **40**, No. 3, 254–260 (1964).

40. G. H. Blake, *Misurata: a market town in Tripolitania*, University of Durham, Department of Geography, Durham, 1968, 1–34.

41. I. M. Lapidus, 'Muslim cities and Islamic societies,' in *Middle Eastern Cities* (Ed. I. M. Lapidus), University of California, Berkeley and Los Angeles, 1969, 60–64.

CHAPTER 7

Problems of Economic Development

7.1 Introduction

The position of the Middle East in the development spectrum is far from clear. Crude indicators (Table 7.1) suggest that only Israel might be termed a 'developed' country, while Jordan, Yemen A.R., and P.D.R. Yemen, for example, appear to be 'underdeveloped'. Kuwait possessed the world's highest per capita income in 1968, but the mere figure disguises the almost total

TABLE 7.1
Crude indices of economic development for the Middle East

Country	G.D.P. per capita Total 1968 (U.S. Dollars)	Average annual growth, 1960–68 (per cent)	Energy consumption Per capita 1970 kgs. of coal equivalent	Percentage change, 1967–70
Bahrain	—	—	9,623	+ 186·7
Egypt	196	4·3	268	+ 1·1
Iran	329	7·8	939	+ 108·2
Iraq	328	4·3	597	+ 7·0
Israel	1,474	7·1	2,278	− 0·4
Jordan	249	6·7	295	+ 9·1
Kuwait	4,933	0·1	9,764	− 10·2
Lebanon	524	4·6	719	+ 14·1
Libya	1,768	57·9	646	+ 35·7
Oman	—	—	46	+ 58·6
P.D.R. Yemen	—	—	449	+ 223·0
Qatar	—	—	1,873	+ 42·5
Saudi Arabia	458	11·0	965	+ 108·4
Syria	253	4·1	483	+ 25·8
Turkey	379	10·4	487	+ 15·4
Yemen, A.R.	—	—	13	+ 44·4
REGION	990	10·7(6·0)*	1,840	+ 54·3
CARIBBEAN & LATIN AMERICA	460	5·5	706	+ 15·2
AFRICA	180	4·8	312	+ 7·9
Sweden	3,412	10·5	6,311	+ 30·6
United Kingdom	1,834	4·5	5,362	+ 9·6
United States	4,300	6·6	11,144	+ 12·8

*without Libya.
Source: U.N. Statistical Yearbook, 1971, New York, 1972, Tables 137 and 186.

dependence of the economy on oil. Per capita income in Libya increased enormously during the 1960's, but the advances were rather abstract, since great efforts are still required to improve real living standards for the majority of the population and to diversify the economic base of the country. Incomes and energy consumption are still comparatively low in Turkey, yet considerable industrial progress over the last fifty years may have produced self-sustaining growth at last. Even Turkey and Israel, though, are a long way from the socio-economic position of the United States, Sweden or even the United Kingdom (Table 7.1). Other countries are further away still, despite, in some cases, high national earnings from petroleum, since these earnings are of comparatively recent origin.

Although the gap is still considerable between the countries of the Middle East and the developed nations of the world, rapid economic growth has been characteristic of Middle Eastern states since the end of the Second World War. Despite the problems of comparison,[1] the region progressed more rapidly than some other less-developed parts of the world, and most Middle Eastern countries are wealthy compared with African and Latin American countries[2] (Table 7.1). This achievement rests on foundations laid during the nineteenth century, when much of the Middle East was drawn firmly within the trading orbit of northwestern Europe as demands for food and raw materials grew. Considerable investment was made in the infrastructure during the otherwise largely stagnant period of the 1920's and 1930's,[3] and this paid dividends later. The Second World War marks something of a watershed, for it provided an important boost to local economies by its pressures for national self-sufficiency and import substitution. High prices created by the subsequent Korean War (1950–1953) helped to sustain growth. Political independence created important stimuli, while additional but localized advantages were realized from oil exploitation and the aid offered by great powers.

Favoured countries naturally wish to maintain their economic growth, while the more backward states of the region feel a need to increase their growth rates, to improve general living standards, as well as secure a greater measure of political independence and world influence. Improved living standards, however, depend upon a more equitable distribution of national wealth, while further economic growth, in many instances, can be achieved only by change in the structure of the economy, away from agriculture and towards more manufacturing industry. Structural changes are not easily secured, and the problems involved are the subject of this chapter. Some problems are peculiar to the Middle East, but many are shared with other developing regions of the world, albeit with a Middle Eastern flavour.

7.2 General problems of economic development

Economic development is promoted by a complex of interacting but poorly understood forces. Much depends upon the roles and relative importance of capital accumulation, past and present, and total factor productivity. Rates

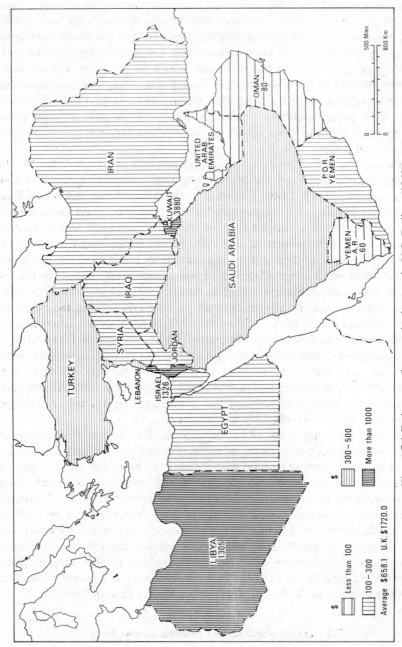

Figure 7.1 Estimates of per capita income in U.S. Dollars (1968)

of saving and investment are crucial, especially where incomes are low (Figure 7.1). Equally important are the choices of techniques and methods employed to achieve the goals. While the temptation is always to borrow answers from more developed countries, problems should be formulated with Middle Eastern conditions specifically in mind. The quality of administrators becomes vital here, as in the rest of the development process, especially since Middle Eastern states almost invariably feel forced to initiate, finance and control socio-economic change themselves. More basic elements in the development complex, though, are the role of agriculture, the influence of population growth, and the existence of regional inequalities.

7.2.1 Agriculture

Agriculture is of considerable importance in the economies of most Middle Eastern states, including the oil giants, Iran, Libya and Saudi Arabia, especially when petroleum earnings are removed from their national accounts (Table 4.1). Local farming produces much of the food consumed in the region, and generally employs the largest part of the labour force. In addition, agriculture provides much of the raw material for manufacturing industry and a great deal of locally-raised development capital. The export of agricultural products is an important source of foreign exchange.

The very dominance and fundamental importance of agriculture create a number of problems for economic development. Most important is the conse-quent dependence of many states upon an unstable and uncertain economic base. Both the growing season and the range of crops are limited by the concen-tration of precipitation into one season and the excessive evapotranspiration characteristic of the summer. For environmental and technological reasons, yields are generally low (Chapter 4), but in the dry-farming areas, which consti-tute the largest farming zone of the region, they also vary considerably from year to year according to the interannual variations in precipitation. Industrial supplies and exports are, therefore, uncertain and fluctuate greatly to the annoyance of the market. Since about 1950, the region's agriculture has not been able to meet demands made upon it for food, industrial raw material and foreign exchange. In fact, trade figures collected by the United Nations showed that Egypt, Iran, Jordan, Labanon, Libya, Saudi Arabia, Syria and P.D.R. Yemen imported considerably greater value of food and live animals during the late 1960's than they exported. Over the same period, however, Iraq and Turkey consistently exported more of these commodities than they imported, while the balance had tended to oscillate for Israel. Bowen-Jones, though, has spoken of the whole Middle East as a food deficit region.[4] At the beginning of the 1970's the region certainly seems more at the mercy of shortages than ever before, should the delicate balance of world trade be disrupted.

Several changes have brought the region to this situation. Population growth has been considerable (Chapter 5), and demand has consequently risen.

At the same time, easily reclaimed land is limited by aridity and, in any case, has been much reduced in the dry-farming zone after more than a hundred years of spatial advance in the farming frontier (Chapter 13). Land use has also changed in favour of high value industrial crops, such as cotton, and fruit and vegetable production, with the result that proportionately less land is devoted to the staple grains. Government investment in agriculture and closely allied activities has continued to be small, despite the basic importance of the sector and the low opportunity costs, which mean that relatively small investments can bring high returns. Some authorities, however, assert that fundamentally agriculture has failed to respond to the demands put upon it because of the retarding effects of 'traditional' socio-economic structures.[5]

Various measures are being taken to develop agriculture still further, but their appropriateness and effectiveness are often debatable. Production might still be raised in the dry-farming areas by ploughing up more land, but so little is now available that further horizontal expansion must largely depend, for example, upon the elimination of draft animals (and hence of pasture and land used for growing fodder) and greater use of tractors. The introduction of tractors has already meant that land is now in production which was once too distant from settlements to be cultivated.[6] Much of this is marginal in terms of precipitation, depth of soil and degree of slope. Any further expansion will be even more hazardous ecologically, and must depend, in any case, upon relatively high agricultural prices, if it is to be financially worthwhile. Cereal prices will inevitably remain above general world levels.

The introduction of crop rotation is another way of increasing production. By this means, wasteful fallow can be eliminated and soil fertility maintained. However, the rotation of crops requires a fundamental change in the entire system of land use. Boserup has argued[7] that land use is closely geared to population levels, and that a given system will change only when population growth reaches a level where there is no longer sufficient land available for the old system to provide basic subsistence at acceptable levels. According to this theory, crop rotation will expand greatly in the Middle East only when the existing system of fallowing and common grazing can no longer support the farming population and employ the labour available. As long as it is still possible to subsist using 'traditional' patterns of land use, there is no incentive to change. Indeed, Middle Eastern farmers often show considerable reluctance to adopt new systems, when the risks inherent to farming in the region are not clearly reduced and the rewards for increasing the drudgery of labour are not obvious.

Such reluctance has often been attributed to the inherent conservatism of 'traditional' socio-economic systems and often blamed specifically on Islam. This is based upon a number of misconceptions, largely stemming from a Euro-American viewpoint.[8] Too much emphasis has been given to the alien features of Islam and its allegedly all-embracing nature as a socio-economic system. Not enough allowance has been made for the elements of life which the Middle East shares with other developing regions. Most important has been a failure to appreciate the fundamental features of 'peasant economy' (Chapter 4). The peasant is not essentially a small-scale capitalist, and his activities are not geared to maximizing profit but to minimizing risk, so as to secure the subsistence needs of his family. He aims to employ all the labour at his disposal, rather than to maintain economic efficiency in a classic sense, while the pattern of work is closely related to the growing season and, accordingly, is characterized in the Middle East by short peaks of enormous activity and long troughs of unemployment. Until recently, economic and social life in the countryside has been dominated by the urban-based landlords, whose favoured position has often meant that they have been the chief beneficiaries of incentives to reclaim, irrigate or fertilize the land. 'Peasant economy' is more likely to change as the rural population grows and the economic structure of the country as a whole changes, rather than by government attempts to fight 'conservatism'. The forcing of socio-economic change on ideological grounds may be expensive and wasteful. This is especially true in countries where land reform has been urged as the basic solution to all rural problems. Land reform may be important in giving the peasant the opportunity to benefit fully from his family's labour, but much depends upon other things. The landlord must be satisfactorily replaced as director of agricultural operations, supplier of credit, protector and entrepreneur. Title to land must be secure, and payment for newly acquired land should not induce debt or new landlords will appear. Commodity prices must be adequate to mediate urban demands satisfactorily to the countryside and encourage new developments, while attention must be given to mechanisms of distribution. Failure to appreciate the difficulties involved in land reform led to agricultural dislocation and falling production in Iraq, to the retrenchment of landlords in Syria and the appearance of a new class of landlords in Iran (Chapters 12, 13 and 18). Lack of protection for the delicate balance in 'peasant economy' resulted in the emergence of landless labourers and a fall in living standards for people in the Çukorova of Turkey when new market forces and modern technology began to influence farming (Chapter 4).

Agricultural output can also be raised without structural change. For example, yields can be increased from existing farm land. Improved strains are more fruitful and more resistant to drought and salinity, but they are expensive to buy, sometimes unpopular to sell and may require greater attention. Greater applications of fertilizer are efficacious in raising yields, but possess similar disadvantages. Chemical fertilizers are expensive to obtain, largely because local production is inadequate and distribution poor, while successful application requires quite sophisticated knowledge on the part of the average farmer.

The extension of irrigation is a further solution to the problem, and it also has the advantage of combatting fluctuations in output due to interannual variations in precipitation. Cultivation can be a carried on all the year round, and a greater diversity of crops can be grown, as Egyptian experience with the extension of perennial irrigation over the last hundred years has shown

(Chapter 19), while arid land can be brought into production. However, silting up of reservoirs and canals is often rapid, and evaporation is high. Management is generally poor, so that much water is lost in transport and innundation. The general neglect of drainage may mean that land is poisoned by salination. Water-carried disease usually increases, undermining the health of the farming population at the very time that the new system requires greater labour inputs to control water, clear irrigation channels and maintain production on a year-round basis. Finally, the introduction of irrigation is relatively expensive, even when simple diesel pumps are used, but especially when spectacular engineering works are necessary. The high cost of irrigation projects virtually dictates that high value crops, for export or local industrial use, are grown instead of cereals. The result is that the vicious circle is not always broken, but often perpetuated.

A fundamental solution to the problem of dependence upon agriculture is offered by a change in the structure of the economy. Manufacturing and service industries have increased their roles since the Second World War,[9] and most states seek to advance them still further. It is often forgotten, however, that industrial development in the Middle East is still partially dependent upon the agricultural sector as a source of raw materials and investment, and that the market is still predominantly rural. Government stimulation of industrial development may even have detrimental affects upon agricultural progress in this situation, and consequently upon the pace of general economic development. Industrial development, and the work opportunities created, either directly or indirectly, are important factors in the drift of people from the countryside to the towns (Chapters 5 and 6). This has been regarded as perhaps inevitable, because of the differences in incomes and living standards, as well as what was thought until recently to be widespread underemployment in rural areas.[10] Removal of labour from the countryside, however, may have hitherto unsuspected results, and the dislocation of agriculture in Iraq following massive emigration to the towns, consequent upon land reform,[11] is simply an extreme case of a more widespread phenomenon. The new developments in farming outlined above, demand more labour, not less. Mechanization is proceeding, but this too may require more human effort, because more land can now be cultivated, more attention may be necessary depending on the crop and a larger harvest has to be reaped, threshed and carried. It might also be argued that the drain of people from the countryside is reducing the pressure for structural change in land use, and thereby retarding the very processes of intensification which governments are seeking to promote. Population, in various ways, begins to look very much the key factor in economic development.

7.2.2 Population

Although the total population of the Middle East is still comparatively small (149 million in 1972), it has been growing at an average rate of 2·8 per cent per annum, which is amongst the highest in the world (Chapter 5). This rate of growth is fairly recent, and, as Cooper and Alexander have pointed out, its economic significance is difficult to determine.[12]

Population increase appears to have been one of the engines of economic growth in the region.[13] There have been increasing numbers of people to feed, clothe and house, and a larger labour force available for employment. Mounting pressure on land in some districts has been instrumental in producing the kind of structural change in agriculture which the Boserup thesis would lead one to expect, though in others the necessary changes have failed to materialize and there is overpopulation. Migration contributes to the manpower needed for manufacturing and service industries; indeed, economic growth along the Gulf, for example, would have been difficult without it. Further, the youthfulness of the population, with its improving health and education, represents a considerable economic potential for the future. At the moment, though, a young population (40 per cent of the population under 15 years of age) means that a large proportion of the people is not economically active to any extent, even though child labour is still common, and, in a climate of modernization, requires considerable investment for its education. The high rate of population increase itself means that a considerable investment is necessary to maintain current living standards, let alone produce advances. However, structural changes in national economies may be expected to reduce crude birth rates, so that some of the problems associated with high rates of increase may be temporary.

Perhaps more serious is the rapid expansion of towns in this already comparatively urbanized region (Chapters 5 and 6). Much investment has to be put into maintaining the viability of towns—providing work, housing, transport and education, as well as maintaining public health and public order. Although this may promote general economic development in a state, the need to support the towns emphasizes two important development problems. One is the problem of increasing agricultural production, which has already been discussed. The other is the need for improving distribution. Improvements here are normally brought about by extending national road networks, but road building eats up capital in this region. Distances are often considerable, the terrain is difficult to surmount, even using modern engineering techniques, and large numbers of bridges and culverts are required to deal with seasonal floods, while many of the areas crossed generate little or no trade. But roads are not the only need. Marketing and storage facilities are often inadequate and need to be improved, though they receive proportionately less attention.

Despite these problems, some would see urban growth as forcing the economy along.[14] An opposite view is that rapid urban growth may be creating fundamental economic stresses, which may be more difficult to tackle than those so far discussed in this chapter. Immigration is an important element in urban growth, though its role can be exaggerated. Kinship networks appear to help the migratory and settling processes, but, because of the rate at which people are now moving to the larger towns, they may be weakening absorptive mechanisms found in 'traditional' urban communities. Rural attitudes are being maintained amongst the immigrants,[15] and the character of many larger towns appears to be changing. Dwyer has argued that this trend, observable throughout the developing world, could destroy the innovating role of the city, thereby retarding economic development.[16] The braking effect appears to be reinforced by the strongly primate character of city-size distributions in the Middle East, and the gap between the largest city and the rest of the hierarchy may now be too large to be effectively bridged.[17] The problem is compounded by the 'traditional' attractions of urban life, and the perpetuation of the service character of most towns. These mean that there is a tendency to neglect the economic development of the countryside, where agricultural change requires expert assistance. A further element is the possible retarding effects of releasing rural pressures by draining people to the towns. If the long term effects of rapid growth are somewhat speculative, there is no doubt that, in general, the larger towns are increasing in population and economic activity more rapidly than the smaller ones. They lie at the heart of comparatively developed, growing regions and the rest of the country lags behind.

7.2.3 Regional inequalities

Little work has so far been done on regional inequalities in the Middle East, but, in general, the growth regions appear to be those which already have the advantages of standing astride major routes, and possess physical conditions which support a flourishing agriculture. On rather subjective grounds, examples of such *core* areas appear to include the northwestern region of Turkey, the delta region of Egypt, the Aleppo-Damascus axis in Syria, and the capital city regions of practically all countries (Figure 7.2). The external economies achieved by continuing to locate new activity in these areas are very powerful, but the rest of the country appears to suffer when they are obeyed. Core areas not only draw upon the rest of the country for their food and raw materials, and thus assist regional growth; they also take a disproportionate share of infrastructural investment and drain the more backward regions of their manpower, especially its young, enterprising elements, as well as much of its wealth. Thus, the continued growth of the core may have a weakening effect upon the periphery, which seems to fall back, at least relatively.[18] Alonso argued that regional imbalance may be no more than an early phase in the development process, which will be followed by diffusion effects out towards the backward areas, leading to greater equalization of prosperity across national space.[19] In the short term, though, economic growth seems to be promoted at the expense of socio-economic equity. National aspirations may not be fully realized until greater equity has been achieved, in spatial as well as socio-political terms. Spread effects, so far, are not only weak, but are more important in promoting overall growth. The structural changes necessary to national economic development are not being achieved. Progress in the peripheral regions requires substantial government intervention

Educational opportunities have improved greatly in recent years (top): a roadside scribe giving reading lessons in the Doha sūq, (The Press Association Ltd.); (bottom): Bahrain secondary school in 1960 (Central Office of Information)

Middle East settlements have long suffered insecurity from natural and man-made causes (top): Nabatieh Camp for Palestine refugees in Lebanon, after Israeli attacks in May 1974, (UNRWA photograph by F. Samia); (bottom): earthquake damage at Gediz in Turkey (Turkish Embassy, London)

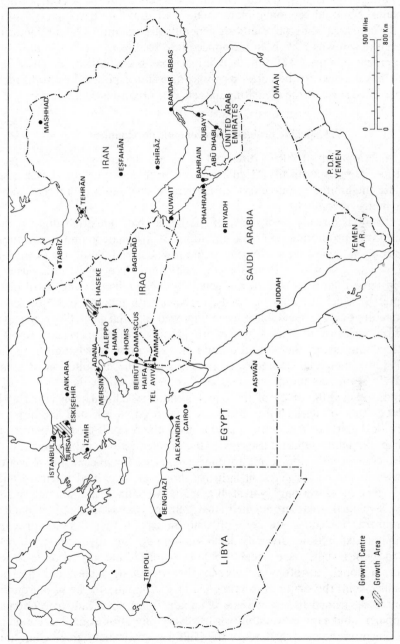

Figure 7.2 Growth Centres and areas in about 1970

in the economic process, and the injection of large amounts of capital if the disadvantages of distance, terrain, climate and resources are to be even partially overcome. National economic plans attempt to stimulate development away from the core areas, but the results are generally disappointing. Dams, factories and even new towns have been introduced into backward regions to promote development (Chapter 17), but their impact has been limited; much of the benefit has accrued to the cores, partly as a result of political centralization and partly because of the mediating influence of urban-based landlords.

7.3 Specific problems of economic development

The development problems discussed so far are shared by most developing countries. Three specifically Middle Eastern problems must be raised now. They are the limited resource base of the region, the use of oil revenues, and the existence of conflict.

Mention has already been made of the belief that industrialization is the best means of promoting economic development. Ultimately, industrialization depends upon the availability of power and raw materials. With the exception of oil, which, it should be remembered, is not found in every Middle Eastern state in large quantities, the region generally lacks minerals and fossil fuels (Chapter 8). Fuel and raw materials, together with manufactured or semi-manufactured components, have to be imported, but the costs throw a heavy strain on agricultural exports, which provide much of the necessary foreign exchange, and distort the pattern of land use. Attention is being given to the search for commercial quantities of minerals and the exploitation of comparatively scarce commodities, such as chrome, for which there is a world demand. Meanwhile, much of the region's industry remains concerned with the processing of agricultural products into food, drink and clothes for largely local markets. Agricultural land is, thus, the region's greatest industrial resource, though its efficient use creates the problems already discussed.

Petroleum exploitation seems to offer a panacea for ancient ills to many countries in the region. The oil industry, however, is capital intensive and directly generates little employment. It is spatially confined, and, though small, highly developed areas are created, they remain islands in a sea of under-development. Revenues are certainly enormous (Chapter 9), and provide the capital required to diversify local economies, but there are problems here, too. Oil revenues are a highly political subject, and any increase is the subject of tough negotiation between the producing states and the oil companies, with the major consuming countries looming in the background. The increases gained in recent years (Chapter 9) are important to economic development, but capital availability is not everything. For example, economic development in the oil-rich states of the Gulf was somewhat hampered at first by the shortage of raw materials, apart from oil, and a scarcity of labour; today, the economic structure is precariously balanced on imported goods and immigrant labour. The availability of oil and natural gas has encouraged the foundation of petrochemical industries, but their survival must depend upon successful competition for markets, even if these appear to be expanding at the moment (Chapter 11). Even when new industries have been established and ambitious programmes of social welfare have been launched, capital often remains available for investment abroad. There is no doubt that surplus funds from Arabia could be used for the general benefit of the Middle East, where a fundamental problem is shortage of capital. Kuwait, in particular, has realized the potential.[20] However, advance along these lines is dependent upon the relationships between states and the competing demands raised in the political arena.

A characteristic of the Middle East, particularly marked in recent years, though by no means new, has been the existence of conflict within and between states (Chapter 10). The existence of actual or potential conflict has a number of consequences for economic development. It is an important determinant of how resources, manpower and even national space are used. The geographical manifestations are particularly clear in the settlement and regional development schemes pursued in Israel, but they are also apparent elsewhere, for example in the continued existence of refugee camps, the navigational problems of the Shaṭṭ al'Arab and the emphasis in Dhufar placed on forts and airstrips rather than on roads or agricultural improvement. On occasions, conflict is deliberately used by politicians to direct attention away from development issues and to explain why commitments have not been fulfilled. The time lost, however, may be crucial, especially in dealing with such things as population growth.[21] Ordinary development capital, like tourists with their valuable foreign exchange, is discouraged. War has brought the loss of industrial plant (e.g. oil refineries at Suez), and economic assets such as the Suez Canal, or the agricultural land and tourist resorts of western Jordan.[22] People have been driven from their homes in large numbers, and become something of a political and economic liability to their hosts. Conflict also means that Middle Eastern states maintain large defence forces, and throughout the 1960's generally allocated increasing and sizeable proportions of their G.N.P.

TABLE 7.2
Defence expenditure as a percentage of G.N.P.

State	1965	1966	1967	1968	1969	1970	1971
Egypt	8·6	11·1	12·7	12·5	13·0	19·6	21·7
Iran	4·4	3·6	5·5	5·6	6·0	7·1	8·5
Iraq	10·2	10·5	10·3	9·1	9·6	9·4	6·5
Israel	11·7	12·2	13·8	15·4	24·1	26·5	23·9
Jordan	12·9	12·2	12·8	14·7	21·0	16·4	11·3
Saudi Arabia	8·6	12·1	11·9	8·9	8·8	9·4	8·9
Syria	8·4	11·1	11·9	12·1	11·6	12·1	9·8
Turkey	4·3	4·4	4·6	4·5	4·2	3·7	3·3

Source: International Institute for Strategic Studies, The Military Balance, London, 1973, pp. 71–72.

to military purposes, though decline was apparent in some cases from 1969 (Table 7.2). This drain on resources seems detrimental to general economic development. On the other hand, the existence of conflict may have distinct advantages. Unemployment is probably kept down to the currently estimated level of 5 to 10 per cent by this means, while military service provides many men with modern technical skills otherwise difficult to acquire. Capital is attracted to the region in an attempt to tip the political balance in favour of one bloc or the other, and this might not be available but for the possibilities inherent in a conflict situation. In a perverse sort of way, conflict even appears to facilitate economic development by providing a solvent, again through military service, for traditional prejudices and regional separatism, as well as acting as an acceptable explanation for otherwise unplatable development schemes.[23] It is not without significance that socio-economic change in the region, for good or ill, has often been initiated by soldiers, whether Turkish mercenaries during the early Middle Ages or Egyptian colonels in the 1950's.

7.4 Conclusion

Military and political dimensions serve to underline the complexity of economic development and the interdependency of contributary or retarding forces. Simplistic solutions to the problem of development are clearly inappropriate, especially when so little is really known about the existing socio-economic structures of the region. Change, if it is to be humane, requires greater knowledge, even of the constraints imposed by the physical environment. Development plans, which are important in ordering priorities and allocating investment, must be carefully conceived and flexibly implemented. In particular, the planners should be aware of the spatial dimension to economic development. Investment is applied in certain places, rather than others. The existence of growth areas is perhaps inevitable, but further growth in them increases regional imbalance. To some extent, then, economic growth and equality of regional development are incompatible, at least in the short run. Finally, attention should probably be given to indigenous forces of change and to domestic assets, such as population, rather than to the uncertain panaceas of imported solutions and investment. Peoples who have already created some of the world's great civilizations have the capacity, and ought to possess the nerve, to build a reasonable economic future for themselves.

References

1. S. Kuznets, 'Problems in comparing recent growth rates for developed and less developed countries', *Economic Development and Cultural Change*, **20**, 185–209 (1971–72).
2. P. George, R. Grigliolino, B. Kayser, and Y. Lacoste, (Eds.), *La Géographie Active*, Presses Universitaires de France, Paris, 1964, 82–83, 88, 90–92, 94.
3. C. Issawi, 'Growth and structural change in the Middle East', *Middle East Journal*, **25**, 309–324 (1971).

4. (a) United Nations, *Yearbook of International Trade Statistics, 1969*, New York, 1971.
(b) H. Bowen-Jones, 'Agriculture', in *The Middle East: A Handbook* (Ed. M. Adams), Anthony Blond, London, 1971, 415–426.
5. For example, on the role of Islam, Z. Y. Hershlag, *Introduction to the Modern Economic History of the Middle East*, E. J. Brill, Leiden, 1964, 23–24.
6. For example, W. Hütteroth, 'Getreidekonjunktur und jüngerer Siedlundsausbau im südlichen Inneranatolien', *Erdkunde*, **16**, 249–271 (1962).
7. E. Boserup, *The Conditions of Agricultural Growth: The Economics of Agrarian Change under Population Pressure*, George Allen and Unwin, London, 1965.
8. A. Abdel-Malek, 'Sociology and economic history: an essay on mediation', in *Studies in the Economic History of the Middle East*, (Ed.M.A.Cook), Oxford University Press, London, 1970, 268–282.
9. C. Issawi, 'Growth and structural change in the Middle East', *Middle East Journal*, **25**, 309–324 (1971).
10. C. A. Cooper and S. S. Alexander (Eds), *Economic Development and Population Growth in the Middle East*, American Elsevier Publishing Co., New York, 1972.
11. (a) F. Baali, 'Social factors in Iraqi rural-urban migration', *American Journal of Economics and Sociology*, **25**, 259–364 (1966).
(b) F. Baali, 'Agrarian reform in Iraq: some socio-economic aspects', *American Journal of Economics and Sociology*, **28**, 61–76 (1969).
12. C. A. Cooper and S. S. Alexander (Eds), *Economic Development and Population Growth in the Middle East*, American Elsevier Publishing Co., New York, 1972, 11.
13. C. Issawi, 'Growth and structural change in the Middle East', *Middle East Journal*, **25**, 309–324 (1971).
14. W. Alonso, 'Urban and regional imbalances in economic development', *Economic Development and Cultural Change*, **17**, 1–14 (1968–69).
15. P. J. Magnarella, 'From villagers to townsmen in Turkey', *Middle East Journal*, **24**, 229–240 (1970).
16. D. J. Dwyer, 'The city in the developing world and the example of South East Asia', *Geography*, **53**, 353–364 (1968).
17. J. I. Clarke, 'Population in movement', in *Studies in Human Geography* (Ed. M. Chisholm and B. Rogers), Heinemann, London, 1973, 85–124.
18. G. Myrdal, *Economic Theory and Undeveloped Regions*, Duckworth, London, 1957.
19. W. Alonso, 'Urban growth and regional imbalances in economic developments', *Economic Development and Cultural Change*, **17**, 1–14 (1968–69).
20. (a) R. el Mallakh, 'Kuwait's economic development and her foreign aid programmes', *World Today*, **22**, 13–22 (1966).
(b) J. O. Ronall, 'Banking developments in Kuwait', *Middle East Journal*, **24**, 87–90 (1970).
21. C. A. Cooper and S. S. Alexander (Eds.), *Economic Development and Population Growth in the Middle East*, American Elsevier Publishing Co., New York, 1972, 14.
22. E. Kanovsky, 'The economic aftermath of the Six Day War', *Middle East Journal*, **22**, 131–143, 278–296 (1968).
23. E. Kanovsky, 'The economic aftermath of the Six Day War', *Middle East Journal*, **22**, 131–143, 278–296 (1968).

CHAPTER 8

Industry and Trade

8.1 Industrial resources

The resource base of a country or region largely conditions its patterns of industry and trade. Raw materials often control the form of industrial activity, while surpluses and deficiencies dictate the commodities of trade. The location, size and wealth of markets are also important, together with the qualities of the population, the availability of energy and the degree of transport development. On a world scale, and with the exclusion of petroleum, the Middle East is poorly endowed with resources, and this single fact goes far to explain the region's continuing economic backwardness, despite sustained growth during the period since the Second World War.

The region's greatest single resource, with the current exception of petroleum, is its agricultural land. Agriculture not only produces many of the leading exports of the Middle East (Appendix), but also supplies raw materials to the region's manufacturing industry. Available statistics give an incomplete picture of the agricultural materials available for processing (Table 8.1), but they reveal the importance of cereals and cotton in terms of volume and regional availability. Sugar beet, olive oil, grapes and other crops are significant at a local level (in Aegean Turkey, for example), and often possess high value. The figures also show the concentration of production in the dry-farming zone of the region, as well as the relatively diverse agricultural base available for industrial development in Iran, Syria and Turkey. The arid zone, however, is not without its importance, as the output of Kufra (in Libya) and other oases indicate. Despite the figures in Table 8.1, nomadic herdsmen throughout this section of the Middle East contribute important quantities of wool, hides and skins to their national economies and to international trade (Appendix).

Although a wide range of minerals is found in the Middle East as a whole, including gold and silver, not all of them are now of commercial importance. Petroleum is undoubtedly the most important at the moment, and Chapter 9 described its extraction and use. Clays and building stones, as well as limestones suitable for cement making, are widespread. Salt is also produced in many localities, generally by evaporation (Table 8.1; Figure 8·1), and is important not only for seasoning food, but also for the manufacture of chemicals. Other minerals are more localized in occurrence. Phosphate rock is produced chiefly in the vicinity of the Dead Sea, in Israel and Jordan, though a large quantity is extracted in parts of upper Egypt accessible from the Red Sea or the Nile.

TABLE 8.1
Production of selected raw materials
(Note: Data are incomplete since returns not made by every country, e.g. wool.)

COUNTRY	BARLEY TOTAL[1]	BARLEY %[2]	COTTON LINT TOTAL[1]	COTTON LINT %[2]	RICE TOTAL[1]	RICE %[2]	TOBACCO TOTAL[1]	TOBACCO %[2]	WHEAT TOTAL[1]	WHEAT %[2]	WOOL TOTAL[1]	WOOL %[2]	COAL TOTAL[1]	COAL %[2]	IRON ORE TOTAL[1]	IRON ORE %[2]	CHROMITE TOTAL[1]	CHROMITE %[2]	COPPER ORE TOTAL[1]	COPPER ORE %[2]	LEAD ORE TOTAL[1]	LEAD ORE %[2]	MANGANESE ORE TOTAL[1]	MANGANESE ORE %[2]	ZINC ORE TOTAL[1]	ZINC ORE %[2]	SALT TOTAL[1]	SALT %[2]	PHOSPHATE ROCK TOTAL[1]	PHOSPHATE ROCK %[2]
													AGRICULTURAL PRODUCTS												MINERALS					
EGYPT	83	1·6	509	40	2605	61	—	—	1516	9	—	—	1323	—	227	12·1	—	—	—	—	—	—	1·8*	12·1	—	—	446	28·9	699	26·8
IRAN	880	16·8	160	12·6	1200	28·1	17	9·1	3800	22·6	20	24·4	—	6·6	2	0·1	145·1	33	12·0	26·4	23	83	8·4	56·4	22·5	48·7	368	23·9	—	—
IRAQ	691	13·2	14	1·1	204	4·8	15·6	8·4	1059	6·3	14	17·1	—	—	—	—	—	—	—	—	—	—	—	—	—	—	51	3·3	—	—
ISRAEL	14	0·3	35	2·7	—	—	1·6	0·8	125	0·7	—	—	—	—	—	—	—	—	11	24·2	—	—	—	—	—	—	66	4·2	1000	38·3
JORDAN	42	0·8	—	—	—	—	0·9	0·5	45	0·3	—	—	—	—	—	—	—	—	—	—	—	—	—	—	—	—	—	—	913	34·9
KUWAIT	—	—	—	—	—	—	—	—	—	—	—	—	—	—	—	—	—	—	—	—	—	—	—	—	—	—	4	0·5	—	—
LEBANON	—	—	—	—	—	—	7·2	3·8	50	0·3	—	—	—	—	—	—	—	—	—	—	—	—	—	—	—	—	27	1·8	—	—
LIBYA	—	—	—	—	—	—	—	—	—	—	—	—	—	—	—	—	—	—	—	—	—	—	—	—	—	—	11	0·6	—	—
SAUDI ARABIA	34	0·6	—	—	3	0·1	—	—	150	0·9	—	—	—	—	—	—	—	—	—	—	—	—	—	—	—	—	88	5·6	—	—
P.D.R. YEMEN	—	—	5	0·4	1	·02	6·7	3·6	—	—	—	—	—	—	—	—	—	—	—	—	—	—	—	—	—	—	—	—	—	—
SYRIA	235	4·5	149	11·7	255	5·9	—	—	—	—	—	—	—	—	—	—	—	—	—	—	—	—	—	—	—	—	46	3	—	—
TURKEY	3250	62·1	400	31·4	—	—	137·6	73·7	10081	59·8	48	58·5	4573	93·4	1654	87·8	294·9	67	22·4	49·4	4·7	17	4·7	31·5	23·7	51·3	435	28	—	—
YEMEN, A.R.	—	—	—	—	—	—	—	—	15	·09	—	—	—	—	—	—	—	—	—	—	—	—	—	—	—	—	—	—	—	—
REGIONAL TOTAL	5229	100	1272	100	4268	100	186·6	100	16841	100	82	100	4896	100	1883	100	440	100	45·4	100	27·7	100	14·9	100	46·2	100	1542	100	2612	100

Source: United Nations, *Statistical Yearbook 1971*, New York, 1972.
*cf. 82 in 1964, the peak before June War of 1967 in which Egypt lost Sinai.
(1) Thousands of tonnes.
(2) Percentage of regional total.

240

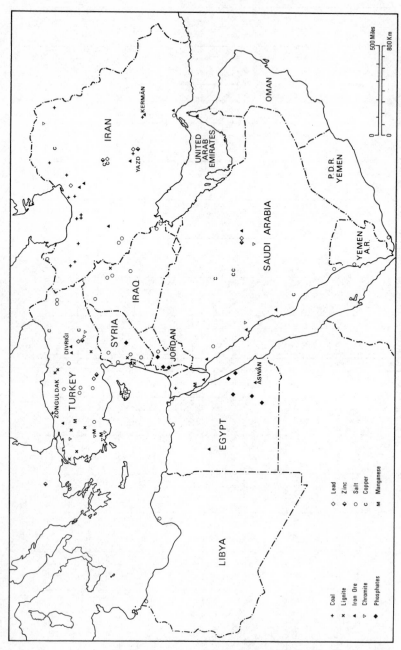

Figure 8.1 Major Minerals (except petroleum)

Metal ores, which are basic to a comprehensive industrial structure, are mainly associated with the fold mountains sweeping through Iran and Turkey, though a small concentration is also found in the gently folded area of central Arabia and some sizeable deposits are situated in Libya and Egypt (Figure 8.1). Access is a great problem everywhere, and much of the mining is on a very small scale. Chromite is widespread in the northern part of the region, and production from Iran and Turkey together formed 15·5 per cent of the world's output in 1970, making chrome the region's second most important mineral in world terms after petroleum. Deposits of other non-ferrous metals are more concentrated, with the Elâziğ (Turkey) and Yazd (Iran) districts as currently the most productive (Figure 8.1). Although iron ores are found in several parts of the Middle East, Iran and Turkey are the greatest producers (Table 8.1). Lignite is largely confined to Turkey, but poor quality coal is found not only there (in the Ereğeli–Zonguldak area) but also at various generally remote locations in Iran. Reserves are only about 0·03 per cent of the estimated total for the world. However, the variety of minerals and the scale of extraction mean that Iran and Turkey have the most diverse resource bases in the region. They are approached only by Egypt. The other countries of the region possess fewer minerals, and their industrial base lies in a range of agricultural produce; everything else required has to be imported.

Energy is important to modern industrial activity. Waterwheels and windmills (especially in eastern Iran) have been used for centuries to grind corn and lift water, but their power was little used for manufacturing purposes, mainly because of their dependence upon the seasons. When modern industrial development began, lack of coal was an important limitation on development in the region, and most of the fuel actually consumed down to the Second World War was imported. The situation has been transformed with the development of electricity generation. A relatively cheap and potentially ubiquitous form of power became available, and one which eased locational constraint for manufacturing industry, though the location of generators at first assisted an association with the larger towns. Electricity is now the most important source of power in the region. Production increased by 56 per cent between 1962 and 1970, from 16,500 million kWh to 37,589 million kWh (Table 8.2). The amount of increase, however, has varied considerably across the region. With the exception of Yemen, the greatest increases took place in the oil-rich states of Kuwait, Libya and Saudi Arabia, while the smallest changes (with the exception of P.D.R. Yemen) occurred in those countries already comparatively well endowed with generators before 1962. This pattern emphasizes two facts. First, it accents the low level of development and the limited industrial potential of the desert states before the petroleum era. At the same time, the pattern of increase stresses the importance of regional oil production in the generation of electricity. Oil provides the basic fuel in most countries and is a vital commodity in intraregional trade. Regional variations in fuel availability, however, are equally reflected in the dominant role still played by low-grade coal and lignite in the production of Turkey's

TABLE 8.2
Output of electricity (million kWh)
1962–1970

Country	Output 1962	Output 1970	Increase 1962–70 (per cent)	Per cent of regional output in 1970
Egypt	4,110	7,134	73·6	18·9
Iran	3,120	7,044	125·7	18·7
Iraq	995	2,115	112·6	5·6
Israel	2,936	6,838	132·9	18·2
Kuwait	414	2,213	434·5	5·9
Lebanon	551	1,230	123·2	3·3
Libya	93	426	358·1	1·1
P.D.R. Yemen	163	194	19·0	0·5
Saudi Arabia	55	770	1,300·0	2·0
Syria	502	947	88·6	2·5
Turkey	3,560	8,616	142·0	22·9
Yemen, A. R.	1·2	6·2	416·7	0·2
TOTAL	16500·2	37589·2	56·0	100·0

Source: United Nations, Statistical Yearbook, 1971, New York, 1972, Table 139.

electricity. Hydro-electric power is well developed in Turkey (35 per cent of the total output for 1970) and Egypt (56 per cent of the total output for 1970), where again there are distinct natural advantages, but many of the dams now being constructed throughout the region have electricity generation as one of their prime purposes. The greatest potential obviously lies where precipitation is high and where there is a reasonable flow all the year round, that is, chiefly in the northern countries of the region. At the moment, the greatest amounts of electricity potentially available to manufacturing industry are in Turkey (22·9 per cent of the regional total in 1970), Egypt, Iran and Israel (each with 18·0 per cent of the regional total in 1970). Libya, Saudi Arabia and the two Yemeni states have the least energy available, though Libya and Saudi Arabia may be expected to make up this deficiency.

A similar dichotomy to that in energy availability is found in manpower resources. Largely because of the origin of its people, Israel is fortunate in possessing a concentration of highly skilled people. Turkey, Egypt and Iran have the largest populations in the region (Chapter 5) and potentially the largest number of industrial workers. The other countries have considerably smaller populations and, to that extent, lower potential. In all populations, however, illiteracy is still considerable, while technical skills are limited. Industrial employment is thus curtailed. At the same time, the types of industry which can be developed are restricted and the methods of production tend to be cheap and simple. The number of potential industrial workers is reduced still further by the current youthfulness of the population (Chapter 5), 'traditional' social pressures against women working outside the home or the fields, the recent burgeoning of the service sector consequent upon the expansion of the socio-economic role of governments, and the continued dominance of agriculture, which will shed labour only as farming structures change.

The relative poverty of the great mass of the Middle East's population also influences industrial development. Except where oil royalties are available, capital for investment in industry is relatively scarce. Since capital cannot readily be raised at home, it is sought abroad, either as foreign aid or by selling those very raw materials which Middle Eastern countries require for their own industries. Generally low purchasing power, even where national populations are large, tends to limit the division of labour characteristic of modern industrial economies, as well as effectively reducing the size of the market.

In fact, the number of workers in extractive and manufacturing industries is quite small (Table 8.3). Again, important intraregional differences emerge. Egypt, Iran and Turkey have the largest shares of the region's industrial population, while the gap between them and the other countries is considerable. However, about 10 per cent of the active population of the larger states is employed in industry. Israel (25 per cent) and Iran (17 per cent) have greater proportions than that, while Iraq, P.D.R. Yemen and Yemen A.R. have considerably smaller ones, reflecting the relatively poor development of their economies, though the reasons are partly related to political events rather than to resource endowment alone.

TABLE 8.3
Industrial employment

Country	Mining and quarrying about 1969		Manufacturing, 1968 to 1969		Percentage of active population in industry	
	Numbers ('000)	Percentage of regional total	Numbers ('000)	Percentage of regional total	Year	Percentage
Egypt	16·8	38·5	551·3	26·2	1965	10·0
Iran	—	—	684·6	32·6	1966	17·0
Iraq	0·7	1·6	74·6	3·6	1963	5·0
Israel	4·1	9·4	201·8	9·6	1967	25·0
Jordan	4·9	11·2	32·8	1·6	1961	10·7
Lebanon	—	—	—	—	1961	10·0
Libya	6·4	14·7	7·0	0·3	—	—
P.D.R. Yemen	—	—	—	—	1965	3·0
Syria	3·0	6·9	103·2	4·9	1966	11·0
Turkey	7·7	17·7	445·0	21·2	1965	9·0
TOTAL	112·9	100·0	2100·3	100·0	—	100·0

Source: United Nations, Statistical Yearbook, 1971, New York, 1972, Tables 49 and 77. M. Adams (Ed.), The Middle East: A Handbook, Anthony Blond, London, 1971, p. 5.

8.2 Manufacturing industry

Craft industries have made use of the region's resources for many centuries, but a diversity of trades[1] was particularly well developed in Turkey, Syria and Iran, where the resource endowment was relatively great and the population comparatively large. Traditional crafts still survive,[2] especially in certain metal trades (coppersmithing, for example), while carpet-making in Iran has steadily increased following a revival of European interest in oriental carpets which began towards the end of the nineteenth century. Competition from European goods, which were not only cheaper but also given preferential treatment under capitulatory systems, brought about a change in fashion, then weakened and ultimately destroyed much of the Middle East's craft industry during the late eighteenth and early nineteenth centuries, even in textiles where the region possessed the advantage of producing raw cotton and silk and had earlier exported finished cloth to Europe. Decline was never complete, while Persia seems to have fared better than the Ottoman Empire. Attempts were also made to resist the decay. In western Asia Minor and in Egypt new industries were established during the nineteenth century along western lines, using mechanical power and based upon machines collected into factories. The experiments were not particularly successful in the face of foreign competition and foreign control of the economy.[3] Sustained industrial development was initiated between the two World Wars, but the great advance has taken place only since the Second World War.

During the 1960's industrial production increased markedly in all the countries for which data are available (Figure 8.2). The pattern of advance, however, varied. The greater achievements registered by Iran and Turkey were a reflection of their diversified resource base and higher potential for industrial development, but owed much to the expansion of agriculture and rural incomes during the decade (Chapters 17 and 18). Jordan's achievement was largely the combined result of increased mining and construction activity, on the one hand, and the relatively low level of industrial development in the base year, on the other (Chapter 15). The upsurge in Saudi Arabia's manufacturing industry can be at least partially attributed to the very low threshold of industrial development at the beginning of the period, but the major explanation was the comparatively recent date at which massive investment of oil revenues in local industry actually began (Chapter 11). The relatively poor performances of Egypt, Iraq and Syria during the 1960's are not so much the result of limited resources as the product of politico-economic policies which caused considerable internal dislocation.

A common temporal pattern of sectorial development can be discerned within the general pattern of growth,[4] though the detailed experience of each country has varied according to its resource endowment and its political evolution. The first stage of industrialization involved the extraction of minerals and the processing of agricultural products, chiefly for export. It began in Egypt and other parts of the Ottoman Empire during the nineteenth century, but

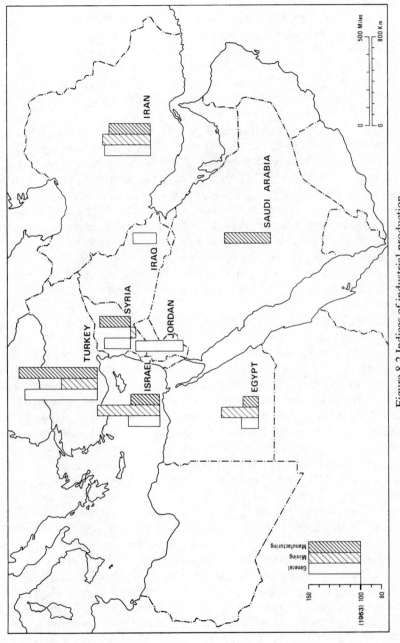

Figure 8.2 Indices of industrial production

was not experienced by Iran until the beginning of the twentieth century,[5] and then only in petroleum. Important advances had to wait until the 1930's or even the 1950's or 1960's. Iraq, though part of the Ottoman Empire until the First World War, contained very few modern industrial plants by 1900,[6] but experienced two forward surges, one in the 1930's and another in the 1950's. Both were associated with the exploitation of petroleum and stimulated by political changes in the country. Industrialization in Arabia was effectively delayed by the almost total lack of resources and investment capital until the 1960's, or even 1970's in the case of Oman.

Amongst the earliest developments in the region were cotton ginning in Egypt (about 1821), the application of steampower to silk winding at Bursa (1845), the use of steam engines in milling and olive crushing in many places within reach of the sea, and the mining of chromite in Asia Minor. Expansion and spread of new techniques and modern machines went hand-in-hand with the expansion of cash cropping in many districts, so that, for example, mechanized cotton ginning was not taken up in Syria until the second cotton boom after the Second World War (Chapter 13). However, the most rapid, as well as the largest developments have taken place over the last 25 years with the expansion of petroleum exploitation. Although much of the region's oil is still shipped as crude, refineries and associated petrochemical industries have been established in several places, with a notable concentration on the Arabian side of the Gulf, where the oil fields lie (Chapter 9).

It is probably true to say that the industrial structure of all Middle Eastern countries has now moved beyond the first stage of development. The south Arabian states are perhaps still closest to it, since industrial development has been very limited (Chapter 11). Most states have reached at least the second stage of industrialization, while retaining aspects of the first phase which are basic to the viability of the entire industrial structure. The second stage may be described as one in which local raw materials are transformed into goods for the domestic market. It is associated with political independence and growth in national and per capita incomes, which produce an expanding domestic market. Manufacturing plants are normally small because risk capital is scarce, due to attractive alternatives in a developing agricultural sector and in construction, and it often has to be raised from the family or in the shape of short-term, high-interest bank loans. The state is not greatly involved at this stage, other than to provide tariff protection against imports, as for example in Egypt after 1930 when duties of up to 30 per cent *ad valorem* were applied to imported manufactured goods.[6] Most states received some benefit from the self-sufficiency enforced by the Second World War and the availability of allied expertise. Local industry was virtually free from external competition, and use had to be made of local materials (the coordinating role of the Middle East Supply Centre was important here).[7] Allied forces not only had to be supplied, but also provided a large pool of additional purchasing power, especially in Egypt where, at its peak, Allied expenditure formed 25 per cent of the national income.[8]

Food processing, including flour miling, is characteristic of the second stage of development. It is largely free from foreign competition because of its perishable raw materials, while demand is strong and generally rising. The production of beverages, such as soft drinks and beer, is an associated development, together with the manufacture of the necessary bottles and glasses. Cigarette making and textile production are normally early developments, either because raw materials are locally available (cotton, for example) or are of such relatively high value that transport costs form a small proportion of the total costs, as in the case of the tobacco imported into Egypt for cigarette making before the First World War. Increasing populations mean that there is an expanding demand for clothing, while rising living standards, as well as Middle Eastern traditions of hospitality, are expressed in an increased consumption of cigarettes. In addition, textile and cigarette making involve technically simple operations, and are relatively easy to man with semi-skilled labour. Difficulties are experienced in all of these lines of development by several states in the Arabian peninsula where the volume and variety of agricultural production are limited by shortage of water. In consequence, imported raw materials are essential, as in the case of flour milling in Kuwait, and even simple industrial activity is possible only because of the large amounts of capital available.

Rising incomes, political independence and industrial and commercial development give rise to an expansion in construction. Transport costs relative to bulk and value make local manufacture of the necessary materials profitable, especially since limestones are available for making cement-based products, while clays can often be found which are suitable for fired bricks. Cement making and associated industries are widespread today. Nails, rivets and pipes are usually worth making in workshops dependent upon local scrap, imported ores, or, in favoured countries, indigenous ores. In this connection, it is interesting to note that Egypt's iron and steel industry was founded in the late 1940's on scrap from the battlefields of the Western Desert, though it soon became more firmly based on local ores. Libya is now following the Egyptian example. The use of motor vehicles and diesel pumps has created an extensive and flourishing repair industry, while agricultural improvements have led to the manufacture of simple steel ploughs and other agricultural implements in many market towns.

Thus, the second stage of industrial development is characterized by a diversity of light industries. This stage was possibly reached by Turkey before the outbreak of the First World War, and was certainly well established by 1939 (Chapter 17). Egypt had moved into the same position by the outbreak of the Second World War, and the existing patterns of industry were strengthened after the Revolution of 1952. The other states of the region, however, lagged behind. Iran, Iraq, Israel, Jordan and Syria may be said to have reached the second stage of development during the 1950's, while Libya and the oil-rich states of the Gulf attained it during the following decade and are consolidating their new position at the start of the 1970's.

Development into the third stage of industrialization has been dependent upon a definite and marked intervention by the state in economic affairs. State involvement is not new, but practically everywhere in the region its scale and nature are now massive.[9] The aims are rapid, soundly-based industrialization, further diversification of the industrial sector and, by a restructuring of the economy, the improvement of living standards for the mass of the population. State intervention became necessary, regardless of ideology and political regime, because these desirable goals were not being achieved under a private entrepreneurial system. Only governments have the will and power to raise the necessary capital at home or abroad and to ensure the required patterns of investment. Protective measures are still continued, and imports of machinery and equipment are often subsidized, but some new devices have been adopted since the Second World War. Nationalization of much private and foreign industry has been carried out in the extreme socialist countries, beginning with Egypt from 1956, so that the benefits would accrue to the people. Various approaches have also been adopted for starting new and desired industrial activities. State companies have been set up in several countries, starting with republican Turkey during the difficult years of the 1930's (Chapter 4), but spreading to monarchical Saudi Arabia in 1962, when Petromin was established with the general responsibility for sponsoring industrial development (Chapter 11). Joint ventures with foreign firms have become increasingly common, since they appear to be successful in providing foreign expertise and technical training, as well as in establishing new lines of activity. But whatever the devices adopted, and regardless of the ideology of the political regime, practically all Middle Eastern states now make use of economic development plans to structure and allocate investment in favour of industry. The plans vary greatly in scope, sophistication, realism and effectiveness, but the type of investment goals can be illustrated with examples from Egypt, Turkey and Saudi Arabia. Egypt's first Five Year Plan (1960 to 1965) estimated that 33·7 per cent of the total investment would be allocated to industry, compared with perhaps 12 per cent under private enterprise. In Turkey's first post-war Five Year Plan (1963 to 1967), 16·9 per cent of the investment from both public and private sources was scheduled for manufacturing industry, though in the event it received 19·1 per cent of the total. At the time Saudi Arabia's Development Plan was launched in 1966/67, government allocations to industry were 0·3 per cent of the total, compared with 1·8 per cent allocated to agriculture and 4·7 per cent to the private treasury.[10]

State intervention has produced three lines of development.[11] Established food processing, textile manufacturing and construction goods industries have continued to be promoted everywhere. The degree of skill required is usually small, while markets and raw materials are available, either from local resources or through imports. Simple consumer goods, like soap, sugar and footwear, are also produced. At the same time, a second line of development has been followed, especially by the more industrialized countries, Egypt, Iran and Turkey. This has been the extension of import substitution to a range of high value consumer durables which are demanded by the increasing numbers of affluent townsmen. Although imported components are used to assemble such things as radios, television sets, refrigerators, washing machines and motor vehicles, local parts are increasingly being used. This is the case, for example, with car assembly in Iran, where only the engine and steering gear were being imported by 1967.[12] Pharmaceuticals are another large and expanding field where import substitution has advanced markedly.

The third line of development which is being actively pursued is the creation of basic heavy industry. Although plants producing industrial chemicals have been established, the production of iron and steel has been particularly pressed as providing the basis for a whole range of metal industries, where demand is expanding, and as being, it is thought, the surest way to transform the economy. Turkey was the leader in this field and began the establishment of the Karabük complex during the 1930's (Chapter 17), using her own coal and iron ore. No other country followed her lead until after the Second World War, partly because they lacked the essential raw materials and partly because the vast capital expenditure involved was prohibitive to private enterprise. Only the state has been able to make the necessary provision, and then usually with foreign help. Iran is the only other country where a full-scale iron and steel industry can rest upon local resources, but development was comparatively late (1966), since the state put emphasis on infrastructure provision. Elsewhere the establishment of smelters and rolling mills seems less soundly based. Some of the raw materials have to be imported, even to the plants at Helwân in Egypt and Jiddah in Saudi Arabia where at least iron ore is available. In the case of Jiddah, local ores are not yet being mined, while in Egypt ore is 800 kms away, near Aswân. Lebanon's smelters are almost entirely dependent upon scrap. The smelter at Acre, in Israel, is dependent upon imported materials, but demand from a sophisticated and diversified economy with access to large amounts of external capital is perhaps sufficient to justify this expensive development.

Egypt, Iran, Lebanon, Syria, Turkey and Israel dominate the industrial patterns of the region. The contribution of manufacturing industry to G.D.P. in these states is now more than 15 per cent of the total (Table 8.4), while the 16 indicators tabulated for 11 states (Table 8.5) show a division into two groups. Egypt, Iran, Israel and Turkey have a diversified industrial structure combined food processing, textile manufacture, fertiliser and chemical production, cement making and associated developments and vehicle assembly. The manufacture of iron and steel is well established. The structure of the other group of leading industrial countries (Lebanon and Syria) is dominated by simple transformation, mainly involving food, beverages, cigarettes and construction materials. Iraq, Jordan and Saudi Arabia have similar structures, but their manufacturing industries contribute less than 10 per cent to G.D.P. The least industrialized countries in 1969 were Libya and Oman. Even though these economies are dominated by oil production and capital is abundant,

TABLE 8.4

Contribution of manufacturing industry
to G.D.P. 1969 (per cent)

Egypt	20
Iran	32
Iraq	9
Israel	22
Jordan	9
Kuwait	4
Lebanon	15
Libya	2
Saudi Arabia	8
Syria	18
Turkey	15
U.K.	30

Source: United Nations, *Statistical Year-book, 1971*, New York, 1972, Table 181.

industrialization has not progressed very far, partly because of a late start, and the contribution of non-petroleum based industry to G.D.P. is less than five per cent. There is scarcely any industry at all in P.D.R. Yemen, Yemen A.R. and most of the United Arab Emirates, although these states do not appear in Tables 8.4 and 8.5.

Scarcity of capital and the low purchasing power of the local market largely explain the present size structure of manufacturing concerns in the region. Most manufacturing units are small, employing fewer than 50 people each, though a few really large plants generally account for most of the production. Size of employment varies according to the type of industry and the circumstances in which it was established. Sugar refining, petrochemicals and cement making are generally recent introductions and use modern techniques in large, purpose-built plants, but consequently, employ relatively few workers. Textile firms vary more widely in equipment and number of workers employed. Large state-sponsored units, as a Tanta in Egypt and Aleppo in Syria, have thousands of employees, but everywhere small and medium-sized units, founded by private enterprise and using second-hand machinery, are common. Metal working and engineering are generally dominated by workshop units in a spectrum merging into large assembly plants, at one end, and single-man booths in the bazaar, at the other. In all industries vertical integration is widespread, particularly in the larger firms, and all stages of production may be carried out on the same site. This is an indication of the low level of industrial development in the region. Competition for production factors, which are normally scarce, and for control of the generally limited home market have similarly ensured that horizontal linkage is well developed.

Horizontal linkage is part of the explanation for the concentration of industry in relatively few centres, chiefly the larger cities. Most of the industries also require locations near the markets, especially since transport is often inade-

TABLE 8.5
Production in selected manufacturing industries, c 1970 (Some figures are for 1968 and 1969)

COUNTRY	WHEATFLOUR		SUGAR		BEER		CIGARETTES		COTTON YARN		WOOLLEN YARN		SULPHURIC ACID		HYDROCHLORIC ACID		CAUSTIC SODA		NITROGENOUS FERTILISERS		COKE		CEMENT		PIG IRON and FERROUS ALLOYS		CRUDE STEEL		CARS[5]		COMMERCIAL VEHICLES	
	TOTAL[1]	%[2]	TOTAL[1]	%[2]	TOTAL[3]	%[2]	TOTAL[4]	%[2]	TOTAL[1]	%[2]	TOTAL[1]	%[2]	TOTAL[1]	%[2]	TOTAL[1]	%[2]	TOTAL[1]	%[2]	TOTAL[1]	%[2]	TOTAL[1]	%[2]	TOTAL[1]	%[2]	TOTAL[1]	%[2]	TOTAL[1]	%[2]	TOTAL[6]	%[2]	TOTAL[5]	%[2]
EGYPT	1093[a]	9·5	495	27·7	243	16·9	12137	15·8	164·5	50·8	10·5	26·1	298	56·3	2·6	17·1	20	42·5	109	2·9	355	18·6	3694	20·1	454	30·5	227	63·4	2·3	5·9	1·8	4·9
IRAN	1944	16·9	560	31·5	258[b]	17·9	11898	15·4	71·5	22·1	24·6	61·2	—	—	9·2[b]	60·5	7	14·9	282	7·6	21[b]	1·1	2577	14	—	—	—	—	28	71·8	9·3	25·5
IRAQ	570[b]	4·9	15	0·8	68[b]	4·7	4917	6·4	0·9[b]	0·3	0·3[b]	0·7	—	—	—	—	—	—	—	—	—	—	1381[b]	7·5	—	—	—	—	—	—	—	—
ISRAEL	6580[a]	57·4	29	1·6	324	22·5	3868	5·0	20·2	6·2	—	—	203	38·4	—	—	16	34·1	269	7·3	—	—	1384	7·5	—	—	110[b]	30·7	4·8	12·3	6·3	17·3
JORDAN	—	—	—	—	15	1·1	1610	2·1	—	—	—	—	—	—	—	—	—	—	—	—	—	—	—	—	—	—	—	—	—	—	—	—
KUWAIT	69	0·7	—	—	—	—	—	—	—	—	—	—	—	—	—	—	—	—	856	23·2	—	—	—	—	—	—	—	—	—	—	—	—
LEBANON	173	1·6	13	0·7	—	—	1281	1·7	—	—	—	—	—	—	—	—	—	—	14	3·8	—	—	1339	7·3	—	—	—	—	—	—	—	—
LIBYA	35	0·4	—	—	53[b]	3·7	1575	2	—	—	—	—	—	—	—	—	—	—	—	—	—	—	—	—	—	—	—	—	—	—	—	—
SAUDI ARABIA	—	—	—	—	—	—	—	—	—	—	—	—	—	—	—	—	—	—	—	—	—	—	675	3·8	—	—	—	—	—	—	—	—
SYRIA	—	—	30	1·7	31	2·2	2429	3·1	20	6·2	1·7	4·2	—	—	—	—	4	8·5	23	6·2	—	—	964	5·2	—	—	—	—	—	—	—	—
TURKEY	990[b]	8·6	643	36	445	31	37253	48·4	46·8*	14·4	3·1*	7·7	28	5·3	3·4	22·4	—	—	82	22·2	1531	80·3	6374	34·7	1034	69·5	21[a]	5·8	3·9	10	19·1	52·3
TOTAL	11454	100	1785	100	1437	100	76968	100	323·9	100	40·2·0	100	529	100	15·2	100	47	100	3687	100	1907	100	18388	100	1488	100	358	100	39	100	36·5	100

1. Thousands of tonnes
2. Percentage of the regional total
3. Thousand hectolitres
4. Millions of cigarettes
5. Assembly
6. Thousands of units

a Figures for 1968
b Figures for 1969

Source: United Nations Statistical Yearbook 1971, New York, 1972.
*Production from state factories only
(Total output of woollen yarn in 1968 was 28·2 tonnes)

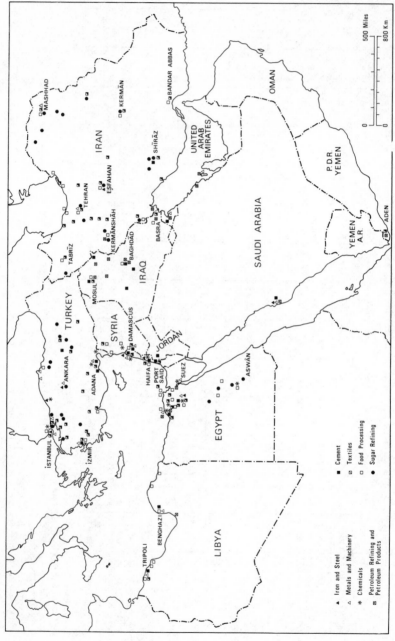

Figure 8.3 Major types of manufacturing industry in about 1970

quate. In addition, factories require labour and access to such public utilities as clean water and electricity which, until recently, were confined to the larger centres of population. Major concentrations of industry on a regional scale are shown in Figure 8.3. They include the inland capitals of Tehrān, Baghdād, Damascus and Cairo, with their large and wealthy markets, as well as the major ports, such as Beirūt, Haifa, Alexandria and İzmir, where imports arrive and primary products are processed. Other concentrations exist in major provincial towns, like Eṣfahān, Mosul and Eskişehir, which are situated in the more productive agricultural areas of the region and frequently close to important minerals. Small towns often contain a group of workshops, but, if their employment structure contains any significant degree of industrial work, it is usually provided by a single, comparatively large plant where local raw materials are processed or transformed. In such a case, the market seems to be essentially provincial, rather than national. It is the larger units, generally situated in the major cities, which appear to contribute most to internal, as well as international trade.

8.3 Foreign trade

'Trade is the acid test of industrialization.'[13] By this test, the Middle East is scarcely industrialized at all. With the partial exception of petroleum, the Appendix shows the items traded in 1970 by ten countries in the region. The export figures reveal that only Israel exported a considerable and diversified quantity of industrial products, though polished diamonds were by far the most valuable item (43·0 per cent of all exports). Lebanon appeared to come second as an industrial country, but this is misleading. Although she did export some of her own manufactured goods, textiles especially, the other manufactured items listed in her trade figures were mainly goods in transit. Lebanon's major exports were, in fact, fruit and vegetables. Egypt's exports of cotton yarn (12·9 per cent) and cotton piece goods (4·8 per cent) earned her, not Lebanon, the position of the region's second industrial country. Iran, where carpets formed 31·8 per cent of her non-petroleum exports by value, ranked third. However, exports of raw cotton and other agricultural products were collectively more valuable than the export of industrial goods from these countries. Even Turkey's exports were still largely agricultural (cotton, fruit and nuts, and tobacco together formed 79·6 per cent of all exports by value), despite the country's considerable industrial developments. Jordan and Syria exported some manufactured goods, but were mainly suppliers of primary products. Apart from petroleum and a small amount of cement, Iraq exported only agricultural produce, of which dates were still the most important (58·7 per cent). Libya and Saudi Arabia exported only petroleum, and mostly crude at that.

It is clear that primary products were the dominant exports from the region in 1970, as they had been in 1958,[14] and that agriculture and extraction are the most important sectors of the economy. Industrialization seems to have a

TABLE 8.6

Foreign trade as a percentage of
G.N.P., 1966

Country	Imports	Exports*
Egypt	21·1	11·9
Iran	14·5	20·4
Iraq	22·0	41·8
Israel	22·0	13·1
Jordan	36·3	7·0
Kuwait	27·2	77·6
Lebanon	43·8	10·7
Saudi Arabia	33·8	90·8
Syria	26·7	15·4
Turkey	7·7	5·2

*includes petroleum.
Source: L. E. Preston, *Trade Patterns in the Middle East*, (American Enterprise Institute for Public Policy Research, Washington, 1970), Table I–1.

long way to go before a diverse and valuable range of manufactured goods becomes dominant in the Middle East's exports. On the other hand, the pattern of imports (Appendix) indicates that the most valuable items brought into the region were industrial raw materials and machinery intended for equiping industry. Industrialization is obviously underway.

The pattern of imports in 1970 also revealed another important aspect of the Middle East's regional economy. Chapter 7 referred to the region as one of food deficit. This is spelt out in the value of food imports into the region. Food imports constituted between 18·0 (Egypt) and 31·9 (Saudi Arabia) per cent of all imports by value for the Arab countries surveyed. Iran, Israel and Turkey were in a more favourable position with food imports valued at less than 10 per cent of the total. The amount of food imported into the region varies from year to year according to weather conditions and the state of the harvest, but the region as a whole is always in competition with the major industrial powers for a share of the world's agricultural surplus.

All Middle Eastern countries are very dependent upon trade. A recent study has shown that imports contributed more than 20 per cent of G.N.P. during 1966 in seven out of the nine countries examined (Table 8.6).[15] Only in Iran and Turkey, with their diversified economies and high import tariffs, did imports contribute less than this, while the large figures for Kuwait and Saudi Arabia reflect their need to import practically everything consumed. Exports contributed more than 10 per cent to G.N.P. everywhere in 1966, except in Jordan and Turkey, but several of their main exports are of relatively low value. The dominant role of petroleum was responsible for the very high proportions of G.N.P. afforded by exports in Iran, Iraq, Kuwait and Saudi

Arabia. Petroleum exports were also responsible for the favourable balance of trade enjoyed by these countries and for the ability of the Middle East as a whole to maintain its position in world trade with about three per cent of all imports and four per cent of all exports in a situation increasingly unfavourable to less-developed countries. By contrast, the role of imports and exports in the G.N.P.'s of Lebanon and Syria is probably due to the mutual interdependence of these countries and their need to import considerable quantities of manufactured goods.

The pattern of trade for 1970 has been analysed by means of a matrix designed to show the extent of intraregional trade as well as the major trading partners (countries or blocs) outside the region (Table 8.7). The matrix was originally designed by Preston and Nashasnibi to examine trade patterns for 1958 and 1966.[17] As far as possible, the original form has been kept. The imports of a country are read vertically in the table and the exports horizontally. Thus, Turkey imported goods worth 67·5 million U.S. Dollars from the U.K. (column 1, row 16) out of a total of 558·6 million U.S. Dollars, but exported goods worth only 25·8 million U.S. Dollars to the U.K. (column 16, row 1) out of total exports worth 384·3 million U.S. Dollars. Although petroleum has been largely excluded from the analysis of the 1970 situation and is discussed in Chapter 9, the oil exports from Libya and Saudi Arabia are included partly because these states export little else and partly to illustrate the importance of petroleum exports to the regional economy. It is oil exports which keep the Middle East's trading balance comfortably in surplus, despite the poor performance of several countries, and reduced the proportion of imports in total regional trade for 1970 down to 46·4 per cent.

Trade patterns in 1970 were dominated by the extraregional component, which comprised 89·1 per cent of all imports and 90·6 per cent of all exports. The situation was not very different in 1966 or 1958, though the extraregional component was slightly larger.[17] Although this chiefly reflects the region's massive exports of petroleum, and is exemplified in Table 8.6 by Libya and Saudi Arabia, it also arises from the dominance of all primary products in exports and the leading roles of machinery and food in imports. The largest exporters were the oil states, and this was the position in 1966 and 1958, though the rank order changed. Egypt has been an important exporter, chiefly of cotton, since 1958 and indeed since the middle of the nineteenth century. Israel emerged as an important exporting state in the 1950's soon after foundation, and in Table 8.6 occupied third place in the regional ranking. She is the leading importer, since many of the raw materials required for her manufacturing industry cannot be produced within Israeli territory, but the high value of uncut diamonds is something of a distorting factor. Egypt used to import the greatest value of commodities, but though she remained dependent upon imports, especially of raw materials, machinery and food, she had fallen back to third place in the ranking by 1970. Iran and Saudi Arabia occupied first and second place respectively as importers. Both are industrializing rapidly and the necessary equipment is being imported in large quantities. Saudi Arabia

TABLE 8.7
Middle East trade matrix, 1970

	1 TURKEY	2 EGYPT	3 JORDAN	4 SYRIA	5 LEBANON	6 YEMEN A.R.	7 P.D.R. YEMEN	8 IRAN	9 IRAQ	10 LIBYA	11 SAUDI ARABIA	12 KUWAIT	13 *GULF STATES	14 ISRAEL	15 USA	16 UK	17 JAPAN	18 EEC	19 OTHER WEST EUROPE	20 LATIN AMERICA	21 AFRICA	22 ASIA	23 USSR	24 YUGOSLAVIA	25 OTHER EAST EUROPE	26 CHINA	27 OTHER	28 INTRA REGIONAL EXPORTS	29 TOTAL EXPORTS	30 28/29 AS %
1 TURKEY														3.7	42.0	25.8	14.9	189.7	34.8									14.0	364.3	3.8
2 EGYPT	6.8		5.9								4.0	1.4			6.8	15.5	26.5	66.1								19.3		34.2	668.0	5.1
3 JORDAN	1.0			4.2	5.0				3.4		7.7	2.8					12.6	24.0				0.7		2.3	0.8	0.6		24.1	28.3	85.1
4 SYRIA		7.9	7.9		16.6				7.3	16.8	1.0	3.1			8.7	0.8							15.7		3.8			35.9	106.9	33.6
5 LEBANON			13.3	17.9			1.8		7.3		258.7	49.8	4.5		8.7	6.8		45.4	1.2				3.8					370.3	436.2	85.0
6 YEMEN A.R.					8.3												0.4						1.1					1.1	3.4	32.3
7 P.D.R. YEMEN						8.3		38.0			27.8						21.9	0.1			7.6		1.1					8.3	75.2	11.0
8 IRAN		11.0		12.7	21.1						12.0		2.4	2.7	37.4	9.6	9.3	46.5	127.9			1.7	57.3					55.1	216.1	25.5
9 IRAQ			7.6									9.3			25.3							4.4	6.8					54.1	70.1	77.2
10 LIBYA								2.1							74.2	425.6		1970.0										0.0	2547.2	0.0
11 SAUDI ARABIA		1.5	7.6		7.6		27.8					13.0	77.7		24.0	200.0	906.0	112.0			114.0	807.0						107.4	2370.4	4.7
12 KUWAIT											11.0		7.5		2.9	4.0				107.0		7.5						37.4	158.8	23.5
13 *GULF STATES											11.0+	9.2+																20.2+		
14 ISRAEL								22.3							149.1	81.4	32.3	205.3	62.1		10.7	3.7		9.4	11.0	38.8	20.6	22.3	587.3	3.8
15 USA	132.2	52.3	21.1	11.0	75.1			209.3	21.8	91.0	137.0	98.6	41.6	324.3															1215.3	
16 UK	67.5	87.3	25.2	12.6	81.8	3.4	11.4	187.4	72.7	61.4	56.0	88.0	26.9	227.7															956.3	
17 JAPAN	14.7	13.0	11.1	18.6	28.0	2.3	2.2	116.1	18.7	37.1	18.1	11.3	68.3	61.9															473.2	
18 EEC	237.4	196.3	31.6	69.0	214.0	3.0	2.1	459.1	119.7	144.4	18.1	11.8	39.2	447.0															1968.8	
19 OTHER WEST EUROPE	35.0				86.1						1.0	11.8		115.5															288.6	
20 LATIN AMERICA				7.9				2.1			71.0	160.5	18.8	10.2															241.5	
21 AFRICA		58.0					14.2				31.0			1.7															41.2	
22 ASIA	29.4		4.7	25.6		4.8		41.7	60.3	4.4	148.0	27.8	49.5	1.7															415.9	
23 USSR			6.7	25.6	81.8			115.6	64.2		148.0			15.8													20.6	22.3	333.6	3.8
24 YUGOSLAVIA	38.8	22.1			12.0			16.6	4.4					26.5				15.8											42.3	
25 OTHER EAST EUROPE	38.8	171.4	4.0		12.0			16.6		5.1		24.2		26.5														20.2	333.4	
26 CHINA	3.6	14.3	4.3			5.1					1.0		17.0	18.6															59.8	
27 OTHER																												20.6	20.6	
28 INTRA REGIONAL IMPORTS	3.6	12.5	34.7	34.8	60.6	8.3	79.1	22.3	31.5	18.8	282.0	100.6	92.6	6.4															785.1	
29 TOTAL IMPORTS	558.6	661.0	143.5	179.5	557.6	26.9	126.6	1218.1	507.1	365.8	744.5	540.4	353.4	1255.6	370.4	769.5	117.9	3453.1	338.0	107.0	470.3	870.0	412.6	32.2	176.0	38.8	20.6	7238.8	8367.1	10.9
30 28/29 AS %	0.6	1.9	24.2	19.4	10.9	30.8	62.2	1.8	6.2	5.1	37.9	18.6	26.2	0.5																9.0

*Bahrain, Qatar and United Arab Emirates
+Re-exports only.

NOTES

1) Compiled from trade statistics in, "The Middle East and North Africa, 1972–73" (Europa Publications) standardized in U.S. dollars.

2) Where imports and exports did not tally the figures have been adjusted by taking a mean of the two figures.

3) The imports of a country are read vertically in the table and exports horizontally. E.g.: Turkey imported goods worth 67·5 million U.S. dollars from the U.K. (Col. 1. row 16), out of a total of 558·6 million U.S. dollars (row 29) and exported goods worth 25·8 million U.S. dollars to the U.K. (Col. 16, row 1) of a total of 364·8 million U.S. dollars (Col. 29).

is also dependent upon food imports (Appendix). By contrast, Yemen A.R. consistently imported and exported less than any other state in the period 1958 to 1970, a clear indication of the country's low level of economic development.

The European Economic Community has been the region's major trading partner since it began in 1958. In 1970, the E.E.C. accounted for 48·1 per cent of the region's exports as presented in Table 8.6, and 30·5 per cent of the Middle East's imports. The exports are largely, but on a regional scale not exclusively, oil, as the Egyptian and Turkish figures demonstrate, for they contain no significant amount of petroleum or petroleum products. The various countries of the E.E.C. are traditional markets for many of the region's agricultural products. So important are these markets that in 1963 Iran, Israel and Lebanon negotiated special trading privileges for themselves, while Turkey actually entered into a form of transitional association with the Community in 1964. The effects exerted by the E.E.C. on the economy of the region have been considerable and have given some rise to some concern,[18] especially when the Community was expanded in 1973 to include the U.K., Ireland and Denmark.

The region's second-ranking export market is Asia, where India and Pakistan were the largest customers in 1970. Oil, proximity and traditional contacts are important factors in stimulating Asian trade.

The U.S. and U.K. have retained their positions as important markets and sources of manufactured goods. Significant recent developments, however, have included the appearance of Japan, the U.S.S.R. and now China into the Middle East's trading sphere. Japan is the major consumer of Middle Eastern oil (Chapter 9) and exported 473·2 million U.S. Dollars worth of goods to the region in 1970, chiefly to Iran and the other Gulf States which produce most of her 'black gold'. In 1970 the U.S.S.R. received 5·7 per cent of the region's exports compared with 2·5 per cent in 1966 and 2·9 per cent in 1958. At the same time, the Soviet Union provided 5·4 per cent of the region's imports, instead of 3·4 per cent in 1966 and 4·0 per cent in 1958. Much of the increase can be attributed to political opportunism.[19] Smaller, but otherwise similar changes took place in trade with Eastern Europe over the same period. China had a comparatively small share in Middle Eastern trade in 1958, but this both increased in value and diversified its points of contact during the 1960's, largely as a means of securing political influence.

Intraregional trade has been much smaller than extraregional trade over the period 1958–1970. Between 1958 and 1966 it tended to decline as a proportion of total exports (from 9·5 to 8·6 per cent), but remained virtually static as a proportion of total imports (6·1 to 6·5 per cent).[20] The 1970 figures suggest an improvement in the intraregional component, but this may be misleading because not all the region's oil trade is considered in Table 8.6.

Similarity between the various national economies seems a plausible explanation for the generally poor development of intraregional trade since this would reduce the opportunities and need for exchange. In reality, though, the exports of each country tend to be dominated by either a single product or a small group of products (Appendix). For example, carpets formed 31·8 per cent of Iran's non-petroleum exports in 1970 and phosphates, with fruit and nuts, accounted for more than 50 per cent of Jordan's total sales abroad, while Libya exported little else but crude petroleum. Clearly, there ought to be scope for a good deal of intraregional trade. The explanation for its poor development must be sought elsewhere. It lies in the character and traditions of the region's trade. Many of the region's exports are primary products and the major demand for these lies largely outside the region, in the more developed regions of the world. These commodities were first sought by the industrializing countries of Western Europe, which exported manufactured goods to the Middle East in return. The patterns of trade established in the late nineteenth century were reinforced, on the one hand, by the break-up of the Ottoman Empire into autarchically-inclined states and, on the other hand, by various forms of western political presence in the region during the first half of the twentieth century. Only since about 1950 have the links with Britain and France, for example, begun to break down with shifts in the distribution of world economic and political power.

The importance of intraregional trade varies from country to country (Table 8.6). Egypt, Israel and Turkey were the least involved in trade with the rest of the region, but for very different reasons. Although Israel occupies a position towards the centre of the region, contacts with contiguous Arab countries were severed when the state came into existence in 1948, and she is virtually isolated. Israel's main intraregional trading partners are the peripheral states of Iran, from which she imports oil, and Turkey. Egypt also occupies a rather central position in the region, but her intraregional trade has decreased since 1958. Two reasons may be suggested. Cotton is Egypt's major export and has always been sold outside the region, where in any case it is in competition with other producers. The second reason is growing debt to the U.S.S.R. and Eastern Europe which has arisen from political changes within the country, the financing of the Aswân High Dam and the continuing war with Israel. Turkey, by contrast, lies on the edge of the region and has deliberately strengthened the 'traditional' contacts between Asia Minor and the West.[21] In any case, apart from oil, there is little which the Turks require from the rest of the region.

Jordan, Lebanon, Syria and Yemen A.R. were the states most involved in intraregional trade in 1970. In the case of Yemen A.R., the explanation lies in the relatively large amount of trade with her slightly more wealthy neighbour to the south and her continued use of the port of Aden. Jordan, Lebanon and Syria form an interacting spatial system which lies at the core of the much-heralded, but as yet little developed, Arab Common Market.[22] Not only are the countries contiguous, but the economies of Lebanon and Syria are to some extent complementary. Jordan is virtually landlocked and consequently dependent upon transit trade across her neighbours, while her loss of the West Bank has meant even greater dependence upon agricultural imports which are possible only because of heavy subsidies from within and without the region. The closure of the Suez Canal not only increased the amount of trade within this system, but also reinforced existing trading contacts with Iraq, Kuwait and Saudi Arabia. For example, Lebanon's major markets were Saudi Arabia and Kuwait in 1970, instead of the E.E.C. and Western Europe in general, as in 1966, or Syria and the E.E.C., which was the position in 1958.[23] As well as using Beirūt as an entrepot, Kuwait and Saudi Arabia draw fresh fruit and vegetables from Lebanon, Jordan and the West Bank of the Jordan, as well as some manufactured goods. Iraq is in a similar, though poorer position with respect to both Syria and Lebanon. In addition to being involved in normal forms of trade, Jordan, Lebanon and Syria also secure valuable royalties and necessary oil from the pipelines which cross their territories from the Iraqi and Saudi Arabian oil fields.

Oil is vital to Middle Eastern industry. It accounted for about half of the total intraregional trade in the period 1958 to 1966,[24] and this continued to be the position in 1970. Not only do Jordan, Lebanon and the Yemeni states so far lack their own oil, but production from Egyptian, Syrian and Turkish fields is comparatively recent and, in Turkey's case, is not yet sufficient to meet national needs.[25] Imports, therefore, have been necessary, and it was natural that these should be drawn from close at hand. The major suppliers have been Iran, Iraq, Kuwait and Saudi Arabia. Libya and the Gulf States have played comparatively little part in this aspect of intraregional trade. Another aspect of the region's oil trade is the provision of crude to the refinery at Aden by Iran and Kuwait, and its subsequent sale to the rest of the world and, though not noted in Table 8.6, to ship's bunkers. Without this trade, P.D.R. Yemen would scarcely enter regional, let alone world trade at all. Its internal trade also appears to be very limited.

8.4 Transport and internal trade

Although the transport and internal trade systems of Middle Eastern countries are amongst the least studied aspects of the region's economic geography, sufficient information is available for a number of general observations to be made for further testing by research. Railways are still of considerable importance in the region, as statistics for passenger- and net tonne-km show (Table 8.8). Another demonstration of their continuing importance has been the construction and improvement of railway lines during the 1960's. The section of the Hejāz railway within Jordan has been reconstructed as far south as Ma'ān, while a branch was started to Aqaba in 1972. The Baghdād to Basra line was converted to standard gauge by 1971, and an extension is being constructed to the new port of Umm Qaṣr. Syria is building a completely new line from Latakia, on the Mediterranean, to Aleppo, across to the Euphrates and then down the river to Deir ez Zōr, with the objects of servicing the Tabqa Dam project and tapping the agricultural wealth of the Jezira more effectively. Meanwhile, Iran and Turkey have been joined by a railway line and ferry (on

TABLE 8.8
Railway traffic, 1957 to 1971

State		1953	1963	1966	1970	1971
Egypt	Passenger-km	3,060	4,584	6,170	6,529	6,772
	Net tonne-km	1,215	2,914	3,387	3,333	3,340
Iran	Passenger-km	377	1,440	1,161	1,800	1,991
	Net tonne-km	450	1,447	1,991	2,720	3,008
Iraq	Passenger-km	525	484	431	467	n.a.
	Net tonne-km	855	758	1,079	1,310	n.a.
Israel	Passenger-km	169	412	368	358	381
	Net tonne-km	97	317	318	468	463
Lebanon	Passenger-km	6	5	7	7	7
	Net tonne-km	44	43	46	20	27
Saudi Arabia	Passenger-km	—	24	34	39	n.a.
	Net tonne-km	—	77	52	34	n.a.
Syria	Passenger-km	37	56	64	86	84
	Net tonne-km	130	88	85	102	125
Turkey	Passenger-km	3,016	3,631	4,189	5,561	5,738
		3,071	3,748	5,494	5,618	5,748

Source: United Nations, *Statistical Yearbook, 1972*, New York, 1973, Table 149.

Lake Van) sponsored by CENTO and completed in 1970 (Figure 8.4). In effect, these developments continue policies of national integration developed between the two World Wars when Turkey's railway system was elaborated into a network across the whole country and Iran was traversed by axial routes from Gorgān to Bandar-e-Shāhpur and from Tabrīz to Mashhad. Other parts of the Middle East's railway network were constructed earlier to

TABLE 8.9
Densities of roads and railways, about 1970[26]

State	Area km²	Railways		Metalled roads	
		Length km	km/100 km²	Length km	km/100 km²
Egypt	1,002,000	2,830	2·28	8,125	0·81
Iran	1,648,000	4,560	0·28	11,000	0·67
Iraq	438,446	1,098	0·25	9,240	2·11
Israel	20,700	388	1·87	1,625	7·85
Jordan	96,610	366	0·38	3,255	3·37
Lebanon	10,400	1,990	19·13	162	1·56
Libya	1,759,540	—	—	3,210	0·18
P.D.R. Yemen	195,000	—	—	88	0·01
Saudi Arabia	2,150,000	610	0·03	8,759	0·41
Syria	185,180	844	0·45	7,300	3·94
Turkey	780,576	9,831	1·26	94,564	5·71
Yemen, A.R.	464,000	—	—	450	0·10
		Mean	2·66		2·23
	Mean without Lebanon 0.83				

Sources: Various.

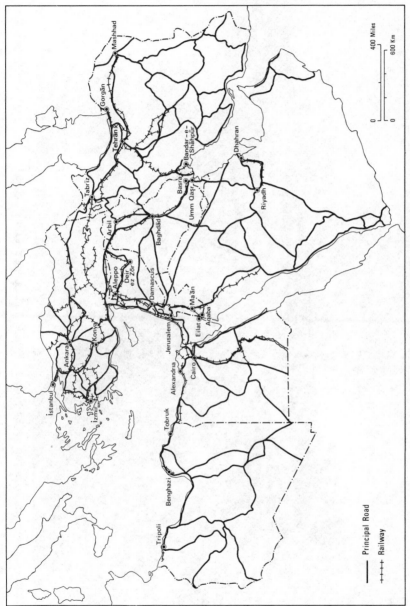

Figure 8.4 Major road and rail systems in about 1970

Coastal shipping remains important, particularly in the Gulf. Loading a dhow at Sharjah. (Central Office of Information)

further imperialist ideals. This was the case especially with the extension of the Anatolian railway from Konya to Aleppo and Ras el'Ain (1918) as part of the Berlin to Baghdād railway project and with the building of the Hejāz railway from Damascus to Medina (1906). The earliest line of all were built in the second half of the nineteenth century to move goods from the interior to the Mediterranean coast for the benefit of western commercial interest, and began with the Smyrna to Aydin railway which was completed in 1867. Despite a long history, railways in the region are not particularly dense in terms of km/100 km² (Table 8.9), while their functions are increasingly being confined to the transport of cereals, minerals and some bulky industrial goods, chiefly because trains are relatively slow and the system is not particularly well-adapted to current economic needs. The net tonne-km ratio has even been falling in Lebanon and Saudi Arabia, while passenger-km have grown slowly nearly everywhere and declined slightly in Israel (Table 8.8).

Much of the traffic lost by the railways has passed to the roads, though statistics comparable with those presented in Table 8.8 are not available. The number of cars and commercial vehicles has increased enormously since 1953 (Table 8.10), and most states have embarked upon ambitious programmes

TABLE 8.10
Number of motor vehicles in use ('000)

State		1953	1963	1966	1970	1971
Egypt	Cars	69·4	86·0	105·3	130·7	141·5
	Commercial vehicles	19·5	22·5	27·5	30·1	34·7
Iran	Cars	22·4	107·8	142·4	278·2	331·2
	Commercial vehicles	20·5	43·8	49·4	73·5	79·6
Iraq	Cars	13·0	50·9	58·2	67·4	71·8
	Commercial vehicles	11·5	24·5	37·0	42·0	44·6
Israel	Cars	14·0	49·3	91·5	151·2	174·5
	Commercial vehicles	17·4	30·7	48·4	70·7	77·5
Jordan	Cars	3·4	8·2	13·6	15·4	15·2
	Commercial vehicles	2·6	4·8	6·2	5·9	5·5
Kuwait	Cars	—	45·2	69·6	120·7	—
	Commercial vehicles	—	18·4	25·3	40·4	—
Lebanon	Cars	16·6	73·1	105·4	136·0	146·3
	Commercial vehicles	4·2	11·4	14·1	16·6	17·5
Libya	Cars	4·4	28·7	53·0	100·1	—
	Commercial vehicles	2·8	15·5	25·2	45·4	—
P.D.R. Yemen	Cars	3·1	10·0	13·1	10·2	13·0
	Commercial vehicles	1·0	2·1	3·1	2·4	3·9
Saudi Arabia	Cars	—	39·5	37·5	64·9	—
	Commercial vehicles	—	32·3	27·6	50·4	—
Syria	Cars	7·2	21·3	37·5	64·9	—
	Commercial vehicles	6·0	32·3	27·6	50·4	—
Turkey	Cars	27·7	72·0	91·5	147·0	—
	Commercial vehicles	33·5	100·0	102·3	164·4	—

Source: United Nations, *Statistical Yearbook, 1972,* New York, 1973, Table 150.

TABLE 8.11
Merchant fleet, 1953–1971
('000 gross registered tonnes)

State	1953	1970	1971
Egypt	110	238	241
Iran	—	129	132
Iraq	—	37	46
Israel	119	714	646
Kuwait	—	592	647
Lebanon	—	182	127
Turkey	478	697	714

Source: United Nations, Statistical Yearbook, 1972, New York, 1973, Table 153.

of road building. Roads are not only cheaper to build and maintain than railways, but they also have the great advantage of providing a very flexible transport system which can reach into practically all parts of a country. Various standards of road now exist in the region, with the extremes represented by paved mule-tracks and multi-lane modern highways. Dirt roads are particularly common, but generally link the villages to the national system of circulation so that there are now very few rural communities which are wholly isolated.[27] The density of metalled roads per 100 kms^2 is still surprisingly small (Table 8.9). Although this may genuinely reflect the degree of economic development in the region, it is also a function of the large amount of unproductive land within national territories. Both the road and rail networks, in fact, are densest in the most closely settled parts of the region (Figure 8.4). Maritime trade is even more limited in its location.

Merchant fleets grew considerably during the 1960's (Table 8.11), but their importance lies in the international rather than the internal trade of the countries concerned. To accommodate increasing foreign trade, harbour works have been extended at ports like Beirūt and Jiddah, new general-purpose ports have been built at, for example, Ashdod in Israel and Umm Qaṣr in Iraq, while the hostility between Israel and her Arab neighbours has helped to revive the ancient ports of Aqaba and Eilat. Oil terminals have increased in number in the Gulf and around the Gulf of Sirte in Libya, while national and international pipelines feeding to them have become numerous (Chapter 9). However, coastal shipping remains important to the Gulf States and in the internal trade of Turkey, where the domestic element formed about 73 per cent of cargoes loaded and unloaded at the six leading ports in 1970.[28] Trade along the Black Sea coast is particularly well developed.[29] By contrast, inland waterways are of very little importance in the region. The Nile is still a major artery of Egypt, while the estuaries at the head of the Gulf are of importance to the international trade of Iran and Iraq. A small amount of traffic is found on the Caspian Sea.

Air transport is a comparatively recent development, though Turkey

TABLE 8.12
Domestic civil aviation, 1971

State	Passenger-km	tonne-km
Egypt	33	113
Iran	337	1,610
Iraq	21	72
Israel	112	6,800
Libya	102	814
Saudi Arabia	281	2,536
Syria	29	556
Turkey	433	1,763

Source: Calculated from figures in United Nations, Statistical Yearbook, 1972, New York, 1973, Table 155.

organized an internal airways system as early as 1933.[30] It is particularly important to the larger countries like Iran, Saudi Arabia and Turkey (Table 8.12), where surface distances are sufficiently great for air transport to become competitive. The urban nature of the nodes in the system is also particularly clear,[31] and emphasizes the importance of large towns in generating traffic.

Small towns, however, play a more basic role in the internal trading patterns of Middle Eastern states. Agricultural goods flow into them for distribution up the urban hierarchy or export abroad, while the small towns distribute nationally manufactured goods and foreign imports to the countrywide. Shops are found in the larger villages, though generally they are not specialized and sell goods in immediate demand (tea, sugar, cigarettes, plates, glasses) and in small quantities. The greatest variety of specialized shops, backed to some extent by specialist wholesalers, are found in the towns. A distinctive spatial arrangement appears to recur.[32] In the old core of the town, often near the citadel and the Friday Mosque, are the shops dealing with high-value non-perishable goods with a low turnover. Semi-perishable commodities and goods in everyday demand are sold in a zone outward from the first. Further away from the centre are shops specializing in cloth and clothing, but mixed in with them are often traders in perishable goods. These three zones, which are not rigidly defined, constitute the traditional bazaar of the typical Middle Eastern town where all the commodities essential to traditional life-styles in the region may be found. Its physical characteristics are narrow alleyways, old property, small open-fronted shops and workshops and a degree of spatial concentration in the various types of activity. A fourth shopping zone lies outside the traditional bazaar, along modern streets and at major intersections. This generally consists of western-style shops selling modern consumer goods, whether imported or manufactured locally. Large cities also contain suburban shopping centres, where the old and new types of shops are frequently mixed together. The residential areas of all towns are further supplied, especially with fresh fruit and vegetables, by peddlars.

Peddlars are still important in a different way to the remoter villages. They bring a selection of goods, like printed cloth and ready-made clothes, which are normally only available in the towns. Periodic markets and fairs are found in rural areas, though they do not appear to have been studied in the Middle East, unlike their counterparts in the Maghreb.[33] The more important weekly markets, as well as the major fairs, appear to take place in the towns. Although fresh food from the countryside is probably the most important item traded, a diversity of manufactured goods can also be seen displayed for sale by travelling salesmen.

Villagers often travel to the towns on foot or on the backs of their animals, but the village bus has become an important institution in most countries, especially for purchasers. Goods for sale are usually taken by truck or tractor trailer, and large items are brought home in the same way. The amount of freight moved between towns seems surprisingly small to the traveller used to western conditions. The flow seems reciprocal between the provincial towns, on the one hand, and the capital, chief port and major manufacturing centres, on the other. One would expect that distance, time and cost would be basic determinants of the type and volume of freight moved, but this remains to be investigated. Goods are often moved by individual merchants in their own trucks, but carrying firms run large trucks on something like regular weekly or even daily schedules, and appear to flourish. The distribution of petroleum is vitally important to the operation of the whole transport system today, and to the health of the various national economies. The volume and direction of oil movements, however, are difficult to determine, as are the quantities and flows of other goods within Middle Eastern states. The wider pattern of petroleum production is discussed in the following chapter.

References

1. H. E. Wulff, *The Traditional Crafts of Persia*, M.I.T. Press, Cambridge, Mass. and London, 1966.
2. (a) A. L. Minkes, 'A note on handicrafts in under-developed areas', *Economic Development and Cultural Change*, **1**, 156–160 (1952).
   (b) X. de Planhol, 'Small-scale industry and crafts in arid regions', in *Arid Lands: A Geographic Appraisal* (Ed. E. S. Hills), Methuen, London, 1966, 273–285.
3. (a) Z. Y. Hershlag, *Introduction to the Modern Economic History of the Middle East*, E. J. Brill, Leiden, 1964, 42–154.
   (b) C. Issawi (Ed), *The Economic History of the Middle East, 1800–1914*, University of Chicago Press, Chicago and London, 1966.
4. R. E. Mabro, 'Industrialisation', in *The Middle East: A Handbook* (Ed. M. Adams), Anthony Blond, London, 1971, 442–449.
5. C. Issawi, 'Iran's economic upsurge', *Middle East Journal*, **21**, 447–461 (1967).
6. A. Lazoni, 'La Mesopotamia economica', *Boll. Soc. geogr. ital.*, **47**, 23–37 (1910), translated in C. Issawi (Ed), *The Economic History of the Middle East, 1800–1914*, University of Chicago Press, Chicago and London, 1966, 179–185.
7. G. Hunter, 'The Middle East Supply Centre', in *The Middle East in the War* (Ed. G. Kirk), Oxford University Press, London, 1952, 169–193.
8. C. Issawi, *Egypt in Revolution: An Economic Analysis*, Oxford University Press, London, 1963, 44–45.

9. C. Issawi, 'Growth and structural change in the Middle East', *Middle East Journal*, **25**, 309–324 (1971).
10. (a) D. G. Edens and W. P. Snavely, 'Planning for economic development in Saudi Arabia', *Middle East Journal*, **24**, 16–30 (1970).
    (b) M. M. El-Kammash, *Economic Development and Planning in Egypt*, Praeger, New York, Washington and London, 1968.
    (c) OECD, *Economic Surveys, Turkey*, Paris, 1968, 18–26, especially Table 8.
11. R. E. Mabro, 'Industrialisation', in *The Middle East: A Handbook* (Ed. M. Adams), Anthony Blond, London, 1971, 442–449.
12. C. Issawi, 'Iran's economic upsurge', *Middle East Journal*, **21**, 447–461 (1967).
13. R. E. Mabro, 'Industrialisation', in *The Middle East: A Handbook* (Ed. M. Adams), Anthony Blond, London, 1971, 448.
14. L. E. Preston, *Trade Patterns in the Middle East*, American Enterprise Institute for Public Policy Research, Washington, D.C., 1970.
15. L. E. Preston, *Trade Patterns in the Middle East*, American Enterprise Institute for Public Policy Research, Washington, D.C., 1970, Table I–1, 6.
16. L. E. Preston, *Trade Patterns in the Middle East*, American Enterprise Institute for Public Policy Research, Washington D.C., 1970, 15–23.
17. L. E. Preston, *Trade Patterns in the Middle East*, American Enterprise Institute for Public Policy Research, Washington D.C., 1970, Tables II–1 and II–2, 18 and 19.
18. For example, R. K. Ramazani, *The Middle East and the European Common Market*, University Press of Virginia, Charlottesville, 1964.
19. W. Laqueur, *The Struggle for the Middle East: The Soviet Union and the Middle East 1958–70*, Penguin Books, Harmondsworth, 1972.
20. L. E. Preston, *Trade Patterns in the Middle East*, American Enterprise Institute for Public Policy Research, Washington, D.C., 1970, Tables II–1 and II–2, 18 and 19.
21. E. J. Cohn, *Turkish Economic, Social and Political Change: The Development of a More Prosperous and Open Society*, Praeger, New York, Washington and London, 1970, 16–41.
22. (a) E. Kanovsky, 'Arab economic unity', *Middle East Journal*, **21**, 213–235 (1967).
    (b) J. E. McConnell, 'The Middle East: competitive or complementary?', *Tijdschr. econ. soc. Geogr.*, **58**, 82–93 (1967).
    (c) A. G. Musrey, *An Arab Common Market: A Study in Inter-Arab Trade Relations, 1920–67*, Praeger, New York, Washington and London, 1969.
23. L. E. Preston, *Trade Patterns in the Middle East*, American Enterprise Institute for Public Policy Research, Washington D.C., 1970, Tables II–1 and II–2, 18 and 19.
24. L. E. Preston, *Trade Patterns in the Middle East*, American Enterprise Institute for Public Policy Research, Washington, D.C., 1970, 34–40.
25. J. C. Dewdney, *Turkey*, Chatto and Windus, London, 1971, 130.
26. Method from N. Ginsburg, *Atlas of Economic Development*, University of Chicago Press, Chicago, 1961, maps XXIV and XXIX. Ginsburg's figures are not strictly comparable with those in Table 8.9 because of different sources for the basic data.
27. J. F. Kolars, 'Types of rural development' in *Four Studies on the Economic Development of Turkey* (Ed. F. C. Shorter, J. F. Kolars, D. A. Rustow and O. Yenal), Frank Cass, London, 1967, 63–88.
28. United Nations, *Statistical Yearbook, 1972*, New York, 1973, Table 154.
29. J. C. Dewdney, *Turkey*, Chatto and Windus, London, 1971, Figure 40, p. 144.
30. V. Eldem, 'Turkey's transportation', *Middle Eastern Affairs*, **4**, 324–336 (1953).
31. A. S. Abdo, 'Domestic passenger air transport in Saudi Arabia', *Bulletin of the Faculty of Arts, University of Riyadh*, **1**, 21–39 (1970).
32. D. Potter, 'The bazaar merchant', in *Social Forces in the Middle East* (Ed. S. N. Fisher), Cornell University Press, Ithaca, New York, 1955, 99–115.
33. Bibliography in R. J. Bromley, 'Markets in the developing countries, a review', *Geography*, **56**, 131–132 (1971).

CHAPTER 9

Petroleum

9.1 Introduction

One of the most spectacular economic achievements of the past 100 years has been the growth and development of the petroleum industry. In 1850, world oil production was virtually non-existent. Then, following discoveries in both the U.S.A. and Russia, total output began to rise rapidly after 1860 until by 1890 world production had reached 10 million tonnes per annum (Figure 9.1). From this date to the present, crude oil production has continued to expand, with world output doubling approximately every 10 years. The U.S.A. and U.S.S.R. still remain the largest producers, although their relative importance has tended to decline with the very rapid growth of crude oil output from the Caribbean, the Middle East and Africa.

At the beginning of the twentieth century oil and natural gas supplied less

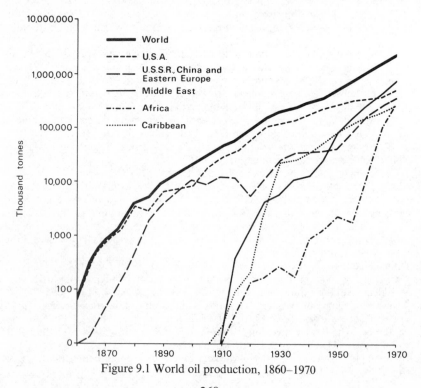

Figure 9.1 World oil production, 1860–1970

268

than four per cent of the total energy requirements of the Western world, while coal accounted for approximately 90 per cent. This picture quickly changed, however, with the share of oil and natural gas in total energy production rising to 12 per cent in 1920, 26 per cent in the mid-1930's, and 36 per cent following the Second World War in 1948. Since this time, the importance of petroleum and its products to the world's economy has continued to grow, so that by 1970, approximately 70 per cent of the total energy requirements of the West were being supplied by oil and natural gas.[1]

The major users of petroleum and related products are the industrialized nations of Western Europe, North America and Japan, which together consumed 70 per cent of the total production in 1970.[2] These same countries, however, produce only 26 per cent of the world's oil and natural gas, and have to satisfy their demands by importing petroleum. As a result, a symbiotic relationship has grown up between the major producing and consuming countries.

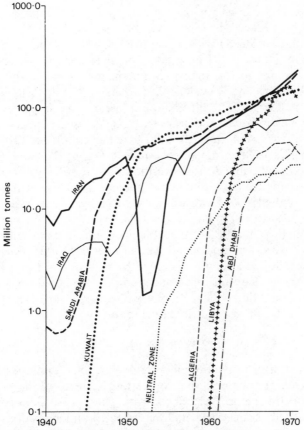

Figure 9.2 Oil production in the Middle East and
North Africa

9.2 The Middle East as an oil producing region

At the present time, the Middle East is a region where the output of petroleum is considerably in excess of demand. The oil production of this area, in terms of the total world output, has increased markedly during the twentieth century. In the 1930's and early 1940's it averaged between two and five per cent of total world production, but, following the rapid post-war revival and expansion of the industry in the Gulf region, it had reached 15 per cent by 1950. Since that date, the relative importance of Middle Eastern and North African oil and natural gas in world production has continued to grow, passing the 25 per cent mark in 1960 and reaching 40 per cent in 1971, when the total oil output of the region surpassed the 1,000 million tonnes mark.[3]

Although oil production in the Middle East first began in Iran in the early part of the twentieth century, it has only been since the Second World War that output has begun to increase rapidly (Figure 9.2). During the early 1940's, Iran was the largest oil producer in the Middle East, followed by Iraq and Saudi Arabia. After intensive oil exploration and development, petroleum output from both Kuwait and Saudi Arabia increased greatly until, by 1950, the production from the Saudi Arabian fields almost equalled that from Iran. In 1951, the oil industry of Iran was nationalized and, as a result, crude oil production slumped to less than two million tonnes in the following year, leaving Saudi Arabia and Kuwait as the two major Middle Eastern producers. During the decade 1955 to 1965, Kuwait became the largest oil producer followed by Saudi Arabia and Iran. A tremendous production increase in Iran occurred from 1954 onwards, after a settlement of the dispute between the oil companies and the Iranian government. During the late 1960's, output from both Iran and Saudi Arabia overtook that from Kuwait and these two countries vied for leadership of Middle Eastern oil production. The real success story of the 1960's, however, belongs to Libya, where production leapt from zero in 1960 to 150 million tonnes in 1969, when Libya ranked second equal with Saudi Arabia.[4] Since that time its production has fallen. With the dawn of the 1970's, Iran and Saudi Arabia now comfortably head the production table followed a long way behind by Kuwait and Libya (Table 9.1). Iran, Saudi Arabia, Kuwait, Libya and Iraq produce about four-fifths of the total output of the Middle East, a fact which clearly emphasizes the low level of production in the other countries of the region.

9.3 Oil concessions

In the period prior to the Second World War, the oil producing countries around the Gulf granted exclusive concessions for exploration and development of their petroleum to Western oil firms. These concessions covered most or all of the countries concerned, and were granted for long periods of 50 to 75 years.[5] At this time, eight foreign parent companies, controlled by American, British, Dutch and French interests, produced all the oil output of the region.

These companies were Standard Oil (New Jersey), Standard Oil (California), Mobil Oil, Texaco, Gulf Oil, British Petroleum, Royal Dutch/Shell and the Compagnie Française des Petroles.[6] Although the situation has changed markedly since this time, even in the late 1960's these same eight companies accounted for more than 90 per cent of the petroleum production of the region.

The first major concession in the Middle East was granted in 1901 by Iran to the English entrepreneur, W.K. D'Arcy. This was acquired by the Anglo-Persian Oil Company in 1909. It covered the whole country, with the exception of the five northern provinces. Since 1954, following nationalization of the Iranian oil industry in 1951, production has been carried out by an inter-

TABLE 9.1
Crude oil production in the Middle East and North Africa

	1970		1971		1972	
	tonnes × 10⁶	per cent	tonnes × 10⁶	per cent	tonnes × 10⁶	per cent
Saudi Arabia	176·9	19·1	223·5	22·3	285·5	26·6
Iran	191·7	20·7	227·3	22·7	254·0	23·7
Kuwait	137·4	14·9	146·8	14·7	152·0	14·2
Libya	159·2	17·2	132·3	13·2	105·0	9·8
Iraq	76·6	8·3	84·0	8·4	67·0	6·2
Algeria	47·3	5·1	36·3	3·6	52·0	4·8
Abū Dhabi	33·3	3·6	44·8	4·5	50·0	4·7
Kuwait/Saudi Arabia 'Neutral Zone'	26·7	2·9	29·1	2·9	30·3	2·8
Qatar	17·3	1·9	20·2	2·0	23·3	2·2
Oman	17·2	1·9	14·1	1·4	13·6	1·3
Egypt	16·4	1·8	14·7	1·5	11·0	1·0
Dubayy	4·3	0·5	6·3	0·5	7·5	0·7
Sinaı	4·5	0·5	6·0	0·6	6·0	0·6
Syria	4·4	0·5	5·3	0·5	5·3	0·5
Tunisia	4·2	0·5	4·1	0·4	4·1	0·4
Bahrain	3·8	0·4	3·7	0·4	3·5	0·3
Turkey	3·5	0·4	3·3	0·3	3·4	0·3
Israel	0·08	0·01	0·06	0·01	0·05	—
Morocco	0·05	0·01	0·02	—	0·03	—
Total Middle Eastern and North African production:	924·83		1,001·88		1,073·58	
Total World production:	2,366·2		2,472·3		2,598·9	
Middle Eastern and North African as percentage of world total:	39·6		40·5		41·3	

Source: Petroleum Press Service 1973 'Output recovers', *The Petroleum Economist*, January, Vol. XL, No. 1, p. 10.

national consortium with 14 participants, including the eight major companies already listed, as well as a number of others.[7] In the agreement reached between the companies and the Iranian government, the concession area was reduced to 259,000 km². The negotiated contract was to run for 25 years until 1979, with the consortium having an option on three further extensions of five years, each under stated conditions.[8]

In Iraq, the first concession was granted to an international consortium in 1925, the first to operate in the Middle East. This consortium, known as the Iraq Petroleum Company, was controlled by British Petroleum, Shell, Compagnie Française des Petroles and the Near East Development Corporation (Standard Oil of New Jersey and Mobil Oil). Its concession, following a number of extensions, covered the whole of the country, except for a narrow strip in the east, close to the Iranian border. In 1961 more than 99 per cent of the original concession territory was re-appropriated by the unilateral action of the Iraqi government, leaving the Iraq Petroleum Company with only those regions actually in production. The dispute between the Government and the Company which this action caused had not been settled prior to the nationalization of the company's assets in 1972.

The other two major producers of the region, Kuwait and Saudi Arabia, both granted concessions during the 1930's. The Kuwait concession, covering the whole country, was granted in 1934 to the Kuwait Oil Company, jointly owned by Gulf Oil and British Petroleum. In Saudi Arabia, the original concession was awarded to Standard Oil of California in 1933 and later taken over by the Arabian American Oil Company (ARAMCO), controlled by four parent companies. In this case, the concessional area covered huge tracts in the central and eastern parts of the country. Parts of this region have since been relinquished.

Since the Second World War, the concessions which have been granted have become much more beneficial for the host countries. This is particularly well illustrated in the case of Libya, where oil production first commenced in 1961. Here, a very different plan of exploration and development took place from that in the older producing countries. Following the enactment of the Petroleum Law in 1955, the oil companies were invited to bid for concessions. At first, a number of attractive inducements were offered to encourage the international companies to participate. The concession areas were large, 30,000 to 100,000 km², and there was a depletion allowance of about 25 per cent besides other attractions.[9] As a result, many companies, representing American, British, French, Italian and German interests, joined in the search for oil. Once it was obvious that the potential for petroleum production was great, the Libyan government began to demand greater benefits. In 1960, the depletion allowance was abolished, and the companies were required to reduce the size of their concessions to between a quarter and one third of the original size within a period of 10 years. Libya joined the Organization of Petroleum Exporting Countries (OPEC) in 1962, two years after its formation, and was coerced into putting her petroleum tax system onto a similar basis to those of the other member states. Pressure was brought to bear on the companies with older concessionary rights, and eventually these were made to conform to the new proposals. Despite these stiffer terms, the demand for concessions remained strong owing to the positional advantage possessed by Libyan oil compared with other Middle Eastern crudes, the low density and low sulphur content of the oil, and the fact that even the new concession terms were still less onerous than those in the Gulf region.

9.4 The oil fields

The distribution of oil in the Middle East is strictly controlled by geological conditions. Almost all the earlier finds were made in the deep sedimentary basins along the margins of the Zagros Mountains and the Gulf. For many years, it was believed that oil would not be discovered in commercial quantities outside this region. More recent work, however, has proved that thick sedimentary sequences with oil reserves are also found in other parts of the Middle East and North Africa, for example in Libya. Thus it is quite likely that other major discoveries of oil may be made elsewhere, once the detailed geology of the area has been worked out. There can be little doubt, however, that none of these discoveries will match the huge oil fields already exploited in the Gulf region.

9.4.1 Libya

The first commercial discovery was made by Esso-Standard at Atshan, in the Fezzan in 1958 (Chapter 20). Since that time, several new fields have been proved, but nearly all of these are located inland from the Gulf of Sirte, far from the original find. The Zelten field, discovered in 1959, has so far been Libya's largest single producer. It was connected by pipeline in 1961 to a tanker terminal at Marsa-el-Brega, and has since been joined by a feeder system to adjacent fields. Large quantities of natural gas were also discovered in this field. A large gas liquefaction plant has now been established at Marsa-el-Brega (1968), fed by a gas pipeline. Export of gas began in 1969, with two-thirds of the planned output expected to go to Italy and the rest to Spain.

East of Zelten lies the large Intisar field from which export began in 1968, less than a year after the initial discovery. The crude oil from this field is transported by a large pipeline to a new tanker terminal at Zuetina. More recently this system has been extended inland to tap adjacent fields at Samah and Waha. Production from the Amal field is transported by pipeline to a terminal at Ras Lanuf, while output from the very isolated Sarir field is piped to the Marsa-el-Hariga terminal, near Tobruk.

In western Libya, a number of smaller fields have been discovered, but owing to the isolation and lack of a pipeline system, commercial development has not taken place. Plans for a new terminal at Zuara are being considered for the future. Considerable interest is currently being shown in a search for oil in the Mediterranean offshore zone.

Little refinery capacity exists within Libya, with several small plants having a combined capacity of only one million tonnes per annum. The largest of these in operation is at Marsa-el-Brega. Three new refineries are being planned, including one at Sirte and another near Tripoli. The development of a petrochemical industry based on the gas resources is also under consideration.

In late 1969, the regime of King Idris was overthrown, and a new republican government established. Difficulties arose between this government and the oil companies, and, as a consequence, production dropped markedly. In 1970, a new-state owned firm, the Libyan National Oil Company, was formed, and in 1972 the foreign oil interests in the country were nationalized.

9.4.2 Egypt

Drilling for oil began in Egypt in the late nineteenth century at Gemsa, on the western side of the Gulf of Suez, and a producing well was sunk in 1908. A second field was discovered nearby in 1913, followed by the proving of other small fields on the Gulf of Suez after the First World War. The discovery of petroleum in the Sinai Peninsula was made at Sudr in 1946.

The Egyptian oil industry was nationalized in 1956, and after this grew rapidly. The first offshore field in the Gulf of Suez was discovered at Belayim Marine in 1961, followed during the mid-1960's by a series of finds in the western desert region at El 'Alamein, Umbaraka and Bîr Abu Gharâdiq. The commercial possibilities of these fields have not yet been fully evaluated. Following the 1967 Arab-Israeli War, Egypt lost the crude oil production from the fields of Sinai at a result of Israeli occupation. These losses have been made up by the development of the offshore El Morgan field in the Gulf of Suez.

The major refineries in Egypt are situated at Alexandria and Suez. The latter was the larger, but was severely damaged by Israeli shelling after the war of June 1967. Parts of this plant have subsequently been moved to Musturud, near Cairo. In the future, it is hoped to construct a crude oil pipeline system (SUMED) from the Gulf of Suez to the Mediterranean at Alexandria, and a new refinery is being completed (1973) there.

9.4.3 Iraq

Oil was discovered by the Turkish Petroleum Company at Kirkūk in 1927. Two years later the name of the original company was changed to the Iraq Petroleum Company. The company later gained further concessions west of the Tigris and in south Iraq, and established the Mosul Petroleum Company and the Basra Petroleum Company respectively to develop them. Production began from the Ayn Zāleh field of the Mosul Petroleum Company in 1952, and the Zubayr field of the Basra Petroleum Company in 1951. Subsequently, new fields have been brought into production at Butmah in the north and Rumaila in the south. Since 1969, the Rumaila field has been developed by the

Iraq National Oil Company (INOC) with the aid of Russian technical assistance.

Owing to the isolated nature of the Kirkūk oil field, which still remains the major production unit of the Iraq petroleum industry, output was unable to begin until pipelines were constructed to the Mediterranean coast at Haifa and Tripoli. Following the closure of the Haifa pipeline, with the establishment of the state of Israel, a new line was constructed to Tripoli, and in 1952 a pipeline was completed to Baniyās. A further line was commissioned in 1962.

Output from the fields belonging to the Basra Petroleum Company was transported by pipeline initially to a terminal at Al Fāw on the Gulf and later to a deep water terminal at Khor-al-Amaya which is capable of handling tankers of more than 100,000 tonnes capacity. The only production of petroleum in Iraq outside the jurisdiction of IPC was at Naft Khaneh, a small field which was geologically a continuation of the Iranian Naft-e Shāh field.

In 1961, the Iraq government passed a law which expropriated all concession areas of companies not in production. This amounted to about 99·5 per cent of all concessions, and was naturally resisted by the companies involved. The government-owned Iraq National Oil Company was formed and given the task of exploiting these expropriated areas. Discussion went on between the companies and the government for more than a decade without any resolution of the problems. Finally, in 1972, the Iraqi Government nationalized all foreign oil interests within the country.

All the refinery capacity of Iraq, with the exception of a small plant belonging to IPC at Kirkūk, has been operated by the National Company. A number of producing units exist, but by far the largest is at Doura, near Baghdād.

9.4.4 Saudi Arabia (Figure 9.3)

Oil was discovered in Saudi Arabia at Ad Dammām, in 1938. Development of this resource was hindered by the Second World War, but, from the mid-1940's onwards, a series of further finds were made. Crude oil production in Saudi Arabia is carried out by the Arabian American Oil Company (ARAMCO), originally jointly owned by Standard Oil of California (30 per cent interest), Standard Oil (New Jersey) (30 per cent), Texaco (30 per cent) and Mobil (10 per cent). In 1971, crude oil was produced from nine onshore fields: Abqaiq, Abu Hadriyah, Berri, Bammam, Fādhilī, Ghawār, Khurays, Khursaniyah and Al Qatīf, and four offshore fields; Abu Safah, Manīfa, Marjan and Safiniya. Most of the output is carried by pipeline from the fields to the large tanker terminal at Ras Tannūrah, but some is carried by submarine pipeline to Bahrain, where it is refined. A further portion of the petroleum production is transported by the Trans-Arabia Pipeline (Tapline) to the Mediterranean coast at Sidon.

The largest refinery in Saudi Arabia is situated at Ras Tannūrah with a capacity of 18 million tonnes/annum, and is owned by ARAMCO. A much smaller refinery is operated at Jiddah by Petromin, the nationally owned oil company, and another is planned at Riyadh. Petromin handles internal marketing of petroleum products, and also has an interest in fertilizer production. Currently, it is exploring jointly with foreign companies regions outside the ARAMCO concessions, but as yet no commercial discoveries have been made. Recent activity along the Red Sea coast of Saudi Arabia suggests the possibility that petroleum deposits may exist in this region also.

9.4.5. Kuwait (Figure 9.3)

Although petroleum was discovered in Kuwait in 1938, the first exports of crude oil did not begin until 1946. The initial discovery was made at Burgan, which still remains the largest single producing field. Subsequently, several other major fields have been developed, of which the largest are at Rawdhatain, Ahmadī-Magwa and Minagish. No significant new discoveries have been made in recent years. The problems with Kuwait crude oil are a high sulphur content and a high specific gravity, which mean that it is less acceptable in the western European and Japanese markets than the lighter, low sulphur crudes. To some extent, this is compensated for by the low production costs of Kuwait oil.

Crude oil is exported from the terminal of Mīnā' al Ahmadī which is an artificial island 15 km offshore, equipped to handle tankers of 300,000 tonnes. Kuwait was one of the countries most severely handicapped by the closure of the Suez Canal in 1967, especially since at the same time there was an increasing demand for oil with low sulphur content. The Kuwait Oil Company has a major refinery at Mīnā' al Ahmadī, with a throughput of 12 million tonnes/ annum. An important desulphurization plant is also in use there. Other refineries are situated at Shuaiba, 50 km south of Kuwait City, operated by the Kuwait National Oil Company (capacity 4·65 million tonnes/annum) and at Mīnā'al Abdullah (capacity five million tonnes/annum). Chemicals made from petroleum are produced by the Kuwait Chemical Fertilizer Company, jointly owned by Kuwait and foreign interests.

The Kuwait National Oil Company, a government concern, is currently exploring jointly with Spanish interests in areas which have been relinquished by the Kuwait Oil Company, but so far without success.

9.4.6 Saudi Arabia/Kuwait Neutral Zone (Figure 9.3)

In the Neutral Zone, established in 1922, Saudi Arabia and Kuwait had equal undivided rights with regard to petroleum production until recently. Oil was first discovered in this region in 1953, at the Wafra field, following the granting of exploration concessions in 1948 to 1949. Production from this field is now declining. New fields have since been discovered at Fuwaris, producing since 1964, and at South Umm Gadair, an extension of one of the Kuwait fields. Most of the crude oil of the region has a high sulphur content.

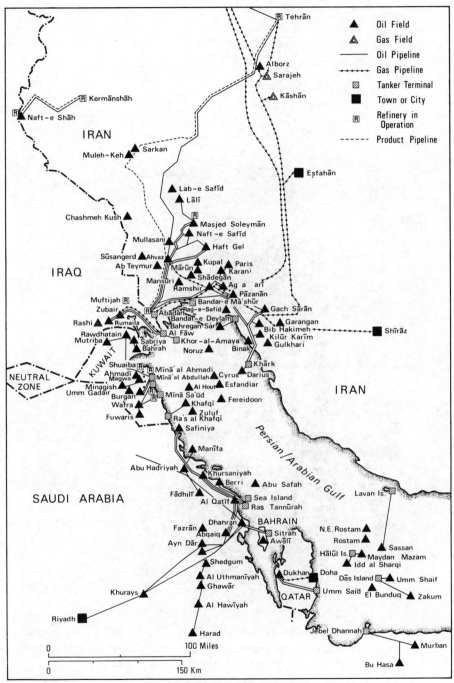

Figure 9.3 Oil fields around the Gulf

Increasing quantities of oil come from offshore fields. Wellheads in the Zakum field, Abū Dhabi marine areas (British Petroleum Co. Ltd.)

In 1960, an important offshore field was discovered at Khafqī by the Arabian Oil Company, which is mainly Japanese owned. A number of other small finds have also been made.

Most of the crude oil exported from the Wafra field went via the terminal at Mīnā'al Abdullah in Kuwait. Later, another terminal was built in Mīnā Saʿūd, within the Neutral Zone. Output from the offshore Khafqī field is sent by pipeline to a new terminal at Ra's al Khafqī from whence it is shipped to western Europe and Japan. Two refineries are located within the Neutral Zone. The first, at Mīnā Saʿūd, is operated by the Getty Oil Company and second, at Mīnā Khafqī, belongs to the Arabian Oil Company.

9.4.7 Gulf states (Figure 9.3)

Towards the southern end of the Gulf there are a number of small states which produce sizeable amounts of petroleum.

The northernmost of these states is Bahrain, where the oil find in 1932 was the prelude to extensive exploration and discoveries in the neighbourhood. The Awālī onshore field is operated by the Bahrain Petroleum Corporation. An offshore field, Abu Safah, also exists in an area shared equally between Saudi Arabia and Bahrain. Bahrain's real importance, however, is as a refinery centre, rather than as a crude oil producer. The Awālī refinery has a capacity of 12 million tonnes/annum, and handles all the local production together with crude piped oil from Ras Tannūrah in Saudi Arabia.

Oil in Qatar, although discovered in 1939, was not developed, because of the Second World War, until 1949. The only onshore oilfield is at Dukhan on the extreme western side of the peninsula and is operated by the Qatar Petroleum Company. From here the crude is piped to a tanker terminal at Umm Saʿid on the east coast. In the early 1960's two large offshore oilfields, Idd al Sharqi and Maydan Mazam, were discovered by Shell off Qatar. Output is piped to a terminal on Hālūl Island. A number of the companies, including Japanese and American interests, are at present engaged in exploration work in areas not covered by the previous concessions of the Shell and Qatar Petroleum Company, but as yet no commercial finds have been reported.

Following extensive onshore and offshore exploration work in the 1950's, Abū Dhabi became a major oil producer in the 1960's. Onshore, the Murban field was discovered in 1960. Crude oil output began in 1963, and was transported by pipeline to a terminal at Jebel Dhannah. A later discovery at Bu Hasa has already been connected to the distribution system, while a third smaller field at Abu Jidu has yet to be developed. All of these fields are operated by the Abū Dhabi Petroleum Company. In the offshore search for oil, BP and Compaignie Française des Petroles joined to form Abū Dhabi Marine Areas. This concern, working from a base on Dās Island, struck oil in 1958 at Umm Shaif. A pipeline was quickly constructed to Dās Island, where a loading terminal was built, and production began in 1962. Since then, two further offshore fields have been discovered at Zakum, producing since 1967, and El Bunduq.

Crude oil production in Dubayy commenced from the offshore Fateh field in 1969. The operating company is Dubayy Petroleum, owned by an international group of firms headed by Continental Oil. Despite exploration since an initial concession was granted in 1937, no onshore fields have yet been opened up.

In Oman, a concession was granted in 1937 to an associate of the Iraq Petroleum Company to begin exploration. Drilling began in the 1950's, but, following initial dry wells, the IPC partners, with the exception of Shell and Gulbenkien, decided to withdraw in 1960. These two interests, joined later by Compagnie Française des Petroles, continued exploration work, and were rewarded in 1964 by the discovery of oil in the Natih/Fahud region to the west of the Jebel Akhdar. A terminal was built at Mīnā al Fahal and, following the construction of a pipeline, export of crude oil began in 1967. In 1969, the Yibal field also began production, while in 1970 an important new find at Al Huwaisah was announced.

9.4.8 Turkey

Exploration concessions for petroleum were first granted in Turkey in the late nineteenth century, but, following the enactment of the Petroleum Law in 1926, foreign investors were effectively barred from exploration and development work. As a result, a governmental agency carried out all petroleum exploration until the law was amended in 1954. The first oil discovery was made at Raman Dağ, in southeast Turkey, in 1940, and nearly all subsequent discoveries have been made in the same area. Unfortunately, the oil tends to be of the heavy variety, with a high sulphur content. The only major exceptions have been finds at Bulgaz Dağ, near Mersin, and at Kâhta, near the River Euphrates.

The principal producers are the government company TPAO (Türkiye Petrolleri Anomin Ortakligi), Shell and Mobil. Their combined output continues to be less than half of the domestic consumption. Exploration continues, but the complex geology in the fold mountain areas which form most of the country makes the work exceedingly difficult. At the present time, particular attention is being paid to the possibility of oil production from the Black Sea and Aegean coastal zones.

Two major refineries are at present in operation. At Mersin, on the south coast, is a plant with five million tonnes/annum capacity, while at İzmit, near İstanbul, there is a refinery of 5·5 million tonnes/annum throughput. At Iluh (Batman), close to the producing fields, a small plant of 0·7 million tonnes/annum belongs to TPAO, and a new refinery of about 3·3 million tonnes/annum capacity is being built at İzmir. Plans for another refinery at Trabzon on the Black Sea coast, are also under consideration.

9.4.9 Syria

Oil was first discovered at Karachuk, though only in small quantities by a Syrian–American independent operator in 1956. In 1959 petroleum was proved at Es Suweidīya by the German Company, Deutsche Erdoel, but it was never granted a development concession. Subsequently, these concessions were expropriated and the oil fields developed by the General Petroleum Authority, a government agency, with the aid of Russian technical assistance. More recently, the Russians have developed fields at Hanzan and Rumaidan. Crude oil is piped to the coast at Tartūs, with a portion being diverted en route to the small refinery at Homs, which supplies the home market. Plans are also under way to build a second line alongside the existing one.

Syria's major role in the petroleum industry of the region is as the transit country for oil piped from both Iraq and Saudi Arabia. In the case of Iraq, there is at the moment no feasible alternative to the Syrian route. On the other hand, following political troubles in Syria and damage to the Tapline, Saudi Arabia is now considering the future possibility of exporting all her oil directly from the Gulf.

9.4.10 Israel

Israel has spent considerable effort in petroleum exploration since 1948, but so far with little success. Small fields are producing at Ḥeleẓ–Bror–Kokhav, to the southeast of Ashdod, and recently there have been gas finds in the Dead Sea region. Following the occupation of Sinai in 1967, Israel managed to augment her oil supplies by production from the fields in that region. Subsequently, Israeli engineers have developed new wells in the Sinai region, and offshore exploration work in the Mediterranean and Gulf of Aqaba is also being planned.

A pipeline links the port of Eilat, on the Gulf of Aqaba, via the Heleẓ fields to the Haifa refinery. This refinery is now entirely owned and operated by the Israelis, and has a capacity of five million tonnes/annum. A second and much longer pipeline has also been built between Eilat and Ashqelon, with a capacity of about 19 million tonnes/annum with the aim of providing an alternative route to that of the Cape for crude oil movement to western Europe.

9.4.11 Iran (Figure 9.3)

The first discovery of oil in commercial quantities in Iran was made in 1908 at Masjed Soleymān, on the western flanks of the Zagros Mountains. Subsequently, a pipeline was constructed from this field to Abādān, where a tanker terminal and a refinery, with an initial capacity of 6,000 barrels per day, were set up. In the 1920's and 1930's, considerable exploration for oil was carried out, and a number of new fields at Haft Gel, Gach Sārān, Naft-e Safīd, Agha Jārī and Lālī were located.

During the Second World War, following the occupation of Iran by the allied armies, the output from a number of fields was increased to supply the growing need for oil for military purposes. In 1944, the Agha Jārī field was connected by pipeline to the Abādān refinery, which was further expanded to a capacity of 500,000 barrels per day, to become the largest refinery in the world at that time. By 1950, the oil producing regions of Iran could be divided into three major groupings. In the north was a single field at Naft-e Shāh, connected by pipeline to a refinery at Kermānshāh. Further south, were the older Khuzestan fields, centred around the original discovery at Masjed Soleymān, and connected by pipeline to Abādān. Finally, there were the two large fields of Gach Sāran and Agha Jārī, which were linked by pipeline to both the Abādān refinery and to a new tanker terminal at Bandar e Ma'shūr.

In 1951, Iran nationalized the oil industry, and created the National Iranian Oil Company (NIOC). The Anglo-Iranian Oil Company was forced to suspend its operations, but, with the assistance of a number of western countries, it managed to arrange a boycott of Iranian oil. Without any outlets for its oil, Iran had to close down most of its fields, and output slumped to only one to two million tonnes/annum. In 1954, an agreement was reached between Iran and a consortium of British, Dutch, American and French companies, and, as a result, the boycott was lifted and production resumed. Under the new 25 year agreement, the concession area of the Consortium was to be limited to only 259,000 km^2 in southwest Iran, with oil rights for the rest of the country going to NIOC. Oil production picked up rapidly and by 1957 had passed the 1950 total of 30 million tonnes. In 1956, NIOC discovered oil on the central plateau at Qom, well away from the main centres of earlier production, but, unfortunately, the field proved difficult to develop. The Consortium enjoyed greater success when oil was discovered near Ahvāz in 1958. The field was rapidly developed and production, which was fed into the new extensive pipeline system, helped to compensate for the declining production from the older fields at Masjed Soleymān, Naft-e Safīd and Lālī. Several other new fields were discovered by the Consortium in the early 1960's, including a number of offshore fields under the Gulf.

With the continued rise in oil production of the Consortium, the terminal at Bandar e Ma'shūr proved too small, and so a new crude oil shipping point was constructed at Khārk Island in the Gulf. This was connected by pipeline with the Agha Jārī and Gach Sāran fields and the other pipeline systems. When the Khārk Island system was completed, it became the sole crude oil exporting terminal for the Consortium and Bandar e Ma'shūr was converted to handle only refinery products from the Abādān refinery.

Since the late 1950's, NIOC has encouraged oil exploration by companies which were not members of the Consortium. As a result of such work, more than half a dozen new offshore fields beneath the Gulf have been discovered, some with apparently great future potential. In order to provide an outlet for these new fields, a terminal was built on Lavan Island, and inaugurated by the Shah in 1968.

A major problem in Iran associated with the exploitation of petroleum has been the wastage of natural gas. As late as 1960, only about seven per cent of the natural gas was utilized and the rest flared. In 1966 a great step forward was made when an agreement was reached between Iran and the U.S.S.R. As part of the agreement, Iran was to supply 6,200 million m³/annum of natural gas through a pipeline, which would be constructed, partly with Soviet money, from Khuzestan to Astara. In return, the U.S.S.R. agreed to build a steelworks at Eṣfahān, and to accept the natural gas in payment for it. The pipeline, which was completed in 1970, also benefits Iran by supplying gas along small feeder mains to the towns en route.

With the growing internal demand for petroleum, the capacities of a number of refineries, including Abādān, Naft-e Shāh and Kermānshāh have been expanded, and a new refinery supplied with crude oil from the Gulf by pipeline was opened at Tehrān in 1968. Associated with these refineries are a number of petrochemical plants, which have been recently established. At Abādān, in a project started in 1966, PVC, detergents, and caustic soda are produced, while sulphur and liquid petroleum gas are the main items at Khārk. A fertilizer plant has also been constructed at Bandar-e-Shāhpūr.

Since 1964, NIOC has expanded its activities into international spheres, by providing technical assistance to other countries in the Middle East and Africa, and also by making a number of bilateral trade agreements with east European and other countries, in which crude oil is sold in return for capital goods, industrial equipment or food products. In 1972, NIOC announced plans in conjunction with BP for oil exploration in the North Sea.

9.5 Petroleum reserves

One of the most important questions relating to the extraction of petroleum is that of the quantity of crude oil still remaining. Oil is not a renewable resource, and once the reserves are exhausted man will have to turn to other

TABLE 9.2
Estimated proven world reserves of petroleum
— changes with time

	tonnes × 10⁶	barrels × 10⁶
1935[1]	3,330	24,000
1945[1]	9,300	67,000
1955[1]	26,400	190,000
1960[1]	41,400	298,000
1965[1]	48,300	348,000
1970[2]	84,600	617,000

Sources: 1. Petroleum Information Bureau 1967, *Oil—The World's Reserves*, p. 1.
2. Institute of Petroleum Information Service 1971, *Oil—World Statistics*, p. 1.

TABLE 9.3
World petroleum reserves 1970

	Million tonnes	Million barrels	Per cent
Middle East	47,817·7	349,062	56·5
Sino-Soviet area	13,698·6	100,000	16·2
Africa	9,620·6	70,230	11·4
North America	7,400·0	54,020	8·8
Latin America	3,577.0	26,112	4·2
Far East and Australia	1,946·4	14,209	2·3
Western Europe	508·0	3,709	0·6
	84,567·3	617,342	100·0

Source: Institute of Petroleum Information Service 1971, Oil—World Statistics, p. 1.

energy sources to satisfy his requirements. Estimates of the world's oil reserves are made at regular intervals by the petroleum industry. These figures are never constant, owing to the dynamic nature of the industry. The total rises as new oil fields are discovered, but with every year of production the reserves are being depleted. On balance, however, the net total of known reserves has risen steadily each year since records were first made (Table 9.2). Owing to the finite nature of the oil reserves, this trend cannot continue indefinitely.

The distribution of the estimated proven oil reserves throughout the world varies greatly from one region to another (Table 9.3). In particular, the area of Southwest Asia alone contains 56·5 per cent of the world reserves (1970). When North African reserves are added, this figure rises to 62·5 per cent. Even within the Middle East and North Africa the reserves of individual countries exhibit large variations (Table 9.4). For example, Iran, Saudi Arabia and Kuwait together contained 43 per cent of the world reserves in 1970.

Generally the countries with the largest crude oil production at the present day also tend to have large reserves. However, the relative rates at which the reserves are being utilized varies greatly, with a surprisingly large number of countries having supplies for only 40 years or less at 1970 rates of extraction. In particular, it is very noticeable that the big North African producers of crude oil, Libya and Algeria, possess small proven reserves. It is little wonder, therefore, that these nations are now very seriously considering a controlled and lower rate of annual exploitation of the remaining resources. Even in those countries where large reserves are known, such as Saudi Arabia, Kuwait and Iran, there is a growing awareness that petroleum supplies will one day come to an end, and an increasing desire to ensure that the country's economy is on a sound footing before this happens. The days when people assumed that more and greater crude oil reserves would be proved annually are now over.

Any discussion of the problems within the oil industry nearly always returns

TABLE 9.4
Estimated proven oil reserves in the Middle East
and North Africa (1970)

	Million tonnes	Million barrels	Years to exhaustion of *known* (1970) reserves at 1970 production levels
Iran	7,650	55,000	40
Saudi Arabia	19,000	137,069	107
Kuwait	9,860	71,210	72
Libya	4,160	30,000	26
Iraq	3,950	28,505	52
Abū Dhabi	2,080	15,000	63
Neutral Zone	810	13,000	68
Algeria	1,110	8,025	24
Qatar	542	3,900	31
Egypt	416	3,000	25
Oman	416	3,000	24
Dubayy	139	1,000	32
Syria	183	1,320	42
Bahrain	59	427	16
Tunisia	57	410	13
Turkey	28	200	8
Israel	1·8	13	22
Morocco	1·3	9·2	26

Total 52,900–62·5 per cent of world total
Total world reserves 84,600 million tonnes
1 tonne = 7·2 barrels

Source: British Petroleum Company Limited, 1970, *Our Industry Petroleum.* Summaries of individual countries, pp. 431–453.

to the question of the size of world reserves, and a consideration of the reserves/production (R/P) ratio. This term is defined as the ratio between the proved recoverable reserves within the ground and the annual production rate. It can be thought of as the number of years of production remaining at the current rate of oil extraction. Since 1920 a marked decline has occurred to a present R/P ratio of 36, despite the continued discovery of new reserves. Not all the oil which is present within an oil field can be extracted economically, and normally production has to cease when the R/P ratio falls to about 10 : 1.[10] For planning purposes on a world scale a more realistic figure is probably a R/P ratio of 15 : 1.

Given these considerations, it is obviously of crucial importance to attempt to make estimates of the world's ultimate reserves of crude oil, as opposed to proven reserves. Over the last few years, a number of attempts have been made giving values ranging from 1,200 to $2,300 \times 10^9$ barrels.[11] Total proved reserves in 1973 were of the order of 850×10^9 barrels. Assuming that the growth of demand for petroleum continues at the present rate of about 7·5 per cent per annum, Warman (1972) has calculated that by the year 2000 AD, in order to maintain a R/P ratio of 15 : 1, total discovered reserves would have to be of the order of $4,000 \times 10^9$ barrels. This figure is almost double what is at present considered to be the ultimate reserves of the world.

The implication of these figures is that oil is likely to become increasingly scarce in the latter part of the twentieth and early twenty-first centuries. Costs are bound to rise as the oil companies are forced to exploit the more inaccessible fields beneath the continental shelves. Certainly, for the rest of this century, there does not appear to be an alternative to petroleum for energy production, except in terms of perhaps a larger contribution to the energy pool from the other major fossil fuel, coal. Ultimately, however, it seems inevitable that nuclear energy will supply most of our energy needs in the twenty-first century. Until that happens the countries of the Middle East will control most of the world's available energy resources.

9.6 Transport of crude oil and petroleum products

In the Middle East one of the most important aspects of the petroleum industry is the transport of the product from the oil producing countries to the markets in Western Europe and Japan. By far the most important means of transport is the ocean-going oil tanker, which today makes up slightly more than one third of the world's merchant shipping fleet. With the growth of tanker sizes after the Second World War, the patterns of movement between the Middle East and Western Europe began to change. During the 1950's and early 1960's, the main oil routeway between the Gulf fields and Europe was through the Suez Canal. With the advent of super tankers, however, this route was no longer usable for the larger vessels, forcing them to make the long detour around the Cape of Good Hope. Following the war of June 1967, the Suez Canal was closed until June 1975. If the Canal can be widened and deepened, as planned, then, sometime in the future, tankers of about 200,000 tonnes will be able to pass through in ballast, but not fully loaded. This will save time as the round voyage, including loading and unloading, via the Cape is 60 days,[12] compared with 40 days via the Suez Canal.

Hand in hand with the growth of tanker sizes has been the construction of even larger terminals capable of handling these monster vessels at both the producing and market ends of the transportation network. In the Gulf tanker terminals such as Khārk Island (Iran), Mīnā'al Ahmadī and Mīnā'al Abdullah (Kuwait), Sea Island and Ras Tannūrah (Saudi Arabia) and Um Sa'id (Qatar) have been established to cope with the growing exports of crude oil. Similarly, in Western Europe, huge tanker unloading and refining complexes has been constructed at Milford Haven (Wales), Finnart on Loch Long (Scotland) and Europort (The Netherlands).

In 1971, 74 per cent of all tanker voyages were from ports in the Middle East, with a further 6·5 per cent from North Africa.[13] Not surprisingly, Western Europe is the destination of 57 per cent of the world's tanker traffic, with more than three-quarters of this coming from Middle Eastern and North African

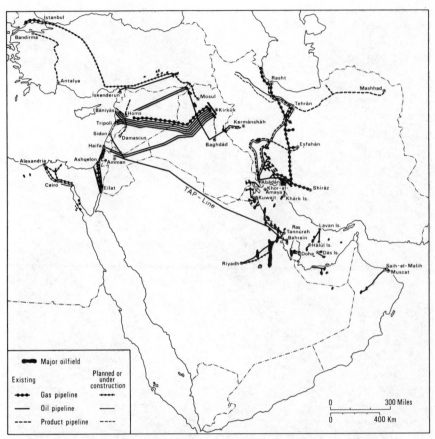

Figure 9.4 Pipelines in the Middle East (Modified from The Petroleum
Publishing Company)

Zelten oilfield in Libya; pipelines converge on the gathering centre at Zelten (An Esso photograph)

sources. Japan, with 18·5 per cent of the traffic, is the second largest destination, and once again the Middle East is the prime supplier.

Besides the ocean going tanker, the commonest means of bulk crude oil transport is by pipeline. When compared with tanker transport, pipelines possess certain advantages and disadvantages. The capital costs of a pipeline are always high, while operating costs are low. A pipeline is also a static feature, and, once constructed it is not easy to change the destination of the carried product. It is difficult to increase the capacity of a pipeline system, and it is, of course, very vulnerable to attack. Over a given distance it is undoubtedly more economical to transport crude oil by large tanker than by pipeline, and, at the same time, one gains benefits associated with greater flexibility, in being able to vary transported amounts in response to market and production fluctuations. Usually, a pipeline can only compete with tankers if its route is shorter than the tanker route, or if sea transport is burdened by heavy port charges or canal dues. With the opening of oil fields in the interiors of the countries of the Middle East in the early part of the twentieth century, the only practical means of getting the crude oil to coastal locations was by pipeline. The first pipeline to be constructed in the Middle East was built by the Anglo-Persian Oil Company in 1911. This was 200 km in length, and linked the newly discovered oil field at Masjed Soleymān with Abādān on the Gulf.

Undoubtedly, the best known pipeline in the Middle East is the Trans-Arabian pipeline (Tapline) connecting the Saudi Arabian oil fields with the Mediterranean Sea (Figure 9.4). At the time of its construction in 1950 this 1,600 km long, 78·7/76·2 cm diameter pipeline with six pumping stations along its route, was the largest in the world and cost £80 million to build. The initial capacity was 15 million tonnes/annum, but this has subsequently been increased to a throughput of 25 million tonnes/annum, which represents about one ninth of Saudi Arabia's current output (1971). Other large pipelines include the Iraq pipelines, connecting the Kirkūk oil fields with Tripoli and Baniyās on the Mediterranean coast, both of which are more than 800 km in length, and the Libyan pipeline from the Sarir oil field to the tanker terminal at Tobruk. This latter is a 86·3 cm line, some 510 km in length and carries up to 15 million tonnes/annum.

A somewhat unusual crude oil pipeline has recently been constructed in Israel between the ports of Eilat, on the Gulf of Aqaba, and Ashqelon, on the Mediterranean. This pipeline, which is 106·6 cm in diameter and 250 km in length, has been built with the aim of by-passing the Suez Canal. The initial capacity of the line is about 12 million tonnes/annum, but it is considered possible that this could be raised to 60 million tonnes/annum, if necessary. The Israelis are hoping that oil will be delivered from Iran, which is friendly towards Israel, by supertankers to Eilat, and then distributed by smaller vessels from Ashqelon. Israel would naturally benefit from toll charges obtained from oil movement.

The destinations of crude oil exports show variations from country to

TABLE 9.5

Destination of crude oil exports from selected countries of
the Middle East (Figures in per cent)

Destination area	Iran[1] (1971)	Kuwait[2] (1971)	Iraq[3] (1970)	Saudi Arabia[4] (1971)
Western Europe	27·2	63·0	82·4	53·2
North America	9·1	1·2 ⎫	6·2	4·0
South America	0·6	2·7 ⎭		6·3
Japan	46·4	13·9 ⎫	2·3 ⎭	30·6
Asia (excluding Japan)	8·9	14·8 ⎬		
Australasia	0·4	2·6 ⎭		1·0
Africa	7·0	—	4·5	4·9

Sources: 1. Iranian Oil Operating Companies, *Annual Review 1971*, p. 39.
2. Kuwait Oil Company Limited, *1971 Review of Operations*, p. 13.
3. Iraq, Basra and Mosul Petroleum Companies, *Review for 1970*, p. 13.
4. Aramco 1971, *A review of operations by the Arabian American Oil Company*.

country within the Middle East. Examples of these differences are included in Table 9.5.

9.7 Revenues

With the earliest concessions, the financial liability of the oil companies consisted of fixed royalty payments to the producing states. These arrangements proved extremely profitable to the oil companies and it was, therefore, almost inevitable that the governments in the producing countries would desire a larger share of the rewards. At first, this was accomplished by increases in royalty payments, but by the early 1950's the oil producing countries increased their demands for the revenues to be related to the profits of the oil companies. Following negotiations, many governments agreed upon a tax formula which gave them 50 per cent of the net profits calculated on the basis of posted prices.[14] This new arrangement greatly increased the revenues of the producing countries and at the same time, produced no extra financial burden for the oil companies, which in most cases were able to offset the larger revenue payments against income tax liabilities in the country where the company was registered.

In the late 1950's, with increasing supplies of petroleum becoming available and increased competition between the producing companies, the posted prices of oil began to decline. This meant that the government oil revenues, which were related to the posted prices, also fell. The producing countries became increasingly worried over this trend, and in 1960 a number of them joined to form the Organisation of Petroleum Exporting Countries (OPEC), with the objective of protecting their interests against the actions of the international oil companies. In its first confrontation with the major companies, OPEC managed to stop the decline in 'posted prices'. From this time forward, 'posted prices' became, to all intents and purposes, nominal in character and of value only for calculating the revenues which the companies had to pay to the host countries. Petroleum taxes became, as far as the companies were concerned, a fixed payment on every barrel of oil which was produced.

During the 1960's, the total revenues collected by the governments of the oil producing countries were further augmented by the introduction of a system known as the 'expensing of royalties'. With the old system, the royalty payment, usually of 12·5 per cent, was included with the 50 per cent of net profits going to the government. Under the new arrangement, the royalties were paid separately from the tax and were classified as a production expense to be deducted before net profits were calculated. The result was to give the governments yet further increased revenues. The implementation of this measure was naturally resisted by the oil companies, but eventually they were forced to accept the principle involved and, by the mid-1960's, most company/country agreements were employing this new method of payment.

The greatest achievement to date, however, was reached by the OPEC countries when new agreements concerning tariffs were drawn up in Tehrān in January 1971, as a result of which the revenues paid by the oil companies to the governments have increased dramatically and will continue to do so in the future (Table 9.6).

TABLE 9.6
Middle East oil exports and revenues

	1962	1965	1968	1971	Percentage increase 1962–71
Kuwait					
Crude oil (million tonnes)	91·7	108·5	121·8	145.0	58
Revenues (million U.S. Dollars)	526·3	671·1	765·6	1,395·3	165
Saudi Arabia					
Crude oil (million tonnes)	76·0	101·2	140·9	222·0	193
Revenues (million U.S. Dollars)	451·1	655·2	965·5	2,159·6	338
Iran					
Crude oil (million tonnes)	66·1	94·3	141·5	227·0	224
Revenues (million U.S. Dollars)	333·8	522·4	817·1	1,869·6	462
Iraq					
Crude oil (million tonnes)	50·2	65·8	73·3	83·0	66
Revenues (million U.S. Dollars)	266·6	374·9	476·2	840·0	214
Libya					
Crude oil (million tonnes)	9·2	61·0	127·0	132·0	1,370
Revenues (million U.S. Dollars)	38·5	371·0	952·0	1.766·6	4,430

Source: Middle East Economic Digest, Vol. 16: 43, 27 October 1972, p. 1251.

One of the most important moves over the last few years has been the growing attempt of the producing countries to obtain some degree of ownership participation in the major producing companies operating the old concessions. Already many Middle Eastern countries have a 25 per cent or greater stake in the western oil companies and they will eventually, it is hoped, obtain at least a 51 per cent controlling interest by 1983.[15] It is quite obvious, therefore, that the roles of the producing country and the oil company are now changing radically.

Of the monies paid by the companies to the governments of the oil-producing nations, by far the largest amount comes from company taxes and royalty payments, mostly in the form of foreign exchange. Another source of income is from payments made locally during actual production for such items as labour, maintenance, and related services. In the early 1960's, such sources accounted for almost one fifth of the payments made to governments, but, by 1970, with increasing production efficiency, this figure has fallen to 10 per cent or less of the total.[16] Nowhere is this increased efficiency witnessed better than in terms of the local employment opportunities provided by the oil industry. In each of the producing countries, local employment has been falling steadily since the beginning of the 1960's, despite continued increases in total production. In Iran 37,000 people were employed by the Consortium in 1961. This had dropped to 26,000 by 1967, and to 17,800 by 1971.[17] Even with this lower figure, some authorities would claim that the numbers are greater than are really needed for efficient production.

One of the great changes which is occurring in the producer countries is that they too, are now becoming significant users of their own petroleum and petroleum products. This change, although started several years ago, has only become of major importance within the last decade, as the local economies have developed rapidly under the impact of growing oil revenues. The three leading producers, Iran, Saudi Arabia and Kuwait, consume the largest absolute amounts of petroleum, with Bahrain and Kuwait heading the list on a per capita basis.

9.8 The future

The future of oil in the world economy is one of the most controversial topics in international affairs at the present time. With the different views held by the producing and consuming countries, it seems inevitable that clashes of interest will occur, with perhaps even greater frequency in the future. The latest and most serious of these occurred following the war of October 1973 between the Arabs and Israel, when oil was used as a political weapon. As a result, crude oil supplies to the United States and the Netherlands were cut off completely and reduced amounts sent to the rest of Western Europe and Japan.

Currently the United States of America is consuming approximately one third of the world's petroleum production. By 1980, as the energy needs of other nations grow, this figure is expected to decline to about one quarter of the world's total, despite an expected 40 per cent rise in absolute demand within the U.S.A. During the late 1960's, imports of petroleum accounted for about 20 per cent of the U.S.A.'s liquid fuel requirements, but of this only a very small fraction was obtained from Middle Eastern sources. One of the major problems facing the United States in the remaining decades of the twentieth century is the question of where oil supplies can be obtained without excessive dependence on foreign and, in particular, Middle Eastern governments. Large oil reserves have already been proved in northern Alaska, but development problems and high costs seem likely to limit severely the pace of exploitation. Less conventional sources of petroleum within North America, such as tar sands and oil shales, have been seriously considered and pilot extraction plants have even been established in a number of areas. However, the high cost of such ventures, compared with conventional methods of crude oil production, has meant that development has been limited, despite the strategic advantages. In this light, one must conclude that in future the economy of the U.S.A. is likely to become more dependent on Middle Eastern oil production to satisfy its growing energy demands.

In contrast to the U.S.A., Western Europe and Japan are already highly dependent on Middle Eastern oil resources. Western Europe consumes about 25 per cent of the world's petroleum production at the present day and this figure is expected to remain relatively constant in the future. Despite the new, and apparently very large finds of natural gas and oil which have been made in the North Sea basin, Western Europe will continue to remain the most important market for world oil and, in particular, for petroleum originating in the Middle East and North Africa. Currently, Japan is consuming about eight per cent of world petroleum production and this figure is expected to rise. In the future the Middle East is likely to continue to be the largest supplier of crude oil for Japan, although recent finds in southeast Asia suggest the possibility of a new and nearer source.

There can be no doubt, therefore, that the Middle East will continue to play a vital role during the remaining years of the twentieth century as a petroleum source for the developed nations of the world. Equally, it also appears likely that by the second or third decade of the twenty-first century, oil will no longer be the pre-eminent source of energy that it is today. Oil will have played an important part in the development of the world's economy, but before the bicentenary of its discovery in commercial quantities in 1858 is reached, its heyday will be well past.

References

1. Actual figures vary slightly dependent upon the source of information.
   (a) *Aramco Handbook*, Dhahran, 1960, 80.
   (b) Shell International Petroleum Company Ltd, *Oil in the World Economy*, London, no date, 33–38.

(c) Institute of Petroleum Information Service, *Oil—World Statistics*, London, 1971, 1.

2. Institute of Petroleum Information Service, *Oil-World Statistics*, London, 1971, 6.
3. *Petroleum Press Service*, XXXIX, 10 (1972).
4. Petroleum Publishing Company, *International Petroleum Encyclopaedia 1971*, Tulsa, Oklahoma, USA, 1971, 76.
5. For a map of concession areas in the Middle East and North Africa in 1958, see Oxford Economic Atlas, *The Middle East and North Africa*, Oxford University Press, 1960, 46–47.
6. S. H. Schurr and P. T. Homan, *Middle Eastern Oil and the Western World*, American Elsevier Publishing Company, New York, 1971, 111.
7. Echo of Iran, *Iran Almanac 1971*, Tehran, Iran, 1971, 330.
8. A. Melamid, 'Industrial activities', in *Land of Iran* (Ed. W. B. Fisher), **1**, The Cambridge History of Iran, Cambridge University Press, Cambridge, 1968, 530.
9. S. H. Schurr and P. T. Homan, *Middle Eastern Oil and the Western World*, American Elsevier Publishing Company, New York, 1971, 118.
10. H. R. Warman, 'The future of oil', *Geogrl. J.*, **38**, 291 (1972).
11. (a) M. K. Hubbard, 'Energy resources', in *Resources and Man: A Study and Recommendations of the Division of Earth Sciences of the United States National Academy of Sciences National Research Council*, Freeman, San Francisco, 1969, 157–242.
    (b) J. D. Moody, 'Petroleum demands of future decades', *Bull. Am. Ass. Petrol. Geol.*, **54**, 2239–2245 (1971).
    (c) H. R. Warman, 'Future problems in petroleum exploration', *Petrol. Rev.*, **25**, 96–101 (1971).
    (d) L. G. Weeks, 'The gas, oil and sulphur potentials of the sea', *Ocean Industries*, **3**, 43–51 (1968).
    (e) L. G. Weeks, 'Marine geology and petroleum resources', *World Petroleum Congress, 8, Moscow Proceedings*, **2**, 99–106 (1971).
12. British Petroleum Company Limited, *Our Industry Petroleum*, London, 1970, 151.
13. British Petroleum Company Limited, *BP Statistical Review of the Oil Industry*, London, 1971, 14.
14. S. H. Schurr and P. T. Homan, *Middle Eastern Oil and the Western World*, American Elsevier Publishing Company, New York, 1971, 120.
15. P. Hillmore, 'Oil producers will take 25 p.c. stake', *The Guardian*, Manchester, Saturday, 17 December, 1972.
16. S. H. Schurr and P. T. Homan, *Middle Eastern Oil and the Western World*, American Elsevier Publishing Company, New York, 1971, 101.
17. Iranian Oil Operating Companies, *Annual Review 1971*, Tehran, 1971, 23.

CHAPTER 10

The Political Map

10.1 Modern political history

Those parts of Africa and Asia selected for detailed consideration in this volume comprise 16 states, together with the seven members of the United Arab Emirates. Some attention is also given to the three states of Morocco, Algeria and Tunisia as constituting the western limb of the Arab world—*Jezira al-Maghreb* to the Arab geographers, 'the island to the west'. The number of political units is not remarkable, but the political and economic interaction between them impinges on almost every aspect of the life of the region. Chapters 11 to 20 form a series of case studies chosen to elaborate some of the outstanding themes of the earlier systematic chapters. In all except Chapter 11 the state itself provides the unit of study, and the configuration, size, and location of the state will frequently be seen as of fundamental importance. It is therefore appropriate to consider the nature and origins of the political map in this chapter. No attempt is made to give a comprehensive account of the political geography of Southwest Asia and North Africa, although a number of key bibliographical references on geopolitical aspects are included.

The gradual decline of the Ottoman Empire in the nineteenth century and the growing ambitions and rivalries of the European powers, provide the background to the emergence of the modern political map. At the height of its power, the Ottoman Empire, like its predecessors the Roman and Arab Empires, embraced huge tracts of Southwest Asia and North Africa. Much of this territory was under Ottoman domination for three or four hundred years, although from the eighteenth century some parts acquired a measure of autonomy.

The broad outlines of the modern political map were established earlier in North Africa than in Southwest Asia. The French conquest of Algeria began in 1830 and was effectively complete by 1845. Tunisia became a French protectorate in 1881, having also previously been under nominal Ottoman rule. Morocco, on the other hand, had managed to remain independent, but in 1912 its Sultan was forced to accept French protection, with Spanish protectorates being proclaimed in the north and south. An International Zone was also established around Tangier to ensure freedom of navigation through the Straits of Gibraltar.

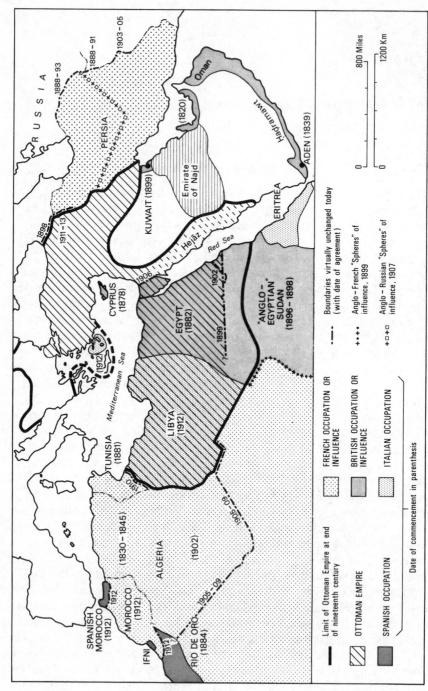

Figure 10.1 The political map on the eve of the First World War

The British occupied Egypt in 1882, although it remained nominally under Ottoman rule until 1914, when a protectorate was formally declared. The chief reason for Britain's intervention was to ensure control of the Suez Canal. Egyptian independence was recognized in 1923, although until 1956 Britain retained the right to station troops in the Canal Zone. Libya became a distinct political unit only in 1912, when it was conquered by the Italians whose dream was to colonize the country and integrate it with the homeland in the way that French had done in Algeria. During the Second World War the Italians were driven out of Libya, and after a brief period of Anglo-French rule, independence was achieved in 1951.

Thus between 1830 and 1914, European powers had gained control of the whole of North Africa, and although the boundaries of individual states were sometimes undefined, particularly in the Sahara, their future shape was already foreshadowed. But in Southwest Asia the political map in 1914 was quite similar to the pattern of previous centuries (Figure 10.1). Two important frontier zones marked the limit of Ottoman control. The frontier with Persia was generally defined according to the loyalties of the tribes, so that in some regions there was a zone some 100 km wide where neither Persia nor Turkey had much influence.[1] In Arabia, Ottoman control had never effectively extended to the interior beyond Al Hasa, Hejāz and Yemen. Most of Arabia's sparse population was ruled by local sheikhs, though in the course of the nineteenth century, two powerful Wahhābi empires were established. In the early years of this century the Wahhābis found a powerful leader in the person of Ibn Saud who had succeeded in imposing his sovereignty over much of Arabia by 1927, although Saudi Arabia was not so named until 1932.

During the latter half of the nineteenth century, new factors became evident in the politics of Southwest Asia. Britain, France, Germany and Russia looked with increasing covetousness at the weakening regimes in the Ottoman Empire and in Persia. British influence was growing as a result of treaties with the Trucial States (1820), the acquisition of Aden (1839) and Cyprus (1878) and the protection of Kuwait (1899). France had long-standing ambitions in Syria, while the Germans sought to promote their interests through railway building notably in Anatolia, Iraq, and the Hejāz. Russia also wanted to build a railway across Persia to the Persian Gulf, and in 1907 Britain and Russia actually agreed on their respective 'spheres' in Persia without reference to local governments (Figure 10.1). Britain's chief concern was still largely to do with imperial strategy, although oil was produced in Iran from 1908. In addition to this jockeying for position by the great powers, Zionist settlement in Palestine began in earnest in 1882, while among a few Arab intellectuals, Arab nationalism was developing as a new and powerful idea.[2] The period 1880 to 1914 in fact, might be described as the time of 'ideas' in Southwest Asia which, according to the theories of S.B. Jones, would lead to the emergence of 'political areas'.[3] The necessary catalyst was provided by the First World War from 1914 to 1918.

The post-war peace settlement created four new political units in Southwest

Asia: Palestine, Transjordan and Iraq, to be administered by Britain under a mandate from the League of Nations, and Syria, mandated to France. This arrangement closely resembled the secret wartime Sykes-Picot agreement between Britain and France for the dismemberment of the Ottoman Empire, and largely disregarded pledges concerning independence apparently made to Arab leaders in the McMahon correspondence.[4] Iraq became independent in 1932, and Transjordan in 1946. (Chapter 15). Lebanon was originally one of seven provinces of Syria intended to be predominantly Christian. After the fall of France in 1941, Lebanon and Syria declared their separate independence, which was recognized at the end of the Second World War.

Events in Palestine from 1918 and the advent of Israel in 1948 are beyond the scope of this book, although one aspect of Zionist expansion is examined in Chapter 16. From 2nd November 1917, when Arthur Balfour, the British Foreign Secretary, sent his declaration to Zionist leaders pledging support for the idea of a Jewish national home in Palestine, the eventual creation of a Jewish state was probably inevitable. Only the shape and timing were uncertain. Several proposals for partition were made (Figure 10.2), but understandably none was acceptable to the Palestine Arabs. These maps themselves, in the view of J.H.G. Lebon, amply demonstrated that the problem was insoluble.[5] The United Nations voted for partition in November 1947 along lines suggested by their Special Committee on Palestine, but during the fighting of the following year, Israel occupied a considerably enlarged area (about 77 per cent of the area of Mandated Palestine), which constituted the de facto state until June 1967. From Israel's point of view, the borders of this state raised many problems, rendering some settled areas highly vulnerable to attack,[6] and making rational use of resources, notably water, extremely difficult.[7] Although a relatively small addition to the political map, Israel is anathema to the Arabs, chiefly on account of injustices to the Palestinians, and the long-term implications of a Jewish state located at the heart of the Arab world.

Modern Turkey was also essentially a creation of the First World War. To begin with, the partitioning of Turkey itself seemed a possibility with Greece, Italy and France gaining footholds, but the deposition of the Sultan and the declaration of a republic under Mustafa Kemal ('Atatürk') in 1922 eventually secured the land for Turkey. Islam ceased to be the state religion, and the national capital was transferred from Constantinople (İstanbul) to the Anatolian plateau at Angora, renamed Ankara.

Apart from the creation of Israel, and events of June 1967 and October 1973, no major changes have occurred in the political map of Southwest Asia in the last fifty years or so. Several minor adjustments have occurred, of which two examples may be given. In 1939, France ceded the Hatay region of Syria to Turkey in recognition of the region's Turkish majority, thus giving Turkey the port of Alexandretta (now İskenderun). More recently, in 1964, an exchange of territory occurred between Saudi Arabia and Jordan which gave the latter enlarged access to its only seaport at Aqaba.[8] In North Africa, the most

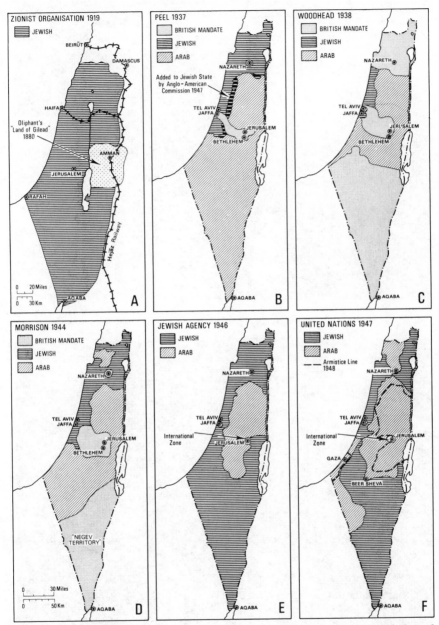

Figure 10.2 Proposals for a Jewish state in Palestine (Reproduced by permission of Keter Publishing House Jerusalem Ltd)

Palestine refugee camps. Top: Dera'a Camp in Syria was established after the war of June, 1967 (UNRWA photograph by Sue Herrick-Cranmer). Bottom: Beach Camp, Gaza, has existed since 1948 (UNRWA photograph)

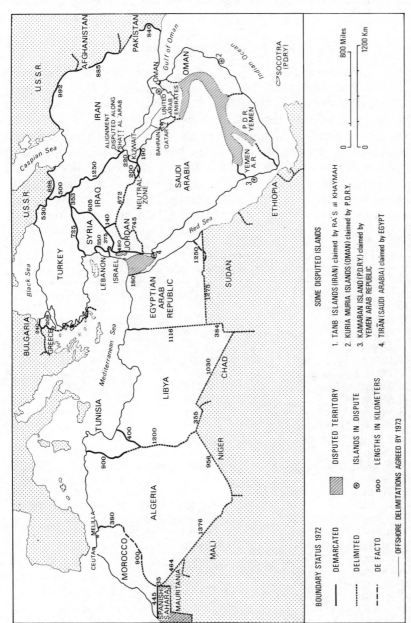

Figure 10.3 The political map in 1972

notable changes have been the disappearance of the Spanish and International
Zones of Morocco in 1956 and the cession of the tiny Ifni enclave to Morocco
in 1969.

10.2 The political map today

The contemporary political map (Figure 10.3) comprises both macro and
micro states. It includes four of the 16 largest countries in the world, while
Israel, Kuwait, Lebanon, Qatar, Bahrain, and six of the Arab Emirates are
among the world's 35 smallest sovereign states (Table 10.1). In view of the
great length of some land boundaries and their comparatively recent imposition by outside powers, the number of active boundary disputes is surprisingly
small. While it remains partially true that '... not a single Middle Eastern
state ... lives at complete ease with its neighbours ...',[9] boundary disputes
are seldom the cause of conflict, although few boundaries are yet properly
demarcated or follow obvious physical features.[10] A high proportion of the

TABLE 10.1
State size and lengths of coastline

Rank	Area (km²)[1]	Coastline (km)[2]
1 Algeria	2,381,741	1,038
2 Saudi Arabia	2,149,690 (approx)	2,474
3 Libya	1,759,540	1,685
4 Iran	1,648,000	1,833
5 Egypt	1,001,499	2,420
6 Turkey	780,576	3,558
7 Morocco	446,500	657
8 Iraq	434,924	19
9 People's Democratic Republic of Yemen	287,683 (approx)	1,211
10 Oman	212,400 (approx)	1,861
11 Arab Republic of Yemen	195,000 (approx)	452
12 Syria	185,180	152
13 Tunisia	164,150	1,027
14 Jordan	97,740	27
15 United Arab Emirates	93,500 (approx)	700 (approx)
16 Israel	20,700	230
(occupied areas 1967–73	68,659)	
17 Kuwait	19,500	250
18 Lebanon	10,400	194
19 Qatar	10,360 (approx)	378
20 Bahrain	598	126
Saudi Arabia/ Iraq Neutral Zone	7,000	nil

Sources: 1. *The Middle East and North Africa 1971–72*, Europa, London, 1972,
pp. 117–757.
2. Geographic Bulletin No. 3, *Sovereignty of the Sea*, U.S. Department of
State, Washington, 1969, pp. 19–22.

boundaries traverse empty or sparsely settled regions, where tribal groups are not divided as in tropical Africa. One notable exception of course is the Kurds, who are divided between five states. The effect of boundaries in restricting the movement of nomads has been overstressed; probably only the U.S.S.R./Iran, and the Israel/Jordan boundaries are impermeable to nomads. Elsewhere, migrations have not been greatly affected, some boundaries being actually delimited to facilitate access to traditional wells and pasture, as in the Saudi Arabia/Iraq Neutral Zone.

In recent years, some boundary disputes have occurred as a result of exploration for oil and other minerals. A number of these have been settled by decisions to share any exploitable resources discovered in disputed territory, regardless of which side of an agreed boundary they occur. Morocco and Algeria, Tunisia and Algeria, and Saudi Arabia and Kuwait have settled differences in this way. In the next decade or so competition of this kind seems likely to shift from land to the Red Sea and the Gulf, where offshore exploration is becoming increasingly intensive. At present (1974) there is no agreement among riparian states as to the limit of territorial waters, most claiming 12 nautical miles (22·2 km), but Israel six (11·1 km) and Jordan, Oman, Qatar and the Arab Emirates except Sharjah, three nautical miles (5·5 km).[11] With the technical possibility of recovering minerals economically from the seabed the whole of the Red Sea and the Gulf could be the scene of future disputes, in which ownership of offshore islands will be an important asset.

Two major river systems are divided by international boundaries. Allocation of Nile waters between Sudan and Egypt has been a problem for many years,[12] but proposed solutions based on the concept of the unity of the Nile valley disregard historical and physical realities.[13] In 1968, Syrian projects on the Euphrates (Chapter 13) similarly had to obtain approval of the Iraqis.

No state is landlocked (Figure 10.3), although the lengths of coastline (Table 1.1) and access to the sea varies greatly from the privileged orientation of Morocco, Egypt and Israel, to the vulnerability of Jordan and Iraq. In geopolitical terms, the maritime orientation of all of the states in the region is of great significance, since land communications tend to converge on coastal locations in concordance with international boundaries, and not transverse to them. Political fragmentation and the interpenetration of the region by seas have given great strategic significance to three waterways; the Turkish Straits (minimum width, 1·8 km), the Red Sea (width of Bāb al Mandab 26 km) and the Gulf (width of Strait of Hormuz 39 km). The Red Sea, in turn, includes two sensitive waterways in the Gulf of Suez and the Gulf of Aqaba.[14]

A further consequence of political compartmentalization is that it multiplies the opportunities for rival external powers to gain influence in the region. S. B. Cohen recognizes two world regions 'occupied by a number of conflicting states and caught between the conflicting interests of the Great Powers'[15]— Southeast Asia and the Middle East. These he calls 'shatterbelts'. His view of the strategic importance of the region has been shared by other political geographers, including N. J. Spykman and D. W. Meinig,[16] for whom it constituted part of a 'Rimland' where Soviet expansion might occur. This view is clearly oversimplified in an age of missiles and growing naval power, but it helps explain the quest for bases in the region for use in cold or hot war situations. The Soviet Union, whose first inroads into the Arab world were noted in 1952, has acquired military interests in Egypt, Syria and Iraq, though the extent of Soviet involvement varies from time to time. Britain maintains a large base in Cyprus and military personnel in the Gulf states, vestiges of her once considerable military power in the region. The Soviet navy has used port facilities in Algeria, Libya, Syria, and Iraq.[17] Turkey, however, is a member of NATO and CENTO, and Iran is a member of CENTO. Units of the United States Sixth Fleet range widely in the Mediterranean Sea and there are United States bases in Turkey. All this is evidence of the strategic importance of Southwest Asia on the southern flank of the Soviet Union, and lying outside a 'ganglion' of land, sea, and air routes second only in density to those of the English Channel.[18] North Africa could also play a crucial role in any major conflict in the Mediterranean or Western Europe. Southwest Asia, in addition, possesses enormous reserves of oil and already supplies a high proportion of European requirements (Chapter 8); it is now clear that the Soviet Union needs to supplement its own production from Middle East sources.[19] While known reserves of oil are more limited in North Africa, oil and natural gas from west of Suez are of particular value of Europe on account of the shorter journey.

10.3 Boundary disputes and territorial claims

One region where the political map has never been clearly defined is in eastern Arabia, where the boundary between Saudi Arabia and neighbouring states is in doubt (Figure 10.4).[20] As late as the 1920's, vast tracts of Arabia, south and east of a line from Aden to Qatar, were still thought of by the British as 'the British hinterland of Aden'.[21] Territorial claims in the region have generally been maintained without military action, but in 1952 a small detatchment of armed Saudis occupied one of the Buraimi group of oases. In 1955, they were ejected by a British-officered force on behalf of the rulers of Abū Dhabi and Muscat. Today six of the nine villages forming the oasis are in Abū Dhabi and three in Oman. Although dormant since 1955, the Buraimi dispute remains unsettled.[22] Saudi Arabia and Abū Dhabi also dispute the region of Az Zafah, a vast area of oil bearing desert on the fringe of the Rub'al Khālī.[23] Elsewhere in southern Arabia there are territorial disputes resulting in frequent armed clashes, usually between tribesmen acting on behalf of rival states. To a large extent, these clashes are evidence of traditional disputes dressed up in ideological terms more than straightforward territorial disputes. Serious disputes thus occurred notably from 1969–1972 involving Saudi Arabia and the Yemen Arab Republic with the neighbouring People's Democratic Republic of Yemen, whose radical regime is pledged to support 'all liberation movements in the Arabian peninsula',[24] including support for left-wing rebels in Oman's Dhufar province since 1968.

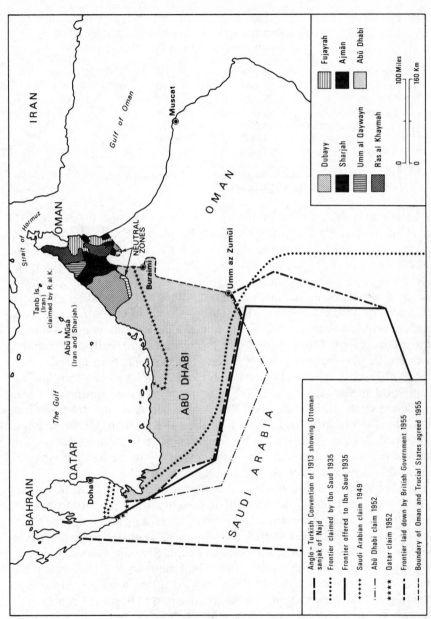

Figure 10.4 The political map of eastern Arabia

TABLE 10.2
The United Arab Emirates

	1970 Population (estimated)	Area km² (approx)	1973 Oil production (tonnes)
1 Abū Dhabi	46,000	83,000	62,700,000
2 Ajmān	4,000	260	—
3 Dubayy	70,000	3,900	12,000,000
4 Fujayrah	10,000	1,170	—
5 Ra's al Khaymah	25,000	1,790	—
6 Umm al Qaywayn	4,000	780	—
7 Sharjah	31,000	2,600	—

Source: Middle East and North Africa 1971–72, Europa, London, 1971, p. 222.
Middle East Economic Digest, 18, p. 84 (1974).

There is also the problem of the United Arab Emirates, formed in 1971 out of six Trucial Sheikhdoms with which Britain previously had treaties of defence and friendship. A seventh, Ra's al Khaymah, joined in 1972. The political viability of the Union may be doubted in a region where the tribes have never achieved unity or much political stability.[25] As in Southwest Asia as a whole, there are marked discontinuities of population and great differences in population size and resources (Table 10.2). With a combined population of less than 200,000, the Union has the smallest population of all Arab states, except Qatar. Moreover, the territories of individual member states are fragmented and internal boundaries have not been agreed.

The situation is complicated by the age old rivalry between Iran and the Arab world in the Gulf region. To some extent this died down when Iran abandoned claims to Bahrain in 1970, but flared up again in 1971 when Iran seized the Tanb islands, also claimed by Ra's al Khaymah. Only one island is inhabited, but they provide a key to the narrow Strait of Hormuz and possible access to offshore oil deposits. Abū Mūsá is held jointly by Iran and Sharjah, and any oil discoveries are to be shared equally between the two states.

The dispute between Iraq and Iran over control of the Shaṭṭ al 'Arab involves no territory apart from a few islands. The present alignment dates from 1913, when Turkey was given control of the estuary, and from 1937, when the boundary opposite Abādān was shifted to the *thalweg* of the river (Figure 10.5). Iran however, wants a mid-stream boundary throughout, while Iraq maintains the right to control its only outlet to the sea. Failure to reach agreement has been costly, since inadequate dredging has led to the need for offshore oil terminals, and the construction of an alternative port to Basra at Umm Qaṣr.[26] The dispute had been dormant for a number of years, but was raised again in 1969 at a time of deteriorating relations between the two states.

10.4 Future changes

It is unlikely that the political map will change as much in the next 50 years as it has in the past 50 years. Minor territorial adjustments will undoubtedly occur, and boundaries will be more precisely delimited. The map of the future

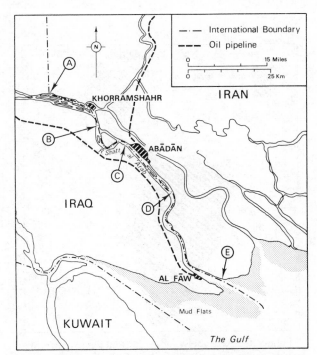

Figure 10.5 The Iran/Iraq boundary along the Shaṭṭ al'Arab.
The boundary follows mid-stream from A to B, and from
E to the sea. From B to C and D to E it follows the low water
mark along the Iranian bank, and from C to D it follows
the *thalweg* to give anchorage to Iran opposite Abādān
(Modified from C. A. Fisher, (Ed.) *Essays in Political
Geography*, Associated Book Publishers Ltd.)

may also show the narrow seas partitioned between riparian states, but the
fundamental pattern of political units will persist. New combinations of states
will doubtless occur for political and economic purposes. The Federation of
Arab Republics (Figure 10.3) may be joined by Sudan, as was originally
planned. Some kind of merger between Egypt and Libya seems possible while
the two Yemens agreed in principle to unite in October 1972. How far the
dream of a united Arab world will become reality is impossible to say. Certainly, there are formidable obstacles to political unity. Charles Issawi has
noted five.[27]

First, the great length of the Arab world, unmatched by corresponding depth;
secondly, the discontinuity of settled population; thirdly, inadequate communications, exacerbated by the fact that most roads and railways were built by
foreigners to facilitate overseas trade rather than link together the constituent
parts of the Arab world; fourthly, the lack of economic integration both within
and between countries despite various attempts to achieve it. Trade has always
been limited because of the shortage of surplus produce for exchange. Several
countries notably in the Maghreb would prefer closer association with the E.E.C.
Fifthly, the lack of social integration for example between town and country
and nomad and peasant. A sixth problem at present is the diversity of political

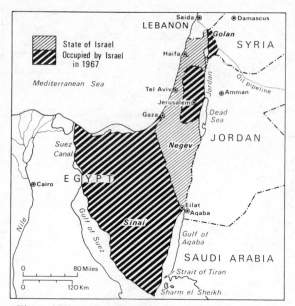

Figure 10.6 Areas of Syria, Jordan and Egypt occupied
by Israel in June 1967

regimes within the Arab world. Indeed, it is arguable that the division of the region into nation states cannot be reversed.[28] Nevertheless, centripetal forces are also powerful, and with a common language and cultural heritage, these could eventually lead to unexpected levels of political cooperation. To begin with however, one can expect to see an increasing awareness of the advantages of close technical and economic cooperation between states. Theoretical studies of trade relations have shown that a good basis for a customs union exists between several states in Southwest Asia and Egypt.[29] Significantly, there has been an increasing interest in more overland pipelines in Southwest Asia in recent years, which could bring about further interdependence, while the completion of the CENTO road and rail links between Turkey and Iran, and the commencement of a North African highway are signs of developing integration between regions.

One region where the political map may be expected to change is in the areas occupied by Israel in June 1967 (Figure 10.6). It would be futile to attempt to predict the shape of future boundaries in these territories, although the Arab military showing in the war of October 1973, and the use of oil as a political weapon, could eventually bring about Israel's withdrawal to the pre-1967 armistice lines, with some minor concessions. The areas still occupied by Israel in 1973 give some very real economic and military advantages, which in the short run will not be willingly forfeited.[30] In the long run however, Israel would probably withdraw from large areas of Arab territory in return for lasting peace, and possibly even encourage the establishment of a national home for the Palestinians.

References

1. A. Melamid, 'The Shaṭṭ al'Arab boundary dispute', *Middle East Journal*, **22**, 350–357 (1968).
2. G. E. Kirk, *A Short History of the Middle East*, University Paperbacks, London, 1964, chapter 5.
3. S. B. Jones, 'A unified field theory of political geography', *Ann. Ass. Amer. Geogr.*, **44**, 111–123 (1954).
4. W. Laqueur (Ed), *The Israel-Arab Reader*, Weidenfeld, London, 1969, 12–18.
5. J. H. G. Lebon, 'South-West Asia and Egypt', in *The Changing Map of Asia*, 5th ed., (Ed. W. G. East, O. H. K. Spate, and C. A. Fisher), Methuen, London, 1971, 120.
6. J. S. Haupert, 'Political geography of the Israel-Syrian boundary dispute 1949–67', *Prof. Geogr.*, **21**, 163–171 (1969).
7. (a) M. Brawer, 'The geographical background of the Jordan water dispute', in *Essays in Political Geography*, (Ed. C. A. Fisher), Methuen, London, 1968, 225–242.
   (b) C. G. Smith, 'The disputed waters of the Jordan', *Trans. Inst. Brit. Geogr.*, **40**, 111–128 (1966).
8. Document: 'Agreement for the delimitation of boundaries between Jordan and Saudi Arabia', *Middle East Journal*, **22**, 346–348 (1968).
9. S. B. Cohen, *'Geography and Politics in a Divided World'*, Methuen, London, 1964, 231.
10. I. W. Zartman, 'The politics of boundaries in North and West Africa', *J. Mod. Afr. Stud.*, **3**, 155–173 (1965).
11. Geographic Bulletin No. 3, *Sovereignty of the Sea*, U.S. Department of State, Washington, 1969, 28–29.
12. J. H. G. Lebon, 'The control and utilization of Nile waters: a problem of political geography', *Rev. Geogr. Institute*, University of İstanbul, İstanbul, No. 6, 1960, 32–49.
13. D. D. Crary, 'Geography and politics in the Nile valley', *Middle East Journal*, **3**, 260–276 (1949).
14. A. Melamid, 'The political geography of the Gulf of Aqaba', *Ann. Ass. Amer. Geogr.*, **47**, 231–240 (1957).
15. S. B. Cohen, *Geography and Politics in a Divided World*, Methuen, London, 1964, 85.
16. N. J. G. Pounds, *Political Geography*, McGraw-Hill, New York, 1963, 402–404.
17. 'The Middle East', in *Strategic Survey 1971*, International Institute for Strategic Studies, London, 1972, 30–45.
18. J. H. G. Lebon, 'South West Asia and Egypt' in *The Changing Map of Asia*, 5th ed. (Ed. W. G. East, O. H. K. Spate, and C. A. Fisher), Methuen, London, 1971, 53–126.
19. W. Laqueur, *The Struggle for the Middle East*, Routledge and Kegan Paul, 1969, Chapter 6.
20. J. B. Kelly, *Eastern Arabian Frontiers*, Faber and Faber, London, 1964.
21. Anon. 'The boundaries of the Nejd: a note on the special conditions', *Geogrl. Rev.*, **17**, 128–134 (1927).
22. (a) D. Hawley, *The Trucial States*, George Allen and Unwin, London, 1970.
    (b) A. Melamid, 'The Buraimi oasis dispute', *Middle East Affairs*, **7**, 56–63 (1956).
23. J. C. Wilkinson, 'The Oman question: the background to the political geography of South East Arabia', *Geogrl. J.*, **137**, 361–371 (1971).
24. N. Ashford, 'Border clashes intensify in border war', *The Times*, 15th March 1972.
25. A. Melamid, 'Political geography of Trucial Oman and Qatar', *Geogrl. Rev.*, **43**, 194–206 (1953).
26. A. Melamid, 'The Shaṭṭ al'Arab boundary dispute', *Middle East J.*, **22**, 355 (1968), V. J. Sevian, 'The evolution of the boundary between Iraq and Iran', in *Essays in Political Geography* (Ed. C. A. Fisher), Methuen, London, 1968, 211–223.
27. C. Issawi, 'Political disunity in the Arab World', in *Readings in Arab Middle East Societies and Cultures* (Ed. A. M. Lutfiyya and C. W. Churchill), Mouton, The Hague, 1970), 278–284.

28. A. H. Hourani, 'Race, religion and nation-state in the Near East', in *Arab Middle East Societies and Cultures* (Ed. A. M. Lutfiyya and C. W. Churchill), Mouton, The Hague, 1970, 1–19.
29. J. E. McConnell, 'The Middle East: competitive or complementary?, *Tijdschr. econ. Geogr.*, **2**, 82–93 (1962).
30. (a) E. Kanovsky, 'The economic aftermath of the Six Day War', *Middle East Journal*, **22**, 131–143 and 278–296 (1968).
    (b) C. G. Smith, 'Israel after the June War', *Geography*, **53**, 315–319 (1968).

CHAPTER 11

Tradition and Change in Arabia

11.1 Introduction

Arabia may be regarded as the heartland of the region studied in this book. Not only does it merge northwards into the uplands at the eastern end of the Mediterranean Sea, the foreland of the high Armenian mountains and the lowlands of the Tigris and Euphrates valleys, which form the modern states of Iraq, Syria and Jordan (Chapters 12 to 15) and lead on to Iran, Turkey and Egypt (Chapters 17 to 19), but Arabia was also the birthplace of two forces which have produced a significant degree of cultural integration in the region, Islam and Arabic (Introduction). The present chapter focuses upon the southern part of the peninsula—a region which may be conveniently defined in terms of its present political units. The Kingdom of Saudi Arabia is the largest state and borders upon all the others. In the southwest lie the Arab Republic of Yemen and its neighbour, the People's Democratic Republic of Yemen. The southeast corner is occupied by the Sultanate of Oman. On the east is the Union of Arab Emirates (the Trucial States before 1971) of Abū Dhabi, Ajmān, Al Fujayrah, Dubayy, Ra's al Khaymah, Sharjah and Umm al Qaywayn. North of these lie the peninsular state of Qatar, the small archipelago of Bahrain, and Kuwait.

Within this immense region, a variety of economies evolved over the centuries in response partly to differences in physical conditions and partly to the degree of isolation from the outside world. An attempt will be made to outline the main features of these 'traditional' economies as they existed around the beginning of the twentieth century, though they are often inadequately documented, despite the vast literature generated by the fascination long exerted by Arabia on the imaginations of north Europeans. The second half of the chapter will be devoted to an account of the modifications and changes brought about during this century. Petroleum exploitation is usually singled out as the sole agent of change. There is no doubt of its importance, but only comparatively recently has petroleum radically altered the patterns of life followed by the majority of people in the peninsula, while the direct impact of the oil industry has been localized. Other forces of change have been at work in Arabia, some of them indigenous, but others emanating from outside, and it is these—perhaps arguably—which have frequently had the most profound effects.

311

11.2 'Traditional' economies

The physical environments of Arabia are generally harsh and uncompromising. Daytime temperatures are high, but there is often a severe diurnal change. Skies are generally clear so that the sun beats down relentlessly, while heat and glare are flung back from bare rock and sand surfaces. The light itself is pure and searing. Scorching blasts of air, dust devils and mirages are frequent during the day. Nights are cool, often cold, and the intensity of starlight and moonshine make them particularly attractive, while the relative comfort turned them into a preferred time for travel. Precipitation is low practically everywhere over the peninsula, and not only extremely variable from one year to the next, but also apparently subject to cycles of drought which might last from 10 to 30 years. However, even a slight fall of rain is sufficient to send fierce and destructive torrents *(seils)* down the wadis and cast a green flush over the desert.

Despite these similarities across the region, there are a number of distinct climates. The coasts of the Red Sea and the Gulf have a broadly tropical climate characterized by stiflingly high humidity (60 to 80 per cent) resulting from onshore winds and precipitation as low as 8 mm per annum. More temperate climates are found in the mountains which form the western, southwestern and southeastern sections of the peninsula. Frosts and snow are frequent in the western mountains, while precipitation ranges from about 500 mm to over 750 mm. Yemen receives most of its rain between July and September, but dew and mist are significant throughout the year. Precipitation is lower and has a late winter maximum over the southern mountains. It declines in amount from west to east, though an accident of exposure raises totals again in Dhufar. Interior Arabia has an mean annual rainfall of between 25 and 150 mm, with a winter maximum. Winter nights here are bitterly cold, due to elevation, low humidity, rapid diurnal cooling and exposure to icy blasts from further north.

Lack of water, steep mountain slopes, lava fields, sand seas and salt marsh (Figure 11.1) have made large parts of Arabia either totally unsuitable for human use or capable of exploitation only at infrequent intervals of time. The scale varies from the local to the regional. Local tracts of uninhabitable country are represented by the lava fields on the inner side of the western mountains, the steep slopes separating the Yemeni plateaus or the Oman valleys, and the salt marshes which impinge upon the east coast. The Rub'al Khālī (The Abode of Emptiness), on the other hand, is a vast, largely uninhabited region, the fringes of which are penetrated only when the rains give a flush of grazing or, mainly in the past, when persecution and banditry made its empty spaces attractive to certain groups. Such desolate tracts have divided the inhabited areas from one another, and enforced a relative isolation which, even with the development of modern means of communication, is still important. In the not too distant past, links were provided only by caravans of dromedaries, with their capacity to cross almost waterless and sandy country. In certain areas, coastal shipping was important.

The inhabited areas were those where some water was available, in the form of precipitation or surface and subterranean flow, and where physical conditions in general combined to produce a resource potential in the shape of, for example, periodic grazing, cultivable land or shoals of fish. It is to the 'traditional' economies based on these and other resources that attention is first given, beginning with the most basic, cultivation.

11.2.1 Cultivation

Although the cultivated area of Arabia was probably unable to feed the entire population at the beginning of the twentieth century, arable farming has been of basic importance for many centuries. Not only were cultivators in a majority, but by sale, exchange and tribute they also helped to support the pastoral and other economies in the peninsula. Some land was worked by owner occupiers and some was in communal ownership, but most belonged to sharecropping estates. Size of holding varied considerably throughout the peninsula, as recent figures for Saudi Arabia indicate (Table 11.1), largely in response to the relative abundance of water, the intensity of cultivation which

TABLE 11.1
Distribution of land holdings in Saudi Arabia in about 1965

Size Group (donums)	Total	Regions							
		South	North	Central	Medina	Jiddah and Mecca	At Ta'if	Eastern	Qasim
0– 5	43,444	19,461	6,186	1,715	5,280	827	4,749	4,201	6,186
5–10	17,236	9,254	1,313	932	1,021	309	1,761	2,232	1,313
10–15	7,515	4,170	306	686	255	93	860	798	306
15–20	3,479	1,670	148	408	144	44	320	538	148
20–25	2,866	1,328	122	445	93	24	323	291	122
25–30	1,308	446	68	275	46	16	120	146	68
30–35	1,204	386	63	265	45	25	99	195	53
35–40	994	539	34	134	25	3	42	109	34
40–45	1,089	199	41	331	20	110	110	60	41
45–50	779	373	35	165	19	4	58	84	35
50–55	565	117	24	176	14	3	49	39	24
55–60	319	72	17	93	—	2	28	21	17
60–65	695	218	24	218	14	16	58	69	34
65–70	289	48	19	89	4	1	31	28	19
70–75	332	108	15	106	3	1	18	15	15
75–80	226	50	10	75	6	—	11	29	10
80–85	454	53	11	152	2	9	53	10	11
85–90	199	31	9	64	2	—	24	9	9
90–95	393	42	6	154	9	11	32	33	6
95–100	215	38	9	89	5	—	20	12	9
100 +	3,510	303	174	1,448	29	104	310	179	174
Total	87,111	38,806	8,624	8,020	7,036	1,501	9,076	9,098	8,624

Source: Kingdom of Saudi Arabia, Ministry of Finance and National Economy, Central Department of Statistics, *Statistical Yearbook, 1387 A.H.* (AD 1967–68), p. 138.

this allows, and the density of population which could thus be carried. Fragmentation was probably commonplace because of the division of property between all the male heirs, but its intensity varied regionally.[1]

Permanent rain-fed cultivation was concentrated where average annual precipitation exceeds 240 mm, that is in the mountains of Asīr, the plateaus of Yemen and the higher valleys of Oman (Figure 11.1). Durah, millet, wheat, barley, legumes and fodder were the most extensive crops grown on stone-built terraces, often laboriously maintained with soil collected from elsewhere and fertilized from middens carefully collected in the settlements. Cash crops were grown mainly in the southwest at the beginning of the twentieth century. Cotton, indigo and later tobacco were important within Arabia, but coffee and qāt *(Catha edulis)* were pre-eminent in Yemen from perhaps the sixteenth century, succeeding to that position long after the collapse of the ancient trade in incense and myrrh from Ḥaḍramawt and Dhufar.[2]

Irrigated cultivation was found throughout Arabia (Figure 11.1), but with particular concentrations in the mountains and along their fringes, as well as in the valleys of the scarp-and-vale country of Najd. A variety of water sources was used, but the greater certainty of water created an altogether more productive form of agriculture than dry-farming. Wheat and barley, maize, millet and durah were grown, together with a variety of fruit and vegetables, but the most important crop, at altitudes below about 1300 m, was dates. More than 70 varieties of date are known.[3] The palm trees, of course, provided vital shade to other crops, useful timber, and leaves for thatching, mat making and basketry. They have the great advantages of tolerating moderately saline water, which is all that is available for irrigation in some areas, of providing more food per unit area than any other crop grown in Arabia, and of being susceptible to several preparations for eating. Mature dates, which are about 58 per cent sugar, are easily preserved, so that they were favoured as an item of commerce and preferred by many nomads as an easily packed food.

11.2.2 Other 'traditional' economies

Around the beginning of the twentieth century, food produced by the cultivators helped to support a number of other economic activities in Arabia. These included fishing, pearling and trading, but the best known—and most typically associated with the interior of Arabia—was nomadic pastoralism.[4] Although animals were kept by cultivators, at least for draught purposes, large herds could only be maintained in the arid environments of the peninsula by a nomadic existence which made fullest use of the scattered and uncertain nature of grazing and of the limited supply of drinking water in seasonal pools and permanent wells. The broad patterns of nomadic pastoralism have been described in Chapter 4 and need not be repeated here. Although sheep and goats were kept to produce butter, cheese and hides, dromedary rearing was the most prestigious of a group of activities, including limited horse breeding,

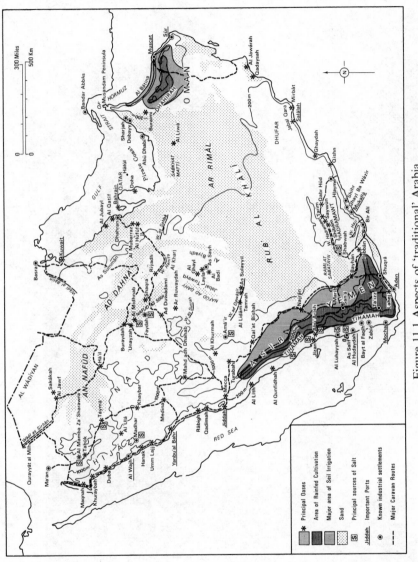

Figure 11.1 Aspects of 'traditional' Arabia

The city of Mecca early nineteenth century. (Radio Times Hulton Picture Library)

which provided the nomads of Arabia with an income to buy food and even tent cloth. Dromedaries were reared not so much for their own produce, though this could be important at times, as for sale to local sedentary communities or, through the great camel fairs, to Iraq, Syria and Egypt where they were used for all manner of draught purposes. Circular and elliptical movements (Chapter 4) were characteristic within tribal territories in northern Arabia and the adjacent parts of Iraq, Syria and Jordan, while constricted-oscillatory movements seem to have been more common in what is now P.D.R. Yemen.

The variety of fish found around the coasts of Arabia supported scattered fishing communities, particularly along the Gulf, where ample fish food was provided through a mixing of local and oceanic waters as well as the discharge from the Shaṭṭ al'Arab.[5] Pearling was also a major activity along the Arabian shore of the Gulf, particularly in water up to 20 fathoms deep in a zone stretching from Ra's al Kaymah to just south of Kuwait. Bahrain was the main centre for this activity.[6] As well as providing bases for fishing and pearling vessels, the coves and creeks of Arabia were also the homes of trading ships. There was always some overseas trade wherever the more fertile parts of the interior impigned directly on the coast or lay close behind it. Trade was facilitated in the Gulf and the Red Sea by the almost parallel nature of the coasts and the relatively short distances between them. But the narrow seas led into the Indian Ocean, which associated Arabia, Egypt, Persia and Iraq with India and East Africa in a single trading system which was worked by various types of lateen rigged ships[7] and powered by the alternation of the monsoons. By the early twentieth century, the African trade was probably the most important, and local commodities like dates, dried fish, salt and coffee were traded, while return cargoes included cloves, ivory but above all mangrove poles which were widely used on the largely treeless coasts of Arabia.[8] Where the ships went, there also the pirate lurked and the migrant travelled. Short-term migration to East Africa or the East Indies was marked in some parts of Arabia in the early twentieth century,[9] but piracy had been suppressed by the British, and communities along the western approaches to the Straits of Hormuz in the lower Gulf were no longer able to exploit the natural advantages of a major trade route passing near the hazards of reefs and shoals along a lee shore.[10]

While cultivation supported all these activities to some extent, it also provided raw materials for local craft industries and some of the commodities for internal, as well as external trade. Pottery making was limited by the lack of suitable clays, but salt production, metal working and textile manufacture were widespread, but with sufficient local specialisms, like the *beedis* (blanket-like coats) of Ta'izz and the shawls of Zabīd or the indigo dyeing of al Hudaydah or Mukallā (Figure 11.1), to generate a degree of trade above that in local agricultural produce, imported cereals and exotic luxuries such as tea, coffee (often from Brazil or the East Indies), sugar and tobacco. Weekly markets and annual fairs provided the basic mechanisms of trade, though simple shops were found in the larger centres and peddlars moved amongst the smaller settlements and nomadic camps. The caravan, generally composed of dromedaries, each capable of carrying up to 180 kg, was the main form of transport. In Yemen and Ḥaḍramawt, caravans were organized by nomads and, changing animals at each stage, followed major routes from the coast to the interior along wadi systems, and then along the interior of the Yemeni or Omani mountains towards the north. Caravans were organized by urban-based merchants in northern Arabia, and draught animals were collected at the various urban termini for use along the entire length of the route. They crossed the territories of the various nomadic tribes safely only when protection money was paid and local escorts hired. The principal routes in the centre and north coincided with the major pilgrim roads throughout Islamic times, and followed lines of wells along the main wadis. They linked the coasts of the Red Sea and the Gulf, and tied the Najd district to Iraq and Syria, but the road system as a whole focused upon Mecca, the pilgrims' goal.

At the beginning of the twentieth century, local pilgrimages to the tombs of saints and prophets were widespread in south Arabia, which was largely unaffected by the Wahhābi 'reformation' of the late eighteenth and early nineteenth centuries or its subsequent revival. Much more important in the whole peninsula, however, was the Great Pilgrimage *(Hadj)* to the Holy Places of Mecca and its vicinity.[11] Mecca is set in a particularly sterile part of Arabia, and for centuries it was virtually dependent upon the Pilgrimage for its livelihood. The other caravan towns also benefited, but it was clear by the early twentieth century that competition from steamships on the sea routes had reduced the size of the Pilgrimage caravans and created something of a crisis for the interior of Arabia.[12] Nevertheless, considerable revenues were collected on goods imported to Jiddah and Mecca for the benefit of pilgrims, and in 1930, before the discovery of oil in what was then Saudi Arabia, the Pilgrimage was the major source of income to Abdul Aziz Ibn Saud. About this time, though, change was already apparent in Arabia, and change is the theme for the second part of the chapter.

11.3 Modification and change

A generalization is often made to the effect that the socio-economic patterns of Arabia changed little between the mission of the Prophet in the seventh century and the discovery of oil in the twentieth. Socio-economic patterns, however, have never been completely fossilized, but have often been much more dynamic than is generally appreciated. This chapter concentrates upon recent changes which appear likely to have lasting and far-reaching consequences. The exploitation of oil has undoubtedly been important in shaping the socio-economic patterns of Arabia in recent years, largely through the vast incomes which it has provided to individual states. Change, however, began before the first oil discoveries were made, stimulated partly by local vision and pressing need, and partly by changes taking place beyond Arabia.

11.3.1 Cultivation

The age-old system of agricultural life and the use of 'traditional' techniques continues in many parts of Arabia today. Change has largely taken the form of an expansion in the cultivated area, almost exclusively by the use of irrigation, and a diversification of cropping patterns, though both have been accompanied by a degree of mechanization. Development started first in Saudi Arabia, but in the last decade it has spread to the Gulf states.

Change in Saudi Arabia was initiated by the father of the state, Abdul Aziz Ibn Saud, himself. The death in 1908 of his great rival, Abdul Aziz Ibn Rashid, allowed him to consolidate his control over the Najd. His policy involved the formation of a confraternity amongst his warrior followers, who became known as *Ikhwān* (Brethren), and were bound together by their devotion to the Wahhābi concept of a purified Islam. The *Ikhwān* were established in permanent military colonies *(hijras)*, containing between 2,000 and 10,000 inhabitants, grouped around a water source used to irrigate cultivated land. Beginning in 1912, with the foundation of al Artāwīyah, Ibn Saud established over a hundred such settlements before the outbreak of the Second World War. Although the *Ikhwān* became something of a political embarrassment, their settlements were important in reviving settled ways of life and extending cultivation. Agricultural development was taken a stage further in 1937 when Ibn Saud's finance minister, Sheikh Abdullah Suleiman, installed a number of pumps, an Iraqi farmer and a Palestinian vegetable grower in the oasis of al Kharj, some 88 km southeast of Riyadh.[13] From small beginnings, the project blossomed into a large-scale experimental farm with the assistance of ARAMCO and successive American agricultural missions. About 12 km^2 are now being cultivated at Al Kharj itself and an additional 3 km^2 at neighbouring Khafs Daghra, largely with the help of machines and primarily for the Riyadh market.

The Al Kharj project was followed in the late 1940's by the establishment of experimental farms in different parts of the country, and an attack was launched on the problems of Saudi Arabia's largest oasis, al Hasa. Al Hasa had been suffering from severe depression. Population pressure had become extreme and was increasing, while the cultivated area was continually being diminished by drifting sand and salinity. Date palms, the main crop, were low yielding, partly because of their age and partly because of a high water table. Prices for dates had slumped as a result of Ibn Saud's ban on the export of dates to the Gulf coast, in order to cheapen this staple for the nomads, and they remained depressed. Water, though abundant, was inefficiently used. Attempts to improve the situation began in 1949. Crop diversification was introduced, improved strains were employed and the use of water improved. Pumps allowed the extension of irrigation, while the construction of the Ad Dammān to Riyadh railway (completed 1951), and the subsequent completion of modern roads, has solved the marketing problem by allowing export to the capital, on one hand, and to the thriving oil settlements, on the other.[14]

Building on these initial successes, and with the capital readily available from oil royalties, Saudi Arabia has initiated a number of further developments. Perhaps the most spectacular to date has been the completion of a large dam near Jīzān in Asīr (1970) to provide irrigation water for some 4,000 to 6,000 ha. Other large dams have been completed at Ad Dīr'īyah, Huraymala, Al Majma'ah, and Milhim,[15] while in 1972 another 4,000 ha of arid land were being reclaimed in Wādī as Sahbā, north of al Hofūf. But it is the many humbler schemes which have been of the greatest significance to the average Saudi farmer. They include the drilling of deep wells to provide extra irrigation water to already established communities, the preparation of land to receive new settlers, as at Harada and in Wādī as Sirhān, the planting of Sudan grass and tamarisk to anchor sand-dunes in districts where blowing sand hazarded cultivation, and the provision of such basic facilities as interest free loans, machine hire at low rates, seedlings and fruit trees at half price, and agricultural extension services. The consequences have been the local expansion of the cultivated area, the opening up of completely new areas, and a vast increase in the number of pumps. The increased wealth of the Saudi population has brought a demand for more fresh fruit and vegetables, which is being met by diversification out of 'traditional' cropping patterns, using the new facilities, and which is now practicable in many districts because of recent improvements in communications.[16]

Despite all the activity, comparatively little of Saudi Arabia's potential agricultural land, optimistically estimated at 15 per cent of the total area of the Kingdom, has been brought into use; only about 0·2 per cent of the surface is actually cultivated. The problems are fundamental and enormous. Water is scarce and much of it saline, while continuous pumping is using up water from the aquifers more quickly than it can be replaced. Cultivable land is limited to discontinuous tracts in the bottoms of wadis, where there is the constant threat of *seils* destroying irrigation works and washing out planted areas, as happened on the Al Kharj project, for instance, in 1945. Marketing is still difficult, despite a large road building programme, because of remoteness and distance. The tenurial situation may also be a brake on change, since *wakf* property is extensive in the country, sharecropping normal and the equal inheritance of property obligatory.

Similar problems beset agricultural development in the United Arab Emirates during the 1960's. They are being solved by the injection of massive amounts of capital into suitable districts, and the measures seem justified by the expanding size and growing wealth of local markets.[17] Relative capital shortage is partly responsible for limited development in Yemen A.R. and P.D.R. Yemen,[18] while Oman's oil wealth has only been effectively used for agricultural development since the coup of 1970.

11.3.2 Pastoralism[20]

While cultivation is expanding and diversifying throughout Arabia, nomadic pastoralism is passing through a grave crisis. This may have a profound effect not only upon the use to which the greater part of Arabia is put in the future, but also upon traditional Arab attitudes and self-esteem. Most of the evidence for the crisis and its socio-economic effects comes from northern Arabia. Almost nothing is known about the situation in south Arabia, but similar developments may be expected.

In northern Arabia, the pastoral crisis has been the culmination of two long-term developments. Sedentarization of the nomads in agricultural communities was pursued by Abdul Aziz Ibn Saud for political and religious reasons very early in the twentieth century, and the policy has been continued by his successors. Implementation began only a few years before falling demand for dromedaries from traditional markets began to be felt as pumps replaced ancient lifting devices and trucks supplanted caravans. Incomes diminished to a level where many nomads were only too glad to accept government assistance and become farmers, though some preferred to find work with the oil companies.

Pastoralism, however, has continued in many districts. A recent estimate put the number of *tents* (the fundamental nomadic units) at about 227,000,[21] that is over one million people. The number of most types of animals actually increased over the period from about 1950 to 1970 (Table 4.4), probably in response to rising demand for meat, wool, hair and hides. Unfortunately, various pressures have concentrated the herds with serious consequences for the pastures. The expansion of arable is one force, since it often takes place in areas which provided good grazing. Even more important have been government policies to control the surviving nomads and to provide them with permanent water sources. Indeed, the provision of secure water in the oil fields and at the pumping stations along Tapline was very effective in concentrating herds, especially during the recurrent droughts in the period 1955 to 1963. Grazing for many kilometres around the permanent water points has been completely destroyed.[22] Fodder must now be imported. Even the distant grazings are threatened by overgrazing since the easy movement of water and stock by truck has produced a kind of motorized nomadism amongst some groups.

11.3.3 Other activities

Maritime activities have probably experienced an even greater change than pastoralism. Seaborne trade is more important to the region than ever before, but few sailing vessels make the voyage to East Africa and oil tankers and large freighters dominate the traffic. To accommodate them, ambitious new facilities have been constructed at ports along the Gulf and at Jiddah and Yanbu'al Bahr on the Red Sea.

Pearling virtually disappeared in the 1920's and 1930's with the perfection of the culturing process by the Japanese, but recently other types of fishing have been transformed. Modern ships and equipment are now used at sea and deep-freezing facilities have been provided on shore, while units of the Kuwait fishing fleet, for example, operate off Somalia, Dahomey, Nigeria, Madagascar, Indonesia and Malaysia. Gulf shrimps are marketed in Western Europe, Japan and the U.S.A.

Internal movement has also been transformed. The motor vehicle, especially with four-wheel drive and sand tyres, has opened up virtually the whole of Arabia, while important networks of roads have been constructed (Figure 11.2). Movement is much more frequent than in the past, and the market areas of the towns have considerably expanded. Partly in consequence, the populations of inland towns appear to be growing, though figures are difficult to obtain. Intra-regional trade is increasing, especially within the diverse territory of Saudi Arabia, where over 6,000 km of surfaced road have been constructed. Crops produced by dry-farming in Asīr now find a ready market in the east of Saudi Arabia, while Ra's al Kaymah trucks fruit and vegetables to Dubayy and even Abū Dhabi. Arabia's only working railway has been important in movements between the Najd and the Gulf coast. The development of air transport has been very significant, especially in spanning the vast distances of Saudi Arabia, as well as in integrating the Gulf states and the different parts of P.D.R. Yemen.

Ease of communication has had two further results of note. It has allowed the more efficient distribution of imported and locally manufactured goods throughout Arabia, and reduced the severe effects of local crop failures which took a heavy toll of life in the past. Improved transportation has been responsible, secondly, for a remarkable revival in the Pilgrimage.[23] In consequence, Jiddah has expanded enormously in both population and areal extent,[24] while Mecca itself has been reshaped. The Great Mosque has been extended, and tall apartment blocks and tree-planted squares have replaced much of the old squalor.

Artisans continue to meet local demands for traditional products, but modern industries are being introduced. Oil revenues are the reason, directly or indirectly. Although increased per capita income has stimulated some development through private initiative, the really large and important introductions have been government sponsored. Oil revenues provide a rich income at the moment, and have raised living standards for many, but the reserves are finite; they will eventually run dry—at Bahrain, before the end of the century. Diversification away from dependence upon the sale of crude oil is thus seen as an absolute necessity by all the oil-rich states in order to safeguard their future and avoid a worse disaster than that which struck the Gulf with the decline of pearling. Most of the development has taken place where the oil industry is situated and where oil revenues are available—that is, largely along the Gulf coast. A common pattern may be detected, in which building supplies, light and consumer-oriented industries predominate, but a number of divergences are also apparent.

Kuwait is dominated by the refinery and associated petrochemical plant at Shvaiba, but a variety of other industries are found. Bahrain has the largest

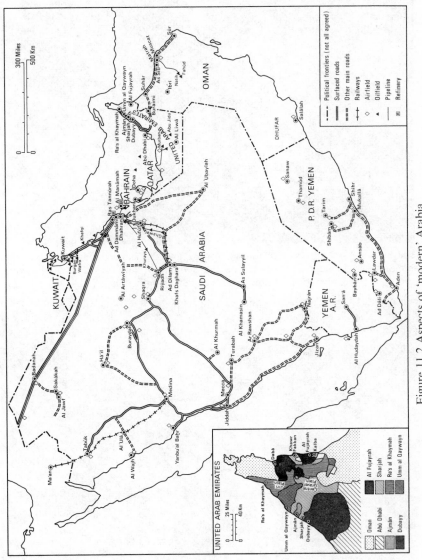

Figure 11.2 Aspects of 'modern' Arabia

The harbour at Dubayy with dhows loading and unloading along the waterfront in the sheltered waters of the creek. The centre of the old town is situated on the peninsula between the creek and the Gulf (Hunting Surveys Ltd.)

The coming of tarmac road to Hili oasis in Saudi Arabia has brought changes in agricultural practice. Date gardens form the core of the oasis, but small holdings growing vegetables and fodder are found on the periphery (Hunting Surveys Ltd.)

ship repair yard between Rotterdam and Hong Kong, though this was being rivalled in 1974 by facilities under construction at Dubayy. Another interesting experiment at Bahrain has been the establishment of an aluminium smelter (1972) using gas from two offshore wells to fuel gas turbines generating the massive quantity of electricity needed, and reducing ore imported from Australia. By contrast, industry in Qatar and the United Arab Emirates is still confined to the manufacture of soft drinks and cement blocks, and a variety of light engineering.

Although industrial developments are so apparent along the Gulf, they are found elsewhere in Arabia, too. Various light industries, such as textile and cigarette manufacturing, were established in Aden under the British, who also established the refinery. Several of the larger towns of Saudi Arabia contain small-scale modern industrial plants producing building materials, furniture and soft drinks or engaged in light engineering (Figure 11.2).[25] Jiddah, however, is fast emerging as the country's leading industrial centre.[26] A new cement plant and refinery were in production by 1968, while the first stage of an iron and steel complex, a 180 m long steel-rolling mill, was in operation by 1970. The mill uses billets imported from West Germany and local electricity, but plans have been laid for the smelting of ore from the mountains between Mecca and Yanbu'al Baḥr. The prospects for further industrial development here and in other parts of Saudi Arabia look very good.

Several problems, however, are involved in industrializing Saudi Arabia and her neighbours still further. The most basic of these is a general lack of raw materials, apart from petroleum and agricultural or pastoral products. Although a number of surveys have shown that Saudi Arabia, for example, possesses a variety of non-ferrous metals, these are situated in remote and difficult country. The result so far has been the importation of most raw materials, thus adding extra costs to manufacturing. In addition, the infrastructure in terms of roads and power is still inadequate, though the position is being remedied by sensible overall development plans. The small size and comparatively low purchasing power of local markets is a great problem, and is intensified by the almost parallel development taking place in each state. Traditional markets in Pakistan, India and East Africa may offer some scope for industrial exports as these countries advance their economies still further. Lack of skill and experience in modern industrial techniques and management are being made good by launching projects in association with foreign companies. Technical education is being pushed ahead rapidly, wherever money is available, but at the moment the Gulf states often recruit skilled manpower from other Arab countries, as well as from India, Pakistan and Iran. These policies, however, are a source of actual or potential friction at home, and make the various states of Arabia even more dependent upon political stability in the region and upon good relationships abroad than the role of petroleum in development would require alone.

11.3.4 Petroleum

Petroleum is so important to modern Arabia that some specific comments on its effects are in order here, though the general situation is surveyed in Chapter 9. The direct effects of petroleum exploitation are confined to a number of small, but drastically changed localities in the eastern parts of the peninsula, where oil is extracted and exported (Figure 11.2). Production sites are characterized by derricks, pipes, tanks and often flares burning off waste gases, while the specially constructed harbour facilities are marked by more storage tanks, and long piers running out into deep water. Between the two areas run pipelines. Refineries are found in Bahrain, Kuwait and Saudi Arabia and petrochemical plants have been added to them (Figure 11.2). Nearby are settlements specially built to accommodate oil industry personnel and company officials. They are marked by regular, grid-iron street plans and air conditioned bungalows surrounded by jasmine and oleander. The prototypes were the ARAMCO settlements in Abqaiq, Dhahran and Ra's Tannūrah in Saudi Arabia, but similar developments may now be seen at Al Ahmadī in Kuwait and on Dās Island, the exporting centre for Abū Dhabi's oil.

The indirect effects of oil exploitation are much more widespread. Some of them have been touched upon already. Exploration for oil, taking place since the 1920's, opened up large parts of Arabia by necessitating at least the grading of tracks, some of them completely new, to supply the drilling sites. The imminence of discovery, and later the finding of oil, led to the abandonment of neutral zones in the United Arab Emirates and between Kuwait and Saudi Arabia, to the allocation of territory definitely to one state or another and to general agreement about boundaries, though with insufficient precision about their lines to be a fruitful source of wrangling.[27] In the same way, offshore drilling now requires the delimitation of claims to territorial waters and areas of seabed. Revenues from the exploitation of oil have led to many changes. Immediate steps have generally involved the improvement of administration, the extension of education at primary and secondary level (in Kuwait and Saudi Arabia, at the higher level, too, with the foundation of universities and technical colleges), the establishment of hospitals, clinics and free medical services, and the gradual introduction of adequate water supplies, especially to the coastal towns. A considerable amount of money, however, is being spent on imported consumer and capital goods, as well as on construction. For example, within ten years of the first shipment of crude from Abū Dhabi (1962), the island town had been transformed into an agglomeration of concrete buildings of standard, international design which line wide, surfaced roads. Kuwait underwent a similar transformation at an earlier date, while a new town of low-cost housing is being built at Issa, in Bahrain, to house some 35,000 workers, largely employed on the industrial estate associated with the port at Mina Sulman.

There is no doubt that wealth from oil has been used to bolster up the 'traditional', patriachal oligarchies of Arabia and, though there have been changes in the exercise of power, political structures remain much the same. It is not by chance that the only revolutionary regimes are found in the two Yemeni Republics, where oil has not been discovered. On the other hand, wealth and the opportunities it has brought, have produced considerable socio-economic strain, especially along the Gulf. Economic development has run ahead of political change. At the same time, a more fundamental crisis has been slowly developing since the end of the Second World War, and affects much more of Arabia than the oases of obvious modernization. Most of the people of Arabia still eat 'traditional' foods and wear 'traditional' clothes. They still conform to age-old customs in behaviour and outlook. Islam is still very much alive. The crisis arises, therefore, in the accommodation of 'traditional' socio-religious patterns to the demands of industrialization and mechanization, which have insidious association with 'westernization'. The position of Saudi Arabia in the crisis, in the search for a new Arab identity, is extremely difficult. Not only has it assumed the prestigious role of Guardian to the Holy Cities, but it owes its very existence to the influence of reformist Wahhābism. It is an open question just how long 'traditional' socio-economic patterns can be maintained even here in the face of rapid and deliberate economic development.

References

1. H. Dequin, *Die Landwirtschaft Saudisch-Arabiens und ihre Entwicklungsmöglichkeiten*, DLG–Verlag–GMBH, Frankfurt am Main, 1963, 48–87.
2. R. L. Bowen and F. P. Albright (Eds), *Archaeological Discoveries in South Arabia*, American Foundation for the Study of Man, John Hopkins, Baltimore, 1958.
3. V. H. W. Dowson, 'The date and the Arab', *Jl. R. cent. Asian Soc.*, **36**, 34–41 (1949).
4. (a) J. L. Burckhardt, *Notes on the Bedouins and Wahabys*, Colburn and Bentley, London, 1831.
   (b) A. Musil, *The Manners and Customs of the Rwala Bedouins*, American Geographical Society, New York, 1928.
   (c) P. G. N. Peppelenbosch, 'Nomadism in the Arabian peninsula: a general appraisal', *Tijdschr. econ. soc. Geogr.*, **59**, 335–46 (1968).
   (d) L. E. Sweet, 'Camel pastoralism in north Arabia and the minimal camping unit., in *Man, Culture and Animals: The Role of Animals in Human Ecological Adjustments*, (Eds. A. Leeds and A. P. Vayda), American Association for the Advancement of Science, Washington D.C., 1965, 129–152.
5. (a) R. Serjeant, 'Fisher folk and fish-traps in al-Bahrain', *Bulletin of the School of Oriental and African Studies*, **31**, 486–514 (1968).
   (b) I. F. Wallen, 'Non-oil trade and resources', in *The Princeton University Conference and Twentieth Annual Near Eastern Conference on Middle East Focus: The Persian Gulf*, (Ed. T. C. Young), Princeton University Conference, Princeton, N. J., 1969, 107–110.
6. (a) C. D. Belgrave, 'Pearl diving in Bahrain', *Jl. R. cent. Asian Soc.*, **21**, 450–452 (1934).
   (b) R. L. Bowen, 'The pearl fisheries of the Persian Gulf', *Middle East Journal*, **5**, 161–180 (1951).
7. J. Hornell, 'A tentative classification of Arab seacraft', *Mariner's Mirror*, **28**, 11–40 (1942).
8. D. N. McMaster, 'The ocean-going dhow trade to East Africa', *East African Geographical Review*, **4**, 13–24 (1966).

328

9. (a) M. S. El Attar, *Le Sous-développement économique et social du Yémén. Perspectives de la révolution yéménite*, Editions Tiers Monde, Algiers, 1964, 65–67.

(b) H. Ingrams, *Arabia and the Isles*, John Murray, London, 1966, 337.

(c) R. Levy, *The Social Structure of Islam*, Cambridge University Press, London, 1957, 43.

10 (a) L. E. Sweet, 'Pirates or politics? Arab societies of the Persian or Arabian Gulf, eighteenth century', *Ethnohistory*, **11**, 262–280 (1964).

(b) R. G. Lander, 'The modernisation of the Persian Gulf: The period of British dominance', in *The Princeton University Conference and Twentieth Annual Near Eastern Conference on Middle East Focus: The Persian Gulf*, (Ed. T. C. Young), Princeton University Conference, Princeton, N. J. 1969, 1–29.

11. (a) Article on the *Hadj* in *The Encyclopaedia of Islam* (Ed. B. Lewis, C. Pellart and J. Schaht), **2**, new ed., E. J. Brill, Leiden, and Luzac and Co., London, 31–38.

(b) R. King, 'The Pilgrimage to Mecca: some geographical and historical aspects', *Erdkunde*, **26**, 61–72 (1972).

12. D. G. Hogarth, *The Nearer East*, William Heinemann, London, 1902, 221–224.

13. (a) D. D. Crary, 'Recent agricultural developments in Saudi Arabia', *Geogrl Rev.*, **41**, 366–383 (1951).

(b) R. H. Sanger, *The Arabian Peninsula*, Cornell University Press, New York, 1954, 58–72.

14. F. S. Vidal, *The Oasis of al-Hasa*, ARAMCO, New York, 1955.

15. Saudi Arabian Monetary Agency, *Annual Report, 1388–89, A. H.* (AD 1969), 37.

16. J. H. Stevens, 'Oasis agriculture in the central and eastern Arabian Peninsula', *Geography*, **57**, 321–326 (1972).

17. (a) J. H. Stevens, 'Arid zone agricultural development in the Trucial States', *J. Soil Wat. Conserv.*, **24**, 181–183 (1969).

(b) J. H. Stevens, 'The changing agricultural practice in an Arabian oasis', *Geogrl J.*, **136**, 410–418 (1970).

18. (a) M. S. El Attar, *Le Sous-développement économique et social du Yémén. Perspectives de la révolution yéménite*, Editions Tiers Monde, Algiers, 1964, 177.

(b) F. Moseley, 'Exploration for water in the Aden Protectorate', *R. Engrs' J.*, **80**, 124–142 (1966).

(c) K. Tan, 'Agricultural problems in southern Arabia', *Wld Crops*, **22**, 397–400 (1970).

19. R. Twisleton-Wykeham-Fiennes, 'Sweetest water for the hottest land', *Geogrl Mag., Lond.*, **42**, 889–893 (1969–70).

20. (a) A. S. Helaissi, 'The Bedouins and tribal life in Saudi Arabia', *International Social Science Journal*, **11**, 532–538 (1959).

(b) P. G. N. Peppelenbosch, 'Nomadism in the Arabian Peninsula: a general appraisal', *Tijdsch. econ. soc. Geogr.*, **59**, 335–346 (1968).

21. H. F. Hendy, 'Ecological consequences of bedouin settlement in Saudi Arabia', in *The Careless Technology*, (Ed. M. T. Farvar and J. P. Milton), The Natural History Press, Garden City, New York, 1972, pp. 683–693.

22. H. F. Hendy, 'Ecological consequences of bedouin settlement in Saudi Arabia' in *The Careless Technology*, (Ed. M. T. Farvar and J. P. Milton), The Natural History Press, Garden City, New York, 1972, 683–693.

23. R. King, 'The Pilgrimage to Mecca: Some geographical and historical aspects', *Erdkunde*, **26**, 61–72 (1972).

24. M. Tomkinson, 'Seaside city for Mecca pilgrims', *Geogrl Mag., Lond.*, **42**, 95–101 (1969–70).

25. Saudi Arabian Monetary Agency, *Annual Report, 1388–89 A. H.* (1969 AD), 37.

26. M. Tomkinson, 'Seaside city for Mecca pilgrims', *Geogrl Mag., Lond.*, **42**, 95–101 (1969).

27. A. Melamid, 'Oil and the evolution of boundaries in eastern Arabia', *Geogrl Rev.*, **44**, 295–296 (1954).

CHAPTER 12

Iraq—A Study of Man, Land and Water in an Alluvial Environment

12.1 The economy

With an area of 434,000 km² and a population of only 10·4 million in 1972, Iraq is one of the least densely populated countries of the Middle East. Yet, in terms of the availability of flat land and water, it has perhaps the greatest agricultural potential of any of the countries within the region. At the present time, the economy of the country rests on the twin pillars of oil production and agriculture. Over the last 15 years or so, although the population has increased markedly, agricultural production has tended to stagnate or even decline in some sectors. As a result, a larger proportion of the oil revenues, needed so urgently for development projects, has had to be diverted to pay for the import of foodstuffs. This situation is in marked contrast to the period before 1955, when Iraq was largely self-sufficient in staple crops and animal products. To comprehend the present position it is necessary to outline the environmental characteristics of the nation, as well as the sequence of land-use changes which have occurred during the historical period.

Four major regions can be identified in Iraq. In the extreme northeast are the high ranges of the Zagros Mountains. This is a barren and harsh environment, with little human activity except for pastoral nomadism in the broad upland basins during summer. At lower altitudes, the foothills of the Zagros provide a much more hospitable landscape for human settlement. This region, the home of the Kurds, once had a natural vegetation cover of forest. Today it is covered by scrub, as the result of centuries of deforestation and overgrazing. Precipitation ranges from 400 mm to 500 mm per annum, so that sufficient moisture is available for rain-fed agriculture, at least in the more northerly and easterly parts. This area, part of the famed 'Fertile Crescent', is one in which most of the country's cereal crops of wheat and barley are grown. Between the rivers Tigris and Euphrates is the Jezira, a barren zone frequented today by nomads, but with considerable agricultural potential if irrigation water can be supplied to it.

Central and southern Iraq is an alluvial plain formed by the deposition of sediment from the rivers Tigris and Euphrates. This is the main agricultural region of the country, and the site of some of the earliest civilizations in the world. Dates, wheat and barley, rice, cotton and vegetables are the principal crops. At the southern end of the alluvial plain lie extensive marshlands, while along the Shatt al'Arab the richest date groves in Iraq are found.

329

To the west of the alluvial plain, covering more than a half of the total area of the country, is the desert stretching away towards Syria, Jordan and Saudi Arabia. In this region, land-use is limited to nomadic pastoralism.

The wealth of Iraq rests upon its oil production, which reached 83 million tonnes in 1971 and provided 840 million U.S. Dollars in revenues (Chapter 9). Most of the oil comes from the Kirkūk fields in the north, but other deposits have been discovered at Ayn Zālah near the Turkish border and also close to the head of the Gulf at Rumaila. About two-thirds of the oil is exported by pipeline through Syria to Baniyās on the Mediterranean Coast, but in future

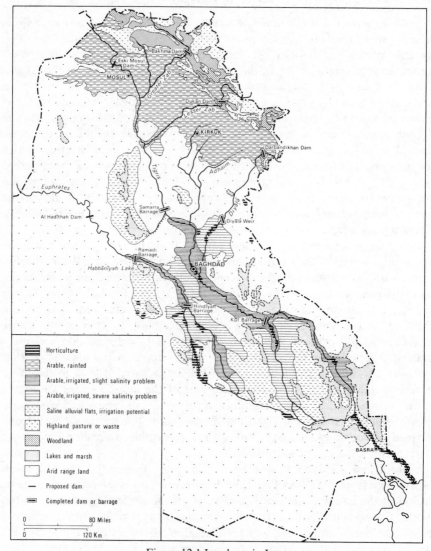

Figure 12.1 Land use in Iraq

it is hoped that a larger proportion will be sent via a new pipeline to a terminal near Basra.

Besides the oil industry, very little large scale industrialization exists in Iraq, and what little there is is concentrated in the capital. Of the 1,200 units employing ten or more people, more than half are located in Baghdād.[1] Food processing and light industries predominate here, though textile industries are found in Mosul and at other centres.

A characteristic feature of the population during the twentieth century has been the drift to the towns.[2] After the Second World War approximately 65 per cent of the population lived and worked in rural areas, while today one half of the population is concentrated in urban centres. Twenty per cent of the total population of the country is now found in the capital, Baghdād.

The total area of cultivable land in Iraq is estimated at 48 million donums (12 million ha), of which only about 12 million donums (3 million ha) are cultivated in any one year (Figure 12.1). Wheat and barley are by far the most important crops and make up about 80 per cent of the total cropped area (Table 12.1). Production is concentrated in the northern, wetter parts of the country, and in the Tigris–Euphrates lowlands (Figure 12.2). Production of wheat and barley, both of which are grown as winter crops, has until recently satisfied most of the domestic demand, but only because very large acreages are devoted to cereal production. Yields are everywhere low (Figure 12.3). The actual costs of wheat and barley production in terms of land, water and labour resources are, therefore, very high. Rice is the only other cereal crop of major significance, with almost all production concentrated in the *Muhafadhas* of Qadissiya, Maysan, Kerbela and Thi-Qar. Over the last ten years

TABLE 12.1
Major crops—areas under cultivation in Iraq
('000 donums)

	1968	1969	1970	1971
Cereals				
Wheat	6,736	6,646	7,034	3,793
Barley	3,614	3,381	2,690	1,584
Rice	435	424	298	436
Industrial crops				
Cotton	63	88	135	136
Tobacco	61	63	61	65
Linseed	62	65	69	38
Sesame	68	68	73	82
Sugar cane	—	6	13	16
Vegetables	750	769	780	855
Orchards of palm trees	585	582	582	583
Orchards of fruit trees and vines	200	202	202	250

Source: Ministry of Planning, Republic of Iraq, Central Statistical Organisation, *Annual Abstract of Statistics 1971*, pp. 108 and 109.

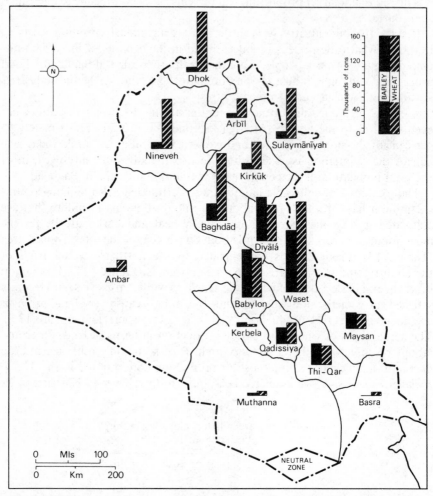

Figure 12.2 Wheat and barley production in the major administrative units of Iraq in 1970

its production has increased, in particular as the result of very marked improvements in yields. The two other major crops are vegetables and dates. The former are grown with the aid of irrigation around all the villages and towns, while the latter tend to be concentrated in the Basra region.

The methods of agricultural production still remain primitive throughout much of the country. Mechanization, although still at a low level, is proceeding and recent estimates suggest that some 10,000 tractors are now in use. About 2,000 combine harvesters were also imported into Iraq during the 1960's. In about 1970, 14,000 irrigation pumps were in use, compared with a figure of only 4,000 in 1950. The use of chemical fertilizers is not widespread. Increasing, though still very small amounts, are utilized in the production of rice, cotton

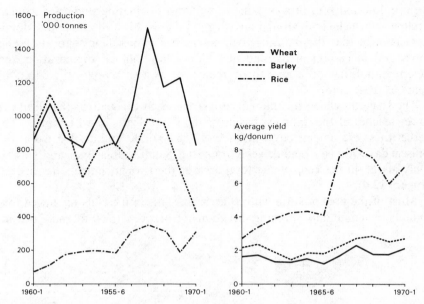

Figure 12.3 Variations in annual production and yields for wheat, barley and rice in Iraq

and vegetables, but almost none is used in the cultivation of wheat and barley. With this continued depletion of nutrients from the soil, which has continued unchecked for thousands of years, it is not really surprising that crop yields are low. Little use is made of weedkillers and pesticides.

An important change in the agricultural structure of the country has occurred since the passing of a Land Reform Law in 1959.[3] This limited the size of private holdings to 1,000 donums (250 ha) of irrigated land, and 2,000 donums (500 ha) of rain-fed land. As a result, large areas have been redistributed amongst landless labourers, but administrative and political difficulties, especially the lack of managerial experience,[4] have limited the overall success of the scheme in terms of agricultural production.

12.2 Agriculture and settlement in the alluvial lowlands

Lowland Iraq provides one of the harshest environments for man in the Middle East. Despite this fact, the riverine lands gave birth to one of the world's earliest civilizations, dating back at least to the fourth millenium BC, when the settlements of Akkad and Sumer were established in the northern and southern parts respectively of the Tigris–Euphrates delta (Chapter 6). Then, as now, agriculture in lowland Iraq was only possible when an assured supply of irrigation water was available, and the growth of these civilizations was entirely dependent upon the life-giving waters of the rivers Tigris and Euphrates. The story of the interrelationships between man and his environ-

334

ment in lowland Iraq provides one of the most fascinating studies of sequent occupance which can be found anywhere in the world. It illustrates the dominant control that the natural environment has imposed on man at certain times and in certain areas, and also shows how human organization and determination has been able to overcome, or at least modify, the effects of some of these controls.

The stage on which this human drama has been enacted is situated in the lower reaches of the drainage basins of the rivers Tigris and Euphrates. Together these catchments cover an area of 785,000 km² and are located at the present day within the boundaries of Iraq, Iran, Saudi Arabia, Syria and Turkey. Only about 46 per cent of the total area of the two catchments lies in Iraq (Figure 12.4).

Most of the precipitation within the basins falls in the belts of rugged fold mountains, commonly reaching elevations of between 1,500 m and 3,000 m,

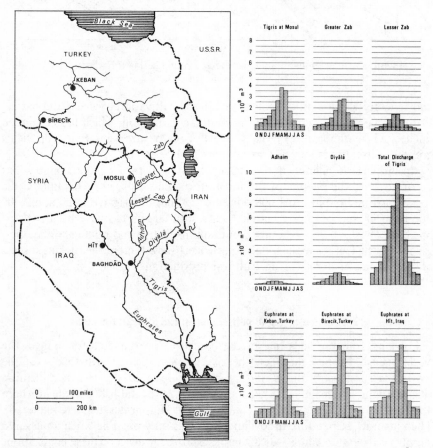

Figure 12.4 The drainage basins of the rivers Tigris and Euphrates, together with selected regime hydrographs

in Turkey and Iran. In these regions, annual totals of more than 1,000 mm are often recorded. Very little of this precipitation occurs during the summer months, and much of it falls as snow.

In Iraq, the alluvial floodplain region, characterized by poor surface drainage and swamps, is found around Baghdād and to the south. Rainfall totals throughout this area are everywhere less than 300 mm, and often below 150 mm per annum. Almost all of the precipitation is concentrated in the period from November to April. Summer temperatures commonly rise to more than 40°C and frosts are rare. Xerophytic vegetation predominates throughout the zone. It is on this alluvial floodplain that human activity has especially been concentrated, although there have been long periods when the lowlands have been virtually uninhabited.

Throughout history, certain related natural hazards have tended to limit man's ability to live successfully in the Tigris–Euphrates lowlands. Four problems stand out as of particular importance. These are floods, often of a sudden and devastating nature; drought, with its slow and relentless pressure on man and his resources; salination, a process which with time renders crop growth impossible; and siltation, causing a progressive deterioration in the efficiency of the man-made irrigation systems.

Floods and droughts in a river system are extreme events of relatively infrequent occurrence. To fully comprehend their environmental significance in Iraq, it is necessary to consider the hydrology and water-balance of the whole of the Tigris–Euphrates basin. In this catchment, an annual water surplus occurs only in the highland region of the north and east, while large water deficits are found elsewhere. This has meant that arable farming is only possible in the lowlands of Iraq if water, which has fallen elsewhere as precipitation, can be imported into the region, either by natural river flow or by irrigation canals. In the case of Iraq, the two largest importing conduits are the rivers Tigris and Euphrates, which transport water surpluses from the highland zone in the northern and eastern parts of the basin to the alluvial lowlands, where water is desperately needed for agricultural activity.

Both the Tigris and Euphrates rivers rise in the mountains of southern Turkey and flow southeastwards into Iraq. The Euphrates possesses only one large tributary, the river Khābūr, which joins the main stream in Syria, while in contrast, the Tigris has four major tributaries, all of which unite with the main stream in Iraq. The largest of these, the Greater Zab, has its source in Turkey, while the Lesser Zab and the Diyālá rise in Iran. All of the catchment of the Adhaim, the smallest stream, is situated in Iraq. In southern Iraq the Tigris and Euphrates rivers unite to form the Shaṭṭ'al Arab, which in turn flows into the Gulf.

Much of the discharge of the Tigris results from the melting of snow accumulated during the winter season in Turkey. However, heavy rains, which are common in late winter and early spring, falling on a ripe snowpack in the highlands, can greatly augment the flow of the main stream and its tributaries, giving rise to the violent floods for which the river Tigris is notorious. The period of greatest discharge on the Tigris system as a whole occurs during March, April and May, and accounts for 53 per cent of the mean annual flow. The highest mean monthly discharge takes place during April. Minimum flow conditions are experienced in August, September and October and make up seven per cent of the annual total discharge.

The total flow of the Euphrates is not as great as that of the Tigris, although the river regimes are similar. It, too, rises in the highlands of Turkey and is fed by melting snows, to an even greater extent than the Tigris, but lacks the major tributaries which the former possesses. In Iraq, the period of maximum flow on the Euphrates is shorter and later than that of the Tigris, and is usually confined to the months of April and May. Discharge during these two months accounts for 42 per cent of the annual total. Minimum flows occur in August, September and October and contribute only 8·5 per cent of the total discharge.

These mean values, however, tend to conceal the fluctuations in discharge which can occur from year to year, for it must be remembered that floods, as well as droughts, are themselves of variable magnitude. Both floods and droughts can have serious effects on the environment, which ancient man, with his limited technology, was unable to control. During the spring floods, although water levels varied from year to year, the effects on the landscape tended to be similar. Natural levees were over-topped, large areas of low-lying ground were flooded and irrigation control works were often seriously damaged by the swirling river waters.

Drought, or water shortage, is caused by long periods of dry weather. Such conditions are, of course, commonplace in lowland Iraq, where annual rainfall totals are so low, although their importance in terms of the water budget of the region is not great. Of far greater importance to the alluvial lowlands is the occurrence of droughts in the upper part of the Tigris–Euphrates basin. In such a case, their effects are always experienced elsewhere, through the transporting agency of the river, and are registered downstream by low spring water levels and insufficient quantities of water for adequate irrigation.

Salinity problems are common in arid and semi-arid regions, especially where soils have high silt and clay contents, and natural drainage is poor. If the water-table is shallow, water is drawn upwards through the soil profile by capillary action. As this water evaporates from the ground surface or is transpired by plants, the less soluble calcium and magnesium salts, already concentrated in the groundwater resources owing to high evaporation, will tend to be precipitated as sulphates and carbonates in the soil profile. Sodium ions tend to be left in the soil solution for the longest period before they too are deposited. It is these sodium ions which have the greatest deleterious effect on the soil, for by deflocculating the clay-sized particles, they cause the structure of the soil to be destroyed. As a result, drainage is further impeded and the ability of the soil to grow crops successfully is seriously reduced. Unfortunately, the process of salination is both progressive and cumulative, and, consequently, the problem tends to worsen from year to year, unless remedial measures are introduced. In the Tigris–Euphrates lowlands, salinity has been introduced into the region largely as the result of human activity. The use of excessive amounts of irrigation water, much of which percolates into the ground, has caused the water-table to rise, and this, coupled with the lack of adequate drainage facilities, partly due to the low natural gradients, has greatly speeded up the concentration of salts within the soils. If irrigation is stopped for a long period and the land withdrawn from cultivation, then the water-table may fall sufficiently by natural processes to permit cultivation to be resumed, following an initial washing of the soil to remove the more soluble sodium salts. Salination, of course, will occur once again, if the environmental controls remain unchanged.

The deposition of silt is a naturally occurring phenomenon in the lowland reaches of most large river systems. Rates of deposition are usually not uniform and tend to be greatest along the margins of the major channels, where levees are built up. The formation and growth of such levees in ancient Iraq often meant that large areas of land had their natural drainage lines to the river blocked, resulting in the development of swamp conditions. Swamps such as these seem to have been transient features in lowland Iraq, with some being drained and new ones created as the rivers changed their courses relatively frequently on the level alluvial flood plains.

In the irrigation canals, sedimentation from the turbid waters over the years greatly reduced the carrying capacity of the system, making periodic cleaning operations essential for the preservation of the irrigation network. Even after passing through the canals, the irrigation water which was led into the fields often still carried large quantities of sediment in suspension. Here the sediment would be deposited under tranquil conditions, causing annually a progressive rise in the level of the fields, which made irrigation increasingly difficult.

The soils of the lowlands are formed entirely from alluvial sediments and, as a consequence of their youth, do not reveal any marked horizon differentiation. They do not possess a well-developed structure and, thus tend to break down to individual particle sizes when wetted. To some extent this absence of a well-defined structure is a reflection of the low organic matter content of the soil. This is due to the general absence of vegetation and the high summer temperatures which promote rapid decomposition of organic material. Throughout the lowlands, calcareous alluvial soils cover by far the largest area. They are often well drained, but, when drainage is poor, more saline alluvial soils predominate. In the larger depressions, which may be continually wet for part of the year, Solonchak soils are found.

12.3 History of land use

Our knowledge of the ancient history of settlement and land-use in the Tigris–Euphrates lowlands is still fragmentary. However, following detailed archaeological work, a reasonably clear picture of the changing patterns of agriculture, irrigation and settlement can be outlined in certain areas.

Research on the Diyālá Plains, near Baghdād, has revealed successive and distinctive patterns of water use and settlement.[5] From the beginnings of cultivation and settlement in the Tigris–Euphrates lowlands during the late fifth millenium BC, to the early first millenium BC, the Diyālá region was characterized by a linear pattern of dispersed settlements along the major water courses and by irrigation works which had little impact upon the natural environment. During this period, irrigation seems to have been achieved by breaching the natural levees of the braided channel system of the lower Diyālá river or by the construction of small canals. One of the chief characteristics at this time appears to have been the durability of the irrigation network, for the

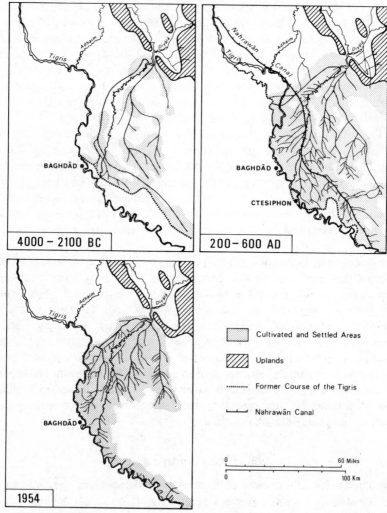

Figure 12.5 Cultivated and settled areas on the lower Diyālá plains
(Reproduced by permission of University of Chicago Press)

same system of canals and distribution channels was in existence at both the beginning and at the end of the period. To some extent, the longevity of the system can be explained by the ease and simplicity with which the maintenance of the levees and canals could be accomplished by the villagers themselves. The settlements which evolved with this pattern of agricultural activity were relatively small, with the majority of the inhabitants apparently engaged in food production for their own consumption. Regional integration of agriculture does not seem to have occurred, and there is little evidence for the existence of coordinated networks of irrigation canals (Figure 12.5).

A second phase of land use, which lasted more than a thousand years, was initiated towards the close of the first millenium BC, following a long period of agricultural decline, and perhaps even the abandonment of land throughout the region. During this new phase, the growth of urban centres commenced and became quite rapid, especially in the period following the conquests of Alexander the Great, and the spread of Greek influence. Later, under Parthian and Sassanian rule, the political capital was established at Ctesiphon, and as a result the Diyálá Plains became the centre of a large and important empire. So great was the expansion of the cultivable area at this time, in an attempt to feed the growing population, that land, as well as water, seems to have been in short supply. With the consequently increased demands for water, the irrigation system had to be enlarged. To ensure that these needs could be met, the central government became increasingly involved in the creation and operation of large integrated canal networks. The supreme example of such a construction was the Nahrawān canal, built during the sixth century AD. This canal, which was 300 km in length and in places more than 50 m in width, abstracted water from the river Tigris near Sāmarrā and transported in southeast to the lower plains of the river Diyálá, where it was used for irrigation purposes. Its water permitted the almost continuous cultivation of the region.

One of the major reasons for the success of this complex irrigation network was the establishment of an efficient system of drainage, which prevented water-logging of the soil and consequent salination of the land. Throughout the lowland as a whole, this drainage was achieved by supplying irrigation water from the Euphrates in the west, and the Nahrawān canal in the east. This permitted the river Tigris, which was situated between the two, to function as a drain, and to collect water from the adjacent agricultural lands. So efficient was this system, that it supported widespread cultivation of the land in the region for many years without a serious decline in land quality.

The crucial disadvantage of this land-use system was that it depended upon a strong central government to ensure that maintenance operations were carried out. On the other hand, the high productivity of the irrigated land enabled the rulers to accumulate large stores of agricultural produce, chiefly of cereals, in the form of taxes from the peasant farmers. With these supplies, they were able to maintain and feed large bodies of soldiers and labourers, who were able to protect and construct new irrigation facilities.

The term 'hydraulic civilization' has been used to describe societies similar to those which existed in the alluvial lowlands of Iraq, and which required large scale management of water supplies by the bureaucracies of central governments for widespread agriculture to be feasible.[6] Such societies, based on government control of complex hydraulic structures and intensive irrigated farming by peasants, seemed to have come into existence through an organizational, rather than a technical revolution, which necessitated the establishment of a new system for the division of labour to ensure that the irrigation network functioned efficiently. The great advantage of the system was that it allowed the production of large quantities of food from a given acreage and so permitted the support of high population densities in what were extremely harsh natural environments.

The maximum limits of agricultural expansion in the Diyālá Plains seem to have been attained during the Sassanian period (226–637 AD) (Figure 12.5).[7] With the collapse of Sassanian rule, a marked deterioration in agricultural conditions occurred, which continued almost unchecked for centuries. One of the characteristic and perhaps surprising features of this period was that, though the rural agricultural economy was in a state of progressive decline, urban growth continued at certain sites. New centres at Baghdād and Sāmarrā quickly outgrew earlier settlements, even through the provincial towns seemed to be stagnating and declining. At its zenith, the imperial capital at Baghdād is claimed to have possessed a population of at least several hundred thousand and perhaps even a million inhabitants, with the majority engaged in non-agricultural pursuits of administration, commerce and service activities.[8] With this marked concentration of power in the capital, little interest was spared for the rural regions which were merely regarded as the sources of tax revenues and food.

The reasons for the agricultural decline are complex, but the major one was probably the decreasing effectiveness of the central government, which meant that the necessary reconstruction and maintenance of the irrigation networks tended to lapse. Progressive siltation of the major canals occurred, reducing the efficiency of water transmission, and the irrigation control works fell into disrepair. These reasons, together with the artificial nature of the complex irrigation system built up during the Sassanian and earlier periods, meant that single destructive acts, or local deterioration at key points in the system, could quickly bring about the complete breakdown of water supply and distribution over wide areas downstream from the affected point. Such events, sometimes of quite small magnitude, were often sufficient to precipitate crises which the local population did not have the resources to remedy without the aid of the central government. The result was that, by the middle of the twelfth century AD, following brief revivals under 'Abbasid rule, large areas of the alluvial lowlands could not be used for arable farming, and the land reverted to poor pasture and range land, which was only capable of supporting a few nomadic peoples. By the time of the Mongul invasions of the twelfth and thirteenth centuries AD, the abandonment of the once fertile land was almost complete. While it is true to say that the Mongols did destroy a number of canal headworks and massacred local populations, their total effect upon the decline of the irrigation system of the alluvial lowlands appears to have been minimal. The irrigation complex to all intents and purposes, had been destroyed by neglect before they arrived.[9]

From the end of the 'Abbasid Caliphate until the later part of the nineteenth century, when some of the old canals were cleaned of silt, irrigation within the Tigris–Euphrates lowlands was carried out only locally on a non-coordinated basis, and agricultural activity was at a particularly low level. Wherever possible, the ancient canals were used to supply water and were even in places repaired, but nowhere was the work undertaken as part of a comprehensive scheme on the scale witnessed in Sassanian or even 'Abbasid times. In summary, for the 600 years prior to the beginning of the twentieth century, it would seem that the physical environment of Iraq dominated the agricultural response of man more strongly than at any time since the first millenium BC (Figure 12.5).

Although the agricultural recovery of the Tigris–Euphrates lowlands began during the late nineteenth century, with the cleaning of a number of the ancient canals, it was not until the early part of the twentieth century that the first modern river control work, the Al Hindīyah barrage (1909–1913) was constructed on the river Euphrates.[10] Its original function was to divert water into the Al Hillah channel, which was running dry, but later, following reconstruction in the 1920's, it was also used to supply other canals. Between the two World Wars, considerable attention was given to the Euphrates canal system, and many new channels were constructed and new control works established. On the river Tigris, development work tended to come later. The building of the Al Kūt barrage commenced in 1934, but was not completed until 1943, while on the Diyālá, a tributary of the Tigris, a weir was constructed in 1927–1928 to replace a temporary earthen dam which had to be rebuilt each year following the winter flood. The weir allowed six canals to be supplied with water throughout the year.

Following the Second World War, river control schemes tended to concentrate on the problems of flood control. Two of the earliest projects, completed in the mid-1950's, were situated towards the upper part of the alluvial valley. The Sāmarrā barrage was constructed on the Tigris river with the objective of diverting flood waters into the Tharthar depression to provide a storage capacity of 30,000 million m³. A similar scheme was also built on the river Euphrates, where the Ar Ramādī barrage diverted floodwaters into the Habbānīyah reservoir and the Abu Dibis depression. It had been hoped that the stored water from these two projects might be used for irrigation during the summer months, but it was discovered that the very large evaporation losses, together with the dissolution of salts from the soils of the depressions, seriously diminished water quality and rendered it unsuitable for irrigation purposes. In conjunction with the barrages on the mainstreams themselves, two major dams were constructed on tributaries of the Tigris. The Dukān dam, with a reservoir storage capacity of 6,300 million m³, was completed on the Lesser Zab river in 1959, while further south, on the Diyālá river, the Darbandikhan dam, with 3,250 million m³ storage was opened in 1961.[11]

12.4 Contemporary environmental problems and their solution

One of the major problems facing Iraq today is the need to improve agricultural production to feed the growing population. Unfortunately, the deterioration of land in Iraq over the last few centuries has been so severe that carefully planned large-scale schemes will be necessary to ensure any major improvement. The extensive and wasteful use of land for cereal production in the alluvial lowlands has been necessitated by the high salt content of the soils and the lack of field drainage. Over the years, a system of agriculture has evolved which at least makes cultivation possible, but which provides no lasting solution to the salt problem. Following the cereal harvest, the land is allowed to remain fallow for at least a year so that it may dry out and so that the water-table, which has risen as the result of percolating irrigation water, may decline. During the hot summer season, the soils dry out to depths of approximately one metre, and deep cracks often develop. Just before the preparation of the ground for the next season's crop, the land is flooded to a depth of a few centimetres in an attempt to dissolve the soluble salts occurring close to the ground surface. These salts are then carried under the influence of gravity to the deeper layers of the soil profile where they enter into the groundwater system. The soil, following preparation, is planted with cereals. Wheat is often the preferred crop, but barley is more salt tolerant and is now widespread throughout the alluvial lowlands. During the early stages of growth, the crop thrives in the salt-free upper layers of the soil, provided that sufficient water is available through irrigation. Unfortunately, as the season progresses, water rises in the soil and is lost through evapotranspiration from the ground surface. The result is a progressive increase in the salt content of the surface layers of the soil. By harvest time, salt levels are often quite high, causing the crop yield to be low.

At present, agricultural water use in the lowlands averages 13,300 m³/ annum/ha, or 1,330 mm/annum in the irrigated regions.[12] This figure is considered to be greater than the amount necessary for plant growth and for the leaching of salts from soil horizons. As a result of this excessive water use, about 60 per cent of the irrigated lands in Iraq now suffer from some form of salinity. Indeed, it has been claimed that since the beginning of modern large-scale irrigation, 20 to 30 per cent of the country's total cultivated land has been abandoned because of this problem.[13]

Despite the serious difficulties which agriculture in Iraq is facing, it is reassuring to know that some of them are capable of solution, at least at a technical level. For example, soil salinity can be overcome simply by surface leaching and an efficient drainage system. Once this is achieved, and provided that adequate water for continued leaching of the soil is available, then crop yields are likely to increase markedly.

Drainage waters with very high salt contents will cause further environmental problems if they are allowed to drain directly into the major rivers. In such cases, the quality of river water can be so seriously reduced that it might become totally unsuitable for irrigation further downstream. A temporary solution to the problem would be to allow the saline waters to drain into enclosed desert basins and there evaporate. Any long-term solution, however, must include the construction of a separate drainage network to ensure that the saline waters are carried directly to the sea without risk of contaminating river waters. At the present time, the waters of the rivers Tigris and Euphrates at the head of the alluvial plain have total dissolved salt contents of between 200 to 400 parts per million (ppm) and, therefore, as yet pose little danger to irrigated farming.

Although soil salinity usually receives most attention in discussions of agriculture, the really crucial problem for the alluvial lowlands of Iraq is the availability of water for irrigation. Without additional water supplies, expansion of arable farming in the region will be impossible. The total amount of water available from the Tigris–Euphrates catchment is still a matter of some dispute. Estimates range from 73,000 million m³/annum to 84,000 million m³/annum.[14] Of these, the higher figure is probably the most accurate, as it is based on the 40 year period 1931 to 1969. With this estimate, the contribution of the individual streams to the total figure is seen in Table 12.2.

To utilize the available water fully, Iraq desperately needs a comprehensive irrigation and water resource development programme which considers the country as a single unit. Better still would be to plan for basin-wide development, but, as this would involve Turkey, Syria and Iran, such a proposal does not appear to be politically practicable at the present time. Any integrated scheme would have to establish efficient methods of water distribution and control at both the local and regional level, bearing in mind the finite amount of irrigation water which is available and ensuring that sufficient water is at hand for leaching the soil and thus preventing salinity build-up.

Today, irrigation water in Iraq is almost exclusively obtained from surface water sources. Over the last thirty years, the average withdrawal of water from

TABLE 12.2
Annual discharges within the Tigris–Euphrates basin

River	million m³/annum
Euphrates (at Hit)	31,820
Tigris (at Mosul)	23,210
Tributaries of the Tigris	29,455
Total	84,485

Source: Ubell K., 'Iraq's water resources', Nature and Resources, 7, 3 (1971), by permission of UNESCO © UNESCO 1971.

TABLE 12.3
Volume of irrigation water abstracted from the major
rivers in Iraq

River	Million m³/annum
Euphrates (Hit to Hindīyah)	17,213
Tigris and tributaries (Mosul to Fathah)	4,190
Tigris (Fathah to Baghdād)	14,052
Diyālá	5,139
Tigris (Baghdād to Kūt)	8,614
TOTAL	49,208

Source: Ubell K., 'Iraq's water resources', *Nature and Resources*, **7**, 4 (1971), by permission of UNESCO © UNESCO 1971.

the Tigris–Euphrates system has increased markedly, although the area of arable lands has only shown a moderate expansion. The available data on water use suggests a withdrawal of about 19,000 million m³/annum between 1940 and 1949; about 28,000 million m³/annum between 1950 and 1959; and a very rapid rise in the 1960's to an average value of about 49,000 million m³/annum.[15] A detailed breakdown of the figures in terms of the individual drainage basins is shown in Table 12.3. The average volume of water which returns to the rivers as the result of drainage is unknown.

These water withdrawals have recently grown to such a scale that the future development of agriculture in Iraq is likely to become increasingly difficult, unless rigorous and strictly enforced controls of water use are introduced. Already the present rate of water abstraction from the Tigris–Euphrates system represents approximately 60 per cent of the average annual flow of the major rivers.

In low flow years, the discharge can fall to 25,000 million m³/annum, a value which is only about one half of the current annual water consumption.[16] This clearly demonstrates the serious nature of the problem facing Iraq in terms of its water resource development. To protect the natural ecosystem of the rivers, as well as to transport agricultural and industrial effluents, it seems necessary to maintain a minimum flow of at least 10,000 million m³/annum. Subtracting this value from the mean annual value of 84,000 million m³/annum suggests that up to 74,000 million m³/annum of water is available for beneficial uses over a long period for the basin as a whole. However, to make full use of this maximum figure, it is essential that storage capacity is available, so that water in years of high discharge can be stored and utilized during periods of drought.

In contrast to earlier times, when the provision of irrigation water was the sole concern of any hydraulic control works, river engineering in the twentieth century has had three major objectives in Iraq. These are the provision of water for irrigation and the reclamation of neglected agricultural land; the prevention of floods; and, wherever possible, the generation of power. All three objectives have necessitated the creation of reservoirs capable of providing sufficient storage capacity to hold the flood water of one year and so allow it to be used in subsequent years. The storage of water within the Tigris–Euphrates system is most efficiently achieved in the region outside the alluvial plain proper, where dam sites are more plentiful and potential evapotranspiration losses lower. Ideally, the location of such sites are to be found in the upland margins of the basin. On the Euphrates, most of the better sites lie within Turkey or Syria, while for the Tigris, Iraq is more fortunate in that a number of suitable locations lie within her territory, along the tributaries of the Greater Zab and the Diyālá. A number of these latter sites have already been developed. The Dukān dam on the Lesser Zab and the Darbandikhan on the Diyālá were primarily planned as flood control structures, but naturally fulfil other needs as well. For example, it is hoped to divert water stored in the Dukān dam southwards to the river Tigris. The Bakhma dam on the Greater Zab could impound flood waters which might be used to supplement the flow of the Tigris, and so compensate for any water which is diverted from the Lesser Zab at the Dukān dam. Any surplus water from the Bakhma dam could also be utilized for irrigation on the lowland around Arbīl. Other potential reservoir sites exist at Eski Mosul, Mosul and Al Fathah. These could supply varying amounts of irrigation water, flood protection and power.

Most of the discharge of the Euphrates originates in Turkey. This has led to considerable dispute arising between Turkey, Syria and Iraq as to how the water resources should be divided, and as yet no satisfactory solution has been reached. In Turkey, construction of the Keban dam is complete, and plans are being made for a considerable use of irrigation water in the southeastern parts of the country, where it is believed that 800,000 ha can be irrigated from the Euphrates. In Syria, the Tabqa dam has recently been opened and proposals drawn up for the utilization of even more irrigation water. Iraq, too, proposes a large dam at Al Hadīthah and a number of small irrigation networks. At the present time, it is difficult to obtain information on the actual amounts of water which are being used in Turkey and Syria. As yet, little seems to be extracted from the Euphrates in Turkey, but up to 3,500 million m³/annum might be being utilized in Syria. If all the water resource development schemes of the three countries are carried out as planned, there can be little doubt that the total amount of water necessary will be well above the mean annual river flow. From this, it should be obvious that some form of international agreement between the three countries must be reached as soon as possible so that scarce capital resources are not squandered on projects which can never produce the designed amounts of water.

In Iraq, the future development of the irrigation system depends basically upon a more efficient use of water. The irrigated area is unlikely to increase significantly, but total agricultural production would rise dramatically if two crops per year were to be cultivated. Emphasis, of course, would be placed on producing more summer crops. Such increased cultivation would require an assured water supply, which in turn means the use of large water storage schemes on the major rivers. At the local level, besides the provision of adequate drains, an important need is the levelling of the fields to ensure adequate and equal irrigation dosages. The results would be the use of smaller amounts of water to cultivate a larger area. Yields would tend to be higher as well, and the amount of labour input should decrease. Water distribution networks can also be improved by providing adequate linings to the larger canals to ensure that water transmission losses are reduced. To a large degree, such losses have been significantly reduced since the Second World War with the introduction of pumps which lift water from the canals and rivers directly to the fields, and so do away with the need for intermediate links in the system.

12.5 Conclusion

Irrigated agriculture in Iraq now seems to be entering yet another crucial stage in its development. Growing populations in all the countries within the Tigris–Euphrates basin are causing increasing pressure on available resources. At the present time, a number of water development projects are being constructed or planned to meet these needs, but little or no coordination of effort is taking place between the various countries involved. Already it would appear that the completion of certain projects on the Euphrates will mean that other schemes downstream will never be able to reach their design potential. Just as the large irrigation networks in ancient Iraq were dependent for successful operation upon a strong central government, so today the increasing size and complexity of environmental problems necessitates the creation of a centralized water authority with complete control of development projects throughout the whole of the Tigris–Euphrates basin. In this context at least, the existing states of the region are of insufficient size to be able to ensure efficient water resource development. In the future, some international authority, with responsibility for the whole of the basin, must come into being to coordinate irrigation, drainage, power generation and land reclamation schemes. Unfortunately, the creation of such an agency does not seem imminent.

References

1. R. A. Fernea and E. W. Fernea, 'Iraq', *Focus, N. Y.*, **20**, 5 (1969).
2. R. I. Lawless, 'Iraq—changing population patterns', in *Populations of the Middle East and North Africa* (Eds. J. I. Clarke and W. B. Fisher), University of London Press Ltd, London, Chapter 4, 97–129.
3. D. Warriner, 'Revolutions in Iraq', in *Land Reform in Principle and Practice*, Oxford University Press, Oxford, 1969, Chapter 4, 78–108.
4. J. L. Simmons, 'Agricultural development in Iraq: planning and management failures', *Middle East Journal*, **19**, 129–140 (1965).
5. R. McC. Adams, *The Land behind Baghdād*, The University of Chicago Press, Chicago, 1965, 187 pages.
6. K. A. Wittfogel, 'The hydraulic civilisations', in *Man's Role in Changing the face*

of the earth (Ed. W. L. Thomas Jr.), University of Chicago Press, Chicago, 1965, 152–164.

7. T. Jacobsen and R. McC. Adams, 'Salt and silt in ancient Mesopotamian agriculture', *Science*, N.Y. **128,** 1256 (1958).

8. R. McC. Adams, *The Land behind Baghdād*, The University of Chicago Press, Chicago, 1965, 116.

9. T. Jacobsen and R. McC. Adams, 'Salt and silt in ancient Mesopotamian agriculture', *Science*, N.Y., **128,** 1257 (1958).

10. Naval Intelligence Division (Great Britain), *Iraq and the Persian Gulf*, Geographical Handbook Series, 1944, p. 438.

11. (a) C. W. Mitchell, 'Investigations into the soils and agriculture of the Lower Diyālá area of eastern Iraq', *Geogrl J.*, **125,** 390–397 (1959).
    (b) C. W. Mitchell and P. E. Naylor, 'Investigations into the soils and agriculture of the Middle Diyālá region of eastern Iraq', *Geogrl J.*, **126,** 469–475 (1960).

12. K. Ubell, 'Iraq's water resources', *Nature & Resources*, **7,** 9 (1971).

13. W. C. Brice, *South-West Asia*, University of London Press Ltd., London, 1966, 379.

14. (a) 73,000 million m^3/annum:—W. H. Al-Khashab, *The Water Budget of the Tigris–Euphrates Basin*, University of Chicago, Department of Geography, Research Paper No. 54, 1958, 39.
    (b) 79,000 million m^3/annum:—M. Clawson, H. H. Landsberg and L. T. Alexander, *The Agricultural Potential of the Middle East*, Elsevier, New York, 1971, 202–205.
    (c) 85,000 million m^3/annum:—K. Ubell, 'Iraq's water resources', *Nature and Resources*, **7,** 3 (1971).

15. K. Ubell, 'Iraq's water resources', *Nature and Resources*, **7,** 4 (1971).

16. K. Ubell, 'Iraq's water resources', *Nature and Resources*, **7,** 9 (1971).

CHAPTER 13

Agricultural Expansion in Syria

13.1 Introduction

Modern Syria (Figure 13.1) was carved out of the Ottoman vilayets of Aleppo, Beirūt, Damascus, and Zōr-and-Jezira in the aftermath of the First World War. Since foundation, its existence has been characterized by political turmoil, though different factors have combined to produce this situation, including the imposition of a French mandate (1920 to 1945), the struggle for independence, the Arab–Israeli conflict, and the emergence since the Second World War of political groups whose socialism is in opposition to the traditions of the old landlord/merchant oligarchy. The stress situation

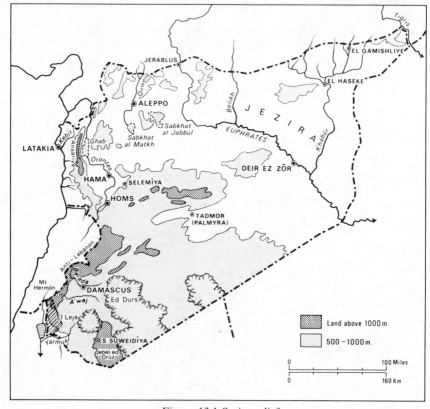

Figure 13.1 Syria: relief

348

has been increased by rapid economic development, especially since the end of the Second World War, which has brought new hopes and new uncertainties to many people. As Warriner pointed out, 'few underdeveloped countries ... made such rapid progress in agriculture and industry as Syria' during the 1950's.[1] Indeed, between 1953 and 1961 the annual growth in G.D.P. was about three per cent. Despite various difficulties in the 1960's, mentioned below, growth attained an annual rate of about five per cent over the period 1963 to 1971.[2] Until the nationalization of the oil industry in 1964, these comparatively high rates of growth were based largely upon increases in agricultural production. Syria's expanding agriculture has been chosen as the theme for the chapter. Agriculture's fundamental role in the Syrian economy is clear. Not only does it provide cereals and cotton for export, but it also furnishes raw materials for much of Syria's manufacturing industry, while employing over 50 per cent of the economically active population. A large proportion of the increased output, however, has resulted from a steady recolonization of cultivable but abandoned land, a process which has been in progress since the early nineteenth century.

The process of expansion has been closely influenced by physical conditions, especially precipitation (Figure 13.2). For many centuries, dry-farming was associated with the wetter areas of the west. The Ansāriye and Anti-Lebanon mountains, which close off much of Syria from Mediterranean influences, constituted one important, though fragmented zone. Steep slopes provided relatively secure situations against the marauders who overran so much of the country, while high ridges, exposed to the rain-bearing winds, raised precipitation to a reliable 750 to 1,000 mm/annum. A more continuous belt of dry-farming stretched across rolling upland between the Orontes

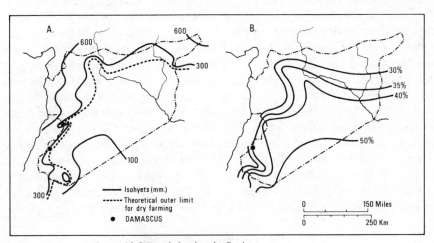

Figure 13.2 Precipitation in Syria
(a) Annual precipitation
(b) Relative interannual reliability
(after de Brichambaut and Wallén 1963)

depression, at the foot of the mountains, and Aleppo, and was made possible by an average precipitation of over 300 mm/annum with a 65 per cent reliability. Smaller areas lay scattered amongst the volcanic mounds and basaltic tracts of the Hauran and in the valleys and hollows of the neighbouring Jebel ed Drūz, where average annual precipitation is over 250 mm. Wheat and barley are basic field crops in all the traditional dry-farming districts, while figs, olives and vines often form extensive plantations.

Opportunities for dry-farming existed northeastwards of the Euphrates, in the hill country of the Jezira, the 'island' between the Euphrates and the Tigris. Here average precipitation totals reach 200 to 400 mm/annum, with interannual variabilities of 20 to 30 per cent. The rivers Belikh and Khābur, as well as the Euphrates, offer scope for irrigation. The potential, however, could not be realized until after about 1930, when the region's nomads had been pacified.

Much of Syria receives less than the critical annual average of 240 mm of precipitation and interannual variabilities are greater than 37 per cent (Figure 13.2). The transition zone runs across rolling country in the north, and permanent rain-fed cultivation becomes impossible with distance south-eastwards. Precipitation, however, is usually sufficient to produce extensive but poor-quality seasonal grazing in various parts of the Syrian desert. The grazing was used by thousands of sheep and camel-rearing nomads until recently. But expansion of cultivation and changes in cropping practice in the crucial base-areas on the margins of the dry-farming zone, or in the oases, combined with government sponsored sedentarization schemes to reduce the number of nomads to an estimated 115,000 by 1960.

Outside the zone of permanent dry-farming, cultivation takes place only where irrigation is possible, as at the famous oasis of Tadmor (ancient Palmyra). The main areas of irrigated farming, however, lie further north and west, either within the dry-farming zone itself or on its margins, since these are the situations where most water is available. An important transitional belt stretched along the Orontes between Homs and Hama, though the widest part of the rift valley, called the Ghab, was little more than a malarial swamp for centuries. Wheat, barley and beans were the main traditional crops here. Further south, the rivers Barada and A'waj flow down from the Anti-Lebanon range to nourish intensive, garden-like cultivation in the oasis of Damascus. Some irrigated farming has always been found along the Euphrates, though the incised nature of the river in many reaches restricted development before the era of the large dam. Technical advances, in fact, now allow the expansion of agriculture to break away from the traditional constraints represented by critical isohyets and interannual variabilities.

13.2 Expansion of cultivation

Western commentators in the second half of the eighteenth century con-stantly drew attention to the number of ruined villages to be seen in what is now Syria. They were found in every region, but appeared most numerous east of the Aleppo–Damascus road and in the Hauran. Inhabited villages and cultivation survived mainly to the west of this axial road, a region corresponding roughly with a narrow tract in which permanent rain-fed cultivation was possible and the risks of dearth comparatively small.

The sorry state of affairs over much of Syria was the result of a long phase of abandonment caused by a complex of interacting factors. Iniquitous taxation, rather than environmental factors, was probably the most important of these. By the second half of the eighteenth century, taxation was not only based on outdated and unadjusted registers of population, but it also varied considerably from year to year, depending upon the advent of a new governor, who had to recoup the price paid for his position, and upon sudden needs for money to meet an emergency. At the same time, the peasant's ability to pay fluctuated with the harvest, which in turn depended upon rainfall conditions. In areas where rainfall variability exceeded 30 per cent a year and rents were accordingly below average, cultivation ceased to yield the landlords any profit. The landlords seem to have withdrawn their tenants to more profitable areas and the land was abandoned. At the same time, Turkish officials did not normally control sufficient force to effectively police the Syrian provinces, and nomads were able to range far and wide across the country. Raiding and demands for protection money increased after the end of the seventeenth century, when indigenous tribes were forced westwards by the northern movement of the Shammar and Anizeh confederations. Many peasants found their burdens excessive and were only too pleased to remove into large villages further west, where the harvest was more certain and agglomerated population offered a degree of protection.

The situation began to improve during the brief period of Egyptian rule, 1831 to 1840. Over 150 villages were reoccupied in the Aleppo district and a similar number in the Hauran. However, some abandonment was reported by British consuls in the 1850's and 1860's. Ruined villages remained common as late as 1920, but the process of reoccupation pushed ahead sporadically and locally throughout the second half of the nineteenth century. By 1860 the frontier of settlement and cultivation had moved to a point about halfway between Aleppo and the Euphrates. At the start of the First World War it had reached the river.

Several parallel developments assisted the expansion. Nomads, defeated in the tribal wars of the eighteenth and early nineteenth centuries, gradually gave up their old habits and became permanently settled in the fringes of the cultivated area. This was especially marked around Aleppo. Here, as elsewhere, little colonies of cultivators also gradually established themselves away from large parent villages. They began to reclaim land, either on their own account or for some city magnate or nomadic chief. During the 1870's, numbers of Circassians were deliberately settled on the cultivation frontier to help contain the nomads.

A classic example of the reoccupation process is afforded by the Selemīya district southeast of Hama[3] (Figure 13.1). Despite the fame of its water in medieval times, when *qanāts* were used for irrigation, the whole district lay abandoned at the beginning of the nineteenth century. In 1854, a group of

Ismāʿīlīs (a Shīʿa sect, some of whom were known as 'The Assassins') moved into it from the Ansāriye mountains and settled on the site of the old town. They partially reactivated the old irrigation system by cleaning out the *qanāts* so that within twenty years the cultivated area stretched outward for about 13 km from Selemīya. Two daughter settlements were founded on old sites in the 1860's and a further seven in the 1870's. Circassians joined the original colonists in 1885, adding a further three villages of their own. Other colonists moved to the district subsequently. After the First World War, semi-nomads, originally driven eastwards by the expansion of cultivation around Selemīya, began to make cultivation a major activity and built a number of permanent settlements.

The recolonization of the Jebel ed Drūz was somewhat different. During the eighteenth century much of the Jebel Hauran, as it was known, was exposed to nomadic raiding and many villages had been abandoned. The situation, however, had already begun to change. From about 1711, small groups of Druzes, defeated in clan wars in the Lebanon, began to make their way eastwards and to establish themselves, against weaker opposition, in the vicinity of Es Suweidīya (Figure 13.1). In the early nineteenth century they were joined by larger groups driven from the Lebanon when Emir Bashīr (1789–1840) broke the power of their chiefs. Fighting between Christians and Druzes in the 1840's and early 1860's added more colonists. These tended to settle away from Es Suweidīya and gradually brought the whole Jebel under control. About 120 villages are currently inhabited.

Reclamation and expansion were facilitated by economic and political developments both within and beyond the Turkish Empire during the second half of the nineteenth century. The most important single factor was a rising demand for agricultural produce, especially for cereals. This seems to have begun during the Anglo-French wars of 1793 to 1815, when large numbers of foreign, principally British, troops were garrisoned around the Mediterranean and required supplies. Despite an Ottoman ban on cereal exports, Greek merchants were able to buy grain from landowners in the coastal provinces of the Turkish Empire and, with the connivance of local governors, ship it to the foreign garrisons. Coastal Syria was, no doubt, tapped. Cereal production was further stimulated by rising demand from the increasing population in northwestern Europe and by evolving regional specialization within the Turkish Empire. Although Britain imported much of her grain from the Baltic and the Ukraine until the 1870's, a small amount was also taken from Syria, which enjoyed the advantage of a harvest at least a month in advance of European suppliers. Syrian grain even replaced that from the Ukraine during the Crimean War. During the nineteenth century, some of the provinces of the Turkish Empire began to develop agricultural specialities. Mount Lebanon, for example, specialized increasingly in the production of silk, and the planting of mulberry trees reduced the area available for cereals. Since Lebanese harvests were already inadequate to feed the growing population, grain had to be imported and Syria was close at hand and able to meet the demand.

The cereals exported principally represented the landlords' share of the normal crop, although it was marketed by merchants. Long-established landlords and credit-giving speculators were able to acquire extensive properties by manipulation of the Ottoman Land Law of 1858. Designed to secure the peasant's title to land, this resulted in property being registered under the names of powerful individuals. They realized that profits could be made from cereal farming, and, accordingly, were prepared to introduce colonists to their newly acquired land. In some cases, the chiefs of semi-nomadic tribes, whose collective property was registered in one name, were able to follow suit and persuade their tribesmen to expand cultivation. Somewhat later on, the Sultan himself encouraged the settlement of imperial domain lying on the then existing frontier of cultivation.

Colonization was assisted by a general tightening-up of Turkish local government. Central direction became more effective as the nineteenth century advanced and distant provinces were brought within the range of the telegraph and railway. Active steps were taken to contain and pacify nomads. Regular, well-armed troops were sent on expeditions against them, garrisons were maintained at strategic points, such as Tadmor and Deir ez Zōr, and a network of police posts was established.

The First World War may have stimulated further expansion of the cultivated area to meet the needs of Turkish armies campaigning in Mesopotamia and Palestine, though the subject has not been investigated.

Sporadic expansion of the cropped area certainly continued in some districts between the World Wars, while infilling with daughter settlements was more characteristic in others. Altogether some 7,000 km² were added to the cultivated area of Syria between about 1850 and 1940, and about 2,000 villages were created.

The outbreak of the Second World War meant that the countries of the Middle East were forced to provide all their own food. At the same time, large numbers of British and French troops were garrisoned in the region or were operating in adjacent parts of North Africa and had to be fed. Syrian response to the situation was to initiate reclamation in the recently pacified Jezira. Economic exploitation was facilitated by a government decision to grant immense areas of fertile but uncultivated state land to tribal sheikhs. Sheikhs leased out their rain-fed land to town-based entrepreneurs for 10 to 15 per cent of the crop, but sold their irrigable property. The entrepreneurs often came from families which had arrived in the Jezira as refugees from Turkey. Low population forced them to adopt mechanized methods, as is shown by a rise in the number of tractors from about 30 in 1942 to 500 in 1950 and in the number of harvesting and threshing machines from about 20 to 430.* The area of cultivated land rose from about 20,000 ha in 1942 to over 243,000 ha in 1946.

Capital accumulation during the War, a rising national population and increasing urbanization and industrialization allowed developments in the

*Figures refer to Haseke province, which covers much of the *high* Jezira.

Jezira to continue. By 1951, about 500,000 ha were cultivated. The total reached 1,400 km² in 1960, representing an increase of nearly 500 per cent since the War. In 1961 the cultivated area of the whole country was estimated at about 6,000,000 ha, though at least 40 per cent of the total probably lay fallow. Nevertheless, the figure represents the attainment of an optimum situation and the physical limits were reached, apparently even in the Jezira, where attempts to extend rain-fed cultivation south of El Haseke have proved disastrous.

Expansion in the Jezira is worth further consideration because of its results. Speculative mechanized farming in the region has resulted in the monoculture of cereals or cotton, or an alternation of the two. Fertility accumulated through centuries of disuse has been mined, and declining yields were commented upon by the International Bank Mission as early as 1955,[4] though they became more noticeable under drought conditions at the end of the decade. Extensive mechanization has also increased the effects of wind erosion, so that parts at least of the Jezira are in danger of resembling an American dust-bowl.

Ploughing has reduced the grazing available to nomads. Some have moved southwards into Iraq, but others have attempted to maintain their old way of life, though on herds reduced to sizes incompatible with a satisfactory standard of living and at the cost of more extensive wandering. Many tribesmen, however, have become cultivators for their sheikh. Others have found work as labourers in the expanding towns and villages of the region or as tractor and lorry drivers.

At the end of the First World War, the population of the Jezira was low and the settled element minimal. Armenian and Kurdish refugees from Turkey and Iraq in the 1920's increased the population, as did the arrival of some 9,000 Assyrian Christians from Iraq in 1933. By 1938, the settled population was about 103,500. This was too small to meet the needs of the 'merchant-tractorists', as the entrepreneurs have been called.[5] Labour had to be imported from the western parts of the country. Unlike earlier colonists in other districts, these were paid regular wages, though attempts to introduce a modified form of share cropping were reported by Warriner.[6] Colonization and the settlement of nomads brought the established population of the Jezira to about 340,000 in 1960. There has been as yet little spontaneous migration to the region from the congested areas of the west; emigrants from the now backward and congested districts of the Ansāriye mountains and the Jebel ed Drūz have preferred to settle in neighbouring large towns.

Population growth in the Jezira has been accompanied by an increase in the number of settlements and the development of towns. There were scarcely any permanent settlements east of the Euphrates at the end of the First World War, but within ten years there were about 280 and by 1960 there were at least 2,000. Some villages were built by the 'merchant-tractorists' to house their workers. Others have crystallized around filling stations and cafés established on routes leading westwards out of the Jezira. The leading towns are El Haseke and El Qamishliye. Both were little more than military posts in the 1920's and began to grow with the influx of refugees. They subsequently enjoyed boom conditions as centres for mechanized farming and marketing. An atmosphere of frontier rawness still persists, despite apartment houses, modern shops and populations now in excess of 10,000.

The Jezira appears to have been affected comparatively little by the troubled history of attempted land reform which had such a disruptive impact on the agricultural sector of Syria's economy during the 1960's. This may have been due to two special reasons. Much of the region was not worked by share-cropping tenants, like the traditional dry-farming areas, since labour was in short supply, and successive governments may have been reluctant to assist the numerically dominant community in the Jezira, namely the Kurds.

As elsewhere in the Middle East, land reform appeared to aim at breaking the power of the great landlords and redistributing confiscated property to landless families. In 1958, when reform was initiated, about 0·6 per cent of the rural population was estimated to own about 35 per cent of the cultivated land, while some 240,000 rural families, at a minimum, were said to be in need of land. Although the scope of the programme remained comparatively modest throughout the vicissitudes of the reform, considerable resistance was encountered from the landlords, many of whom resorted to violence and refused to cultivate their surviving properties. Not only were they aggrieved at the actual loss of their estates, where they did in fact lose them, but they felt that the proposed reforms were unrealistic in that they fixed the maximum holdings at levels which were too low (initially 80 ha of irrigated and 300 ha of unirrigated land) for Syrian conditions, where extensive dry-farming is charac-teristic and not intensive irrigated farming, as in Egypt, whence many of the original reformist ideas were derived. There were further problems attendant on land reform. Title to land became insecure for many families at all levels of the rural social hierarchy, while credit and extension services were inade-quate to the tasks required of them in the new circumstances. Moreover, reform was launched at an unfortunate time, during a period of severe drought, when repeated crop failure drove many dispirited people from the land. Alto-gether, then, it is not surprising that even in 1970 as much as 62 per cent of the normally cultivated land lay idle, though it must be remembered that this figure still included a large amount of fallow. By the same date, the contri-bution of agriculture to G.D.P. had fallen to about 20 per cent, compared with about 32 per cent in 1962, before severe disruption was widely felt in the countryside. The decline was due not only to precipitation conditions, but also to the direct effects of the land reform programme. Structural changes in the economy of the country were of little consequence. Some recovery took place after 1970, when rainfall conditions again improved and, more parti-cularly, when the landlords began to receive more sympathetic attention from the government, and the agricultural contribution to G.D.P. in 1972 had risen to about 26 per cent.

13.3 Cropping (Figure 13.3)

The expansion of cultivation in the 1950's was designed principally to increase the quantity of cereals available. Recent figures indicate the trend with

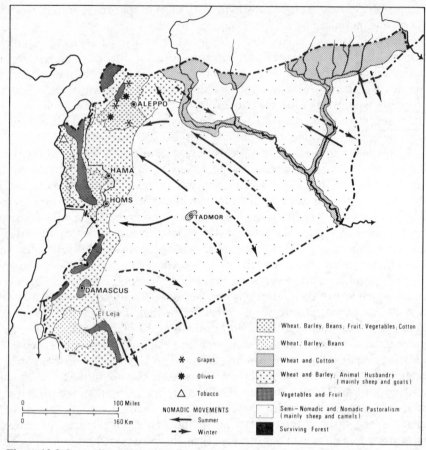

Figure 13.3 Generalized land use in Syria about 1970 (Updated from Hudson, *Focus* **18,** 1963, published by the American Geographical Society)

respect to wheat and barley, the leading cereals, and show quite clearly the decline associated with land reform in the early 1960's (Table 13.1). Wheat and barley between them have occupied about 75 per cent of the cultivated area of the country since before the Second World War, and may be assumed to have done so in the second half of the nineteenth century. The precise proportion of cultivated land devoted to the two crops varies regionally. It is smaller (up to 60 per cent) in the western provinces, where polyculture of olives, vines, fruit trees and cotton is important, and much greater (up to 90 per cent and over) in the Jezira where monoculture of cereals and cotton is frequent. Legumes, vegetables and fodder crops take up about eight per cent of the cultivated area nationally, but are rather more important in the west (Figure 13.3).

In terms of area and economic importance, cotton is the second rank crop at present. Its fortunes, however, have fluctuated over the last 140 years.

TABLE 13.1
Areas devoted to major crops

Year	Wheat ha	Barley ha	Cotton ha
1938[1]	538,000	300,000	37,000
1945[2]	751,000	348,000	17,500
1950	992,000	416,000	78,000
1955	1,463,000	614,000	228,000
1960	1,549,000	742,000	260,000
1965[3]	1,213,000	682,000	295,411
1970[3]	1,340,000	1,126,000	299,072

Sources: 1. Naval Intelligence Division, Geographical Handbook Series *Syria*, London, 1943, p. 259.
2. Figures for 1945–1960 from M. Rosciezewski, Méditerranée **6**, 1965, 179–180.
3. L'Office Arabe de Presse et de Documentation, *Rapport 1971–1972, sur l'Economie Syrienne*, Damascus, n.d., A33, B61.

Some cotton has been grown in Syria since medieval times. In the eighteenth century, it was used in the textile industries of Aleppo and Damascus. During the brief period of Egyptian rule in the early nineteenth century, it enjoyed the first of three relative booms. By 1840, production had doubled and exports quadrupled, but from that year production slumped as a result of the effects of European competition on local industry and the displacement of Syrian by Egyptian cotton in foreign markets. Large scale production revived in 1924, and increased rapidly until the outbreak of the Second World War, despite the Great Depression (13,200 ha in 1934; 37,000 in 1938). Prices fell during the War and there was a large contraction, mainly to the advantage of wheat, for which prices rose. The third boom began about 1949, and prices rose rapidly under the stimulus of the Korean War (1950–1953). In 1951 the price of cotton at Damascus was about twice as high as it had been in 1949, an increase much steeper (28 per cent) than that in the price of wheat for the same period. From a total area of about 25,000 ha, representing about 0·6 per cent of the cultivated area, cotton growing expanded to cover 228,000 ha in 1955 or about 4·5 per cent of the total cultivated area. The 260,000 ha of cotton grown in 1960 represented about seven per cent of the cultivated area of the country. Production rose over the period 1949 to 1960, with fluctuations, from 38,100 tonnes to 295,000 tonnes. In 1968, production was 394,193 tonnes. The sale of cotton abroad accounts for about 40 per cent of the total revenue earned by exports, though this has fluctuated from year to year.* Such dependence must lead to some apprehension in view of price fluctuations on the world market. On the other hand, it is clear that Syrian production is flexibly related to price and demand variations.

Some of the recent cotton expansion has taken place in its traditional growing area round Aleppo. Much of it, however, has been in the coastal strip and

*E.g. 1965, 43·0 per cent; 1966, 53·5 per cent; 1968, 41·8 per cent.

between Homs and Hama, so that now up to 20 per cent of the cultivated area of the western provinces is under cotton. Considerable expansion has also taken place in the Jezira, which today produces more than 60 per cent of the total crop. Here, as in other areas, both dry and irrigated methods are used, depending on water availability, though the use of irrigation is expanding. Excessive use of water has been reported from the central hill and steppe region, where monoculture of cotton is carried out on some estates. Not only has salination developed in the soil, but the water-table has dropped locally also so that some villages are reported short of drinking water.

13.4 Expansion of irrigation

Much of the expansion of cultivation up to the Second World War was achieved in the rain-fed zone using traditional dry-farming methods. Since the Second World War, irrigation has become increasingly important. Reserves of cultivable rain-fed land have almost been used up and the need to increase yield and to control its fluctuations has also been realized. Experience of severe drought in 1958 to 1961 may have increased the sense of urgency.

Until the Second World War, irrigated farming was found in four distinct areas. It was especially characteristic of the Damascus Oasis, where river-fed canals were used. On the Orontes at Homs and Hama, the current turned enormous wooden wheels which lifted water into high-level canals. Similar devices were also found along the Euphrates. The Aleppo district was a fourth irrigated area. Here a variety of sources was tapped—the Orontes west of the town, the Quweiq in its immediate vicinity, the Euphrates to the east and a number of scattered wells. Small and dispersed patches of irrigation were found elsewhere in the country, in the coastal strip, for example, and at oases such as Tadmor. *Qanāts* and springs were tapped, often by systems of great antiquity, in favourable districts, while elsewhere water was lifted from wells by wheels similar in design to those on the Orontes and Euphrates but worked by animal power *(challuf* or *doulab)*. These traditional lifting devices were steadily being replaced by pumps during the interwar period, though the process was to gather momentum after the Second World War. Pumps were also used to expand the strips of cultivated land along the Euphrates and Khābūr.

Despite local expansion, less than 10 per cent of the cultivated area of the country was irrigated in 1947. Between 1947 and 1959 an increase of over 97 per cent was achieved to bring the irrigated area to a total of 584,000 ha. By 1967, some 640,000 ha were irrigated, although the proportional increase which this represents is minimal. Much of the expansion took place in the western provinces (the amount of irrigated land in Hama and Homs provinces increased by about 300 per cent from 1947 to 1959). As in the interwar period, the greater part of it is the result of small-scale developments. Improvements in pumping techniques, the reduction of seepage by lining canals and an increase in the number of pumps have all made more water available.

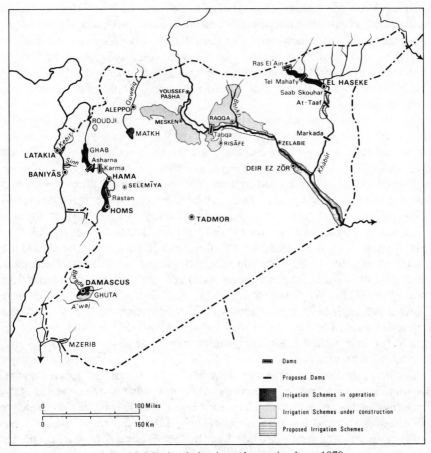

Figure 13.4 Syrian irrigation schemes in about 1970

A number of government schemes have also helped (Figure 13.4). The earliest scheme was actually begun in 1930, under the mandate. It involved raising the level of the ancient dam retaining Lake Homs and the cutting of a canal for some 70 km along the western side of the Orontes. This was completed in 1944 and an additional 21,600 ha were irrigated. Six other schemes have been completed. The copious and perennial Sinn river, which enters the sea between Latakia and Baniyās, has been dammed to irrigate a small area of coastal plain, primarily for the benefit of Palestinian refugees. Further along the coast, the northernmost of the two Kebīr rivers has been regulated by a dam to prevent flooding in the coastal marshes south of Latakia and irrigation works are proceeding. On the Mzerib, a tributary of the Yarmuk, a small dam diverted water into canals along both banks to irrigate some 3,460 ha before the war of June, 1967: its fate is unknown. At Matkh, south of Aleppo, flood water is diverted from January to April to irrigate some 14,400 ha of good valley land, whilst farther west, at Roudi, mountain streams have been regulated and a swamp area drained to provide some 3,840 ha of irrigated land. Work has also been begun on a scheme to make fuller use of the Khābūr. The plan is to use the head spring of the river, at Ras el'Ain to irrigate about 39,000 ha of the valley above its junction with the Euphrates at El Haseke. A diversionary dam has been built near the spring and use made of Roman foundations at Tel Mahafy for a barrage. About 10,000 ha are currently being irrigated.

The most ambitious scheme completed to date has involved making greater use of the Orontes and reclaiming the Ghab. Work began in 1954. Flow has been improved by deepening and widening the river bed at the point where it cuts through the basalt sill at the north end of the Ghab (Kārkūr). Drainage has been further assisted by cutting a new and short course for the river through low ground to the west of the swamp. A large concrete dam at the divergence near Asharna directs water to two main irrigation canals. The river has been regulated in the gorges above the Ghab by the construction of dams at Karma and Rastan, and thus rendered the flow too low to turn the traditional water wheels. By 1968, when the original project was virtually complete, some 43,200 ha of swamp had been reclaimed and irrigation extended to a total of 68,000 ha. Work is now in hand to extend irrigation to a similar area. These developments have been accompanied by the construction of new roads and settlements. The range of crops has been extended by adding rice, cotton, and sugar beet to the traditional winter combination of wheat and barley alternating with vetch or clover.

Further extension of irrigation requires fuller use of the Euphrates and Khābūr. Since each flows in a deep inner valley for much of its course, expensive irrigation works are required. Plans for the Khābūr involve the construction of additional dams downstream from Tel Mahafy at Saab, Skouhar and At-Taaf to irrigate about 120,000 ha. On the Euphrates an earth dam has been built at Tabqa, which is about 2,500 kms long and 60 m high and will retain a lake of some 40,000 million m³ of water, rather less than one third of the amount to be retained ultimately by the Aswân High Dam. The water is being used to irrigate the Raqqa plateau above the east bank of the river and the district of Resafe on the west, in all about 550,000 ha. Syria herself is providing part of the enormous amount of capital required (about £100 million, estimated in 1966), but the rest must come from abroad. The U.S.S.R. made an initial offer of assistance, but this was turned down and a West German offer, made in 1963, was preferred. Only the first part of the payment was made before political instability and the nationalization of industry caused the West German government to hold back. The U.S.S.R. stepped in again and, by a protocol signed in May 1966, agreed to provide capital and technical assistance for the first stage, completed in 1970. Final completion is planned for 1975. Construction has already had an enormous impact on the region. Nomads have been settled, population has increased and a town of about 40,000 inhabitants has been created at Tabqa itself, while communications have been improved by the construction of road and rail links to Aleppo.

Use of the Euphrates and its major tributary, the Khābūr, has international ramifications (Chapter 12). It is estimated that if Syria were to provide irrigation water to all the irrigable land within her portion of the Euphrates catchment, about 75 per cent of the usable flow of the river would be required. However, Turkey and Iraq are also extending their irrigation schemes along the river. Turkey will take some of the flow from the headwaters of the main river, whilst Iraq hopes to benefit from combined flow downstream. Iraq will probably suffer, not only from a reduced flow, but also from increased salt in the water. Agreement about these matters has not been reached.

13.5 Communications and industry

Part of Syria's increasing agricultural production has been consumed directly by her rising rural population; some has been exported. Agricultural products formed over 60 per cent of Syria's exports by value in 1972. Her leading trading partner is still the Lebanon, though Western Europe constitutes the largest market outside the region. Trade with the Eastern bloc is improving its position (Chapter 8). The rest of Syria's agricultural production has gone to the towns, either to feed the urban population (about 36 per cent of the total in 1960) or as industrial raw material.

The leading towns are all located in the west, the traditional core of cultivation in the country. Food, raw materials and important exports are drawn from this region, but their flow is hampered by poor communications, and correspondingly high transport costs. Polarization of production, resulting from developments in the Jezira, is exacerbating the situation, for the distances involved are considerable and communications scarcely adequate to the need.

Railways are limited largely to lines built in the last decades of Turkish rule. The old Baghdād railway reaches Aleppo from Turkey and then turns northeastwards to run along the frontier between the two countries. Much of its use is international, and political complications between three countries have meant that it has played little part in the development of the Jezira. From Aleppo, a line runs south to Hama and Homs, but the original connection down to Damascus is severed by the Lebanese frontier. Design studies for a direct line from Homs to Damascus have been completed. South of Damascus, the Hejāz railway has been rebuilt after partial destruction in the First World War, but is largely used by Jordan. From Homs, another old line leads through Tripoli to Beirūt, thereby completing the link between Aleppo and the Mediterranean Sea. The whole line is important to Syria, for along it flows much of her grain and cotton exports.

Roads have been much more important than the railways to Syria's recent economic development. They have carried practically all the increase in freight since the Second World War. In 1961, some 13,818 kms were in existence but only 5,305 km, including the axial link from Aleppo to Damascus, were metalled. The network is densest in the western provinces and is very poorly developed in the Jezira and in the desert, though hard ground in the latter region is something of a compensation and was quite negotiable by trucks and buses running between Damascus and Baghdād before the completion of the surfaced road in 1974. Apart from integrating the western urbanized region, the roads are important in two other ways. They provide the main link with Syria's leading port, Latakia, though a railway from the port to Aleppo and ultimately to El Qamishliye is being built. Secondly, roads provide the main outlet for the products of the Jezira. A spinal road joins El Qamishliye and El Haseke and then goes south to Deir ez Zōr where it divides, one branch running northwest to Aleppo and the other southeast to Damascus. Not only is this road difficult to negotiate, but its feeders are mere tracks, often impassable in winter.

As well as containing the largest urban populations in the country, the western towns are the principal centres of manufacturing industry. Although inertia has played a part in this, for the tradition of handicraft industry is very ancient here, it is largely a result of the consumer orientation of most modern industry. Some development took place between the wars, but the main stimulus came with the Second World War. Imported manufactured goods became scarce and prices rose, with the result that local industry enjoyed a unique advantage. Import substitution largely came to an end about 1950, though tariffs and embargoes fostered local enterprise. Capital was diverted into construction and agriculture, and little new industrial development took place. In fact, the profitability of agricultural development acted as something of a brake on the rate of industrial development in the 1950's. Nationalization in 1964 and 1965 caused considerable dislocation in industry and a serious flight of capital abroad, though, according to official indices, output continued to rise from 100 in 1963 to 129 in 1966 and 238 in 1970.[7]

Manufacturing industry is squarely based on agriculture. Food processing (olive oil production and refining, sugar and tobacco processing) contributed about 33 per cent of industrial output in 1971 and textiles and clothing about 32 per cent. Textiles provided about seven per cent of Syria's exports by value in 1970. Cotton textiles, in which Syria is now self-sufficient, are made from local material, chiefly in Aleppo and Damascus, though new printing and dyeing plants have been established at Hama and Homs. The woollen industry consists largely of carpet making at Aleppo and Damascus, but there is also some knitting, especially in the capital. Although Syria exports wool, much of the raw material used in this branch of her textile industry is imported. A small amount of silk weaving is still found in Aleppo, where imported yarn is used and most of the production is for export.

Other industries include cement making at Damascus, Aleppo and Homs, furniture, glass, matches, plastic items, refrigerators, soap, washing machines, and tractor assembly (at Aleppo). Salt is made at a number of places, but is especially important around the salt marshes south of Aleppo. Natural asphalt is exploited in the Ansāriye mountains near Latakia. Other minerals exist but are of doubtful commercial value, though recent discoveries of rock phosphate and iron by Russian technicians have already changed the picture.

Plans were made to mine 300,000 tonnes of phosphate south of Tadmor by 1970, and increase production to 1·3 million tonnes during the following year, but all the production is for export to eastern Europe. An iron and steel plant is planned for a site near Hama.

A large part of Syrian industry is mechanized. It draws its power almost exclusively from electricity. About 14 per cent is produced by water power, though this will increase as the hydro-electric schemes associated with irrigation dams come into full operation. Great hopes are attached to the Euphrates dam which is expected to produce between 80 and 100,000 kW on completion for the west of the country. Nationalization of the industry in 1965 allowed the first stage of an electricity grid to be completed between Aleppo, Homs, Hama and Damascus. Many factories, however, still use their own diesel generators. In the past, fuel was obtained from international pipe lines crossing Syria. The ARAMCO Tapline runs through the southern part of the country on its way to the Mediterranean coast at Saida (Sidon). The Iraq Petroleum Company's system of pipes runs directly across the centre of the country through Tadmor to Homs, where the system divides. One pipe line runs through Lebanon to the coast at Tripoli and the other to a Syrian terminal at Baniyās. A refinery has been in operation at the Homs junction since 1959 and refined products have been distributed from it to Aleppo, Damascus and Latakia since 1964 by pipeline. Refining capacity has been expanded to handle Syria's own crude. The major field was discovered in 1956 at Karachuk–Hamzah, southeast of El Qamishliye in the Jezira, but production had to await the completion in 1968 of a pipeline to Homs and a new terminal at Tartūs. Production reached about five million tonnes in 1971, though Syria has experienced some difficulty in marketing her own low-quality, sulphur-rich crude that year. Smaller fields were discovered near Es Suweidīya in 1959 and at Rumaidan in 1962, while there is a field of natural gas to the south at El Haseke. However, now that Syria has its own source of petroleum, the whole economy is likely to experience more rapid restructuring than in the 1960's. Already, there is a moving away from considerable and traditional dependence upon agriculture towards a greater reliance upon manufacturing industry. Any further advance in agriculture will involve mechanization, greater use of irrigation and the application of more fertilizers. It will be very dependent upon Syria's manufacturing industry, thus binding even more closely the two basic sectors of the economy.

References

1. D. Warriner, *Land Reform and Development in the Middle East. A Study of Egypt, Syria and Iraq*, Oxford University Press, London, 2nd ed., 1962, 71.
2. United Nations, *Statistical Yearbooks*, New York.
3. N. E. Lewis, 'The frontier of settlement in Syria: 1800–1950', *International Affairs*, **31**, 48–60 (1955).
4. International Bank for Reconstruction and Development, *The Economic Development of Syria*, John Hopkins, Baltimore, 1955, 300.
5. D. Warriner, *Land Reform and Development in the Middle East. A Study of Egypt, Syria and Iraq*, Oxford University Press, London, 2nd ed., 1962, 89.

6. D. Warriner, *Land Reform and Development in the Middle East. A Study of Egypt, Syria and Iraq*, Oxford University Press, London, 2nd ed., 1962, 91–92.
7. L'Office Arabe de Presse et de Documentation, *Rapport 1971–1972 sur l'Economie Syrienne*, Damascus, n.d., B. 83.

CHAPTER 14

Lebanon: Community Structure

14.1 Introduction

Most countries of the Middle East contain linguistic and religious minorities. Whilst Arabic is the dominant language for everyday purposes in Lebanon, the numbers of Christians and Muslims appear to be roughly equal. Each major religious group, however, is divided into different sects, or, as they are called in Lebanon, *communities*, which vary greatly in size. In addition, Lebanon is one of the few Arab states to have retained a large part of its traditional Jewish community, to which the government gave protection during and after the Six Days War of June, 1967. This chapter seeks to analyse the spatial distribution of Lebanon's various communities and to show how fragmentation of the population has affected the life of the country. The distribution of the different communities and their relative power within the state have been greatly affected by physical conditions, while the present mixture of communities owes much to the way in which the republic was created. An outline of both aspects is, therefore, a necessary preliminary to the exploration of the main themes.

France, as the mandatory power, created the modern state of Lebanon in 1920 by adding the Ottoman vilayet of Beirūt and part of the vilayet of Damascus to the autonomous Mutesarrifate of Lebanon. The Mutesarrifate, which included Mount Lebanon itself, originated in 1861 with the intervention of the Western Powers in the region following some two decades of inter-community strife which had culminated in the 'massacres' of 1860. Lebanon is now divided for administrative purposes into five *mohafazets* (provinces, but including the city of Beirūt as a distinct unit) subdivided into *cazas* (Figure 14.1). The *cazas* correspond to some extent with traditional districts, the feudal fiefs of earlier times, and will be used as units of reference in later discussions.

The relief of Lebanon is easily summarized. It consists basically of two roughly parallel mountain ranges, Mount Lebanon (Arabic *Lubnān*, meaning *white*, from the snow cover) and Jebel esh-Sherki (Anti-Lebanon with Mount Hermon), separated by a broad upland valley known as El Beq'a (Biqu or Bekaa). Mount Lebanon itself is essentially a limestone plateau, crowned by a number of peaks (up to 3,083 m) on which snow lies for much of the year. Above about 1,600 m, the so called *jurd* contains typical karst scenery and looks distinctly bare and bleak, except where a few tattered remnants of the famous cedar forest have survived. The vegetation now is largely spiky shrub, grazed in summer by herds from El Beq'a and the hill country of 'Akkar in the north-

365

west. The mountain slopes below about 1,600 m are characterized by huge cirque-like features lying at the head of deep valleys and ravines which cut to the coast and offer considerable obstruction to north-south communication. These are separated by crags, great tabular blocks and truncated pyramids, all of which combine to give the western slopes an irregular stepped appearance. The middle section of the eastern slopes is more precipitous, as a result of faulting, though the lower slopes are fairly gentle. Middle slopes throughout the mountain, the so called *wusut*, are fortunate in containing a narrow outcrop of clays, marls and sandstones where water, absorbed by the higher limestones from a winter precipitation of 700 to 1,500 mm and considerable snow melt, is forced to the surface in a number of often copious springs. The outcrop also provides relatively fertile soils, where cereals and fruit trees of various kinds (vines, olives, apples and some mulberries) are grown. Terracing has been necessary to exploit these conditions on the western side of the mountain and spectacular flights of terraces may be seen, though their higher levels have often fallen out of use. On the eastern side, slopes are either too precipitous even for terracing or, at lower levels, are sufficiently gentle for it to be unnecessary. Woodland survives in a ravaged condition in many places, but is most extensive on northeastern slopes. Loosely clustered, stone-built villages are numerous on defensive sites at an average height of 1,400 to 1,500 m and close to springs. Population densities are fairly high (about 177 person km,^{2} on the western side), especially in the central area near Beirūt.

The mountain falls steeply to the coast for much of its length, making access to the inhabited zone fairly difficult, but in the north and south it descends through a series of ridges to merge with undulating plateau areas—the 'Akkar plateau in the north, which affords communication between the coast and the plain of Homs in Syria, and Upper Galilee in the south. Extensive tracts of chalky marl occur in Upper Galilee and form such a hard crust that cultivation is difficult. Along the coast, mountain spurs separate small plains where low cliffs and sand-dunes alternate with areas of intensive cultivation. Bananas, citrus, cotton and olives are grown, while market gardening is important around the country's principal towns of Beirūt, Tripoli, Saida (Sidon) and Sūr (Tyre) which are linked by a coastal road making use of old wave-cut terraces to move from plain to plain. The towns were once fortified against both land and sea attack, and threat of the latter perhaps explains the clustered form of old rural settlements and their preference for cliff-top sites. Dispersion is characteristic of comparatively new settlement in the plains.

Anti-Lebanon consists of a series of mountain ranges which form a considerable barrier to east-west communication for much of their length. The main ridge is a broad, barren limestone upland with an average height of 2,100 m. It falls steeply into El Beq'a on the west and is scored by wild and rocky ravines. Although average annual precipitation over the whole mountain is about 700 mm, the northern parts are so sheltered by the highest peaks of Mount Lebanon that they receive much less. Springs are scarce and there are few villages and little cultivation, though some transhumance takes place.

South of the Zebdani depression, which is followed by the Beirūt to Damascus road, rises the whale-back of Mount Hermon. Its oval-shaped summit is topped by three small peaks (2,814 m), which are snow covered except at midsummer. The western slopes are exposed to rain-bearing winds, and their lower levels are composed of sandstones and basalts with the result that copious springs are found, together with vineyards, orchards and patches of deciduous oak woodland. Villages are relatively numerous in a zone up to about 1,000 to 1,100 m, and a few larger agglomerations occur.

El Beq'a is a high valley some 112 km long and up to 26 km wide. It is divided into northern and southern sections by the watershed (1,080 m) between the Āsi (Orontes) and the Lītāni in the vicinity of Ba'albek. The north is crossed by low ridges strewn with loose stone, though patches of productive land exist near springs along the foot of the Anti-Lebanon range and, to a lesser extent, at the contact of the plain with the foothills of Mount Lebanon. Mount Lebanon shuts out the westerly winds, reducing average annual precipitation to an unreliable 300 mm. South of Ba'albek the valley floor is undulating and its red alluvial soils prove more fertile under a slightly higher rainfall. Wheat is a traditional crop but maize and, increasingly, cotton and apples, are also grown under irrigation. Large, highly compacted villages are fairly numerous, both along the Lītāni itself, where they occupy elevated sites to avoid flooding, and along spring lines at the foot of the mountains to west and east.

The main valley is closed to the south by the limestone ridge of Jebel al-Arabi. However, the Lītāni continues southwards through a series of deep gorges along the western side of the mountain before finally turning sharply westwards through a sequence of small plains to reach the sea eventually near Sur. The line of El Beq'a itself is continued southward by the Wādī el-Taym. Despite being drained by the Hasbani, one of the head streams of the Jordan, this is a remote and largely inaccessible area with a low density of population. Its villages are poor, since possession of elevated, defensible sites has deprived them of adequate water and cultivable land.

14.2 Distribution of the communities

In an attempt to maintain a political balance based on community size, no census as such has been made in Lebanon since 1932. Its place is taken by a periodic official reassessment of the 1932 figures on the basis of birth and death registration. One of the most recent of these (1963) revealed that Christians formed the majority of the population (53 per cent), as they have done in Greater Lebanon since estimates were first made in 1846.[1] The true situation, however, may be different. Official population estimates make no clear distinction between permanent emigrants, on the one hand, and residents and temporary emigrants, on the other, nor between permanent emigrants who have retained their Lebanese citizenship and those who have not. Since Christians are believed to form a majority of the emigrants, their numbers in Lebanon are probably fewer than officially represented, while Muslims are probably more numerous. Not only have fewer Muslims emigrated, but they also have a much higher birth rate than the Christians, largely because of a lower average age of marriage. Muslims, in fact, may now form a majority of the population. This would almost certainly be the case if Palestinians were enfranchized, as was suggested during the 1950's.[2]

Seventeen religious communities are recognized by the Lebanese authorities, though some of them are extremely small (Table 14.1). Each is an exclusive, closely integrated socio-political unit, which has been given identity not only by a common set of beliefs but also by the Muslim tradition of classifying people into groups *(millas)* by their faith and conceding groups of the 'People of the Book' (Christian sects and Jews) limited autonomy, a development especially characteristic of Ottoman rule, though such recognition was not extended to heretical Muslim groups by the dominant Sunnīs. The sense of solidarity, particularly of Christian communities, was strengthened by persecution and attack and, rather later, by the manipulative protection extended by one or other of the western powers. This may have been an important element in the early development of Arab nationalism in Lebanon.

Maronite Christians, followers of the hermit Maron, form the largest single community in the country. They split from the universal church in the seventh century over the doctrine of the will of Christ*,[3] and came to be ruled by their own Patriarch 'of Antioch and all the East'. Separated from Rome by the Great Schism, like other Eastern churches, the Maronites re-established relations during the Crusades when they supported the Franks. Further rapprochement was fostered by political and commercial contacts with France

TABLE 14.1
Communities in Lebanon

Community	Percentage of the total population
Christians	53
Maronites	29
Greek Orthodox	10
Greek Catholics	6
Armenians	6
Others	2
Muslims	46
Sunnīs	20
Mitwālis	18
Druzes	6
Others	2
Jews	1

Source: E. de Vaumas, 'La répartition confessionelle au Liban et l'équilibre de l'état Libanais', *Revue Géogr. alp.*, **43**, 511–604 (1955).

*Maronites adopted the Monothelite position that He had a single will.

and Italy and by clerics studying abroad. Reunion of the two churches took place as a result of the synods of Qannūbin and Luwayza, held in Lebanon in 1596 and 1736 respectively and attended by papal delegates. Ancient Syriac, however, is still the language of the liturgy, not Latin. Although Maronites are found in a variety of occupations, most of them are freehold farmers, a result of a social revolution in the middle of the nineteenth century. They are moderately wealthy as a result of both of their own enterprise at home and remittances from relatives abroad.

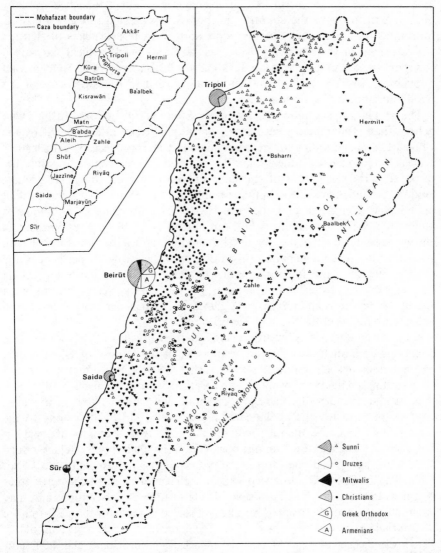

Figure 14.1 Distribution of 'communities' in Lebanon (Reproduced by permission of Institute de Géographie Alpine)

Maronites are found in most parts of the country (Figure 14.1), but their core area is Mount Lebanon, especially the section lying between Tripoli and Beirūt. In Batrūn *caza* they constitute about 76 per cent of the population, rising to about 85 per cent in Kisrawān and about 90 per cent in Zghorta. Their numbers decline southwards in territory which they share with Druzes (e.g. about 19 per cent of the population of Aaley *caza*), but increase again at the southern end of the mountain where, in Jezzine *caza*, they form about 63 per cent of the population. Comparatively few Maronites live in the plains and plateau of 'Akkar or in El Beq'a. They are solidly established in many of the small towns of the country, but poorly represented in the main ones. Maronites form a majority of the population in eastern districts of Beirūt,[4] where priests in their flowing black cassocks and black conical hats are a common sight, but constitute only about eight per cent of the city's total population. In Tripoli they amount to no more than three per cent of the population, but are localized in district clusters.[5]

The next largest community is that of the Sunnī or 'Orthodox' Muslims who believe that Muhammad's successors, or caliphs, were either elected by the whole Muslim community or were nominated by their predecessors. Its leaders are easily recognized by their long, dark brown or grey coats and white be-turbaned tarbushes. Most of the laity fall into two broad social groups, landowners and their share-cropping tenants, but some Sunnīs find employment in industry, commerce and the professions. The distribution of Sunnīs is almost the converse of that of the Maronites (Figure 14.1). They are almost entirely absent from Mount Lebanon, but predominate in the plains and plateau of 'Akkar in northern Lebanon (in 'Akkar *caza* they form 52 per cent of the total population) and fairly numerous in the foothills behind Saida (Saida *caza* 18 per cent of the total population; Shūf *caza* 22 per cent), and near the Beirūt–Damascus road in El Beq'a (e.g. in Zahle *caza* 24 per cent). A few Sunnī villages are found in the Wādī el-Taym.

Almost as numerous as Sunnī Muslims are the Mitwālis. They belong to one of the major branches of the Shī'ite division of the 'House of Islam' which originated in a socio-political revolt during the first Muslim century and soon became a religious movement with heretical doctrines. The Shī'a advanced, in particular, the idea that there was 'an infallible Imām in every age to whom God alone entrusted the guidance of his servants'.[6] Mitwālis belong to the largest Shī'a sect, the Imāmis, which recognizes twelve Imāms in the 'Ali-Fātima line,* the last of whom disappeared in AD 800 but will one day return as Mahdī (the 'guided one') to restore justice and righteousness to the world. Shī'a Muslims as a whole accept that a believer may practice *taqiya*, that is, concealment of his beliefs to save his life in time of persecution, and may enter into a form of trial marriage. The sect is also notable for the performance of a miracle play depicting the death of 'Ali's brother, Husayn, at Karbalā.**

*'Ali was the son-in-law of Muhammad by marriage with Fātima, and the Fourth Caliph.

**in Iraq and one of the major shrines of Shī'a pilgrimage, as well as the major setting for the miracle play.

The play is the climax of ten days mourning, but is enacted in few places, one of them a village in central Lebanon studied by E. L. Peters who showed the symbolic importance of the drama in maintaining traditional social structure.[7]

Mitwālis were not accorded any legal recognition within the Sunnī Turkish Empire, but attained it when the constitution of the Lebanese Republic was drawn up in 1926. They live away from the main lines of communication, in fairly remote districts. In south Lebanon, the community, consisting of land-lords and sharecroppers, forms between about 60 and 80 per cent of the population and in the northern part of El Beq'a between 60 and 70 per cent. Mitwālis are scarce in the southern part of El Beq'a and very rare in Mount Lebanon itself, though a few Mitwāli villages are found in the valley of Nahr Ibrahim and around Arfa, at its head. Although Mitwālis predominate in Sūr, there are few of them in the other coastal towns, and most of those are recent immigrants employed in menial and casual work. The community is entirely absent from the predominantly Sunnī district of the northwest (Figure 14.1).

Greek Orthodox Christians form the next most numerous community. Its members have been separated from Rome since the Great Schism, but have remained in communion with Constantinople, and use the Byzantine liturgy, often in an Arabic translation. As wealthy traders and artisans in the main, though there are some peasants, the Greek Orthodox have gathered in the towns and larger villages of the country. About 20 per cent of the entire com-munity live in Beirūt, where they form about 11 per cent of the population. They are particularly numerous in the traditional Maronite areas, but some are found in the Sunnī dominated northwest, the southern part of El Beq'a and even in the Wādī el-Taym. They are completely absent from Upper Galilee.

Greek Catholic Christians (now known as the *Melkites* or 'Royalists'), Armenian Christians and Druzes form communities of about equal size. Greek Catholics separated from the Orthodox church under the influence of Jesuit missionaries and came into communion with Rome in 1683, though the division of the Greek church was not complete until 1724. The community consists largely of peasant farmers, and is particularly strong along the foothills of the Anti-Lebanon range in the northern section of El Beq'a (Hermel *caza* 30 per cent of the population) and around Zahl *caza* (23 per cent of the population). Small numbers are found amidst the Maronites in Mount Lebanon south of Beirūt, but practically none live in 'Akkar. Although there are few Greek Catholics in the two main towns, they are fairly numerous in such second order ones as Saida and Sūr on the coast and Zahle on the edge of El Beq'a.

Armenian Christians differ from the rest of the population in speaking a language other than Arabic, a fact which has helped to make them unpopular with the local population. Most Armenians belong to the Gregorian church, one of the monophysite groups which separated from the universal church over the doctrine of Christ's nature in the fifth and sixth centuries, and whose Patriarch lives in the Soviet Union, but a few of them are attached to the Armenian Catholic church which separated from the Gregorian and re-established communion with Rome in 1740. Although some Armenians were known in Lebanon from at least the eighteenth century, the majority came as refugees from southeastern and Aegean Turkey in the aftermath of the First World War, following repressive measures and a series of 'massacres' (1895, 1909 and 1922). Their numbers were increased in 1939, when the sanjak of Alexandretta was finally ceded to Turkey, and again in 1946–1947, as a result of Russian interference in the Armenian Soviet Socialist Republic. The refugees settled mainly on the eastern edge of Beirūt, where they form some 24 per cent of the city's population, and especially in the quarter known as Medawar, behind the docks. Their original settlements were shanty-towns bearing names evocative of their homes in Turkey, but these are gradually being transformed as the Armenians improve their position in commerce and the professions. Smaller Armenian groups are found in the Zahle and Sūr districts where refugee camps existed in the past.

Compared with the Armenians, Druzes are an indigenous community. They hold religious gatherings on Thursday evenings in inconspicuous, small buildings *(khalwahs)* and make pilgrimages to local shrines, but their beliefs have been successfully kept secret. It is known, however, that they are derived from the Ismā'īlīya branch of the Shī'a family of Islam and take their name from a Bokhara Turk named Muhammad ibn Ismā'il al-Darazī who worked in the court of the sixth Fatimid Caliph of Cairo, al-Hākim ibn-Armri'llah. The Caliph disappeared in mysterious circumstances in AD 1021, and soon afterwards Darazī appeared in Syria preaching the divinity of the one, al-Hākim, who was still alive but in concealment.

The Druzes today are a very enclosed and largely rural community. They live alongside Maronites in the south–central part of Mount Lebanon, especially in the Shūf and Matn districts (18 and 46 per cent of the population) where they were once so predominant that the area was called Jebel ed Drūz. Another concentration is found along the western slopes of Mount Hermon, above the Wādī el-Taym, and where they constitute about 37 per cent of the population of Riyāq caza. A small number of Druzes live in Beirūt, but they are virtually absent from the rest of the country.

Other Muslim communities, such as the Alawīs, are very small and unimportant. The remaining Christian communities are also small in size, but some of them have played a significant part in fostering the friction which now exists between Christian and Muslim in Lebanon. Two of the Christian communities are relics of ancient and once extensive churches. The Syrian Orthodox (Jacobites), a monophysite church, use Syriac in the liturgy and retain a few Syriac speaking villages in the northern part of Mount Lebanon. Some of their number returned to Rome in 1662. The Chaldean or Assyrian church has been in communion with Rome since 1552, though originally a Nestorian church which believed in the separate personalities of Christ, human and divine. Chaldeans form a very poor group at the bottom of the urban social hierarchy. The other Christian communities are introductions from the West. The Latin or Roman Catholic church is composed of western teachers and missionaries resident in the country, and has a history going back to the seventeenth century at least. Although separate from the Uniate churches,* the community has had a profound effect upon them through its educational activities. Although some of Lebanon's Protestants are westerners, many are converts, won as a result of western, largely American, missionary activity since 1823. Like the Latins, the Protestants have exerted a great influence on the country through their schools and colleges, principally the American University of Beirūt, which was established in 1866 as the Syrian Protestant College.

Finally, mention should be made of the Jewish community in Lebanon. Although somewhat reduced by emigration to Israel since 1948, it now consists of about 6,000 people, mainly artisans and small traders, who live near the Grand Serail in Beirūt.

14.3 Evolution of the community structure

Although Christianity came early to what is now Lebanon, perhaps beginning with the activities of Jesus himself as mentioned in the Gospels, most of the present communities confessing it came from outside the country. The main exceptions are the Syrian Orthodox peasants of northern Lebanon and some of the Greeks, who trace their ancestry to an Orthodox community known to have existed in the Kurā district during the early eighth century, but whose members were scattered across the country as a result of migration during the seventeenth and eighteenth centuries. Much of the Greek Christian community, however, originated outside Lebanon. The first group sought refuge there from Syria and Palestine during the persecutions which followed the final defeat of the Crusaders (1291), whom the Greeks had supported. During the eighteenth century, persecution by the Greek Orthodox of their Catholic brethren forced many of the latter to leave Aleppo and other towns of what is now Syria, while the appearance of Wahhābi** raiders in Syria, from 1805 until their defeat in 1811–1818, led to further emigration from both communities because Turkish governors tried to conciliate the fanatical tribesmen by reviving old restrictions and constraints on Christians. Many of the later Greek exiles were townsmen and naturally established themselves in the coastal towns and large villages of Lebanon, acting as middlemen in the trade which was flourishing on the twin bases of growing contact with the West and the production of silk in Mount Lebanon. Greek migrants from other parts of Lebanon, as well as from Syria, were important to the rapid growth of Zahle in the nineteenth century, when it developed as a collecting point for grain from El Beq'a destined for the mountain villages, a market for bedouin from further east and a staging point on the road from Beirūt to Damascus when this was opened in 1858.

*Indigenous churches in communion with Rome but retaining separate hierarchies and customs.

**A reformist, almost fundamentalist, Muslin sect originating in Central Arabia.

The major Christian community, the Maronites, also came to Lebanon as refugees. During the seventh century they had a wide distribution in what are now Syria, northern Iraq and southern Turkey but with concentrations along the Orontes and at Aleppo and Urfa. Their doctrine of the will of Christ brought conflict with the Jacobites, then much stronger in the Orontes area, and led to sporadic migration to Mount Lebanon. The drift westwards was reinforced when the Caliph, 'Umar ibn-'Abd-al-'Azīz (AD 717–720), introduced thoroughgoing discrimination against Christians by which they were excluded from the administration, prevented from building new churches, and required to wear distinctive dress.

In Mount Lebanon itself Maronites established themselves first of all in the Batrūn district, where the Patriarch, Yuhanna Marun (d.c. 707) established his seat at Kafarhayy, and along the Qadisha (Abou Ali) valley, near which the earliest known Maronite church was built at Ehden in AD 749. Settlement spread in this core area, now regarded as something of a Maronite holy land, because it contained only a small indigenous population and, despite its defensibility, because it possessed cultivable soils and numerous springs. The availability of similar, poorly exploited resources and the remnants of the forests, together with a decimated Mitwāli population, allowed Maronite farmers to spread southwards into Kirawān during the early fourteenth century. Further expansion of this energetic peasantry took place throughout Mount Lebanon during the seventeenth and eighteenth centuries, when the community enjoyed the protection of the Druze Ma'n and Shibāb emirs (the latter were Christians from 1770). They were favoured not only because their higher standard of education made some of them useful to the emirs in their administration, but also because of their proven ability to turn waste land to profit by building terraces, cultivating cereals and producing silk, for which there was a rising demand abroad. At the same time, the Maronites were helped by their own social customs. Their system of land holding was looser than that prevailing amongst other groups, especially the Druzes, whilst inheritance within the nuclear family, rather than the wider kin, and a ban on marriage within the patrilinear group meant that they were not tied to one locality, like Muslim sharecroppers. Maronites also spread into the coastal plains, El Beq'a and Wādī el-Taym—a process of colonization perhaps growing from the mountaineer's habit of finding seasonal work on the large estates of the lower land. Wherever the Maronite farmers went, Greek middlemen followed, and the two enjoyed a beneficial relationship. However, Maronite expansion into traditional Druze districts was one of a number of factors which changed the centuries old balance of power between Druze and Maronite, and led to a deterioration of their previously good relations which culminated in the 'massacres' of 1860. There has been friction between the communities ever since, aided and abetted by various outside interests.

Turning to the Muslim communities, we find that the oldest one in Lebanon is Shī'ite. By the time of the First Crusade (1096), apart from the Maronite districts of Batrūn and Jebeil and the Druze areas of Shūf and Wādī el-Taym, the whole country belonged to one or other of the Shī'ite communities. The distribution of Mitwālis today is largely a relic of this early predominance. Pressure from the Sunnī Mamluks (1291 to 1516), continued by the Ottoman Turks (1516 to 1918), drove them from 'Akkar, most of the coastal plain and Kisrawān. It is hardly surprising, then, that the community has survived principally in the refuge and largely uncoveted areas of Upper Galilee and El Beq'a; the few Mitwāli villages on the eastern side of Mount Lebanon are the relics of an attempt to move into an even more secure district during the sixteenth to eighteenth centuries. The dominance of Mitwālis in Sūr is the result of a more successful attempt at expansion about the same time.

Another factor in the ending of Shī'a predominance in Lebanon was the spread of Druze doctrines amongst the communities during the eleventh and twelfth centuries. Druzes, however, were also severely persecuted in their early days, and this may account for their association with the remote area of Wādī el-Taym, and the difficult Shūf district. Persecution turned the sect in upon itself and produced a tightly knit, highly disciplined community organized for war. These social developments, together with an expertise in guerrilla warfare which was used by successive Sunnī governments to good effect, confirmed the position of Druze feudal chieftains, and allowed them to exert control over the rest of Mount Lebanon's population and to provide its first semi-independent rulers. Feuding within the community, however, reduced its numbers, since defeated factions moved eastwards to settle in the Syrian Jebel ed Drūz (Chapter 13).

Lebanon's Sunnī community is of comparatively recent development. Mamluk persecution of the Shī'ites and Christians following the final expulsion of the Crusaders led to conversions in areas along the main lines of communication through the coastal plain and 'Akkar. Some Druze and Shī'a communities in El Beq'a, Wādī el-Taym and Shūf also practised taqiya for such a long time during Sunnī domination that they ceased to make the necessary mental reservation. However, the introduction of Turkoman and Kurdish nomads during the fourteenth century accounts for the Sunnī predominance in 'Akkar as well as for some of the groups in El Beq'a. The Sunnī element in El Beq'a was also increased by the voluntary sedentarization of some bedouin groups. Finally, the predominance of Sunnī governments from 1291 to 1918 saw the establishment and reinforcement of loyal coreligionist administrators in the important coastal towns. These were augmented from the seventeenth century onwards by numbers of Sunnī merchants attracted by the rising prosperity of the Lebanese seaboard based on its western contacts.

14.4 Effects of community fragmentation

Probably the most publicized effect of the fragmentation of Lebanon's population into distinct communities has been upon its political life. To maintain Lebanon as an independent entity, the communities have agreed to a form of proportional representation which penetrates every aspect of government. The system was evolved during the nineteenth century when the cooperation of Druze and Maronite, which had maintained the semi-independence of Mount Lebanon from the sixteenth century, finally broke down. Arrangements made then were extended in a modified form to embrace the Sunnī and Mitwāli communities brought into the state at the end of the First World War. Proportional representation was enshrined in the constitution of 1926, if only as a temporary measure, and was reiterated during the 1930's. In 1943, it formed the basis of the unwritten National Pact which, though severely strained, is still the agreed foundation of Lebanese government. Under these arrangements, the President of the Republic, the key post with tenure for six years, is a Maronite, his Prime Minister a Sunnī Muslim and the President of the Chamber of Deputies a Mitwāli, and so on through the government. Seats in the Chamber are allocated in the proportions of six Christians to five non-Christians, but are filled by a complex system of list-voting from constituencies which often have mixed populations. Administrative posts used to be filled in a similar way, though recognition of the inefficiencies involved here has produced a move towards appointment on merit. Muslims contest the population basis on which this discriminatory structure depends, while the vested interests of Christians have prevented a new census from being taken.

Political parties, though often mixed, tend to be dominated by one community and are led by a group of its powerful individuals—feudal chiefs, absentee landowners and financiers. The community basis also means that the parties are very weak and ineffective, a fact which Suleiman has argued has been important in preserving Lebanon's presidential democracy.[8] Party politics reflect community and hence locality interest, but 'the close balance between Christians and Muslims ties internal problems to an increasing struggle on the level of international politics, between westward-orientated Christians and Arab-oriented Muslims, between conflicting images of Lebanon as a Christian 'foyer' to the Middle East and as a province of an Arab state'.[9] The continuing conflict with Israel and the presence of Palestinian refugees and guerrilla organizations in the country, together with Syrian interference, have done much to exacerbate the situation.

The community structure has had equally well-known effects upon migration patterns, though precise statistics for emigration are not available after 1932. The 1932 census showed that Christians formed a majority of the emigrants (Table 14.2), with Maronites and Greek Orthodox as the most important groups. It has been suggested that the number of Maronites abroad now balances that of those remaining in Lebanon, while the number of Greek Orthodox emigrants may be twice that of residents.[10] The volume of emigration is a function of numbers in the different communities, but, on the push side of the casual equation, it was stimulated by population growth which, by the 1880's, when the first migrants left for Egypt, had resulted in the fragmentation of property down to sizes insufficient to support a family and in the emergence of large numbers of seasonal labourers. Similar developments have not necessarily

TABLE 14.2
Emigration from Lebanon, 1932 Census

Communities		1	2
A. Christians		54·0	85·0
i. *Old-established Communities*			
	Maronites	54·0	48·0
	Greek Orthodox	73·0	22·0
	Greek Catholics	63·0	11·0
ii. *Recently-established Communities*			
	Armenians	7·0	1·0
	Latins	—	—
	Protestants	42·1	1·0
iii. *Other Christian Communities*		7·0	—
B. Muslims		9·0	14·0
	Sunnīs	9·0	6·0
	Mitwālis	7·0	4·0
	Druzes	16·0	3·0
C. Jews and Other Groups		16·0	—
D. Total		32·0	

1 : Emigrants as a percentage of the community remaining in Lebanon.
2 : Community emigrants as a percentage of the total number of emigrants.
Source: E. de Vaumas, 'La répartition confessionelle au Liban et l'équilibre de l'état Libanais', *Revue Géogr, alp.*, **43**, 511–604 (1955).

resulted in large-scale emigration from other countries of the Middle East, and it is therefore necessary to seek other influences peculiar to Lebanon. One of them was the early availability of roads, both the paved mule tracks built by Emir Bashīr II (1788 to 1840) and the carriage roads laid out by the French, beginning with the Beirūt–Damascus road of 1858. Much more important was a tradition of Christian contact with the West through religion, education and trade. Lebanese Christians came to admire the West and to feel that they could find work and security there, while their Western-oriented education and their business acumen gave them personal qualities which they could utilize better abroad than at home. Some emigrants went to Egypt at the end of the nineteenth century and found work under the British dominated administrations, but increasingly Lebanese Christians went to Roman Catholic Latin America, especially Brazil, the U.S.A. and the British territories of West Africa.

Muslim emigrants have been comparatively few, though proportionate to their total strength in the country, more Druzes have gone abroad than any other community. Druze emigration may have been stimulated by their deteriorating position in independent Lebanon during the nineteenth and twentieth centuries, but it is probably significant that the Druzes are the only Muslim community to have had much contact with the West, either directly with Britain in the game of great power influence in the region or through the Maronites, with whom they were tolerantly associated for so long. As the establishment community of the Turkish Empire, Sunnīs had little incentive to emigrate, unlike the Mitwālis. Both communities, however, had few contacts with westerners, whom they despised as infidels, and have subsequently felt that the West's Christian-influenced culture would offer an unsympathetic environment to them, an attitude which Khuri believed lay behind the preference of Shī'a emigrants for West Africa rather than the U.S.A.[11] Muslim emigration has also been curtailed by the patterns of inheritance and marriage, as well as by social structure. Inheritance takes place on a kinship rather than a single family basis, while early marriage, preferably between cousins, is essential to male status. Most of the Muslim community consists of sharecroppers and they are tied to the land by debt.

Khuri has shown that community affiliation has to some extent conditioned whether rural migrants choose to go abroad or try to settle in Lebanon's towns.[12] The large towns have grown rapidly since the end of the Second World War and members of the various communities have moved to them, especially Beirūt, but it does seem that the preference is greatest amongst Muslims. One explanation is the urban orientation of Islam, and the rhythm of work which is still adjusted to the needs of daily prayer, but another is the widespread lack of skill and education amongst the Muslim communities which tends to make their members suitable only for the unskilled labour market of construction and certain manufacturing industries. Christians are better educated through missionary schools and colleges, and find that their skills are more readily marketable abroad. In addition, Beirūt, Tripoli and Saida have been and still are dominated by Sunnīs, and are centres of pan-Arab and Islamic sympathy with its anti-Christian, anti-Western colouring.

The economic effects of community fragmentation cannot easily be demonstrated, though they appear to be very real. An attempt will be made here to isolate the effects upon agriculture, industry, commerce, finance and planning.

Only about 38 per cent of the country's area is cultivated, and in the past Maronites and Druzes controlled the most productive part of it in the form of the well-watered fertile soils of Mount Lebanon, the rugged slopes of which offered all-important security (Figure 14.2). Although methods and crops were labour intensive and the cereal harvest inadequate to local needs, the two communities grew crops which provided a valuable cash element to their economies. Wine and spirits, olives and olive oil were sold in neighbouring regions, and from the seventeenth century until the First World War increasing amounts of silk were shipped abroad. The relief, with its demand for terraces, even proved advantageous to aboriculture, for it allowed vertical as well as horizontal spacing and thus 25 per cent more trees than on flat land.[13] In addition to crops, charcoal, timber and firewood were moved from the depleted forests to the towns and the coast. The Maronites and Druzes also had comparatively easy access to Beirūt, an important factor as traffic built up during the nineteenth century and increasingly with the improvements made to the port by French engineers in 1890 to 1895 and 1934 to 1939.

In recent times, the agricultural advantage enjoyed by Maronites and

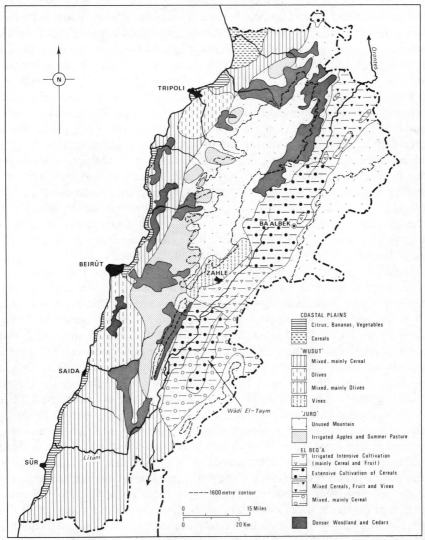

Figure 14.2 Land use in Lebanon in about 1970 (Reproduced by permission of Societé de Géographie de lyon)

Druzes has declined (Figure 14.2). The most active elements now leave the villages to work abroad or in the towns, and their remittances are so important to many families that they can afford to neglect their land. Accordingly, farming is becoming less important to the economy of Mount Lebanon, and terraces, especially those where only cereals were grown at uneconomic costs, fall out of use. In some districts, they have collapsed to such an extent that coastal areas are locally threatened with flooding. Remittances also encourage domestic construction, often with a view to summer letting, and though many families undoubtedly enjoy a comparatively high standard of living, its basis is precarious, as the First World War showed when payment was not possible and there was widespread famine. Falling demand for silk, as rayon and nylon were developed, affected Mount Lebanon's traditional communities between the wars. Expansion of apple growing appears at first sight to have been a compensation for this, but is not so in reality, since many of the mountain orchards are the property not of peasant farmers but of city businessmen. In any case, the mountain is not well adapted to apple growing because of competition from established crops and the critical requirements of the apple, especially for irrigation water which, with the vast demands being made upon it, is often in short supply during the summer. At the same time, other agricultural areas are competing fairly successfully with the Druze-Maronite area in the production of cash crops. Banana, citrus, cotton and vegetable growing has expanded along the Sunnī dominated coast, whilst cereal monoculture in El Beq'a has been diversified with cotton and apples, where new land has been brought into cultivation by drainage, the eradication of malaria and some extension of irrigation. These areas have the advantage of comparatively flat land, where expensive terracing is unnecessary, to which drilling and dam building techniques can bring the necessary water in ample quantities.

Although Lebanon is one of the most industrialized countries of the Middle East, with about 20 per cent of its active population employed in manufacturing, it has few resources and industrial development is further hampered by the smallness of the national market. A little lignite and iron are mined, but the most important domestic resources are agricultural products. Foodstuffs and textiles are the leading industrial sectors, though the refineries at Tripoli and Saida, processing Iraq and Saudi Arabia oil respectively, are the largest single employers. These are followed by the production of beverages, leather goods, soap, cigarettes and metal items (a steel furnace was opened in 1962), while plants to produce paper and cardboard, cosmetics and pharmaceuticals, superphosphates, car batteries and sugar have been introduced. Most of these industries are concentrated in the coastal towns where there is a mixed labour force but a Muslim predominance. The individual firms, however, are generally very small and often Christian managed, so there is ample scope to select employees on the basis of community affiliation, with the result that all the available skill cannot be fully used. Lack of resources and a regional inequality of incomes virtually restricts the home market to Beirūt and its hinterland, though Druze and Maronite families receiving remittances from abroad often prefer to buy foreign goods.

Commerce, finance and services are much more important to the Lebanese economy than either agriculture or manufacturing industry, and account for its comparatively high per capita income ($480 in 1969). All involve exploitation of the country's location and have been stimulated by Lebanon's poverty in natural resources. They depend upon stability and good will to such an extent that the upheavals of 1958 in Lebanon itself and elsewhere in the Middle East saw a 15 per cent decline in national income and a 25 per cent fall in income earned from tertiary sectors.

The most important service industry is tourism, for Lebanon benefits from the close relationship of beaches and snowfields, ancient ruins and a cosmopolitan city. Middle Easterners are attracted to the country by the summer coolness and greenery of Mount Lebanon and the developed pleasures of Beirūt. Westerners enjoy not only the sun and sea but also winter sports; they visit the splendid ruins and attend the Ba'albek festival. Lebanon is accessible to both groups, for it lies on major great circle air routes across the world. Khalde Airport, near Beirūt, has developed as a major international airport handling 1,510,000 passengers in 1968, of whom some 270,861 were in transit. Tourism suffered a set back as a result of the war of June, 1967, when Jordan's loss of the West Bank meant that package tours of the Holy Land could no longer be arranged. The Israeli raid on Beirūt airport in December, 1968 did not help matters. The benefits of tourism, however, are comparatively localized in the country. Beirūt profits most, as the point of access and central place to the country, but it is followed by neighbouring districts, principally inhabited by Druzes and Maronites. It is also these communities who have the initial capital, often in the form of remittances, to reap most benefit from tourism by building hotels and villas and by developing other facilities.

Lebanon exports mainly fruit, vegetables, some textiles and a few light metal products on its own account, about half of which go to the neighbouring Arab countries of Saudi Arabia, Iraq, Jordan, Kuwait and Egypt. Much of the country's trade, however, is goods in transit: grain and flour, hides, cotton and wool from Syria, Iraq and Jordan; vehicles, machines and manufactured goods of all kinds from Britain, the E.E.C. and the U.S.A. Oil also crosses the country to the refineries at Tripoli and Saida. Beyond these bare facts, few details are available on commodity composition, while monetary conversions are made at varying rates, and numbers of unrecorded transactions are said to be involved. The traffic is obviously considerable, and cargo handled by the overcrowded port of Beirūt has increased officially from 2·17 million tonnes in 1965 to 2·58 million tonnes in 1968. A third basin is under construction, together with a new quay, silos and cold stores. The growth of Beirūt's trade since about 1950 has been assisted by the continuance of the Arab–Israeli conflict which has prevented competition from neighbouring Haifa, and, since 1967, by the closure of the Suez Canal, which has diverted goods to land routes.

Community structure appears to affect the trade situation in two ways. Although transit trade depends upon the port of Beirūt (especially its free zone), the absence of currency control and good communications with the Arab hinterland, political stability is also important. This depends upon good relationships between the communities. When intercommunal friction breaks the surface in open strife, as in 1958, transit trade suffers. In 1954, goods in transit amounted officially to some 574,000 tonnes but had dropped to 317,000 tonnes by 1965, only to rise to 642,750 tonnes in 1967. The effects of political friction in the country, exacerbated by the Arab–Israeli conflict, were offset by the benefits derived from the closure of the Suez Canal, so that, in official figures, the amount of goods in transit rose to 832,000 tonnes in 1968. The second effect of the community structure is more direct. Much of Lebanon's trade is handled by small firms and, like finance, depends upon a network of reliability and trust. There is, therefore, a tendency to employ relatives or, failing them, members of the same community. Christian firms appear to be numerous, perhaps because the communities are better educated than the Muslims and have traditional ties with the major trading countries of the world. There are, however, a number of Druze and Sunnī merchants, some of them very successful.

Beirūt's role as a financial centre has developed since the end of the Second World War. In 1945, there were only nine banks in the city, but the number rose rapidly to 85 by 1966, 68 of which were Lebanese and the rest foreign, including one of the few branches of the Narodny Bank outside the U.S.S.R. There are, in addition, numerous money changers and finance houses. Beirūt's rise to prominence depended upon a number of factors. The most basic of these included the legal confidentiality of accounts, free convertibility and free import of gold. But these would have made little difference without the flood of wealth coming from the Gulf and Saudi Arabia after the exploitation of oil resources there during the 1950's. Political instability in other Arab countries was also an important factor, for wealthy individuals and the new political leaders had so little trust in their own people that they thought it wise to move their resources abroad. Cairo might have been preferred, but Egypt's growing socialism diverted the funds to Beirūt. Lebanon's political stability was again of crucial importance and this depended upon community relationships. Its importance was shown when the failure of the Intra Bank in 1966 led to the withdrawal of deposits and threatened the whole financial structure of the country as other banks failed and the scale of Intra's involvement in the national economy—through controlling interests in such enterprises as Middle East Airlines, the Port of Beirūt Company, Radio Orient and the Casino du Liban—was realized. At one stage, it was reported that the Maronite Patriarch had put the not inconsiderable resources of the church at the government's disposal to weather the crisis.[14] The community implication seems clear, for many banks and finance houses are dependent upon family and community connections for the success of their operations. Confidence was partially restored when the government passed a new banking law which insisted upon minimum capital reserves and urged the merger of the smaller and weaker banks. Several banks closed immediately, ten were subsequently nationalized but only two merged. The number of registered banks in 1969 was 74, with foreign ones handling most of the big business, since they are thought to be more reliable. Beirūt's share of Middle East banking has declined as competition has drawn substantial deposits direct to financial centres outside the Middle East, leaving the city as just one of a range of possibilities considered by Arabs with money to invest.

Although Lebanon's economy has been run along almost classic *laissez-faire* lines, planning machinery has existed since 1953. The first Five Year Plan was launched in 1958, only to be ended by political upheaval in the country during the same year. A new plan was drawn up with foreign assistance and implementation began in 1962. As a result, several large developments began, including an extension to the port Beirūt, the construction of a coastal motor-way, the provision of domestic water supplies and electricity to more rural areas and, as part of the *Green Plan*, the reclamation of 100,000 ha of arid land. For the most part, though, the projects initiated under these plans were small scale, involving individual settlements or particular localities and were not clearly integrated into an overall strategy for national development. Several factors worked together to create this situation. Financing was not adequate to support many large-scale and well-integrated projects, largely because of an antiquated tax structure, which favours wealthy individuals at the expense of the community, but partly because of Lebanon's refusal until recently to contract loans from outside for fear of jeopardizing her financial credibility. Some of the capital shortage was made good under the new Five Year Plan (1965 to 1970) with a loan from Kuwait to improve roads and services in Greater Beirūt, the anarchic growth of which since the Second World War has caused rising concern. Another weakness in Lebanese planning has been a certain naivety about planning itself, in particular the emphasis laid on partner-ship between the state and private sectors in a situation where most private firms are extremely small, probably under-capitalized and engaged in forms of enterprise depending upon confidentiality, as well as sensitivity to external conditions and great flexibility. A third factor is the community situation. Each community is haunted by the fear that another will come to dominate government planning and exploit its machinery for sectional gain. The result is that all the communities seek to restrict the role of government, but this seems especially true of the Christians. The Muslims, who are in general less economi-cally privileged, appear more sympathetic to central planning, for they see it not only as the method of development chosen by Arab nationalist regimes in neighbouring countries, which they admire, but also as a great equalizer and social leveller. Government has tried to deal with the situation by distribut-ing improvements as evenly as possible about the country—and hence amongst the communities. Unfortunately, it is clear that resources in land and water are unevenly distributed and that the coastal plains, El Beq'a and the southern districts adjacent to the Lītāni—all Muslim areas—have the greatest potential for development. The coastal plains, with access to the major towns, also enjoy distinct locational advantages for further industrial and commercial growth, even when compared with neighbouring parts of Mount Lebanon. Recognition of these facts has reinforced the friction between the communities. The Lītāni development scheme is probably the best case in point. It was launched in 1957, with the aim of extending irrigation to a number of small plains along the river, especially that of Merj Ayon on the great westward bend of the Lītāni where cotton already does comparatively well, and of doubling the output of electricity in the country by the time of completion, originally scheduled for 1982. Much of the territory through which this section of the river runs is inhabited by Mitwālis, and it has been unofficially suggested that fear of upsetting the communal balance in the country, by favouring that community, was responsible for various modifications made to the plan after work was resumed in 1961 following the blocking of a crucial tunnel by a rock fall in August, 1959.[15] The modifications would have deprived the south of a large proportion of the water and much of the electricity on which its development will depend. New modifications were made to the benefit of the south only after strong Mitwāli protests and the threat of violence. Further developments to close the gap between the different parts of the country will probably be affected by the community situation in the future, even if Muslims succeed in altering the traditional balance of political power.

References

1. E. de Vaumas, 'La répartition confessionelle au Liban et l'equilibre de l'état libanais', *Revue Géogr. alp.*, **43**, 511–604 (1955).
2. The exact number of Palestinians resident in Lebanon is difficult to compute but UNRWA put the figure at 163,904 in 1967.
3. A convenient summary of the doctrinal differences between the Eastern Churches may be found in A. Schmemann, *The Historical Road of Eastern Orthodoxy*, Harvill, London 1963, especially Chapter 3. See also P. Rondot, *Les Chrétiens d'Orient*, Peyrounet, Paris, 1955.
4. S. Chehabe-ed-Dine, *Géographie humaine de Beyrouth*, Beirut 1960, 204–205.
5. J. Gulick, *Tripoli: A Modern Arab City*, Harvard Middle Eastern Studies, 12, Cambridge, Mass., 1967, 67.
6. A. Guillaume, *Islam*, 2nd ed. reprinted, Penguin, Harmondsworth, 1964, 117.
7. E. L. Peters, 'Aspects of rank and status among Muslims in a Lebanese village', in *Mediterranean Countrymen, Essays on the Social Anthropology of the Mediterranean*, (Ed. J. Pitt-Rivers), Mouton, Paris and The Hague, 1963, 159–200.
8. M. W. Suleiman, 'The role of political parties in a confessional democracy: The Lebanese case', *Western Political Qtly.*, **20**, 682–693 (1967).
9. D. Lerner, *The Passing of Traditional Society, Modernising the Middle East*, The Free Press, New York, 1964, 205–206.
10. E. de Vaumas, 'La répartition confessionalle au Liban et l'équilibre de l'état libanais', *Revue Géogr. alp.*, **43**, 511–604 (1955).
11. F. I. Khuri, 'A comparative study of migration patterns in two Lebanese villages', *Hum. Org.*, **26**, 206–213 (1967).
12. F. I. Khuri, 'A comparative study of migration patterns in two Lebanese villages', *Hum. Org.*, **2b**, 206–213 (1967).
13. N. N. Lewis, 'Lebanon. The mountain and its terraces', *Geogrl Rev.*, **43**, 1–14 (1953).
14. 'The church uses funds to beat Lebanon's bank crisis', *The Times*, 19 November, 1966.
15. N. Raphaeli, 'Development planning; Lebanon', *Western Political Qtly.*, **20**, 714–728 (1967).

CHAPTER 15

Jordan—The Struggle for Economic Survival

15.1 Introduction

From the sixteenth century to the end of the First World War, the territory occupied by Jordan formed part of the Ottoman Empire. Towards the end of these times, Damascus vilayet, with its western boundary on the Jordan, extended from Hama to Aqaba, while the country west of the Jordan, Palestine, was divided between the independent sanjak of Jerusalem in the south, and the vilayet of Beirūt in the north. Following capture by British and Arab forces, and the defeat of Turkey in 1918, Britain became responsible for the region under Mandate from the League of Nations. Under British administration, the area was divided in 1923 into the territories of Palestine, west of the Jordan river, and Transjordan to the east under the rule of the Emir Abdullah (Chapter 10). After a relatively uneventful period of indirect British rule in Transjordan, the Mandate ended on 22 May 1946, and in 1948 the country became known as the Hashemite Kingdom of Transjordan, under King Abdullah. When the British Mandate of Palestine ended on 14 May 1948, the Jews in Palestine proclaimed the establishment of the State of Israel, and widespread fighting broke out between Jews and Arabs. Eventually, a cease fire was established, and an armistice on 3 April 1949 demarcated *de facto* borders for the new state of Israel. As a result of this armistice, Transjordan obtained a portion of former Palestine, and, to acknowledge this fact, the country was renamed in 1950 as the Hashemite Kingdom of Jordan.

15.2 Transjordan

The main theme of this chapter is an examination of the economic life of the state of Jordan. The economic position of Transjordan in the 1940's will first be examined and then the changes since this date. Transjordan covered an area of 89,300 km². Although no census of the population was taken under British Mandate, it was estimated to be between 300,000 and 350,000 in the early 1940's.[1] This population was overwhelmingly Arab, although small and distinct groups of Circassians, Chechens, Turkomans, and Armenians, were present. The vast majority of the people were Muslim. The Arabs were descendants of nomadic tribes which had moved northwards in a slow migration from the Arabian peninsula. In their movements to the north, some of the groups settled when they reached favourable agricultural areas on the southern fringe of the

Fertile Crescent in northern Transjordan. Others took up a semi-normadic type of existence.

The population of Transjordan clearly showed this threefold division into sedentary, semi-nomadic and fully nomadic groups. The settled inhabitants, including all the non-Arabs, lived in towns and villages concentrated in the northwest of the country, with main centres at Irbid, Ajlūn, and Jarash. In the districts to the south, centred around the towns of Amman and Salt, approximately half of the population could be classified as settled. Elsewhere in Transjordan, sedentary populations were only found near Karak, Ma'ān and Aqaba. The semi-nomadic population, numbering 130,000 to 150,000, a figure similar to that of the sedentary population, was organized in tribal groupings and lived in tents. These people, besides their pastoral activities, cultivated the land and occupied the highland areas around Amman and southwards towards Ma'ān. The bedouin, numbering between 40,000 and 50,000, were scattered throughout the rest of the country. These people were entirely dependent on their flocks of sheep and goats and herds of camels, and cultivated no land whatsoever. Living on the fringe of the desert, these tribes undertook seasonal migrations in the search for pastures. During the wet winter months they moved eastwards into the desert, or downwards to the Jordan valley, while in summer, movement was westwards and upwards into the better watered highlands.

During the period of the British Mandate, there was little market activity within Transjordan with the majority of the population dependent upon subsistence arable farming or nomadic pastoralism. The total cultivated area was estimated at 445,000 ha, and was concentrated in the highlands of the northwestern part of the country. Of the cultivated area, only some 91,000 ha received an annual rainfall of more than 500 mm. Much of the land which was cultivated was really unsuited for this type of activity. Soil erosion was widespread, and a large area of formerly arable land had lost its top soil cover. Irrigated land comprised about seven per cent of the total cultivated area, and was found mainly in the Jordan valley. Even in the 1940's it was estimated that most of the easily available water in the valley was already being used, although the distribution systems were often wasteful. In the highland areas, little irrigation was practised except to supply the villages with fruit and vegetables. On the plateau and uplands of the north and west, wheat and barley were the main winter cereals, often grown in conjunction with leguminous crops, such as vetches, kersennah peas, and lentils. The chief summer crop was durra, a form of millet, but melons and cucumbers were also grown. On the slopes overlooking the Jordan valley, fruit cultivation was more important, with vineyards being common round Salt and Ajlūn. Finally, in the Jordan valley, besides the production of wheat and barley, bananas and other tropical fruits were grown under irrigation. Throughout the country, livestock, particularly flocks of sheep and goats, formed an essential part of the agricultural economy.

With regard to the mineral resources of the country, no mines were worked at this period, and apart from the huge salt resources of the Dead Sea, no minerals, other than phosphates, had been proved in large quantities. Rock with a rich phosphate content was known to occur at Er Ruseifa, to the north-west of Amman, and in 1936 a company was formed to exploit these reserves, with the result that by the early 1940's the quarried phosphatic rock was being used for the manufacture of fertilizers in Palestine. The only other mineral activity was the local quarrying of limestones, around Jarash and Amman for building purposes, and the sporadic digging of the salt deposits at El Azraq.

Industrial activity, in the western sense, was practically non-existent and was confined to two small tobacco factories at Amman, and three small distilleries near Salt. In the larger towns, tailoring and dyeing were of some importance but were concentrated in extremely small units. Some processing of agricultural products did take place. *Samne*, a clarified butter, was manu-factured, while rugs and sacks were made from locally produced wool and hair when prices were low.

With the low level of economic activity in Transjordan, commercial activity was very restricted and little trade passed over the country's frontiers. That which did occur was mostly confined to the neighbouring states of Palestine, Syria, Iraq, and Saudi Arabia, but no accurate statistics of the amount of trade exist. Exports were largely agricultural products such as wheat, barley, sheep and fresh fruit, while imports were dominated by products which could not be produced in Transjordan. Chief among such items were textiles, sugar, petroleum, rice and kerosene. From this short description, it is clear that Transjordan in the early 1940's was a very poor country, with very few natural resources, a low level of economic activity, and already, evidence of population pressure.

15.3 Jordan (Figure 15.1)

With the *de facto* partition of Palestine following the establishment of the state of Israel, Transjordan acquired the West Bank territory, which increased its area from 89,300 km^2 to 96,600 km^2. At the same time, the state received a massive influx of population. Some 460,000 people were residents of the West Bank when Transjordan was enlarged to become the Hashemite Kingdom of Jordan, but besides these people, a further 350,000 to 500,000 refugees from Palestine had already fled into the West Bank area and Trans-jordan, while the fighting was going on. When the armistice was signed in 1949, these refugees were never allowed to return to their lands in Israel. So by 1952, while the area of Transjordan had been enlarged by about 10 per cent to form the new state of Jordan, the population had risen 130 per cent from 375,000 in 1946 to at least 1·1 million[2].

Since 1950, the population of Jordan, including refugees, has risen steadily at the rate of about 3 per cent per annum. As a result, the population had grown to approximately 2·1 million in 1967, prior to the June War. Of this total 720,000 were registered as refugees with the United Nations Relief

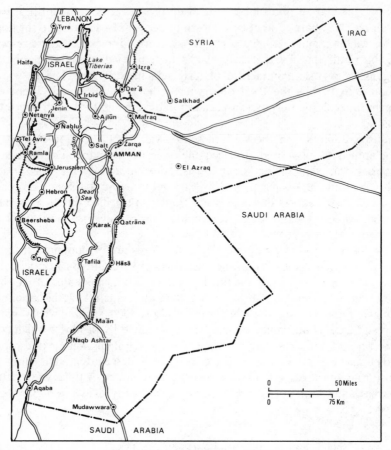

Figure 15.1 The Kingdom of Jordan

and Works Agency.[3] The 1961 census revealed that 45 per cent of the refugees were less than 15 years of age. The population density for the country as a whole is approximately 21 people per km². Unfortunately, owing to the harshness of the environment the population is markedly concentrated in a very small portion of the total area, and in this zone population densities are more than 190 people per km².

From the time of the formation of the state of Jordan, there has been a steady drift of population from the West Bank to the East Bank, so that by the early 1960's a slight majority of Jordan's population were residents of the East Bank. Many reasons help to account for this population drift, but the main one would seem to be the concentration of industrial development in the larger towns of the East Bank, especially Amman and Zarqa, and it has been here that opportunities for employment have been greatest. In all rural areas, population pressure on the land has increased markedly, in itself giving rise to a drift of population to the urban centres. Unfortunately, however, unemployment rates in cities are high and underemployment of labour is everywhere common. Following the war of June 1967, when Israel took over Jordan's West Bank region, another 200,000 refugees fled from the area to the East Bank of the Jordan and so made a bad situation even worse.

On the West Bank of the Jordan, still occupied by Israel in 1974, a number of local urban centres were found around which population was concentrated. None of these centres were, however, so large as to dominate the whole region. In the northern part, Nablus was the dominant centre of population and also especially of industry. To the south, Jordanian Jerusalem, Jericho, and Hebron were the main centres. Jericho, in the Jordan valley, was an agricultural centre and possessed very little industrial activity.

On the much larger East Bank, the capital Amman and the nearby town of Zarqa dominate the country as a population and industrial centre. In the extreme north, Irbid is the local market and centre of industrial activity for the country's most productive agricultural region. South of Amman, population densities are very low and only a few towns are found along the main routes to the port of Aqaba. Among these, the chief centres are Mādaba, Karak, Tafila and Ma'ān.

15.3.1 Agriculture

Of all the problems facing Jordan in the early 1950's, none was more immediate than the problem of feeding its new citizens and of placing its agricultural production on a sound basis. If one was willing to accept a risk, the former of the two problems could be at least eased by the cultivation of those areas which were not really suited for this task, due either to the uncertainty of precipitation or the instability or insufficiency of the soil. In many cases this happened, but the result of such a practice has been to further worsen the overall situation by substantially increasing the processes of land degradation and soil erosion. Therefore, any food increase resulting from this practice has been bought at the price of potentially less food production in the future. Although the new Jordanian government realized the problem, it was unable to initiate conservation schemes owing to a lack of funds.

Utilization of the waters of the Jordan valley has been hindered since 1948 by the political difficulties of the area.[4] Four states, Lebanon, Syria, Jordan and Israel, control the Jordan catchment, and although a number of schemes for the rational utilization of the water resources of the region have been proposed, none have been implemented. Instead, each state has gone ahead with its own plans, often to the detriment of other nations. In Jordan, the major irrigation scheme which has been implemented is known as the East Ghor project.[5] This consists of the diversion of the waters of the Yarmuk, a tributary of the Jordan, to irrigate land in the northern part of the Ghor (Figure 15.2).

The Ghor is a terrace feature which occurs some 50 m above the present river, and forms the main area of level land in the Jordan valley. It is found on both sides of the flood plain of the Jordan, and at its outer margin abruptly

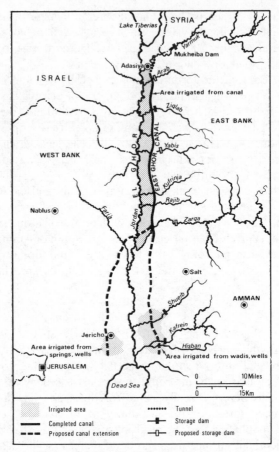

Figure 15.2 The East Ghor irrigation project

meets the fault escarpments which delimit the valley. It is well developed over the 120 km between Lake Tiberias and the Dead Sea. Composed largely of alluvial material, the soils developed upon it are well suited to agricultural production. Unfortunately, precipitation in the Jordan valley is low and unreliable. At the northern end of the valley near Lake Tiberias, rain-fed agriculture can occur, but further south, towards the Dead Sea, where precipitation totals are less than 100 mm, arable farming cannot be undertaken without irrigation. As a result, pastoral farming was the primary economic activity. Very little of the Ghor was brought under cultivation for the first time by the East Ghor project, as irrigation using the waters of the streams flowing down into the rift valley had been practised over a long period. Unfortunately, such water sources have always proved unreliable, especially in spring and summer, during the period of maximum irrigation demand.

Work on the East Ghor project was initiated in August 1958, and by the summer of 1966, water was being delivered through the system to most of the land supplied from the main canal.[6] The canal taps the water of the Yarmuk at a point approximately eight kilometres above its confluence with the Jordan and conveys it through a concrete-lined canal parallel to the Jordan river for a distance of some 70 km. Lateral canals then distribute the water by gravity flow to fields situated between the canal and the Jordan river.

The scheme has had a tremendous effect on farming practices, and has resulted in a land-use change from the traditional cultivation of cereals to a more commercially orientated agriculture. Vegetables, including tomatoes, eggplants, melons, cucumbers and peppers now occupy more than half the cultivated area, while the acreage devoted to fruits, especially citrus and bananas, has also increased. All of these provide a high financial return, and possess export potential to the Gulf area. It should be noted, however, that wheat is still the most important single crop, as many farmers are reluctant to change their traditional patterns of farming. It is also true that, although a new marketing centre is being constructed in the Wadi Yabis, storage facilities for perishable crops are lacking in the Jordan valley at the present time.

The natural resistance to change of the farmer has been combated in this region by the valuable work of the Jordanian Agricultural Extension Service. This organization has helped farmers experiment with new crops, fertilizers and pesticides, and, at the same time, has provided cash loans and incentive grants through recently established cooperative societies. The wasteful traditional methods of irrigation have been discouraged, and largely replaced by efficient distribution techniques involving the levelling of fields and the controlled flow of water. Without adequate drainage in this area, the build-up of soil salinity would pose a considerable problem.

A detailed programme of land reform also accompanied the implementation of the East Ghor project, and was the first of its kind in Jordan. Before the initiation of the project, much of the land throughout the East Ghor area was owned by absentee landlords residing in the larger urban centres or by smaller landlords often owning and cultivating uneconomic units. A large proportion of the population, however, owned no land at all and lived as tenant farmers or as farm labourers. With the sudden increase in the population of the country in the early 1950's, pressure on the land intensified and resulted in a decrease of farm size and higher rents. Under such conditions of fragmentation and insecurity, efficient farming was difficult to establish.

Under the Canal Law, all the land within the area of the scheme was appropriated and compensation paid to landowners at pre-project land values. New rectangular units, better suited for irrigation, were demarcated and re-alloted to the former owners, on the basis that no individual landowner could now own more than 20 ha or less than three hectares.[7] The minimum figure of three hectares was regarded as the smallest unit capable of providing a family with a reasonable standard of living and at the same time being capable of repaying the construction costs. This ruling allowed a redistribution of property with the virtual abolition of both very large and very small farms. The overall effect of this policy was a 20 per cent reduction in the total number of landlords. As a result, the scheme did not provide any opportunity for the tenant farmers or farm labourers to obtain land of their own, and, indeed, many were worse off than before, owing to the lower labour requirements.

Associated with the East Ghor scheme was a programme of soil conservation and farming modernization in the Ajlūn and Amman Highlands.[8] These highlands form a dissected upland area between Amman and Irbid, bounded on the west by the Rift valley of the Jordan, and on the east by the Syrian Desert. The two highland masses, each rising to more than 1000 m, are separated by the valley of the Wadi Zarqa. The eastern part of the area is a plateau sloping gently eastwards, while the western part has been deeply dissected by a series of steep-sided wadis which flow down into the Jordan. The rocks of these highlands are mainly terrestrial and marine sediments dating from Jurassic to Tertiary times.

With an altitudinal range of more than 1,500 m, temperature variations within the area can be considerable. From the limited data available it would seem that frosts occur on between five and 15 days/annum on the plateau around Amman, while they are only rarely recorded in the Jordan valley. Summers are everywhere hot. Almost the whole region receives more than 300 mm of precipitation, with the two areas of highest elevation recording totals of more than 600 mm. A feature of the precipitation of the region is its annual variability, with a number of stations recording maximum annual values four times greater than the minimum ones. Approximately 95 per cent of the precipitation falls in the winter season from November to March, and within this period the three months of December to February account for about 70 per cent of the total. As a result, the number of rain days is surprisingly small, averaging between 30 to 50 over most of the higher ground.

Soils tend to correlate closely with the geological outcrop. Terra Rossa soils cover the greatest area in the Ajlūn and Amman Highlands, and occur almost exclusively on hard crystalline limestones, while Rendzinas occur on the chalky or marly formations. Slope and alluvial soils are common throughout the area. A significant proportion of the land surface is bare rock. The natural vegetation of the region was forest, but, at the present time, only stunted remnants of the original cover are found.[9]

The most important problem of this region is undoubtedly that of soil erosion, which, although caused largely by human activity, has certainly been intensified by natural conditions. The soils, owing to a lack of structural stability, tend to break down to individual particles when subjected to wetting. This means that the pores in the upper layers become clogged by these particles and so an impermeable surface crust is formed. In turn, this reduces infiltration rates, and promotes increased runoff and water erosion. Another important environmental feature is the steepness of the slopes, with much of the region possessing gradients greater than 15 per cent (Figure 15.3).[10] On such slopes runoff is both rapid and erosive.

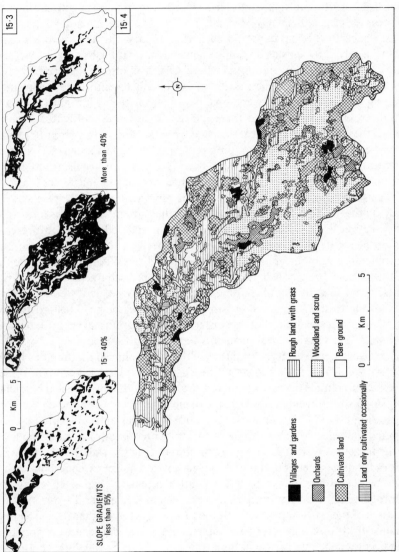

Figure 15.3 Steepness of slopes in the Wadi Ziqlab, northern Jordan (Reproduced by permission of Soil Conservation Society of America)

Figure 15.4 Land use in the Wadi Ziqlab, northern Jordan

Over the centuries, deforestation has been practised to provide additional agricultural land, as well as timber and fuel supplies. This activity is particularly difficult to correct, as forest regrowth is such a long-term process. Deforestation continues, but fortunately at a much reduced rate, while the replanting of forest areas is now official government policy. The overgrazing of pasture land dates back to Biblical days and earlier. In theory, this is a problem that can easily be solved by legislation, and in some areas goat husbandry is severely limited. Unfortunately, in a country where wealth is often measured by the number of animals owned, such a decree is difficult to enforce. As a result, overgrazing continues in many regions. Throughout the Ajlūn and Amman Highlands, between one half and three quarters of the total cultivated area is devoted to the cultivation of cereals, especially wheat and barley (Figure 15.4). The most serious effect of this cropping pattern is that the soil surface is bare of vegetation during the winter months, when precipitation totals are highest. This, coupled with the lack of soil stability when wet, means that sheet erosion of soil is extremely widespread throughout the region.

As all of the westerly drainage of the Northern highlands flows into the Jordan valley in a series of short wadis, flooding and sedimentation present serious problems to the success of the East Ghor canal scheme. To minimize these problems, a number of dams at the mouths of the Wadis Ziglab, Shueib, and Kafrein have been constructed to regulate the discharges. These dams, of course, are susceptible to sedimentation and consequent reduction in capacity owing to the severe soil erosion within the watersheds behind them. It was, therefore, essential that a conservation programme be initiated in this area if Jordan's agricultural problems were to be alleviated.

Conservation measures were initiated within the Ajlūn and Amman High-lands as part of a large scale project in the early 1960's. The prime aim of these measures was to reduce the rate of soil removal by introducing physical barriers to downslope soil movement and, at the same time, increasing the density of the vegetation cover. Contour walling, gradoni terraces and gully plugs were constructed in selected areas in association with an afforestation policy. While the measures were clearly successful in reducing the rate of soil erosion, the lack of funds has meant that the programme could not be extended through-out the whole area. So far, relatively little attention has been paid to the improvement of agricultural practices, which are, after all, one of the main causes of the erosion problem. In the future, it is hoped that the emphasis will change from direct government implementation of conservation projects to schemes of village and area rehabilitation carried out by the villagers them-selves, under the guidance of trained conservationists. At the same time, it is planned to introduce new cropping practices and to increase the area devoted to fruit crops, such as olives, vines and citrus. As a result of these changes, it is hoped that a more stable agricultural pattern can be developed in the area.

On the West Bank, the agricultural system was similar to that of the East Bank, and was dominated by the cultivation of wheat and barley, and the grazing of sheep and goats. However, this region has always had a much higher proportion of crops such as vines and olives than the East Bank, and many areas have been terraced. As a general rule, the West Bank gave the impression of being more prosperous and the soil better conserved than on the East Bank. However, the possibilities of increasing agricultural production within this area were not high.

At the margin of the desert on the East Bank, much land has recently been brought under cultivation for cereal production. Unfortunately, most of this land is at best marginal for any type of cultivation and crop yields have been very dependent on rainfall totals. Indeed, in some years, crop failures have been extensive. Coupled with the uncertainty of production is the added hazard of soil erosion by strong winds blowing across the desert. Following ploughing, the soil is extremely friable and particularly susceptible to wind blow. Given a reliable source of water and the provision of windbreaks, however, this land could be very productive. Further south, in the region around Qatrāna, a number of projects have been initiated to explore the possibility of building small check dams in local wadis to impound the winter runoff. Precipitation is low, and so no large scale increase in the cultivated area can occur. It is hoped that the result of such schemes will be to ensure a more reliable agricultural yield for the population. Considerable groundwater supplies may also be available in this region.

About one third of Jordan's labour force is engaged in agricultural activities, and yet the net income from agriculture averages only about one fifth of the G.N.P. The prime aim of the agricultural modernization programme is to attempt to produce sufficient food to feed the local population. In Jordan's

TABLE 15.1
Agricultural production in Jordan ('000 tonnes)

Major crops	1964*	1966*	1968	1970	1972
Wheat	294·7	101·1	95·1	54·1	211·4
Barley	97·2	22·8	19·7	5·3	34·0
Lentils	25·1	11·0	10·8	5·0	22·4
Vetch	13·2	6·9	2·3	2·5	6·8
Tomatoes	227·8	144·6	127·3	137·4	152·7
Eggplant	41·7	50·4	27·0	23·1	32·5
Cauliflowers and cabbages	35·9	21·6	10·8	10·9	13·2
Water melon and melon	159·8	47·7	36·4	22·5	63·0
Cucumbers	64·3	39·6	2·5	6·8	18·7
Broad beans	16·2	10·7	7·1	5·1	5·1
Olives	97·1	32·7	12·6	3·0	35·0
Bananas	8·2	16·8	5·5	8·2	6·7
Lemons, Oranges and other citrus fruits }	37·1	57·2	17·6	3·8	4·9
Grapes	76·9	61·9	7·6	6·2	18·1

*Includes West Bank
Source: Department of Statistics, The Hashemite Kingdom of Jordan, Amman, *Statistical Yearbooks*, 1969, 1970 and 1972.

TABLE 15.2
Livestock numbers in Jordan—'000 head

Livestock	1964*	1966*	1968	1970	1972
Sheep	803	1136	792	664	723
Goats	651	766	400	350	405
Cattle	65	78	40	32	46
Camels	10	17	13	10	16

*Includes West Bank
Source: Department of Statistics, The Hashemite Kingdom of Jordan, Amman,
Statistical Yearbooks, 1969, 1970 and 1972.

case, crop yields have been improved markedly for a number of crops in specific areas, and more drought resistant plants have been introduced into the drier regions. With these measures, and the conservation measures already outlines, Jordan's agriculture is on a much sounder footing than it was in 1950.

The major crop in Jordan today is wheat. It covers an area of 2·2 million donums (0·22 million ha), and 1972 production was 211,000 tonnes (Table 15.1). This crop, as with barley, is mostly grown without the aid of irrigation and, consequently, total production varies from year to year in response to the amount of precipitation which has fallen in the preceding winter period. The most important vegetable crops are tomatoes, water melons and melons, and cucumbers. These crops are often grown with the aid of irrigation and, as a result, production does not reveal marked annual fluctuations, as do cereals. Of the tree crops olives, grapes and citrus fruits are the most important. Sheep and goats are the most numerous livestock (Table 15.2). They are generally reared on poor marginal pastures, and their numbers fluctuate annually in response to precipitation conditions.

15.3.2 Mineral resources

Jordan is poorly endowed with minerals. Oil has so far not been discovered in any quantity, though seepage of liquid petroleum from the base of the Nubian Sandstone on the eastern shore of the Dead Sea has been known for centuries. Elsewhere, bituminous limestone has been discovered, but nowhere is it rich enough to warrant exploitation. Iron ore has been worked sporadically near Ajlūn, and ores are known to exist in the Zarqa region. In the south, copper was mined in early times in the Wadi Araba near Aqaba, but recent exploration has not yet revealed any ores suitable for modern commercial mining. Small deposits of manganese also occur in the Wadi Danā, south of Tafila.

High grade phosphate deposits were discovered at Er Ruseifa, close to Amman, in the 1930's, and quarrying of this material began in the early 1940's. Detailed exploration revealed that the phosphate rock outcropped in a broad band from Er Ruseifa, to the northeast of Amman, through Amman and southwards to Hāsā. Large scale workable deposits however, were confined to the Er Ruseifa and Hāsā areas. In the early 1950's, production was low with a total of 25,000 tonnes being mined in 1952. This figure had risen to 250,000 tonnes in 1960, and then, with the development of the Hāsā deposits, a further increase to more than one million tonnes occurred prior to the war of June 1967 (Figure 15.5). Following this war and the internal troubles of the country in 1970, production dropped to below 700,000 tonnes in 1971. By 1975, it had been hoped that total production from Er Ruseifa and Hāsā would exceed two million tonnes, but this no longer seems a feasible target. The deposits at Hāsā are suitable for mining by opencast methods and, therefore, production costs are considerably cheaper than at the older Er Ruseifa works. This fact, linked with its proximity to Aqaba, means that the Hāsā production is likely to grow rapidly in the future. At the moment, phosphate is transported by road from both Er Ruseifa and Hāsā to Aqaba for shipment. Additional storage and handling facilities are under construction at Aqaba to cope with the anticipated increase in phosphate exports. Most of the phosphates are exported to India and to the eastern European countries of Yugoslavia, Czechoslovakia and Poland.

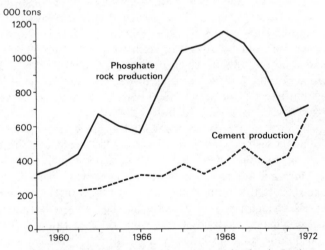

Figure 15.5 Phosphate and cement production in Jordan

The salt resources of the Dead Sea, in particular potash, were exploited commercially by the Palestine Potash Company between 1929 and 1948 at its two plants at the northern and southern ends of the Dead Sea. As a result of fighting in 1948, the northern plant at Kallia (on the West Bank) was destroyed. Under its present development plan, Jordan intends to construct a potash plant on the southeast shore of the Dead Sea at Safi, with an annual production of 500,000 tonnes. A new road is to connect this plant with the port at Aqaba but, owing to the 1967 hostilities, neither of these projects has been completed so far.

The only other kind of natural resources exploited are high quality limestones, chiefly in the Amman and Jarash districts. Such material is widely used for building in the larger urban centres, and it seems likely that demand in the future will increase. The export potential of this product, owing to high transport costs, is not likely to be great. In the Amman area, limestone is also quarried for use as the raw material in cement manufacture.

15.3.3 Industry

The establishment of the state of Israel, and the subsequent closing of the frontiers, helped to stimulate industrial activity in Jordan. The demands of the domestic market for building material, basic household goods and food-stuffs could no longer be supplied from what was formerly Palestine, and, as a result, local production increased. The opportunities for large-scale industrialization within Jordan, however, were severely limited, owing to the restricted range of raw materials and the small size and low purchasing power of the domestic market. Heavy industry is still only poorly represented in the country. A cement plant using local limestone was constructed near Amman in the mid-1950's and a new plant has recently been constructed near Suweilih, to the north of Amman. Total production had risen from 110,000 tonnes in 1959 to 480,000 tonnes in 1969 (Figure 15.5). In 1970, production fell to 377,000 tonnes, but by 1972 had risen to more than 650,000 tonnes. At Zarqa there is an oil refinery which obtains its crude oil from the Trans-Arabian pipeline (Tapline), which, crosses Jordan. By western standards, it is only small, with a capacity of about 7,500 barrels per day, but it is capable of supplying the present needs of the country.

Other main industries are concerned with the processing of agricultural produce. Olive oil, largely pressed in small local mills, was of great importance on the West Bank, although it tended to be of a poor quality, with a high acid content. Only one modern vegetable oil plant was operating prior to the war of June 1967, to the south of Nablus, but in the future, with an increase in the number of such factories, it would seem that both the quality and quantity of the product could be increased. Using olive oil as a raw material, there was a small but important soap industry centred in the Nablus region which used to supply most of Jordan's requirements. The milling of flour is another important industrial activity based on agricultural production, and is centred around Irbid, Nablus and Jerusalem.

A number of small clothing factories exist, especially in the main urban centres, such as Amman. These manufacture goods of a high quality but in very small quantities. At many places throughout the Kingdom, tanning of goat and sheep skins takes place under primitive conditions, but nowhere as yet, has this been commercially organized into a large scale modern industrial activity. A dairy industry exists to supply the urban centres, but again on a very small scale. Associated with all the larger urban centres are a whole range of service industries, including automobile repairing, building and contracting, and similar activities. In many centres, but particularly close to the main tourist sites, the production of handicrafts for sale to overseas visitors is an important part of the local economy. Most of the work is done in small individual units, still largely by hand labour, but the quality of the product is often high. Jerusalem pottery, mother-of-pearl brooches from Bethlehem, olive wood carvings, and embroideries are known and appreciated by tourists from all over the western world.

The future large scale development of industry within Jordan does not at the present appear to be a realistic proposition. On the other hand, it does seem likely that a number of new small industries might be profitably established and present ones expanded. One of the greatest hopes would seem to lie in the development of a fertilizer industry, using the local raw materials of phosphate and potash. Already in Jordan there is a demand and need for fertilizers to improve the agricultural situation. Future demand will, undoubtedly, be greater within the country with the development of irrigated areas, and it also seems likely that an export trade could be developed to the surrounding Arab countries.

With the development of the East Ghor project, and the initiation of commercial agriculture within the region, the possibility exists for new industries dependent on agricultural produce. One of the most obvious industries in this field would be sugar refining from sugar beet. This would help reduce the sizeable import of sugar, thereby saving important foreign exchange, and, at the same time, the processed beet could be utilized as animal fodder. A food canning and packaging industry, dealing with the new crops developed in the region, especially tomatoes, and possibly later citrus fruits and grapes, also seems to be a potentially profitable venture with an export potential. The growth of the dairy industry appears likely as well, with increasing urbanization and a rise in standards of living. Plans have also been discussed for the establishment of a large clothing and textile industry based on local wool and cotton grown in the Jordan valley. Such an industry would undoubtedly save considerable foreign exchange. Prospects for a modern tanning and leather industry also appear to be good. The possibility of a petrochemical industry growing up around the Zarqa refinery is conceivable, but unlikely in the near future. Plastics production would be an obvious development.

When Jordan became independent in 1950, her economic development depended largely on the provision of better communications and transport facilities. One of the main needs was to reduce the dependence of the country on the port of Beirūt, because of the high costs of crossing the Syrian and Lebanese frontiers now that the outlets of Haifa, Jaffa and Gaza had been lost. This has been achieved by the development of Jordan's only port at Aqaba into an important shipping, commercial and tourist centre. As late as 1950, Aqaba was only a small fishing village and yet, by 1962, it was handling more than 500,000 tonnes and more than one million tonnes by 1966. Since then, port activity slumped to a mere 380,000 tonnes handled in 1970, but has subsequently risen dramatically to more than 1·2 million tonnes in 1972.

When the port facilities are completed, it is hoped to be able to deal with three million tonnes per annum. Over the last decade, land communications have been greatly improved. A new 'Desert Highway' links Aqaba with Amman, and modern motor roads link Amman with Jerusalem and the West Bank, and with Irbid in the north. Even at the village level, the network of all-weather roads, often with a asphalt topping, is excellent in the more densely peopled areas. The Hejāz railway provides a rail link north to Damascus from Amman, and southwards to Naqb Ashtar, south of Ma'ān. The railway is being rebuilt in the stretch from Ma'ān into Saudi Arabia. This portion of the railway was never profitable in Ottoman times, even for transportation of pilgrims, and now with air and bus competition, it does not seem that it will be in the future either. The airports at Amman and Jerusalem (before 1967) have been developed and are now capable of handling large commercial aircraft. Jordan also possesses its own airline—ALIA.

Perhaps the greatest resource of all which Jordan possesses, is the unique collection of historical remains stretching back over more than 10,000 years. Unfortunately, many of these, including the great Christian shrines, are situated on the occupied West Bank. As a result, the future growth of the tourist industry has become less certain than appeared likely prior to 1967. During the 1950's, the tourist industry, although important, did not play a crucial part in the economy of the country. In the early 1960's, however, the number of tourists increased by almost 100,000 a year from 210,000 in 1962 to a record 616,000 in 1966, and revenues from tourism increased proportionately in the same period from 5·05 million U.S. Dollars to 31·6 million U.S. Dollars. Tourists from North America and Western Europe numbered about 150,000 per annum in the mid-1960's (Figure 15.6). New hotels, catering for the wealthy western, tourist were opened during this period and the number of small businesses dealing with the tourist trade greatly increased. The tourist industry appeared to be entering a boom period, and it was hoped, according to the Seven Year Plan of 1966, that the annual number of tourists would reach more than a million by the early 1970's. Following the 1967 hostilities, the sector of the Jordanian economy which was hit most was tourism, with numbers dropping to as low as 257,000 in 1971. This was due partly to the physical loss of many of the historical sites on the West Bank, but perhaps more importantly, owing to the political uncertainty and instability which existed within the country. As a consequence, western tourists, who provided most of the tourist revenue, have dwindled in numbers to only 20,000 in the late 1960's compared to more than 150,000 in 1966. Until political stability is established throughout the region as a whole, it would appear unlikely that the tourist industry of Jordan, which in the early 1960's had made such a positive contribution to the country's balance of payments position, will return to its former importance. Nevertheless, even without the religious shrines of the West Bank, Jordan still possesses, in sites such as Petra and Jarash, historical remains of tremendous significance.

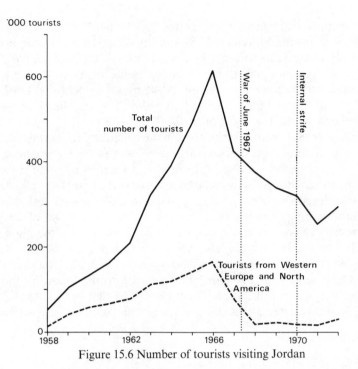

'000 tourists

600 —

400 —

200 —

0 —

Total
number of tourists

War of June 1967

Internal strife

Tourists from Western
Europe and North
America

1958   1962   1966   1970

Figure 15.6 Number of tourists visiting Jordan

15.4 Conclusion

A useful index of the viability of a state is its balance of trade. This is, unfortunately, weighed heavily against Jordan, with imports in the late 1960's
approximately five times the value of exports (Figure 15.7). Although the
ratio of this deficit is large, when the actual figures are studied, it is seen that
the absolute cash amounts involved are, by western standards, relatively small.
For example, in 1972, exports from Jordan, made up largely of fruit, vegetables
and phosphates, brought in a revenue of 17 million Jordanian Dinars. The
main destinations of these goods were as follows: Saudi Arabia 17 per cent;
Kuwait 12 per cent; Lebanon 12 per cent; Iraq 12 per cent and India 11 per
cent. On the other hand, the cost of imports, mainly petrol, textiles, capital
goods, motor vehicles and foodstuffs, amounted to 95 million Jordanian
Dinars. Here the major supplying countries were U.S.A. 17 per cent; West
Germany nine per cent; United Kingdom eight per cent; Lebanon five per cent
and Japan 4·5 per cent. Revenue from the tourist industry of course, did help
to reduce the balance of payments deficit. As late as the end of the 1950's,
it was thought that Jordan had little economic future owing to the paucity
of the natural resources of the country and the political difficulties of the King.
Then, during the early 1960's, prior to the June War, there occurred a period
of rapid economic growth, made possible by the wise use of foreign economic

assistance, mainly from the United States and Great Britain. As a result, the G.N.P. rose from 140 million U.S. Dollars in 1954 to 575 million U.S. Dollars in 1967, a rate of increase of about nine per cent per annum. This period of rapid economic growth had given rise to the hope that Jordan would be able to reach the economic 'take-off' point by the mid-1970's, but hopes of still achieving this aim have been greatly reduced by the effects of the war of June 1967 and the internal strife of 1970.

The future of Jordan would appear to be in the balance. If the United Nations Security Council resolution of November 1967 was to be implemented and a 'just and lasting peace' concluded, there would seem to be some reason to hope that the Jordanian economy could be restored to the potentially favourable position which existed in 1967. Certainly, there would be a long period before full economic viability was reached, but with the rationalization of farming, the development of commercial agriculture, the exploitation of the phosphate and potash reserves, and the expected growth of the tourist industry, most of the economic portents of the future would appear propitious. The chances of such a political settlement between Israel and the Arabs following the war of October 1973 are still uncertain. It could even be that part of Jordan will be passed to the Palestinians as part of a regional 'peace package'. Between

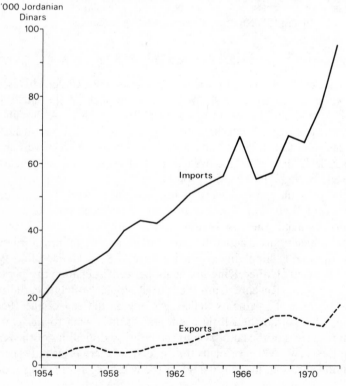

Figure 15.7 Jordan's foreign trade—exports and imports.

the war of June 1967 and the war of October 1973, the 'open bridges' policy of the Israelis along the river Jordan cease-fire line did mean that some contact occurred between the two nations, and this in itself offers hope for the future. Within Jordan itself, although King Hussein seems to be in full control, tensions are growing and the danger of a breakdown of government might well occur should the King be assassinated. In the event, the longer the settlement is delayed between Jordan and Israel, the more difficult it is likely to be to establish Jordan as a viable economic unit in the future. Meanwhile, the West Bank is developing beneficial economic relations with Israel, though somewhat against the wishes of much Arab political opinion.

References

1. Naval Intelligence Division (Great Britain), *Palestine and Transjordan*, Geographical Handbook Series, BR 514, 1943, 465.
2. P. G. Phillips, *The Hashemite Kingdom of Jordan: Prolegomena to a Technical Assistance Program*, Department of Geography, University of Chicago, Research Paper No. 34, 1954, 70.
3. For a detailed study of the population of Jordan see W. B. Fisher, 'Jordan—a demographic shatterbelt', in *Populations of the Middle East and North Africa* (Ed. W. B. Fisher and J. I. Clarke), University of London Press, 1972, Chapter 9, 202–219.
4. C. G. Smith, 'The disputed waters of the Jordan', *Trans. Inst. Br. Geogr.*, **40**, 111 128 (1966).
5. (a) J. L. Dees, 'Jordan's East Ghor canal project', *Middle East Journal*, **13**, 357–372 (1959).
   (b) R. A. Smith and B. P. Birch, 'The East Ghor irrigation project in the Jordan valley', *Geography*, **48**, 407–409 (1963).
6. I. R. Manners, 'The East Ghor irrigation project', *Focus*, N.Y., **20**, 8–11 (1970).
7. (a) I. R. Manners, 'The East Ghor irrigation project', *Focus*, N. Y., **20**, 11 (1970).
   (b) J. S. Haupert, 'Recent progress on Jordan's East Ghor canal', *Prof. Geogr.*, **18**, 9–13 (1966).
8. K. Atkinson and P. Beaumont, 'Watershed management in northern Jordan', *Wld Crops*, **19**, 62–65 (1967).
9. K. Atkinson and P. Beaumont, 'The forests of Jordan', *Econ. Bot.*, **25**, 305–311 (1971).
10. P. Beaumont and K. Atkinson, 'Soil erosion and conservation in northern Jordan', *J. Soil Wat. Conserv.*, **24**, 144–147 (1969).

CHAPTER 16

Israel: Pre-State Jewish Colonization

16.1 Introduction

Although one of the smallest states in Southwest Asia and North Africa, Israel has been the subject of a torrent of literature covering almost every conceivable aspect of its life, and geography is no exception. The problem of compiling even a limited selection of references on Palestine and Israel is illustrated by a bibliography of the Middle East and North Africa prepared for undergraduate libraries by the New York State Education Department in 1969; out of some 3,000 entries, 330 are listed for Israel, and the list is far from complete.[1] The Central Bureau of Statistics in Jerusalem also publishes much valuable information, particularly in its annual *Statistical Abstract of Israel* and *Israel Government Yearbook*, which appear in English and Hebrew.

In view of the considerable quantity of useful material already available on the contemporary geography of Israel, it would be difficult to contribute anything fresh on the subject in a single chapter. The story of pre-1948 Jewish colonization in Palestine is less well known, and has been chosen as the theme of this chapter. Events in Palestine during the preceding 70 years provide the key to an understanding of modern Israel. The configuration of Israel's pre-1967 boundaries were determined largely by the location of Jewish rural settlement, and the distribution of the Jewish population was the basis of proposals for partition. During the years before 1948, national institutions and types of settlement were evolved which survive today, while the nation's future leaders acquired an understanding of the potentialities and limitations of the land. In all this, geographical factors played an important part.

Ottoman–Turkish rule in Palestine lasted from 1517 until British troops captured Jerusalem in 1917. After the First World War the Mandate for Palestine was entrusted to Britain and continued until the eve of the birth of Israel in 1948. The boundaries of Palestine in the east followed the natural divide of the Jordan valley and the Araba depression. In the southwest the 1906 boundary between the Ottoman Empire and Egypt remained, from the Gulf of Aqaba to the Mediterranean Sea south of Gaza. This border, with the Gaza enclave on the coast, was Israel's border with Egypt until 1967. The northern and northeastern boundaries of Palestine were established by Anglo-Fresh agreements in 1920 and 1923, and remained unchanged until Israel seized the Golan heights in June 1967. Although substantially larger than the area commonly referred to as Biblical Palestine, the Mandated territory was one of the smallest political units in Southwest Asia. Its total population was only 752,000 at the 1922 census. Yet throughout history, control of this part of the earth's surface has been the ambition of succeeding powers, not only because of its unrivalled strategic significance at the crossroads of Asia, Africa and Europe, and between the Mediterranean and Red Sea, but also because Palestine is revered by millions of Christians, Jews, and Muslims for its religious associations.

16.2 The personality of Palestine

Palestine is part of a physiographic region consisting of marine sedimentary formations lying along the western margins of the ancient Arabian landmass, which were folded in Miocene and early Pliocene times to form a long anticline running roughly parallel with the Mediterranean coast. Through most of Palestine the axis lies almost north to south, curving southwest towards the Sinai frontier in southern Palestine. Heights range from 600 m to 1,000 m. Strong vertical movements have occurred, resulting in the formation of the deepest inland depression on earth, containing the Jordan valley, the Dead Sea depression (over 790 m below the level of the Mediterranean Sea in some places), the Araba, and the Gulf of Aqaba. Other minor transverse faults have created a number of smaller depressions, including notably the 'Emek Yizre'el in the north. Volcanicity was often associated with these vertical movements, and basalt outcrops widely in eastern Galilee. The almost straight, harbourless shoreline may also be attributable to faulting, but uplift of the land and regression of the sea have also been suggested as possible causes.[2] Surface drainage is largely by a few east and west flowing streams, some of which have cut deeply into the highlands with their numerous headstreams. Throughout the southern half of Palestine streams are ephemeral. The largest river, the Jordan, is entirely an inland river terminating in the Dead Sea.

The structure and topography of Palestine are thus complex and varied. At least three dozen subregions have been recognized by geographers, but the following fourfold division will serve to illustrate the personality of the country.

16.2.1 The coastal plains and the 'Emek Yizre'el

The great spur of Mount Carmel interrupts the coastal plain just south of the Bay of Haifa. To the north lies the small plain of 'Akko; to the south are the wider plains of Sharon and the southern coastal plains. They nowhere exceed 20 km in breadth. The coast itself as far north as Caesarea is fringed by sand dunes, in places more than five km inland, covering good agricultural soils. The soils of the coastal plains are formed largely from alluvial deposits brought down from the highlands. The fertile Red Mediterranean Soils (Arabic 'Hamra') of the western parts are particularly suitable for citrus cultivation. Irrigation is commonly practised on these soils, and erosion has been severe in the past. In recent geological times they were enriched and darkened by swamp vegetation associated with streams blocked at their mouth by sand dunes. Soils of the eastern plains and the plain of 'Akko are heavier, formed by deposits of Terra Rossa from the eastern highlands; these soils have also been partially darkened by swamp vegetation in Pleistocene times. Certain crops can be cultivated on these heavier soils without irrigation. The coastal plain is rich in water resources from wells and springs. Up to 700 mm of precipitation may be received over the hills and permeable strata dipping westward yield valuable groundwater for the coastal plains which gave the early Jewish settlers a wide choice of sites for their villages. The aquifer supplying the majority of settlements lies at depths of 18 to 120 m.

The 'Emek Yizre'el is a tectonic trough formed by subsidence, floored by a thick layer of alluvium weathered from the limestone and basalt dykes of the surrounding hills. The soils are dark, heavy, and rich in organic matter derived from the thick swamp vegetation which flourished locally until Jewish colonization in the 1920's.

16.2.2 The mountains and hills

This division includes the historic areas of Upper and Lower Galilee, Samaria, and Judaea. Upper Galilee is structurally part of the mountains of Lebanon—a picturesque limestone plateau dominated by Mount Hermon (2,814 m). Lower Galilee to the south, is broken into many smaller hills of lower altitude with gentler slopes. Galilee as a whole is the wettest region of Palestine, receiving over 1,000 mm of precipitation annually in places, and both springs and streams are more numerous than in Judaea.

The hills of Samaria roughly correspond with the heartland of the ancient Kingdom of Israel, between the 'Emek Yizre'el and the plateau of Judaea. Samaria is lower in elevation than Galilee or Judaea, and the climate and vegetation is transitional. Although rainfall reaches 630 to 750 mm, surface water is not plentiful. Both Galilee and Samaria were well populated with Arab Muslim villages before 1948, and Galilee also supported a number of Christian Arab and Druze communities.

The boundary between Samaria and Judaea is not physically well defined, but may be thought of as passing some 15 km north of Jerusalem. Samaria is dissected into hills and valleys, whereas Judaea is more like a high pleateau between 450 m and 900 m high. The Judaean landscape is bleaker and bare rocks and loose stones dominate the scenery. Apart from a few valley floors, the possibilities for cultivation are limited. Three parallel subregions of Judaea can be identified; the foothills in the west which receive up to 500 mm of precipitation, and contain several wide fertile valleys; the Judaean hills themselves in the centre rising to nearly 1,000 m, with precipitation of up to 700 mm; and, to the east, the dry virtually uninhabited Wilderness of Judaea, with under 300 mm of precipitation.

The commonest soil type throughout these mountain regions is the reddish brown Terra Rossa, enriched in parts of Galilee by the weathering products from the basalt dykes. Where it has sufficient depth, Terra Rossa is excellent for cultivation, but highly susceptible to erosion so that large areas have lost nearly all their top soil. Nevertheless, the mountains and hills contained the majority of the Arab rural population of Palestine. Good defensive sites were plentiful and cisterns for water storage could easily be hewn out of the soft limestone rocks to supplement springs and wells. In the lowlands on the other hand, where defensive sites are scarce, Arab settlement was sparse until improved security during the nineteenth century encouraged the founding of a number of new villages.[3] Even so, the prevalence of malaria continued to be a strong disincentive to settlement.

16.2.3 The rift valley

By far the most impressive physical feature of Palestine, the rift valley, extends the entire length of the country from beyond the Lebanon border to the Gulf of Aqaba. Its width varies from three to 25 km. The lowest point in the Dead Sea depression is some 790 m below sea level. The water level, which fluctuates, is about 390 m below sea level. Although clearly belonging to a single structural region bounded by steep faulted sides, the rift has several subregions. In the north is the Hula basin, about one third of which was formerly occupied by the shallow Lake Hula where papyrus and other reeds formed malarial swamps. It is now an area of fertile farmland. Both Lake Hula and Lake Tiberias to the south were originally formed by basalt flows across the rift valley. Beyond Lake Tiberias, the Jordan river meanders some 100 km to the Dead Sea through the Ghor. The flood plain of the Jordan was often inundated and covered in parts by thick vegetation, though much has now been cleared. Although rainfall is generally under 300 mm, irrigation sustains successful agriculture in parts of the Jordan valley. The Dead Sea region and the Araba further south have never been important for settlement, though some experimental *kibbutzim* have been established there by the Israelis. The chief importance of the Dead Sea is its vast mineral wealth including large quantities of potash, common salt, bromide, magnesium chloride and calcium chloride.

16.2.4 The Negev

This large triangular desert region constituted about half the area of Palestine and over six tenths of Israel before June 1967. Its limits in the north are somewhat indeterminate, but the traditional margin between the closely settled lowlands to the north and the semi-desert steppe to the south is an accepted guide, corresponding roughly with the 300 mm isohyet.

The only possibility for extensive agricultural settlement in the Negev is in the northwest, adjacent to the congested Gaza strip. It is a depression covered with a thick deposit of loess soil and considerable areas of desert sand. The loess is potentially fertile but, being liable to serious erosion, sometimes degenerating into 'badlands', it requires skilful management. The northwest also receives a fair but unreliable rainfall; the rest of the Negev receives from 200 mm to less than 50 mm of rainfall annually. A ridge of mountains and hills runs across the central Negev at heights between 500 m and 600 m, rising towards the pre-1967 Sinai frontier to above 900 m in places. The Eilat hills in the extreme south expose the ancient basement rocks of the Arabian block—a variety of crystalline and metamorphic rocks which have been sculpted into an impressive arid landscape.

The Negev was never thickly populated. Even in Nabatean times, the population was probably no more than 50,000 (Chapter 5). The present population is under 200,000, most of whom are urban dwellers. There are 20,000 or so semi-sedentary Arab bedouin in the Negev. Its economic significance however is considerable, since almost all Israel's important minerals such as copper, phosphates, natural gas, and glass sand are found there.

Climatically, Palestine lies in a transitional zone between the Mediterranean and the deserts of Asia and Africa. The chief features are the rainy and dry seasons, and the regional contrasts in climate due in part to the variety of topography outlined above.

The rainy season begins in October or November and ends in April; for the rest of the year there is very little rain, three or four summer months being completely rainless. Thus rain is received during the cool winter months when evaporation is low. The amount varies, decreasing generally from north to south (Table 16.1). Westerly winds bring rain to the western slopes of the highlands, but in the Negev they carry little moisture, having passed over the deserts of North Africa and Sinai. Annual precipitation totals also fluctuate considerably; in wet years the total may be more than twice that of a year of

TABLE 16.1
Israel: selected climatic data

Region and station	Altitude	Average annual rainfall (1931–1960)	Monthly mean of daily minimum & maximum temperatures (°C)				Mean relative humidity (per cent)	
			January		August		January	August
			Min	Max	Min	Max		
Coastal plain:								
Tel Aviv	20 m	564 mm	8	18	22	31(1949–58)	74	73
Hill:								
Har Kenaan	934 m	718 mm	4	10	18	29(1940–49)	—	—
Jerusalem	810 m	486 mm	6	13	20	30(1951–60)	65	54
Rift valley:								
Sedom	− 390 m	47 mm	12	21	29	39(1961–70)	56	38
Deganya	− 200 m	384 mm	9	18	24	37(1949–58)	70	54
Negev:								
Beersheba	280 m	204 mm	7	17	19	33(1961–70)	65	58
Eilat	12 m	25 mm	10	21	26	40(1956–65)	46	28

Source: State of Israel, *Statistical Abstract of Israel*, Vol. 23, Jerusalem, 1972, pp. 8–10.

low rainfall. Some rain comes in the form of violent storms and cloud bursts, in the course of which up to 100 mm may fall in 24 hours. Snow is quite common in the highlands in winter.

Temperatures also show great regional contrasts, the chief determinants being distance from the sea and altitude. On the whole, conditions are pleasant and healthy (Table 16.1). Fresh westerly breezes off the Mediterranean moderate temperatures by day, and at night breezes blow from the great deserts to the east and south towards the sea. Winters are cool on the coast but are colder inland. Occasional frosts occur in winter, though rarely at low altitudes. While citrus trees are in no danger from frosts, deciduous fruits and vines on the hills experience moderate cold spells from which they actually benefit. Daily ranges of temperature are greatest in the rift valley and in the southern and central Negev, with the greatest ranges recorded during summer. For most of the year relative humidity is high in the coastal plains, averaging from 65 to 70 per cent. In the rift valley, it is sufficiently high to add to the discomfort of heat in summer, but the air in the central and southern Negev is agreeably dry.

Perhaps the outstanding feature of the geographical personality of Palestine is the rich variety of its landscapes and physical environments. Within the compass of an area measuring some 420 km by 100 km, seas, lakes, mountains, valleys, lowland and desert are all found. The climates range from Subalpine through Temperate to Mediterranean and Tropical, with corresponding contrasts in vegetation and agricultural potential. The effect of these contrasts on the historic events narrated in the Bible for purposes of moral instruction and communicating the divine revelation are remarkable.[4] Although not among the most favoured regions for human settlement, Palestine has many beautiful landscapes and a certain quality of light and air which engender deep and lasting affection among its inhabitants. The nature of relief, soils, and climate offer man an environment capable of high productivity, but liable to serious ecological deterioration if neglected or mismanaged. In recent centuries the land had indeed become pitifully impoverished. The hillsides which may have seen the invention of the art of terracing, aided by the natural structure of their step-like slopes[5], became stony and barren. It has even been suggested that over one metre of soil has been carried away since the breakdown of terrace agriculture from the seventh century AD.[6] Parts of the central coastal plain and the northern Negev were also severely eroded in places. Forests of oak and Aleppo pine were once extensive, but by 1918 following a great wave of destruction by the Turks which was the climax to centuries of cutting and burning, they had almost entirely disappeared. On the coastal plains between Haifa and Tel Aviv many west-flowing streams were choked with sand, forming swamps in their lower courses. Parts of 'Emek Yizre'el had degenerated into pestilential swamps, though according to several European travellers in the late nineteenth century other parts were under regular cultivation. The Beyt Shean and central Jordan valleys, once extensively cultivated, were the domain of pastoral nomads.[7] Altogether, the land bore of the scars of centuries of neglect and insecurity, and of the incursions of nomadic groups from the east.

16.3 Jewish rural settlement, 1882–1948

During the latter half of the nineteenth century more than half the Jews in the world lived in Eastern Europe and Tsarist Russia, where their conditions were as miserable as they had been anywhere in Europe for several centuries. In the 1880's their distress was added to by a series of anti-Jewish riots in southern Russia which resulted in the exodus of many thousands of Jews. Among these was the first wave of Zionists to reach Palestine in modern times. It was their conviction that the only possible solution to the plight of Jewish communities in the east, and the threat of assimilation in the west, was the creation of a Jewish state. By 1903 altogether 20,000 to 30,000 immigrants had arrived, chiefly from Russia, Rumania and Poland.[8] In 1882 there were already 24,000 Jews in Palestine out of a total population of 450,000,[9] but these were chiefly devout urban dwellers in the towns of Jerusalem, Safad and Tiberias who had been in the land for many centuries. The newcomers, on the other hand, were determined to establish rural settlements in Palestine, as being the only practical way of laying the foundations of a Jewish society free from interference, and of restoring the land itself.

16.3.1 1882 to 1903 (Figure 16.2)

The first period of immigration lasted from 1882 until 1903, during which time 20 Jewish villages were successfully founded in Palestine, though not without several disasters. These early Zionist settlements ('*moshava*', plural '*moshavot*') strongly resembled the grain-growing villages of eastern Europe in their layout. Farmsteads were arranged along both sides of a broad village street. A proportion of each holding was attached to the farmyard at right angles to the street. The rest of the village farmland was divided into several large blocks on the basis of their suitability for particular crops, each farmer being allocated a plot in each, an imitation of the practice in Palestine Arab villages. Gedera, founded on the southern coastal plain in 1884, provides a good example (Figure 16.1). The form of tenure was always private ownership and partnerships were very rare. The number of holdings in the early *moshavot* varied with the location and in accordance with the type of farming practised. Zikron Ya'akov (1882) and Petah Tiqva (1883) were exceptionally large with 150 to 200 holdings by the turn of the century, but 30 to 40 units was much more typical.[10] The small number of holdings was partly due to the difficulties of purchasing large blocks of continuous land from the Arabs, and the fact that the type of farming adopted required large holdings, particularly to begin with, when cereal growing was the main branch. As far as possible, farm units were of comparable size in individual villages, but varied considerably between villages from less than 10 ha to 30 ha each. Central services were not well

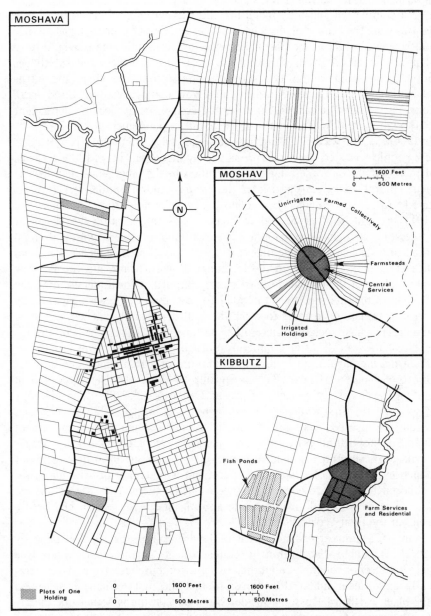

Figure 16.1 Gedera, a *moshava* founded in 1884 (After 1:5,000 Survey of Palestine, 1943). **Inset:** layout of typical *kibbutz* and *moshav*

developed in most *moshavot*, though Gedera had a flour mill, olive press and school, as well as a pharmacy and synagogue.

For a number of reasons, including the inexperience of the settlers, the *moshavot* were not economically a great success, and but for financial assistance from the Jewish millionaire Baron Edmond de Rothschild, many would have collapsed altogether. Baron Edmond was keen to make these Jewish villages economically sound, and was responsible for introducing vines and citrus fruit, which meant that few families could now manage without hired Arab labour, particularly at harvest time. In due course, many became dependent on Arab labour and began to assume the habits of gentlemen-farmers.

In 1904, a second wave of immigrants began to arrive in Palestine from Russia. These people regarded the *moshavot* as wholly incompatible with their ideals, and their search for something better resulted in the emergence of both the *kibbutz* (plural, *kibbutzim*) and later the *moshav* (plural, *moshavim*) as alternative forms of settlement. The second period of immigration, which ended in 1914 brought another 35,000 to 40,000 Jews to Palestine. Unlike their predecessors, a high proportion of these immigrants were young manual workers and students, often penniless, but with a passionate concern for social justice derived, it seems, from the teachings of Karl Marx and the Hebrew prophets. Two of their ideas are particularly important for understanding the *kibbutz* movement. First, they intended to revitalize the Jewish personality by creating a class of farmers to work the soil for themselves. Secondly, they would create a just society, unlike other nations, which could be a model for the rest of the world. After competing unsuccessfully with Arab labour for work in the *moshavot*, and following the failure of a number of experiments with large commercial farms, a small group of these idealists succeeded in founding the first fully collective farm at Deganya in 1910.[11] The ideology and spirit of this first *kibbutz**, 'from each according to his ability, to each according to his need' remains essentially the ideal of the *kibbutz* movement today. Six important principles are generally recognized: (a) no wages are paid; (b) everything is held in common; (c) farming and other forms of production are fully collective; (d) government is by consent of the majority; (e) children live and are educated collectively; (f) there is no use of outside labour. The *kibbutz* had an immediate appeal, nine being established before the end of the First World War.

Figure 16.2 summarizes the extent of Jewish colonization in Palestine by 1918. The scattered distribution of Zionist villages in these early years was largely a reflection of the availability of land for purchase from Arabs, frequently on or near malarial swamps. In fact the first settlers, accustomed to the black earths of Russia, considered the dark swampy soils to be ideally suited to grain growing. Most villages founded in the first decade were within 35 km of the only port at Jaffa, but villages also appeared on the North Sharon plain and in eastern Galilee. Groundwater supplies were generally plentiful

*The earliest collectives were called *Kvutsot*, but they were in all essential aspects, small *kibbutzim*.

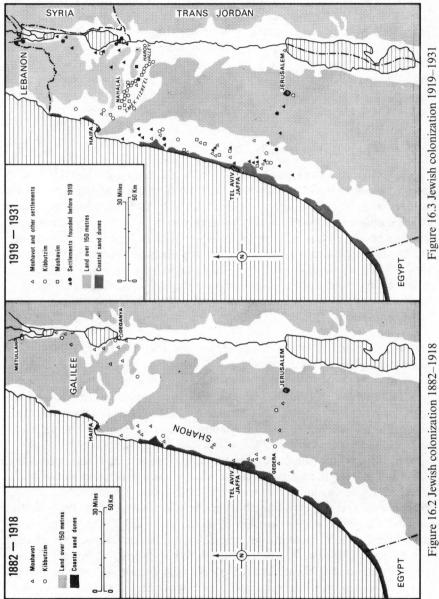

Figure 16.3 Jewish colonization 1919–1931

Figure 16.2 Jewish colonization 1882–1918

in the lowland areas colonized at first. Yesud Hama'ala was founded on the shores of Lake Hula as early as 1892, and Metullah appeared in the extreme north in 1896. Penetration of these remote districts was not as yet politically motivated, but it had political results. For example, the extreme north of the Hula basin was included within Palestine by an Anglo-French agreement in 1923 (Figure 16.3). Although the *kibbutzim* were at an early stage of development in 1918, their suitability for isolated and difficult locations was already being demonstrated. In time, this unique form of rural settlement was to become the spearhead of Zionist colonization, and its ability to survive in pioneer situations was a big factor in extending Jewish influence.

16.3.2 1919 to 1931 (Figure 16.3)

Two further waves of immigration reached Palestine during this period. From 1919 until 1923, following the optimism created among Jews by the Balfour Declaration and the commencement of the British Mandate, some 35,000 immigrants arrived, chiefly pioneer elements from several European countries, many of them already prepared by Zionist organizations to undertake any tasks required of them. A second wave began to arrive in 1924, chiefly from Poland, where Jews were now being effectively excluded from certain trades. Many were middle class immigrants chiefly interested in settling in the towns. By 1931, they numbered some 82,000. Thus the 1931 census of Palestine revealed 175,000 Jews in a total population of 1,036,000, some 17 per cent.[12]

This was a period of great significance for Jewish rural settlement since it saw the emergence of the *moshav*, an entirely new type of village designed to provide an alternative to the *kibbutzim* and *moshavot*. More than 70 *moshavim* were founded before 1948, compared with twice as many *kibbutzim*, but since 1948 the *moshav* has become numerically more important. By 1971 there were 347 *moshavim* Israel containing 4·2 per cent of the total Jewish population, compared with 229 *kibbutzim* containing 2·8 per cent.[13]

Even during the earliest years of the *kibbutz* movement there were those who wanted more individual initiative than collective farming would allow, and others who favoured more normal family life. To meet these serious objections and yet preserve something of the spirit and security of the *kibbutz*, Eliezer Yaffe proposed the creation of *moshavim* in 1919. The *moshav* would be governed by four fundamental principles: (a) national ownership of land, with inheritable leases; (b) self-labour on family farms; (c) mutual aid and responsibility among members; (d) cooperative purchasing and marketing. A fifth unwritten principle was equality of opportunity in the size and quality of holdings. Two developments had taken place during the previous few years to make these proposals feasible. The Jewish National Fund had begun work in Palestine, purchasing large blocks of land, not for resale to private individuals but for letting at low rents and held in trust on behalf of the Jewish people. The shortages of the First World War had forced many Jewish settlements to take to mixed farming, adding dairying, poultry and vegetables to the previous main branches of production—citrus, cereals, and vines. The new type of production was common in Jewish villages all over Palestine, and persisted almost unchallenged until the mid-1950's. Its importance lay in providing a relatively even labour schedule throughout the year, intensive production leading to a reasonably high standard of living, and self-sufficiency. At the same time, a rapidly growing Jewish urban community in the 1930's created a demand for dairy products and vegetables.

Mixed farming, with dairying as the mainstay, became the economic basis of the new *moshavim*. The first *moshav*, Nahalal, was founded in the 'Emek Yizre'el in 1921 and was quickly followed by several more. The number of holdings was generally between 70 and 100, small enough to permit a reasonably compact groundplan yet large enough to support central services such as school, dairy, cold store, tractor station, granary and so on. The size of farm units was small by comparison with the *moshavot*, but much of the income was derived from irrigated crops and dairy products. In Nahalal for example, holdings comprised 10 ha of irrigated land, together with a share of the income from non-irrigated land farmed collectively for cereals. In all pre-1948 *moshavim*, the main irrigated plots were attached to the farmsteads. Since cows were stall-fed with irrigated fodder cut daily, this was clearly the most efficient arrangement. The typical *moshav* plan, with holdings grouped around a closed village street containing services at the centre, provided a great sense of community and a measure of security, but it left no way of increasing the number of holdings for a second generation.

The period 1919 to 1931 also saw changes in the *kibbutz* movement. Many new *kibbutzim* were established, sometimes as large settlements from the beginning, whereas previously they had tended to acquire land and members gradually. The use of machinery was greatly increased. Mixed farming became predominant, so that by the end of the period the agricultural income of all *kibbutzim* was divided between dry farming (40 per cent), animal husbandry (28 per cent), poultry (16 per cent) and vegetables and outside employment on neighbouring farms (15 per cent).[14]

The activities of the Jewish National Fund led to the purchase, reclamation and colonization of large areas by almost continuous chains of Jewish villages. The most notable developments before 1931 were the draining and reclamation of the 'Emek Yizre'el and Harod valleys, which now came to have the greatest concentration of *kibbutzim* and *moshavim* (Figure 16.3). Most were highly successful settlements. A few more privately owned villages were also founded, chiefly by middle class immigrants for the purpose of citrus production for export. However, Jewish rural settlement was still largely confined to the lowlands of central and northern Palestine.

16.3.3 1932 to 1939 (Figure 16.4)

The fifth and final pre-1948 wave of immigration began to reach Palestine in 1931 as a result of the rise of the Nazis in Germany. By the end of 1939, 230,000 immigrants had entered Palestine, chiefly from Germany and Austria, with smaller numbers from Poland and Rumania where anti-Semitic policies were also being followed. The estimated population of Palestine in 1940 was 1,530,000, of which 457,000 (22 per cent) were Jews.[15] Once again, many immigrants in this period were middle class Jews, with capital and skill, who preferred life in Tel Aviv, Haifa or Jerusalem to pioneering in rural areas. Nevertheless, a sufficient number, particularly the young, took to agriculture, making this a period of rapid increase in the number of all kinds of rural settlements. More than 50 *kibbutzim* were founded, many of them between 1937 and 1939. Almost as many *moshavim* were established, the largest number between 1932 and 1935.

From the beginning of the British Mandate in Palestine, the Arab population had understandably become anxious about the political future of the country. They feared that their interests and aspirations were secondary to those of the Jewish minority and that they had been cheated by the great powers, but most of all they deplored the growing number of Jewish immigrants from 1919. After 1936, when the numbers increased markedly, their exasperation, hitherto expressed by rioting and isolated acts of terrorism, broke out into full-scale rebellion against the British authorities. A Royal Commission under Lord Peel was sent to Palestine to investigate the causes of Arab unrest; this was the fourth official inquiry since 1919.[16] Lord Peel's Commission recommended the partitioning of Palestine into Jewish and Arab states under British sovereignty, with certain regions retained under direct British control.[17] Figure 16.4 shows the relationship of the proposed arrangements with existing Jewish settlements; no Zionist village was to be in the Arab State, though large numbers of Arabs would be in the proposed Jewish State. The Arabs rejected the Peel Commission, and violence was renewed. The idea of partition was examined more closely by the Woodhead Commission which reported in 1938.[18] Although regarding partition as unworkable, the Commission reluctantly drew up several alternative plans, all of which assigned less of northern Palestine to the Jewish state, which was now reduced to a narrow coastal strip. The whole of the south would be either part of an Arab state, as in the Peel proposals, or would remain under British administration. The British government however also rejected partition, at least for the time being, but announced new policies for Palestine in a White Paper published in 1939.[19] Palestine was to become an independent Arab–Jewish state within ten years. Jewish immigration would be limited to 75,000 over the next five years, enough to bring the Jewish population to one third of the total. Any subsequent immigration would require the consent of the Arabs. Finally, the purchase of land by Jews was restricted to a small part of western Palestine.

Jewish settlement in the period 1932 to 1939 took place against this disturbed and tragic political background, and many of the developments shown in Figure 16.4 were politically motivated. The most striking example was the acquisition and settlement of the Beyt Shean valley, settled by *kibbutzim* after

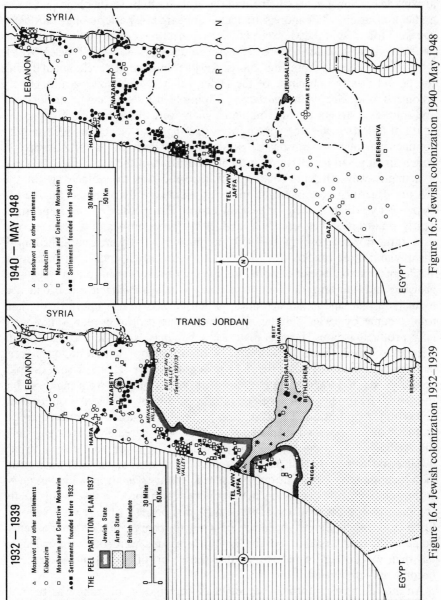

Figure 16.5 Jewish colonization 1940–May 1948

Figure 16.4 Jewish colonization 1932–1939

the 1937 Peel proposals had excluded it from the Jewish state. Attempts were also made to consolidate settlement of the Hula basin by further land purchases and colonization, while more settlements appeared in western Galilee. *Kibbutzim* were founded in the Menashe Hills to connect Jewish centres in the Sharon, generally designated as the core of any future Jewish state, with 'Emek Yizre'el, whose future seemed more ambiguous. Another important development during the period was the purchase of the Hefer valley, which now became closely colonized by *kibbutzim* and *moshavim*, linking Jewish settlement in the northern and southern parts of the Sharon plain. There were also signs of activity in the south of Palestine with the appearance of a *kibbutz* at Negba in 1933, and the commencement of operations at Sedom by the Palestine Potash Company, which already had installations at the northern end of the Dead Sea, at Kallia.

In many ways the immediate pre-war period was the golden age of the *kibbutz*. Recruits were plentiful, many of them already prepared for the life by pioneer youth movements in east and central Europe. The *kibbutz* population nearly quadrupled between 1931 and 1936. The number of *kibbutzim* rose from three dozen to over 50 by 1939, and most of these were established more cheaply and more quickly than in previous years, often in difficult situations. While production became more intensive with the expansion of vegetable growing and dairying, the economic base of most *kibbutzim* was broadened to include light industrial activities, which earned nearly one fifth of their total income by 1936.[20] Some *kibbutzim* in the central Jordan valley were now producing dates, pomegranates and bananas, and the first fish ponds were established there. Experiments with new crops and techniques were being undertaken. At *kibbutz* Beit Ha'arava north of the Dead Sea, for example, record yields of winter vegetables and fruit were obtained from highly saline soils after treatment with large quantities of Jordan water. A countrywide marketing organization, TNUVA, was set up, which greatly improved access to the growing Jewish urban markets. This was extremely important since the Arabs could produce more cheap food for the towns, but Jewish urban dwellers purchased Jewish products for nationalistic reasons and as a result of a 'campaign of persuasion'.[21] Indeed, many *kibbutzim* and *moshavim* at this time were non-economic, in that many of their products were not strictly competitive and the real cost of settlement was borne by the Jewish National Fund and other Zionist agencies content to charge non-economic rents. Some settlements established for political reasons were never intended to pay their way; others, chiefly engaged in the export of citrus fruit, had quickly become self-supporting.

An interesting new form of settlement to emerge at this time was the collective *moshav* or *moshav shitufi*, an attempt to combine the best principles of the *kibbutz* and *moshav*. While family life was preserved in individual households, collective production was undertaken on the farm. The first collective *moshavim* were founded by German and Bulgarian Jewish immigrants in 1936, but in spite of their theoretical merits, only seven such villages appeared before 1948 and only a further 15 between 1948 and 1970. Precisely why the *moshav shitufi* has not proved more popular remains obscure. It is a sound proposition economically, combining the social advantages of the *moshav* with the economic advantages of the *kibbutz*. The usual explanations that it combines the disadvantages of both, or that existing farms provide sufficient choice, seem somehow unconvincing.[22]

16.3.4 1940 to May 1948 (Figure 16.5)

Between 1940 and May 1948 Jewish immigration into Palestine was officially restricted, but in practice more than 110,000 people managed to enter the country, the vast majority of whom were refugees from Nazi Europe. Although the British also attempted to enforce the land purchase regulations, the Jewish National Fund acquired more land, though some holdings purchased before 1939 had not yet been colonized. Some 60 *kibbutzim* were established during this period, and about 20 *moshavim*. Many of the new *kibbutzim* were strategically located in the upper Hula basin and throughout the north and centre of Palestine, but above all in the south. This was the period of 'tower and stockade' settlement in which *kibbutzim* (and one or two *moshavim*) were established literally in a day, at first with crude wooden defences, and later with more permanent structures. The objective was frankly political and strategic, to establish a Jewish presence on land already in Jewish ownership. The most extraordinary instance of the technique was in 1946 when 11 settlements were founded in the northern Negev in the course of one night. The region is near the southern extremity of a Pleistocene aquifer which supplied all the pre-1948 settlements with water delivered in a network of six-inch pipes. Three Jewish observation posts had been conducting experiments in the region since 1943, and their conclusion was that irrigated agriculture in the Negev could provide a sound economic basis for permanent settlement. Their views have proved economically justified since 1948, but in the period immediately preceding the birth of Israel, they also proved politically justified from a Zionist point of view. When the United Nations resolved to partition the country in November 1947, the whole of the northwestern Negev, excluding Beersheba, was included within the Jewish state, together with the southern Negev. Apart from the Haifa Bay district, the whole of western Galilee was to become part of an Arab state.

The British Mandate in Palestine terminated on May 14, 1948, and the State of Israel was proclaimed by the Jews on the same day. Several months of desperate fighting between Israel and surrounding Arab states followed. In 1949 armistice lines were agreed with Egypt, Jordan, Syria and Lebanon, roughly reflecting the front lines when military operations ceased. The area contained within Israel, which remained unaltered until June 1967, included all but six Jewish settlements established before 1948 (Figure 16.5). Its total area was 20,700 km,[2] about one fifth larger than that proposed by the United Nations. The only radical difference between the new armistice lines and the old frontiers of Palestine were the Gaza strip and the West Bank territory of

Jordan. The Gaza region was dealt a serious blow since its population was now swollen by many thousands of refugees, and its economic links with the rest of Palestine were severed. The West Bank of Jordan fared little better. Jerusalem was a divided city. Many Arab villages found themselves cut off from their lands, and the region was overwhelmed by refugees. Transjordan now no longer had access to the ports of Jaffa and Haifa through which to pursue a modest trade (Chapter 15).

From Israel's point of view, the armistice lines constituted more of a security risk than an economic problem. Two particularly vulnerable corridors had been created in the south between Gaza and the West Bank of Jordan, and in central Israel, where Jordanian territory came within 17 km of the Mediterranean sea. Elsewhere, Israeli settlements were overlooked by Arab highlands, notably from the Golan district of Syria. For nearly 70 years geographical factors seem to have invited Jewish settlement of lowland areas, leaving the highlands to their Arab inhabitants. In this sense, geography can be said to have played a part in the Palestine tragedy, as always seeming to hold out the prospect of partition or physical separation of Arabs and Jews, whereas greater integration in town and country might conceivably have forced some kind of enduring cooperation.

The population of Palestine would have reached about 2,065,000 by May 1948, including 650,000 Jews, about 31 per cent. Just under six per cent of the total land area, or 15 per cent of the cultivable land, was owned by Jews.[23] In November 1948, following the flight and expulsion of approximately 650,000 to 700,000 Arabs from within the borders of Israel, and the immigration of over 100,000 Jews, the population of the young state was 873,000, 82 per cent of whom were Jews.

16.4 The Jewish urban population, 1882 to 1948

In spite of their immense political significance in laying the foundations of the Jewish state, rural settlers were generally no more than a small proportion of the total Jewish population in Palestine. The reasons for this are fairly obvious. In the first place, few Jews in the dispersion were farmers, and the decision to take to the soil was based upon an ideological desire to build a Jewish peasant class, in order to recreate the Jewish personality corrupted by centuries of oppression in Europe, and to found a Jewish community independent of interference by other people. During the 1920's, no more than four per cent of the economically active Jews in Europe were farmers; in 1907, the proportion for Germany was 1·3 per cent[24] and for Russia in 1897 it was less than four per cent.[25] Moreover, a high proportion were engaged in occupations least calculated to prepare them for arduous pioneer agriculture, in the professions, commerce, and industry. Agricultural colonization in Palestine offered a life of unremitting toil, and in some cases ill-health and death. Nor was land available in unlimited quantities; it had to be purchased piecemeal, chiefly by Zionist agencies, and the number of suitable settlers usually exceeded the sites available. Finally, it should be remembered that the Jewish urban population grew most rapidly with the advent of Polish German and Austrian refugees, the first large-scale influx occasioned more by 'push' factors than 'pull' factors, and for whom Tel Aviv, Haifa or Jerusalem provided attractive and welcome refuge.

The level of the Jewish urban population in Palestine from 1900 to 1948 appears to have been between 10 and 15 per cent. The proportion in 1948 was 16 per cent, slightly lower than the proportion in 1968. Overall, the proportion of rural dwellers has remained surprisingly low. At the beginning of Zionist activity in 1882, Jewish communities were confined to Jerusalem, Safad, Tiberias and Hebron. These were chiefly devout Orthodox Jews, descendents of ancient communities, or a few who had migrated to the Holy Land to pray and die there. Most were supported by charity. An attempt to found an agricultural village had been made in 1870, but in 1882 Jewish rural settlement was confined to the small Mikwe Israel farm school. The Jewish population was therefore effectively 100 per cent urban in the early 1880's.

Jerusalem, Tel Aviv and Haifa were responsible for attracting the great majority of urban immigrants (Table 16.2). Together they contained 68 per cent of the Jewish population of Palestine, and 56 per cent of the total population in 1948. Although the historic and religious associations of Jerusalem had an emotional appeal, and the city functioned both as administrative capital and the headquarters of a number of Jewish organizations, it grew relatively slowly. Tel Aviv and Haifa on the other hand grew rapidly. Tel Aviv, founded in 1909, was the only purely Jewish city in the world, and rapidly assumed the role of cultural and commercial capital of Palestine. Many small industries

TABLE 16.2
Jewish populations of Jerusalem, Tel Aviv–Jaffa,
and Haifa, 1914 to 1948

	Jerusalem	Tel Aviv–Jaffa	Haifa
1914	45,000	1,400	?
1922	?	22,000	6,200
1931	53,000	46,000	16,000
1935	70,000	135,000	50,000
1941	85,700	180,000	57,100
1948 (November)	84,000*	244,300	95,400

(*Israeli Jerusalem only)

Sources: (a) A. Bein, The Five Aliyot and Their Achievements, South African Zionist Federation, Johannesburg, 1943–44, pp. 17–19. (b) Naval Intelligence Division (Great Britain), Palestine and Transjordan, Geographical Handbook Series, BR 514, 1943, pp. 184–186.
(c) State of Israel, Statistical Abstract of Israel, 12, Jerusalem, 1961, pp. 36–37.

grew up, and a jetty and lighter harbour began operations in 1936, following disturbances in the neighbouring Arab port of Jaffa. About 24,000 Jews lived in Jaffa itself, on the border with Tel Aviv. Haifa enjoyed two advantages: a beautiful setting, and a good harbour which stimulated its industrial expansion. Economically, Haifa was the leading city of Palestine, with an oil refinery, railway workshops, foundries, cement works, and a variety of other industrial activities after the end of the First World War.

Approximately 15 per cent of the Jews in Palestine lived in eight small towns in 1948, the largest of which, Petah Tiqva, had scarcely more than 20,000 inhabitants. Five others possessed over 10,000 inhabitants and two 9,000 inhabitants. Three of these towns had been founded during the 1920's as satellite townlets for Tel Aviv, but engaging in some agriculture. The remainder were *moshavot* which had become increasingly urbanized since the late 1920's, so that by the early 1940's approximately four-fifths of their active populations were engaged in non-agricultural activities,[26] chiefly light industries such as textiles, food processing, wine making and diamond polishing. The process of urbanization was made possible in the *moshavot* by private ownership of land, and was stimulated by their favourable location within the populous coastal zone near Tel Aviv or Haifa. Apart from these eight centres, there were no towns of any size in Palestine, except the Arab town of Nazareth with nearly 17,000 inhabitants.[27] The population of Palestine, particularly the Jews, was thus polarized between the large cities on the one hand and the small agricultural villages on the other. Centres of intermediate size were few, and by no means all of these functioned as intermediaries in the provision of services. In 1925, 'Afula was founded as a regional town for the 'Emek Yizre'el, but proved a great disappointment. Its population in 1948 was only 2,500. The failure of 'Afula was largely due to the nature of the *kibbutz* and *moshav*, which were almost self-sufficient for most services, and depended largely on nationwide Jewish marketing organizations to sell their products in the towns. Indeed, the absence of medium-sized towns in the pre-state era presented no real problem, but it clearly had important implications for the planners of Israel's future settlement pattern. It is interesting to note that the British drew up a proposed hierarchy of settlement for Samaria in 1942 (revised in 1946), including rural centres and regional centres along the classic lines later adopted in Israel.[28]

16.5 Conclusion: the foundations of Israel

The State of Israel is sometimes regarded as a kind of youthful prodigy among the nations by virtue of its remarkable achievements, particularly in land reclamation and settlement, the absorption of immigrants, and economic development. In reality, the foundations of Israel were laid during 66 years of Zionist endeavour before 1948. Rightly or wrongly, Zionist villages staked out the Jewish claim to a national home in Palestine, and when conflict occurred between Arabs and Jews in 1948, Jewish rural settlements proved the decisive factor in Israel's victory. The area and shape of Israel until June 1967 was largely a reflection of the course of pre-1948 Jewish colonization. The borders themselves were long and difficult to secure adequately, but, on the other hand, the *kibbutz* had emerged as one effective form of defence against infiltration and sabotage. The *kibbutz* had also proved its worth in areas where soils and climatic conditions precluded any other form of settlement and has since spearheaded Israel's rural settlement in the Negev and added greatly to scientific knowledge of difficult environments. From 1967 to 1973, over 40 *kibbutz*-type settlements were established in the Occupied Territories of the West Bank and Golan. The *moshav* has complemented the *kibbutz*. Less suited to a semi-military role and to pioneering in extreme conditions, the *moshav* has proved to be an effective medium for the production of vegetables, poultry products and industrial crops which superseded mixed farming in new *moshavim* during the 1950's. *Moshavim* are also more easily integrated into schemes of regional settlement than are *kibbutzim*, and above all, have been successful in the absorption of immigrants. In other words, the hard won experience of pre-state days presented Israel with two ready made forms of settlement, both of which became vital in the life of the state. Both have experienced problems, principally in connection with the use of hired labour, while recent immigrants from Africa and Asia have not always taken to the idea of mutual and cooperation in the way envisaged by its originators. In future, both *kibbutzim* and *moshavim* may change, but their importance during Israel's first decade has been inestimable.

The pre-state era established a Jewish population distribution presenting two fundamental problems to Israel. The first was the concentration of nearly 80 per cent of the Jewish population in the Haifa–Tel Aviv coastal zone, more than half of them in the Tel Aviv district. The whole of the south contained less than one per cent of the Jewish population, the north only eight per cent, and the Jerusalem district 12 per cent. Northern Israel also had a substantial Arab majority. Secondly, there was a dearth of medium-sized urban centres which would be a vital part of any plan for the dispersion of population. Since 1948, therefore, Israel has embarked on a vigorous campaign of decentralization, dispersal of population chiefly by directing new immigrants to developing regions, and the construction of a network of new towns. These efforts have not been quite as successful as hoped; some new towns have grown very slowly, while the Tel Aviv district has continued to expand. Nevertheless, by 1970, the south of Israel contained nearly 12 per cent of the Jewish population and the north 10 per cent.

In 1948, nine-tenths of the Jewish population of Palestine was of European origin, and its institutions and culture were largely European. Since 1948, large-scale immigration of Jews from North Africa and Asia has occurred, resulting in radical changes in the composition of the population which can scarcely have been anticipated in 1948. Although European immigrants still constitute a majority of the foreign-born population, children born to African and Asian parents in Israel have been sufficiently numerous to bring about approximate numerical equality between the two groups. The cultural and educational gulf between 'European' and 'Oriental' Jews living together in a country whose foundations were western, has created many problems in Israel. In time, no doubt, assimilation will be complete, but meanwhile it is still possible to detect pre-1948 influences in the demographic pattern of Israel. The central, lowland regions tend to be inhabited by literate, Hebrew-speaking, European Jews, and the peripheral areas and new towns with a high proportion of dark-skinned immigrants; Hebrew is less prevalent, levels of education are lower, and birth rates somewhat higher.[29]

References

1. E. Ehrman, K. Hale, and W. Morehouse (Eds). *Preliminary Bibliography on the Middle East and North Africa for Undergraduate Libraries*, New York State Education Department, New York, 1969, 621 pages.
2. E. Orni and E. Efrat, *Geography of Israel*, Israel Universities Press, Jerusalem, 1971, 37.
3. A. Granott, *The Land System in Palestine*, Eyre and Spottiswoode, London, 1951. 35–36.
4. (a) G. Adam–Smith, *Historical Geography of the Holy Land*, Hodder and Stoughton, London, 7th edn. 1900, 713 pages.
   (b) D. Baly, *The Geography of the Bible*, Lutterworth, London, 1957, 303 pages.
5. E. Orni and E. Efrat, *Geography of Israel*, Israel Program for Scientific Translations, Jerusalem, 1964, 2.
6. W. C. Lowdermilk, *Palestine Land of Promise*, Victor Gollancz, London, 1946, 14.
7. (a) D. Nir, *La vallée de Beth-Chéane*, Librarie Armand Colin, Paris, 1968, 176 pages.
   (b) Y. Ben-Arieh, 'The changing landscape of the central Jordan valley', *Scripta Hierosolymitana*, Jerusalem, **15,** Pamphlet 3, 1–131 (1968).
8. S. N. Eisenstadt, 'Israel', in *The Institutions of Advanced Societies* (Ed. A. M. Rose), University of Minnesota Press, Minneapolis, 1958, 385–386.
9. E. Orni and E. Efrat, *Geography of Israel*, Israel Program for Scientific Translations, Jerusalem, 1964, 157.
10. A. Granott, *The Land System in Palestine*, Eyre and Spottiswoode, London, 1951, 259.
11. J. Baratz, *A Village by the Jordan*, Ichud Habonim, Tel Aviv, 1960, 174 pages.
12. Naval Intelligence Division (Great Britain), *Palestine and Transjordan*, Geographical Handbook Series, BR 514, 1943, 172.
13. State of Israel, *Statistical Abstract of Israel*, **23,** Jerusalem, 1972, 31.
14. U. Paran, 'Kibbutzim in Israel: their development and distribution', *Jerusalem Studies in Geography*, **1,** Hebrew University, Jerusalem, 1970, 1–36.
15. Naval Intelligence Division (Great Britain), *Palestine and Transjordan*, Geographical Handbook Series, BR 514, 1943, 172–181.
16. Cmd. 1540: *Disturbances in May 1921: Reports of the Commission of Inquiry*, H.M.S.O., London, 1930 (The 'Shaw Commission').
   Cmd. 3686, and Cmd. 3687 (Maps): *Report on Immigration, Land Settlement and Development in Palestine*, H.M.S.O., London, 1930 (The 'Hope-Simpson Commission').
17. Cmd. 5479: *Palestine Royal Commission Report*, H.M.S.O., London, 1937 (The 'Peel Commission'), 380–395.
18. Cmd. 5854: *Palestine Partition Commission Report*, H.M.S.O., London, 1938 (The 'Woodhead Commission').

19. Cmd. 6019: *Palestine—Statement of Policy*, H.M.S.O., London, 1939 (The 'Macdonald White Paper').
20. U. Paran, 'Kibbutzim in Israel: their development and distribution', *Jerusalem Studies in Geography*, **1,** Hebrew University, Jerusalem, 1970, 13.
21. A. Rubner, *The Economy of Israel*, Frank Cass, London, 1960, 99.
22. Klatzmann, *Les enseignements de l'expérience Israélienne*, Presses Universitaires de France, Paris, 1963, 163–177.
23. Y. A. Sayigh, *Palestine in Focus*, Palestine Research Center, Beirūt, 1968, 27–28.
24. A. Granott, *Agrarian Reform and the Record of Israel*, Eyre and Spottiswoode, London, 1956, 19–20.
25. *Jewish Encyclopedia*, **1,** Funk and Wagnalls, New York and London, 1901, 246–252.
26. H. Halperin, *Changing Patterns in Israel Agriculture*, Routledge and Kegan Paul, London, 1957, 75–76.
27. For populations of settlements in 1948 see: State of Israel, *Statistical Abstract of Israel* **12,** Jerusalem, 1961, Tables 9 and 10.
28. H. Kendall and K. H. Baruth, *Village Development in Palestine During the British Mandate*, Crown Agent, London, 1949, 18.
29. R. Bachi, 'Effects of migration on the geographic distribution of population in Israel', *International Union for Scientific Study of Population*, Conference Papers, Sydney, 1967, 737–751.

CHAPTER 17

The Industrialization of Turkey

17.1 Introduction

All the countries of the Middle East are attempting to industrialize (Chapter 9). Turkey was one of the first to begin the process, and by 1970 manufacturing industry employed about 12 per cent of the active population of 13,519,000 and contributed 14 per cent of G.D.P., but scarcely any exports. Instructive comparisons may be made with Japan, which began to industrialize about the same time.[1] About 27 per cent of Japan's 50,940,000 active population was engaged in manufacturing industry in 1970. Manufacturing contributed about 33 per cent of G.D.P. and produced all the country's exports, except for a small amount of raw silk. This chapter outlines the spatial aspects of Turkey's struggle to industrialize and distinguishes four phases of development, two of them virtually new beginnings. Each phase was characterized by different combinations of productive factors and marked by particular socio-political circumstances.[2] Some elements, however, remained more or less permanent and exerted profound influences upon industrial development.

The chapter is concerned with the Asiatic section of the Turkish Republic, though it is impossible to leave aside the İstanbul conurbation which covers a considerable area on both sides of the Bosphorus. Asiatic Turkey will frequently be called by its traditional name, Anatolia (Turkish *Anadolu*), partly to avoid confusion when discussing industrialization under the Ottoman Turkish Empire and partly to retain the subregional terminology currently in use. This region has presented formidable barriers to national economic development by its size, shape and physical variety.

Anatolia is a rectangular peninsula stretching more than 1,600 kms from the Aegean coast to the eastern frontier, but generally less than 800 kms between the Black Sea and the Mediterranean, distances which in 1915 would have taken about 13 and seven days of continuous motoring to traverse respectively.[3] The area of 755,681 kms² is framed on the north and south by chains of fold mountains which merge in the east to form a tangled knot (Figure 17.1) through which communications are difficult. Between the great mountain chains is a belt of terrain within which movement is comparatively easy. Its north-western corner is an upland mass fringed by plains. To the south lies a series of horsts separated by long, wide rift valleys which afford communication with the interior. The 'Grey Country' *(Bozkır)* of Interior Anatolia consists of high-level plains (up to 1,000 m) separated by mountain ranges.

Although the rocks of Anatolia contain a variety of minerals, these were

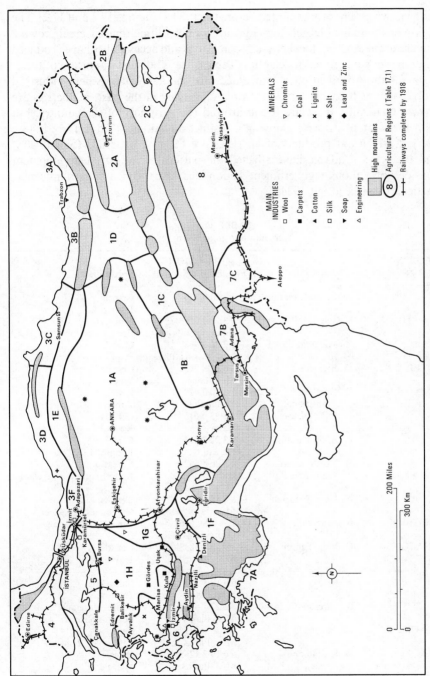

Figure 17.1 Distribution of factory industry and mineral production in Turkey (1914–18)

little known and poorly exploited before the 1930's (Figures 17.1 and 17.2). The region has remained largely agricultural from Neolithic times. Cereal growing still predominates, but local physical conditions and accessibility have produced a number of subregional specialities (Table 17.1). The most important of these, as far as industrialization is concerned, are the subregions where industrial crops, such as tobacco, olives, cotton and, largely in the past, mulberries are grown. Generally, these are found around the periphery of the country, but with the western districts enjoying a distinct advantage, (Table 17.1; Figure 17.1). Agricultural products of all types are the raw materials for industry, and the types available have affected the pattern of industrial development considerably, though government action has also been a major influence, particularly since about 1934.

TABLE 17.1
Agricultural regions of Turkey

REGION	Name	SUB REGION Physical conditions	Specialities
I	A Central Anatolia	− 0·2 20·0 360 Plateau	Cereals Livestock
	B Kayseri–Niğde	0·3 22·7 357 Volcanic Soils	Cereals (rye) Fruit Vines
	C Malatya–Elâzığ	− 1·2 26·8 368 Mts., Basins, Plateaus	Cereals Fruit, Cotton, Rice, Tobacco
INTERIOR	D Erzincan	− 3·6 23·8 365 Mountains	Cereals Vines
ANATOLIA	E Northern Transitional	− 1·3 20·3 438 Mountains	Cereals Tobacco, Rice, Sugar beet
	F Lake District	1·7 23·0 615 Karst	Cereals Roses
	G Afyonkarahisar	0·3 22·0 461 Plateau	Cereals Poppies, Livestock
	H Northwestern Transitional	0·2 20·5 552 Hilly	Cereals Maize, Tobacco, Vegetables
II	A Kars–Erzurum	− 8·6 15·0 476 Mts., Depressions	Cereals Vegetables, Livestock
EASTERN	B Aras Valley	− 10·1 20·9 546 Depressions	Vines, Rice, Cotton
ANATOLIA	C Van–Tunceli	− 3·4 22·1 383 Mts., Valleys	Cereals Livestock
III	A Rize	6·9 19·8 2440 Mts., Plains	Maize, Tea, Citrus Tobacco
	B Giresun–Ordu	7·2 22·7 836 Mts., Plains	Maize, Hazelnuts Beans, Tobacco
BLACK	C Samsun	6·9 20·0 731 Mts., Plains	Cereals Vegetables, Tobacco
SEA	D Kastamonu–Kocaeli	6·0 19·2 1245 Mts., Basins	Cereals Maize
	E Istranca	5·5 22·3 735 Mountains	Cereals Maize
	F Düzce–Adapazari	6·6 23·1 774 Basins, Plains	Cereals, Maize, Potatoes Fruits, Sugar beet, Tobacco

TABLE 17.1 (Contd.)

REGION		Name	SUB REGION Physical conditions	Specialities
IV INTERIOR THRACE			2·0 21·9 609 Plateaus, Basins	Cereals, Maize, Hemp Sugar beet, Tobacco, Vines
V MARMARA			5·4 21·6 740 Plateaus, Basins	Fruit, Vegetables, Cereals Tobacco, Olives, Vines
VI AEGEAN			8·6 24·8 693 Mountains, Valleys	Cereals, Tobacco, Cotton Vines, Figs, Olives
VII MEDITERRA- NEAN	A	Muğla–Mersin	10·0 25·0 1030 Mountains, Plains	Cereals Cotton, Flax, Sesame, Citrus
	B	Seyhan–Ceyhan (Çukorova)	9·1 25·0 611 Plains	Cereals Cotton, Early fruit, Citrus
	C	Hatay–Gaziantep	8·0 26·9 1141 Mountains, Valleys	Cereals Vines, Olives, Pistachios
VIII SOUTH EAST			5·0 27·7 452 Plateaus, Valleys	Cereals, Livestock Rice, Vegetables, Vines, Fruit

Key to physical conditions
Jan. mean temp. (°C), July mean temp. (°C); Average annual precipitation (mm) for representative stations.

Sources: Devlet Meteoroloji İşteri Genel Mürdürlüğü, *Ortalama ve Ekstrem Kiymetler*, İstanbul, 1962; S. Erinç and N. Tunçdilek, 'The agricultural regions of Turkey', *Geogrl. Rev.*, **42** 189–203 (1952).

17.2 Phase I: the beginnings, about 1800 to 1914

The Ottoman Empire may have been the 'Sick Man of Europe' during the nineteenth century, but her vast territories contained valuable minerals, which could be exploited for the benefit of European and American industry, and produced a diversity of crops, some of which could be transformed in the place of origin either for export or for sale in a market estimated at over 20 million people,[4] even if many of them were impoverished.

In Anatolia itself, mining was carried on in an haphazard and sporadic way by a number of foreign companies, mainly in the west and comparatively near the coast (Figure 17.1).[5] Handicraft industry was badly affected by imports during the first half of the nineteenth century, but it survived.[6] About 1,000 workshops were listed in the Turkish Trade Annual for 1900,[7] and this number is probably a vast underestimate of the true position, even for Anatolia. Local demand for traditional products remained strong, while distance and poor communications blunted the competitive edge of imports in the interior of the empire.

Power-driven factory industry forms the subject of this chapter, and at the end of the nineteenth century it was much more restricted than handicrafts in both scale and location (Figure 17.1). An industrial census of 1913 revealed that there were 269 manufacturing establishments in the whole empire using machinery with five HP or more, and 76 of these processed food and 75 produced textiles.[8] Food processing was probably the most widespread modern industry in Anatolia, but there was a marked concentration in the west, particularly at Üsküdar, across the Bosphorus from İstanbul, and around İzmir. The mechanical branch of the textile industry was much more concentrated, almost without exception in the raw material districts, chiefly in the west but with a small outlier in the Çukorova. Closely related to the textile industry was the production of soap in the olive-growing districts, with Ayvalik, north of İzmir, the main centre. Machine building and repairing were found in the two main cities, İzmir and İstanbul.[9]

Concentration in western Anatolia owed much to the region's range of industrial crops and its comparatively dense and wealthy population. Accessibility was also important. İzmir was the focus of natural routeways in the Aegean region and had been linked with major agricultural areas by foreign-built railways (Figure 17.1). Railways opened up much of western Anatolia in a way which was not achieved by the meandering eastern sections of the Anatolian railway or the Baghdād railway.[10] A well-developed system of sea communications was focused on İzmir and İstanbul and allowed the ready export of goods in demand in Europe (silk thread and carpets, for example) and the import of coal from the Zonguldak area, though western Anatolia itself possessed reserves of lignite which were already being exploited at the end of the century (Figure 17.1). In addition, both great ports were long-standing centres of western commercial activity.

Foreign enterprise laid the foundations of mechanical industry in Turkey. The Capitulations, a series of agreements granting specific privileges in the empire, had been extended to such an extent after the Anglo-Turkish Commercial Convention (1838) that foreigners enjoyed almost unrestricted freedom of movement and activity, as well as preferential tariff rates. Not only did this allow an increase in imports, but it also allowed foreign capital to penetrate deeply into the economy. Industrial entrepreneurs were attracted by the availability of raw materials, low wages, some skilled labour, a potential market of about 10 million people in Anatolia alone, and savings in transport costs. Their agents were often Armenian and Greek Christians to whom the privileges of the Capitulations were extended, and the 'Europe Merchants' *(Avrupa Tüccari)* soon became industrialists in their own right.

A comparatively small part was played in industrialization by the state during the nineteenth century, though much attention has been given to it by commentators.[11] Unsuccessful attempts were made to protect industry against foreign competition and government help was given to silk making. Efforts were made to establish new industries, particularly during the reign of Sultan Abdülmecit I (1839–1861), but most of them failed after a short time. The privileges enjoyed by foreigners meant that they could not compete with imports, and adequate protection could not be provided in the face of great power opposition and the apparent logic of free trade. Those factories which did survive were located near the capital and supplied largely military equipment, for which there was a guaranteed, non-competitive market. From these modest beginnings the state sector expanded considerably during the next phase of industrialization which began after the First World War.

17.3 Phase II: a new state, about 1920 to 1940

The First World War shattered the Ottoman Empire but, together with the War of Liberation (1919 to 1923), fought against a Greek invasion in the west of Anatolia and a French occupation of Cilicia in the south, it produced the Turkish Republic. The first task of the new government in Ankara was to rebuild a country torn by more than a decade of war which had decimated the population, virtually ruined the economy and strained the communications system. The long-term aims were the transformation of the suppressed and exploited people of Anatolia into an independent, western, industrial nation.[12]

Much attention had to be given to reconstruction and to laying the legal foundations of the new order, but industrialization was encouraged in various ways which began to fruit in the 1930's. Communications were gradually restored and improved, chiefly by building railways (Figure 17.2). The silk industry was saved by government action. Sugar production was started when the government introduced beet and built refineries at Apullu (in Thrace) and Uşak (in western Anatolia). Two other government measures were important. The İş Bankasi was established in 1924 to finance private business enterprises, including industrial ventures, and the 'Law for the Encouragement of Industry' was passed in 1927 so that industrialists could enjoy various privileges.

Industrialization, however, made comparatively little progress down to 1930. Food processing and textile manufacturing dominated the industrial structure, and the chief industrial regions remained in the west. Development was restricted by the economic and political situation of the 1920's. War losses had to be made good, and the unity of the state had to be maintained against dissension and rebellion. Entrepreneurial skill was scarce after the removal of most of the Armenians and Greeks, capital was short, while low customs duties and foreign concessions were maintained by the Treaty of Lausanne (1923).[13]

By 1939, the situation had changed. The number of industrial establishments covered by the 'Law for the Encouragement of Industry' had risen to 1,144. Agricultural industries remained of first importance with 468 establishments and were followed by textiles with 249 establishments, but several new industries had appeared. The most important were artificial silk (at Gemlik and Bursa), cement, paper, chemicals and iron and steel (at Karabük). Mining, which had been stagnant during the 1920's, received substantial encouragement (Figure 17.2).[14]

A marked feature of the 1930's was the spread of modern industry to the Central Anatolia and Kayseri—Niğde subregions of Interior Anatolia. Single modern plants were established near railways on the outskirts of several towns with populations of 10,000 or more at the census of 1927. Small concentrations

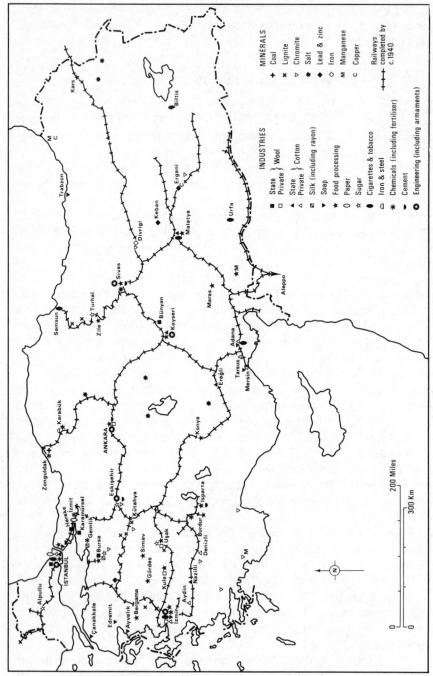

Figure 17.2 Distribution of factory industry and mineral production in Turkey (1940)

of industrial activity emerged in major provincial cities such as Eskişehir, Kayseri and Sivas, which were important railway nodes, whilst new industrial regions began to emerge along the Gulf of İzmit and around the ends of the Karabük–Zonguldak axis (Figure 17.2). The general effect, though, was to disperse industry in a way which was socially and politically justifiable, but which was often economically inefficient and could not prevent the Aegean, Marmara and Northwestern Transitional regions from retaining their advantage. Only Ankara could compete as an attractive industrial location with İstanbul and İzmir. The town's increasing and wealthy population provided a valuable market for industrial goods, while developing centrality gave access to the national market. A vast building programme stimulated the local production of construction materials, though the state took a hand by its investments in infrastructure and the making of cement and armaments.

The government, in fact, was responsible for all the new industrial developments away from the western parts of the country, apart from some at Ankara. The 'Brasilia approach' could be used only once, and the main impetus came from direct action. The new approach, usually called *Etatism* (Turkish *Devletçilik*), was never adequately defined, but the aim was clearly 'to initiate and develop projects in fields which were of vital concern to the strength and well-being of the nation'.[15] Various influences produced this policy. Despite the encouragements, private investment had not gone into industry to any great extent during the 1920's, while the world depression emphasized the lack of industrial development in Turkey and her dependence on exports of primary products. The ending of tariff restrictions in 1929 allowed the government to implement a national economic policy, while an example of what state action could achieve was available in the first Soviet Five Year Plan, launched in 1927. Finally, the Ottoman legacy was strong, for the Republic inherited not only several state enterprises but also a long tradition of state intervention in economic affairs.[16]

Investment was structured by two Five Year Plans (1934 to 1939, 1938 to 1942). The first aimed at import substitution by using local raw materials to establish consumer industries, while the second emphasized energy provision as well as producer and capital goods. Both plans were very unsophisticated by modern standards, and were really little more than 'listings of industry, mines and infrastructure which the government considered desirable'.[17] Only state industry was covered. The previous arrangements were continued for the private sector, but agriculture, despite its basic relationships to industry, was almost completely neglected. Funds were channelled through two, originally three, development corporations.* The Sümer Bankası was established in 1933 with the major responsibilities of operating the existing state concerns, as well as planning and ultimately running new industrial enterprises. The Eti Bankası was founded in 1935 to develop mining in accordance with a special Five Year Plan launched in 1936. Capital continued to be raised from

*The Deniz Bankası did not operate effectively and its responsibilities were transferred to the Ministry of Communications.

government monopolies on tobacco, spirits and salt, as well as from confiscated *evakf* properties, but new sources were also tapped. High taxes were applied internally, customs duties were raised, prices were fixed at high levels and loans were contracted from Britain and Russia.

Industrial development was further assisted by the type of activity promoted by the government and, to some extent, by a favourable combination of socio-economic conditions within the country. Several of the new activities, like iron making and construction, had important linkages, while an expansion in textile production was well adapted to national circumstances, particularly the income elasticity of demand, the availability of raw material and the great mobility of the products. A population increase of 1·8 per cent per annum and a slight improvement in agricultural incomes over the period 1927 to 1940 increased the national market, especially for processed foods, cigarettes and textiles, while small-scale and often seasonal migration provided the labour force for the emerging industrial towns. Migration was to become one of the main socio-political problems of the 1950's, and brought a renewed government commitment to industrialize the less-developed provinces.

17.4 Phase III: experiment, 1950 to 1960

Although Turkey was not involved in the Second World War, the emergency produced a decade of virtual stagnation, particularly in industry. The post-war period, particularly the years of Democratic Party rule, 1950 to 1960, was marked by four changes which had considerable effect upon the industrialization of Turkey. These were the encouragement given to private enterprise, the availability of large amounts of foreign aid, the relative prosperity of agriculture and a rapid rise in population.

Private enterprise had not been neglected under the Etatist system, but its scope had certainly been restricted by the priorities and privileges given to state economic enterprises (S.E.E.s). Post-war criticism of the state sector produced a series of measures designed to encourage private enterprise in industry.[18] The main instrument of government assistance was the *Türkiye Sinai Kalkınma Bankasi* (Industrial Development Bank of Turkey), established in May, 1950 by a consortium including the Central Bank, the International Bank, which had suggested the idea, and private business.[19]

The availability of large amounts of capital through the International Bank and direct from the United States (after 1947) allowed Turkey to embark upon a vast investment programme. Industry was helped by direct investment and loans, but it was also assisted by expenditure on infrastructure. The road network was greatly extended and opened up the country as never before (Figure 17.3),[20] while new power stations were built to realize some of the country's considerable thermal and hydro potential. In the west, an electric grid was completed. Agriculture prospered during the 1950's, particularly in the wet years 1951 to 1953, but prosperity was achieved mainly by ploughing up marginal land in Interior Anatolia with the help of tractors. Mechanization

Examples of modern communications in the Middle East: Intersection of Vata and Millet Avenues, İstanbul (Turkish Embassy, London) (see over)

The new Bosporus bridge, opened in 1973. (Freeman Fox and Partners)

integrated agriculture more firmly into the industrial market economy, while improved rural incomes produced something of a boom in consumer goods and encouraged some landlords to invest in industry, especially in food processing.[21] Population increase also appeared to assist industry by expanding the potential market. However, an increase of more than three per cent per annum had the effect of reducing the arable land available to the average rural family. Increased pressure on the land, together with mechanization, which tended to end sharecropping arrangements and create unemployment,[22] promoted migration. Migration increased to a level equivalent to about 30 per cent of the estimated rural increase, compared with an estimated 10 per cent over the previous 23 years.[23] Towns expanded rapidly, especially Ankara, İzmir and Istanbul where *gecekondus* (shanties) proliferated alarmingly. Eventually, the influx of people from the countryside brought a modification in government industrial policy.

The encouragement of private industry helped to achieve an average growth rate in industrial output of eight per cent. It also maintained textiles and food processing as the main lines of activity, though 40 per cent of the Industrial Development Bank's investments were in engineering, chemical and metallurgical industries. At the same time, the encouragement of private enterprise concentrated activity in the already industrialized regions. More than 1,000 of the 5,000 private enterprises using more than 10 HP and/or employing more than 10 workers in 1957 were situated in İstanbul vilâyet (province) and about 500 were found in İzmir, about 350 in Bursa and 234 in Ankara vilâyets. Seventy-five per cent of the plants sponsored by the Industrial Development Bank were similarly located in the Aegean, Marmara and Northwestern Transitional regions.[24] Concentration was due to the locational advantages already enjoyed by these regions. İstanbul and İzmir offered not only the largest and wealthiest markets in the country but also the ones in which purchasing power was increasing most rapidly. The government's promotion of the three leading cities as show places stimulated construction, thus expanding the market for building materials of all kinds. The second advantage enjoyed by the growth regions was in transport. İstanbul and İzmir remained the most important ports and their harbours were improved. The road building programme emphasized their nodality, together with that of Ankara, easing the flow of goods between them as well as to and from the provinces. At the same time, the improvement of communications in western Turkey reduced any need for manufacturers to locate their factories away from existing industrial regions, while the relative paucity of transport links in the eastern regions, as well as their remoteness and general backwardness, were positive disincentives to any one seeking to set up a factory there. Capital availability was the third advantage possessed by the already industrialized regions. Private wealth, whether generated by trade or drained from the land, was concentrated in the three main cities. Ankara, İstanbul and İzmir were the main banking centres, and entrepreneurs in the provinces had great difficulty in securing access to investment capital. The Industrial Development

438

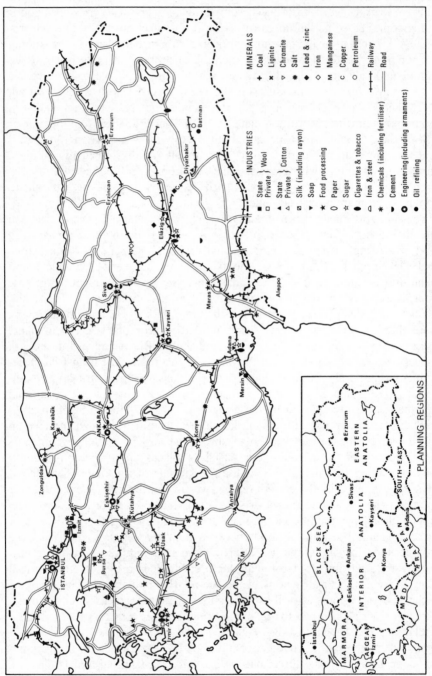

Figure 17.3 Distribution of factory industry and mineral production in Turkey (1960)

Bank was a prime example here. Its sole office was in İstanbul, so that while industrialists in, say, the Northwestern Transition region had fairly ready access, their counterparts in Diyarbakır were 16 hours drive or 2·5 hours flight away.* Finally, the leading industrial regions possessed the advantages of external economies because so many industries already existed there and the necessary infrastructure had been developed.

Direct government intervention in industrial development was revived largely by the migration of large numbers of people to the towns which had resulted from the continued regional imbalance. All but 12 of the 40 new S.E.E.s were located outside the Aegean, Marmara and Northwestern Transitional regions in towns with populations of 10,000 or more. The pattern was dispersed, as during the 1930's, but even less clearly related to local resources or markets, while lack of coordination with other development activities meant that plants were incapable of acting as the foci for industrial concentrations. In general, the counter-magnets to Ankara, İstanbul and İzmir, which these *ad hoc* developments might have produced, failed to emerge. Interior Anatolia benefited to some extent from government industrial activity, but Eastern Anatolia, the Mediterranean coastlands between Muğla and Mersin and much of the Black Sea region were still neglected.

17.5 Phase IV: the return to planning, 1960 to 1970

Extensive investments designed to develop the peripheral regions of the country were instrumental in causing the Turkish economy to overheat during the second half of the 1950's. Mounting inflation and a serious trade deficit resulted. Rigid government controls were introduced in 1958 in an attempt to curb inflation and restore international confidence, but growing economic dislocation and increasing social frustration produced a political upheaval culminating in a military coup d'état on 27 May, 1960. Civilian rule was soon restored, but the army continued to loom large in the background as the guarantor of democracy and socio-economic justice.

The Revolution produced a return to planned economic development. Not only was the principle of planning enshrined in the new constitution, but planning machinery was also set up. The ministerial High Planning Council determined the broad planning strategy, but the preparation and implementation of development plans was left to the State Planning Organization. The first Five Year Plan was launched in 1963 and the second in 1968. Formulated within a 15 year development perspective, these were based on a macro-economic growth model relating 'income levels to gross investment with relevant capital-output ratios'[25] and, consequently, were more comprehensive than the industrial development plans of the 1930's. Nonetheless, the plans were really sets of desirable objectives, projected on the basis of previous trends and related to each other in a consistent way, rather than detailed investment programmes.[26]

*But the flight is available only once a weak, Türk Hava Yollari, *Yaz Tariferi*, (Summer timetable), 1973.

TABLE 17.2
Aims and achievements of the Five Year Plans

| Selected aspects | First Plan (1963–67) | | Second Plan (1968–72) |
	Planned	Achieved	Planned
1. Growth of G.N.P. per annum	7·0	6·7	7·0
2. Gross capital formation per annum	10·7	13·2	11·2
3. Gross fixed investment as per cent of G.N.P.	19·0	18·0	22·9
4. Foreign investment as per cent of G.N.P.	3·5	1·5	1·5
5. Per cent growth in agriculture per annum	4·2	3·3	4·1
6. Per cent growth in industry per annum	12·3	9·7	12·0

Source: OECD, Economic Surveys, Turkey, Paris, 1968, Tables 8 and 10.

Selected aims and achievements of the first Five Year Plan are given in Table 17.2. Although the overall achievement was impressive, industry fell short of its target, despite investment rates higher than planned. This poor performance is probably related to the retardive effects of output fluctuations in agriculture and the continued inefficiences of the S.E.E.s, but also influential were the migration of labour abroad, the poor performance of agriculture and the greater than expected growth of services (8·1 instead of 6·1 per cent) which was partly due to work opportunities created by the planning organization itself.

In the industrial sector, growth was most rapid in steel, oil and textiles. A new steel mill was started at Ereğli, near Zonguldak, in 1961, while the output of cotton textiles increased considerably, partly by a growth in the number of private firms and partly by improved state production. Motor vehicles increased by 97 per cent between 1960 and 1967, with about 30 per cent of the total being built in Turkey itself by foreign firms. Economies of scale were lost, however, by the fragmentation of the industry between 15 enterprises, most of which were located in the Aegean, Marmara and Northwestern Transitional regions. Rising demand for oil ensured the continued growth of the petroleum industry, and new refineries came into operation at İzmit (1961) and Mersin (1962). These subsequently became the centres for petrochemical industries, as did the İzmir refinery, completed in 1971.

Despite overall progress, the western regions have remained the most industrialized in the country. Subordinate concentrations exist at Ankara, where the market and capital availability are important, and in the Çukorova, where the availability of oil and cotton gave industry a firm base in raw materials. Eastern Anatolia and the Black Sea region were relatively neglected, though new cement works at Tabzon and Van and superphosphates plants at Elâzığ and Samsun may be seen as further attempts to 'seed' industry in these backward parts of the country. The most important single project, the Keban dam on the upper Euphrates, has been completed, and is scheduled to produce almost as much electricity as is currently consumed in the whole of Turkey thus facilitating the establishment of a variety of manufacturing industries in the towns of Eastern Anatolia.[27] However, the old problems of remoteness, lack of communications in difficult country, poverty and inadequate supplementary investments will be powerful countervailing forces.

17.6 Regional imbalance

The impact of industrialization on Turkey is difficult to demonstrate. Some indication is given by the development of urbanization over the period 1927 to 1960 (Table 17.3). Although the increase in services and the expansion of communications have been important to urban growth in Turkey, as elsewhere in the Middle East, the introduction of industry has been an important catalyst, especially in Interior Anatolia.

The Aegean and Marmara administrative regions were the most urbanized in 1927. İstanbul and İzmir were nodes of industrial concentration which had remained strong since late Ottoman times and which were firmly based on access to raw materials, fuels and relatively wealthy markets. Interior Anatolia was the third most urbanized region, but this was largely the result of Ankara's development as the capital of the new republic. At this date, urbanization in Interior Anatolia was probably not significantly related to industrial development. The

TABLE 17.3
Urbanization of Turkey by regions, 1927–1960

Administrative regions	Towns with populations of 10,000 or more						Towns with populations of 50,000 or more					
	Per cent of regional population			Per cent of national urban population			Per cent of regional population			Per cent of national urban population		
	1927	1950	1960	1927	1950	1960	1927	1950	1960	1927	1950	1960
Marmara	36·5	37·0	42·5	43·0	35·7	31·3	29·0	28·5	35·0	72·0	50·0	39·5
Aegean	20·5	24·5	29·5	14·1	13·8	12·5	49·0	10·9	14·9	14·6	11·0	9·3
Interior Anatolia	11·1	17·2	25·0	15·4	20·7	22·8	21·5	11·8	17·5	7·1	25·6	24·5
Mediterranean	19·3	21·5	33·0	9·8	11·4	13·7	33·0	9·2	21·7	0	8·7	13·8
Black Sea	5·7	7·6	12·0	8·1	8·9	9·8	0	1·3	4·1	0	2·7	5·0
South East	15·0	15·2	16·0	5·1	4·3	4·0	0	0	8·4	0	0	2·8
Eastern Anatolia	7·6	8·5	13·0	5·4	5·2	5·9	0	2·2	7·8	0	2·0	5·1
National average	16·4	18·8	25·0	100	100	100	7·7	10·5	16·6	7·7	10·5	16·6

Source: R. Keleş, *Türkiyede Şehirleşme Hareketleri, (1927–1960)*, Faculty of Political Science, Ankara, 1961 (mimeographed)

Mediterranean came close behind, mainly because of the development of cotton manufacturing in the towns of the Çukorova but also because of a long tradition of urban life in this zone. By contrast, low levels of urbanization were found in the Black Sea region, the Southeast and Eastern Anatolia, where modern industry had scarcely penetrated.

Urban population increased throughout Turkey in the period after 1927, and was accompanied by a spread in modern industry. The Marmara region retained its predominance as the already strong agglomerative tendencies continued to assert themselves and republican aversion to the old capital diminished. İstanbul emerged by 1960 as the major concentration of leather, paper, electrical and engineering industries in the country.[28] Despite continued investment by both public and private enterprise, the Aegean region had fallen behind Interior Anatolia by 1950 as state measures began to fruit. Although growth in the number of industrial enterprises slackened in Ankara after 1960, the existence of an expanding market made the capital the great industrialization success of the previous thirty years. The period was also marked by the emergence of Eskişehir, Kayseri and Konya, joined later by Sivas, as, industrial cities with populations of about 100,000 or more. Clearly, industrially-promoted urbanization was spreading eastwards. Although Erzurum became a significant industrial centre and attained a population of about 100,000 by 1960, the rest of Eastern Anatolia remained in the same relative position as in 1927. The Black Sea and Southeast regions were even further behind.

The most urbanized regions are those which received heavy public investment. Communications were improved and electricity was provided, but the greatest beneficiaries were the Aegean, Marmara and Interior Anatolia regions. Nineteen of the 21 towns over 50,000 in population in 1960 (excluding Ankara, İstanbul and İzmir) possessed one major state factory and 15 of them possessed several. Only one of the towns (Denizli) was in the Aegean administrative region, while three (Isparta, Kīrīkkale and Kütahya) were situated in Interior Anatolia. One town of 50,000 population was found in each of the Black Sea (Karabük) and Eastern Anatolia (Erzincan) regions, indicating the relatively low degree of capital investment in the peripheral regions. By contrast, private enterprise was important in spreading industry only in the Çukorova section of the Mediterranean region. Even there, though, state investment in roads, drainage and irrigation was fundamental to the expansion of cotton growing on which the region's economy depended. In fact, the lack of private investment in anything but cotton was striking.

This illustrates a fundamental weakness of Turkish private enterprise. Generally, capital is invested only where turnover is rapid and profits high. Commerce and construction are thus favoured instead of industry, but where capital does enter industry it is mainly for the production of consumer goods. As elsewhere in the Middle East, state investment is essential for the production of capital and even intermediate goods. It is vital if there is to be industrial development in the peripheral provinces. The Turkish S.E.E.s, however, suffer from being used as pioneers. Their locations are often uneconomic and expensive new infrastructure often has to be provided. They are not competitive and drain state resources. The constant shortage of development capital, despite large-scale aid from abroad and improved fiscal measures at home, raises the question of whether Turkey is wise to continue a policy of dispersing industry. Concentrated investment might be more effectively used in creating counter-magnets to Ankara, İstanbul and İzmir. This is where the facts of distance and uneven distributions of people and resources become of basic importance to successful economic and social planning.

References

1. R. E. Wary and D. A. Rustow (Eds), *Political Modernization in Japan and Turkey*, Princeton University Press, Princeton, 1964.
2. R. Stewig, 'Die industrialisierung in der Türkei', *Erde*, **103**, 21–47 (1972).
3. B. Darkot, *Türkiye İktisadî Coğrafasi*, Bermet, İstanbul, 1958, 165.
4. V. Cuinet, *La Turquie d'Asie. Géographie Administrative, Déscriptive et Raisonée de Chaque Provence de l'Asie Mineure*, Ernest Leroux, Paris, T. 1, 1890.
5. G. P. Meriam, 'The regional geography of Anatolia', *Econ. Geogr.*, **2**, 86–107 (1926).
6. O. C. Sarç, 'Tanzimat ve sanayimiz', in *Tanzimat*, İstanbul, 1941, 423–440, translated as 'The Tanzimat and our industry' in *The Economic History of the Middle East, 1800–1914* (Ed. C. Issawi), Chicago University Press, Chicago and London, 1966, 48–59.
7. Z. Y. Hershlag, *Introduction to the Modern Economic History of the Middle East*, E. J. Brill, Leiden, 1964, 70.
8. Z. Y. Hershlag, *Turkey: The Challenge of Growth*, E. J. Brill, Leiden, 1968, 52.
9. V. Cuinet, *La Turquie d'Asie*, Ernest Leroux, Paris, T. 3, 1893, 406–12; **4**, 1894, 619f.
10. V. Eldem, 'Turkey's transportation', *Middle Eastern Affairs*, **4**, 324–336 (1953).
11. O. C. Sarç, 'Tanzimat ve sanayimiz', in *Tanzimat*, İstanbul, 1941, 423–440, translated as 'The Tanzimat and our industry' in *The Economic History of the Middle East, 1800–1914* (Ed. C. Issawi), Chicago University Press, Chicago and London, 1966, 48–59.
12. B. Lewis, *The Emergence of Modern Turkey*, 2nd ed., Oxford University Press, London, Oxford and New York, 1968.
13. Z. Y. Hershlag, *Turkey: The Challenge of Growth*, E. J. Brill, Leiden, 1968, 16–27.
14. (a) E. Tümertekin, 'The iron and steel industry in Turkey', *Econ.Geogr.*, **31**, 174–184 (1955). (b) Z. Y. Hershlag, *Turkey: The Challenge of Growth*, E. J. Brill, Leiden, 1968, 97.
    (c) Naval Intelligence Division, *Geographical Handbook Series, Turkey*, **2**, London, 1943, 109–130.
15. B. Lewis, *The Emergence of Modern Turkey*, 2nd ed., Oxford University Press, London, Oxford and New York, 1968, 286.
16. (a) Z. Y. Hershlag, *Turkey: The Challenge of Growth*, E. J. Brill, Leiden, 1968, 72. (b) O. Okyas, 'The concept of Etatism', *Economic Journal*, **75**, 98–111 (1965).
17. M. D. Rivkin, *Area Development for National Growth. The Turkish Precedent*, Praeger, New York and London, 1965, 68.
18. R. W. Kerwin, 'Private enterprise in Turkish industrial development', *Middle East Journal*, **5**, 21–38 (1951).
19. W. Diamond, 'The Industrial Development Bank of Turkey', *Middle East Journal*, **4**, 349–351 (1950).

20. R. W. Kerwin, 'The Turkish roads programme', *Middle East Journal*, **4**, 196–208 (1950).
21. A. P. Alexander, 'Industrial entrepreneurship in Turkey: origins and growth', *Economic Development and Cultural Change*, **8**, 349–365 (1960).
22. R. D. Robinson, 'Turkey's agrarian revolution and the problem of urbanisation', *Public Opinion Quarterly*, **22**, (1958), quoted by M. D. Rivkin, *Area Development for National Growth, The Turkish Precedent*, Praeger, New York and London, 1965, 104.
23. M. D. Rivkin, *Area Development for National Growth, The Turkish Precedent*, Praeger, New York and London, 1965, 98–100.
24. (a) J. Hiltner, 'The distribution of Turkish manufacturing', *J.Geogr.*, **61**, 251–258 (1962).
    (b) M. D. Rivkin, *Area Development for National Growth. The Turkish Precedent*, Praeger, New York and London, 1965, 115.
25. I. I. Poroy, 'Planning with a large public sector: Turkey (1963–1967)', *International Journal of Middle East Studies*, **3**, 348–360 (1972).
26. W. W. Snyder, 'Turkish economic development: the First Five Year Plan, 1963–67', *Journal of Development Studies*, **6**, 58–71 (1969).
27. Ministry of Reconstruction and Resettlement, *The Elâzīğ-Keban Region*, Ankara, 1965.
28. E. Tümertekin, 'L'activité industrielle à İstanbul', *Rev. geogr., Inst. Univ. Istanb.*, **7**, 35–52 (1961).

CHAPTER 18

Iran—Agriculture and its Modernization

18.1 Introduction

Until recently agriculture has provided the major source of national income in all the countries of the Middle East. Indeed, it is only in the last 30 years, with the growth of oil revenues and industrialization, that the relative importance of agriculture in the economies of a few favoured countries has begun to decline. One of the characteristic features of all the countries of the region has been that agricultural activity has changed little over the past 1,000 years. In Iran, agriculture has been dominated by production of cereal crops for small scale local economies. This has been characterized by a high labour input, low levels of mechanization, little seed selection and only minor use of fertilizers. Under these conditions, agricultural productivity has been largely dependent upon the vagaries of local weather, in particular the availability of water, rather than on the labour input of the individual farmer. In an attempt to lessen the degree of environmental control on farming activity, Iran has initiated programmes of agricultural modernization, financed by oil revenues which have provided a large and assured source of national income since the late 1950's.

In addition to the environmental controls on agricultural development, there are also those imposed by human or cultural conditions. The old system of land tenure, with farming activity strictly controlled by landlords, has stifled innovation. The continued low level of income of the rural peasant has meant that, until recently, farming implements have had to remain simple, cheap, and capable of being fabricated locally. Similarly, the only sources of power in the fields were provided by man or animal. Rural education in any formal sense was almost totally lacking, and this, coupled with the relative isolation of most communities owing to poor communications, meant that new ideas and beneficial farming practices diffused slowly, or not at all.

With an estimated population of 30·2 million in 1972, a 2·8 per cent growth rate and a projected population in 1985 of 45 million, one of the most pressing problems facing Iran is the establishment of a sound and productive agricultural system which can feed these growing numbers.[1] Approximately 60 per cent of the population are classified as rural dwellers. These live scattered throughout the country in more than 45,000 villages which have populations of less than 5,000. Nearly everywhere incomes are low and illiteracy is high. All of these people are dependent upon agriculture, often in very difficult environments. The introduction of medical care has meant that peasant numbers are no longer strictly controlled by disaster or disease, as was the case in the past. The result has been rapid population growth during the last two decades. Associated with this has been a definite shift of population from rural to urban centres. At the present time, about 46 per cent of the population is under the age of 15.[2]

Agriculture has always been important to the Iranian economy in terms of G.N.P., although recently it has tended to decline relatively as industrial activity expanded. At the beginning of the twentieth century, agricultural production appears to have made up at least 80 per cent of the G.N.P.[3] By the early 1960's, it had fallen to about 28 per cent and to 22 per cent in 1968. During the Fourth Development Plan (1968–1972), it was estimated that it would decrease still further to about 16 per cent by 1973.

Of the total area of Iran, only 11·5 per cent is considered to be agricultural land and only 4·3 per cent is under crops at any one time[4] (Table 18.1). Approximately 19 per cent of the land is usually classified as being capable of reclamation and development. Unfortunately, this is a somewhat misleading category since lack of use is indicative of severe environmental restrictions. To bring such land under cultivation would often require considerable capital investment, and might well cause a soil erosion or soil salinity problem. Indeed, it is probably the case that many areas which are at present being cultivated are at best marginal land and, ideally, ought to be withdrawn from arable farming.

The fundamental basis of Iranian agriculture is cereal production aimed at supplying local needs. Wheat is by far the most important crop, occupying 56 per cent of the cultivated area, as against 17 per cent for barley. Rice is

TABLE 18.1
Land use in Iran

Type of land use	Area ('000 hectares)	Percentage of total land area of country
Total land under cultivation, including:	19,000	11·5
(a) Area under annual and permanent cultivation	(7,100)	(4·3)
(b) Area temporarily fallow	(11,900)	(7·2)
Permanent pastures and meadows	10,000	6·1
Forests and copses	19,000	11·5
Uncultivated land capable of reclamation and development	31,000	18·8
Uncultivatable land (mountains, deserts, lakes, swamps, cities, roads, etc.)	86,000	52·1
TOTAL	165,000	100·0

Source: Echo of Iran, Iran Almanac 1971, Echo of Iran, Tehrān, 1971, p. 364.

the only other significant cereal, and this is grown on about five per cent of the area. Most of this production is confined to the Caspian Sea lowlands. Together these three crops occupy more than three-quarters of the total cultivated area of the country. Most of these cereals are produced for local or national consumption, with only a small fraction of the total production being exported in an average year. The other mainstay of the peasant diet is food obtained from animals, particularly whey, milk and cheese, and to a much lesser extent, meat. Sheep and goats are the most important animals, and are raised on generally poor quality pastures around the villages. Cattle and donkeys are used chiefly for draught purposes.

Agricultural land in Iran has always tended to belong to urban residents.[5] Unlike western Europe in medieval times, no hereditary landed aristocracy ever developed, owing mainly to frequent conquests and the Islamic laws of multiple-inheritance. As a result, there were frequent changes in the families composing the landowing class, although the privileges and functions of this class as a whole continued unchanged. The dominant type of landownership has always been that of the large landowner, and such people have usually been absentees. Many of the large estates have become fragmented, and it was not uncommon for an owner to possess parts of different villages in different areas. At the same time, aggregation of holdings did occur as a man or family gained more power. The relationship between the peasant working the fields and the landlord was, in most cases, in the form of a sharecropping agreement which involved the payment of 'rents' in kind. Five elements—land, water, seeds, draught animals and labour—often formed the basis of fixing the shares between landlord and peasant. Frequently, the landowner provided the first three of these, so that the peasant received only two-thirds of the crop. Locally, however, other practices were found which were influenced by the nature of farming and the type of crops grown. Under a sharecropping agreement, the peasant possessed no permanent right to the land he farmed, though customary and hereditary rights were often recognized. Redistribution of the land amongst the peasants was practised by the landlords from time to time. This was done partly to stop the peasant acquiring any real interest in the land he worked, but also to adjust the amount of land to the size of the peasant's family. Under such conditions, there was little security of tenure for the peasant, and little incentive to improve the land.

18.2 Factors influencing agricultural activity

The distribution of agricultural activity in Iran reflects the availability of certain natural resources. Amongst the most important are the presence of a long enough growing season for a particular crop, good soil, flat land and, above all, water. Only rarely in Iran do these four factors combine to produce optimum conditions for agricultural production, and in most regions one or more of these environmental parameters fall well below optimum development. The result is that farming activity reveals a very patchy distri-

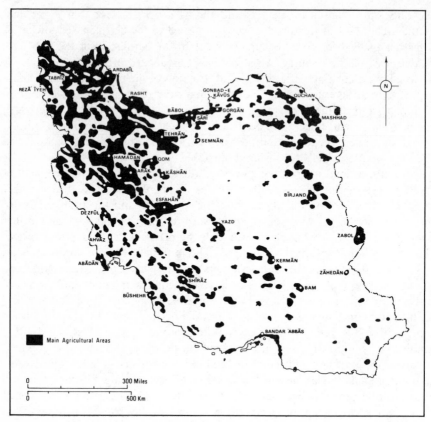

Figure 18.1 Main agricultural areas in Iran

bution within the framework of the country as a whole (Figure 18.1). Indeed, on the central plateau and in the highlands, the pattern of settlement and agriculture is one of regional oases separated by barren wildernesses. Only in one part of the country, the Caspian lowlands, does agricultural land-use provide an almost unbroken mosaic over a very large area.

Water, or more correctly, its absence, is the overriding control of agricultural activity throughout most of Iran. Successful agriculture without irrigation requires at least 240 mm annual precipitation and an interannual variability of 37 per cent. Unfortunately, about half the total area of the country receives annual totals of less than this amount[6] (Figure 18.2). Those regions where annual precipitation totals are greatest tend to be the highland areas, where farming is made difficult by shallow soils, the scarcity of flat land and a restricted growing season (Figure 18.3). A compromise, therefore, has to be reached in which water is transported from the uplands of water surplus to the dry fringing basins and alluvial plains, which possess a longer growing season and more fertile soils. In the natural environment, such water movement is accomplished by rivers which convey water surpluses from one region to

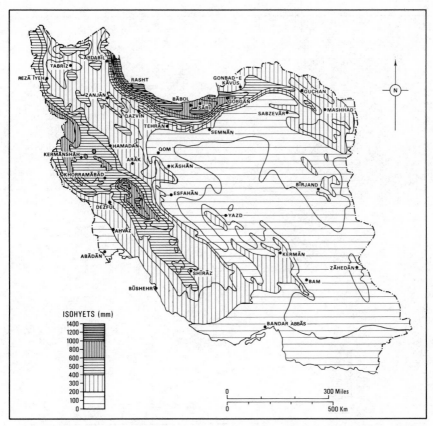

Figure 18.2 Annual precipitation totals in Iran (After *Climatic Atlas of Iran*, 1965, Plan Organization, Tehran)

another under the influence of gravity. Once the water reaches a zone amenable to agricultural activity, it is immediately utilized by the rural farming community. This is achieved by the construction of small, hand-dug canals which lead the water to the fields in which the crops are to be planted. Such canals, from 0·5 m to more than 5·0 m in width, are generally unlined and, as a result, percolation losses through the bed and banks can be up to one half or more of the total intake volume. They usually commence at a point where the river leaves its upland course and radiate like the veins of a leaf to all parts of the cultivated area. In the individual fields breaches are made in the canal banks to permit flood or furrow irrigation.

Rivers flowing from highland regions are also the major sources of ground-water replenishment in the adjacent plains and basins. This recharge of underground water reservoirs takes place mainly where rivers form large alluvial spreads and fans at the margin of the upland zone. Use of groundwater for irrigation is common throughout the plateau region of central Iran and in the Zagros Mountains. Unlike many other parts of the Middle East, these

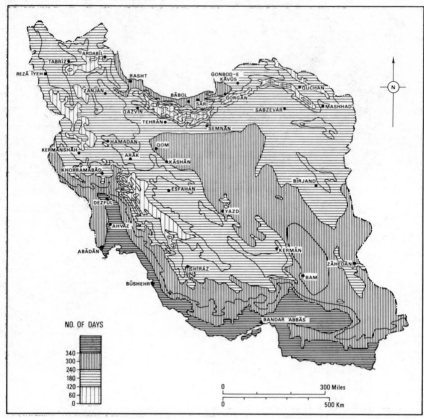

Figure 18.3 Length of growing season in Iran (After *Climatic Atlas of Iran*, 1965 Plan Organization, Tehran)

water resources have not until recently been exploited by wells, but by the highly individual engineering constructions known as *qanāts*[7] (Chapter 2). Groundwater possesses the advantage over surface water supplies in that it is commonly available throughout the year.

In one respect, Iran is fortunate in possessing a crescent of high mountain ranges, since most of the precipitation occurring during the period from October to March is in the form of snow. Owing to the altitude, the snow does not melt immediately, but rather remains as deep snowpacks. Snowmelt begins in the spring, swelling the streams and rivers to provide maximum water discharges during April and May, at a time which coincides with the beginning of the growing season.[8] Water supply is, therefore, not as much out of phase with the season of maximum crop growth as precipitation data alone would at first suggest. Once the early summer discharge peak has passed, the availability of water from surface sources diminishes rapidly. Unfortunately, this is at a time when water demand for the growing crops is reaching a maximum. Where water cannot be supplied from alternative sources during this period arable farming is impossible.

18.3 Agricultural production

The major changes in agricultural production in Iran during the twentieth century have largely been due to the increased and changing demands of an expanding population. Table 18.2 indicates the changes in production of selected major crops over the last 40 years, and reveals marked increases for most of the crops. Wheat and rice production, two of the bases of agriculture, has more than doubled during the period, while barley output has remained relatively stable. The most dramatic increases have been witnessed by sugar beet production, which has grown by almost 300 times, and tea, which has registered an increase of 60 fold during the same period. The extremely rapid rise in output of these latter crops has been the result of deliberate government policy since the 1920's, in an attempt to cut down on the high level of imports.

Data on the number of livestock in Iran are particularly unreliable. In general, it seems that the numbers of cattle, sheep and goats have increased markedly since the Second World War, while the number of camels appears to be decreasing, owing to the increasing use of mechanized transport throughout the country and the sedentarization of nomads. Estimates for the late 1960's reveal 32 million sheep, 15 million goats, 6·2 million cows and oxen, and 2·2 million asses. The number of poultry is thought to be about 48 million.

The only comprehensive survey of agriculture in Iran was made in October, 1960, when the first national census of agriculture was undertaken. Although this census preceded the land reform measures of the early 1960's, which resulted in a re-allocation of land amongst rural dwellers, the actual distribution of the different crops has changed little since this time. The census revealed a land tenure system which had prevailed with little change for centuries. The sizes of individual holdings were small, with four-fifths of the total number composed of less than 10 ha and with more than half less than three hectares. By way of contrast, two-thirds of the total agricultural area was included in holdings of between five to 50 ha in size and less than 10 per cent in holdings smaller than three hectares. The type of power used for agricultural activity

TABLE 18.2
Agriculture in Iran—crop production

'000 tonnes	1934–38	1950	1958	1960	1965–66	1967–68	1972
Wheat	1,869	2,263	3,050	2,570	3,648	4,970	3,750
Barley	638	875	1,280	684	935	1,036	900
Rice	423	450	670	651	681	941	1,000
Sugar Beet	17	62	805	588	1,411	2,857	3,198
Cotton	103	70	90	94	417	360	n.a.
Tea	1	7	7	9	50	63	65
Tobacco	15	15	n.a.	n.a.	25	4	18

Sources: 1. *Iran Almanacs*, Echo of Iran, Tehran (various years).
2. *The Middle East and North Africa*, Europa Publications (various years).
3. Bharier J., *Economic Development in Iran 1900–1970*, Oxford University Press, 1971.

452

on these holdings was mostly animal, with mechanical power being of importance only in areas close to the larger urban centres or adjacent to the major routeways. The use of human labour as the only power source reached its highest values in the agricultural regions of central and southern Iran.

The distribution of agricultural activity within Iran, as revealed by the 1960 census, showed considerable variation between the different administrative units. Of the total area of agricultural land, by far the largest proportion was concentrated within the wetter northern and western parts of the country, with only minor amounts in the central drier regions. Temporary crops made up from five to 60 per cent of this total area in the different census units, while permanent crops contributed only 0·2 to 14 per cent. In the arid central portions of Iran, temporary fallow land was from a fifth to a half of the total agricultural area, with particularly low values of less than 10 per cent concentrated along the Caspian lowlands. Permanent pastures, accounting for two to 60 per cent of the total area, showed more varied distributions. The major areas of land classified as potentially cultivable following improvements were found in the eastern regions, bordering the central deserts.

The proportion of temporary crops which are irrigated varies widely, dependent upon climatic conditions together with the types of crop cultivated. In the wetter parts of the north and west, between a fifth and a quarter of the temporary crops are irrigated, while towards the east and south the figure rises to between a half and four-fifths of the total area. Interestingly, in the wettest part of Iran, the western margin of the Caspian Sea lowlands, irrigation of temporary crops accounts for three-quarters of the total area. Here rice, with its high water need, and not wheat or barley, is the major cereal produced. Irrigation of permanent crops is of crucial importance to cultivation in almost every part of the country, with the sole exception of the Caspian Sea lowlands.

Almongst the temporary crops, wheat and barley dominate the picture in

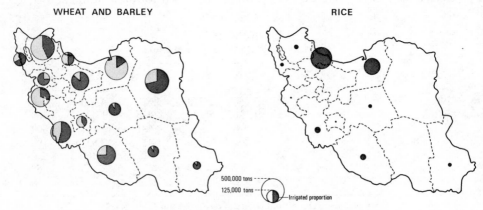

Figure 18.4 Wheat and barley production in Iran (left):
rice production in Iran (right).

terms of the total area under production, and reveal a distribution which closely parallels that of population (Figure 18.4). Taken together, these two crops account for between 50 and 94 per cent of the area devoted to temporary crops in all the administrative units, with the exception of the western part of the Caspian lowlands, where rice production is particularly important (Figure 18.4). Rice is also cultivated outside the Caspian Sea lowlands region in places where water supplies are available. In particular the Khuzestan lowlands, the Gulf coastal region, parts of Sistan–Baluchistan and interior desert oases all produce significant, though small amounts. Cotton, one of the major cash crops of Iran, although requiring an assured water supply, demands smaller quantities than rice. As a consequence, its production is chiefly concentrated in the drier eastern parts of the Caspian Sea lowlands, where it is grown without irrigation (Figure 18.5a). Locally important centres of cultivation are also found in Khurasan, the plateau region around Tehrān and in the southern parts of the Zagros Mountains.

The distribution of permanent crops exhibits much greater regional variations than temporary crops. This is largely because of a more pronounced suscepti- bility to environmental conditions shown by many of these crops. A variety of fruits form an important sector of agricultural production in Iran, and one that appears destined to grow even larger, as standards of living increase. The growth of some of these crops is closely controlled by environmental conditions. Date cultivation, which requires a long and hot growing season, is confined almost solely to the dry southerly *Ostans* (administrative regions), especially the Khuzestan lowlands and Sistan–Baluchistan (Figures 18.3 and 18.5b). Citrus fruits, sensitive to frosts, are concentrated along the Caspian Sea littoral and in the southern *Ostans* bordering the Gulf. In contrast, the vine is somewhat less demanding of its environment, although it, too, is sensitive to late frosts during the spring and early summer. As a result, the distribution of the vine is more evenly spread through the country than either the date or citrus fruit. Apples, pears, quinces and the stone fruits are more temperate crops and their production is concentrated in the northerly *Ostans* of Azerbaijan and Khurasan (Figure 18.5c). Tea is almost exclusively confined to the wetter western parts of the Caspian Sea lowlands (Figure 18.5a). Other tree crops, almond, hazel, pistachio and walnut, show a concentration in the Caspian lowlands, Azerbaijan, and parts of central and southern Iran.

18.4 Modernization of agriculture

Significant changes in the traditional agricultural system of Iran have occurred only since the end of the Second World War, and particularly from the late 1950's. Resistance to any change has often been great, both from landlords and peasants, though for very different reasons. The greatest changes have been brought about by government action through a programme of economic planning and land reform, financed largely by oil revenues.[9]

The first Iranian economic plan was introduced more than 20 years ago,

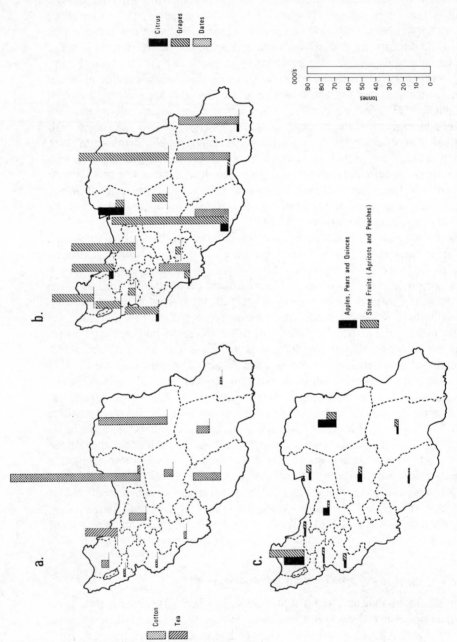

Figure 18.5 (a) Cotton and tea production in Iran, (b) Citrus fruit, grape and date production in Iran, (c) Apple, pear, quince and stone fruit production in Iran

with one of its main aims being the 'westernization' of methods of agricultural production. This First Seven Year Plan (1949–1956), originally proposed to devote about 25 per cent of its income to agriculture, 24 per cent to transport, and 19 per cent to industry. Administration and implementation of the schemes and objectives was to be carried out by Plan Organization, a newly established government agency. Unfortunately, owing to the Iranian expropriation of the Anglo-Iranian oil company's installations in 1953, and the subsequent world boycott of Iranian oil, government oil revenues dropped sharply. As a consequence, many of the objectives of this first plan had to be changed or at least postponed, and the money that was available concentrated in small capital projects.

The initiation of the Second Plan (1956–1962) began with the resumption of oil revenues in 1954, and it is this plan which laid the base for the rapid economic growth of the country. Lack of experience and shortage of accurate statistics created considerable difficulties during the course of the plan, which was not really working satisfactorily until 1957. Some of its greatest achievements were the construction of a number of large multi-purpose dam schemes aimed at providing irrigation and flood control, domestic and industrial water production and the generation of electricity. Four large projects—the Mohammed Reza Shah Pahlavi dam on the Dez river, the Empress Farah dam on the Safīd river, the Amir Kabir dam on the Karaj river, and the Shahnaz dam near Hamadan—were all completed during the plan period. At the same time, a number of smaller projects were built, and studies began for the construction of other large dams throughout the country. Attempts were also made to improve the low yields of all crops grown in Iran through the greater use of fertilizers. The consumption of chemical fertilizer, which was first used on a large scale in Iran in 1956, when 3,000 tonnes were imported, increased markedly to more than 25,000 tonnes by 1960, as a result of this stimulus. A fertilizer factory was set up near Shīrāz during this plan. Funds were set aside in the field of animal husbandry to reduce disease by large scale vaccination programmes and efforts were made to increase the amount and quality of meat production.

The Third Plan (1962–1968) was concerned with more specific objectives, building on the foundations established by the Second Plan. This Plan coincided with the enactment of the new land reform laws and, therefore, its aims in the agricultural sector concentrated upon the development of regionalism, the formation of cooperatives, and rural development. Numerous structural projects, such as public baths, schools and water wells, together with sanitation and water improvement projects, were carried out in village communities, while almost 9,000 km of feeder roads were built to improve rural communications. Finally, to provide education for the villagers, a number of what became known as 'revolutionary corps' were set up: Literacy Corps, Health Corps, Extension and Development Corps. During the Third Plan, the government decided upon the nationalization of forest and water resources in order to permit more rational and efficient use. Within this context, the supply of irrigation water became one of the main aims of the plan, and this was implemented by the drilling of deep wells, the repair and improvement of *qanāts*, the construction of irrigation networks and the completion of projects begun under the Second Plan. New construction work also began on the Mahābād, Darius-the-Great and Cyrus-the-Great dams. With the construction of these multi-purpose water resource projects, it had been hoped that a four per cent growth rate of agricultural production could be achieved during the Third Plan. However, owing to adverse weather conditions and the dislocation of land ownership through land reform, less capital investment in farming took place than had been envisaged by the plan, and the average rate of growth was actually only 2·6 per cent.

The Fourth Development Plan (1968–1973) had, as its main objective, the raising of the average economic growth of the country to nine per cent per annum.[10] This, it was hoped, would be achieved by an annual growth rate of five per cent in the agricultural sector and of 13 per cent in the industrial sector. Once again, a large proportion of the funds of this plan were devoted to rural development. In the agricultural sector, the plan placed special emphasis on the greater use of chemical fertilizers, mechanization, the improvement of seeds and plants, better crop protection and further agricultural research.

Chemical fertilizer consumption had already risen from 40,000 tonnes in 1962 to 250,000 in 1969, and was expected to rise to 350,000 tonnes by the end of the Fourth Plan. A new tractor plant is being completed at Tabrīz, and the number of tractors in use increased from about 17,500 at the beginning of the plan to almost 23,000 in 1973. At Atrek, a heavy engineering works has recently commenced the production of agricultural implements, such as ploughs, disc harrows, and seeders. The Ministry of Agriculture has been successfully developing better wheat and rice seeds at its research stations. Largely as a result of the introduction of new rice strains, production rose to a new record of 1·2 million tonnes in 1969, while a recently developed strain of Mexican wheat, has proved highly suitable for Iranian conditions. The cultivation of a wide variety of oil seeds, especially soya beans, has been encouraged, and the area of land under oil seed production rose from 16,000 ha in 1968 to 68,000 ha in 1969. At the same time, storage facilities are being developed to handle agricultural produce, for at the present time approximately 40 per cent of perishable crops is thought to be lost because of the lack of adequate storage.

During the plan, it was hoped to be able to increase the availability of irrigation water by 15 per cent from the 1969 volume of about 29,000 million m^3/annum to 33,000 million m^3/annum 1973, as the result of further water resource development schemes. With this water, it was hoped to bring some 400,000 ha of new land under cultivation and also to improve the irrigation of a further 500,000 ha. The provision of greater water supplies for industrial use was envisaged, and programmes for sea water desalination and cloud seeding were to be developed and tested. Several multi-purpose reservoir dams have been either completed or initiated during the Fourth Plan. Related to the above dam schemes was a commitment to the electrification of rural areas in a further attempt to raise rural living standards. During the Third Plan, there was a 250 per cent increase in total electric output to 4,500 million kW hours, and a similar increase to 12,000 million kW hours was expected during the Fourth Plan. At present, only about one fifth of total capacity is being utilized, but this position is expected to change markedly as standards of living begin to rise and a more complex local distribution network is installed.

Finally, in an attempt to utilize Iran's agricultural potential more efficiently on a large scale, the government is now pursuing a policy of agricultural polarization by the formulation of large agro-business concerns to develop the lands irrigated by large dams. Such schemes, financed in part by foreign capital, are initially planned to operate on about 8,000 ha of land, with possible expansion up to 10,000 ha. In the future, it seems likely that these projects will become of greater importance.

Undoubtedly, one of the most important aspects of the agricultural revolution in Iran has been the government-instigated programme of land reform which has resulted in the transfer of land from wealthy landowning families to the smaller farmers. Reform measures were initiated in 1950 by the Shah, with the distribution of some crown property amongst the farmers, and this was followed in 1955 by the similar distribution of government land. However, the redistribution of other privately owned land proved more difficult, and the government found that, while it was easy to make a law, it was considerably more trouble to apply it. This was especially so when the law was in conflict with the interests of the privileged classes, who possessed almost all the political power and influence.[11]

With an outmoded agricultural structure and with absentee landlords controlling the lives of the farmers, it was imperative that something was done to improve the farmers' lot. In the villages, the landlords were usually represented by agents, often unscrupulous men who victimized and pressured the farmers. As a result, few were interested in improving agricultural conditions. The farmers had neither incentive nor ability to work harder owing to poor health or lack of labour. They also did not have the knowledge to improve techniques. The agents had no reason to improve conditions or to see changes introduced, while the landlords themselves were also generally satisfied with prevailing conditions. The problem was essentially one of a satisfied minority and a mass of ill-informed farmers who did not realize just how badly off they were.

The First Phase of land reform proper began in the early 1960's, with the passing of a law which allowed landowners to possess only one village and its land. All other lands were to be taken over by the government and compensation paid to the owners. This land was then sold to the farmers who had been working the land. The Second Phase of land reform, which began in 1964, was much more difficult to implement, as this dealt with the 100,000 or so smaller landowners who held 63 per cent of the farmlands of Iran. These were people who possessed one village or less. Landlords were allowed to retain a maximum of 30 to 150 ha of non-mechanized land, depending on the region. They were given three options, later increased to five, for dealing with the lands affected by the new laws. The three major options were as follows. First, they could rent the land to the farmers; secondly, they could sell the land to the farmers by a mutually agreed contract; or, finally, they could divide the land amongst themselves and the farmers in the same proportion as that in which the crops had previously been shared.

The Third Phase of land reform began in 1966, and is still continuing. In this, emphasis has been laid on modernization and mechanization schemes in the agricultural sector, and the full implementation of the reforms already initiated. One of the main aims of this modernization was to promote the establishment of rural cooperatives. The idea behind the cooperative was to form groupings of peasant families into production and consumption units, in order to give them more control over their livelihood. At the same time, it was realized that some organization had to be set up to take over the administrative role which had been performed by the landlords. The number of cooperatives grew rapidly, and by the end of 1968 there were more than 8,600. Cooperatives had the immediate advantage of increasing the purchasing power of the farmers, and also provided them with access to information on modern farming techniques. Over a longer period of time, it was hoped that the cooperatives would increase the political maturity of the rural areas and so allow a greater delegation of responsibility from the central government.

To gain even greater economies, a grouping of the cooperatives has taken place in some areas, to form regional cooperative unions. About 100 of these were in operation in 1971. At the local level, farm corporations were set up to modernize farming techniques and encourage large-scale reclamation schemes.[12] At the same time, these act as a means of concentrating small capital sums and allowing the economic administration of many small farms. In a region where a corporation is planned, the landowners are faced with the choice of joining or not. If the majority elect to form a corporation, the others have to join, sell or rent their land to others who are willing to do so. Once the corporation has been established, the landowners transfer their rights of exploitation to the corporation in perpetuity. Shares are then issued to each stockholding farmer in relation to the value of the land he contributes. Dividends are paid out on each share from the net profits, as are wages. These corporations operate with about 1,000 ha of land under cultivation per annum. Such units usually include several villages, resulting in the abandonment of the village as the main local economic unit. In the late 1960's, some 20 corporations were in existence cultivating more than 15,000 ha. Other schemes to benefit the farmers were the establishment of 'Rural Cultural Houses' to teach people the solution of modern problems and the principles of social discipline and cooperation, and, in 1969 the formation of a Rural Research Centre to cope with rural problems. An Agricultural Bank has also been set up to deal with the financing of agricultural production, marketing, distribution and development.

The official results of land reform are impressive. Under the First Phase of land reform up to July 1969, 15,710 villages had been purchased by the government and redistributed to 730,000 farmers. In all, it is claimed that 3·6 million people were affected by these changes. With the Second Phase up to the same date, it is stated that 2,457,982 farmers benefited, making with their families a total of 12 million people. Finally, as a result of the Third Phase, 8,550 rural cooperatives had come into existence by mid-1969. Some scholars however, have claimed that the official statistics have been in some cases too optimistic, and that many problems still remain in rural areas which are often overlooked. As the land reform law gives priority in allocating land to cultivators, but does not ensure that they actually work the land either before or after reform, this has meant that the higher status farmers, possessing instruments of production, were the ones who benefited most from the land reform measures.[13] In contrast, the sharecropper with only his labour to sell, the labourer with regular wages in cash or kind, and the casual labourer did not benefit at all. An agricultural sample survey in 1960, undertaken by the Iranian Government and FAO workers found that 14·4 per cent of the employed rural population were wage labourers and that 33·1 per cent were family workers. Thus about 47·5 per cent of the rural employed population received no land in either the First or Second Phase of land reform. These people still remained dependent on the landowners, whether new or old, for their employment or else they must continue to migrate to the cities where unemployment and underemployment are still prevalent. In summarizing the available data, both from official and unofficial sources, it has been estimated that about eight per cent of Iran's farmers obtained land during the First Phase of land reform, while during the Second Phase another six to seven per cent of the farmer population received some land, making a total of 14 to 15 per cent of Iran's farmers as new landowners.[14]

A. K. S. Lambton has noted that the farmer in many areas is becoming politically more mature, with a growing belief in himself and his importance in the community.[15] In almost every area where land has been transferred to small peasant farmers, it is now better cultivated. More diverse cropping patterns are beginning to appear and cash crops are of growing importance in the rural economy. The traditional indebtedness of the peasant farmer, although very definitely still present appears to be decreasing in some regions. These are the positive results, but problems still remain. The chief of these is the plight of the landless and agricultural labourers. Also of concern, is the fact that many of the holdings appear to be too small to provide adequate returns, no matter how efficiently they are managed. Only further government initiative can provide solutions to these problems.

18.5 Case studies

Although Iran can be divided into a number of geographic or environmental regions, the types and practices of agriculture are often similar in different areas. The aim of this section is to provide outlines of three differing environ-

460

mental and farming regions in Iran, and to try and show how modernization of agriculture has affected them.

18.5.1 Caspian lowlands (Figure 18.6)

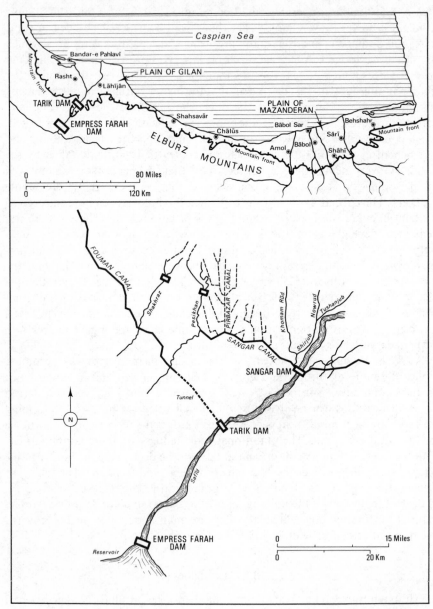

Figure 18.6 The Caspian lowlands and the irrigation network downstream from the Empress Farah dam

The only regionally intensive type of agricultural production in Iran is to be found in the Caspian lowlands and is based on the cultivation of rice. These lowlands comprise a linear belt, approximately 700 km long, which have been largely formed by alluvial deposition of material eroded from the Elburz Mountains. Two large plains can be delimited, separated by a narrow coastal fringe where the mountains reach almost to the sea. The Plain of Gilan is a triangular-shaped area of more than 3,000 km² formed by the deposition of sediment from the river Safīd, while the Plain of Mazandaran, in the east, is the result of deposition from the rivers Heraz, Bābol, Talar and Tejan. Other lowland areas are small and confined to the mouths of the larger rivers, as around Chālūs and Shahsavār. All of these rivers rise in the mountains at high altitudes, and are fed by melting snows in spring and early summer. Most are utilized for irrigation purposes, as soon as they leave their mountain courses, by a complex system of canals.

Climatically, these lowlands are characterized by warm humid winters and hot humid summers, which produce an almost subtropical climate reminiscent of southeast Asia. The annual range of temperature is low, with mean values in the warmest month, July or August, of 24°C to 28°C, and in the coldest month, February, between 5°C and 8°C. Extreme temperatures, which are rare, are usually associated with the penetration of the influence of the Continental Eurasian climate and range from about −10°C to 37°C. Frosts are not of common occurrence except in the foothill zone. The highest precipitation in Iran is recorded in the region, and this is also the only area of the country which receives considerable precipitation during the summer months. Annual totals of between 800 and 1900 mm occur in Gilan, decreasing eastwards to values of between 600 and 800 mm in Mazandaran. Most of the precipitation is brought by eastward moving depressions from the Mediterranean or the Atlantic. Rainfall occurs in every month, although the period September to December is usually the wettest. Snow fall at sea level is exceptional, but can occur when a depression in winter brings cold Siberian air into the region. In summer, evaporation rates are high and usually exceed precipitation totals between May and August. Humidity is almost always high, and the cloud cover often dense.

Soils are developed mainly on fine-grained alluvial material and lack well developed horizons in many places. In the damper areas, waterlogging phenomena are found, with gleyed horizons and acid reactions. On the more freely draining soils, calcareous accumulations are sometimes found at depth. In the foothill zone, the vegetation consists of dense deciduous forest, while on the plains themselves and in parts of the foothills, the actions of man have removed the original forest and dense scrub vegetation completely in some districts. Agricultural crops now provide the most important vegetation cover.

The Caspian lowlands are one of the most densely peopled areas of Iran, and include more than 15 per cent of the country's total population. The plain of Gilan and the surrounding area has a population of more than one million, concentrated in small compact villages, and a high rate of population growth. The resulting demographic pressures have ensured that, wherever land and water are available, they are used for the intensive cultivation of rice. Rice covers more than 40 per cent of the total area of the plain, and is the only irrigated crop of any significance.[16] Tea, tobacco and fruits are the principal non-irrigated crops and these tend to be confined to those areas which are difficult to irrigate because of relief. In Gilan, most of the water requirements for irrigation are supplied directly from canals. The population of Mazandaran is similar in number to that of Gilan, and lives in more than 1,000 villages scattered across the plain. In contrast to Gilan, it is water and not land which is the limiting factor for rice cultivation in the area. When precipitation totals are low, shallow surface reservoirs have been constructed to conserve water supplies. These reservoirs increase in average size in an easterly direction, as low precipitation necessitates greater water storage capacity.

Both long and short-grain varieties of rice are cultivated, with the short-grain variety being grown mainly for local consumption. The higher quality, long-grain rice, comprising approximately 75 per cent of the total production, is exported from the region to the major urban centres of Iran.

The traditional pattern of farming activity in the Caspian lowlands is thus seen to be highly dependent on the production of rice, with other crops tending to be grown in quantity only in those areas where rice cultivation is impracticable. Although the Caspian Lowlands are the wettest parts of Iran, the major problem which has faced rice cultivation in the past has always been the uncertainty of water supply during the growing season. The water requirements for rice are high, usually between 9,000 and 12,000 m^3/ha, and irrigation is essential to ensure growth. In the western parts of the area, in Gilan, the river Safīd provides the largest source of water for agriculture, while in Mazandaran, to the east, the rivers Heraz, Bābol, Talar and Tejan provide similar water resources. All of these streams, however, exhibit considerable variations in discharge from year to year, and after peaking in April or May possess much lower discharges during the summer. As a consequence, the growing rice in the fields can often become parched through inadequate water for irrigation. In an attempt to provide a more assured water supply to the plain of Gilan, the central government commissioned the construction of the Empress Farah dam on the Safīd river at the point where the river breaks through the Elburz range of mountains. This dam, like the others constructed during the Second Development Plan, is a multi-purpose scheme combining flood control, water storage and electricity generation. Since its completion in the mid-1960's, it has provided a controlled supply of water to the Plain of Gilan during the summer months, and even allowed an extension of the cultivated area of rice by the introduction of more efficient water control and distribution systems. Of the electricity produced, most is transmitted to Tehrān, but an increasing amount is being consumed in rural electricification schemes in the Caspian lowlands themselves.

One of the highest priorities of the Development Plans of Iran was the improvement of communications, both on a regional and local level. In the Caspian lowlands, the high rainfall and soft alluvial material meant that surface communications were difficult and, as a consequence, many villages suffered from considerable isolation. This position is now being rapidly improved as all-weather roads are constructed throughout the region. Fast motor roads now connect Gilan and Mazandaran with Tehrān. Such schemes have greatly eased the problem of marketing agricultural products.

Agricultural practices have been improved by the setting up of agricultural research institutes at Rasht and Amol, and the diffusion of modern farming techniques through the creation of an agricultural extension service. New rice varieties have been tested, and a breeding programme is under way to try and produce a rice plant with a shorter growing season than the average of 160 days available. By so doing, it is hoped to avoid the problem of harvesting during the wet month of September. New crops are also being experimented with and introduced to cut down dependence on rice. Citrus fruit production in particularly, appears to have great potential in the region.

Traditionally, all work in the rice fields has been carried out by human or animal labour. Men and women planted and harvested the crop, while animals were solely used for the preparation of the ground prior to planting. Over the last 10 years, the picture has changed with the introduction of two-wheeled, petrol-driven tractors. These have greatly eased the task of preparing the land before hand planting of the seedlings. The machines have proved relatively cheap to buy and run, and possess the added advantage that they can be utilized as power sources for threshers and polishers of the rice.

Modernization of agriculture has come quickly to the Caspian lowlands, with many significant advantages being gained, especially as the result of multiple-use water schemes. In the future, it seems certain that this area will continue to be the most important agricultural region in the country.

18.5.2 The Varāmīn plain

The Varāmīn plain illustrates the general pattern of agricultural activity which is carried on throughout the central basins of Iran. It is situated on the margin of the Dasht-e-Kavir basin and the Māsileh basin, some 40 km to the southeast of the capital, Tehrān. It covers an area of some 1,300 km^2 and was formed by alluvial deposition from the river Jaji. Annual precipitation totals in the centre of the plain average around 150 mm, with almost all of this falling between December and April. Winters are cold, with frosts common in December and January. Summers are hot and dry. The population of the plain totals approximately 100,000, distributed in about 200 villages. Only two towns of any size, Varāmīn and Pīshva, are found on the plain and of these Varāmīn, with a population of about 6,000, acts as the regional centre. More than 75 per cent of the total population are engaged in agricultural activities. The main subsistence crops are wheat and barley, with cotton the main cash crop.

The pressures for the modernization of agriculture were felt earlier on the Varāmīn plain than in many other parts of Iran. A location close to the capital, Tehrān, meant that new ideas imported from abroad spread rapidly and this tendency was reinforced by the establishment of an agricultural research institute near the town of Varāmīn. The rapid growth of the population of Tehrān from the beginning of the 1950's demanded an increased supply of vegetables and fruits which the Varāmīn plain was well suited to produce. At the same time, the region was one of the first areas in the country to feel the effects of the land reform programme, which had commenced on the Varāmīn plain with the redistribution of crown lands by the Shah in the 1950's.

Owing to the low annual precipitation totals experienced on the Varāmīn plain, arable farming is only possible with the aid of irrigation. All water for irrigation is obtained directly or indirectly from the river Jaji. The traditional pattern of water supply consisted of the distribution of surface water by hand dug canals radiating from the apex of the plain, and of underground water by an extensive and complex *qanāt* system (Figure 18.7). Most of the water was obtained from surface sources, with ground-water production being of greatest relative importance in dry years. In such years, *qanāts* might supply as much as 40 per cent of all the irrigation water which was utilized.[17] During the 1960's, changes occurred which greatly altered the water supply pattern of the region. A large number of pumped deep wells were sunk on the plain by private individuals in an attempt to increase local water supplies. Ground-water production increased considerably, so that in the drier years it was supplying about 60 per cent of the total irrigation needs. Water production from these deep wells meant that the water-table dropped markedly, in places by as much as 0·5 m per annum. The result was that many *qanāts* had their discharges greatly reduced and large numbers dried up completely, causing considerable social and economic problems. Fortunately the government soon realized the danger of overpumping the ground-water reserves, and banned private well drilling without prior issue of a permit.

Besides their growing demands for food, the population of Tehrān also required increasing amounts of water and electricity which could not easily be supplied from the area immediately adjacent to the capital. As a partial solution to this problem, a scheme was proposed to construct a multi-purpose dam on the river Jaji at Latian. This would supply water and electricity to Tehrān and also provide flood control and an assured water supply for the Varāmīn plain. The scheme was eventually approved and the dam completed in the late 1960's. Associated with the dam was a plan to ensure a more efficient water distribution network on the Varāmīn plain and a more rational use of agricultural land in response to the economic demands from Tehrān. The implementation of this plan is now well under way and agricultural activity on the Varāmīn plain is rapidly becoming more mechanized, more market conscious and employing sounder techniques and practices.

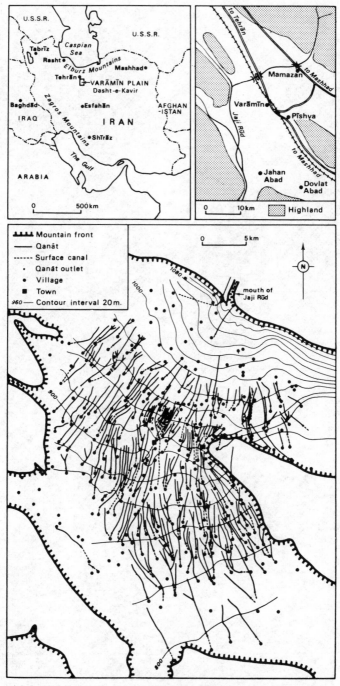

Figure 18.7 Qanāts on the Varāmīn plain (Reproduced by permission of the Institute of British Geographers)

Circular earth mounds around the ventilation shafts mark the lines of *qanāts* to a village near Mashhad, Iran (National Cartographic Centre, Iran)

18.5.3 Khuzestan lowlands

One of the highest priorities of the Iranian government during the First Seven Year Development Plan was given to a scheme to revitalize the Khuzestan lowlands. These lowlands, once the home of the Elamite civilization based on irrigated agriculture, had become, after long periods of misuse and neglect, wilderness regions characterized by the three interrelated problems of aridity, salinity, and waterlogged soils. In 1959, Plan Organization commissioned the Development and Resources Corporation of New York, to draw up a master-plan for the region similar in overall concept to that executed by the Tennessee Valley Authority of the United States of America.

The result was an integrated scheme to control and utilize the waters of the five major streams of the region—the Karkheh, the Dez, the Kārūn, the

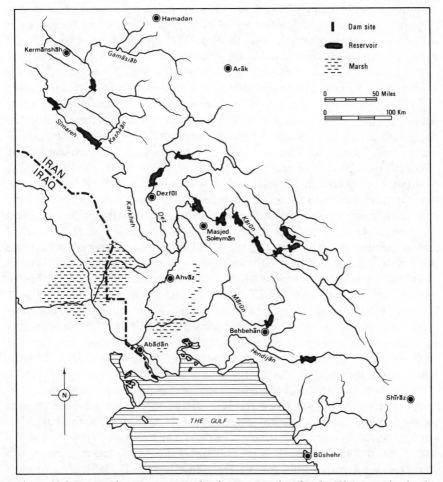

Figure 18.8 Proposed water resource development project for the Khuzestan lowlands

Jarrāhī, and the Hendijān. In total, about 35,000 million m³/annum of water were estimated to be available, and 14 sites for the construction of dams were (Figure 18.8). Seven of those were on the Kārūn, three on the Karkheh and two on the Dez. When the project is completed, it is hoped that at least one million hectares can be irrigated, and 6·6 million kW of electricity produced.

The first dam which was constructed was the Mohammed Réza Shah dam on the Dez river, with a reservoir capacity of 3,950 million m³. The water from the lake impounded by the dam will eventually be utilized to irrigate 125,000 ha in the Khuzestan lowlands and to produce 520,000 kW of electricity. Before the construction of the dam, about 91,000 ha had been irrigated within the region, and a further 33,000 ha dry farmed. Whcat and barley formed the major non-irrigated crops, and wheat, barley, beans, rice and sesame the irrigated ones. Yields of all crops were poor, and rural standards of living were generally low.

With the construction of the dam, a new cropping pattern for the area was prepared, providing a diversification of crop types, together with changes in the areas of crops already cultivated. With the improvement of agricultural methods, crop yields were raised by large amounts.

The implementation of the Khuzestan lowlands project however, does not seem to have been without its problems. The distribution of water and power from the Dez dam is controlled by the Khuzestan Water and Electricity Authority, and it is this authority which supervised land reform within the region. As agricultural practices are also supervised by the same organization many of the farmers felt that with land reform they had merely exchanged one landlord for another.[18] Unfortunately, despite the fact that careful planning based on sound economic criteria had gone into the agricultural organization, the human element had tended to be neglected. In many cases, there was little contact or understanding between the officials and the farmers. The problem was compounded by the fact that a number of the officials were the sons of former landowners, and many of them had been trained abroad, so making them even more out of touch with the feelings of the local farmers.

To use the water resources of Khuzestan more efficiently a number of agro-business enterprises have been established under the Agro-Industrial Act. These undertakings are an attempt to create intensive farming on a commercial basis. So far they have been established on waste or little used land in proximity to water resource projects. In Khuzestan the oldest and most advanced of such enterprises is the government's sugar-cane plantation at Haft Tappeh, which began production during the Third Development Plan. By 1986, it is hoped that cane production will have reached 200,000 tonnes/annum.

The rest of the 68,000 ha of the Dez irrigation project has been divided amongst a number of concerns. These are Iran California with 10,000 ha; Hashim Narraghi Agro-Industries of Iran and America with 20,000 ha; Dezkar with 5,000 ha; Iran Shellcott with 15,000 ha; the Ahvāz sugar refinery with 1,000 ha and a corporation for the Dez farmers with 17,000 ha.[19] For their right to farm the land, the companies have to pay a high water and ground rent and are also compelled to make a fixed investment per hectare. Government organizations are responsible for the supply of water through large scale canals to project areas, but the individual business concerns have to arrange and provide the field distribution and irrigation systems at their own expense.

One of the most advanced projects is that belonging to Iran Shellcott, which is owned jointly by Shell, the Agricultural Development Fund of Iran, the Bank Omran, and Mitchell Cotts. To date, over £4 million have been invested, and the project is expected to be completed in seven years. When the agro-business enterprises are in full operation a steady stream of agricultural supplies should be available for the Iranian market. These will include oil seeds, alfalfa, sorghum and milo, tomatoes, cereals, meat and dairy products and sugar beet.

References

1. Population Reference Bureau Inc., *1972 World Population Data Sheet*, Population Reference Bureau Inc., Washington D.C., 1972.
2. For a detailed study of the population of Iran see B. D. Clark, 'Iran: changing population patterns', in *Populations of the Middle East and North Africa* (Ed. W. B. Fisher and J. I. Clarke), University of London Press, London, 1972, 68–95.
3. J. Bharier, *Economic Development in Iran 1900–1970*, Oxford University Press, London, 1971, 131.
4. Echo of Iran, *Iran Almanac 1971*, Echo of Iran, Tehrān, 1971, 364.
5. For a detailed study of rural life in Iran see A. K. S. Lambton, *Landlord and Peasant in Persia*, Oxford University Press, Oxford, 1953, 459 pages.
6. For a detailed study of the climate of Iran see M. H. Ganji, 'Climate', in *The Land of Iran* (Ed. W. B. Fisher), The Cambridge History of Iran, **1,** Cambridge University Press, Cambridge, 1968, 212–249.
7. P. Beaumont, 'Qanat systems in Iran', *Bull. int. Ass. scient. Hydrol.*, **16,** 38–50 (1971).
8. P. Beaumont, *River Regimes in Iran*, Occasional Publications (New Series) No. 1, Department of Geography, University of Durham, 1973, 29 pages.
9. (a) K. S. McLachlan, 'Land reform in Iran', in *The Land of Iran* (Ed. W. B. Fisher), the Cambridge History of Iran, **1,** Cambridge University Press, Cambridge, 1968, 684–713.
   (b) A. K. S. Lambton, 'Land reform and co-operative societies in Persia', *Jl. R. cent. Asian Soc.*, **LVI,** 1–28 (1969).
10. Plan Organisation, *Fourth National Development Plan, 1968–72*, Plan Organisation, The Imperial Government of Iran, Tehrān, 1968, 335 pages.
11. Ministry of Land Reform and Rural Co-operation, *Land Reform Programme in Iran*, Rural Research Center, Ministry of Land Reform and Rural Co-operation, Tehrān, 1970, 20 pages.
12. Ministry of Information, *Farm Corporations in Iran*, Ministry of Information, Tehrān, Iran, 1970, 10 pages.
13. N. K. Keddie, 'The Iranian village before and after land reform', *Journal of Contemporary History*, **3,** 69–91 (1968).
14. N. K. Keddie, 'The Iranian village before and after land reform', *Journal of Contemporary History*, **3,** 87 (1968).
15. A. K. S. Lambton, *The Persian Land Reform*, Clarendon Press, Oxford, 1969, 386 pages.
16. P. Beaumont and J. H. Neville, 'Rice cultivation in Iran's Caspian lowlands', *Wld Crops*, **20,** 70–73 (1968).

470

17. P. Beaumont, 'Qanats on the Varamin Plain, Iran', *Trans. Inst. Br. Geogr.*, **45,** 169–179 (1968).
18. A. K. S. Lambton, *The Persian Land Reform*, Clarendon Press, Oxford, 1969, 280.
19. M. Field, 'Agro-business and agricultural planning in Iran', *Wld Crops*, **24,** 68–72 (1972).

CHAPTER 19

Egypt: Population Growth and Agricultural Expansion

19.1 Introduction

The Arab Republic of Egypt is one of the best documented countries in the Arab world, and one of the least understood. With a highly distinctive geographical personality, the country's complex social and economic problems have been the subject of much oversimplification, often resulting in undue pessimism about the future. The aim of this chapter is to give some perspective to one of the most geographical aspects of Egypt's development problems—the expansion of agricultural production, seen against the background of a rapidly increasing population, approximately six tenths of whom are still essentially rural dwellers.

There is still much truth in the old saying of Herodotus that Egypt is the gift of the Nile. Although located in the great Saharan–Arabian desert belt, the Nile valley and delta support 99 per cent of Egypt's population. Within this settled region communications are easy and centralized political control is relatively simple to impose, which partially accounts for the many centuries during which Egypt was successfully dominated by external powers and also the cultural homogeneity of the country. The physical environment of the valley and delta is also highly favourable for intensive agriculture and settlement. The nature of the valley itself, enclosed by scarps sometimes rising to over 400 m above the valley floor, enables the river to flow without serious losses by seepage and evaporation. The alluvial soils of the valley and delta are also favourable to agriculture (Chapter 2). Crops can be grown all the year round in three main growing seasons—winter *(shitwi)*, summer *(seifi)* and autumn *(nili)*—because of the continuous warmth and high levels of isolation. The temperature regime throughout is ideal for crop development, without extremes of heat or cold. In the past, the annual flood added a valuable layer of silt to the land, thus contributing to its perpetual fertility. For a high proportion of the population the physical environment remains of paramount importance, but the economic life of the country is also vastly more complicated than in the time of Herodotus.

Before the war of June 1966 deprived Egypt of the Sinai peninsula, it had the unique distinction of being an African state with a foot in Asia, and the Palestine question thrust Egypt to the forefront of Arab politics as being the most powerful neighbour to Israel. The Arab–Israeli war of 1973 gave Egypt a vital toe-hold once more in Sinai, which is not likely to be lost again. The

471

modern political boundaries of the state, like most in the Middle East and North Africa, were largely the product of European influence; the Sudan boundary was fixed in 1899, the Palestine boundary in 1906, and the Libyan boundary in 1925. In 1948 Egypt also acquired the Gaza strip, which had been part of Palestine, and administered it until 1967. The total area thus outlined was 1,002,000 km², or 940,456 km² without the Sinai peninsula and Gaza strip. Until the last two or three decades, Egypt's territories beyond the Nile valley and delta were regarded largely as negative areas, but the discovery of a range of important raw materials, including petroleum, iron ore, manganese and phosphates, has changed this attitude, and the possibility of desert reclamation and settlement are now known to be considerable.

19.2 Population growth 1800 to 1970

In 1800 the population of Egypt was probably about two and a half million.[1] The first population census was in 1882, but it is not regarded as reliable. Subsequently, eight censuses have been conducted, so that Egyptian population statistics are more plentiful than for most developing countries. Table 19.1 summarizes the results. The accelerating rate of population growth is entirely the result of natural increase since immigration is negligible in Egypt. If sustained, the present rate of increase would lead to a doubling of the population in 25 years time. The remarkable decline in death rates has been chiefly responsible for this increase (Figure 19.1).

Before the Second World War, Egyptian death rates (25 to 29 per thousand) were among the highest in the world as a result of several related factors. To begin with, the peasants and their families suffered appallingly poor health. Many endemic diseases in Egypt are waterborne and affect a high proportion of the rural population because of the dense network of irrigation canals and ditches, and such diseases increased with the spread of perennial irrigation.

TABLE 19.1
Population of Egypt 1897 to 1970

Census year	Population total	Rate of increase per annum (per cent)
1897	9,714,500	—
1907	11,190,000	—
1917	12,718,300	1·3
1927	14,177,900	1·1
1937	15,920,700	1·2
1947	19,038,500	1·8
1960	26,085,300	2·4
1966	30,083,400	2·5
1970 (Estimate)	33,900,000	2·8
1972 (Estimate)	35,500,000	2·8

Source: United Nations, Demographic Yearbook, New York (various years).

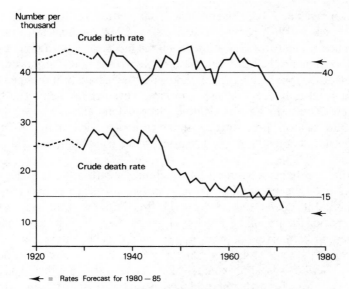

Figure 19.1 Crude birth rates and death rates for Egypt
1920–1972

Several common diseases such as bilharziasis and malaria, were a constant source of misery and reduced efficiency. Ankylostomiasis (hookworm) and trachoma, which results in partial or total blindness were also very widespread. The chief killers however, were bronchitis, heart diseases, tuberculosis and all kinds of liver diseases. Cholera epidemics spread through Egypt several times from 1816, the final epidemic being in 1947 when over 20,000 people died.[2] Resistance to disease in rural areas was also low because of widespread undernourishment; in the 1950's it was estimated that as many as 75 to 80 per cent of the population received an inadequate diet.[3] The intake of animal protein and protective foods, such as calcium and vitamins, was found to be extremely low, particularly in some of the poorer rural areas. Some 80 per cent of the rural population's calories still come from maize or millet bread, the rest of the diet largely comprising a variety of vegetables. Cheese, dates or melons are sometimes available but rarely any meat or fish. Another underlying cause of so much disease is poor housing and inadequate sanitation. The low houses, built of sun-dried Nile mud bricks generally consist of one or two dark rooms which the family sometimes share with their animals. Villages consist of closely-knit groups of houses with twisting narrow lanes; the great majority have less than 5,000 inhabitants. While a considerable effort has been made to improve conditions since the days when the Egyptian village was reputedly one of the most insanitary places in the world to live,[4] the majority are still unhealthy and depressing. Everyday life in such villages has been graphically described in three classic books.[5]

The establishment of medical facilities in rural areas began on a modest scale before the Revolution of July 1952, but the most impressive developments have occurred since then. There were 1,750 medical centres of various kinds in rural areas in 1969, compared with 289 in 1952, and at least a further 750 are planned.[6] The provision of these centres has clearly been one of the chief factors in reducing the death rate, notably by reducing infant mortality which was previously appallingly high. In addition, the installation of piped drinking water in practically every village is an impressive achievement. The spread of education has also had a considerable effect in combatting disease; during the 1960's new schools were opened at the rate of 11 a month.[7] Free midday meals for all schoolchildren are also doing much to build up natural resistance to disease.

Another probable cause of the declining death rate is the increasing proportion of the population living in urban areas where incomes tend to be higher, and social services superior to those in rural areas. In 1937, 25 per cent of the population of Egypt were classed as urban compared with 43 per cent in 1970. Even so, the average annual growth of the urban population from 1960 to 1969 was 4·6 per cent. The overall rate of natural increase in the same period was approximately 2·5 per cent per annum, which means that even allowing for higher natural increase in the towns, rural-urban migrants were an important component in the urban growth. Their contribution was greatest in the large cities of Cairo and Alexandria, and to a lesser extent in other towns with over 100,000 inhabitants. Many small towns have recorded modest growth rates during the past two or three decades. Thus, it is in the largest towns that the greatest concentration of migrants occurs, and where problems of unemployment are most severe. Despite rapid industrialization, insufficient jobs have been created, and urban slum conditions are multiplying on the outskirts of many large urban centres.

The crude birth rate in Egypt has remained high at between 37 and 43 per thousand, compared with 40 to 44 in the pre-Second World War period (Figure 19.1). Besides strong economic incentives to have large families in some rural areas, where children can work in the cotton fields and provide security for ageing parents, the practice of young marriages and very high divorce rates also accounts for high birth rates.[8] Although evidence exists to support the view that eventually birth rates will fall in the towns, there is as yet no sign of this except among the middle classes. The Egyptian government is meanwhile officially committed to a family planning campaign, which it is hoped will reduce natural increase to 1·7 per cent per annum by 1978.[9] A Supreme Council for Family Planning has existed since 1965, and family planning advice is widely available in all the towns and also many of the newly established rural health centres. The campaign has met with some success in the towns but as yet has had little impact in the villages.

The social and economic implications of rapid population growth in any developing country are well known. With some 43 per cent of the population of Egypt under the age of 15, a high proportion are in the 'dependent' age group. Every year there are 800,000 more people to feed, resulting in heavy expenditure on imported food: at its peak in 1967 food imports cost Egypt

TABLE 19.2
Value of food imports, excluding
international economic aid (£E millions)

1910	5·1	1964	119·8
1920	20·8	1965	110·2
1930	8·8	1966	126·1
1940	4·8	1967	137·7
1950	50·2	1968	91·9
1960	47·9	1969	66·2

Source: National Bank of Egypt, Cairo, *Economic Bulletin* **23**, No. 4, Table 3.4 (a) (1970).

nearly £E138 million, in addition to food imported through international economic aid schemes (Table 19.2). In most years approximately half the imported food by value is cereals and milling products. The government also has to build more schools, hospitals and houses to keep pace with the rising population, while every year thousands of school leavers seek jobs in the towns. It has been calculated that the annual investment necessary to achieve Egypt's economic growth would fall by £E85 millions if the birth rate could be reduced by 15 per thousand.[10]

19.3 Man and the land

The rate of population growth in Egypt is not exceptionally high compared with several other Middle East countries (Table 5.1), but against a background of limited resources of cultivable land and water, the growing population has serious implications. Only 35,800 km² or 3·5 per cent of the country is settled and cultivated, with the Nile valley and delta supporting the bulk of the population, three-fifths of them more or less directly by agriculture. Rural population densities are already high, averaging around 700 persons per km² rising to 1,200 per km² in parts of the delta. In some regions, holdings are already too small to yield a reasonable standard of living and present levels of production could be generally achieved by a greatly reduced labour force. Moreover, productivity is already high. Each cultivated feddan* produces an average of 1·7 crops a year, and over 99·5 per cent of farmland is irrigated. More fertilizer is used in Egypt than in the whole of the rest of North Africa, and levels of application are high compared with Britain and the United States.

Table 19·3 shows that both cultivated area and crop area per capita are declining. An unnecessarily gloomy picture is sometimes given by quoting the figures in column (v) whereas column (viii) is a far more realistic indicator. Thus, while the *cultivated* area per capita has fallen by about two-thirds since 1897, the *cropped* area per capita of the *rural* population has only declined by just over one third. Certainly there is no room for complacency; these figures do not reveal that a high proportion of proprietors own less than one feddan,

*1 Feddan = 1·038 acres = 042 ha.

TABLE 19.3
Man and the land; some statistics

	(i) Total population (millions)	(ii) Urban population (per cent)	(iii) Cultivated area (million feddans)	(iv) Cropped area (million feddans)	(v) (vi) Feddans per capita of total population		(vii) (viii) Feddans per capita of rural population	
					Cultivated	Cropped	Cultivated	Cropped
1820	2·5	12	3·0	3·0	1·2	1·2	1·4	1·4
1897	9·7	20	5·0	6·8	·51	·70	·64	·87
1907	11·2	19	5·4	7·7	·48	·68	·60	·85
1917	12·7	21	5·3	7·7	·41	·60	·53	·77
1927	14·2	23	5·5	8·7	·39	·61	·50	·79
1937	15·9	25	5·3	8·4	·33	·53	·44	·70
1947	19·0	31	5·8	9·2	·31	·48	·44	·70
1960	26·0	38	6·1	10·3	·30	·38	·49	·64
1966	30·0	40	6·5	10·5	·27	·35	·36	·58
1970	33·9	42	7·4	10·7	·22	·32	·37	·54
1982	44·7	50	8·3	14·0	·18	·31	·36	·61

Sources: E. Garzouzi, *Old ills and new remedies in Egypt*, Dar al Ma'aref, Cairo, 1958, 15.
P. O'Brien, 'The long-term growth of agricultural production in Egypt: 1821–1962', in *Political and Social Change in Modern Egypt*, (Ed. P. M. Holt), Oxford University Press, London 1968, 162–195.
Daily Telegraph, Report, 15 January 1971
Statistical Handbook of the U.A.R. 1952–1966, Cairo, 1967, 22–25.
Statistical Abstract of the U.A.R., Cairo, 1971, 26–28.

and that output per capita has declined markedly. Hired labour is also in less demand than a few decades ago partly as a result of mechanization on the large estates. During the next two or three decades the proportion of Egypt's population living in rural areas will continue to decline, while the overall rate of population increase could be slowed down by a successful family planning programme. Nevertheless, by the end of this century Egypt's non-urban areas might still have to support at least another 15 million people. The challenge of absorbing such numbers in the rural areas, while raising the living standards of the rural population as a whole, is a formidable one. The following sections examine the two chief ways in which this challenge is being met—by extending the cultivated area, and by increasing production from existing farmland.

19.3.1 Expansion of the cultivated areas

Until the construction of the Aswân High dam (1958 to 1970) the water from the Nile could irrigate little more than six million feddans. Apart from some minor cultivated areas in the oases and along the northwest coast, this figure was approximately equivalent to the cultivated area of Egypt in the early 1960's. The additional water made available by the Aswân High dam will add a further 1·3 million feddans to the cultivated areas of the Nile valley and delta, and ensure the conversion of 900,000 feddans in Upper Egypt from basin to perennial irrigation (Chapter 2). In 1972, 800,000 feddans had already been reclaimed using Nile water, and much of this was already producing crops.

The balance of additional land arising from the High dam waters is expected to have been taken up by 1980.

Figure 19.2 shows the chief features of the expansion of cultivated land in Egypt from 1960 to 1980. Seven major projects are shown in and around the delta and western Sinai:[11]

(1) *Tahrir ('Liberation') Province*, one of the earliest large scale settlement schemes in Egypt was begun in 1957. Over 150,000 feddans had already been reclaimed by 1972 and 25,000 people had been established in seven villages[12] A further 50,000 feddans remain to be taken up. Water is

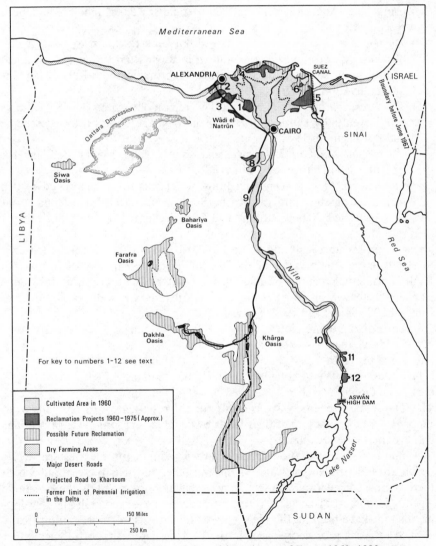

Figure 19.2 Expansion of the cultivated area of Egypt 1960–1980

obtained from the Nile by canal, but in the southern sector it is also supplemented by local groundwater. A number of problems have arisen in the management of the calcareous soils of this region, which are gradually being overcome.

(2) *The Maryût region.* This scheme, eventually covering some 115,000 feddans, includes the draining and reclamation of lake Maryût and adjacent land near Alexandria. A feature of this project is the use of processed sewage water to supplement water from the Nile. The reclamation of 68,000 feddans was completed in 1972.

(3) *The Nûbârîya desert scheme*, southwest of Alexandria, is being undertaken using Nile waters on some 217,000 feddans: 75,000 feddans had been reclaimed by 1970.

(4) *The northern delta*, south of Lakes Idku and Burullus. A vast region of lakes, swamps and lagoons known locally as *Barari* has been drained and the saline soils reclaimed at great cost, bringing about 120,000 feddans into cultivation.

(5) *The desert southwest of Ismâ'ilîya.* This region of perhaps 300,000 feddans could eventually support dozens of new villages; the projected scheme had not begun in 1972.

(6) *The region south of Lake Manzala* should yield 135,000 feddans for agriculture when drained and irrigated.

(7) *The western Sinai scheme.* Irrigation water was to be conducted to this region by pipeline underneath the Suez Canal. Over 2,000 feddans out of a projected 20,000 feddans had been reclaimed in 1967, but not yet settled.

These seven schemes will add some 1,107,000 feddans to the cultivated area of Egypt, largely as a result of the 'century' storage capacity of the Aswân High Dam, supplemented by local ground-water. There are in addition five smaller schemes in or near the Nile valley utilizing Nile water, amounting to some 142,000 feddans in 1972. These are:

(8) The Faiyūm depression	—	9,500 feddans
(9) El Minya region	—	58,500 feddans
(10) Kena province	—	17,000 feddans
(11) Radesia and Wadi Abbady	—	13,000 feddans
(12) Kom Ombo	—	44,000 feddans

The Kom Ombo scheme was primarily for the resettlement of Nubians from Upper Egypt dispossessed of their lands by lake Nasser; some 115,000 feddans will eventually be reclaimed.

A number of reclamation schemes are scheduled for the western desert which are independent of waters from the Nile, and it is these about which there is most speculation. These schemes are being organized by the Executive Agency for Desert Projects (EADP). The chief areas for research and development so far have been in 'the New Valley', the name sometimes optimistically applied to a chain of depressions in the western desert supporting a number of small oases. The total area is about eight million feddans, about 25 per cent of which could one day perhaps be reclaimed and cultivated, given sufficient water. Water supplies in these oases are obtained from artesian wells 300 to 600 m deep drawing on the vast natural reservoirs which exist in the Nubian sandstones. The irrigation potential of this water may have been exaggerated[13], but there seems a reasonable prospect of cultivating some 400,000 feddans of the level sandy soils of the New Valley. A proposal to bring water to the southern parts of El Khârga direct from lake Nasser by underground canal could greatly increase this amount if implemented. In 1972 only about 50,000 feddans had been reclaimed and cultivated, chiefly in the El Khârga and Dakhla oases. The first new villages established in El Khârga show great promise: in the late 1960's, some settlers were already earning £E200 per annum from four or five feddans.[14] In 1968, Egypt and the Sudan agreed to link Cairo and Khartoum by road through the New Valley (Figure 19.2), thus overcoming the problem of remoteness in part at least.

It is also hoped to irrigate up to 200,000 feddans in Wâdi el Natrûn using local groundwater. Orchards and crops are already being raised by local bedouin settlers on some 16,000 feddans. There are thus altogether some 600,000 feddans of immediately cultivable land in western Egypt, about one tenth of which was already irrigated and settled in 1972. Figure 19.2 therefore, shows a total of over 1·9 million feddans made up of 1,320,000 feddans in and around the Nile valley and delta, and a further 600,000 in the New Valley and Wâdi el Natrûn. When this programme is complete it is difficult to foresee any further major reclamation schemes, though with advances in technology and the possibility of a share in Libya's huge oil revenues, further horizontal expansion cannot be completely discounted. One possibility being studied in 1971 was the revival of the Jonglei scheme, a project for cutting a canal through the swamps of the Sudd Region in southern Sudan to save 18 million m^3 of water each year. Divided equally between Egypt and the Sudan this could irrigate over one million feddans in Egypt.

Besides such large scale schemes, there will be increasing emphasis upon efficient use of cultivable land in Egypt. The most significant of these measures is the conversion of open drainage systems to a covered network of underground pipes. Nearly three million feddans will have been converted in Lower Egypt by 1980. Pilot schemes of closed drainage have reportedly shown increased production of 30 to 50 per cent.[15] Such schemes should also result in more efficient drainage, which is important particularly in the delta where increasing levels of salinity in the soils are a serious problem. The use of sprinkler irrigation, already practised on 80,000 feddans in Tahrir Province could also be adopted more widely, reducing water requirements by half compared with flood irrigation.[16]

Finally, in connection with extending the cultivated area, projects to develop rain-fed cultivation deserve mention. In the northwestern coastal zone from Alexandria to the Libyan frontier at Salum, some 17,000 feddans are being systematically prepared for the permanent settlement of Egypt's 100,000 bedouin population. Wind pumps have been erected and small dams built by

EADP; olives, almonds and figs have been planted. Rainfall varies from 100 to 200 mm near the coast, and here barley is grown using fast tractor plough-ing, while further inland special desert grasses are being sown from the air to improve the pastures.[17] So far, settlement of the bedouin has met with mixed success, but the final outcome can be in little doubt. Over 9,000 feddans had also been prepared for cultivation in northern Sinai before 1967.

19.3.2 Intensification of agricultural production

The 'vertical' expansion of agricultural production can be achieved by improving yields of traditional crops and by introducing new crops yielding higher incomes or more food. Thus, the introduction of cotton, rice, sugar-cane and fruit at different times in Egypt have given the *fellaheen* higher incomes, but most effort today is concentrated on increasing yields of the most widely grown staple crops (Table 19.4). Clearly, the most significant impact would be made if the yields of the five major crops could be increased, since they represent the staple foods of man and animal, and by far the most impor-tant cash crop. Together they occupy nearly four fifths of the crop area. With the exception of rice, they are grown almost universally throughout the Nile valley and delta, whereas most of the less important crops are more localized in their distribution, usually in response to differences in temperature and types of soil. Egyptian clover (or *berseem*) is a quick growing variety peculiar to Egypt and known since Pharaonic times. It is a staple fodder for animals, and its ability to fix nitrogen from the atmosphere has played an important

TABLE 19.4
Chief crops and orchards, 1970

	Area in '000s of feddans	Per cent of total area under crops
Clover (or *berseem*)	2,734	25·5
Cotton	1,627	15·2
Maize	1,509	14·0
Wheat	1,304	12·2
Rice	1,140	10·6
Vegetables	706	6·6
Millet	501	4·6
Beans	330	3·0
Sugar cane	186	1·7
Barley	83	0·8
Other crops	380	3·5
Oranges	113	1·1
Other fruit	119	1·1
TOTAL:	10,732	100·0

Source: Statistical Abstract of the U.A.R., Cairo, 1971, 27–28.

part in maintaining soil fertility.[18] Cereals for human consumption, including barley, which is gradually declining in area, occupied 42 per cent of the area under crops in 1970. The area under rice has more than trebled since 1952 and it could soon become the third crop in importance by area. Meanwhile, it is already a significant earner of foreign exchange, half the annual crop being exported. Vegetable and fruit production has also increased greatly in recent years as urban demands have grown.

There is some argument as to how far Egyptian crop yields can be increased. It is certainly true that remarkable progress has already been made. Between 1820 and 1880, the *volume* of Egyptian agricultural output increased just over twelvefold, per capita production rose nearly sixfold, and average yields per unit of land rose substantially. The causes of this revolution are well known—the use of new implements, barrages, canals and drains. Precise figures of the increasing yields are not available but these were clearly considerable, possibly due in part to the reserve of soil fertility maintained under basin agriculture.[19] Early this century however, the yields of most crops began to decline because of a number of unforeseen problems associated with perennial irrigation—insects, pests, overcropping, waterlogging and salinization among them. After the First World War, yields once again rose as a result of the utilization of new inputs such as chemical fertilizers, selected seeds, machinery and better systems of drainage and crop rotation. Most crops showed steady gains; the average yield of cotton rose 21 per cent from 1913 to 1954, rice by 17 per cent, wheat by 14 per cent and sugar-cane by 13 per cent. Some crops, however, showed little or no increase during this period including maize, beans, lentils and onions. Since 1952, further increases have been achieved, including several crops which showed no increases in yield in previous years (Table 19.5).

Table 19.5 gives only the crudest indication of the possibilities for increasing yields in Egypt. Those for cotton, wheat, rice and sugar are already high and

TABLE 19.5
Yields (in 100 kg per ha) of selected crops,
1948–1952 and 1968

	Average		Ranking in 1968	
	1948–1952	1968	Afro–Asia	World
	(in 100 kg per ha)			
Cotton	5·2	7·1	2nd	4th
Maize	20·9	35·2	2nd	13th
Wheat	18·4	25·6	3rd	11th
Rice	37·9	51·1	3rd	5th
Millet	27·1	40·5	1st	1st
Sugar cane	771·0	923·0	3rd	6th
Lentils	15·0	16·3	1st	1st

Source: United Nations, FAO, *Production Yearbook, Vol. 23, 1969,* Rome, 1970, pp. 37–286.

could probably not be greatly increased short of a scientific revolution in agriculture, though the gap between Egyptian yields and those of the top country are quite large. Other crops could undoubtedly be improved as experiments on model farms have proved. The measures accompanying land reform discussed in the next section will also achieve a great deal, notably the new triennial crop rotation and the spread of cooperatives. Another possibility is the adoption of new patterns of crop production, in which cereals would be substantially replaced by high value crops for local consumption and export to Europe in winter and spring. Egyptian flowers, tomatoes, mangoes, onions and melons, for example, are already marketed in Europe, and this trade might be greatly expanded. In time, agricultural production might also become less dominated by the need to export cotton in return for essential goods and services, thus releasing land for food production.

The high proportion of cultivated land devoted to fodder for animals is shown in Table 19.4. The bulk of this is for cattle and buffaloes kept for milk, meat and draft purposes. There were about two million of each in Egypt in 1969, one third more than in 1960.[20] With increasing mechanization, some of these animals could be replaced by more suitable strains of beef and dairy cattle capable of producing more meat and milk. On the other hand, the use of machinery on small holdings is of limited value, particularly where intensive labour can be as effective for most operations, and animal power is likely to remain important for a long time, even on holdings of up to 20 feddans. Clover is also an important part of the crop rotation, and its total removal could result in falling yields.

The Ten Year Programme of National Action aims at increasing agricultural production by 50 per cent by 1981. The programme includes measures which could radically influence future patterns of land ownership in Egypt. An Agricultural Land Development Organization has been created to organize 'agro-companies' to exploit newly reclaimed lands for the large scale commercial production of cash crops, the settlement of landless peasants no longer being the primary objective.

19.3.3 Agrarian reform

Agrarian reform is another way of increasing the efficiency of agricultural production, but it is of such fundamental importance in Egypt as to warrant separate consideration.

Agrarian reform bills had been introduced in 1945 and 1950, but were decisively rejected by the landlord dominated parliament. In September 1952 scarcely six weeks after the Revolution, the Young Officers implemented the First Agrarian Reform. It had four main objectives: first, to break the power of the landlords; secondly, to improve the living conditions of the rural population; thirdly, to divert capital from agriculture to industry and finally, to raise agricultural output. In 1952, out of a total cultivated area of 5·9 million feddans, 40 per cent was held by less than one per cent of owners, while 72

TABLE 19.6
Landownership in 1952 and 1965 (Figures are in thousands)

Size group (Feddans)	Before land reform (1952)				After land reform (1965)			
	Owners	Area	Per cent of total Owners	Area	Owners	Area	Per cent of total Owners	Area
Less than 1	2,018	788	72·0	13·0	3,033	3,693	94·5	57·1
1– 4	624	1,344	22·2	22·5				
5– 9	79	526	2·8	8·8	78	614	2·4	9·5
10–19	47	638	1·8	10·7	61	527	1·9	8·2
20–29	13	309	0·5	5·0	29	815	0·9	12·6
30–49	9	344	0·3	5·7				
50–99	6	429	0·2	7·2	6	392	0·2	6·1
100–199	3	437	0·1	7·3	4	421	0·1	6·5
200 and over	2	1,177	0·1	19·8	0	0	0	0
TOTAL	2,802	5,982	100	100	3,211	6,462	100	100

Sources: E. Garzouzi, *Old Ills and New Remedies in Egypt*, Dar al Ma'aref, Cairo, 1958, p. 79. *Statistical handbook of the U.A.R. 1952–1969*, Cairo, 1970, pp. 54–57.

per cent of owners together held no more than 13 per cent of the cultivated area, and the average size of their holdings was less than half a feddan (Table 19.6). Since two feddans was generally regarded as the minimum required to yield a reasonable standard of living in Egypt, many *fellaheen* were clearly in great poverty. Some of course were able to supplement their incomes through hired employment on estates or by selling craft work. The average size of holdings had shown a steady decline since the nineteenth century; before 1900, there were still no owners with less than one feddan in their possession, but by 1913 there were nearly one million, farming over seven per cent of the cultivated area of Egypt.[21] The chief reasons for this progressive decline were the division of property between all the male heirs, and the growing importance of large estates. There were also large numbers of tenant farmers and landless wage earners in Egypt, probably as many as 1·5 million families.[22] Generally, rents were exorbitant and wages extremely meagre. The very high price of land, furthermore, precluded its purchase by any but a few. Between the Second World War and 1952, land prices rose fourfold. The eagerness of capitalists to purchase agricultural land was largely due to the promise of a guaranteed income, and the absence of attractive alternatives.

The implications of the maldistribution of land in 1952 are obvious enough. Tenants and wage earners were readily exploited by landowners or their middlemen. On the other hand many small landowners experienced a decline in real income as their holdings diminished in size. The First Agrarian Reform of 1952 was a cautious attempt to deal with these problems. The maximum size of individual holdings was reduced to 200 feddans, though landowners were permitted to transfer up to 100 feddans to their children. Expropriated land was given to landless labourers and to owners with less than five feddans where possible. As a condition of his land grant, each new peasant–proprietor was required to join one of the newly-formed land reform cooperatives.

Maximum rents were fixed for all agricultural land, reducing them in effect by about 40 to 50 per cent. Written tenancy agreements, with a minimum tenure of three years became compulsory, and a minimum agricultural wage was to be fixed; the yearly earnings of an agricultural labourer stood at £E25·3 in 1953.[23] While wages have undoubtedly risen, the improvement has not been as great as originally planned. Agricultural workers were authorized to form trade unions, and fragmentation of holdings into lots of less than five feddans was henceforth forbidden.

Under the law of 1952, about one tenth of the cultivated area was eligible for redistribution. This was complete by 1956. The area involved was not great, but the social and economic implications to reform, the first in the Arab world, were colossal. The transfer of land occurred without bloodshed, and the legal status and human rights of the *fellaheen* had been proclaimed. A Second Reform Law in 1961 reduced the maximum size of holdings to 100 feddans per person, though the ceiling on family owned land remained at 300 feddans. Compensation was paid in government bonds, but in 1964 these were cancelled. In 1962, all foreign-owned land in Egypt was expropriated for redistribution, while in 1969 the maximum size of holding per individual was reduced to 50 feddans, and family holdings to 100 feddans. When complete, this latest reform will considerably affect the figures shown in Table 19.6. In 1965 nearly 13 per cent of the cultivated area was in holdings of over 50 feddans, most of which will be divided into holdings of between two and five feddans. Nevertheless, it is worth noting that the fundamental character of land ownership in Egypt remains unchanged, with the vast majority consisting of small properties. Even if the entire cultivated area could be equally divided between all cultivators, each would have less than two feddans of land. By the end of 1969, some 17 per cent of the 1952 cultivated area had been transferred to peasant proprietors and another 10 per cent, awaited transfer.

One of the most important achievements of the Land Reform Authority has been the introduction of multi-purpose cooperatives. Several hundred cooperatives already existed in 1952, largely for the provision of credit, and the wholesale purchase of seeds and fertilizers, but their membership was limited and they did not undertake marketing. The new-style cooperatives perform similiar services, but in addition, offer technical and practical advice, arrange for the marketing of produce, and generally supervise farm production through a resident manager. The most striking feature, however, is the introduction of a consolidated triennial crop rotation. Under the traditional system in Egypt farms typically consisted of several strips of land scattered throughout three or more large blocks of land. Within each block, individual farmers could grow any crop on their own strips, resulting in inefficient application of irrigation water and waste of land in paths, boundaries and ditches. Some crops were watered insufficiently, others too much, as when cotton was planted next to rice. Insect and plant diseases spread easily from crop to crop, and the application of fertilizers and pesticides was difficult. The traditional system also relied on a biennial crop rotation which had an adverse effect on soil fertility since the land lay fallow for only two months every two years. Clover, which is essential for restoring nitrogen to the soil, could only be grown once in every two years.

Under the new system the lands of the village are divided into three large consolidated blocks, each being assigned annually to one of three main groups of crops, which can now be ploughed, watered, drained, sprayed and harvested as a unit. Sowing, weeding and tending crops remain individual activities which the *fellaheen* continue to conduct on their own plots as before. Farming is thus a mixture of collective and individual enterprise. Crop consolidation permits the adoption of a triennial crop rotation which enables soil to rest for eight months, with clover cultivation twice every three years. As a result, yields may increase by up to one fifth. In some villages, land consolidation as well as crop consolidation is being carried out, with plots belonging to individual *fellaheen* being consolidated on an exchange basis. Under both systems it will be noted, land remains in private hands, and no attempt is made to standardize the size of ownership. Where land consolidation is complete, the farmer's share of the crop is calculated in proportion to his holding after deductions for production costs.

Participation in the scheme is obligatory for all recipients of redistributed land, and attempts are being made to introduce it more generally in other villages. In association with all-purpose cooperatives the new triennial rotation could foreshadow a revolution in Egyptian agriculture. There are naturally some drawbacks; thus the individual is restricted in his choice of crop, but the benefits are marked. In one village, a 58 per cent increase in cotton yields occurred after consolidation and all crop yields were at least 20 per cent higher than in neighbouring villages.[24] There are many reasons for such higher yields: more efficient farming techniques; land saved from ditches and boundaries; a scientific crop rotation; and the fact that family workers tend to farm plots more intensively than hired labourers on the old estates.

A modest improvement in the average net incomes of small landowners has occurred since 1952, in spite of rising costs and frequently diminishing holdings, largely as a result of greatly increased yields. The beneficiaries of land distribution, for example, showed increased net incomes *per feddan* from £E27 in 1953 to £E64 in 1965.[25] Tenant cultivators are also better off due to lower rents and higher yields. The most unfortunate group remain the landless labourers. The statutory minimum wage proved unenforceable because of the large surplus of unemployed. In some regions, there was hardship because the break-up of large estates reduced the demand for casual labour; possibly five or ten per cent remain unemployed.[26]

It would be a mistake to assess Egypt's development programmes simply in the light of crop yields and incomes. Hand in hand with the economic and technical programme, a substantial social programme designed to improve the quality of life in rural areas has been pursued. The most outstanding aspect of this has been the construction of combined rural centres throughout the country, providing comprehensive social services catering for approximately

15,000 persons. Typically, these centres include a health unit, school, and training centre for rural crafts, a social unit with library and assembly hall, cooperative society offices, and housing for the professional employees of the centre. There will eventually be over 800 such centres. In selecting villages for the new centres, communications and centrality were key considerations. It has been suggested that, if urban industry cannot absorb Egypt's surplus rural population, handicrafts and light industries, such as food processing, might be widely established outside the towns.[27] If this concept was to become reality, the service centres might provide ideal locations for such activities.

Mention has been made of the coming of fresh water to most villages. Rural electrification is also going ahead very rapidly in Egypt. By 1976 over 3,500 villages will have electricity, at a total cost of £E183 million. The demand for electricity in rural areas will eventually absorb all the spare capacity of the turbines of the High Dam at Aswân. Egypt therefore will need to increase the production of electricity in the near future, and one possibility is the construction of a nuclear power station jointly with Libya. Another interesting possibility is the generation of hydro-electric power by conducting Mediterranean water to the Qattâra depression.[28]

19.4 Conclusion

While any firm predictions would be folly, it seems reasonable to conclude that increased agricultural production in Egypt during the next three or four decades should be sufficient to maintain present standards of living, or even raise them. Nevertheless, the long-term solution will depend upon the successful development of all sectors of the national economy, in addition to agriculture. A programme of industrialization has been instituted, and in spite of many set-backs this has already met with considerable success. Some useful industries were inherited from the Farouk regime in 1952, but the 1956 Suez War began a serious drive towards self-sufficiency which was greatly accelerated by the First Five Year Plan of 1960. Industry now generates a higher proportion of the G.D.P. than agriculture. The value of industrial production has more than doubled since 1960, and the number of workers in manufacturing industry and electricity production has more than trebled to around one million. Nevertheless, over half the active labour force is still engaged in agriculture.

Industrialization is undoubtedly the right policy for Egypt, particularly in those sectors where local resources are most suitable—food processing, textiles, and chemicals. Though the number of jobs directly created is modest, varying between one-third and one-sixth of the annual increase in population, much more employment is created indirectly in the services sector and in construction. Industrialization however is no panacea. Egypt's economic future will depend on both agriculture and industry, together with the fullest possible exploitation of every other potential source of revenue. Petroleum production, which was 11 million tons in 1972 (to which may be added 6 million tons from the Sinai wells), will certainly increase, possibly to large proportions. The tourist industry could eventually revive to its pre-1967 levels when some 580,000 visitors entered Egypt annually. A steady income might also be derived from transit trade. The new SUMED pipeline from Suez to Alexandria could eventually bring in £E70 million annually in transit dues,[29] which may be compared with £E95 million earned by the Suez Canal in 1966, the last full year of operations before closure. Whatever measures are taken, and however much effort is expended, no really significant economic progress will be made in Egypt without a lower rate of population increase and permanent peace with Israel, which seemed a real possibility in 1974.

References

1. P. O'Brien, 'The long-term growth of agricultural production in Egypt: 1821–1962', in *Political and Social Change in Modern Egypt* (Ed. P. M. Holt), Oxford University Press, London, 1968, 174.
2. L. D. Stamp, *The Geography of Life and Death*, Fontana, London, 1964, 35.
3. J. M. May and I. S. Jarcho, *The Ecology of Malnutrition in the Far and Near East*, Hafner, New York, 1961, 651.
4. W. A. Hance, *Geography of Modern Africa*, Columbia University, New York, 1964, 119.
5. (a) H. M. Ammar, *Growing up in an Egyptian Village*, Routledge and Kegan Paul, London, 1954.
   (b) H. H. Ayrout, *The Egyptian Peasant*, Beacon Press, Boston, 1963.
   (c) W. S. Blackman, *The Fellahin of Upper Egypt, their Religious, Social and Industrial Life*, New impression, Frank Cass, 1971 (First published 1927).
6. P. Mansfield, *Nasser's Egypt*, Penguin Books, 1965, 110.
   United Arab Republic, *Statistical Handbook 1952–1969*, Cairo, 1970, 136.
7. United Arab Republic, *Statistical Handbook 1952–1969*, Cairo, 1970, 179–181.
8. D. N. Wilber (Ed.), *The United Arab Republic, its People, its Society, its Culture*, Human Relations Area Files, New Haven, 1969, 88.
9. S. Galal, 'Plan to cut birth rate', in Supplement on Egypt, *The Times*, London, 24 July 1969, xiv.
10. R. Pettengill, 'Population control to accelerate economic progress in the Middle East', *Middle East Economic papers*, American University, Beirūt, 1961, 85.
11. Compiled from the following:
    (a) *The Guardian*, Manchester, 14 April 1966, 14–15.
    (b) H. Hopkins, *Egypt, the Crucible*, Secker and Warburg, London, 1969, 129–139.
    (c) Ministry of Land Reclamation: *Land Reclamation Development in the Arab Republic of Egypt*, Cairo, 1972, 18–36.
    (d) R. R. Platt and M. B. Hefny, *Egypt: a Compendium*, American Geographical Society, New York, 1958, 17, 61–78.
    (e) Supplement on Egypt, *The Times*, London, 24 July 1969, i–xx.
    (f) Economist Intelligence Unit, *Annual Supplement on Egypt*, London, 1970, 9.
12. A. B. Mountjoy, 'Egypt cultivates her deserts' *Geogr. Mag.*, **44**, 241–250 (1972).
13. H. Y. Hammad, *Groundwater Potentialities in the African Sahara and the Nile Valley*, Arab University, Beirūt, 1970, 41.
14. H. Hopkins, *Egypt the Crucible*, Secker and Warburg, London, 1969, 320.
15. *Middle East Economic Digest*, London, 23 April 1971, 442.
16. Ministry of Land Reclamation, *Land Reclamation Development in U.A.R.*, Cairo, 1970, 36.
17. H. Hopkins, *Egypt the Crucible*, Secker and Warburg, London, 1969, 323.
18. D. N. Wilber (Ed.) *The United Arab Republic, its People, its Society, its Culture*. Human Relations Area Files, New Haven, 1969, 310.

19. G. Hamdan, 'Evolution of irrigation agriculture in Egypt', in *History of Land Use in Arid Regions*, UNESCO, New York, 1961, 128.
20. United Arab Republic *Statistical Abstract, 1951/52 to 1969/70*, Cairo, 197, 47.
21. A. Granott, *Agrarian Reform and the Record of Israel*, Eyre and Spottiswoode, London, 1956, 208.
22. E. Eshag and M. A. Kamal, 'Agrarian reform in the United Arab Republic', *Bull. Oxf. Univ. Inst. Statist.* **30,** 81–1968).
23. E. Garzouzi, *Old Ills and New Remedies in Egypt*, Dar al Ma'aref, Cairo, 1958, 91.
24. G. S. Saab, *The Egyptian Agrarian Reform 1952–62*, Oxford University Press, London 1967, 192.
25. E. Eshag and M. A. Kamal, 'Agrarian reform in the United Arab Republic', *Bull. Oxf. Univ. Inst. Statist.* **30,** 87–93 (1968).
26. E. Eshag and M. A. Kamal, 'Agrarian reform in the United Arab Republic', *Bull. Oxf. Univ. Inst. Statist.* **30,** 97 (1968).
27. M. Adamowicz, 'Transformation of agricultural structure in the United Arab Republic', *Africana Bulletin*, **43,** University of Warsaw, 76 (1970).
28. *Middle East Economic Digest*, London, 12 November 1971, 1302.
29. *Middle East Economic Digest*, London 13 August 1971, 933.

CHAPTER 20

Libya: The Impact of Oil

20.1 Introduction

With a total area of 1,759,500 km², Libya is among the world's 15 largest states, yet its population (2,257,000 at the 1973 census) is among the smallest. The underlying cause of this sparse population is aridity. Nearly 95 per cent of the country receives less than 100 mm of rainfall per annum, and even in the well watered areas such as the Gebel el Akhdar in Cyrenaica and the Gefara plains in Tripolitania, where rainfall may be as high as 350 to 500 mm per annum, serious drought can occur. Throughout the south practically no rain falls and there are no perennial surface streams. Groundwater, however, is relatively plentiful in Libya and soils are potentially fertile over large areas, including some parts of the desert. Altogether probably no more than five to 10 per cent of the land can be put to economic use[1] and only two per cent is suitable for settled cultivation. Table 20.1 summarizes land use in 1970, when 1·4 per cent was cultivated and less than five per cent of the cultivated area was irrigated.

Population distribution reflects the scarcity of cultivable land in Libya and the paucity of alternative economic opportunities. Most of the people are concentrated in a northern coastal belt, three quarters of them within 30 km of the sea,[2] while the oases of the Saharan zone support no more than 100,000 to 150,000 inhabitants. In 1972, the two largest cities of Tripoli (280,000 inhabitants) and Benghazi (240,000 inhabitants) contained some 26 per cent of the population of Libya, while other urban centres accounted for a further three or four per cent. The proportion of nomads and semi-nomads among

TABLE 20.1
Land use in 1970 in km²

Arable—irrigated	1,240
Arable—unirrigated	24,510
Vines, orchards etc.	1,400
Pasture	11,300
Forest	5,320
TOTAL:	41,770

Source: United Nations, FAO, *Production Yearbook 1971*, **25**, Rome, 1972, p. 6.

489

the rural population has greatly declined in recent years as a result of employment in the cities and oil camps and government efforts to bring about sedentarization. In 1964, 17 per cent of the population was classified as nomadic or semi-nomadic, but it is doubtful whether the proportion now exceeds 10 per cent.

Libya was one of the poorest countries in the world when granted independence in 1951, with an average per capita income of less than £14 a year and a total budget of about £7 million.[3] Over 70 per cent of the indigenous population were farmers or herders, and in Cyrenaica half were nomadic. Most were illiterate. With such a poor, scattered internal market, local manufacturing industry had hardly developed at all. There were almost no known mineral resources. The chief exports were esparto grass, olive oil and scrap metal collected from the desert battlefields of the Second World War. Altogether the common view that Libya was 'chained by a harsh environment to never-ending poverty'[4] seemed amply justified. Economic problems were compounded by internal political rivalries between the three federal provinces of Tripolitania, Cyrenaica and Fezzan, and a top-heavy administration. In 1963, Libya became a unitary state with 10 administrative districts (or *mohafaza*) in an attempt to overcome these difficulties.

In some ways Libya's backwardness in 1951 was surprising. The Italians conquered Tripolitania in 1912 and had acquired control of the whole of the country by 1929. During the short period of colonial rule, some impressive developments were begun, including road building, town planning, and land reclamation. Altogether they invested the equivalent of 150 million per-war U.S. Dollars in Libya.[5] Unfortunately their efforts were primarily for the benefit of Italian colonists, who numbered 110,000 by 1940, while Libyan welfare was largely neglected.[6] The Italians were greatly influenced by the fact that in Roman times the coastal areas of Libya may have supported two or three times more people than today and magnificent cities such as Leptis Magna and Sabratha. Much destruction occurred during the Second World War and the exodus of many Italians and Jews after the war left the country with a shortage of personnel in key positions.

Until 1959, Libya received massive international aid partly in return for the use of military bases by the United States and Great Britain. Possibly the only optimists in Libya in the 1950's were the oil companies. Some oil exploration took place after the Second World War, but intensive exploration only began in 1955 after the passing of the Libyan Petroleum Law, whose terms appealed to the oil companies.[7] The first strike occurred in 1958 at Atshan in the Fezzan, but the first really big discovery was at Zelten in the Sirte Basin in April 1959. Libyan oil was exported for the first time in September 1961. Few areas have ever been explored so intensively. Between 1957 and 1958 alone £42 million was spent on exploration,[8] and by 1961 the whole northern half of Libya and much of the coastal waters were under concession. Companies were obliged to relinquish one quarter of their blocks after five years and another quarter after eight. These blocks were awarded again and success by one

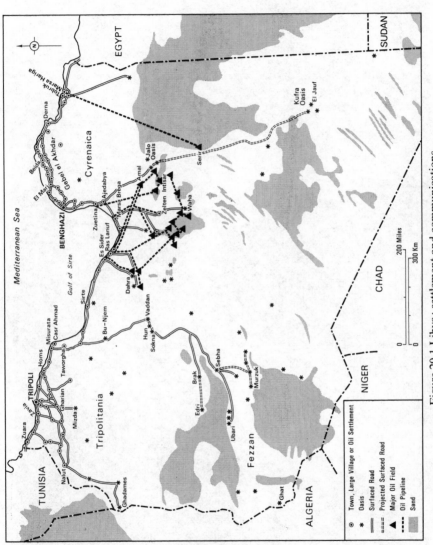

Figure 20.1 Libya : settlement and communications

An exploration well drilled in the Libyan desert by Esso, 1967 (An Esso photograph)

company sometimes followed failure by another. Thus exploration was rapid, and a fragmented pattern of concessions emerged quite unlike the huge blocks familiar in the producing areas of Southwest Asia. Many difficulties were encountered in exploration. To begin with, thousands of mines left over from the Second World War had to be cleared. Distances were great, and vast expanses of sand and rocky desert made movement of heavy equipment difficult. Nor was there any guarantee of success. The Shell Company, for example, drilled 70 wells over a period of 20 years at a cost of over 100 million U.S. Dollars without success.[9]

There were, however, powerful incentives for the oil companies in their search for Libyan oil. The most important was the immense advantage enjoyed by Libya in proximity to western Europe, then the fastest growing oil market in the world. In 1971, 49·3 per cent of all international oil imports were to western Europe. Libya's freight advantage greatly increased after June 1967 with the closure of the Suez Canal, culminating in the astonishing 49 per cent increase in production in 1968. This advantage is illustrated by the relative cost in 1971 of shipping one barrel of crude oil from the Gulf to Rotterdam (9·18 U.S. Dollars) compared with the cost from Libya (2·95 U.S. Dollars).[10] This advantage could diminish with the completion of the SUMED pipeline (Chapter 19) and other possible transit pipelines in Israel, Turkey, and Lebanon, or the reopening of the Suez Canal. For the time being however, Libya's largest customers are all European; Italy, West Germany, the United Kingdom, France and the Netherlands. In 1970, Libya marketed oil in 21 countries, but delivered 90 per cent of the total to E.E.C. countries, Spain and the United Kingdom.[11] Libyan crude is attractive to the pollution conscious customers of western Europe since it has low sulphur content (one per cent compared with 3·5 per cent from the Gulf) and a relatively low residue (29 per cent compared with 36 per cent).

Libya's major oilfields are quite near the Mediterranean coast where the Gulf of Sirte penetrates far inland (Figure 20.1). As a result, most pipelines are relatively short, one notable exception being from Serir to Tobruk (560 km), though even this does not compare with distances covered in Algeria and other producing countries. Although several strikes have been made in western Libya, the region has been neglected in favour of the more prolific fields of the Sirte Basin. The rivalry of the nine major groups of companies and their desire to begin exports as quickly as possible explains the existence of so many pipelines, not all of which take the shortest route to the sea. The complex of parallel and interlacing pipelines might look very different if based on subsequent knowledge of oilfield locations. Each of the five oil terminals was originally established by groups of producers for their own use.

Table 20.2 shows the pattern of crude oil production in Libya from 1962 to 1972. Oil revenues of LD 51,000* were received as early as 1955, with the first concessions.[12] In 1963 Libya achieved a favourable balance of payments for

*1 dinar (LD) = £1·36 sterling, June 1973.

TABLE 20.2
Crude oil production in Libya 1962 to 1972

	Production million tonnes	Per cent of world total	Government receipts in U.S. cents per barrel	Revenue in millions of U.S. Dollars
1962	9·6	0·7	64·7	38·5
1963	22·1	1·8	64·1	109·0
1964	41·5	2·9	62·9	197·0
1965	61·0	3·9	83·8	371·0
1966	72·2	4·4	87·0	476·0
1967	83·5	4·8	101·6	631·0
1968	125·0	6·3	100·7	952·0
1969	149·0	7·0	100·0	1132·0
1970	159·3	6·8	109·0	1295·0
1971	132·0	5·3	178·6	1766·6
1972	105·0	4·0	201·0	1614·1

Source: Petrol. Pr. Serv., **39**, No. 9, p. 322 (1972), and Institute of Petroleum Information Service, London.

the first time and in the next 10 years despite rising levels of imports, the surplus climbed to become one of the largest in the world, at LD 710 millions in 1971.[13] The cut back in production in 1971 and 1972 was largely the result of government determination to strengthen its position in negotiations with the oil companies and to conserve Libya's reserves. One estimate is that at a production rate of 110 million tonnes a year, reserves would last another 20 to 30 years.[14] The early 1970's were also marked by successful government efforts to improve Libya's share of oil revenues. Their success is shown by the fact that while production fell between 1970 and 1971, government receipts increased substantially, enabling it to embark upon even more ambitious development plans. The climax came in September 1973, when the government finally took control of all companies operating in Libya.

Libya has one of the highest G.N.P's. per capita in the world and a very large surplus of foreign exchange. In 10 years, the country has truly progressed from rags to riches. Libyan dependence on oil is indicated by the fact that 99·9 per cent of exports by value are crude oil and petroleum products, while traditional commodities (hides and skins, castor seeds, and certain foodstuffs) are valued at under LD one million. Over half the total revenue from oil has been devoted to development expenditure, the scale of which is the envy of other developing countries. These funds are being used to provide improved social facilities of all kinds, including fresh water, electricity and sewerage in every major settlement, an adequate network of surfaced roads, proper housing, and basic educational and medical services. At the same time, large sums are being spent in an attempt to prepare for the day when oil runs out by developing alternative sources of income, notably from agriculture and industry. The Three Year Development Plan (1973 to 1975), costing LD 1,012

TABLE 20.3
Objectives of the Three Year Development Plan 1973 to 1975

	1972	1975	Annual rate of growth
Gross income from oil	LD 957 million	LD 1,191 million	7·5 per cent
Gross income from non-oil activities	LD 552 million	LD 818 million	14·0 per cent
G.N.P. per capita	LD 651 million	LD 786 million	6·7 per cent

Source: 'The Libyan Arab Republic', The Times (Supplement), p. IV, 6 June, 1973.

million in particular is designed to achieve rapid growth in non-oil activities (Table 20.3).

20.2 Changes in agriculture

Arable and pastoral farming both suffered greatly during the early years of the oil industry in Libya. The decline actually began in about 1956 when exploration was at its height, but before the export boom had begun. Between 1956 and 1962 agricultural production fell at about four per cent per annum, largely as a result of the movement of farmers to the towns in search of work, and the general assumption that the country could now afford to import its foodstuffs. In 1963 Libya already imported £10 million worth of foodstuffs, including olive oil which was once produced locally. By 1968 the figure had risen to £27.6 million, though this increase partly reflects a higher standard of living among the urban population, and the needs of a large expatriate population.

The neglect of the agricultural sector was already being tackled in 1962, and output was increasing by about 4.5 per cent per annum from 1963.[15] Since the 1969 revolution, the government has placed an altogether higher priority on agriculture, with over LD 50 million allocated annually. The aim is to bring all Libya's 3.7 million ha of cultivable land into production, compared with 2·5 million ha actually in use in 1973.[16] Eventually, Libya could be self-sufficient in agricultural products, and the aim is to develop a modest export trade. By raising rural incomes and providing access to social services, the government hope to check migration to the towns, and raise the standard of living of two-thirds of the population. They also hope to bring an end to pastoral nomadism, which is regarded as incompatible with national unity and efficient administration. In time, the most favourable areas of pasture on the margins of the desert will be used for livestock production by modern techniques of range management, but meanwhile the number of livestock has fallen as nomadism has declined (Table 20.4).

A large number of land reclamation schemes are being undertaken to increase the cultivated area. Details of four of the projects are summarized below to to illustrate the variety of techniques being adopted to make best use of local environments.[17]

TABLE 20.4

Livestock in Libya

	1960	1971
Sheep	2,509,000	2,284,000
Goats	2,391,000	1,141,000
Cattle	223,000	101,000
Camels	345,000	120,000

Source: The Middle East and North Africa, Europa Publications, London, p. 391 (1965–1966) and p. 534 (1972–1973).

The Taworgha project, half complete in September 1973, will result in the creation of 300 new farms on 3,000 ha of irrigated land at a cost of some LD 8·5 million. A central services village, offering all basic amenities is being built, and some 75,000 saplings are being planted as windbreaks. The functional relationship of the village to the regional market town of Misurata will be a matter of some interest,[18] particularly in view of the limited success of similar centres in other parts of the world. The Taworgha region was being colonized by the Italians until the early 1940's.

The Gebel el Akhdar project is a remarkable integrated plan to develop a whole region, consisting at present of 2,000 farms. The aim is also to convert semi-nomadic tribal groups from shifting cultivation to modern cereal farming and orchards. Eventually, 8,000 ha of land will be reclaimed and irrigated, fruit and nut trees will be planted, and hundreds of new houses, grain silos and water reservoirs will be built. There are also plans for forestry, road construction, and electrification of the whole district. The project was due to begin in 1974.

The Collina Verde (Hadaba el Khadra) project uses approximately six million gallons of purified sewage water from Tripoli each day to irrigate 600 ha supporting 100 farms. The chief products are fruit and vegetables for the local urban market, but the scheme also includes extensive tree planting and cereal production on a further 400 ha. There is a similar scheme in operation at Kawarsha, using purified sewage water from Benghazi.

The Kufra project is the best known of Libya's land reclamation schemes both on account of its scale and the wide interest shown in the possibilities for desert agriculture which it demonstrates.[19] The development of Kufra was originally initiated in 1968 by the Occidental Oil Company, following their discovery of huge quantities of groundwater in the region, but in 1972 the project was taken over by the government-owned Kufra Agricultural Company. The immediate aim is to reclaim and irrigate 10,000 ha, with possible further extension in future. The soils of Kufra are sandy but productive when fertilized and irrigated. One hundred wells have been drilled, each of which is the centre of a circle one km in diameter irrigated by an electrically controlled rotating sprinkler. These circles of 100 ha are principally used for the production of fodder for sheep. In 1972, there were 25,000 sheep, about one tenth of the projected size of the flock when complete. Eventually, Libya's northern cities will be supplied with mutton from Kufra, thus reducing the country's enormous meat imports. This huge experiment in large-scale commercial production in the desert is operated by a labour force of less than 450 men. The Kufra settlement project, now being implemented adjacent to the agricultural scheme (Figure 20.2), will have far more impact on the local population, since the aim is to resettle farmers from the outlying oases of Kufra. The settlement will eventually have a population of about 4,500.[20] El Jauf will be the major urban centre for the whole Kufra region, which in time could develop into an enterprise of significance for the whole Middle East.

There were also several large land reclamation schemes in the planning stage in 1973, including parts of the Gefara plains, Serir and Jalo in the eastern desert, amounting to 50,000 ha, and the southwestern Fezzan, where 30,000 ha are to be reclaimed. Reclamation schemes in progress in 1972 amounted

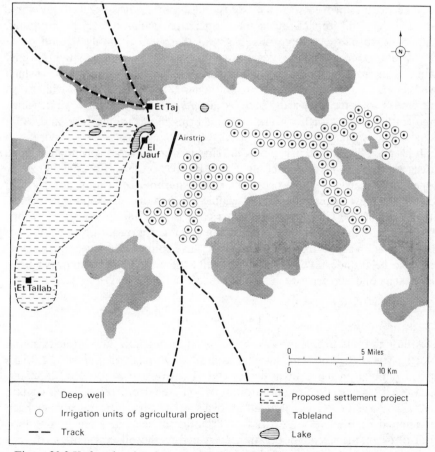

Figure 20.2 Kufra, showing the agricultural project and proposed settlement scheme
(Reproduced by permission of *Middle East International*)

to 100 to 200,000 ha, while those now being planned could add a further 400 to 500,000 ha. Altogether, more than one million ha of cultivable land remain for development. The availability of water will clearly be a critical factor in future projects, and water resource management figures prominently in agricultural planning. A number of dams and barrages are being built to store water and prevent flooding, seven of which were complete in 1973.

Large sums of money are being spent to improve existing farms, and every branch of agricultural production is being modernized with the best advice and equipment that money can buy. A countrywide campaign to combat pests has begun. Machinery is being provided for cooperatives by the government at half price, and maintenance workshops are being set up. Veterinary and extension services are now operating. In the field of research, a variety of experiments have been conducted, including attempts to induce rain by 'seeding' clouds. Long-term loans and credit are available to farmers, and marketing of all major crops is assisted by the government. All these developments, together with improved strains of seeds and imported livestock, will take time to have their full impact, but some farmers, particularly near the big cities, should be able to earn high incomes. But there will certainly remain many for whom farming will be less rewarding than urban employment. Many workers in the new factories can earn LD 900 to 1,000 per annum,[21] which would be a very good net income from the land. Farming in Libya will always be subject to natural hazards, such as the *ghibli*, a hot southerly wind, which frequently sweeps northern Tripolitania, bringing scorching heat and sand, dessicating cereals and other crops.

If between five and 10 per cent of the land is ever to become productive, large areas will have to be afforested or devoted to pastoralism. Forestry has developed only slowly, largely because of unfavourable conditions for trees in Libya, but new techniques should enable much more afforestation. In 1951, there were 459,000 ha of forest, compared with 532,000 ha in 1970.[22] In one experiment, sand dunes were halted after being sprayed with a coating of synthetic rubber and planted with eucalyptus saplings. Pasture improvement has also been undertaken with success, and there are plans to improve some 400,000 ha of desert pasture in the Sirte region

20.3 Urban growth

Although rapid urban growth has occurred throughout the Middle East and North Africa (Chapter 6), even in countries with no oil industry, Libya's urban population has grown almost entirely in response to the oil industry. Between 1954 and 1966 the urban population grew from 18 to 25 per cent;[23] in 1972 it was nearly 30 per cent. Libya's urban structure has always been dominated by the two large cities of Tripoli and Benghazi, which contained four-fifths of the urban population even before the oil era. This share has increased in recent years, and the two cities now contain over one quarter of the entire population. During the intercensal period 1954 to 1964, Tripoli grew from 130,000 to 213,000 and Benghazi from 70,000 to 137,000, an average annual growth rate of 6·3 per cent and 9·6 per cent respectively. These rates have fallen in recent years, but both towns continue to grow more rapidly than the natural rate of increase, as a result of migration.

During the first decade of the oil industry, Tripoli and Benghazi grew largely as a result of the mushrooming of an enormous tertiary sector in response to the needs of the industry. As the chief ports and administrative centres of the country, they could hardly escape these benefits. Transport, catering, retailing, construction, light engineering, and government services all created opportunities for employment, and migrants were drawn to the towns by the usual myths of fortunes to be made. In the early years, ugly shanty accommodation sprang up on the outskirts, but these have been largely replaced by modern housing estates. The secondary sector is now beginning to grow in these towns, and in spite of government plans to locate industry elsewhere whenever feasible, many of the latest developments are in or near Tripoli and Benghazi.

While the oil industry has had its chief impact in the large towns, most small urban centres have also been affected. All towns have been subject to some replanning and the provision of basic services. Many, like Misurata and Sebha, have grown as increasingly important regional centres. Of the settlements associated with the production and export of oil, only Marsa Brega has a permanent population of any size (4,500 in 1972). Indeed, the total number of persons employed in the petroleum industry is surprisingly small. After reaching a peak of 12,600 in 1963, the number had declined to 9,900 in 1973, although the proportion of Libyans had increased to 70 per cent.

20.4 Industrial development

Industries associated with petroleum were slow to develop in Libya, partly because of the high degree of expertise required for petrochemicals. A small refinery supplying all Libya's fuel oil and about half the country's petroleum products began operation at Marsa Brega in 1963, and a plant for liquefied natural gas opened there in 1969. A second refinery opened at Zavia in 1973 operated by the government controlled LINOCO. Crude oil is taken by coastal tanker to Zavia and refined products are piped 44 km to storage tanks near Tripoli. A third refinery is planned for Tobruk. A large petrochemical complex is to be constructed at Marisa, 30 km south of Benghazi. Other petrochemical developments for additional liquefied gas and methanol are planned for Marsa Brega, which will necessitate the construction of a proper harbour for the first time.

Besides making funds available for investment in manufacturing industry, the oil boom encouraged it in other ways, particularly by creating a demand for a whole range of hardware, and creating an urban population with money to spend on consumer goods. The first Five Year Plan of 1963 sought to expand and diversify manufacturing industry to meet local demands. By 1967, there

TABLE 20.5
Libya: some industrial projects completed or under construction
January 1971–December 1972

Industry	Location	Industry	Location
Dairying	Benghazi	Asbestos	Zanzur
	Zanzur	Bricks	Benghazi
Date processing	Hun	Cement	Benghazi
Fish canning	Tripoli		Homs
Flour milling	Tripoli, El Marj,	Ceramics and pottery	Gharian
	Sebha, Zuetina		
Fruit and vegetable	Tripoli	Lime	Benghazi
processing		Prefabricated housing	Tripoli
Sardine canning	Homs, Zanzur		Benghazi
	Zuara		
Tomato processing	Sebha	Cables and wire	Benghazi
Carpets	Misurata	Oil refinery	Zavia
Cotton and textiles	Zanzur	Petrochemicals	Marsa Brega
Leather	Tripoli	Scrap metal	Tripoli
Paper and boxes	Homs	Steel pipes	Benghazi
Shoes	Tripoli	Desalination plants	Zuetina
Woollen mill	Gebel al Akhdar		Jawara
			Tuara

Source: Middle East Economic Digest (weekly), 1971–1972.

were 587 industrial establishments employing 12,600 workers. The most important branches were food processing and chemicals, with metal work and light engineering taken together also important. Shoes, furniture and textiles were also represented. Manufacturing industry now accounts for about 10 per cent of the national income and employs about one sixth of the working population. The current 1973 to 1975 Development Plan will create over 60,000 additional jobs. The variety of industrial units established, particularly since 1970, is impressive, and almost all are soundly based on local raw materials. There have been relatively few failures, since Libya has the resources to conduct meticulous feasibility studies for such projects, and technical assistance has been sought from over a dozen countries.

Table 20.5 lists some of the industrial units completed or under construction with government funds in 1971 to 1972. There are, in addition, a large number of smaller units established by private enterprise with loans from the Industrial Bank. Among products proposed for the 1973 to 1975 Development Plan are iron and steel, tyres, bicycles and bottles. All this expansion has resulted in large imports of capital goods, causing serious congestion in the two major ports. Their expansion and modernization is under way and other minor ports are to be developed, notably at Casr Ahmed near Misurata and Marsa Brega.

20.5 Conclusion

It is scarcely an exaggeration to say that in less than a decade and a half the geographical face of Libya has been transformed, while in the next twenty years it could change beyond recognition. Nine-tenths of the land surface, it is true, remains unaffected by the activities of man, but in the populated regions, change is the keynote. With the decline of nomadism, the growth of the urban population, and schemes for the resettlement of cultivators, the population is undergoing gradual restructuring and redistribution. With the extension of irrigation, tree planting schemes, and the rehabilitation of ex-Italian farms, landscapes are undergoing visual and functional change. Similarly in the towns, modern and often costly redevelopment is replacing traditional townscapes. The need to create national unity is being met chiefly by improving communications. The network of surfaced roads (Figure 20.1) is being greatly extended and telephone systems and broadcasting and television transmitters have been installed to give national coverage. A series of airports is under construction, even in some of the remote oases. The ill-fated attempt to create a focus of national unity in a new capital at Beida was a costly mistake, but it is surprising that with so much wealth to spend there have been relatively few major failures of this kind.

Libyan oil has given the country considerable political influence, assisted by the favourable geopolitical position of Libya in relation to Europe, the Mediterranean Sea, and the Arab world.[24] Libya has exerted political pressure in countries such as Uganda, Chad, Malta, Sudan and Jordan, and a number of other groups, notably the Palestinians, are in receipt of Libyan funds. More significant however, is the possibility that the attraction of sharing Libya's oil revenues could eventually bring about an effective union with Egypt.[25] If successful, union might solve the one really major development problem remaining—shortage of manpower, particularly of highly qualified personnel which Egypt has in abundance. Libyan plans for agriculture, industry, tourism, and mining will require a labour force far beyond the country's capacity, even with increasing participation of women in economic activities. Thus Libya will have to rely on expatriate assistance for many years to come.

References

1. International Bank for Reconstruction and Development, *The Economic Development of Libya*, John Hopkins Press, Baltimore, 1960, 29.
2. R. G. Hartley, 'Libya: economic development and demographic response', in *The Populations of the Middle East and North Africa* (Ed. J. I. Clarke and W. B. Fisher), University of London Press, London, 1972, 319.
3. R. S. Harrison, 'Libya', *Focus*, **17**, 1 (November 1966).
4. J. D. Farrell, 'Libya strikes in rich', *Africa Report*, **12**, 8 (April 1967).
5. International Bank for Reconstruction and Development, *The Economic Development of Libya*, John Hopkins Press, Baltimore, 1960, 27.
6. W. B. Fisher, 'Problems of modern Libya', *Geogr. J.*, **119**, 183–199 (1953).
7. J. I. Clarke, 'Oil in Libya: some implications', *Econ. Geogr.*, **39**, 41 (1963).
8. G. Furlonge, 'Libya: putting the oil to work', *Middle East International*, No. 25, 9, (July 1973).
9. 'Crisis of confidence in Libya', *Petrol. Pr. Serv.*, **39**, 282 (August 1972).

502

10. 'Tough bargaining in Tripoli', *Petrol. Pr. Serv.*, **38,** 122 (April 1971).
11. 'Libya trade shows record surplus', *Middle East Economic Digest*, 1237–1239 (29 October 1971).
12. Ministry of Petroleum Affairs, *Libyan Oil 1954–1967*, Tripoli, 51, n.d.
13. 'Libya', *The Middle East and North Africa 1972–73*, Europa Publications London, 1972, 536.
14. 'Libya', *Middle East Economic Digest*, 606 (25 May 1973).
15. E. Penrose, J. A. Allan, & K. S. McLachlan (Eds.) *Agriculture and the Economic Development of Libya*, Universities of Libya and London, and British Petroleum, **1,** 1970, 11.
16. 'The Libyan Arab Republic', *The Times* (Supplement) 6 June 1973, 111.
17. Details of agricultural reclamation from *Middle East Economic Digest*, and Ministry of Information and Culture, *Achievements of the First of September Revolution*, Tripoli, 1972, 21–29.
18. See G. H. Blake, *Misurata, a Market Town in Tripolitania*, Department of Geography, University of Durham, Durham, 1968.
19. K. Atkinson, M. Bovis, and D. Johnson, 'Man-made oases of Libya', *Geogr. Mag.*, **45,** 112–115 (November 1972).
20. A. R. George, 'Kufra: the desert's hidden resources', *Middle East International* No. 25, 15–18 (July 1973).
21. Ministry of Information and Culture, *Achievements of the First of September Revolution*, Tripoli, 1972, 46–50.
22. United Nations, FAO, *Production Yearbooks*, Rome, **25,** 1971, 6 and **11** (i), 1957, 6.
23. R. G. Hartley, 'Libya: economic development and demographic response', in *The Populations of the Middle East and North Africa*, (Ed. J. I. Clarke and W. B. Fisher), University of London Press, London, 1972, 325.
24. S. A. Hajjaji, *The New Libya*, Ministry of Information and Culture, Tripoli, 1967, 5.
25. G. H. Blake, 'Desert marriage of convenience', *Geogr. Mag.*, **45,** 851–855 (September 1973).

Appendix

IMPORT AND EXPORT FIGURES FOR TEN MIDDLE EASTERN COUNTRIES, 1970

Source: Original figures from *The Middle East and North Africa, 1972–73* (Europa Publications Ltd., London, 1972), converted into U.S. Dollars, arranged in descending value and calculated as percentages.

Egypt		Value in million U.S. Dollars	Percentage of Total
Imports			
Machinery		142,700	17·6
Chemical products		104,700	12·9
Mineral products		86,200	10·6
Transport and equipment		81,200	10·0
Cereals and milling products		76,200	9·4
Iron and steel		62,200	7·7
Wood, hides and rubber textiles		59,700	7·4
Textiles		48,000	5·9
Animal and vegetable oils		42,200	5·2
Paper and paper products		30,500	3·8
General grocery		27,700	3·4
Tobacco		18,700	2·3
Crude petroleum		15,700	1·9
Pottery and glassware		8,500	1·0
Clocks, watches, scientific apparatus		7,000	0·9
	TOTAL	811,200	100·0
Exports			
Raw cotton		369,700	53·7
Cotton yarn		89,000	12·9
Rice		85,500	12·4
Crude oil		38,200	5·6
Edible fruits		36,700	5·3
Cotton piece goods		32,700	4·8
Onions		18,200	2·6
Potatoes		9,200	1·3
Cement		4,200	0·6
Manganese and phosphates		3,500	0·5
Benzine, kerosene and mazout		1,000	0·1
	TOTAL	687,900	100·0

Iran, 1969–1970		Value in million U.S. Dollars	Percentage of Total
Imports			
Boilers and other machinery		357,400	28·4
Iron and steel		272,200	21·7
Electrical machinery and apparatus		151,400	12·1
Motor vehicles and parts		138,600	11·1
Chemicals and pharmaceuticals		114,000	9·1
Textiles		99,400	7·9
Rubber and products		36,700	2·9
Paper, paperboard, etc.		36,700	2·9
Animal and vegetable fats		28,300	2·3
Wood and animal hair		13,000	1·0
Sugar and confectionary		5,900	0·5
Cereals		0,400	0·03
	TOTAL	1254,000	100·0
*Exports**			
Carpets		59,000	31·8
Raw cotton		49,300	26·5
Fruit		36,700	19·9
Hides and leather		16,800	9·0
Mineral ores		11,800	6·4
Oil-bearing seeds		6,200	3·0
Gum tragacanth		4,800	2·9
Wool		1,200	0·6
	TOTAL	185,800	100·0

Iraq

Imports			
Boilers and engines		96,000	45·1
Automobiles and parts		40,200	18·9
Sugar		26,400	12·4
Tea		20,200	9·5
Pharmaceuticals		18,300	8·6
Timber		9,700	4·5
Clothing		2,200	1·0
	TOTAL	213,000	100·0
*Exports**			
Dates		30,900	58·7
Cement		8,600	16·2
Hides and skins		5,700	10·7
Raw wool		5,100	9·7

*excluding petroleum

Iraq *(Contd.)*		Value in million U.S. Dollars	Percentage of Total
Barley		1,800	3·4
Raw cotton		0,600	1·1
Straw and fodder		0,100	0·2
	TOTAL	52,800	100·0

Israel

Imports			
Diamonds, rough		174,785	18·9
Boilers, machinery and parts		172,355	18·6
Iron and steel		133,705	14·4
Electrical machinery		88,368	9·6
Vehicles		87,569	9·4
Cereals		81,846	8·8
Textile and textile articles		64,609	7·0
Crude oil		64,568	7·0
Ships, boats, etc.		58,437	6·3
	TOTAL	926,442	100·0

Exports			
Diamonds, polished		244,543	43·5
Textiles and textile articles		102,278	18·2
Edible fats		97,941	17·4
Fruit and vegetable products		39,447	7·0
Fertilizers		25,552	4·5
Rubber, including synthetic		16,820	3·0
Organic chemicals		13,982	2·5
Resins and plastics		9,312	1·7
Plywood		6,673	1·2
Mineral products		5,356	1·0
	TOTAL	561,904	100·0

Jordan

Imports			
Grains and legumes	17,606	13·6
Clothing	13,899	10·6
Animals and products	12,967	10·1
Transport equipment	12,865	10·0
Non-electric machines	12,183	9·4
Textiles	10,361	8·0
Wood and cork	6,598	5·1
Electrical machinery	6,247	4·8

Jordan *(Contd.)*		Value in million U.S. Dollars	Percentage of Total
Petroleum (refined)		6,205	4·8
Fruits		5,465	4·2
Spices		4,834	3·7
Mining and quarrying products		3,840	3·0
Others		16,135	12·7
	TOTAL	129,205	100·0
Exports			
Phosphates		6,391	29·4
Vegetables and fruit		5,239	24·1
Tomatoes		4,485	20·7
Lentils		1,534	7·1
Cigarettes		1,483	6·8
Electric accumulators		868	4·0
Olive oil and prepared olives		603	2·8
Raw hides and skins		475	2·2
Bananas		422	1·9
Water melons		215	1·0
	TOTAL	21,715	100·0

Lebanon

Imports			
Precious metals, stones Jewellery and coins		136,810	22·6
Machinery and electrical apparatus		72,981	12·1
Vegetable products		72,381	12·0
Textiles and products		67,866	11·2
Non-precious metals and products		56,212	9·3
Industrial chemicals		46,601	7·7
Mineral products		41,059	6·8
Animals and animal products		40,900	6·8
Transport vehicles		39,368	6·5
Beverages and tobacco		29,962	5·0
	TOTAL	604,141	100·0
Exports			
Vegetable products		32,187	20·8
Machinery and electrical apparatus		21,262	13·7
Precious metals, stones, jewellery and coins		20,148	13·0
Textiles and products		18,527	12·1
Beverages and tobacco		17,721	11·4
Non-precious metals and products		17,245	11·1
Transport vehicles		15,628	10·1
Animals and animal products		12,067	7·8
	TOTAL	154,785	100·0

Libya		Value in million U.S. Dollars	Percentage of Total
Imports			
Machinery		243,210	37·6
Manufactures		141,280	21·8
Food and live animals		131,087	20·3
Beverages and tobacco		87,107	13·2
Mineral fuel		12,060	1·9
Animal and vegetable fats and oils		9,257	1·4
Chemicals		3,805	0·5
Inedible crude materials, including fuel		2,100	0·3
	TOTAL	646,806	100·0
Exports			
Crude petroleum		2,803,780	99·9
Others		2,317	0·1
	TOTAL	2,806,097	100·0

Saudi Arabia, 1969–1970

Imports			
Machinery and transport		247,000	37·7
Foodstuffs		209,000	31·9
Building materials		104,000	15·9
Chemical products		57,000	8·7
Textiles and clothing		38,000	5·8
	TOTAL	655,000	100·0
Exports			
Crude oil		1,835,000	85·3
Refined oil		315,000	14·7
	TOTAL	2,150,000	100·0

Syria

Imports		
Base metals and manufactures	48,000	20·4
Machinery, apparatus and electrical materials	40,000	16·7
Cereals	34,000	14·2
Cotton textiles, other textiles and silk	28,000	11·6
Mineral fuels and oils	25,000	10·6
Chemical and pharmaceutical products	17,000	7·1
Preserved food and beverages	16,000	6·7

Syria *(Contd.)*		Value in million U.S. Dollars	Percentage of Total
Vegetables and fruit		14,000	5·9
Vehicles		13,000	5·4
Lime, cement and salt		2,000	0·8
Oil seeds and medical plants		1,000	0·4
Precious metals and coins		1,000	0·4
	TOTAL	239,000	100·0
Exports			
Cotton (raw, yarn, textiles)		77,200	59·6
Live animals		16,500	12·8
Non-cotton textiles		13,000	10·1
Preserved foods, beverages and tobacco		11,000	8·5
Vegetables and fruit		5,600	4·3
Cereals		5,200	4·0
Dairy products		0,600	0·6
Precious metals		0,100	0·1
	TOTAL	129,200	100·0

Turkey

Imports			
Machinery		204,163	28·4
Chemicals		111,071	15·9
Base metals		95,904	13·3
Vehicles		72,185	10·0
Mineral products		55,898	7·8
Vegetable products		44,371	6·2
Animal and vegetable oils and fats		37,227	5·2
Textiles		29,161	4·0
Plastics and rubber		27,426	3·8
Paper-making material		14,094	1·9
Measuring instruments		13,024	1·8
Glassware and ceramics		6,806	0·9
Wood		2,574	0·3
Hides and skins		1,402	0·2
Live animals and animal products		1,273	0·2
Foodstuffs, beverage and tobacco		0,839	0·1
	TOTAL	717,418	100·0
Exports			
Cotton		147,932	37·2
Fruit and nuts		107,261	27·8
Tobacco		55,858	14·5
Iron, chrome, manganese and other ores		16,636	4·3
Cattle cake and foodstuff residues		16,235	4·2
Livestock		14,085	3·6
Oilseeds		8,237	2·1
Others		19,814	5·0
	TOTAL	386,058	100·0

Bibliography

Introduction

Adams, M. (Ed.) (1971).   *The Middle East: A Handbook*, Anthony Blond, London.

Bacon, E. E. (1946).   A preliminary attempt to determine the culture areas of Asia, *Southwestern Journal of Anthropology*, **2**, 117–132.

Bacon, E. E. (1953).   Problems relating to delimiting the culture areas of Asia, *Memoirs of the Society for American Archaeology*, **9**, 17–23.

Beckington, C. F. (1960).   *Atlas of the Arab World and the Middle East*, Djambatan, Amsterdam.

Birot, P. et J. Dresch (1955).   *La Méditerranée et le Moyen Orient*, 2 vols., Presses Universitaires de France, Paris.

Brice, W. C. (1966).   *South-West Asia*, University of London Press, London.

Chirol, V. (1903).   *The Middle East Question, or Some Political Problems of Indian Defence*, John Murray, London.

Coon, C. S. (1951).   *Caravan: The Story of the Middle East*, Henry Holt and Co., New York.

Cressey, C. B. (1960).   *Crossroads: Land and Life in South-West Asia*, Lippincott and Co., Chicago.

Daniel, N. (1960).   *Islam, Europe and Empire*, Edinburgh University Press, Edinburgh.

Davison, R. H. (1960).   Where is the Middle East? *Foreign Affairs*, **38**, 665–675.

Encyclopaedia of Islam, E. J. Brill, Leiden and Luzac and Luzac and Co., London, 1954.

English, P. W. (1973).   Geographical perspectives on the Middle East: the passing of the ecological trilogy. In M. W. Mikesell (Ed), *Geographers Abroad*, Department of Geography, Research Paper 152, Chicago, pp. 134–164.

Europa Publications (1973).   *The Middle East and North Africa, 1973–74*, 20th ed., Europa Publications, London.

Fisher, W. B. (1947).   Unity and diversity in the Middle East, *Geogrl Rev.*, **37**, 414–435.

Fisher, W. B. (1971).   *The Middle East*, 6th ed., Methuen, London.

Hale, G. A. (1969).   Maps and atlases of the Middle East, *Middle East Studies Association Bulletin*, **3**, 17–39.

Hogarth, D. G. (1902).   *The Nearer East*, William Heinemann, London.

Hopwood, D. and D. Grimwood-Jones (Eds). (1972).   *Middle East and Islam. A Bibliographical Introduction*, Bibliotheca Asiatica, 9.

Keddie, N. R. (1973).   Is there a Middle East? *International Journal of Middle Eastern Studies*, **4**, 255–271.

Landen, R. G. (1970).   *The Emergence of the Modern Middle East: Selected*

Readings, Van Nostrand-Reinholt, Princeton.

Le Lannou, M. (1966).   L'isthme du Proche et Moyen-Orient, *Revue Géogr. Lyon*, **41**, 289–302.

Laqueur, W. (1972).   *The Struggle for the Middle East. The Soviet Union and the Middle East*, Penguin, Harmondsworth.

Lewis, B. (1964).   *The Middle East and the West*, Weidenfeld and Nicolson, London.

Ljungqren, F. and M. Hamdy, (1964).   *Annotated Guide to Journals Dealing with the Middle East and North Africa*, American University of Cairo Press, Cairo.

Longrigg, S. H. and J. Jankowski (1970).   *The Middle East: A Social Geography*, Duckworth, London.

Lorraine, P. (1943).   Perspectives of the Near East, *Geogrl J.*, **102**, 6–13.

Manners, I. R. (1971).   The desert and the sown: an ecological appraisal of the Middle East, *Focus*, **22 (2)**, 1–8.

Mansfield, P. (Ed) (1973).   *The Middle East: A Political and Economic Survey*, Oxford University Press, London.

Martin, L. (1947).   The miscalled Middle East, *Geogrl Rev.*, **37**, 414–435.

Oxford Regional Economic Atlas (1960).   *The Middle East and North Africa*, Oxford University Press, London.

Patai, R. (1952).   The Middle East as a culture area, *Middle East Journal*, **6**, 1–21. Reprinted in A. M. Lutfiyya and C. W. Churchill, (Eds), *Readings in Arab Middle East Society and Culture*, Mouton, Paris and The Hague, 1970, pp. 187–204.

Patai, R. (1969).   *Golden River to Golden Road. Society, Culture and Technical Change in the Middle East*, 2nd ed., University of Philadelphia Press, Philadelphia.

Peretz, D. (1971).   *The Middle East Today*, 2nd ed., Holt, Rinehart and Winston, New York.

Reifenberg, A. (1958).   *The Struggle between the Desert and the Sown. Rise and Fall of Agriculture in the Levant*, Government Press, Jerusalem.

Smith, C. G. (1968).   The emergence of the Middle East, *Journal of Contemporary History* **3**, 3–17.

Chapter 1: Relief, Geology, Geomorphology and Soils

Asfia, S., E. B. Bailey and R. C. B. Jones (1948).   Notes on the geology of the Elburz mountains, north-east of Tehran, *Q. Jl geol. Soc. Lond.*, **104**, 1–42.

Atkinson, K. (1969).   The dynamics of Terra Rossa soils, *Bulletin of the Faculty of Arts, University of Libya*, **3**, 15–35.

Atkinson, K. (1970).   Fossil limestone soils in north-west Turkey, *Palaeogeography, Palaeoclimatology, Palaeoecology*, **8**, 29–35.

Barton, D. C. (1938).   The disintegration and exfoliation of granite in Egypt, *J. Geol.*, **46**, 109–111.

Beaumont, P. (1968).   Salt weathering on the margin of the Great Kavir, Iran, *Bull. geol. Soc. Am.*, **79**, 1683–1684.

Beaumont, P. (1972).   Alluvial fans along the foothills of the Elburz Mountains, Iran, *Palaeogeography, Palaeoclimatology, Palaeoecology*, **12**, 251–273.

Berry, L. (1961).   Large scale alluvial islands in the White Nile, *Revue Géomorph. dyn.*, **12**, 105–109.

Beug, H. J. (1967).   Contributions to the postglacial vegetational history of northern Turkey. In E. J. Cushing and H. E. Wright Jnr. (Eds), *Quaternary Palaeoecology*, Yale University Press, New Haven and London, pp. 349–356.

Birman, J. H. (1968). Glacial reconnaissance in Turkey, *Bull. geol. Soc. Am.*, **79**, 109–126.

Blandford, W. T. (1873). On the nature and probable origin of the superficial deposits in the valleys and deserts of Central Persia, *Q. Jl geol. Soc. Lond.*, **29**, 495–503.

Bobek, H. (1937). Die Rolle der Eiszeit in Nordwestiran, *Z. Gletscherk. Glacial geol.*, **25 S**, 130–183.

Bobek, H. (1959). *Features and Formation of the Great Kavir and Masileh*, Arid Zone Research Centre, University of Tehrān, Publication No. 2, Tehrān, 63 pages.

Bobek, H. (1963). Nature and implications of Quaternary climatic changes in Iran. In UNESCO & WMO Symposium, *Changes of Climate*, UNESCO, Rome, pp. 403–413.

Brown, G. F. (1960). Geomorphology of western and central Saudi Arabia, *Report 21st International Geological Congress*, Copenhagen, Pt. 21, pp. 150–159.

Brown, G. F. (1970). Eastern margin of the Red Sea and the coastal structures in Saudi Arabia, *Phil. Trans. R. Soc.*, *A*. **267**, 75–87.

Buringh, P. (1960). *Soils and soil conditions in Iraq*, Ministry of Agriculture, Republic of Iraq, Baghdād, 322 pages.

Butzer, K. W. (1958). *Quaternary stratigraphy and climate in the Near East*, Bonner Geogr. Abhandl. 24, 157 pages.

Butzer, K. W. (1959). Contribution to the Pleistocene geology of the Nile Valley, *Erdkunde*, **2**, 46–67.

Butzer, K. W. (1960). Archaeology and geology in ancient Egypt, *Science, N. Y.*, **132**, 1617–1624.

Butzer, K. W. (1960). On the Pleistocene shorelines of Arabs' Gulf, Egypt, *J. Geol.*, **66**, 626–637.

Butzer, K. W. (1965). Desert landforms at the Kur̄kur Oasis, Egypt, *Ann. Ass. Am. Geogr.*, **55**, 578–691.

Butzer, K. W. (1967). Late Glacial and Post Glacial Climatic Variation in the Near East, *Erdkunde*, **11**, 21–35.

Butzer, K. W. and C. L. Hansen (1965). On Pleistocene evolution of the Nile Valley in Southern Egypt, *Canadian Geographer*, **9**, 74–83.

Butzer, K. W. and C. L. Hansen (1967). Upper Pleistocene stratigraphy in Southern Egypt. In W. W. Bishop and J. D. Clark (Eds), *Background to African Evolution*, University of Chicago Press, Chicago, pp. 329–356.

Butzer, K. W. and C. L. Hansen (1968). *Desert and River in Nubia*, The University of Wisconsin Press, Madison, 562 pages.

Clapp, F. G. (1930). Tehran and the Elburz, *Geogrl Rev.*, **29**, 69–85.

Cooke, R. U. (1970). Stone pavements in Deserts, *Ann, Ass. Am. Geogr.*, **60 (3)**, 560–577.

Dan, J. and H. Koyumdjisky (1963). The soils of Israel and their distribution, *J. Soil Sci.*, **14**, 12–20.

Dewan, M. L. and J. Famouri (1964). *The Soils of Iran*, Food and Agricultural Organization, United Nations, Rome, 319 pages.

De Ridder, N. A. (1965). Sediments of the Konya Basin, central Anatolia, Turkey, *Palaeogeography, Palaeoclimatology, Palaeoecology*, **1**, 225–254.

512

Dietz, R. S. and J. C. Holden (1970).
The Breakup of Pangaea, *Scient. Am.*, **223**, 30–41.

Dresch, J. (1959).
Le piémont de Tehéran. In J. Dresch et al (Eds), Expedition de 1958 en Iran, *Bull. Ass. Géogr. fr.*, **284–285**, 35–64.

Elgabaly, M. M., I. M. Gewaifel, N. N. Hassan and B. G. Rozanov (1969).
Soil map and land resources of U.A.R., Institute of Land Reclamation, Alexandria University, Research Bulletin, No. 22, 14 pages.

Emery, K. O. (1960).
Weathering of the Great Pyramid, *J. sedim. Petrol.*, **30**, 140–143.

Evans, G. (1966).
The recent sedimentary facies of the Persian Gulf region, *Phil. Trans. R. Soc.*, A. **259**, 291–298.

Evans, I. S. (1969–1970).
Salt crystallization and rock weathering: a review, *Revue Géomorph. dyn.*, **No. 4, 19** Année, 153–177.

FAO (1968).
Definitions of Soil Units for the Soil Map of the World, Soil Map of the World: FAO/UNESCO Project, World Soil Resources Office, Land and Water Development division, FAO, Rome, 72 pages.

FAO (1970).
Key to Soil Units for the Soil Map of the World, FAO/ UNESCO Project, Soil Resources, Development and Conservation Service, Land and Water Development Division, FAO, Rome 16 pages.

Federov, P. V. (1969).
The marine terraces of the Black Sea Coast of the Caucasus and the problem of the most recent vertical movements, *Dokl. Acad. Nauk. U.S.S.R.*, **144**, 431–434, (In Russian).

Fleisch, H. and M. Gigout (1966).
Révue du Quaternaire marin Libanais, *Bull. Geol. Soc. France*, **8**, 10–16.

Fookes, P. G. and J. L. Knill (1969).
The application of engineering geology in the regional development of northern and central Iran, *Engineering Geology*, **3**, 81–120.

Freznel, B. (1959–60).
Die Vegetations und Landschaftszonen Nord-Eurasien während der letzten Eiszeit und während der postglazialen Wärmezeit, *Abh. Akad. Wiss. Liter, (Mainz) Math.-Naturw. Kl. 1959*, No. 13, 164 pages and 1960 No. 6, 167 pages.

Ghaith, A. M. and M. Tanious (1965).
Preliminary Soil Association Map of the United Arab Republic, Soil Department, Soil Survey Division, Ministry of Agriculture, U.A.R., Cairo, 9 pages.

Guilcher, A. (1955).
Géomorphologie de l'extrémité septentrionale du Banc Farsan (Mer Rouge), *Ann. Inst. Océanog.*, **30**, 55–100.

Hamdi, H. (1972).
The Soils of Egypt, Soil Science Society of Egypt, International Symposium on Salt Affected Soils, 4 pages.

Harrison, J. V. (1943).
The Jaz Murian depression, Persian Baluchistan, *Geogrl J.*, **101**, 206–225.

Harrison, J. V. and N. L. Falcon (1937).
The Saidmarreh landslip, Southwest Iran, *Geogrl J.*, **89**, 42–57.

Hey, R. W. (1971).
Quaternary Shorelines of the Mediterranean and Black Seas, *Quaternaria*, **15**, (VIII Congrés INQUA—Les Niveaux Marins Quaternaires II-Pleistocene), 273–284.

Hutchinson, G. E. and U. M. Cowgill (1963).
Chemical examination of a core from Lake Zeribar, Iran, *Science N. Y.*, **140**, 67.

Jelgersma, S. (1966).
Sea-level changes during the last 10,000 years. In,

World Climate from 8000 to 0 B.C., Royal Meteorological Society, London, 54–71.

Jenny, H. (1941). *Factors of Soil Formation*, McGraw-Hill Book Co., New York, 281 pages.

Jewitt, T. N. (1966). Soils of arid lands. In E. S. Hills (Ed), *Arid Lands— A Geographical Appraisal*, Methuen–UNESCO, pp. 103–125.

Kinsman, D. J. J. (1966). Gypsum and anhydrite of recent age, Trucial Coast, Persian Gulf, *Second Symposium on Salt*, 1, Northern Ohio Geological Society, Cleveland, Ohio, pp. 302–325.

Krinsley, D. B. (1968). Geomorphology of Three Kavirs in Northern Iran. In: J. T. Neal, (Ed), *Playa Surface Morphology: Miscellaneous Investigations*, USAF, Office of Aeorspace Research, Environmental Research Papers, No. 283, pp. 105–130.

Krinsley, D. B. (1970). *A Geomorphological and Palaeoclimatological Study of the Playas of Iran*, Parts I and II, Geological Survey, United States Department of the Interior, Washington D.C., 486 pages.

Krinsley, D. B. (1972). The paleoclimatic significance of the Iranian playas, *Palaeoecol. Afr.*, **6**, 114–120.

McKee, E. D. (1962). Origin of the Nubian and similar sandstones, *Geol. Rdsch.*, **52**, 551–587.

McKenzie, D. P. (1970). Plate tectonics of the Mediterranean Region, *Nature, Lond.*, **226**, 239–243.

McKenzie, D. P., D. Davies and P. Molnar (1970). Plate tectonics of the Red Sea and East Africa, *Nature, Lond.*, **226**, 243–248.

Messerli, B. (1966). Das Problem der eiszeitlichen Vergletscherung am Libanon und Hermon, *Z. Geomorph.*, **10 (1)**, 36–68.

Messerli, B. (1967). Die eiszeitliche und die gegenwärtige Vergletscherung im Mittelmerraum, *Geographica helv.*, **3**, 105–228.

Moorman, F. (1959). *The Soil of East Jordan*, FAO, Rome, Report, No. 1132.

Oakes, H. (1957). *The Soils of Turkey*, Republic of Turkey, Ministry of Agriculture, Soil Conservation and Farm Irrigation Division, Ankara, Division Publication No. 1, 180 pages.

Oberlander, T. M. (1965). *The Zagros Streams: A New Interpretation of Transverse Drainage in an Orogenic Zone*, Syracuse Geographical Series, Syracuse, No. 1, 168 pages.

Quennell, A. M. (1958). The structural and geomorphic evolution of the Dead Sea *rift*, *Q. Jl geol. Soc. Lond.*, **114**, 1–24.

Ravikovitch, S. (1960). *Soils of Israel—Classification of the Soils of Israel*, (In Hebrew—English summary), The Hebrew University of Jerusalem, Faculty of Agriculture, Rehovot, Israel, 89 pages.

Reifenberg, A. (1947). *The Soils of Palestine*, (Translated by C. L. Whittles), London, Thomas Murby & Co., 179 pages.

Rieben, E. H. (1955). The geology of the Tehran Plain, *Am. J. Sci.*, **253**, 627–639.

Rieben, E. H. (1960). *Les terrains alluviaux de la région de Tehran*, Arid Zone Research Centre, University of Tehran, Publication No. 4, 41 pages.

Rieben, E. H. (1966). *Geological Observations on Alluvial Deposits in Northern Iran*, Geol. Surv. Iran, Report 9, 41 pages.

Sanlaville, P. (1967). Sur les niveaux marins quaternaires de la région de

514

| | Tabarja (Liban), *Comptes Rendues. Somm. Soc. Geol. Fr.*, 157–158. |

Sanlaville, P. (1971). Sur le Tyrrhènien Libanias, *Quaternaria*, **15** (VIII, Congrès INQUA—Les Niveaux Marins Quaternaires), 11–Pleistocene, pp. 239–248.

Scharlau, K. (1958). Zum Problem der Pluvialzeiten in nordost Iran, *Z. Geomorph.*, **2**, 258–277.

Sharon, D. (1962). Hammadas in Israel, *Z. Geomorph.*, **6**, 12–147.

Soil Survey Staff, Soil Conservation Service, United States Department of Agriculture (1960). *Soil Classification: A Comprehensive System (7th Approximation)*, U.S. Government Printing Office, Washington D.C.

Stevens, J. H. (1969). Quaternary events and their effect on soil development in an arid environment—The Trucial States, *Quaternaria*, **10**, 73–81.

Takin, M. (1972). Iranian geology and continental drift in the Middle East, *Nature, Lond.*, **235**, 147–150.

Van Liere, W. J. (1961). Observations on the Quaternary of Syria, *Ber. Rijkdienst oudheidk. Bodemonderz.*, **10–11**, 1–69.

Vita-Finzi, C. (1968). Late Quaternary alluvial chronology of Iran, *Geol. Rdsch.*, **58**, 951–973.

Vita-Finzi, C. (1969). *Mediterranean Valleys*, Cambridge University Press, Cambridge, 140 pages.

Wellman, H: W. (1966). Active wrench faults of Iran, Afghanistan and Pakistan, *Geol. Rdsch.*, **55**, 716–735.

Wright, H. E. (1961). Pleistocene glaciation in Kurdistan, *Eiszeitalter Gegenw.*, **12**, 131–164.

Wright, H. E. (1962). Late Pleistocene geology of coastal Lebanon, *Quaternaria*, **6**, 525–540.

Yaalon, D. H. (1970). Parallel stone cracking, a weathering process on desert surfaces, *Geological Institute Technical and Economical Bulletins*, Series C, Pedology No. 18, Bucharest, 107–111.

Zeist, W. van and H. E. Wright Jnr. (1963). Preliminary pollen studies at Lake Zeribar, Zagros Mountains, southwestern Iran *Science, N.Y.*, **140**, 65–69.

Chapter 2: Climate and Water

Aberbach, S. H. and A. Sellinger (1967). Review of artificial groundwater recharge in the coastal plain of Israel, *Bull. int. Ass. scient. Hydrol.*, **12**, 65–77.

Addison, H. (1959). *Sun and Shadow at Aswan*, Chapman & Hall, London, 166 pages.

Aelion, E. (1958). A report on weather types causing marked storms in Israel during the cold season, *Israel Meteorological Service*, Series C. Miscellaneous Papers 10, 7 pages.

Al-Khashab, W. H. (1958). *The Water Budget of the Tigris-Euphrates Basin*, University of Chicago, Department of Geography, Research Paper, No. 54, 105 pages.

Amiran, D. H. K. and M.Gilead, (1954). Early excessive rainfall and soil erosion in Israel, *Israel Explor. J.*, **4**, 286–295.

Arab Report and Record, (1970). Dam devastates Mediterranean fishing, *Arab Report and Record*, Issue 23, 1–15 December, p. 677.

Arab Republic of Egypt, Ministry of Culture & Information, State Information Service, (1972).
The High Dam, State Information Office, Cairo, Egypt, 54 pages.

Arad, A. (1966).
Hydrogeochemistry of groundwater in central Israel, *Bull. int. Ass. scient. Hydrol.*, **11**, 122–146.

Atkinson, K., M. Bovis and D. Johnson (1972).
Man-made oases of Libya, *Geogrl Mag.*, **45**, 112–115.

Austin, E. E. and D. Dewar (1953).
Upper Winds Over Mediterranean and Middle East, Great Britain, Meteorological Research Committee, MRP. 811, 10 pages.

Barbour, K. M. (1957).
A new approach to the Nile Waters problems, *International Affairs*, **33**, 319–330.

Baum, W. A. and L. B. Smith (1953).
Semi-monthly mean sea-level pressure maps for the Mediterranean area, *Arch. Met. Geophys. Bioklim.*, *Serie A: Meterologie und Geophysik*, **5**, 326–345.

Beaumont, P. (1968).
Qanats on the Varamin Plain, Iran, *Trans. Inst. Br. Geogr.*, **45**, 169–179.

Beaumont, P. (1968).
The Road to Jericho: A climatological traverse across the Dead Sea lowlands, *Geography*, **53**, 170–174.

Beaumont, P. (1971).
Qanat systems in Iran, *Bull. int. Ass. scient. Hydrol.*, **16**, 39–50.

Beaumont, P. (1973).
River Regimes in Iran, Department of Geography, University of Durham, Occasional Publications, New Series No. 1, 29 pages.

Beaumont, P. (1973).
A Traditional method of groundwater extraction in the Middle East, *Ground Water*, **11**, 23–30.

Beaumont, P. (1974).
New uses for ancient water. In Saudi Arabia—Financial Times Survey, *The Financial Times*, London, June 10th.

Beaumont, P. (1974).
Water resource development in Iran, *Geogrl J.*, **140**, 418–431.

Beckett, P. H. T. (1951).
Waters of Persia, *Geogrl Mag.*, **24**, 230–240.

Beckett, P. H. T. (1952).
Qanats in Persia, *Iran Society Journal*, London, **1**, 125–133.

Beckett, P. H. T. (1953).
Qanats around Kirman, *Jl R. cent. Asian Soc.*, **40**, 47–58.

Beckett, P. H. T. and E. D. Gordon (1956).
The climate of Kerman, south Persia, *Q. Jl R. met. Soc.*, **82**, 503–514.

Bell, B. (1970).
The oldest records of the Nile floods, *Geogrl J.*, **136**, 569–573.

Bémont F. (1961).
L'irrigation en Iran, *Annls Gèogr.*, **70**, 597–620.

Bleeker, W. (Ed), (1960).
The UNESCO/WMO Seminar on Mediterranean Synoptic Meteorology, Rome 24th November–13th December 1958, Frien Universität, Berlin, Institut für Meteorologie und Geophysik, Meteorologische, Abhandlungen. Vol. 9, 226 pages.

Brawer, M. (1968).
The geographical background of the Jordan water dispute. In C. A. Fisher (Ed), *Essays in Political Geography*, Methuen, London, pp. 225–242.

Bromehead, C. E. N. (1942).
The early history of water supply, *Geogrl J.*, **99**, 142–151 and 183–195.

Budyko, M. I., N. A. Yefimova, L. I. Aubenok and L. A. Strokina (1962).
The heat balance of the surface of the earth, *Soviet Geogr.*, **3**, 3–16.

Butzer, K. W. (1960). Dynamic climatology of large-scale European circulation patterns in the Mediterranean area, *Met. Rdsch.*, **13**, 97–105.

Cantor, L. M. (1967). *A World Geography of Irrigation*, Praeger, New York and Washington, 252 pages.

Caponera, D. A. (1954). *Water Laws in Moslem Countries*, FAO, Rome, Agricultural Development Paper, No. 43, 202 pages.

Carter, D. B., C. W. Thornthwaite and J. R. Mather (1958). *Three Water Balance Maps of Southwest Asia*, Publs. Clim. Drexel. Inst. Technol., **11**, 57 pages.

Caton-Thompson, G. and E. W. Gardner (1939). Climate, irrigation and early man in the Hadhramaut, *Geogrl J.*, **93**, 18–38.

Cederstrom, D. J. (1971). Ground water in the Aden Sector of Southern Arabia, *Ground Water*, **9 (2)**, 29–34.

Clapp, G. R. (1957). Iran, a TVA for the Khuzestan Region, *Middle East Journal*, **11**, 1–11.

Colvin, I. (1964). Sharing the water of the Jordan, *Jl R. cent. Asian Soc.*, **51**, 245–250.

Cressey, G. B. (1957). Water in the desert, *Ann. Ass. Am. Geogr.*, **47**, 105–124.

Cressey, G. B. (1958). Qanats, karez and foggaras, *Geogrl Rev.*, **48**, 27–44.

Duvdevani, S. (1964). Dew in Israel and its effects on plants, *Soil Sci.*, **98**, 14–21.

Ebert, C. H. V. (1965). Water resources and land use in the Qatif oasis of Saudi Arabia, *Geogrl Rev.*, **55**, 496–509.

Eldblom, L. (1967). Notes on the problems of irrigation in three Libyan Oases, *Ekistics*, **24 (137)**, 199–202.

El-Fandy, M. G. (1952). Forecasting thunderstorms in the Red Sea, *Bull. Am. met. Soc.*, **33**, 332–338.

English, P. W. (1968). The origin and spread of qanats in the old world, *Proc. Am. phil. Soc.*, **112**, 170–181.

Field, M. (1973). Developing the Nile, *Wld Crops*, **25**, 11–15.

Fitt, R. L. (1953). Irrigation development in central Persia, *Jl R. cent. Asian Soc.*, **40**, 124–133.

Flohn, H. (1965). *Contributions to a Synoptic Climatology of the Red Sea, Trench and Adjacent Territories*, University of Bonn, Institute of Meteorology, U.S. Department of Army Contract No. DA 91–591-EUC-3201, Technical Report, 33 pages.

Flower, D. J. (1968). Water use in North-East Iran. In W. B. Fisher (Ed), *The Cambridge History of Iran*, Vol. 1, Cambridge University Press, Cambridge, pp. 599–610.

Ffrench, G. E. and A. G. Hill (1971). *Kuwait: Urban and Medical Ecology*, Geomedical Monograph Series, No. 4 Geomedical Research Unit of the Heidelberg Academy of Sciences, Springer-Verlag, Berlin, 124 pages.

Gabriel, K. R. (1965). *The Israel Artificial Rainfall Stimulation Experiment, An interim Statistical Evaluation of Results*, Hebrew University, Department of Statistics, Jerusalem, Israel, 23 pages.

Ganji, M. H. (1955). The climates of Iran, *Société Royale de Géographique d'Egypt Bulletin*, **28**, 195–299.

Gilead, M. and N. Rosenan, (1954). Ten years of dew observation in Israel, *Israel Explor. J.*, **4**, 120–123,

Gleeson, T. A. (1953). Cyclogenesis in the Mediterranean region, *Arch. Met.*

	Geophys. Bioclim., Serie A. Meteorologie und Geophysik, **6**,.153–171.
Gleeson, T. A. (1956).	A comparison of cyclone frequencies in the North Atlantic and Mediterranean regions, *Arch. Met. Geophys. Bioclim., Serie A. Meteorologie und Geophysik,* **9**, 185–190.
Goblot, H. (1962).	Le Problème de l'eau en Iran, *Orient,* **23**, 43–60.
Gordon, A. H. and J. G. Lockwood, (1970).	Maximum one day falls of precipitation in Tehran, *Weather, Lond.,* **25**, 2–8.
Hare, F. K. (1961).	The causation of the arid zone. In *A History of Land-use in Arid Lands,* Arid Zone Research, Vol. 17, UNESCO, Paris, pp. 35–50.
Hollingworth, C. (1971).	Egypt's Aswan balance-sheet, *The Times, London,* 15 January.
Holz, R. K. (1968).	The Aswan High Dam, *Prof. Geogr.,* **20**, 230–237.
Houseman, J. (1961).	Dust haze at Bahrain, *Met. Mag.,* **19**, 41–51.
Hurst, H. E. (1952).	*The Nile,* London, Constable, 326 pages.
Ionides, M. G. (1937).	*The Regime of the Rivers Euphrates and Tigris,* E. & F. Spon, London, 255 pages.
Israel Embassy, (1964).	*Israel Water Project,* Washington D. C.
Jiabajee, N. A. (1957).	Saudi Arabia—water supply of important towns, *Pakist. J. Sci.,* **9**, 189–201.
Johns, R. (1970).	The Aswan High Dam—power for war torn Egypt, *The Financial Times, London,* 23rd July.
Kanter, H. (1967).	*Libya,* Vol. 1, Geomedical Monograph Series, Geomedical Research Unit of the Heidelberg Academy of Sciences, Springer-Verlag, Berlin, 188 pages.
Kassas, M. (1971).	The river Nile ecological system: A study towards an international programme, *Biological Conservation,* **4**, 19–25.
Katnelson, J. (1964).	The variability of annual precipitation in Palestine, *Archiv für Meteorologie, Geophysik und Bioklimatologie, Serie B,* **13**, 163–172.
Kenyon, K. (1969).	The origins of the Neolithic, *Advmt Sci., Lond.,* **26**, 144–160.
Khalaf, J. M. (1956).	The climate of Iran, *Union Géographique International Congrès International de Géographie, 18ᵉ, Rio de Janeiro, 1956, Comptes Rendus,* **2**, 507–525.
Knill, J. L. and K. S. Jones, (1968).	Groundwater conditions in greater Tehran, *Quaterly Journal of Engineering Geology,* **1**, 181–194.
Lamb, H. H. (1972).	*Climate: Present, Past and Future, Vol.* 1, *Fundamentals of Climate Now,* Methuen, London, 613 pages. The
Levi, M. (1963).	dry winter of 1962–63; a synoptic analysis, *Israel Explor. J.,* **13**, 229–241.
Little, T. (1965).	*High Dam at Aswan,* Methuen, London, 242 pages.
Little, T. (1971).	Why cry havoc at Aswan? *Middle East International,* June **No. 3**, 5–6.
Lloyd, J. W. (1965).	The hydrochemistry of the aquifers of North-Eastern Jordan, *Journal of Hydrology,* **3**, 319–330.
Lomas, J. (1972).	Forecasting wheat yields from rainfall data in Iran, *World Meteorological Organisation Bulletin,* **21**, 9–14.
Lowdermilk, W. C. (1944).	*Palestine—Land of Promise,* Victor Gollancz, London, 167 pages.

Main, C. T. (1953). — The Unified Development of the Water Resources of the Jordan Valley Basin, Boston, Massachusetts.

McCaull, J. (1969). — Conference on the ecological aspects of international development, Nature and Resources, (UNESCO), 5, 5–12.

Meigs, P. (1964). — Classification and occurrence of Mediterranean-type dry climate. In Land Use in Semi-arid Mediterranean Climates, UNESCO, Paris, Arid Zone Research, v. 26, 17–21.

Meteorological Office, (1962). — Weather in the Mediterranean, Vol. 1, (Second edition), General Meteorology, Her Majesty's Stationery Office, London, 362 pages.

Ministry of Information, Tehrān, Iran (1970). — Nationalisation of Water Resources of Iran, Tehrān, 20 pages.

Murray, G. (1951). — The water beneath the Egyptian desert, Geogrl J., 117, 422–434.

Murray, G. W. (1951). — The Egyptian climate: an historical outline, Geogrl J., 117, 422–434.

Murray, R. (1960). — Mean 200-millibar winds at Aden in January 1958, Met. Mag., 89, 156–157.

Noel, E. (1944). — Qanats, Jl R. cent. Asian Soc., 31, 191–202.

Oppenheimer, H. R. (1951). — Summer drought and water balance of plants growing in the Near East, J. Ecol., 39, 356–362.

Orsenan, N. (1963). — Climatic fluctuations in the Middle East during the period of instrumental record. In Changes of Climate, UNESCO, Arid Zone Research, Vol 20, 67–74.

Otkun, G. (1969). — "... and the search for supplies underground is extensive", The Financial Times, London, June 23rd, 1969.

Otkun, G. (1970). — A thirsty nation looks underground, The Financial Times, London, December 28th, 1970.

Otkun, G. (1969). — Outlines of Ground Water Resources of Saudi Arabia, Presented at International Conference on Arid Lands in a Changing World, Tucson, Arizona, U.S.A., June 3rd–13th, 1969, 16 pages.

Pedgley, D. E. and P. M. Symmons (1968). — Weather and the locust upsurge, Weather, Lond., 23, 484–492.

Penman, H. L. (1948). — Natural evaporation from open water, bare soil and grass, Proc. R. Soc. Series A., 193, 120–145.

Perrin de Brichambaut, G. and C. C. Wallén (1963). — A Study of Agroclimatology in Semi-arid and Arid zones of the Near East, World Meteorological Organisation, Technical Note No. 56, Geneva, 64 pages.

Plan Organisation (1969). — Dam Construction in Iran, Bureau of Information and Reports, Tehran, 87 pages.

Prushansky, Y. (1967). — Water Development, Israel Digest, Israel Today, No. 11, Jerusalem, 40 pages.

Raikes, R. L. (1967). — Water, Weather and Prehistory, John Baker, London, 208 pages.

Ramage, C. S. (1966). — The summer atmospheric circulation over the Arabian Sea, Journal of Atmospheric Sciences, 23, 144–150.

Ramaswamy, C. (1965). — On a remarkable case of dynamical and physical interaction between middle and low latitude weather systems over Iran, Indian J. Met. Geophys., 16, 177–200.

Ray Choudhuri, A. N., — A climatological study of storms and depressions in

Y. H. Subramanyan and R. Cehllappa (1959). the Arabian Sea, *Indian J. Met. Geophys.*, **10**, 283–290.

Rieben, E. H. (1953). *Les Resources en Eaux Souterraines de la Plaine Alluviale de Tehran*, FAO, rapport No. 168, Rome, 18 pages.

Rosenthal, S. L. and T. A. Gleeson (1959). Sea-level anticylcogenesis affecting Mediterranean weather, *Arch. Met. Geophys. Bioklim.*, *Serie A*, *Meteorologie und Geophysik*, **9**, 185–190.

Royal Meteorological Society, (1966). *World Climate from 8000 to 0 B.C.* Royal Meteorological Society, London, 229 pages.

Scott, K. F., W. T. N. Reeve and J. P. Germond (1968). Farahnaz Pahlavi dam at Latiyan, *Proc. Instn civ. Engrs*, **39**, 353–395.

Serjeant, R. B. (1964). Some irrigation systems in Hadramaut, *Bulletin of the School of Oriental and African Studies*, **27**, 33–76.

Sherbrook, W. C. and P. Paylore (1973). *World Desertification: Cause and Effect*, Arid Lands Resource Information Paper No. 3., University of Arizona, Office of Arid Lands Studies, Tucson, Arizona, 168 pages.

Sivall, T. (1957). Sirocco in the Levant, *Geogr. Annlr.*, **39**, 114–142.

Smith, C. G. (1966). The disputed waters of the Jordan, *Trans. Inst. Br. Geogr.*, **40**, 111–128.

Smith, C. G. (1970). Water resources and irrigation development in the Middle East, *Geography*, **55**, 407–425.

Stevens, J. H. (1972). Oasis agriculture in the central and eastern Arabian Peninsula, *Geography*, **57**, 321–326.

Storke, C. (1959). Evapotranspiration problems in Iraq, *Neth. J. agric. Sci.*, **7**, 269–282.

Striem, H. L. (1967). Rainfall groupings in the Middle East, *Bull. int. Ass. scient. Hydrol.*, **11**, 59–64.

Taylor, G. (1955). *Australia*, Methuen, London, 490 pages.

Thatcher, L., M. Rubin and G. Brown (1961). Dating desert·ground water, *Science, N.Y.*, **134**, 105.

Thornthwaite C. W. and J. R. Mather (1957). *Instructions and Tables for Computing the Potential Evapotranspiration and the Water Balance*, Publs. Clim. Drexel. Inst. Technol., Vol. 10, 311 pages.

Thornthwaite, C. W., J. R. Mather and D. B. Carter (1958). *Three Water Balance Maps of South-West Asia*, Publs. Clim. Drexel, Inst. Technol., Vol 11, 57 pages.

Twisleton-Wykeham-Fiennes, D. (1970). Sweet water for the hottest land, *Geogrl Mag.*, **42**, 889–893.

Twitchell, K. S. (1944). Water resources of Saudi Arabia, *Geogrl Rev.*, **34**, 365–386.

UNESCO/FAO (1963). *Bioclimatic Map of the Mediterranean Zone*, Explanatory notes, UNESCO, Paris, Arid Zone Research, Vol. 21, 58 pages.

UNESCO/FAO (1963). *Environmental Physiology and Psychology in Arid Regions*, Reviews of Research, Aric Zone Research, Vol. 22, UNESCO, Paris, 345 pages.

UNESCO/FAO (1963). *Changes of Climate*, Arid Zone Research, Vol. 20, UNESCO, Paris, 488 pages.

UNESCO (1969). *Discharge of Selected Rivers of the World (Vol. 1)*, UNESCO–IASH, Paris, 70 pages.

UNESCO (1971). *Discharge of Selected Rivers of the World (Vol. 2)*, *Monthly and Annual Discharges Recorded at Various*

520

	Selected Stations (from start of observations up to 1964), UNESCO, Paris, 194 pages
UNESCO (1971).	*Discharges of Selected Rivers of the World (Vol. 3), Mean Monthly and Extreme Discharges (1965–1969)*, (Part 1), UNESCO, Paris, 98 pages.
United Arab Republic, Ministry of the High Dam, Aswân High Dam Authority (1972).	*Aswan High Dam—Commissioning of the First Units— Transmission of Power to Cairo*, Ministry of the High Dam, Aswân, Egypt, 76 pages.
United Arab Republic, Information Department (1963).	*The High Dam—Bulwark of our Future*, Information Department, Cairo, 36 pages.
Vahidi, M. (1968).	*Water and Irrigation in Iran*, Plan Organisation and Bureau of Information and Reports, Tehrān, 79 pages.
Van Riper, J. E. (1971).	*Man's Physical World*, McGraw-Hill, New York 713 pages.
Weickmann, L. (1961).	*Some Characteristics of the Sub-tropical Jet Stream in the Middle East and Adjacent Regions*, Meteorological Department, Iran, Meteorological Publications, Series A, No. 1, 29 pages.
Weickmann, L. (1963).	Meteorological and hydrological relationships in the drainage area of the Tigris River north of Baghdad, *Met. Rdsch.*, **16**, 33–38.
Wiener, A. (1972).	*The Role of Water in Development*, McGraw-Hill, New York, 483 pages.
Wilcox, L. V. (1955).	*Classification and Use of Irrigation Waters*, U.S. Dep. Agric. Circular No. 969, Washington, 29 pages.
Wittfogel, K. A. (1956).	The hydraulic civilisation. In W. L. Thomas (Ed), *Man's Role in Changing the Face of the Earth*, University of Chicago Press, Chicago, pp. 152–164.
World Meteorological Organisation (1964).	*High-level forecasting for turbine-engined aircraft operations over Africa and the Middle East*, Proc. of the Joint ICAO/WMO Seminar, Cairo-Nicosia 1961, World Meteorological Organisation, Technical Note 64.
Wulff, H. E. (1968).	Qanats of Iran, *Scient. Am.*, **218**, 94–105.

Chapter 3: Landscape Evolution

Abu-Lughod, J. (1972).	*Cairo: 1001 Years of the City Victorious*, Princeton University Press, Princeton.
Adams, R. M. (1960).	Factors influencing the rise of civilisation in the alluvium illustrated by Mesopotamia. In C. H. Kraeling and R. M. Adams (Eds), *City Invincible. A Symposium on Urbanism and Cultural Development in the Ancient Near East*, University of Chicago Press, Chicago and London, 1960, pp. 24–34.
Adams, R. M. (1962).	Agriculture and urban life in early south-western Iran, *Science, N.Y.*, **136**, 109–122.
Adams, R. M. (1965).	*Land Behind Baghdad. A History of Settlement on the Diyala Plains*, University of Chicago Press, Chicago and London.
Aharoni, Y. (1968).	*The Land of the Bible: An Historical Geography*, Burns and Oates, London.
Atlas des Centuriations romaines de Tunisie, Institut Geographiques National, Paris, 1954.	

Baradez, J. (1949). *Fossatum Africae*, Arts et Métiers Graphiques, Paris.

Benevisti, M. (1970). *Crusaders in the Holy Land*, Israel Universities Press, Jerusalem.

Boserup, E. (1965). *The Conditions of Agricultural Growth: The Economics of Agrarian Change under Population Pressure*, Allen and Unwin, London.

Braidwood, R. J. and C. A. Reed, (1957). The achievement and early consequences of food production: a consideration of the archaeological and natural–historical evidence, *Cold Springs Symposium on Quantitative Biology*, **22**, 19–31.

Brice, W. C. and A. N. Balci (1955). The history of forestry in Turkey, *Orman Fakültesi Dergisi İstanbul Üniversitesi*, **5**, 19–42.

Butzer, K. W. (1961). Archaelogy and geology in ancient Egypt, *Science, N.Y.*, **132**, 1617–1624.

Butzer, K. W. (1972). *Environment and Archaeology*, 2nd ed., Methuen, London.

Caillemer, A. et R. Chevalier, (1954). Les centuriations romaines de l'Africa vetus, *Annales, E.S.C.*, **9**, 433–460.

Caillemer, A. et R. Chevalier, (1957). Centuriations romaines de Tunisie, *Annales, E.S.C.*, **12**, 275–286.

Clark, J. D. (1962). The spread of food production in sub-Saharan Africa, *Journal of African History*, **3**, 211–228.

Clark, J. D. (1964). The prehistoric origins of African culture, *Journal of African History*, **5**, 161–183.

Clark, J. D. (1967). *Atlas of African Prehistory*, University of Chicago Press, Chicago and London.

Cuinet, V. (1890–94). *La Turquie d'Asie. Géographie Administrative, Statisique, Déscriptive et Raisonée de Chaque Provence de l'Asie Mineure*, 4 vols., Ernest Leroux, Paris.

Despois, J. (1961). Development of land use in northern Africa. In L. D. Stamp (Ed), *A History of Land Use in Arid Regions*, Arid Zone Research, Vol. 17, UNESCO, pp. 219–237.

Dostal, W. (1959). The evolution of bedouin life. In F. Gabrielli (Ed), *L'Antica Società Bedounia, Studi Semitici* No. 2, Centro de Studi Semitici, Universita di Roma, Rome, pp. 11–34.

Edwards, I. E. S., C. J. Gadd, and N. G. L. Hammon, (Eds) (1970). *The Cambridge Ancient History*, 3rd ed., Vol. 1, Cambridge University Press, London.

Eisma, D. (1962). Beach ridges near Selçuk, Turkey, *Tijdschr.K.ned.aardrijksk. Genoot.*, **79**, 234–246.

English, P. W. (1966). *City and Village in Iran. Settlement and Economy in the Kirman Basin*, University of Wisconsin Press, Madison.

Fisher, S. N. (1968). *The Middle East: A History*, 2nd ed., Knopf, New York.

Fowler, G. L. (1972). Italian colonisation of Tripolitania, *Ann. Ass. Am. Geogr.*, **62**, 627–640.

Frank, T. (Ed), (1933–40). *An Economic History of Ancient Rome*, 5 vols., John Hopkins, Baltimore.

Goodwood, R. G. (1952a). Farming in Roman Libya, *Geogrl Mag.*, **25**, 70–80.

Goodwood, R. G. (1952b). The mapping of Roman Libya, *Geogrl J.*, **118**, 142–152.

Grünebaum, G. E. von, (1955). The Muslim town and the Hellenistic town, *Scientia*, **90**, 364–370.

Hachicho, M. A. (1964). English travel books about the Arab Near East in the eighteenth century, *Die Welt der Islam*, **9**, 1–206.

522

Hamdan, G. (1961).   Evolution of irrigation agriculture in Egypt. In L. D. Stamp (Ed), *A History of Land Use in Arid Regions, Arid Zone Research*, Vol. 17, UNESCO, 119–142.

Harris, D. R. (1967).   New light on plant domestication and the origins of agriculture: a review, *Geogrl Rev.*, **57**, 90–107.

Hasan, M. S. (1958).   Growth and structure of Iraq's population, 1867–1947, *Bull. Oxf. Univ. Inst. Statist.*, **20**, 339–352.

Hershlag, Z. Y. (1964).   *Introduction to the Economic History of the Middle East*, E. J. Brill, Leiden.

Heyd, U. (1960).   *Ottoman Documents on Palestine, 1552–1615*, Oxford University Press, London.

Higgs, E. S. and M. R. Jarman (1969).   The origins of agriculture: a reconsideration, *Antiquity*, **43**, 31–41.

Holt, P. M., A. K. S. Lambton, and B. Lewis (Eds) (1970–71).   *The Cambridge History of Islam*, 2 vols., Cambridge University Press, London.

Hourani, A. (1957).   The changing face of the Fertile Crescent in the eighteenth century, *Studia Islamica*, **8**, 89–122.

Hütteroth, W. (1962).   Getreidekonjunktur und jüngerer Siedlungsausbau im südlichen Inneranatolien, *Erdkunde*, **16**, 249–271.

Hütteroth, W. (1969).   Schwankungen von Siedlungsdichte und Siedlungsgrenze in Palästina und Transjordanien seit dem 16 Jahrhundert, *Deutscher Geographentag. Kiel 21–26 Juli*, pp. 463–475.

Isaac, E. (1970).   *Geography of Domestication*, Prentice-Hall, Englewood Cliffs, N.J.

Issawi, C. (Ed) (1966a).   *The Economic History of the Middle East, 1800–1914*, University of Chicago Press, Chicago and London.

Issawi, C. (1966b).   *Egypt in Revolution: An Economic Analysis*, Oxford University Press, London.

Jacobsen, T. and R. M. Adams, (1958).   Salt and silt in ancient Mesopotamia, *Science, N.Y.*, **128**, 1251–1257.

Jones, A. H. M. (1966).   *The Decline of the Ancient World*, Longmans, London.

Knight, M. M. (1952–53).   Economic space for Europeans in French North Africa, *Economic Development and Cultural Change*, **1**, 360–375.

Kraeling, C. H. and R. M. Adams, (Eds) (1960).   *City Invincible. A Symposium on Urbanism and Cultural Development in the Ancient Near East*, University of Chicago Press, Chicago and London.

Lamb, H. H. (1968).   Climatic background to the birth of civilisation, *Advmt Sci., Lond.*, **25**, 103–120.

Lebon, J. H. G. (1955).   The new irrigation era in Iraq, *Econ. Geogr.*, **31**, 47–59.

Le Strange, G. (1890).   *Palestine under the Muslims: A Description of Syria and the Holy Land from A.D. 650 to 1500*, Palestine Exploration Fund, London.

Lewis, N. E. (1949).   Malaria, irrigation and soil erosion in central Syria, *Geogrl Rev.*, **39**, 278–290.

Lewis, N. E. (1955).   The frontier of settlement in Syria, 1800–1950, *International Affairs*, **31**, 48–60.

Lombard, M. (1959).   Les bois dans la Méditerranée musulmane, *Annales, E.S.C.*, **14**, 234–254.

Margalit, H. (1964).   Some aspects of the cultural landscape of Palestine during the first half of the nineteenth century, *Israel Explor. J.*, **13**, 208–223.

Marthelot, P. (1965).   Bagdād: notes de géographie humaine, *Annls Géogr.*, **74**, 24–37.

Matson, F. R. (1966).   Power and fuel resources in the ancient Near East, *Advmt Sci., Lond.*, **23**, 146–153.

Mikesell, M. W. (1955).   Notes on the dispersal of the dromedary, *Southwestern Journal of Anthropology*, **11**, 231–245.

Mikesell, M. W. (1969).   The deforestation of Mount Lebanon, *Geogrl Rev.*, **58**, 1–28.

Owen, E. R. J. (1969).   *Cotton and the Egyptian Economy, 1820–1914: A Study in Trade and Development*, Oxford University Press, London.

Proudfoot, V. B. (1971).   Man's occupance of the soil. In R. H. Buchanan, E. Jones and D. McCourt (Eds), *Man and his Habitat. Essays presented to Emyr Estyn Evans*, Routledge and Kegan Paul, London, pp. 8–37.

Reifenberg, A. (1958).   *Struggle between the Desert and the Sown: Rise and Fall of Agriculture in the Levant*, Government Press, Jerusalem.

Rosenam, N. (1963).   Climatic fluctuations in the Middle East during the period of instrumental record. In *Changes in Climate. Proceedings of the Rome Symposium Organised by UNESCO and the World Meteorological Organisation, Arid Zone Research*, Vol. 20, UNESCO, pp. 67–73.

Rostovtzeff, M. I. (1941).   *The Social and Economic History of the Hellenistic World*, 3 vols., Oxford University Press, London.

Rowton, M. B. (1967).   The woodlands of ancient Asia, *Journal of Near Eastern Studies*, **26**, 261–277.

Russell, R. J. (1954).   Alluvial morphology of Anatolian rivers, *Ann. Ass. Am. Geogr.*, **44**, 363–391.

Thomas, W. L. (Ed) (1956).   *Man's Role in Changing the Face of the Earth*, Chicago University Press, Chicago and London.

Tignor, R. L. (1966).   *Modernisation and British Colonial Rule in Egypt, 1882–1914*, Princeton University Press, Princeton.

Ucko, P. J. and G. W. Dimbleby (Eds) (1970).   *The Domestication and Exploitation of Plants and Animals*, Duckworth, London.

Ucko, P. J., R. Tringham and G. W. Dimbleby, (Eds) (1972).   *Man, Settlement and Urbanism*, Duckworth, London.

Vita-Finzi, C. (1969).   *The Mediterranean Valleys. Geological Changes in Historical Times*, Cambridge University Press, London.

Volney, M. C. F. (1786).   *Voyage en Syrie et en Egypte pendant les années 1783, 1784 et 1785*, 2 vols., Desenne and Volland, Paris.

Whyte, R. O. (1961).   Evolution of land use in south-western Asia. In L.D. Stamp (Ed), *A History of Land Use in Arid Regions, Arid Zone Research*, Vol. 17, UNESCO, pp. 57–118.

Wright, H. E. (1968).   Natural environment of early food production north of Mesopotamia, *Science, N. Y.*, **161**, 334–339.

Chapter 4: Rural Land Use: Patterns and Systems

Allan, J. A., K. S. McLachlan and E. T. Penrose (Eds) (1973).   *Libya: Agriculture and Economic Development*, Frank Cass, London.

Baer, G. (1964).   *Population and Society in the Arab East*, Routledge and Kegan Paul, London.

Beaumont, P. (1968).   Qanats in the Varamin Plain, *Trans. Inst. Br. Geogr.*, **45**, 169–180.

524

Beckett, P. H. T. (1953). Qanats around Kerman, *Jl R. cent. Asian Soc.*, **40**, 47–57.

Bensidoun, S. (1970). *Les Modes d'aménagement des Terroirs et le Dynamisme de la Civilisation de l'Oasis*, Armand Colin, Paris.

Bharier, J. (1972). The growth of towns and villages in Iran, 1900–66, *Middle East Studies*, **8**, 51–62.

Caponera, D. A. (1954). *Water Laws in Moslem Countries*, FAO Development Paper No. 43, FAO, Rome.

Clawson, M., H. H. Landsberg and L. T. Alexander (1971). *The Agricultural Potential of the Middle East*, American Elsevier Publishing Co., New York, London, Amsterdam.

Crist, R. (1957–60). Land for the fellahin, *American Journal of Economics and Sociology*, **17**, 21–30, 157–166; **18**, 83–90, 193–201, 313–320, 415–428; **19**, 81–91, 207–216, 311–322, 427–433; **20**, 118–126.

Eldblom, L. (1961). *Quelques Points de Vue Comparatifs sur les Problèmes d'Irrigation dans les Trois Oases Libyennes de Brâk, Ghadamès et particulièrement Mourzouk*, Lund Studies in Geography No. 22, Royal University of Lund, Sweden.

English, P. E. (1967). Urbanites, peasants and nomads: the Middle Eastern ecological trilogy, *J. Geogr.*, **61**, 54–59.

Filali, M. al, (1967). Sedentarisation and land problems. In M.R. el Ghomemy (Ed), *Land Policy in the Near East*, FAO, Rome, pp. 38–52.

Fattah, F. (1972). Farming cooperatives in Egypt, *World Marxist Review*, **18**, 96–99.

Freivalds, J. (1972). Farm corporations in Iran: an alternative to traditional agriculture, *Middle East Journal*, **26**, 185–194.

Ghonemy, M. R. el (1967). The economic and social development of nomadic populations before and after settlement. In M.R. el Ghonemy (Ed), *Land Policy in the Near East*, FAO, Rome, pp. 317–326.

Ghonemy, M. R. El (1968). Land reform and economic development in the Near East, *Land Econ.*, **44**, 36–49.

Goblot, H. (1963). Dans l'ancien Iran, les techniques de l'eau et la grande histoire, *Annales, E.S.C.*, **18**, 499–520.

Ibrahim, A. (1968). Classification and characteristic patterns of rural settlements (Egypt), *Mediterranea*, **23–24**, 332–345.

Issawi, C. (1971). Growth and structural change in the Middle East, *Middle East Journal*, **25**, 309–324.

Hinderink, J. and M. B. Kiray (1970). *Social Stratification as an Obstacle to Development. A Study of Four Turkish Villages*, Praeger, New York, Washington and London.

Hütteroth, W. (1971). Anadolu'da sosyal yapinin arazi bölünumesi ve iskân üzerindeki etkileri. In *Türkiye: Coğrafi ve Sosyal Araştırmalar*, pp. 55–86.

Johnson, D. L. (1969). *The Nature of Nomadism. A Comparative Study of Pastoral Migrations in Southwestern Asia and Northern Africa*, Department of Geography, Research Paper No. 118, Chicago.

Kolars, J. (1966). Locational aspects of cultural ecology: the case of the goat in non-western agriculture, *Geogrl Rev.*, **56**, 577–584.

Kolars, J. F. (1967).   Types of rural development. In F. C. Shorter, J. F. Kolars, D. A. Rustow and O. Yenal (Eds), *Four Studies on the Economic Development of Turkey*, Frank Cass, London, pp. 63–87.

Latron, A. (1936).   *La Vie Rurale en Syrie et au Liban*, Beirūt.

Mitchell, W. A. (1971).   Turkish villages in interior Anatolia and von Thünen's "Isolated State"; a comparative analysis, *Middle East Journal*, **25**, 355–369.

Nieuwenhuijze, C. A. O. van (1962).   The Near Eastern village: a profile, *Middle East Journal*, **16**, 295–308.

Noel, E. (1944).   Qanats, *Jl R. cent. Asian Soc.*, **31**, 191–202.

O'Brien, P. (1966).   *The Revolution in Egypt's Economic System, from Private Enterprise to Socialism, 1952–1965*, Oxford University Press, London.

Planhol, X.de (1968).   Geography of settlement. In W. B. Fisher (Ed), *The Cambridge History of Iran*, Vol. 1, *The Land of Iran*, Cambridge University Press, London.

Raphaeli, N. (1966).   Agrarian reform in Iraq: some political and administrative problems, *Journal of Administration Overseas*, **5**, 102–111.

Ron, Z. (1966).   Agricultural terraces in the Judean mountains, *Israel Explor. J.*, **16**, 33–49; 111–122.

Shanin, T. (Ed) (1971).   *Peasants and Peasants Societies*, Penguin Books, Harmondsworth.

Smith, C. G. (1970).   Water resources and irrigation development in the Middle East, *Geography*, **55**, 407–425.

Stauffer, T. R. (1965).   The economics of nomadism in Iran, *Middle East Journal*, **22**, 284–302.

Tanoglu, A. (1954).   The geography of settlement, *Rev. geogr. Inst. Univ. Istanb.*, **1**, 3–27.

Taylor, D. C. (Ed) (1968).   *Research on Agricultural Development in Selected Middle Eastern Countries*, Agricultural Development Council, New York.

Tuma, E. H. (1970).   Agrarian reform and urbanisation in the Middle East, *Middle East Journal*, **24**, 163–177.

Tümertekin, E. (1962).   Some maps of agricultural holdings in Turkey, *Prof. Geogr.*, **14**, 21–22.

Turkowski, L. (1969).   Peasant agriculture in the Judean hills, *Palestine Exploration Quaterly*, **101**, 21–33, 101–112.

Tute, R. C. (1927).   *The Ottoman Land Laws*, Jerusalem.

Vieille, P. (1972).   Les paysans et l'état après le reforme agraire en Iran, *Annales, E.C.S.*, **27**, 347–372.

Warriner, D. (1962).   *Land Reform and Development in the Middle East*, 2nd Ed., Oxford University Press, London.

Weulersse, J. (1946).   *Paysans de Syrie et du Proche Orient*, Gallimard, Paris.

Wulff, H. E. (1966).   *The Traditional Crafts of Persia*, M.I.T. Press, Cambridge, Mass. and London.

Chapter 5: Population

Amani, M. (1972).   La population de l'Iran, *Population*, **27**, 411–418.

Barkan, O. L. (1958).   Essai sur les données statistiques des registres de recensemement dans L'Empire Ottoman aux XVe et XVle siècles, *J. Econ. Soc. Hist. Orient*, **1**, 9–36.

Bharier, J. (1972). Growth of towns and villages in Iran, *Middle East Studies*, **8**, 51–61.

Clarke, J. I. and W. B. Fisher (Eds) (1972). *Populations of the Middle East and North Africa*, University of London Press, London.

Clarke, J. I. (1971). *Population Geography and the Developing Countries*, Pergamon, Oxford.

El-Badry, M. A. (1965). Trends in the components of population growth in the Arab countries of the Middle East: a survey of present information, *Demography*, **2**, 140–186.

English, P. W. (1967). Urbanites, peasants and nomads: the Middle East ecological trilogy, *J. Geogr.*, **66**, 54–59.

Etterna, W. A. (1970). Female fertility in the Kingdom of Jordan: a statistical analysis, *Tijdschr. econ. Geogr.*, **61**, 195–206.

George, A. R. (1973). Processes of sedentarisation of nomads in Egypt, Israel and Syria, *Geography*, **48**, 167–169.

Hartley, R. G. and J. M. Norris, (1969). Demographic regions in Libya, *Tijdschr. econ. Geogr.*, **60**, 221–227.

Hill, A. (1969). The population of Kuwait, *Geography*, **54**, 84–88.

Holler, J. E. (1964). *Population Growth and Social Change in the Middle East*, George Washington University, Washington.

Hourani, A. H. (1947). *Minorities in the Arab world*, Oxford University Press, Oxford.

Hurewitz, J. C. (1963). The politics of rapid population growth in the Middle East, *Journal of International Affairs*, **19**, 26–38.

Lebon, J. H. G. (1953). Population distribution and the agricultural regions of Iraq, *Geogr. Rev.* **43**, 223–228.

May, J. M. and I. S. Jarcho, (1961), *The Ecology of Malnutrition in the Far and Near East*, Hafner, New York.

McClure, H. A. (1971). *The Arabian Peninsula and Prehistoric Populations*, Field Research Projects, Coconut Grove, Florida.

Mitchell, W. A. (1971). Turkish villages in interior Turkey and von Thünens "Isolated State": a comparative analysis, *Middle East Journal*, **25**, 355–369.

Nieuwenhuijze, C. A. O. van (1962). The near eastern village: a profile, *Middle East Journal*, **16**, 295–308.

Patwardhan, V. N. and W. J. Darby, (1972). *The State of Nutrition in the Arab Middle East*, Vanderbilt University, Nashville.

Percial, D. A. (1949). Some features of a peasant population in the Middle East, *Popul. Stud.* **5**, 192–204.

Phillips, D. G. (1959). Rural to urban migration in Iraq, *Economic Development and Cultural Change*, **7**, 405–421.

Ritter, G. (1972). Landflucht und Städtewachstum in der Türkei, *Erdkunde*, **XXVI**, 177–196.

Rondot, P. (1959). The minorities in the Arab Orient today, *Middle East Affairs*, **10**, 214–228.

Shnaiberg, A. (1970). Rural–urban residence and modernism: a study of Ankara province, *Demography*, **2**, 71–85.

Stechman, S. (1965). Map of population distribution in Libya. *Africana Bulletin*, No. 3, Polish Institute of African Studies, Warsaw.

United Nations (1969). Notes on some demographic characteristics. In *Studies on Selected Development Problems in Various Countries of the Middle East*, New York, pp. 47–69.

United Nations (1970). Demographic characteristics of youth in the Arab

	countries: present situation and growth prospects. In *Studies on Selected Development Problems in Various Countries of the Middle East*, New York, pp. 71–103.
United Nations (1971).	Population distribution and urbanisation in selected countries of the Middle East. In *Studies on Selected Development Problems in Various Countries of the Middle East*, New York, pp. 59–78.
Vallin, J. (1970).	Les populations de l'Afrique du Nord du Sahara, Maroc, Algérie, Tunisie, Libye, Egypte, *Population*, **25**, 1212–1235.
Waal, E. H. van de (1968).	Setting in Silifke, Turkey, *Tijdschr. econ. Geogr.*, **59**, 347–358.
Wickwar, W. H. (1965).	Food and social development in the Middle East, *Middle East Journal*, **19**, 177–193.
Yaukey, D. (1970).	Fertility differences in a modernising country. In *Readings in Arab Middle East societies and cultures*, (Ed. A. M. Lutfiyya and C. W. Churchill), Mouton, The Hague, pp. 162–167.

Chapter 6: Towns and Cities

Geographical studies of individual towns and cities are not given here, though a number of useful articles and monographs have been published, particularly on major cities.

Amin, G. A. (1972).	*Urbanisation and Economic Development in the Arab World*, Beirūt Arab University, Beirut, 38 pages.
Azeez, M. M. (1968).	Geographical Aspects of Rural Migration from Amara Province, Iraq, 1955–1964. Ph.D. thesis, University of Durham, Durham, England. (Source of Figure 6.9).
Benet, F. (1963).	The ideology of Islamic urbanisation. *International Journal of Contemporary Sociology*, **4**, 221–226.
Brown, L. C. (Ed) (1972).	*From Madina to Metropolis: Heritage and Change in the Near Eastern City*, Darwin Press, Princeton, New Jersey, 343 pages.
Berger, M. (Ed) (1963).	*The New Metropolis in the Arab World*, Allied Publishers, New York.
Chandler, T. and G. Fox (1974).	*3,000 Years of Urban Growth*, Academic Press, New York and London.
Clark, B. D. and V. F. Costello (1973).	The urban system and social patterns in Iranian cities, *Trans. Inst. Br. Geogr.*, **59**, 99–128.
Costello, V. F. (1973).	The industrial structure of a traditional Iranian city, *Trans. Inst. Br. Geogr.*, **64**, 108–120.
Darwent, D. F. (1965).	Urban Growth in Relation to Socio-economic Development and Westernisation. A Case Study of the City of Mashhad, Iran. Ph.D. thesis, University of Durham, Durham, England (Source of Figure 6.5).
de Planhol, X. (1968).	Geography of settlement. In W. B. Fisher (Ed), *Cambridge History of Iran: The Land of Iran*, Vol. 1, Cambridge University Press, Cambridge, pp. 438–440.
Dunham, D. (1960).	The courtyard house as a temperature regulator. *New Scient.*, **8**, 663–666.
English, P. W. (1966).	*City and Village in Iran: Settlement and Economy in*

528

	the *Kirman Basin*, University of Wisconsin Press Madison.
Fowler, G. L. (1972).	Development of city size distributions for the Egyptian urban system 1897–1960, *Prof. Geogr.*, **24**, 317–320.
French, G. E. and A. G. Hill (1971).	*Kuwait: Urban and Medical Ecology*, Geomedical Monograph Series No. 4, Springer-Verlag, Berlin.
Gordon-Childe, V. (1950).	The urban revolution, *Town Plann. Rev.*, **21**, 3–17.
Hamdan, G. (1962).	The patterns of medieval urbanism in the Arab world, *Geography*, **47**, 121–133.
Hassan, R. (1972).	Islam and urbanisation in the medieval Middle East, *Ekistics*, **33**, 108–112.
Hourani, A. H. and S. M. Stern (Eds) (1970).	*The Islamic City*, Bruno Cassirer, Oxford.
Ismail, A. A. (1972).	Origin, ideology and physical patterns of Arab urbanisation, *Ekistics* **33**, 113–123.
Lampl, P. (1971).	*Cities and Planning in the Ancient Near East*, Studio Vista Ltd., London.
Landay, S. (1971).	The ecology of Islamic cities: the case for the ethnocity, *Econ. Geogr.*, **47**, 303–313.
Lapidus, I. M. (Ed) (1969).	*Middle Eastern Cities*, University of California, Berkeley and Los Angeles.
Lebon, J. H. G. (1970).	The Islamic City in the Near East, a comparative study of Cairo, Alexandria and İstanbul, *Town Plann. Rev.*, **41**, 179–194.
Mallowan, M. E. L. (1967).	The development of cities from Al 'Ubaid to the end of Uruk 5, *Cambridge Ancient History*, Vol. 1, Cambridge University Press, Cambridge, Chapter VIII.
Sauvaget, J. (1941).	*Alep*. (Album), Librairie Orientaliste Paul Geunther, Paris (Source of Figure 6.3).
Shiber, G. S. (1968).	*Recent Kuwait City Growth*, Kuwait Planning Board, Kuwait.
Shiber, G. S. (1964).	*The Kuwait Urbanisation*, Kuwait Planning Board, Kuwait.
Shnaiberg, A. (1970).	Rural-urban residence and modernism: a study of Ankara Province, *Demography*, **7**, 71–83.
Spiegal, E. (1967).	*New Towns in Israel*, Praeger, Stuttgart and Bern.
Tuma, E. H. (1970).	Agrarian reform and urbanisation in the Middle East, *Middle East Journal*, **24**, 163–177.
United Nations Economic and Social Office in Beirut (1973)	Problems and policy implications of Middle East urbanisation. In *Studies on Selected Development Problems in Selected Countries of the Middle East 1972*, New York, pp. 42–63.
United Nations Economic and Social Office in Beirut (1971).	Population distribution and urbanisation. In *Studies on Selected Development Problems in Various Countries of The Middle East*, New York, pp. 59–78.
Wirth, E. (1966).	Damaskus–Aleppo–Beirut; Ein geographischer Vergleich dreir nahöstlicker Städte im Spiegel ihrer sozial und wirtschaftlich tonangebenden Schichten, *Erde*, **97**, 96–137.

Chapter 7: Problems of Economic Development

| Abdel-Malek, A. (1970). | Sociology and economic history: an essay on mediation. In M. A. Cook (Ed), *Studies in the Economic History* |

of the Middle East, Oxford University Press, London, pp. 268–282.

Agarwala, A. N. and S. P. Singh (Eds) (1963). *The Economics of Underdevelopment*, Oxford University Press, New York.

Alonso, W. (1963–69). Urban and regional imbalances in economic development, *Economic Development and Cultural Change*, **17**, 1–14.

Amiran, D. H. K. (1965). Arid zone development: a reappraisal under modern technological conditions, *Econ. Geogr.*, **41**, 189–210.

Baali, F. (1966). Social factors in Iraqi rural-urban migration, *American Journal of Economics and Sociology*, **25**, 359–364.

Baali, F. (1969). Agrarian reform in Iraq: some socio-economic aspects, *American Journal of Economics and Sociology*, **28**, 61–76.

Boserup, E. (1965). *The Conditions of Agricultural Growth: The Economics of Agrarian Change under Population Pressure*, Allen and Unwin, London.

Clark, C. and M. Haswell (1964). *The Economics of Subsistence Agriculture*, Macmillan, London.

Clarke, J. I. (1968). World population and food resources: a critique. In *Land Use and Resources: Studies in Applied Geography*, Institute of British Geographers, Special Publication 1, pp. 53–70.

Clarke, J. I. (1973). Population in movement. In M. Chisholm and B. Rogers (Eds), *Studies in Human Geography*, Heinemann, London, pp. 85–124.

Cooper, C. A. and S. S. Alexander (Eds) (1972). *Economic Development and Population Growth in the Middle East*, American Elsevier Publishing Co., New York, London, Amsterdam.

Dresch, J. (1966). Utilisation and human geography of the deserts, *Trans. Inst. Br. Geogr.*, **40**, 1–10.

Dwyer, D. J. (1968). The city in the developing world and the example of South-east Asia, *Geography*, **53**, 353–364.

Elkan, W. (1973). *An Introduction to Development Economics*, Penguin Books, Harmondsworth.

Flinn, P. (1968). The impact of the technological era, *Journal of Contemporary History*, **3**, 53–68.

George, P., R. Grigliolino, B. Kayser, et Y. Lacoste, (Eds) (1964). *La Géographie Active*, Presses Universitaires de France, Paris.

Hershlag, Z. Y. (1964). *Introduction to the Modern Economic History of the Middle East*, E. J. Brill, Leiden.

Hershlag, Z. Y. (1970). *Contemporary Economic Structure of the Middle East*, 2nd ed., E. J. Brill, Leiden.

Holler, J. E. (1964). *Population Growth and Social Change in the Middle East*, George Washington University, Washington, D.C.

Hütteroth, W. (1962). Getreidkonjunktur und jüngerer Siedlungsausbau im südlichen Inneranatolien, *Erdkunde*, **16**, 249–271.

Issawi, C. (1971). Growth and structural change in the Middle East, *Middle East Journal*, **25**, 309–324.

Jansen, A. C. M. (1970). The value of the growth pole theory for economic geography, *Tijdschr. econ. soc. Geogr.*, **61**, 67–76.

Joyce, J. (1972). Planning prospects in the Middle East, *Contemporary Review*, **220**, 113–117.

530

Kammash, M. el (1968).   *Economic Development and Planning in Egypt*, Praeger, New York, Washington and London.

Kanovsky, E. (1968).   The economic aftermath of the Six Day War, *Middle East Journal*, **22**, 131–143, 278–296.

Kuznets, S. (1971–72).   Problems of comparing recent growth rates for developed and less-developed countries, *Economic Development and Cultural Change*, **20**, 185–209.

Magnarella, P. J. (1970).   From villagers to townsmen in Turkey, *Middle East Journal*, **24**, 229–240.

Myrdal, G. (1957).   *Economic Theory and Underdeveloped Regions*, Duckworth, London.

Ortiz, S. R. de (1972).   *Uncertainties in Peasant Farming*, Athlone Press, London.

Shorter, F. C. (1966).   The application of development hypotheses in Middle Eastern studies, *Economic Development and Cultural Change*, **14**, 340–354.

Ward, R. J. (1970).   The long run employment prospects for Middle East labour, *Middle East Journal*, **24**, 147–162.

Wheeler, G. (1972).   Factors in the process of modernisation in Asian countries, *Asian Affairs*, **59**, 41–46.

Wickwar, W. H. (1965).   Food and social development in the Middle East, *Middle East Journal*, **19**, 177–195.

Chapter 8: Industry and Trade

Abdo, A. S. (1970).   Domestic passenger air transport in Saudi Arabia, *Bulletin of the Faculty of Arts, University of Riyadh*, **1**, 21–39.

Barbour, K. M. (1972).   *The Growth, Location and Structure of Industry in Egypt*, Praeger, New York, Washington and London.

Boxer, B. (1967).   *Israeli Shipping and Foreign Trade*, University of Chicago, Department of Geography, Research Papers, No. 48, Chicago.

Chapman, A. S. (1957).   The economic regions of Turkey as characterised by railway shipments, *Northwestern University Studies in Geography*, (Evanston. Ill.), **2**, 71–75.

Cohen, E. J. (1970).   *Turkish Economic, Social and Political Change: The Development of a More Prosperous and Open Society*, Praeger, New York, Washington and London.

Collard, E. (1972).   Trade relations between the E.E.C. and the Arab World, *Middle East International*, **14**, 16–20.

Edens, D. G. and W. P. Snavely, (1970).   Planning for economic development in Saudi Arabia, *Middle East Journal*, **24**, 16–30.

Eldem, V. (1953).   Turkey's transportation, *Middle Eastern Affairs*, **4**, 324–336.

Encle, W. (1966).   Iraks Industrieentwicklung in Problemen und Zielen, *Orient (Hamburg)*, **7**, 115–120.

Garnick, D. H. (1961).   Regional integration and economic development in the Middle East, *Middle Eastern Affairs*, **12**, 294–300.

Ginsburg, N. (1961).   *Atlas of Economic Development*, University of Chicago Press, Chicago and London.

Grunwald, K. and J. O. Ronall, (1960).   *Industrialisation in the Middle East*, Council for Middle Eastern Affairs Press, New York.

Hindle, P. (1966).   Aqaba: an old port revived, *Geogrl J.*, **132**, 64–68.

Hunter, G. (1952).   The Middle East Supply Centre. In G. Kirk (Ed), *The Middle East in the War*, Oxford University Press, London, pp. 163–193.

Issawi, C. (1963).   *Egypt in Revolution: An Economic Analysis*, Oxford University Press, London.

Issawi, C. (Ed) (1966).   *The Economic History of the Middle East, 1800–1914*, University of Chicago Press, Chicago and London.

Issawi, C. (1967).   Iran's economic upsurge, *Middle East Journal*, **21**, 447–461.

Kammash, M. M. el (1968).   *Economic Development and Planning in Egypt*, Praeger, New York, Washington and London.

Kanovsky, E. (1967).   Arab economic unity, *Middle East Journal*, **21**, 213–235.

Karmon, Y. (1963).   Eilath, Israel's Red Sea port, *Tijdschr. econ. soc. Geogr.*, **54**, 117–126.

Karmon, Y. (1966).   Ashdod: a new Mediterranean port, *Geography*, **51**, 254–258.

Kerwin, R. W. (1950).   The Turkish roads programme, *Middle East Journal*, **4**, 196–208.

Kleiman, E. (1967).   The place of manufacturing in the growth of the Israeli economy, *Journal of Development Studies*, **3**, 226–248.

Kolars, J. F. (1964).   Types of rural development. In F. C. Shorter, J. F. Kolars, D. A. Rustow and O. Yenal (Eds), *Four Studies on the Economic Development of Turkey*, Frank Cass, pp. 63–88.

Kolars, J. F. and   Population and accessibility: an analysis of Turkish
  H. J. Malin, (1970).   railroads, *Geogrl Rev.*, **60**, 229–246.

Kreinin, M. (1968).   Israel and the European Economic Community, *Quart. J. of Econ.*, **82**, 297–312.

Langley, K. M. (1961).   *The Industrialisation of Iraq*, Harvard University Press, Cambridge, Mass.

Mabro, R. E. (1971).   Industrialisation. In M. Adams (Ed), *The Middle East: A Handbook*, Anthony Blond, London.

McConnell, J. E. (1967).   The Middle East: competitive or complementary?, *Tijdschr. econ. soc. Geogr.*, **58**, 82–93.

Minkes, A. L. (1952).   A note on handicrafts in under-developed areas, *Economic Development and Cultural Change*, **1**, 156–168.

Musrey, A. G. (1969).   *An Arab Common Market: A Study in Inter-Arab Trade Relations, 1920–67*, Praeger, New York, Washington and London.

Planhol, X.de (1966).   Small-scale industry and crafts in arid regions. In E. S. Hills, (Ed), *Arid Lands: A Geographic Appraisal*, Methuen, London, pp. 273–285.

Potter, D. (1955).   The bazaar merchant. In S. N. Fisher (Ed), *Social Forces in the Middle East*, Cornell University Press, Ithaca, New York, pp. 99–115.

Preston, L. E. (1970).   *Trade Patterns in the Middle East*, American Enterprise Institute for Public Policy Research, Washington D.C.

Ramazani, R. K. (1964).   *The Middle East and the European Common Market*, University of Virginia, Charlottesville.

Wulff, H. E. (1966).   *The Traditional Crafts of Persia*, M.I.T. Press, Cambridge, Mass., and London.

Chapter 9: Petroleum

Assah, A. (1969).   *Miracle of the Desert Kingdom*, Johnson Publications Ltd., London, 330 pages.

Alnasrawi, A. (1967).   *Financing Economic Development in Iraq—The Role of Oil in a Middle Eastern Economy*, Praeger, New York, 188 pages.

Arabian American Oil Company (1965).   *Aramco's Role in the Development of the Eastern Province*, Dammam.

Arabian American Oil Company (1970).   *Aramco 1970—A Review of Operations by the Arabian American Oil Company*, ARAMCO, Dammam, 22 pages and tables.

Arabian American Oil Company (1971).   *Aramco 1971—A Review of Operations by the Arabian American Oil Company*, ARAMCO, Dammam, 7 pages and tables and foldouts.

Berry, J. A. (1972).   Oil and soviet policy in the Middle East, *Middle East Journal*, **26**, 149–161.

Bill, J. A. (1971).   The challenge of change: petroleum and planning in the Middle East, *Focus*, **22 (1)**, 1–5.

British Petroleum Company Ltd. (1970).   *Our Industry Petroleum*, British Petroleum Company Ltd., London, 528 pages.

British Petroleum Company Ltd. (1972).   *BP Statistical Review of the World Oil Industry 1971*. British Petroleum Company Limited London, 24 pages.

Caroe, O. (1951).   *Wells of Power, the Oil Fields of S.W. Asia*, Macmillan, London, 240 pages.

Cattan, H. (1967).   *The Evolution of Oil Concessions in the Middle East and North Africa*, Dobbs-Ferry Oceana Publications, New York, 173 pages.

Cheney, M. S. (1958).   *Big Oil Man from Arabia*, Heinemann, London, 320 pages.

Darmstadter, J., P. D. Teitelbaum and J. G. Polach (1971).   *Energy in the World Economy: A Statistical Review of Trends in Output, Trade, and Consumption Since 1925*, Johns Hopkins Press for Resources of the Future, Baltimore, 876 pages.

Echo of Iran, (1971).   *Iran Almanac 1971*, Echo of Iran, Tehrān, 808 pages.

Finnie, D. H. (1958).   *Desert Enterprise*, Harvard University Press, Cambridge (USA), 224 pages.

Finnie, D. H. (1958).   Recruitment and training of labour. The Middle East oil industry, *Middle East Journal*, **12**, 127–143.

Frank H. J. (1966).   *Crude Oil Prices in the Middle East*, Praeger, New York, 209 pages.

Frenkel, P. H. (1962).   *Oil: The Facts of Life*, Weidenfeld and Nicolson, London,

Ghalayini, A. K. (1970).   Drilling techniques and cost in Saudi Arabia, *Seventh Arab Petroleum Congress, Beirūt*, **2**, 267–284.

Gordon, R. L. (1970).   *The Evolution of Energy Policy in Western Europe: The Reluctant Retreat from Coal*, Praeger, New York, 330 pages.

Hamilton C. W. (1962).   *Americans and oil in the Middle East*, Gulf Publishing Company, Houston, 307 pages.

Hartshorn, J. E. (1967).   *Politics and World Oil Economics*, Praeger, New York.

Hirst, D. (1966).   *Oil and Public Opinion in the Middle East*, Faber and Faber Ltd., London, 127 pages.

Hillmore, P. (1972).   Oil producers will take 25 pc. stake, *The Guardian*, Manchester, 17 December 1972.

Hubbert, M. K. (1969).   Energy Resources. In *Resources and Man: A Study and Recommendations of the Division of Earth Sciences of the United States National Academy of Sciences National Research Council*, Freeman, San Francisco, 157–242.

Institute of Petroleum Information Service (1971).   *Oil—World Statistics*, Institute of Petroleum, London, 8 pages.

Institute of Petroleum Information Service (1971).   *Oil—The Middle East*, Institute of Petroleum, London, 13 pages.

Iranian Oil Operating Companies (1971).   *Annual Review 1971*, Iranian Oil Operating Companies, Tehrān, 40 pages.

Iraq, Basrah and Mosul Petroleum Companies (1971).   *Review for 1970*, Iraq Petroleum Company Ltd., London, 32 pages.

Issawi, C. and M. Yeganeh, (1962).   *The Economics of Middle Eastern Oil*, Faber and Faber, London, 230 pages.

Khatib, A., H. Munif and F. Ruwayha, (1963).   Aramco's participation in Saudi Arabian development, *Fourth Arab Petroleum Congress, Beirūt*, 1, 53 (A-1).

Kubbah, A. A. Q. (1964).   *Libya—its Oil Industry and Economic System*, The Arab Petro-Economic Research Centre, Baghdād, 274 pages.

Kuwait Oil Company (1971).   *1971 Review of Operations*, Kuwait Oil Company, Kuwait, 32 pages.

Lebkicher R., G. Rentz., M. Steineke et al. (1960).   *Aramco Handbook*, Arabian American Oil Company, Dhahran, 343 pages.

Leeman, W. A. (1962).   *The Price of Middle East oil, an Essay in Political Economy*, Cornell University Press, Ithaca, 274 pages.

Lenczowski, G. (1960).   *Oil and State in the Middle East*, Cornell University Press, Ithaca, 379 pages.

Lockhart, L. (1953).   The causes of the Anglo-Persian oil dispute, *Jl R. cent. Asian Soc.*, **40**, 134–150.

Longrigg, S. H. (1949).   The liquid gold of Arabia, *Jl R. cent Asian Soc.*, **36**, 20–33.

Longrigg, S. H. (1968).   *Oil in the Middle East; its Discovery and Development*, Oxford University Press, London, 519 pages.

Lubbell, H. (1962).   *Middle East Oil Crises and Western Europe's Energy Supplies*, A RAND Corporation Study, Johns Hopkins Press, Baltimore, 233 pages.

Lutfi, A. (1968).   *OPEC Oil*, The Middle East Research and Publishing Centre, Beirūt, Middle East Oil Monographs No. 6., 120 pages.

Lutfi, A. (1965).   Royalty oil economics—key to Arab participation in the international oil industry, *Fifth Arab Petroleum Congress*, Cairo, 1 1 (A-4).

McLachlan, K. (1972).   *Spending Oil Revenues—Development Prospects in the Middle East to 1975*, Q.E.R. Special No. 10, Economist Intelligence Unit Ltd., London, 36 pages.

Manners, G. (1964).   *The Geography of Energy*, Hutchinson University Library, London, 205 pages.

Marlowe, J. (1962).   *The Persian Gulf in the Twentieth Century*, The Cresset Press, London, 278 pages.

Melamid, A. (1959).   Geographical pattern of Iranian oil development *Econ. Geogr.*, **35**, 199–218.

Melamid, A. (1968).   Industrial activities. In W. B. Fisher (Ed), *The Cambridge History of Iran, Vol. 1—The Land of Iran*, Cambridge University Press, Cambridge, pp. 517–551.

534

Mikdashi, Z. (1966).   *A Financial Analysis of Middle Eastern Oil Concessions 1901–1965*, Praeger, New York, 341 pages.

Moody, J. D. (1970).   Petroleum demands of future decades, *Bull. Am. Ass. Petrol. Geol.*, **54**, 2239–2245.

O'Dell, P. R. (1963).   *An Economic Geography of Oil*, G. Bell & Sons Ltd., London, 219 pages.

O'Dell, P. R. (1970).   *Oil and World Power—A Geographical Interpretation*, Penguin Books, Harmondsworth, 188 pages.

Oxford Regional Economic Atlas (1960).   *The Middle East and North Africa*, Oxford University Press, London, 135 pages.

Penrose, E. T. (1968).   *The Large International Firm in Developing Countries: The International Petroleum Industry*, George Allen & Unwin Ltd., London, 311 pages.

Petroleum Information Bureau (1967).   *Oil—Drilling Techniques*, Petroleum Information Bureau, London, 7 pages.

Petroleum Information Bureau (1967).   *Oil—The World's Reserves*, Petroleum Information Bureau, London, 5 pages.

Petroleum Information Bureau (1968).   *Oil—Refining*, Petroleum Information Bureau, London, 5 pages.

Petroleum Information Bureau (1968).   *Oil—Pipelines*, Petroleum Information Bureau, London, 8 pages.

Petroleum Information Bureau (1969).   *Oil—Africa*, Petroleum Information Bureau, London, 9 pages.

Petroleum Publishing Co. (1970).   *International Petroleum Encyclopedia 1971*, Tulsa, Oklahoma, 367 pages.

Petroleum Publishing Co. (1972).   *International Petroleum Encyclopedia 1972*, Tulsa, Oklahoma, 448 pages.

Pratt, W. E. and D. Good (Eds) (1950).   *World Geography of Petroleum*, American Geographical Society, Special Publication, 31, Princeton University Press, 134 pages.

Roosevelt, K. (1949).   *Arabs, Oil and History*, Gollancz, London, 271 pages.

Rouhani, F. (1971).   *A History of O.P.E.C.*, Praeger, New York, 281 pages.

Sayegh, K. S. (1968).   *Oil and Arab Regional Development*, Praeger, New York, 359 pages.

Schurr, S. H. and P. T. Homan (1971).   *Middle Eastern Oil and the Western World—Prospects and Problems*, American Elsevier, New York, 206 pages.

Shwadran, B. (1956).   *The Middle East, Oil and the Great Powers*, Atlantic Press, London, 500 pages.

Snow, C. (1972).   The emerging giant of world oil, *The Financial Times*, London, December 19, p. 17.

Stevens, G. P. (1949).   Saudi Arabia's petroleum resources, *Econ. Geogr.*, **25**, 216–225.

Stocking, G. W. (1970).   *Middle East Oil: a Study in Political and Economic Controversy*, Vanderbilt University Press, Nashville, 485 pages.

Tayim, H. A. (1960).   Utilisation of natural gas in Saudi Arabia, *Second Arab Petroleum Congress,·Beirūt*, **2**, 308–321.

United States, Department of the Interior, (1968).   *United States Petroleum Through 1980*, Washington, July 1968.

Warman, H. R. (1971).   Future problems in petroleum exploration, *Petroleum Review*, **25**, 96–101.

Warman, H. R. (1972).   The future of Oil, *Geogrl J.*, **38**, 287–297.

Weeks, L. G. (1968).   The gas, oil and sulphur potentials of the sea, *Ocean Industry*, **3(6)**, 43–51.

| Weeks, L. G. (1971). | Marine geology and petroleum resources, *World Petroleum Congress*, 8, Moscow, Proceedings, 2, 99–106. |

Chapter 10: The Political Map

Abir, M. (1972).	Red Sea Politics. In *Adelphi Papers* No. 93, International Institute for Strategic Studies, London, pp. 24–41.
Alexander, L. M. (1954).	*World Political Patterns*, John Murray, London, pp. 279–313.
Boyd, A. and P. van Rensburg. (1962).	*An Atlas of African Affairs*, Methuen, London.
Brawer, M. (1968).	The geographical background of the Jordan water dispute. In *Essays in Political Geography*, (Ed. C. A. Fisher,) Methuen, London, pp. 225–242.
Crary, D. B. (1949).	Geography and politics in the Nile Valley, *Middle East Journal*, 3, 260–276.
Haupert, G. S. (1969).	Political geography of the Israel–Syrian boundary dispute 1949–67, *Prof. Geogr.*, 21, 163–171.
Haupert, G. S. (1971).	Jerusalem: aspects of reunification and reintegration, *Prof. Geogr.*, 23, 312–318.
Hawley, D. (1970).	*The Trucial States*, George Allen and Unwin, London.
Hourani, A. H. (1970).	Race, religion and nation-state in the Near East. In, *Arab Middle East Societies and Cultures*, (Ed. A. M. Lutfiyya and C. W. Churchill). Mouton, The Hague, pp. 1–19.
International Institute for Strategic Studies, (1966).	*Sources of Conflict in the Middle East*, Adelphi Paper No. 26, London.
Issawi, C. (1970).	Political disunity in the Arab World. In *Readings in Arab Middle East societies and cultures*, (Ed. A. M. Lutifiyya and C. W. Churchill), Mouton, The Hague, pp. 278–284.
Kanovsky, E. (1968).	The economic aftermath of the Six Day War, *Middle East Journal*, 22, 131–143 and 278–296.
Kelly, J. B. (1964).	*Eastern Arabian Frontiers*, Faber and Faber, London.
Kingsbury R. C. and N.J.G. Pounds, (1964).	*An Atlas of Middle Eastern Affairs*, Methuen, London.
Kirk, G. E. (1964).	*A Short History of the Middle East*, University Paperbacks, London, Chapter 5.
Laqueur, W. (Ed) (1969).	*The Israel–Arab Reader*, Weidenfeld, London.
Laqueur, W. (1969).	*The Struggle for the Middle East*, Routledge and Kegan Paul, London.
Lebon, J. H. G. (1960).	The control and utilisation of Nile waters: a problem of political geography, *Rev. Geogr. Inst. Univ. of İstanb.*, 6, 32–49.
Lebon, J. H. G. (1971).	South-West Asia and Egypt. In *The Changing Map of Asia*, 5th ed., (Ed. W. G. East, O. H. K. Spate, and C. A. Fisher), Methuen, London, pp. 53–126.
Lenczowski, G. (1962).	*The Middle East in World Affairs*, Cornell University Press, New York.
Melamid, A. (1953).	Political geography of Trucial Oman and Qatar, *Geogr. Rev.* 43, 194–206.
Melamid, A. (1956).	The Buraimi oasis dispute, *Middle East Affairs*, 7, 56–63.

536

Melamid, A. (1957).	The political geography of the Gulf of Aqaba, *Ann. Ass. Amer. Geogr.*, **47**, 231–240.
Melamid, A. (1968).	The Shaṭṭ al'Arab boundary dispute, *Middle East Journal*, **22**, 350–357.
McConnell, J. E. (1962).	The Middle East: competitive or complementary?, *Tijdschr. econ. Geogr.*, **2**, 82–93.
Middle East Journal (1968). Document:	Agreement for the delimitation of boundaries between Jordan and Saudi Arabia, *Middle East Journal*, **22**, 346–348.
Sevian, V. J. (1968).	The evolution of the boundary between Iraq and Iran. In *Essays in Political Geography*, (Ed. C. A. Fisher), Methuen, London, pp. 211–223.
Shaw, W. B. K. (1935).	The international boundaries of Libya, *Geogrl J.*, **85**, 50–53.
Smith, C. G. (1958).	Arab nationalism: a study in political geography, *Geography*, **43**, 229–242.
Smith C. G. (1966).	The disputed waters of the Jordan, *Trans. Inst. Br. Geogr.*, **40**, 111–128.
Smith C. G. (1968).	Israel after the June War, *Geography*, **53**, 315–319.

U.S. Dept. of State (1961–1972). Boundary Studies:

No. 1   Algeria–Libya 1961
No. 2   Libya–Niger 1961
No. 6   Afghanistan–Iran 1961
No. 9   Morocco–Spanish Sahara 1961
No. 10   Libya–Sudan 1961
No. 18   Sudan–Egypt 1962
No. 25   Iran–U.S.S.R. 1963
No. 27   Iraq–Turkey 1964
No. 28   Iran–Turkey 1964
No. 29   Turkey–U.S.S.R. 1964
No. 41   Greece–Turkey 1964
No. 46   Israel–U.A.R. armistice line 1965
No. 49   Bulgaria–Turkey 1965
No. 60   Jordan–Saudi Arabia 1965
No. 66   Libya–U.A.R. 1966
No. 75   Israel–Lebanon 1967
No. 88   Algeria–Mauritania 1970
No. 94   Jordan–Syria 1969
No. 96   Algeria–Mali 1970
No. 99   Algeria–Niger 1970
No. 100 Iraq–Syria 1970
No. 103 Kuwait–Saudi Arabia 1971
No. 111 Iraq–Saudi Arabia 1971
No. 121 Libya–Tunisia 1972,
Bureau of Intelligence, Washington D.C.

Wilkinson, J. C. (1971).	The Oman question: the background to the political geography of south east Arabia, *Geogrl J.*, **137**, 361–371.
Willats, E. C. (1946).	Some geographical factors in the Palestine problem, *Geogrl J.*, **108**, 146–179.
Wilson, A. (Ed) (1971).	*The Observer Atlas of World Affairs*, George Philip, London.
Zartman, I. W. (1965).	The politics of boundaries in north and west Africa, *Journal of Modern African Studies*, **3**, 155–173.

Chapter 11: Arabia: Tradition and Change

Abdul-Ela, M. T. (1965).   Some geographical aspects of Al Riyadh, *Bull. Soc. Géogr. Egypte*, **38**, 31–72.

Amps, L. W. (1953).   Kuwait town development, *Jl R. cent. Asian. Soc.*, **40**, 234–240.

Anthony, J. (1972).   The Union of Arab Emirates, *Middle East Journal*, **26**, 271–287.

Attar, M. S. el, (1964).   *Le Sous Développement Economique et Social du Yémén. Perspectives de la Révolution Yéménite*, Editions Tiers Monde, Algiers.

Belgrave, C. D. (1934).   Pearl diving in Bahrain, *Jl R. cent. Asian. Soc.*, **55**, 450–452.

Belgrave, C. D. (1968).   Persian Gulf: past and present, *Jl R. cent. Asian. Soc.*, **55**, 28–34.

Bowen, R. L. (1951a).   Marine industries of eastern Arabia, *Geogrl Rev.*, **41**, 384–400.

Bowen, R. L. (1951b).   The pearl fisheries of the Persian Gulf, *Middle East Journal*, **5**, 161–180.

Burckhardt, J. L. (1831).   *Notes on the Bedouins and Wahabys*, Colburn and Bentley, London.

Crary, D. D. (1951).   Recent agricultural developments in Saudi Arabia, *Geogrl. Rev.*, **41**, 366–383.

Decandle, E. A. V. (1965).   Kuwait today, *Jl R. cent. Asian Soc.*, **52**, 31–37.

Dequin, H. (1963).   *Die Landwirtschaft Saudisch-Arabiens und ihre Entwicklungs möglichkeiten*, DLG-Verlag-GMBH, Frankfurt am Main.

Dickson, H. H. P. (1951).   *The Arab of the Desert: A Glimpse of Badawin Life in Kuwait and Saudi Arabia*, 2nd ed., *Allen and Unwin*, London.

Dowson, V. H. W. (1949).   The date and the Arab, *Jl R. cent. Asian Soc.*, **36**, 34–41.

Ebert, C. H. V. (1965).   Water resources and land use in the Qatif oasis of Saudi Arabia, *Geogrl Rev.*, **55**, 496–509.

Edens, D. G. and W. P. Snavely, (1970).   Planning for economic development in Saudi Arabia, *Middle East Journal*, **24**, 16–30.

Fenelon, K. G. (1971).   *The United Arab Emirates: An Economic and Social Survey*, 3rd Ed., Longmans, London.

Haupert, J. S. (1966).   Saudi Arabia, *Focus*, **16(4)**, 1–6.

Heard-Bey, F. (1972).   The Gulf states and Oman in transition, *Asian Affairs*, **59**, 14–22.

Helaissi, A. S. (1959).   The bedouins and tribal life in Saudi Arabia, *International Social Science Journal*, **11**, 532–538.

Hendy, H. F. (1972).   Ecological consequences of bedouin settlement in Saudi Arabia. In M. T. Farvar and J. P. Milton (Eds), *The Careless Technology*, The Natural History Press, Garden City, New York, pp. 683–693.

Hill, A. G. (1972a).   Clouds over Kuwait: threatened aftermath of an oil boom, *Geogrl Mag.*, **44**, 753–758.

Hill. A. G. (1972b).   Bahrain is independent; efforts to retain Gulf supremacy, *Geogrl Mag.*, **44**, 846–852.

Hopwood, D. (Ed) (1972).   *The Arabian Peninsula*, Allen and Unwin, London.

Hornell, J. (1942).   A tentative classification of Arab seacraft, *Mariners' Mirror*, **28**, 11–40.

538

Ingrams, H. (1966).   *Arabia and the Isles*, John Murray, London.

Johnstone, T. M. and   Some geographical aspects of Qatar, *Geogrl J.*, **126**,
    J. C. Wilkinson (1960).   442–450.

Kelly, J. B. (1964).   *Eastern Arabian Frontiers*, Faber and Faber, London.

King, R. (1972).   The Pilgrimage to Mecca: some geographical and historical aspects, *Erdkunde*, **26**, 61–72.

Küpper, H. (1965).   Kuwait. Entwicklungszentrum am "arabischen" Golf, *Mitt. Ost. geogr. Ces.*, **107**, 138–144.

Lander, R. G. (1969).   The modernisation of the Persian Gulf: the period of British dominance. In T. C. Young, (Ed), *The Princeton University Conference and Twentieth Annual Near Eastern Conference on Middle East Focus: The Persian Gulf*, Princeton University Conference, Princeton, pp. 1–29.

Leidlmair, A. (1961).   *Hadramaut*, Bonner Geog. Abhandlungen No. 30, Geographische Institute, Universität Bonn, Bonn.

Machie, J. M. (1924).   Hasa: an Arabian oasis, *Geogrl J.*, **63**, 189–207.

Mallakh, R. el (1966a).   Kuwait's economic development and her foreign aid programmes, *World Today*, **22**, 13–22.

Mallakh, R. el (1966b).   Planning in a capital surplus economy: Kuwait, *Land Econ.*, **42**, 425–440.

Mallakh, R. el (1970).   The challenge of affluence: Abu Dhabi, *Middle East Journal*, **24**, 135–146.

Melamid, A. (1953).   Political geography of Trucial Oman and Qatar, *Geogrl Rev.*, **43**, 194–206.

Melamid, A. (1954).   Oil and the evolution of boundaries in eastern Arabia, *Geogrl Rev.*, **44**, 295–296.

Melamid, A. (1957).   Boundaries and petroleum development in southern Arabia, *Geogrl Rev.*, **47**, 589–591.

Melamid, A. (1962).   Transportation in eastern Arabia, *Geogrl Rev.*, **52**, 122–124.

Melamid, A. (1965).   Political boundaries and nomadic grazing, *Geogrl Rev.*, **55**, 287–290.

Melamid, A. (1967).   Eastern Arabia, *Focus*, **18(3)**, 1-6.

Melamid, A. (1968).   South Yemen, *Focus*, **18(5)**, 1-6.

Mosely, F. (1966).   Exploration for water in the Aden Protectorate, *R. Engrs'. J.*, **80**, 124–142.

Musil, A. (1928).   *The Manners and Customs of the Rwala Bedouins*, American Geographical Society, New York.

Peppelenbosch, P. G. N. (1968).   Nomadism in the Arabian peninsula: a general appraisal, *Tijdschr. econ. soc. geogr.*, **59**, 335–346.

Pourcelet, F. (1968).   Notes de géographie urbaine: l'expansion recente de la ville de Kuwayt, *Cahiers de l'Orient Contemporain*, **71**, 4–8.

Raswan, C. R. (1930).   Tribal areas and migration lines of the North Arabian bedouins, *Geogrl Rev.*, **20**, 494–502.

Ronall, J. O. (1970).   Banking developments in Kuwait, *Middle East Journal*, **24**, 87–90.

Saigh, Y. A. (1971).   Problems and prospects of development in the Arabian peninsula, *International Journal of Middle Eastern Studies*, **2**, 40–58.

Serjeant, R. B. (1964).   Some irrigation systems in Hadramawt, *Bulletin of the School of Oriental and African Studies*, **27**, 32–76.

Serjeant, R. B. (1968).   Fisher-folk and fish-traps in Al-Bahrain, *Bulletin of*

	the School of Oriental and African Studies, **31**, 486–514.
Stevens, J. H. (1969).	Ariz zone agricultural development in the Trucial States, *J. Soil Wat. Conserv.*, **24**, 181–183.
Stevens, J. H. (1970).	The changing agricultural practice of an Arabian oasis, *Geogrl J.*, **136**, 410–418.
Stevens, J. H. (1972).	Oasis agriculture in the central and eastern Arabian peninsula, *Geography*, **57**, 321–326.
Sweet, L. E. (1964).	Pirates or politics? Arab societies of the Persian or Arabian Gulf, eighteenth century, *Ethnohistory*, **11**, 262–280.
Sweet, L. E. (1965).	Camel pastoralism in north Arabia and the minimal camping unit. In A. Leeds and A. P. Vayda (Eds), *Man, Culture and Animals: The Role of Animals in Human Ecological Adjustments*, American Association for the Advancement of science, No. 78, Washington D.C., pp. 129–152.
Tan, K. (1970).	Agricultural problems in southern Arabia, *Wld Crops*, **22**, 397–400.
Tomkinson, M. (1969).	Seaside city for Mecca pilgrims, *Geogrl Mag.*, **42**, 95–101.
Twisleton-Wykeham-Fiennes, R. (1970).	Sweet water for the hottest land, *Geogrl Mag.*, **42**, 889–893.
Twitchell, K. S. (1958).	*Saudi Arabia, with an Account of the Development of its Natural Resources*, 3rd ed., Oxford University Press, New York, 1958.
Vidal, F. S. (1955).	*The Oasis of Al-Hasa*, Arabian-American Oil Co., New York.
Watt, W. W. (1968).	Traditional Arab communities in the modern world, *International Affairs*, **44**, 494–500.
Wallen, I. F. (1969).	Non-oil trade and resources. In T. C. Young (Ed), *The Princeton University Conference and Twentieth Annual Near Eastern Conference on Middle East Focus: The Persian Gulf*, Princeton University Conference, Princeton, pp. 107–110.

Chapter 12: Iraq: Man, Land and Water in an Alluvial Environment

Adams, R. M. (1958).	Survey of ancient water courses and settlements in central Iraq, *Sumer*, **14**, 101–103.
Adams, R. McC. (1965).	*Land Behind Baghdād*, The University of Chicago Press, Chicago, 187 pages.
Al-Barazi, N. K. (1961).	*The Geography of Agriculture in Irrigated Areas of the Middle Euphrates Valley*, Vol. 1 and 2, College of Arts Baghdād University, Baghdād, 183 pages.
Al-Khashab, W. H. (1958).	*The Water Budget of the Tigris and Euphrates Basin*, University of Chicago, Department of Geography, Research Paper, No. 54, 105 pages.
Baali, F. (1969).	Agrarian reform in Iraq: some socio-economic aspects, *The American Journal of Economics and Sociology*, **28**, 61–76.
Buringh, P. (1957).	Living conditions in the lower Mesopotamian plain in ancient times, *Sumer*, **13**, 30–57.
Buringh, P. (1960).	*Soils and Soil Conditions in Iraq*, Directorate General

540

	of Agricultural Research and Projects, Baghdad, Republic of Iraq, Ministry of Agriculture.
Clawson, M., H. H. Landsberg and L. T. Alexander (1971).	*The Agricultural Potential of the Middle East*, Elsevier, New York, 312 pages.
Davies, D. H. (1957).	Observations on land use in Iraq, *Econ. Geogr.*, **33**, 122–134.
Fernea, R. A. (1959).	*Irrigation and Social Organisation Among the El Shabana—a Group of Tribal Cultivators in Southern Iraq.* Ph.D. Thesis, University of Chicago.
Fernea, R. A. (1969).	Land reform and ecology in post-revolutionary Iraq, *Economic Development and Cultural Change*, **17**, 356–381.
Fernea, R. A. and E. W. Fernea (1969).	Land reform in modern Iraq, *Focus*, **20(2)**, 9–12.
Fernea, R. A. and E. W. Fernea (1969).	Iraq, *Focus*, **20(2)**, 1–8.
Gulick, J. (1967).	Baghdad, portrait of a city in physical and cultural change, *Journal of the American Institute of Planners*, **34**, 339–350.
Harris, S. A. and R. M. Adams, (1957).	A note on canal and marsh stratigraphy near Zubediya, *Sumer*, **13**, 157–163.
Harris, S. A. (1958).	The Gilgaied and bad-structured soils of central Iraq *J. Soil Sci.*, **9**, 169–185.
Ionides, M. G. (1937).	*The Regime of the Rivers Euphrates and Tigris*, London, 255 pages.
Issawi, C. (1969).	Economic change and urbanisation in the Middle East. In I. M. Lapidus (Ed), *Middle Eastern Cities*, University of California Press, Berkeley, 102–121.
Jacobsen, T. and R. M. Adams (1958).	Salt and silt in ancient Mesopotamian agriculture, *Science, N. Y.*, **128**, 1251–1258.
Jones, L. (1969).	Rapid population growth in Baghdad and Amman, *Middle East Journal*, **23**, 209–215.
Kaul, R. N. and D. C. P. Thalen, (1971).	Range ecology at the Institute for Applied Research on Natural Resources, Iraq, *Nature and Resources*, **7(2)**, 10–15.
Kingsman, J. (1970).	Kurds and Iran: Iraq's changing balance of power, *The New Middle East*, **22**, 25–27.
Laessøe, J. (1953).	Reflection on modern and ancient oriental waterworks, *Journal of Cuneiform Studies*, **7**, 5–26.
Langley, K. M. (1964).	Iraq: some aspects of the economic scene, *Middle East Journal*, **18**, 180–188.
Langley, K. M. (1967).	*The Industrialization of Iraq*, Harvard Middle East Monographs, Cambridge, 313 pages.
Lawless, R. I. (1972).	Iraq—changing population patterns. In J. I. Clarke and W. B. Fisher (Eds), *Populations of the Middle East and North Africa*, University of London Press, London, 97–129.
Lebon, J. H. G. (1953).	Population distribution and the agricultural regions of Iraq, *Geogrl Rev.*, **43**, 223–228.
Lees, G. M. and N. L. Falcon, (1952).	The geographical history of the Mesopotamian plains, *Geogrl J.*, **118**, 24–39.
Longrigg, S. H. and F. Stokes, (1958).	*Iraq*, Praeger, New York, 256 pages.

Millon, R. (1962). Variations in social responses to the practice of irrigation and agriculture. In R. B. Woodbury (Ed), *Civilisations and Desert Lands*, University of Utah, Anthropological Papers, Salt Lake City, **62**, pp. 56–88.

Mitchell, R. C. (1957). Recent tectonic movement in the Mesopotamian plains, *Geogrl J.*, **123**, 569–571.

Mitchell, C. W. (1959). Investigations into the soils and agriculture of the lower Diyala area of eastern Iraq, *Geogrl J.*, **125**, 390–397.

Mitchell, C. W. and P. E. Naylor, (1960). Investigations into the soils and agriculture of the middle Diyala region of eastern Iraq, *Geogrl J.*, **126**, 469–475.

Naval Intelligence Division (Great Britain) (1944). *Iraq and the Persian Gulf*, Geographical Handbook Series BR 524, London,524 pages.

Phillips, D. G. (1959). Rural to urban migration in Iraq, *Economic Development and Cultural Change*, **7**, 405–421.

Quint, M. N. (1958). The idea of progress in an Iraqi village, *Middle East Journal*, **12**, 369–384.

Simmons, J. L. (1965). Agricultural development in Iraq, planning and management failures, *Middle East Journal*, **19**, 129–140.

Smith, C. G. (1970). Water resources and irrigation development in the Middle East, *Geography*, **55**, 407–425.

Smith, H. H. et al. (1971). *Area Handbook for Iraq*, The American University, Washington D.C., 413 pages.

Smith, R. and V. C. Robertson (1962). Soil and irrigation classification of shallow soils overlying gypsum beds, northern Iraq, *J. Soil Sci.*, **13**, 106–115.

Storke, C. (1959). Evapotranspiration problems in Iraq, *Neth. J. agric. Sci.*, **7**, 269–282.

Tamimi, S. A. and M. A. Younis (1972). Effect of CEC and irrigation on wheat yields in Iraq, *Wld Crops*, **24(6)**, 310–311.

Thesiger, W. (1964). *The Marsh Arabs*, Longmans, London, 242 pages.

Treakle, H. C. (1966). *The Agricultural Economy of Iraq*, Washington Foreign Regional Analysis Division, Economic Research Service, U.S.D.A., Washington,D.C., 74 pages.

Ubell, K. (1971). Iraq's water resources, *Nature and Resources.* **7(2)**, 3–9

Warriner, D. (1969). Revolutions in Iraq. In D. Warriner, *Land Reform in Principle and Practice*, Oxford University Press, London, pp. 78–108.

Weickmann, L. (1963). Meteorological and hydrological relationships in the drainage area of the river Tigris north of Baghdad, *Met. Rdsch.*, **16**, 33–38.

Willcocks, W. (1908). *The Restoration of Ancient Irrigation Work on the Tigris*, Cairo.

Willcocks, W. (1917). *The Irrigation of Mesopotamia*, Spon, London,

Wittfogel, K. A. (1965). The Hydraulic Civilisation. In W. L. Thomas Jr. (Ed), *Man's Role in Changing the Face of the Earth*, University of Chicago Press, Chicago, 152–164.

Wright, H. E. Jr. (1968). Natural environment of early food production north of Mesopotamia, *Science, N.Y.*, **161**, 334–339.

Wright, H. E. Jr. (1970). Environmental change and the origin of agriculture in the Near East, *Bioscience*, **20**, 210–212.

Chapter 13: Agricultural Expansion in Syria

Ashton, B. L. (1928). The geography of Syria, *J. Geogr.* **27**, 164–180.

Dresch, J. (1963). Observations sur la région Palmyre en Syrie, *Bull. Ass. Géogr. fr.*, 2–18.

El-Zaim, I. (1968). La réforme agraire en Syrie, *Tiers-Monde*, **9**, 508–517.

Garrett, J. (1936). The site of Damascus, *Geography*, **21**, 288–296.

Garzouzi, E. (1963). Land reform in Syria, *Middle East Journal*, **17**, 83–90.

Gilbert, A. and M. Fevret, (1953). La Djezirah Syrienne et son reveil économique, *Revue Géogr. Lyon*, **38**, 1–15, 83–99.

Hamide, A. H. (1959). *La Région d'Alep* Paris.

Helbaoui, Y. (1963). La Population et la population active en Syrie, *Population, Paris*, **18**, 697–714.

Hudson, J. (1968a). Syria, *Focus*, **18(8)**,1–8.

Hudson, J. (1968b). The role of irrigation (in Syria), *Focus*, **18**, 8–11.

International Bank for Reconstruction and Development (1955). *The Economic Development of Syria*, Johns Hopkins, Baltimore.

Keilany, Z. (1970). Economic planning in Syria, 1960–65; an evaluation, *Journal of Developing Areas*, **4**, 361–373.

Latron, A. (1936). *La Vie rurale en Syrie et au Liban*, Beirūt.

Lewis, N. E. (1949). Malaria, irrigation and soil erosion in central Syria, *Geogrl Rev.*, **39**, 278–290.

Lewis, N. E. (1955). The frontier of settlement in Syria: 1800–1950, *International Affairs*, **31**, 48–60. Reprinted in Issawi, C. (Ed). (1966). *The Economic History of the Middle East, 1800–1914*. University of Chicago, Chicago and London, pp. 259–268.

Mahhouk, A. (1956). Recent agricultural development and Bedouin settlement in Syria, *Middle East Journal*, **10**, 167–176.

Money-Kyrle, A. F. (1956). *Agricultural Development and Research in Syria*. American University of Beirūt, Faculty of Agricultural Science, Publication No. 2.

Muir, A. (1951). Notes on the soils of Syria, *J. Soil. Sci.*, **2**, 163–182.

Orgels, B. (1963). *Contribution a l'Etude des Problèmes Agricoles de la Syria*, Centre Pour L'Etude des Problèmes du Monde Musulman Contemporain, Brussels.

Petran, T. (1972). *Syria*, Nations of the Modern World, Ernest Benn, London.

Peretz, D. (1964). River schemes and their effect on economic development in Jordan, Syria and Lebanon, *Middle East Journal*, **18**, 293–305.

Reifenberg, A. (1952). The soils of Syria and the Lebanon, *J. Soil. Soc.*, **3**, 68–88.

Rolley, J. (1948). Forest conditions in Syria and Lebanon, *Unasylva*, **2**, 77–80.

Rosciszewski, M. (1965). Quelques remarques sur la géotaphie agraire de la Syrie, *Méditerranée*, **6**, 171–184.

Shair, K. A. (1965). *Planning for a Middle Eastern Economy: Model for Syria*, Chapman and Hall, London.

Smilianskaya, I. M. (1958). Razlozhenie feodalnikh otnoshenii v Sirii i Livane v seredine xix v (The distintegration of feudal relations in Syria and Lebanon in the middle of the nineteenth century), *Peredneaziatskii Etnosgraficheskii Sbornik*,

	1, 156–179, Translated in Issawi, C. (Ed) (1966). *The Economic History of the Middle East, 1800–1914*, University of Chicago, Chicago, and London, 227–247.
Thoumin, R. (1936).	*Géographie Humaine de la Syrie Centrale*, Ernest Leroux, Paris.
Tresse, R. (1929).	L'irrigation dans la Ghouta de Damas, *Revue des Etudes Islamiques*, **3**, 459–473.
Vaumas, E. de (1955).	La population de la Syrie, *Annls Géogr.*, **64**, 74–80.
Vaumas, E. de (1956).	Le Djéziré syrienne, *Annls Géogr.*, **65**, 64–80.
Warriner, D. (1962).	*Land Reform and Development in the Middle East. A Study of Egypt. Syria and Iraq*, 2nd ed., Oxford University Press, London.
Weulersse, J. (1936).	Damas, étude de développement urbain, *Bull. Ass. Géogr. fr.*, 5–9.
Weulersse, J. (1938).	La primauté des cités dans l'économie syrienne, *Congres inter. de Géogr.*, *Amsterdam*, **2**, sect. 3A, 233–239.
Weulersse, J. (1946).	*Paysans de Syrie et du Proche-Orient*, Gallimard, Paris.
Wirth, E. (1966).	Damaskus–Aleppo–Beirut; en geographischer Verleich dreier nahöstlicher Städte in Spiegel ihrer sozial wirtschaftlich tanangebenden Schichten, *Erde*, **97**, 96–137; 166–202.
Wofast, R. (1967).	*Geologie von Syria und der Libanon*, Gebrüder Borntraegerm, Berlin.
Zuckermann, B. (1971).	Das Euphratprojekt in der Syrischen Arabischen Republik und sein Einflusch auf die Territorialstruktur der syrischen Volkswirtschaft, *Petermanns geogr. Mitt.*, **115**, 98–101.

Chapter 14: Lebanon: Community Structure

Asfour, E. Y. (1955).	Industrial development in Lebanon, *Middle East Economic Papers*, American University of Beirūt, Beirūt, pp. 1–16.
Asseily, A. E. (1967).	*Central Banking in Lebanon*, Khayat, Beirūt.
Beals, E. W. (1965).	The remnant cedar forests of Lebanon, *J. Ecol.* **53**, 679–694.
Chehabe-ed-Dine, S. (1960).	*Géographie humain de Beyrouth*, Imprimeric Calfat Beirūt.
Churchill, C. (1960).	Village life of the central Beq'a valley of Lebanon, *Middle East Economic Papers*, American University of Beirūt, pp. 1–48.
Crow, R. E. (1962).	Religious sectarianism in the Lebanese political system, *Journal of Politics*, **24**, 489–520.
El-Abdallah, H. (1964).	Plan du développement agricole en cours au Liban, *Méditerranee*, **3–4**, 174–183.
Fevret, M. (1949).	La sériculture au Liban, *Revue Géogr. Lyon*, **24**, 247–260, 341–361.
Fisher, W. B. (1944).	The Lebanon, *Geogrl Rev.* **33**, 235–258.
Gulick, J. (1955).	*Social Structure and Cultural Change in a Lebanese Village*, Viking Fund Publications in Anthropology No 21, New York.
Gulick, J. (1967).	*Tripoli: A Modern Arab City*, Harvard Middle Eastern Studies 12, Cambridge, Mass.
Hess, C. G. and H. L. Bodman, (1954).	Confessionalism and feudality in Lebanese politics, *Middle East Journal*, **8**, 10–26.

544

Hitti, P. K. (1967).   *Lebanon in History*, Macmillan, London,3rd. ed.

Hourani, A. H. (1947).   *Minorities in the Arab World*, Oxford University, London.

Issawi, C. (1964).   Economic development and liberalism in Lebanon, *Middle East Journal*, **18**, 279–292.

Jones, D. R. W. (1963).   Apple production in the Lebanon: a study of agricultural development in an underdeveloped area, *Econ. Geogr.*, **39**, 245–257.

Khuri, F. I. (1967).   A comparative study of migration patterns in two Lebanese villages, *Hum. Org.*, **26**, 206–213.

Khuri, F. I. (1969).   The changing class structure in Lebanon, *Middle East Journal*, **23**, 29–44.

Lewis, N. N. (1953).   Lebanon: The Mountain and its terraces, *Geogrl Rev.* **43**, 1–14.

Marthelot, P. (1963a).   Une ville remplit son site: Beyrouth, *Méditerranée*, **4**, 37–56.

Marthelot, P. (1963b).   L'expansion récente de la ville de Beyrouth, *Bull. Ass. Géogr. fr.*, 74–84.

Mikesell, M. W. (1969).   The deforestation of Mount Lebanon, *Geogrl Rev.*, **59**, 1–28.

Mills, A. E. (1959).   *Private Enterprise in Lebanon*, American University of Beirūt, Beirūt.

Peretz, D. (1964).   River schemes and their effect on economic development in Jordan, Syria and Lebanon, *Middle East Journal*, **18**, 293–305.

Persen, W. (1958).   Lebanese economic development since 1950, *Middle East Journal*, **12**, 277–294.

Peters, E. L. (1963).   Aspects of rank and status among Muslims in a Lebanese Village. In *Mediterranean Countrymen. Essays on the Social Anthropology of the Mediterranean* (Ed. J. Pitt-Rivers), Mouton, Paris and The Hague, pp. 159–200.

Raphaeli, N. (1967).   Development planning: Lebanon, *Western Political Qtly.*, **20**, 714–728.

Rondot, P. (1947).   *Les institutions politiques du Liban*, Institut d'Etudes de l'Orient Contemporain, Paris.

Rondot, P. (1968).   Lebanese institutions and nationalism, *Journal of Contemporary History*, **3**, 37–51.

Rossillion, C. (1968).   Cultural pluralism, equality of treatment and equality of opportunity in the Lebanon, *International Labour Review*, **98**, 225–244.

Safa, E. (1960).   *L'Emigration Libanese*, Université Saint-Joseph, Beirūt.

Salibi, K. S. (1965).   *The Modern History of Lebanon*, Praeger, New York; Weidenfeld and Nicolson, London.

Sanlaville, P. (1963).   Les régions agricoles du Liban, *Revue Géogr. Lyon.* **38**, 47–90.

Sanlaville, P. (1965).   L'electricité au Liban, *Revue Géogr. Lyon.* **40**, 367–369.

Sayigh, Y. A. (1962).   *Entrepreneurs of Lebanon*, Harvard, Cambridge, Mass.

Suleiman, M. W. (1967a).   *Political Parties in Lebanon. The Challenge of a Fragmented Political Culture*, Cornell University, Ithaca.

Suleiman, M. W. (1967b).   The role of political parties in a confessional democracy: the Lebanese case, *Western Political Qtly.*, **20**, 682–693.

Vaumas, E. de (1948).   Les conditions naturelles de l'occupation humaine au Liban, *Annls Géogr.*, **57**, 40–49.

Vaumas, E. de (1953).   La répartition de la population au Liban, *Bull. Soc. Geogr. Egypte*, **26**, 5–76.

Vaumas, E. de (1954).   *Le Liban (montagne libanaise Bekaa. Anti-Liban-Herman. Haute Gaililee libanese). Etude de géographie physique*, Firmin-Dibot, Paris.

Vaumas, E. de (1955).   La répartition confessionelle au Liban et l'équilibre de l'etat libanais, *Revue Géogr. alp.*, **43**, 511–604.

Vouras, P. P. and   Lebanon, *Focus*, **15(10)**, 1–6.
A. Taylor (1965).

Wirth, E. (1966).   Damaskus–Aleppo–Beirut; en geographischer Vergleich dreier nahöstlicher Stadte im Spiegel ihrer Sozial und wirtschaftlich tanagebenden Schichten, *Erde*, **97**, 96–137; 166–202.

Chapter 15: Jordan: The Struggle for Economic Survival

Aharoni, Y. (1966).   *The Land of the Bible*, Burns & Oates, London (Translated from the Hebrew by A. F. Rainey), 409 pages.

Atkinson, K. and   Watershed management in northern Jordan, *Wld Crops*,
P. Beaumont (1967).   **19**, 63–65.

Atkinson, K. and   The forests of Jordan, *Econ. Bot.*, **25**, 305–311.
P. Beaumont (1971).

Baly, D. (1958).   *The Geography of the Bible*, Lutterworth Press, London, 303 pages.

Beaumont, P. (1968).   The Road to Jericho: A climatological traverse across the Dead Sea lowlands, *Geography*, **53**, 170–174.

Beaumont, P. and   Soil erosion and conservation in northern Jordan,
K. Atkinson (1969).   *J. Soil Wat. Conserv.*, **24**, 144–147.

Birch, B. P. (1971).   Jordan's geography after the 1967 war, *Tijdschr. econ. soc. Geogr.*, **72**, 45–52.

Birch, B. P. (1973).   Recent developments in agriculture, land and water use in Jordan, *Wld Crops*, **25**, 66–76.

Blake, G. S. and   *Geology and Water Resources of Palestine*, Government
M. J. Goldschmidt (1947). Printer, Jerusalem, 413 pages.

Brawer, M. (1968).   The geographical background of the Jordan water dispute. In C. A. Fisher (Ed), *Essays in Political Geography*, Methuen, London, pp. 225–242.

Browning, I. (1973).   *Petra*, Chatto and Windus, London, 256 pages.

Burdon, D. J. (1959). *Handbook of the Geology of Jordan*, Government of the Hashemite Kingdom of Jordan, Amman, 82 pages.

Casto, E. R. (1937).   Economic geography of Palestine, *Econ. Geogr.*, **13**, 235–259.

Casto, E. R. and   Economic geography of Trans-Jordan, *Econ. Geogr.*,
O. W. Dotson (1938).   **14**, 121–130.

Copeland, R. W. (1965). *The Land and People of Jordan*, J. B. Lippincott Company, Philadelphia, 160 pages.

Davies, H. R. J. (1958). Irrigation in Jordan, *Econ. Geogr.*, **34**, 264–271.

Dees, J. L. (1959).   Jordan's East Ghor canal project, *Middle East Journal*, **13**, 357–371.

Fisher, W. B. (1972). Jordan: a demographic shatter-belt. In J. I. Clarke and W. B. Fisher (Eds), *Populations of the Middle East and North Africa*, University of London Press, London, 202–219.

Garbell, M. A. (1965). The Jordan valley plan, *Scient. Am.*, **212(3)**, 23–31.

Gregory, J. W. (1930).   Palestine and the stability of climate in historic times, *Geogrl J.*, **76**, 487–494.

Hacker, J. M. (1960).   *Modern Amman—A Social Study*, Department of Geography, Research Paper Series No. 3, University of Durham, 144 pages.

Hindle, P. (1964).   The population of the Hashemite Kingdom of Jordan, 1961, *Geogrl J.*, **130**, 261–264.

Haddard, S. M. (1966).   Principles and procedures used in planning and execution of East Ghor Irrigation project, *Sixth NESA Irrigation Practices Seminar, Amman*, 2–6.

Hare, V. C. (1954).   The Jordan valley of the future: desert or garden? *The Near East*, **7**, 8–15.

Hashemite Kingdom of Jordan, Central Water Authority (1962).   Irrigation in Jordan, *Fourth NESA Irrigation Practices Seminar, Ankara*, 56–153.

Haupert, J. S. (1966).   Recent progress on Jordan's East Ghor canal, *Prof. Geogr.*, **18**, 9–13.

International Bank for Reconstruction and Development (1957).   *Economic Development of Jordan*, Johns Hopkins, Baltimore, 488 pages.

Ionides, M. G. and G. S. Blake (1939).   *Report on the Water Resources of Trans-Jordan and their Development: Incorporating a Report on Geology, Soils, and Minerals and Hydrogeological Correlations*, Crown Agents for the Colonies, London, 372 pages.

Ionides, M. G. (1946).   The perspective of water development in Palestine and Transjordan, *Jl R. cent. Asian Soc.*, **33**, 271–280.

Ionides, M. G. (1951).   The Jordan valley, *Jl R. cent. Asian Soc.*, **38**, 217–225.

Ionides, M. G. (1953).   The disputed waters of Jordan, *Middle East Journal*, **7**, 153–164.

Johnston, E. (1954).   Arab-Israel tension and the Jordan valley, *World Affairs*, **117**, 38–41.

Jones, W. E. (1965).   The Jordan river valley: a problem in political geography, *Swansea Geographer*, **3**, 77–90.

Jordan Development Board (1965).   *Programme for Economic Development 1964–1970*, Amman, 360 pages.

Kanovsky, E. (1968).   The economic aftermath of the Six Day War: Part II, *Middle East Journal*, **22**, 278–296.

Khouri, F. J. (1964).   The Jordan river, the U.S., and the U.N., *Middle East Forum*, **40**, 20–24.

Khouri, F. J. (1965).   The Jordan river controversy, *Révue Politique*, **27**, 32–57.

Kirk, G. (1954).   *The Middle East in the War*, Oxford University Press, London, 511 pages.

Kirk, G. (1954).   *The Middle East 1945–1950*, Oxford University Press, London, 338 pages.

Long, G. A. (1957).   *The Bioclimatology and Vegetation of Eastern Jordan*, FAO, Rome.

Mackenzie, M. (1946).   Transjordan, *Jl R. cent. Asian Soc.*, **33**, 260–270.

Manners, I. R. (1970).   The East Ghor irrigation project, *Focus*, **20(8)**, 8–11

Mehdi, M. (1973).   Israeli settlements in the occupied territories, *Middle East International*, **19**, 21–27.

Middle East Economic Digest (1973).   Economic recovery in Jordan, *MEED*, **17 (24)**, 675–679.

Mountfort, G. (1965). *Portrait of a Desert*, Collins, London, 192 pages.

Natur, F. (1962). Farm unit layout, distribution and development in East Ghor canal project, *Fourth, NESA Irrigation Practices Seminar*, Ankara, 300–312.

Naval Intelligence Division (Great Britain) (1943). *Palestine and Transjordan*, Geographical Handbook Series, B. R. 514, British Admiralty, 621 pages.

Notestein, F. W. and E. Jurkat (1945). Population problems of Palestine, *The Milbank Memorial Fund Quarterly (New York)*, **23**, 307–352.

Nuttonson, M. Y. (1947). Agroclimatology and crop ecology of Palestine and Transjordan and climatic analogues in the United States, *Geogrl Rev.*, **37**, 436–456.

Patai, R. (1958). *The Kingdom of Jordan*, Princeton University Press, Princeton, New Jersey, 315 pages.

Peretz, D. (1964). River schemes and their effects on economic development in Jordan, Syria and Lebanon, *Middle East Journal*, **18**, 293–305.

Phillips, P. G. (1954). *The Hashemite Kingdom of Jordan: Prolegomena to a Technical Assistance Program*, Department of Geography, Research Paper No. 34 , University of Chicago, 191 pages.

Poore, M. E. D. and V. C. Robertson (1964). *An Approach to the Rapid Description and Mapping of Biological Habitats*, Sub-Commission on Conservation of Terrestrial Biological Communities of the International Biological Programme, 68 pages.

Randall, R. (1968). *Jordan and the Holy Land*, Federick Muller, London, 243 pages.

Reeçe, H. C., T. D. Roberts, J. P. Coury, S. Cooper, A. E. Farrier, T. Tompkins and N. B. Turk (1969). *Area Handbook for the Hashemite Kingdom of Jordan*, The American University, Washington, D.C., 372 pages.

Schattner, I. (1962). *The Lower Jordan Valley*, Scripta Hierosolymitana, Publications of the Hebrew University, Jerusalem, vol. **11**, 123 pages.

Smith, C. G. (1966). The disputed waters of the Jordan, *Trans. Inst. Br. Geogr.*, **40**, 111–128.

Smith, R. A. and B. P. Birch (1963). The East Ghor irrigation project in the Jordan valley, *Geography*, **48**, 407–409.

Sparrow, J. G. (1961). *Modern Jordan*, Allen & Unwin, London, 180 pages.

Talal, H. (1967). Growth and stability in the Jordanian economy, *Middle East Journal*, **17**, 92–100.

Van Valkenburg, S. (1954). The Hashemite Kingdom of the Jordan: a study in economic geography, *Econ. Geogr.*, **30**, 102–116.

Vouras, P. P. (1967). Jordan, *Focus*, **17(6)**, 1–6.

Whyte, R. O. (1950). The phytogeographical zones of Palestine, *Geogrl.Rev.*, **40**, 600–614.

Chapter 16: Israel: Pre-State Jewish Colonization

Adam-Smith, G. (1900). *Historical Geography of the Holy Land*, 7th ed. Hodder and Stoughton, London.

Bachi, R. (1967). Effects of migration on the geographic distribution of population in Israel, *International Union for Scientific Study of Population, Conference Papers*, Sydney, pp. 737–751.

Baly, D. (1957).   *The Geography of the Bible*, Lutterworth, London.

Ben-Arieh, Y. (1968).   The changing landscape of the central Jordan valley, *Scripta Hierosolymitana*, **15**, 1–131.

Blake, G. H. (1968).   The origins and evolution of Israel's moshav, *Kultur-geografi*,No. 109, 293–311.

Central Bureau of Statistics   *Population Census of 1967: West Bank, Golan Heights,* (1967–1968).   *Gaza Strip, Northern Sinai*, 2 vols. Jerusalem.

Cohen, A. (1964).   *Arab Border Villages in Israel*, Manchester University Press, Manchester.

Dash, H. and   *Israel Physical Master Plan*, Ministry of the Interior, E. Efrat (1964).   Jerusalem.

Elsevier, (1970).   *Atlas of Israel.* Elsevier, London and Amsterdam.

Evanari, M., N. H. Tadmor   *The Negev*, Oxford University Press, London.
and L. Shanan (1971).

Gilbert M., (1974).   *The Arab-Israel Conflict; its History in Maps*, Weidenfeld and Nicolson, London.

Granott, A. (1951).   *The Land System in Palestine*, Eyre and Spottiswoode, London.

Halperin, H. (1957).   *Changing Patterns in Israel agriculture*, Routledge and Kegan Paul, London.

Hopkins, I. W. J. (1970).   *Jerusalem: a Study in Urban Geography*, Baker Book House, Grand Rapids.

Karmon, Y. (1971).   *Israel—a Regional Geography*, John Wiley, Chichester.

Klayman, M. I. (1970).   *The Moshav in Israel*, Pall Mall, London.

Nir, D. (1968).   *La vallée de Beth Cheane*, Librairie Armand Colin, Paris.

Paran, U. (1970).   Kibbutzim in Israel: their development and distribution, *Jerusalem Studies in Geography*, Vol. 1, Hebrew University, Jerusalem.

Roth, C. and   *Encyclopaedia Judaica*, 16 vols. Keter, Jerusalem.
G. Wigoder (Eds) (1971).

Tavener, L. E. (1961).   *The Revival of Israel*, Hodder and Stoughton, London.

UNESCO (1964).   Agricultural planning and village community in Israel. *Arid Zone Research* **23**, United Nations, New York.

Vilnay, Z. (1968).   *The New Israel Atlas, Bible to Present Day*, Israel University Press, Jerusalem.

Wiener, A. (1972).   The development of Israeli water resources, *American Scientist*,**60**, 466–473.

Chapter 17: The Industrialization of Turkey

Aktan, R. (1966).   Turkish agricultural problems, *Mediterranea*, **12**, 266–275.

Albaum, M. and   The spatial structure of socio-economic attributes
C. S. Davies (1973).   of Turkish provinces, *International Journal of Middle Eastern Studies*, **4**, 288–310.

Alexander, A. P. (1960).   Industrial entrepreneurship in Turkey: origins and growth, *Economic Development and Cultural Change*, **8**, 349–365.

Bagna, M. A. (1965a).   La production céréalière en Turquie, *Mediterranea*, **6**, 102–107.

Bagna, M. A. (1965b).   Les conditions de l'élevage en Turquie, *Mediterranea*, **7**, 207–212.

Burgel, G. (1967).   Note sur le development récent de l'agglomeration d'Istanbul, *Bull. Ass. Géogr. fr.*, Nos. 355 to 361, 51–63.

Chapman, A. S. (1957).   The economic regions of Turkey as characterized by railway shipments, *Northwestern University Studies in Geography* (Evanston, Ill.), **2**, 71–75.

Clark, J. (1970–71).   The growth of Ankara, 1961–69, *Rev. geogr. Inst. Univ. Istanb.*, **13**, 119–140.

Cohen, E. J. (1970).   *Turkish Economic, Social and Political Change: Development of a More Prosperous and Open Society*, Praeger, New York, Washington and London.

Crabbe, G. (1944).   Turkey: a record of industrial and commercial progress in the last quarter of a century, *Jl R. cent. Asian Soc.*, **31**, 48–63.

Cuinet, V. (1890–94).   *La Turquie d'Asie. Géographie Administrative, Déscriptive et Raisonée de Chaque Provence de l'Asie Mineure*, 4 vols., Ernest Leroux, Paris.

Darkot, B. (1958).   *Türkiye Iktisadî Coğrafasi*, Bermet, İstanbul.

Dewdney, J. C. (1971).   *Turkey*, Chatto and Windus, London.

Dooren, P. J. van (1969).   Structural and institutional obstacles facing Turkey's peasant farmers, *Tropical Man*, **2**, 107–161.

Dulgarian, M. and E. Tümertekin (1962).   The population of İstanbul: patterns and changes, 1955–60, *Rev. geogr. Inst. Univ. Istanb.*, **8**, 251–258.

Eldem, V. (1953).   Turkey's transportation, *Middle Eastern Affairs*, **4**, 324–336.

Eren, N. (1966).   Financial aspects of Turkish planning, *Middle East Journal*, **20**, 187–195.

Erinç S. (1950).   Climatic types and the variation of moisture regions in Turkey, *Geogrl Rev.*, **40**, 224–235.

Erinç, S. and N. Tunçdilek (1952).   The agricultural regions of Turkey, *Geogrl Rev.*, **42**, 189–203.

Fry, M. J. (1971).   Turkey's first Five-Year Development Plan: an assessment, *Economic Journal*, **81**, 306–326.

Helburn, N. (1955).   A stereotype of agriculture in semi-arid Turkey, *Geogrl Rev.*, **45**, 375–384.

Hershlag, Z. Y. (1968a).   *Turkey: The Challenge of Growth*, E. J. Brill, Leiden.

Hershlag, Z. Y. (1968b).   *Economic Planning in Turkey*, Economic Research Foundation, İstanbul.

Hiltner, J. (1962).   The distribution of Turkish manufacturing, *J. Geogr.*, *N.Y.*, **61**, 251–258.

Hinderink, J. and M. B. Kiray (1970).   *Social Stratification as an Obstacle to Development. A Study of Four Turkish Villages*, Praeger, New York, Washington and London.

Hirsch, E. (1971).   *Poverty and Plenty on the Turkish Farm: A Economic Study of Turkish Agriculture in the 1950s*, Middle East Institute, Columbia University, New York.

Hirsch, E. and A. Hirsch (1963).   Changes in agricultural output per capita of rural population in Turkey, 1927–60, *Economic Development and Cultural Change*, **11**, 372–394.

Hirsch, E. and A. Hirsch (1966).   Changes in terms of trade to farmers and their effect on real farm income per capita of rural population in Turkey, 1927–60, *Economic Development and Cultural Change*, **14**, 440–457.

Keleş, R. Y. (1961).   *Türkiyede Şehirleşme Haraketleri (1927–1960)*, Faculty of Political Science, Ankara, mimeographed.

550

Keleş, R. Y. (1963).   Regional disparities in Turkey, *Ekistics*, **15**, 331–335.
Keleş, R. Y. (1966).   Urbanisation and balanced regional development in Turkey, *Ekistics*, **22**, 163–168.
Kerwin, R. W. (1950).   The Turkish roads programme, *Middle East Journal*, **4**, 196–208.
Kerwin, R. W. (1951).   Private enterprise in Turkish industrial development, *Middle East Journal*, **5**, 21–38.
Kolars, J. F. (1965–68).   Decision and commitment in Turkish agriculture, *Rev. geogr. Inst. Univ. Istanb.*, **11**, 37–46.
Kolars, J. F. and   Population and accessibility; an analysis of Turkish
H. J. Malin (1970).   railroads, *Geogrl Rev.*, **60**, 229–246.
Kolodny, Y. (1968).   Données récentes sur la population urbaine de la Turquie, *Méditerranée*, **9**, 165–180.
Kroner, G. (1969).   Der Bau des Euphrat-Dammes bei Keban (Ostananatolien): Möglichkeiten und Grenzen einer raumplanerischen Lösung, *Raumforschung und Raumordung*, **27**, 156–162.
Kündig-Steiner, W. (1968).   Neueste kulturlandschaftliche Veränderungen in Ostanatolien, speziell in der Region Kars, *Geographica helv.*, **23**, 129–131.
Lewis, B. (1968).   *The Emergence of Modern Turkey*, 2nd ed., Oxford University Press, London.
Louis, H. (1972).   Die Bevölkerungsverteilung in der Türkei 1965 und ihre Entwicklung seit 1935, *Erdkunde*, **26**, 161–177.
Merriam, G. P. (1926).   The regional geography of Anatolia, *Econ. Geogr.* **2**, 86–107.
Morris, J. A. (1960).   Recent problems of economic development in Turkey, *Middle East Journal*, **14**, 1–14.
Okyas, O. (1965).   The concept of Etatism, *Economic Journal*, **75**, 98–111.
Ozuygur, M. (1968).   The place of fertilisers in Turkish agriculture and its development prospects, *Mediterranea*, **23–24**, 512–519.
Planhol, X. de (1960).   Expansion et problèmes de l'agriculture turque, *Revue Géogr. Lyon.*, **35**, 91–103.
Poroy, I. I. (1972).   Planning with a large public sector: Turkey (1963–1967), *International Journal of Middle Eastern Studies*, **3**, 248–260.
Ritter, G. (1972).   Landflucht und Städtewachstum in der Türkei, *Erdkunde*, **26**, 177–196.
Rivkin, M. D. (1965).   *Area Development for National Growth. The Turkish Precendent*, Praeger, New York, Washington and London.
Robinson, R. D. (1967).   *High-level Manpower in Economic Development: The Turkish Case*, Middle East Monographs No. 17, Harvard University Press, Cambridge, Mass.
Sarc, O. C. (1941).   Tanzimat ve sanayimiz. In *Tanzimat*, İstanbul, pp. 423–440. Translated as The Tanzimat and our industry. In C. Issawi (Ed), *The Economic History of the Middle East, 1800–1914*, Chicago University Press, Chicago and London, 1966, pp. 48–59.
Simpson, D. J. (1965).   Development as a process: the Menderes phase in Turkey, *Middle East Journal*, **19**, 141–152.
Snyder, W. W. (1969).   Turkish economic development: the first Five Year Plan, *Journal of Development Studies*, **6**, 58–71.
Stewig, R. (1972).   Die Industrialisierung in der Türkei, *Erde*, **103**, 21–47.

Tanoğlu, A., S. Erinç and E. Tümertekin (1961).
Turkiye Atlasi, Istanbul Üniversitesi Edebiyat Fakültesi Yayinlau, No. 903, Istanbul.

Treadway, R. C. (1972).
Gradients of metropolitan dominance in Turkey; alternative models, *Demography*, **9**, 13–34.

Tümertekin, E. (1955).
The iron and steel industry in Turkey, *Econ. Geogr.*, **31**, 174–184.

Tümertekin, E. (1961).
L'activité industrielle à Istanbul, *Rev. geogr. Inst. Univ. Istanb.*, **7**, 35–52.

Tümertekin, E. (1970–71).
Manufacturing and suburbanisation in İstanbul, *Rev. geogr. Inst. Univ. Istanb.*, **13**, 1–40.

Tümertekin, E. (1970–71).
Gradual internal migration in Turkey: a test of Ravenstein's hypothesis, *Rev. geogr. Inst. Univ. Istanb.*, **13**, 157–169.

Yarruz, J. (1952).
The development of Ankara, *J. T. Plann. Inst. Lond.*, **38**, 251–252.

Chapter 18: Iran: Agriculture and its Modernization

Adams, R. M. (1962).
Agriculture and urban life in early southwestern Iran, *Science, N.Y.*, **136**, 109–122.

Ajami, I. (1973).
Land reform and modernisation of the farming structure in Iran, *Oxford Agrarian Studies*, **2**, 120–131.

Arfa, H. (1963).
Land reform in Iran, *Jl R. cent. Asian Soc.*, **50**, 132–137.

Avery, P. (1965).
Modern Iran, Ernest Benn, London, 527 pages.

Ayazi, M. (1961).
Drainage and reclamation problems in the Garmsar area. In UNESCO, *Salinity Problems in the Arid Zone*, Arid Zone Research, Vol. 14, 285–290.

Banami, A. (1961).
The Modernization of Iran 1921–41, Stanford University Press, Stanford, 191 pages.

Barth, F. (1964).
Nomads of South Persia, The Basseri Tribe of the Khamseh Confederacy, Universitetsforlaget, Oslo, 159 pages.

Barth, F. (1962).
Nomadism in the mountain and plateau areas of South West Asia. In UNESCO, *The Problems of the Arid Zone*, Arid Zone Research, Paris, Vol. 18, 341–355.

Beaumont P. (1968).
Qanats on the Varamin Plain, Iran, *Trans. Inst. Br. Geogr.*, **45**, 169–179.

Beaumont, P. (1971).
Qanat systems in Iran, *Bull. int. Ass. scient. Hydrol.*, **16**, 39–50.

Beaumont, P. (1973).
A traditional method of ground water extraction in the Middle East, *Ground Water*, **11**, 23–30.

Beaumont, P. (1973).
River Regimes in Iran, Occasional Publications (New Series), No. 1, Department of Geography, University of Durham, 29 pages.

Beaumont, P. (1974).
Water resource development in Iran, *Geogrl J.*, **140**, 100–110.

Beaumont, P. and J. H. Neville (1968).
Rice cultivation in Iran's Caspian lowlands, *Wld Crops*, **20**, 70–73.

Beckett, P. H. T. (1953).
Qanats around Kerman, *Jl R. cent. Asian Soc.*, **40**, 47–58.

Beckett, P. H. T. (1957).
Tools and crafts in south central Persia, *Man*, **57**, 145–148.

Beckett, P. H. T. (1958).
The soils of Kerman, south Persia, *J. Soil Sci.*, **9**, 20–32.

Beckett, P. H. T. and E. D. Gordon (1956). The climate of Kerman, South Persia, *Q. Jl R. met. Soc.*, **82**, 503–514.

Beckett, P. H. T. and E. D. Gordon (1966). Land use and settlement round Kerman in southern Iran, *Geogrl J.*, **132**, 476–491.

Bémont, F. (1961). L'irrigation en Iran, *Annls Géogr.*, **70**, 597–620.

Bharier, J. (1968). A note on the population of Iran, 1900–1966, *Population Studies*, **22**, 273–279.

Bharier, J. (1971). *Economic Development in Iran 1900–1970*, Oxford University Press, London, 314 pages.

Bharier, J. (1972). The growth of towns and villages in Iran, 900–1966, *Middle Eastern Studies*, **8**, 51–61.

Bill, J. A. (1963). The social and economic foundations of power in contemporary Iran, *Middle East Journal*, **17**, 400–418.

Black, A. G. (1948). Iranian agriculture—present and prospective, *Journal of Farm Economics*, **30**, 422–442.

Bobek, H. (1968). Vegetation. In W. B. Fisher (Ed), *The Cambridge History of Iran, Vol. 1—The Land of Iran*, Cambridge University Press, Cambridge, pp. 280–293.

Bowen-Jones, H. (1968). Agriculture. In W. B. Fisher (Ed), *The Cambridge History of Iran, Vol. 1—The Land of Iran*, Cambridge University Press, Cambridge, pp. 565–598.

Caponera, D. (1954). *Water Laws in Moslem Countries*, FAO Agricultural Development Papers, No. 43, 202 pages.

Clark, B. D. (1972). Iran: changing population patterns. In J. I. Clarke and W. B. Fisher (Eds), *Populations of the Middle East and North Africa*, University of London Press, London, 68–96.

Clark, B. D. and V. Costello (1973). The urban system and social patterns in Iranian cities, *Trans. Inst. Br. Geogr.*, **59**, 99–128.

Clarke, J. I. (1963). *The Iranian City of Shiraz*, Department of Geography, Research Paper Series No. 7, University of Durham, 55 pages.

Clarke, J. I. and B. D. Clark (1969). *Kermanshah, an Iranian Provincial City*, Department of Geography, Research Paper Series, No. 10, University of Durham, 137 pages.

Development and Resources Corporation (1959). *The Unified Development of the Natural Resources of the Khuzestan Region*, New York, 162 pages.

Dewan, M. L. and J. Famouri (1968). Soils. In W. B. Fisher (Ed), *The Cambridge History of Iran, Vol. 1—The Land of Iran*, Cambridge University Press, Cambridge, pp. 250–263.

Djavid-Pour, E. (1968). Condition of agriculture and farmers before execution of the Iranian Law of Land Reforms, *Mediterranea*, **25**, 572–575.

Echo of Iran (1971). *Iran Almanac 1971*, Echo of Iran, Tehrān, Iran, 808 pages.

Elwell-Sutton, L. P. (1958). Nationalism and neutralism in Iran, *Middle East Journal*, **12**, 20–33.

English, P. W. (1966). *City and Village in Iran*, University of Wisconsin Press, Madison, 204 pages.

Field, M. (1972). Agro-business and agricultural planning in Iran, *Wld Crops*, **24**, 68–72.

Fisher, W. B. (Ed) (1968). *Cambridge History of Iran, Vol. 1—The Land of Iran*, Cambridge University Press, Cambridge, 784 pages.

Fitt, R. L. (1953). Irrigation development in central Persia, *Jl R. cent. Asian Soc.*, **40**, 124–133.

Flower, D. J. (1968).   Water use in north-east Iran. In W. B. Fisher (Ed), *The Cambridge History of Iran, Vol. I—The Land of Iran*, Cambridge University Press, Cambridge, pp. 599–610.

Freivalds, J. (1972).   Farm corporations in Iran: an alternative to traditional agriculture, *Middle East Journal*, **26**, 185–193.

Ganji, M. H. (1960).   *Iranian Rainfall Data*, University of Tehrān, Arid Zone Research Centre, Publication No. 3, 191 pages.

Ganji, M. H. (1968).   Climate. In W. B. Fisher (Ed), *The Cambridge History of Iran, Vol. I—The Land of Iran*, Cambridge University Press, Cambridge, pp. 212–249.

Gastil, R. D. (1958).   Middle class impediments to Iranian modernisation, *Public Opinion Quaterly*, **22**, 325–329.

Gittinger, J. P. (1965).   *Planning for Agricultural Development: the Iranian Experience*, National Planning Association, Washington D.C., 121 pages.

Gittinger, J. P. (1967).   Planning and agricultural policy in Iran—program effects and indirect effects, *Economic Development and Cultural Change*, **16**, 107–117.

Goblot, H. (1962).   Le Problème de l'eau en Iran, *Orient*, **23**, 43–59.

Hadary, G. (1951).   The agrarian reform problem in Iran, *Middle East Journal*, **5**, 181–196.

Harrison, J. V. (1932).   The Bakhtiari Country, S. W. Persia, *Geogrl J.*, **80**, 193–210.

Hayden, L. (1949).   Living standards in rural Iran, a case study, *Middle East Journal*, **3**, 140–150.

Issawi, C. (1967).   Iran's economic upsurge, *Middle East Journal*, **17**, 447–461.

Johnson, V. W. (1960).   Agriculture in the economic development of Iran, *Land Economics*, **36**, 314–321.

Keddie, N. R. (1968).   The Iranian village before and after land reform, *Journal of Contemporary History*, **3**, 69–91.

Kernan, H. S. (1957).   Forest management in Iran, *Middle East Journal*, **11**, 199–202.

Khamsi, F. (1969).   Land reform in Iran, *Monthly Review*, **21(2)**, 20–28.

Lambton, A. K. S. (1953).   *Landlord and Peasant in Persia*, Oxford University Press, London, 459 pages.

Lambton, A. K. S. (1957).   Impact of the West on Iran, *International Affairs*, London, **33**, 12–25.

Lambton, A. K. S. (1969).   *The Persian Land Reform*, Clarendon Press, Oxford, 386 pages.

Lambton, A. K. S. (1969).   Land reform and co-operative societies in Persia, *Jl R. cent Asian Soc.*, **56**, 142–155 and 245–258.

McLachlan, K. S. (1968).   Land reform in Iran. In W. B. Fisher (Ed), *The Cambridge History of Iran, Vol I—The Land of Iran*, Cambridge University Press, Cambridge, 684–716.

Ministry of Information (1970).   *Farm Corporations in Iran*, Ministry of Information, Tehrān, 10 pages.

Ministry of Land Reform and Rural Cooperation (1970).   *Land Reform Programme in Iran*, Rural Research Centre, Ministry of Land Reform and Rural Co-operation, Tehrān, 20 pages.

Naval Intelligence Division (Great Britain) (1945).   *Persia*, Geographical Handbook Series, B.R. 525, 638 pages.

Noel, E. (1944).   Qanats, *Jl R. cent. Asian Soc.*, **31**, 191–202.

Oberlander, T. M. (1968).   Hydrography. In W. B. Fisher (Ed), *The Cambridge*

554

	History of Iran, Vol I—The Land of Iran, Cambridge University Press, Cambridge, pp. 264–279.
Plan Organisation, Iran (1968).	Fourth National Development Plan, 1968–1972, Plan Organisation, The Imperial Government of Iran, Tehrān, 335 pages.
Plan Organisation, Iran (1969).	Dam Construction in Iran, Bureau of Information and Reports, Tehrān, 87 pages.
Planhol, X. de (1966).	Aspects of mountain life in Anotolia and Iran. In S. R. Eyre and G. R. J. Jones (Eds), Geography as Human Ecology, Arnold, London, pp. 291–308.
Sahebdiam-Bunodière, C. (1962).	L'agriculture en Iran, Orient, 21, 33–47.
Smith, A. (1953).	Blind White Fish in Persia, E. P. Dutton & Co., New York, 256 pages.
Spooner, B. (1963).	The function of religion in Persian Society, Iran, 1, 83–95.
Spooner, B. (1966).	Iranian kinship and marriage, Iran, 4, 51–59.
Sunderland, E. (1968).	Pastoralism, nomadism and the social anthropology of Iran. In W. B. Fisher (Ed), The Cambridge History of Iran, Vol I—The Land of Iran, Cambridge University Press, Cambridge, 611–683.
Sykes, C. (1957).	Persian gardens, Geogrl Mag., 30, 326–329.
Vahidi, M. (1968).	Water and Irrigation in Iran, Plan Organisation, published by Bureau of Information and Reports, Tehrān, 79 pages.
Wulff, H. E. (1968).	Qanats of Iran, Scient. Am., 218(4), 94–105.
Young, T. C. (1948).	The problem of westernization in Modern Iran, Middle East Journal, 2, 47–59.

Chapter 19: Egypt: Population Growth and Agricultural Expansion

Abou-Zeid, A. (1959).	The sedentarization of nomads in the western desert of Egypt, International Social Science Journal, 11, 550–558.
Abu-Lughod, J. L. (1963–64).	Rural–urban differences as a function of the demographic transition: Egyptian data and analytical model, American Journal of Sociology, 69, 476–490.
Abdamowicz, M. (1970).	Transformation of agricultural structure in the United Arab Republic. Africana Bulletin, Warsaw, 13, 75–88.
Ammar, H. M. (1954).	Growing up in an Egyptian Village, Routledge and Kegan Paul, London.
Asadi, F. (1972).	Agricultural land in Egypt: the quest for rationale. Geographical Survey, Blue Earth County Geographical Society, 1, 3–24.
Ayrout, H. H. (1963).	The Egyptian Peasant, Beacon Press, Boston.
Baer, G. (1962).	History of Land Ownership in Modern Egypt from 1800–1950, Oxford University Press, London.
Ball, J. (1939).	Contributions to the Geography of Egypt, Government Press, Cairo.
Barbour, K. M. (1970).	The distribution of industry in Egypt: a new source considered, Trans. Inst. Br. Geogr., 50, 155–176.
Barbour, K. M. (1972).	The Growth, Location, and Structure of Industry in Egypt, Praeger, New York.
Besançon, J. (1957).	L'homme et le Nil, Gallimard, Paris.

Crary, D. B. (1949). Irrigation and land use in Zeiniya Bahari, upper Egypt, *Geogrl Rev.*, **39**, 568–583.

Duff, R. E. B. (1969). *One Hundred Years of the Suez Canal*, Clifton Books, Brighton.

Eshag, E. and M. A. Kamal (1968). Agrarian reform in the United Arab Republic, *Bull. Oxf. Univ. Inst. Statist.*, **30**, 73–104.

Field, M. (1973). Developing the Nile. *Wld Crops*, **25**, 11–15.

Garzouzi, E. (1958). *Old Ills and New Remedies in Egypt*, Dar al Ma'aref, Cairo.

George, C. J. (1972). The role of the Aswan High Dam in changing the fisheries of the southeastern Mediterranean. In M. Taghi Farvar and J. P. Milton (Eds), *The Careless Technology*, Natural History Press, New York, pp. 159–178.

Hamdan, G. (1961). Evolution of irrigation agriculture in Egypt. In *History of Land Use in Arid Regions*, Arid Zone Research, Vol. 17., UNESCO, New York, pp. 119–142.

Hammad, H. Y. (1970). *Groundwater Potentialities in the African Sahara and the Nile Valley*, Arab University, Beirūt.

Hansen, B. and G. A. Marzouk (1965). *Development and Economic Policy in the United Arab Republic*, North Holland, Amsterdam.

Haupert, J. S. (1969). The United Arab Republic, *Focus*, **19(7)**.

Holt, P. M. (Ed) (1968). *Political and Social Change in Modern Egypt*, Oxford University Press, London.

Holz, R. K. (1968). The Aswan High Dam, *Prof. Geogr.*, **20**, 230–237.

Hopkins, H. (1969). *Egypt the Crucible*, Secker and Warburg, London.

Hurst, H. E. (1952). *The Nile*, Constable, London.

Issawi, C. (1963). *Egypt in Revolution: an Economic Analysis*, Royal Institute of International Affairs, Oxford.

Mansfield, P. (1965). *Naser's Egypt*, Penguin Books. Harmondsworth.

Mountjoy, A. B. (1958). The Suez Canal at mid-century, *Econ. Geogr.* **34**, 153–167.

Murray, G. (1952). Water from beneath the Egyptian western desert, *Geogrl J.*, **118**, 443–452.

Nasr, N. el Sayed (1955). A sample study of land use in the Nile delta, *Geography*, **40**, 178–190.

Nour el Din, N. (1968). The High Dam and land reclamation in Egypt, *Méditerranée*, **20**, 262–269.

O'Brien, P. (1966). *The Revolution in Egypt's Economic System*, Oxford University Press, London.

Platt, R. R. and M. B. Hefny (1958). *Egypt: a Compendium*, American Geographical Society, New York.

Rizkana, I. and M. S. Abou el Ezz (1964). The High Dam lake in Aswan: a new environment in the making, *Bull. Soc. Geogr. Egypt*, **37**, 101–109.

Rosciszewski, M. (1966). Agricultural geography of Egypt, *Africana Bulletin*, Warsaw, **5**, 33–52.

Saab, G. S. (1967). *The Egyptian Agrarian Reform 1952–1962*, Oxford University Press, London.

Smith, C. G. (1969). The great ditch across the Suez isthmus, *Geogrl Mag.* **41**, 259–270.

Wilber, D. N. (Ed), (1969). *The United Arab Republic, its People, its Society, its Culture*, Human Relations Area Files, New Haven.

Chapter 20: Libya: The Impact of Oil

Atkinson, K., M. Bovis, and D. Johnson. (1972). Man-made oases of Libya *Geogrl Mag.*, **45**, 112–115.

Blake, G. H. (1968). *Misruta, a Market Town in Tripolitania*, Department of Geography, University of Durham, Durham.

Bottomley, A. (1962). Cereal production in a semi-desert community, *J. Agric. Econ.*, **15**, 122–128.

Brown, R. W. (1967). Libya's rural sector. *Africa Report*, **12**, 16–18.

Clarke, J. I. (1963). Oil in Libya: some implications, *Econ. Geogr.*, **39**, 40–59.

Doxiadis Associates, (1965). *Transport in Libya*, 2 vols., Athens.

Eldblom, L. (1961). Quelques points de vue comparatifs sur les problèmes d'irrigation dans les trois oases Libyennes de Brâk, Ghadamès et particulièrement Mourzouk, *Svensk Geografisk Arsbok*, Vol. 37, pp. 124–145.

Farrel, J. D. (1967). Libya strikes it rich. *Africa Report*, **12**, 8–15.

Fowler, G. L. (1972). Italian colonisation in Tripolitania, *Ann. Ass. Am. Geogr.*, **62**, 627–640.

Furlonge, G. (1973). Libya: putting the oil to work, *Middle East International.* No. 25, 9–11.

George, A. R. (1973). Kufra: the desert's hidden resources, *Middle East International*, **25**, 15–18.

Hajjaji, S. A. (1967). *The New Libya*, Ministry of Information and Culture, Tripoli.

Harrison, R. S. (1966). Libya, *Focus*, **17**(3), 1–6.

Heitman, G. (1969). Libya: an analysis of the oil economy, *Journal of Modern African Studies*, **7**, 249–263.

International Bank for Reconstruction and Development (1960). *The Economic Development of Libya*, Johns Hopkins Press, Baltimore.

Isnard, H. (1968). Esquisse du climat de la Libye, *Méditerranée*, **3**, 247–260.

Johnson, D. L. (1973). *Jabal al Ak̲h̲dar, Cyrenaica*, University of Chicago, Chicago.

Kanter, H. (1967). *Libyen–Libya; a Geomedical Monograph*, Springer Verlag, Berlin.

Marthelot, P. (1964). La révolution du petrole dans un pays insuffisamment développé: la Libye, *Cah. d'Outre-mer*, **17**, 5–31.

Ministry of Information and Culture (1972). *Achievements of the First of September Revolution*, Tripoli.

Penrose, E., J. A. Allan, and K. S. McLachlan (Eds) (1970). *Agriculture and the Economic Development of Libya*, University of Libya, University of London, and British Petroleum, London.

Pesce, A. (1968). *Gemini Space Photographs of Libya and Tibesti*, Petroleum Exploration Society, Tripoli.

Willimot, S., and J. I. Clarke. (Eds.) (1960). *Field Studies in Libya*, Department of Geography, University of Durham, Durham.

Index

564